HOSEA 2

Society of Biblical Literature

Academia Biblica

Steven L. McKenzie,
Hebrew Bible/Old Testament Editor

Mark Allan Powell,
New Testament Editor

Number 20

HOSEA 2
Metaphor and Rhetoric in
Historical Perspective

HOSEA 2
Metaphor and Rhetoric in Historical Perspective

Brad E. Kelle

Society of Biblical Literature
Atlanta

HOSEA 2

Copyright © 2005 by the Society of Biblical Literature

Library of Congress Cataloging-in-Publication Data

Kelle, Brad E., 1973–
    Hosea 2 : metaphor and rhetoric in historical perspective / by Brad E. Kelle.
        p. cm. — (Academia Biblica ; no. 20)
    Includes bibliographical references and index.
    ISBN-13: 978-1-58983-189-6 (paper binding : alk. paper)
    ISBN-10: 1-58983-189-6 (paper binding : alk. paper)
    1. Bible. O.T. Hosea II—Criticism, interpretation, etc. 2. Metaphor in the Bible. 3. Rhetoric in the Bible. 4. Syro-Ephraimitic War, ca. 734 B.C. I. Title. II. Series: Academia Biblica (Series) (Society of Biblical Literature) ; no. 20.
    BS1565.52.K45 2005b
    224'.6066—dc22   2005026987

Printed in the United States of America
on acid-free paper

CONTENTS

PART 1: THE *METAPHORS* OF HOSEA 2

ACKNOWLEDGMENTS

The completion of a monograph, especially one that began as a dissertation, is a feat that is never accomplished alone. Teachers, friends, and family contribute to the process of learning and writing in ways that are often as indirect as they are important. Because my life has been so graciously enriched by these people in many and constant ways, it is a joy to express, even in this most limited fashion, my gratitude to them at this moment of my journey.

Pride of place in this regard goes to my teachers and, more specifically, those who served as my original dissertation committee. I am grateful to Dr. Martin J. Buss and Dr. Gail O'Day for serving so aptly in this capacity. I am most deeply indebted to my mentor, Dr. John H. Hayes, not only for his sage counsel and scholarly expertise but also for his good humor and positive encouragement, which often sustained me throughout the writing process. My thanks also go to the other members of the Hebrew Bible Department at Emory University, Dr. Carol Newsom, Dr. David Petersen, and Dr. Brent Strawn, each of whom has shaped my thinking and my life in ways too numerable to count. Thanks are also due to Bob Buller, Dr. Frank Ames, Leigh Andersen, and the other editors and readers associated with the Society of Biblical Literature for providing assistance throughout the production of the manuscript. I would especially like to thank Derek Davis, who served as my assistant during the formatting stage of this project. Although a full-time theology student in his senior year at Point Loma Nazarene University, Derek gave countless hours of effort and expertise to help bring the manuscript into shape.

During the process of writing, I have been reminded that learning takes place not only through interaction with professors but also through rich relationships with friends and colleagues. Among this important group, I would like to thank especially David Casson and Rebecca Duke-Barton, the two colleagues with whom I began a doctoral journey in 1998. Although working on projects (and lives!) of their own, they always had time to talk, read, encourage, and commiserate. Thanks, Rebecca, for reminding me how to keep parish life a part of the process. Thanks, David, for showing me how to be "Daddy" and "Doctor" at the same time. I would also like to thank my colleagues at Colorado Christian University and now at Point Loma Nazarene University for their encouragement to undertake (and complete!) this project.

Since this work began as the culmination of many years of graduate education, it is very appropriate to thank my family. My sisters, Becky and Beth, and their husbands, Dennis and Rick, have shared so many important moments with me and contributed significantly to them all. My parents, Gene and Janet Kelle, have demonstrated time and again the kind of selfless love and open-hearted giving that true parenting entails. Of course, it is to my wife, Dee, and our now five-year old son, Grayson, that I owe the greatest debt. Grayson has so frequently changed my perspective on all things, brightened my life in ways that I could not have imagined, and patiently endured his father's preoccupation with his "work." Dee has sacrificed many of her own goals and desires to make the completion of this process possible. She has repeatedly given me the time (and space) needed, never demanding for herself but always allowing me to pursue any venture. She has too often played the role of a single (working) parent, yet never faltered in being a friend, companion, and lover. For all the days she was alone, for all the times I was too busy, and for all the moments I was too distracted, I express my regret—and gratitude. To her this work is dedicated.

ABBREVIATIONS

AB	Anchor Bible
ABD	*Anchor Bible Dictionary*
ACEBT	*Amsterdamse Cahiers voor Exegese en bijbelse Theologie*
AfOB	Archive für Orientforschung: Beiheft
AJSL	*American Journal of Semitic Languages and Literature*
ANET	*Ancient Near Eastern Texts Relating to the Old Testament*
AOAT	Alter Orient und Altes Testament
AOS	American Oriental Series
ARM	Archives royales de Mari
ArOr	*Archiv Orientální*
ATD	Das Alte Testament Deutsch
BA	*Biblical Archaeologist*
BASOR	*Bulletin of the American Schools of Oriental Research*
Bib	*Biblica*
BibOr	Biblica et orientalia
BDB	Brown, Driver, Briggs, *A Hebrew and English Lexicon*
BETL	Bibliotheca ephemeridum theologicarum lovaniensum
BR	*Biblical Research*
BTB	*Biblical Theology Bulletin*
BWA(N)T	Beiträge zur Wissenschaft vom Alten (und Neuen) Testament
BZ	*Biblische Zeitschrift*
BZAW	Beihefte zur Zeitschrift für die alttestamentliche Wissenschaft
CBC	Cambridge Bible Commentary
CBQ	*Catholic Biblical Quarterly*
ConBOT	Coniectanea biblica: Old Testament Series

DBI	*Dictionary of Biblical Interpretation*
DCH	*Dictionary of Classical Hebrew*
EncJud	*Encyclopaedia Judaica*
ERE	*Encyclopedia of Religion and Ethics*
ErIsr	*Eretz-Israel*
EvT	*Evangelische Theologie*
ExpTim	*Expository Times*
FAT	Forschungen zum Alten Testament
FB	Forschung zur Bibel
FRLANT	Forschungen zur Religion und Literatur des Alten und Neuen Testaments
GBS	Guides to Biblical Scholarship
HBT	*Horizons in Biblical Theology*
HSM	Harvard Semitic Monographs
HSS	Harvard Semitic Studies
HTR	*Harvard Theological Review*
HTS	Harvard Theological Studies
HUCA	*Hebrew Union College Annual*
IB	Interpreter's Bible
IBC	Interpretation Commentary
ICC	International Critical Commentary
IDBSup	*Interpreter's Dictionary of the Bible Supplementary Volume*
IEJ	*Israel Exploration Journal*
Int	*Interpretation*
ITC	International Theological Commentary
JANESCU	*Journal of the Ancient Near Eastern Society of Columbia University*
JAOS	*Journal of the American Oriental Society*
JBL	*Journal of Biblical Literature*
JLA	*Jewish Law Annual*
JNES	*Journal of Near Eastern Studies*
JNSL	*Journal of Northwest Semitic Languages*
JQR	*Jewish Quarterly Review*
JSJ	*Journal for the Study of Judaism in the Persian, Hellenistic, and Roman Periods*
JSOT	*Journal for the Study of the Old Testament*
JSOTSup	Journal for the Study of the Old Testament Supplement Series
JSP	*Journal for the Study of the Pseudepigrapha*
JSS	*Journal of Semitic Studies*
JTS	*Journal of Theological Studies*
KAT	Kommentar zum Alten Testament

LAPO	Littératures anciennes du Proche-Orient
LUÅ	Lunds universitets årsskrift
NAC	New American Commentary
NCB	New Century Bible
NIB	New Interpreter's Bible
NKZ	*Neue kirchliche Zeitschrift*
OBO	Orbis biblicus et orientalis
OBT	Overtures to Biblical Theology
Or	*Orientalia*
OTE	*Old Testament Essays*
OTG	Old Testament Guides
OTL	Old Testament Library
RA	*Revue d'assyriologie et d'archaeologie Orientale*
RB	*Revue biblique*
REJ	*Revue des études juives*
RevExp	*Review and Expositor*
RevScRel	*Revue des sciences religieuses*
RGG	*Religion in Geschichte und Gegenwart*
RHPR	*Revue d'histoire et de philosophie religieuses*
SAA	State Archives of Assyria
SAAS	State Archives of Assyria Studies
SBLDS	Society of Biblical Literature Dissertation Series
SBLMS	Society of Biblical Literature Monograph Series
SBLSymS	Society of Biblical Literature Symposium Series
SBS	Stuttgarter Biblestudien
SBTS	Sources for Biblical and Theological Study
ScrHier	Scripta hierosolymitana
SJOT	*Scandinavian Journal of the Old Testament*
SR	*Studies in Religion*
SSN	Studia semitica neerlandica
SVTQ	*St. Vladimir's Theological Quarterly*
TA	*Tel Aviv*
TBC	Torch Bible Commentaries
TBT	*The Bible Today*
TDOT	*Theological Dictionary of the Old Testament*
TLOT	*Theological Lexicon of the Old Testament*
TOTC	Tyndale Old Testament Commentaries
TSK	*Theologische Studien und Kritiken*
UF	*Ugarit-Forschungen*
UUA	Uppsala Universitetsårskrift

VT	*Vetus Testamentum*
VTSup	Supplements to Vetus Testamentum
WBC	Word Biblical Commentary
WD	*Wort und Dienst*
WMANT	Wissenschaftliche Monographien zum Alten und Neuen Testament
ZAW	*Zeitschrift für die alttestamentliche Wissenschaft*
ZDMG	*Zeitschrift der deutschen morgenländische Gesellschaft*
ZTK	*Zeitschrift für Theologie und Kirche*
ZWT	*Zeitschrift für wissenschaftliche Theologie*

1

APPROACHING HOSEA 2

1. INTRODUCTION

The prophetic discourse in Hos 2 relies on a wealth of metaphorical imagery. This imagery touches the realms of marriage, parenting, adultery, and reconciliation and functions in the service of a complex rhetorical argument in which Yahweh confronts his metaphorical "wife."[1] The first part of the chapter consists of a positive section that describes the reunification and rejuvenation of the people of Israel and Judah represented by the family metaphor of brothers and sisters who speak kindly to one another (2:1–3). This opening is followed by an extended divine oracle in which Yahweh speaks in the first-person and tells the story of his tumultuous metaphorical marriage (2:4–25). Particularly in this portion of Hos 2, one encounters a text that is certainly complex and even unsettling. The passage puts a metaphorical speech into Yahweh's mouth that is multifaceted, violent, and perhaps even pornographic. Yahweh's speech describes marital unfaithfulness, divorce procedures, retributive punishments, and sudden reconciliation. At the conclusion, however, the divine oracle ends with the same positive tone and familial metaphor that punctuate the opening section of 2:1–3.

---

[1] This study follows the MT verse numbers.

The complexity of Hos 2 has generated a large amount of scholarly discussion, yet in spite of all the critical studies devoted to different elements of the chapter, no general agreement exists on any of the major interpretive issues. Even the most basic questions concerning the interpretive thrust of the text's metaphors and images and the significance of possible rhetorical-historical contexts remain unsettled. Additionally, the previous critical analyses of this chapter have rarely taken the form of comprehensive and integrated investigations of the passage's literary, rhetorical, and historical elements. Thus, one can identify several inherent difficulties within the text that are discussed repeatedly in the critical works yet seem to call for further examination:

1. the possible rhetorical-historical situation(s) that gave rise to the text;
2. the extent of the rhetorical unit(s) within Hos 2;
3. the basic form(s) presupposed by and reflected in the text; and
4. the meaning and background of the chapter's major metaphors.

There is also a methodological dimension that warrants a fresh treatment of the prophetic material in Hos 2. Among the many voices in the interpretive conversation about this text that will be outlined in the following pages, one perspective has been largely ignored. The method of analysis that can be called "rhetorical criticism" offers a unique way of thinking about who the prophet Hosea was and how the words now found in Hos 2:1–25 may have functioned in the service of a larger rhetorical project. The rhetorical criticism referred to here does not focus on the study of stylistics but on the classical conception of rhetoric as the art of persuasion undertaken in particular rhetorical-historical situations. A reading of Hos 2 from this methodological perspective works from the notion that the prophets of Israel may have functioned in a manner similar to the orators of ancient Greece. Prophets like Hosea may have delivered extended rhetorical discourses (rather than short, isolated statements) that attempted to discern the meaning of contemporary events, forewarn others, and persuade an audience to a particular viewpoint or course of action. Prophetic speech should thus be investigated specifically in light of its possible persuasive goals and rhetorical-historical circumstances. Such a rhetorical analysis has much to add to the various voices in the interpretive discussion and can offer a fresh, intentionally comprehensive, reading of the entirety of Hos 2:1–25.

2. MAJOR ISSUES IN THE HISTORY OF INTERPRETATION

To help situate this study, it is useful to consider how previous analyses have treated the metaphors and rhetoric of Hos 2. Such treatments have primarily been confined to limited examinations as part of commentaries or in the form of articles, rather than full scale investigations.[2] The scholarly works which have come the closest to such an analysis situate their discussions of Hos 2 within a larger examination of chapters 1–3.[3] This trend is surprising since the majority of the redactional theories for the book of Hosea propose that all or part of Hos 2 originally existed independently of chapters 1 and 3.[4]

The major difficulties within the text outlined above provide helpful categories for reviewing the study of Hos 2.[5]

---

[2] For helpful but dated overviews of the history of interpretation of both chapter 2 and the book as whole, see J. Craghan, "The Book of Hosea: A Survey of Recent Literature on the First of the Minor Prophets," *BTB* 1 (1971): 81–100, 145–70 and G. Yee, *Composition and Tradition in the Book of Hosea* (SBLDS 102; Atlanta: Scholars Press, 1987), 1–25. More recently, see Alice A. Keefe, *Woman's Body and the Social Body in Hosea* (Gender, Culture, Theory 10; JSOTSup 338; Sheffield: Sheffield Academic Press, 2001), 9–103.

[3] See R. Abma, *Bonds of Love: Methodic Studies of Prophetic Texts with Marriage Imagery (Isaiah 50:1–3 and 54:1–10, Hosea 1–3, Jeremiah 2–3)* (SSN; Assen: Van Gorcum, 1999); G. Baumann, *Love and Violence: Marriage as Metaphor for the Relationship between YHWH and Israel in the Prophetic Books* (trans. L. Maloney; Collegeville, Minn.: Liturgical Press, 2003); G. Blankenbaker, "The Language of Hosea 1–3" (Ph.D. diss., Claremont Graduate School, 1976); Keefe, *Woman's Body*; Y. Sherwood, *The Prostitute and the Prophet: Hosea's Marriage in Literary-Theoretical Perspective* (JSOTSup 212; Sheffield: Sheffield Academic Press, 1996); R. Törnkvist, *The Use and Abuse of Female Sexual Imagery in the Book of Hosea: A Feminist Critical Approach to Hos 1–3* (Uppsala Women's Studies A; Women in Religion 7; Uppsala: Acta Universitatis Upsaliensis, 1998); G. Yee, *Poor Banished Children of Eve: Woman as Evil in the Hebrew Bible* (Minneapolis: Fortress, 2003).

[4] See M. Buss, *The Prophetic Word of Hosea* (BZAW 111; Berlin: Töpelmann, 1969), 33–34; W. Harper, *A Critical and Exegetical Commentary on Amos and Hosea* (ICC; Edinburg: T&T Clark, 1905), clxii; J. Jeremias, *Der Prophet Hosea* (ATD 24; Göttingen: Vandenhoeck & Ruprecht, 1983), 18–19; A. Macintosh, *A Critical and Exegetical Commentary on Hosea* (ICC; Edinburg: T&T Clark, 1997), lxiii–lxix; J. Mays, *Hosea* (OTL; London: SCM, 1969), 15; H. H. Wolff, *Hosea* (Hermeneia; Philadelphia: Fortress, 1974), 33. But contrast F. Andersen and D. Freedman, who argue that the events in chapters 1 and 3 gave rise to the "fantasy" of chapter 2 (*Hosea* [AB 24; New York: Doubleday, 1985], 69).

[5] This review makes no effort to be exhaustive. For example, feminist critical readings that focus on images and portrayals of women in Hos 2 have not been covered here since they are not directly relevant to the present examination. For a useful compilation of different feminist readings of Hos 2, see A. Brenner, ed., *A Feminist Companion to the Latter Prophets* (Sheffield: Sheffield Academic Press, 1995). Cf. The Bible and Culture Collective, *The Postmodern Bible* (New Haven: Yale University Press, 1995), 225–32. Works that center on feminist analysis but play a significant role in the argument of this study include the following: P. Day, "The Bitch Had It Coming to Her: Rhetoric and Interpretation in Ezekiel 16," *BibInt* 8 (2000): 231–54; F. van Dijk-Hemmes, "Imagination of Power and the Power of Imagination: An Intertextual Analysis of Two Biblical Love Songs: The Song of Songs and Hosea 2," *JSOT* 44 (1989): 75–88; A. Keefe, "The Female Body, the Body Politic, and the Land: A Sociopolitical Reading of Hosea 1–2," in *A Feminist Companion to the Latter Prophets* (ed. A. Brenner; Sheffield: Sheffield Academic Press, 1995), 70–100; F. Landy, "Fantasy and the Displacement of Pleasure: Hosea 2:4–17," in *A Feminist Companion to the Latter Prophets* (ed. A. Brenner; Sheffield: Sheffield Academic Press, 1995); T. Setel, "Prophets and Pornography: Female Sexual Imagery in Hosea," in *Feminist Interpretation of the Bible* (ed. L.

2.1 Possible Rhetorical-Historical Situation(s)

A first issue that has long occupied scholars deals with the general relationship of Hosea's prophecy to historical events.[6] This issue plays an important part in any discussion of possible rhetorical situations for Hos 2, and the majority of the major commentaries are historically oriented.[7] Among these major commentaries, there is a near consensus concerning the dating of Hosea's prophetic career.[8] Using the references to the kings of Israel and Judah in the superscription (1:1) and the reference to the "house of Jehu" in 1:4, most scholars situate Hosea's activity between the last years of Jeroboam II (ca. 750 B.C.E.) and the time of or just before the fall of Samaria (ca. 722 B.C.E.).[9] This view also usually associates descriptions in the early part of the book (e.g., 1:2–9; 2:4–15) with a time of prosperity believed to have existed during the reign of Jeroboam II.[10] The major exceptions to this consensus are the works of Harper

---

Russell; Philadelphia: Westminster, 1985), 86–95; M. Wacker, *Figurationen des Weiblichen im Hosea-Buch* (Herder's Biblische Studien 8; Freiburg: Herder, 1996); G. Yee, *Poor Banished Children;* G. Yee, "Hosea," in vol. 7 of *The New Interpreter's Bible* (eds. L. Keck, et al.; 12 vols.; Nashville: Abingdon, 1996); G. Yee, "Hosea," in *The Women's Bible Commentary* (eds. C. Newsom and S. Ringe; Louisville: Westminster John Knox, 1992), 195–202.

[6] For two recent articles that directly address the issues involved in reconstructing history from prophetic texts, see E. Ben Zvi, "Studying Prophetic Texts against Their Original Backgrounds: Pre-Ordained Scripts and Alternative Horizons of Research," in *Prophets and Paradigms: Essays in Honor of Gene M. Tucker* (ed. S. Reid; JSOTSup 229; Sheffield: Sheffield Academic Press, 1996), 125–35 and R. Melugin, "Prophetic Books and the Problem of Historical Reconstruction," in *Prophets and Paradigms: Essays in Honor of Gene M. Tucker* (ed. S. Reid; JSOTSup 229; Sheffield: Sheffield Academic Press, 1996), 63–78.

[7] Wolff perhaps best represents this orientation by asserting that historical events are the key to understanding all prophetic texts (*Hosea*, xxi). Clements also stresses that the book of Hosea is "intimately related to historical events" (R. Clements, "Understanding the Book of Hosea," *RevExp* 72 [1975]: 405–23). Cf. B. Anderson, *The Eighth Century Prophets* (Proclamation Commentaries; Philadelphia: Fortress, 1978), vii, xv.

[8] One must, of course, recognize that the various dates given for Hosea's ministry may emerge from the use of different chronological systems, and this fact, more than any other, may explain the variations in scholarly views.

[9] For this view, see B. Birch, *Hosea, Joel, and Amos* (Westminster Bible Companion; Louisville: Westminster John Knox, 1997), 8; T. Cheyne, *Hosea* (Cambridge Bible for Schools and Colleges; London: Cambridge University Press, 1884), 12; G. Davies, *Hosea* (OTG; Sheffield: Sheffield Academic Press, 1993), 14–15; D. Gowan, *Theology of the Prophetic Books* (Louisville: Westminster John Knox, 1998), 37; D. Hubbard, *Hosea: An Introduction and Commentary* (TOTC; Leicester: InterVarsity Press, 1989), 21, 23; Jeremias, *Der Prophet*, 17; G. Knight, *Hosea: God's Love* (TBC; London: SCM, 1960), 13; Macintosh, *Critical and Exegetical Commentary*, lxx; Mays, *Hosea*, 3; C. Pfeiffer, "Hosea," in *The Wycliffe Bible Commentary* (eds. C. Pfeiffer and E. Harrison; Chicago: Moody, 1962), 801; W. Rudolph, *Hosea* (KAT 13.1; Gütersloh: G. Mohn, 1966), 25; N. Snaith, *Amos, Hosea, and Micah* (Epworth Preacher's Commentaries; London: Epworth, 1956), 52; D. Stuart, *Hosea-Jonah* (WBC 31; Waco: Word Books, 1987), 8–14; Wolff, *Hosea*, xxi.

[10] For example, see Mays, *Hosea*, 4 and D. Sellin, *Das Zwölfprophetenbuch übersetzt und erklärt* (KAT; Leipzig: A. Deichertsche Verlagsbuchhandlung, 1922), 18.

and Andersen and Freedman, who significantly restrict Hosea's career to the
years 750 to 740 and exclude the period of the Syro-Ephraimitic war (734–731
B.C.E.).[11] In support of this exceptional view, Andersen and Freedman argue
that, while Hosea does mention Assyria and Egypt, Assyria does not yet play a
major role and remains only "in the wings." On the contrary, Hosea's oracles
focus on conflicts with Israel's immediate neighbors.[12]

Opinions about the date of Hos 2 and its relationship to historical events are
heavily dependent on theories of the formation and redaction of the text. The
consensus view regards at least the bulk of chapter 2 as reflecting the events of
the Syro-Ephraimitic war.[13] For example, Wolff takes the negative parts of Hos
2, which seem to reflect destruction, as representing the situation in Israel after
the Assyrian campaign in 734/733 B.C.E. His evidence involves the use of the
name "Jezreel" in the chapter and its connection with the struggle for the Jezreel
valley during the Syro-Ephraimitic conflict. Wolff asserts that Hosea's picture
of a future restoration in 2:18–25 reflects a present state of deportation and
deprivation that "would not have existed until after the fall of Pekah."[14] He even
maintains this position concerning Hos 2:1–3 and argues that it represents the
eschatological hope that emerged from the despair at the end of the Syro-
Ephraimitic war.[15]

More recent assessments of the importance of history for the book of Hosea
have objected to the notion of a strong relationship between prophetic texts and

---

[11] Harper, *Critical and Exegetical Commentary*, cxli; Andersen and Freedman, *Hosea*, 34–37. Cf. J.
Mauchline, who places the end of Hosea's public ministry just after the Syro-Ephraimitic war
("Hosea," in vol. 6 of *The Interpreter's Bible* [eds. G. Buttrick et al.; 12 vols.; Nashville: Abingdon,
1956], 553–63). McComiskey represents the opposite end of the dating spectrum by extending
Hosea's career down to the period of the accession of Hezekiah, which he dates to 716/15 (T.
McComiskey, ed., *The Minor Prophets: An Exegetical and Expository Commentary* [2 vols.; Grand
Rapids: Baker Book House, 1992], 3).

[12] Andersen and Freedman, *Hosea*, 34.

[13] F. Landy, *Hosea* (Readings: A New Biblical Commentary; Sheffield: Sheffield Academic Press,
1995), 16; Mays, *Hosea*, 3; Stuart, *Hosea-Jonah*, 57; Wolff, *Hosea*, 48.

[14] Wolff, *Hosea*, 48.

[15] Ibid; cf. Stuart, *Hosea-Jonah*, 57. One should note that while Wolff and Stuart situate Hos 2:1–3
in a general historical setting, they do not argue that the text reflects specific historical events.

The other portion of Hosea that has long been identified with the situation of the Syro-
Ephraimitic war is Hos 5:8–6:6. This identification goes back to the work of Alt and uses various
redactional schemes to explain the present arrangement of the book. See A. Alt, "Hosea 5:8–6:6: Ein
Kreig und seine Folgen in prophetischer Beleuchtung," in *Kleine Schriften zur Geschichte des
Volkes Israel II* (München: C. H. Beck, 1959), 163–87; repr. of *NKZ* 30 (1919): 537–68. Cf.
Hubbard, *Hosea*, 23; Mays, *Hosea*, 16; Rudolph, *Hosea*, 25. See also Jeremias (*Der Prophet*, 17),
who dates all of Hos 5:8–9:9 to the Syro-Ephraimitic war. P. Arnold takes a similar view of Hos 5:8–
6:6 but argues that it represents the north attacking the south rather than Alt's view of southern
aggression (P. Arnold, *Gibeah: The Search for a Biblical City* [JSOTSup 79; Sheffield: JSOT Press,
1990], 110–19).

historical events. Melugin has recently advanced this argument for all prophetic texts.[16] He identifies three "forms of doubt" concerning the possibility of using historical criticism on prophetic texts: 1) historical reconstructions often go beyond the available evidence, 2) the recovery of the past from written texts may be epistemologically impossible, and 3) the language of the text itself resists historical investigation because of its metaphorical character. Melugin concludes that interpreters can know the historical background of prophetic texts only at the level of plausibility, that is, only in "the vaguest of terms."[17]

Garrett's recent commentary on Hosea proceeds in a similar vein and argues that an interpreter "cannot easily correlate any text in Hosea with any known event of history."[18] Nissinen also does not try to date Hosea's oracles to events in the eighth century but only attempts to date units by their times of redaction.[19] Like Melugin, Weems notes that important evidence leading to this approach is the poetical and metaphorical nature of the book of Hosea and its failure to yield any clear historical conclusions: "A fundamental feature of poetry is its metaphorical nature; and the fact that it is metaphorical, in many instances, mitigates against one's ability to adduce precise historical data."[20]

One recent study on the whole book of Hosea that attempts to bridge the gap between literary and historical approaches is that of James Trotter.[21] This book offers a reading of the final form of Hosea against the specific historical background of the early Achaemenid period (ca. 539–516 B.C.E.) in Yehud. Trotter tries to reconstruct the historical and social setting of this period and delineate the ways in which the oracles in the book functioned within that context. Several of Trotter's methodological points are relevant to the issue

---

[16] Melugin, "Prophetic Books," 63–78.

[17] Ibid., 64, 69, 72. Similarly, Ben Zvi asserts that the identification of historical settings for prophetic texts leads to restricting their richness, ambiguity, and meanings for other contexts. He specifically argues against the rhetorical-critical methodology that views texts like Hos 2 in terms of "oral proclamation," a "historical audience," and "public speech intended to convince" ("Studying Prophetic Texts," 133). Ben Zvi's arguments revolve around his claim that the implicit and explicit acceptance of the superscriptions of prophetic books as historically reliable has "pre-ordained" the historical interpretation of the texts (ibid., 125).

[18] D. Garrett, *Hosea, Joel* (NAC 19a; Nashville: Broadman & Holman, 1997), 24.

[19] M. Nissinen, *Prophetie, Redaktion und Fortschreibung im Hoseabuch: Studien zum Werdegang eines Prophetenbuches im Lichte von Hos 4 und 11* (AOAT 231; Kevelaer: Neukirchen-Vluyn, 1991), 56, 337–38.

[20] R. Weems, "Gomer: Victim of Violence or Victim of Metaphor?" *Semeia* 47 (1989): 88. This circumspection about the relationship between prophetic texts and history has led to several more recent works devoted to a purely literary approach to Hosea. Landy (*Hosea*) offers a final form study focused on the poetry in Hosea. See also H. Fisch, "Hosea: A Poetics of Violence," in *Poetry with a Purpose: Biblical Poetics and Interpretation* (ed. H. Fisch; Bloomington: Indiana University Press, 1988), 136–57.

[21] J. Trotter, *Reading Hosea in Achaemenid Yehud* (JSOTSup 328; Sheffield: Sheffield Academic Press, 2001).

under consideration here.[22] While asserting that his own reading will focus on the book's final redactional stage and its recontextualization of previous material for a new context, Trotter also acknowledges that the setting in which a prophetic oracle was first spoken and heard does represent a legitimate interpretive context. He also maintains that the problem with historical study of texts like Hosea is not its focus on the historical context or authorial intention but only its traditional practice of identifying the results of historical exegesis with the single, objective meaning of the text.[23] Given this caveat, Trotter has no problem offering an interpretation of how Hosea's speeches functioned within the rhetorical-historical context of the Persian period. In this way, it is difficult to see why the same possibilities could not exist for the prophet's own historical context in the eighth century B.C.E.

The objections to a close correlation of history and prophetic texts have been especially strong concerning the specific block of material in Hos 1–3. Several recent works do see a strong connection with historical events for most of Hosea's oracles but not for Hos 1–3.[24] Abma notes that Hos 1–3 is "not the sort of text to contain many references to a specific historical situation but rather consists of images and symbols and names used as signs. It is a poem and not a commentary to a specific historical situation."[25] The most important of the major commentaries to adopt this view is that of Andersen and Freedman. They offer an interpretation that resists dating the oracles and attempts to describe the literary characteristics of each section. They maintain this position because of the uncertainty concerning the historical framework of Hosea and the fact that one "can rarely identify people and events with any confidence."[26]

In spite of these recent arguments, the scholarly consensus is that texts like Hos 2 do reflect historical events, even if those events are difficult to reconstruct precisely. There are some historical references that yield possibilities for reconstruction and, as this work hopes to show, the text's own metaphors may provide information in this regard. Many arguments, like that of Weems, which stand against a historical understanding of Hosea's oracles, depend on assumptions about the unhistorical nature of metaphor in particular. Yet there are ways of understanding metaphor that allow one to work cautiously with historical references and say that the historical study of prophetic texts is useful "as long as the limitations described above are clearly recognized."[27] This study seeks to build on the long-standing view of the importance of historical

---

[22] See ibid., 9–14.

[23] Ibid., 12.

[24] See Birch, *Hosea, Joel, and Amos*, 9; Davies, *Hosea* (OTG), 39–40; J. Limburg, *Hosea-Micah* (IBC; Atlanta: John Knox, 1988), 3–4.

[25] Abma, *Bonds*, 167.

[26] Andersen and Freedman, *Hosea*, 73.

[27] Melugin, "Prophetic Books," 77.

background to understanding Hosea's prophecy by engaging the text in a rhetorical study that emphasizes the elements of audience and rhetorical situation. This approach to the chapter's metaphors and rhetoric may challenge the notion that Hos 2, a poetic and metaphorical text, cannot also be a discourse that reflects a particular historical situation. Such an investigation may answer some of the objections of Melugin and others by demonstrating that any historical reconstruction begins with the "horizon" put forth by the text itself and emphasizing that historical study is, quite appropriately, the product of a dynamic interaction between text and reader.

2.2 Rhetorical Unit(s) and Composition

A second aspect of the interpretation of Hosea is the formation and composition of the book, an aspect that influences the identification of the rhetorical units in chapter 2.[28] On the question of authenticity, scholarly views cover a wide range. At one end are those who identify a significantly large amount of the book as being from editors and situations in periods after the eighth century. For example, Harper excises many texts as late additions because he operates with the assumption that prophets originally spoke only messages of doom.[29] It is assumed that after Hosea himself wrote down some of his messages of judgment, various exilic and postexilic Judean redactors contributed large amounts of material.[30] Yee represents the most detailed and comprehensive attempt to separate the redactional layers of Hosea and to demonstrate that a large amount of the material in the book is not original to the prophet. She uses the criteria of difficulties in the text (repetitions, changes in person, etc.), contradictory themes, and the presence of later theological ideas to identify those texts from later redactions.[31] This position appears in a different way in the works of Kaufmann and Ginsberg. Observing the differences in content and

---

[28] For a helpful overview of theories of composition of the whole book, see Yee, *Composition*, 1–25.

[29] Harper, *Critical and Exegetical Commentary*, cliii. Cf. N. Snaith, *Mercy and Sacrifice: A Study of the Book of Hosea* (London: SCM, 1953), 15 and P. Borbone, *Il libro del Profeta Osea* (Torino: Silvio Zamorani, 1987), 39.

[30] This notion of Judean redactors is especially significant for consideration of the various references to Judah in the book (e.g., 2:1–3). Scholarly opinions about the authenticity of these references range from complete rejection of all references to acceptance of all references as original to attempts to distinguish between original and later references. Given the fact that the oracles in Hosea do not all come from the same historical situation, it seems best to analyze each reference to Judah on its own terms.

[31] Yee, *Composition*, 49. For instance, Yee (ibid., 77–79) concludes that 2:8–9 is an insertion by the latest redactor because it uses vocabulary that is similar to that of 3:4–5 and suddenly shifts to a second-person address, which she claims is characteristic of the redactor's insertions into received material. Cf. L. J. Regt, "Person Shift in Prophetic Texts: Its Function and Its Rendering in Ancient and Modern Translations" in *The Elusive Prophet: The Prophet as Historical Person, Literary Character, and Anonymous Artist* (ed. J. C. de Moor; OtSt; Leiden: Brill, 2001), 214–31.

themes between Hos 1–3 and 4–14, these scholars argue that the present book consists of the work of two different prophets in the ninth and eighth centuries B.C.E. respectively.[32] Ewald followed a similar position but attributed both parts of the book to the same prophet who worked in two different periods in the north.[33]

On the other end of the spectrum of views regarding authenticity, several scholars argue that the majority, if not the totality, of the oracles in the book are original to the prophet Hosea. These views often consider most or all of the references to Judah in the book to be original. Additionally, these positions tend to view the material in the book as closely preserving the actual oral preaching of the prophet.[34] As evidence in this regard, scholars note that the book contains oracles that are "artfully" composed and reflect prominent covenant curse and restoration blessing forms.[35] The remaining jaggedness of the text perhaps indicates an attempt to preserve original sayings while connecting them artfully (through catchwords, repetitions, etc.) and may thereby favor the material's originality.[36]

The consensus view occupies a middle ground. The majority of scholars see the book of Hosea as consisting partly of the *verba ipsissima* of the prophet from the eighth century B.C.E. but also including salvation oracles and some references to Judah from exilic and postexilic times. This position generally includes the view that an original collection of Hosea's preaching was taken to Judah after the fall of Samaria and was developed by Judean (and perhaps deuteronomistic) editors.[37] Wolff's commentary is representative of this view. He argues that the book developed from three different "transmission

---

[32] Y. Kaufmann, *The Religion of Israel* (abridg. and trans. M. Greenberg; Chicago: University of Chicago Press, 1960), 368–72; H. Ginsberg, "Hosea," *EncJud* 8: 1010–24. This view is also followed by J. Milgrom in *Leviticus 17–22: A New Translation with Introduction and Commentary* (AB 3a; New York: Doubleday, 2000), 1383.

[33] H. Ewald, *Amos, Hosea and Zechariah* (vol. 1 of *Commentary on the Prophets of the Old Testament*; trans. J. Smith; London: Williams & Norgate, 1875), 214.

[34] For example, Stuart suggests that one cannot easily challenge any of the book as inauthentic and that the material in Hosea represents "transcripts of the preaching of an orthodox northern prophet from the latter half of the eighth century B.C." (*Hosea-Jonah*, 14); so also Hubbard, *Hosea*, 31 and E. Pentiuc, *Long-Suffering Love: A Commentary on Hosea with Patristic Annotations* (Brookline, Mass.: Holy Cross Orthodox Press, 2002), 12.

[35] Stuart, *Hosea-Jonah*, 14. See also Macintosh, *Critical and Exegetical Commentary*, lxix. He argues that Hosea withdrew from public life around 733 and reworked and expanded his publicly delivered oracles (ibid., lxxiii). However, Macintosh does not include the references to Judah in this original writing by the prophet (ibid., lxx).

[36] See Buss, *Prophetic Word*, 35–36.

[37] Andersen and Freedman, *Hosea*, 53–59; H. Beeby, *Hosea: Grace Abounding* (ITC; Grand Rapids: Eerdmans, 1989), 1; Birch, *Hosea, Joel, and Amos*, 12; Cheyne, *Hosea*, 38; G. Davies, *Hosea* (NCB; Grand Rapids: Eerdmans, 1992), 36; Garrett, *Hosea, Joel*, 24; Jeremias, *Der Prophet*, 18; Rudolph, *Hosea*, 25; Mauchline, "Hosea," 563–64; Mays, *Hosea*, 15.

complexes" (chs. 1–3, 4–11, 12–14), which contain both Hosea's original words and materials from two different Judean redactions.[38] Emmerson offers the most detailed study of the redactional materials and the way in which they interact with the original materials in the book. She uses historical, linguistic, and theological criteria to identify Judean materials that now overlay the original texts and concludes that the redactional materials do not simply extend the prophet's original message but introduce new elements and change parts of the original materials.[39]

The significance of this issue for Hos 2 involves the question of how much of the text is original to the eighth-century Hosea and thus the question of how to identify the rhetorical units within the chapter. Both extremes, as well as the middle ground consensus, are represented in views of Hos 2. For example, earlier commentaries, like Harper's, considered less than half of the chapter to be original.[40] This view has been followed more recently by Yee, who attributes only 2:4aA, 2:4B–5, 2:7B, and 2:12 to Hosea.[41] On the other hand, there is a strong tradition that understands a large portion, if not all, of Hos 2 to be original. For example, Wolff sees all of Hos 2:4–17 as original to the prophet. Additionally, 2:1–3 and 2:18–25 represent actual words of Hosea that have been editorially placed into their present context.[42] Wolff's specific evidence includes the consistency and uniformity of vocabulary items, like comparisons with כְּ and the children's names, as well as the close connections in imagery and theme among the various parts of chapter 2.[43] One should note, however, that while Wolff does attribute nearly all of Hos 2 to the prophet, he does not argue that the entire chapter comes from the same historical situation. Rather, he takes the imagery in 2:4–17 as reflecting a literal "thriving economic situation" and therefore associates these verses with a period prior to the Syro-Ephraimitic war.[44]

There is somewhat of a consensus view regarding the rhetorical units in 2:4–25. The majority of scholars conclude that this section consists of two major rhetorical units from different rhetorical situations, but the exact divisions

---

[38] Wolff, *Hosea*, xxx–xxxi.

[39] G. Emmerson, *Hosea: An Israelite Prophet in Judean Perspective* (JSOTSup 28; Sheffield: JSOT Press, 1985), 1–5. Cf. T. Naumann, *Hoseas Erben: Strukturen der Nachinterpretation im Buch Hosea* (BWANT 131; Stuttgart: Kohlhammer, 1991).

[40] Harper considers 2:2a, c, d, 3, 5, 8f, 11f, 13, 17 (English versification) as original (*Critical and Exegetical Commentary*, cxliii).

[41] Yee, *Composition*, 55. She splits the remaining parts of chapter 2 between a Judean redactor during the Josianic period and a Judean redactor in the exilic period. For similar conclusions but with seven later supposed redactions of Hos 2, see J. Vermeylen, "Os 1–3 et son histoire littéraire," *ETL* 79 (2003): 23–52.

[42] Wolff, *Hosea*, 33. Cf. Mays, *Hosea*, 5; Stuart, *Hosea-Jonah*, 14. Jeremias's view is similar regarding 2:4–17, but he takes 2:18–25 as a later addition (*Der Prophet*, 19).

[43] Wolff, *Hosea*, 48.

[44] Ibid., 33.

between the units vary. For example, Mays, Stuart, and Wolff assert that 2:4–17 is a single speech from Hosea while 2:18–25 is a collection of various salvation oracles.[45] As evidence of a separate unit, these scholars generally point to a new focus on Baal and a move away from a focus on the wife in 2:18–25. At the same time, some commentators divide the chapter between verses 15 and 16.[46] This alternative division usually considers 2:16–17 part of the salvation section (2:18–25) and emphasizes the marker "oracle of Yahweh" that occurs at the end of 2:15. There are, however, those scholars who take all of 2:4–25 as a single rhetorical unit by stressing the general consistency of theme, imagery, and vocabulary throughout the section.[47]

There is a much stronger scholarly consensus regarding the separation of 2:1–3 from 2:4–25. Virtually all major interpreters consider 2:1–3 to be a separate rhetorical unit, which was subsequently joined to the material in 2:4–25.[48] Batten's assertion is representative and notes the typically cited evidence: "The first section 2 1–3 (Eng. 1 10–2 1) is a beautiful messianic prophecy painting in rosy colors an impressive picture of the restored unity and prosperity of the whole nation as in the days of David, and is usually assigned to the late post-exilic age."[49] This view of the separateness of 2:1–3 often stems from the problem of clearly identifying the conclusion of the story in Hos 1 and is reflected in the different chapter divisions in the Hebrew and English versions. Some scholars see 2:1–3 as the conclusion to the final oracle in chapter 1.[50]

Most interpreters who differ from this consensus do so by connecting Hos 2:3 with 2:4–25.[51] This grouping seems to go back to the LXX and Vulgate and generally considers 2:1–2 to be the conclusion to Hos 1. For example,

---

[45] Mays, *Hosea*, 15; Stuart, *Hosea-Jonah*, 45; Wolff, *Hosea*, 33. See also H. Krszyna ("Literarische Struktur von Os 2, 4–17," *BZ* 13 [1969]: 41–59), who argues that 2:4–17 is unified by a two-part chiastic structure.

[46] Macintosh, *Critical and Exegetical Commentary*, lxix; H. McKeating, *The Books of Amos, Hosea and Micah* (CBC; Cambridge: Cambridge University Press, 1971), 82; Pfeiffer, "Hosea," 803; Rudolph, *Hosea*, 64–65; Vermeylem, "Os 1–3," 28; J. Ward, *Hosea: A Theological Commentary* (New York: Harper & Row, 1966), 29, 41.

[47] For example, Clines asserts that, whether original or not, 2:4–25 now stands as "an integrated poem" (D. J. A. Clines, "Hosea 2: Structure and Interpretation," in *Studia Biblica/Sixth International Congress on Biblical Studies* [ed. E. Livingstone; JSOTSup 11; Sheffield: University of Sheffield Press, 1979], 83). Cf. Birch, *Hosea, Joel, and Amos*, 24–25; Davies, *Hosea* (OTG), 32; Snaith, *Amos*, 56.

[48] See Buss, *Prophetic Word*, 70; Jeremias, *Der Prophet*, 24; Macintosh, *Critical and Exegetical Commentary*, lxix; Mauchline, "Hosea," 565; Mays, *Hosea*, 36; Rudolph, *Hosea*, 55–59; Yee, *Composition*, 55.

[49] L. Batten, "Hosea's Message and Marriage," *JBL* 48 (1929): 269.

[50] Andersen and Freedman, *Hosea*, 201–2; Davies, *Hosea* (OTG), 32; Rudolph, *Hosea*, 26.

[51] Blankenbaker, "Language," 121; Knight, *Hosea*, 48; McComiskey, *The Minor Prophets*, 4; Pfeiffer, "Hosea," 803; M. Sweeney, *The Twelve Prophets* (2 vols.; Berit Olam; Collegeville: The Liturgical Press, 2000), 11–12.

Blankenbaker suggests that the כִּי clause in 2:2 closes off the statement from
2:3, while the imperatives in verses 3 and 4 suggest that they should be
considered together.[52] There are, however, some scholars who assert that all of
Hos 2:1–25 forms one rhetorical unit. Nonetheless, many of those who hold this
position accept 2:1–25 as a single unit only in its final redacted form.[53] The
arguments of Renaud represent the most complete statement of this position.[54]
He notes that the problem with arguments for the original unity of the whole
chapter is that they are often determined by the selection of what one considers
and what one does not when looking at Hos 2. He finds evidence for the
redactional unity of 2:1–25 in the form of a chiasmus that extends throughout
the whole chapter between the inclusio of the children's names in 2:1–3 and
2:23–25.[55]

In comparison with these redactional arguments, only Cassuto and Hubbard
seem to take 2:1–25 as the product of a single act of oral or written
composition.[56] These scholars find their evidence in a consistency in vocabulary
and imagery that runs throughout the whole chapter. For example, Cassuto
emphasizes the striking similarities in both the terms used and the situation
presupposed between 2:1–3 and 2:23–25. From these similarities he concludes
that "the verses mentioned are wonderfully suited to serve jointly as the
beginning and end of an address ... [and] their position should of itself be
evidence of their originality and indicate that they occupied their present place
from the outset."[57]

The open-ended debate concerning the composition and formation of Hos 2
provides an impetus for fresh study of the whole text and the ways in which the
metaphors and rhetoric work throughout. One particular facet of the debate over
composition and formation suggests the fruitfulness of a rhetorical-critical
approach to Hos 2. Many scholars who attribute large portions of the book to
the prophet himself also see these materials as originally having been public
pronouncements.[58] As evidence of this oracular nature, one may note, for
example, the prophet's use of the speech forms of legal contention or public
debate (e.g., רִיב in 2:4; 4:1; 12:3) and the use of a rhythmic parallelism in
many sayings (e.g., 2:4a, 5b, 8).[59] This observation invites an analysis that

---

[52] Blankenbaker, "Language," 122.

[53] Borbone, *Il libro*, 131; Garrett, *Hosea, Joel*, 35, 71; Snaith, *Mercy*, 27.

[54] B. Renaud, "Genèse et unitè redactionnelle de Os 2," *RevScRel* 54 (1980): 1–20.

[55] Ibid., 1–3.

[56] U. Cassuto, "The Second Chapter of the Book of Hosea," in vol. 1 of *Biblical and Oriental Studies* (trans. I. Abrahams; Jerusalem: Magnes, 1973), 101–3; Hubbard, *Hosea*, 31–32.

[57] Cassuto, "Second Chapter," 106.

[58] Buss, *Prophetic Word*, 33; Macintosh, *Critical and Exegetical Commentary*, lxii; Mays, *Hosea*, 5; Stuart, *Hosea-Jonah*, 8; Wolff, *Hosea*, xxii.

[59] See Wolff, *Hosea*, xxii–xxiv.

emphasizes persuasive oral discourse and the elements of speaker, audience, and shared rhetorical situation.

The effort to identify the rhetorical units within Hos 2, however, may perhaps be framed in a more helpful way. Rather than focusing on whether the oracle is "authentic" to a particular prophet, it may be more beneficial initially to consider whether it is the product of a single act of composition by one author/speaker.[60] Thus, a rhetorical analysis of Hos 2 may initially concern itself with the ways in which the rhetorical devices and metaphors run throughout the whole of the chapter, reconsider the dominant view of the isolation of 2:1–3, and explore the ways in which 2:1–25 may or may not be read as a single rhetorical speech in a particular situation.

2.3 Form and Image-base

A third question in research on Hos 2 concerns the form and image-base represented and presupposed by the text. This research usually looks to comparative texts from the ancient Near East and other biblical texts to shed light on the overall form of the chapter as well as on some of the specific imagery used therein. The term "image-base" refers here to the figures and symbols or practices and realities that fund the text's rhetoric. Such literal actions or figurative symbols provide the base from which Hos 2 draws its images.

The two areas of Hos 2 that have most attracted this type of study are the pronouncement in 2:4 and the descriptions of punishments against the wife in 2:5 and 12. A large number of scholars make mention of Akkadian and Elephantine marriage texts in attempting to decide whether Hos 2:4 represents an actual divorce formula. Additionally, many interpreters cite connections between the punishments for adultery mentioned in chapter 2 and those given in ancient Near Eastern legal texts like the Middle Assyrian laws, Nuzi tablets, and Code of Hammurabi. [61] For example, Kruger makes the general assertion that

---

[60] See B. Jones, *Howling Over Moab: Irony and Rhetoric in Isaiah 15–16* (SBLDS 157; Atlanta: Scholars Press, 1996), 89.

[61] Abma, *Bonds*, 16, 170; Buss, *The Prophetic Word*, 88; Cassuto, "Second Chapter," 122; Garrett, *Hosea, Joel*, 77–78; Harper, *Critical and Exegetical Commentary*, 227, 243; Jeremias, *Der Prophet*, 41, f.n. 5; Macintosh, *Critical and Exegetical Commentary*, 41–43; Mauchline, "Hosea," 577; McComiskey, *The Minor Prophets*, 32; E. Nwaoru, *Imagery in the Prophecy of Hosea* (Ägypten und Altes Testament 41; Wiesbaden: Harrassowitz, 1999), 141; Pfeiffer, "Hosea," 804; Stuart, *Hosea-Jonah*, 51; Wolff, *Hosea*, 34–37. Slightly different but similar approaches appear in the works of Braaten and Cheyne. Braaten uses a great deal of comparative study of ancient Near Eastern, Ugaritic, and Elephantine texts to explore the related concept of adoption and disownment of children and its relationship to the imagery in Hos 2 (L. Braaten, "Parent-Child Imagery in Hosea" [Ph.D. diss., Boston University, 1987], 1–5). Cheyne cites comparative German texts that stipulate stripping as a punishment for an adultress (*Hosea*, 48).

knowledge of the juridical principles that govern ancient Near Eastern marriage and divorce arrangements is essential for a proper understanding of the imagery in Hos 2.[62] He then cites evidence like the Babylonian document called the "Ḫana Marriage Text" and notes that it describes three stages of divorce that are similar to the imagery in Hos 2: 1) a divorce formula, 2) symbolic punishment (stripping), and 3) driving away of the wife from the husband's juridical responsibility.[63]

For this study, the conclusions reached by scholars in this area are not as important as the general approach they take. In spite of the attention that has been paid to Hos 2:4–5 and 12, this type of comparative study has not been sufficiently used by commentators. Many major commentaries do not even engage in this type of discussion of the chapter's forms and imagery.[64] The work that has been done has limited itself primarily to the study of divorce formulas in other comparative texts. Even the discussions noted above rarely take the form of an extensive engagement with the extrabiblical texts and often rely on secondary literature and appear only in footnotes. There is a lack of any detailed consideration of the ways in which ancient Near Eastern texts shed light on all the statements, stipulations, punishments, and promises throughout the whole of Hos 2. This gap is especially visible in relation to the evidence from Jewish marriage texts from Elephantine, which scholars seldom engage for more than a discussion of the divorce formula. Careful exploration of these Jewish texts may offer significant insight into the legal stipulations and language that lie behind Hos 2's imagery and inform its rhetoric.

2.4 The Major Metaphors

A final important aspect of the interpretation of Hos 2 is the identification of the main underlying issue or rhetorical focus of the prophet's speech. The interpretation of the text's major metaphors is intimately bound up with this issue. The long-standing and virtually unanimous scholarly consensus is that the text's metaphors characterize Israel's religious apostasy as participation in a fertility cult dedicated to the god Baal. Thus, the main rhetorical focus of Hos 2 is the religious syncretism and conflict between Baal worship and Yahweh worship in eighth-century Israel.[65] Mays's statements are representative: "From

---

[62] P. Kruger, "The Marriage Metaphor in Hosea 2:4–17 against Its Ancient Near Eastern Background," *OTE* 5 (1992): 7.

[63] Ibid., 13. For the original publication of the Ḫana Marriage text, see A. T. Clay, ed., *Babylonian Records in the Library of J. Pierpont Morgan IV* (New Haven: Yale University Press, 1923), 51, text 52, plate 48.

[64] For example, note Anderson, *Eighth Century Prophets*, 87; Knight, *Hosea*, 14–15; Mays, *Hosea*, 8–10; Sweeney, *The Twelve Prophets*, 1–5.

[65] Reconstructions of what was involved in this supposed Baal fertility cult vary greatly, including things like cultic prostitution, the defloration of virgins, ritual sex, etc.

the opening verses of ch. 1 to the concluding oracle in ch. 14, the cult and mythology of the god Baal is the foil of most of Hosea's sayings."[66] Nyberg perhaps represents the strongest statement of the consensus by arguing that the crisis addressed by Hosea was wholly religious and even the references to kings and princes in the book do not represent political leaders but a god named *melek* and associated deities.[67]

This consensus view dominates the interpretation of the text's major metaphors. Scholars generally identify the "wife/mother" with the people of Israel and the "lovers" with various manifestations of the god Baal. Accordingly, the metaphors of "fornication" and "adultery" seem to stand for religious apostasy and syncretism.[68] For example, Wolff specifically argues that the etymology of the verb אהב from a root meaning "to gasp, pant" establishes its metaphorical connection with the "extramarital love" taking place in the Baal fertility rituals condemned by Hosea.[69] Even those interpreters who see Hosea as focusing on political affairs and foreign alliances elsewhere in the book typically deny such a meaning to the major metaphors in Hos 2.[70]

Several recent monographs and articles directly address the study of the major metaphors in Hos 2 in this regard.[71] These works are especially concerned to investigate the metaphors in light of their backgrounds in ancient Near Eastern and biblical metaphorical traditions. Some of the more recent treatments also focus on reconstructing the possible situations behind the text's imagery. These works offer a more comprehensive, comparative, and wide-ranging examination of the metaphors, but they do not sufficiently explore or critique the dominant religious interpretation of those metaphors within the discourse of Hos 2. For example, both Stienstra and Abma stress the importance of exploring

---

[66] Mays, *Hosea*, 8. A large but still not comprehensive list of scholars who hold the common view includes the following: Andersen and Freedman, *Hosea*, 431–44; Beeby, *Grace Abounding*, 2; Birch, *Hosea, Joel, and Amos*, 9; M. Buss, "Tragedy and Comedy in Hosea," *Semeia* 32 (1984): 74; Davies, *Hosea* (OTG), 39–40; Garrett, *Hosea, Joel*, 80; Harper, *Critical and Exegetical Commentary*, cli; Knight, *Hosea*, 15; Limburg, *Hosea-Micah*, 11; Macintosh, *Critical and Exegetical Commentary*, xiii, 49; Mauchline, "Hosea," 554; McKeating, *Books*, 71; Pfeiffer, "Hosea," 801; Rudolph, *Hosea*, 81; Snaith, *Mercy*, 35; Stuart, *Hosea-Jonah*, 47–48; Sweeney, *The Twelve Prophets*, 30–32; Wolff, *Hosea*, 33–34; Yee, "Hosea" (*NIB*), 198.

[67] H. Nyberg, *Studien zum Hoseabuch* (UUA 6; Uppsala: A. B. Lundqvistska, 1935). Cf. A. Gelston, "Kingship in the Book of Hosea," in *Language and Meaning: Studies in Hebrew Language and Biblical Exegesis* (OtSt 19; Leiden: Brill, 1974), 72–73.

[68] For examples, see Stuart, *Hosea-Jonah*, 48 and Wolff, *Hosea*, 33–34. Scholars often assert that sexual rites like cultic prostitution lie at the heart of Hosea's metaphors. For example, see Stienstra, *YHWH Is the Husband of His People* (Kampen: Kok Pharos, 1993), 98–100; 139–41.

[69] Wolff, *Hosea*, 35.

[70] See Andersen and Freedman, *Hosea*, 431–44; Cheyne, *Hosea*, 22; Jeremias, *Der Prophet*, 40; Mauchline, "Hosea," 555; Mays, *Hosea*, 12; Ward, *Hosea*, 30.

[71] Abma, *Bonds*; Baumann, *Love and Violence*; Keefe, *Woman's Body*; Nwaoru, *Imagery*; Stienstra, *YHWH*; Törnkvist, *Use and Abuse*; Yee, *Poor Banished Children*.

the historical, cultural, and social background of metaphors like wife, husband, and marriage, as well as the importance of the influence of biblical traditions like covenant on the chapter's imagery.[72] They still maintain, however, the typical religious interpretation of the metaphors.[73]

The works of Keefe and Yee come the closest to presenting new perspectives by offering complex sociological readings. In studies that are similar in many ways to the present analysis of Hos 2, Keefe and Yee argue that there is no evidence to support the existence of a Baal fertility cult in Hosea's day nor did Hosea's metaphors of fornication and adultery refer to cultic sin or apostasy. Keefe sees the story of chasing after lovers as a reflection of Israel's acceptance of a new social organization based on royal land accumulation and the consequent dispossession of land owners.[74] In contrast to this study, Keefe uses an intertextual approach to link Hosea's sexual imagery with *social* conflicts in Hosea's day. She takes Hosea's unfaithful wife as a reference to social conflict in the body politic caused by increasing monarchical power and land consolidation going on in the time of Jeroboam II.

Yee operates with this sociological emphasis but suggests that the marriage and sexual metaphors in Hos 1–2 are condemnations of the ruling elite that address the interrelated areas of socioeconomics, politics, and cult.[75] She emphasizes much more than other recent interpreters the role of politics and foreign policy in the background of Hos 2's metaphors. Yee remains convinced, however, that Hosea primarily denounces an agricultural "mode of production" and that Baal worship and foreign policy are only expressions of this socioeconomic injustice. While Israel's rulers are the ultimate target of the prophet's discourse, Hosea is interested, it is argued, in the socioeconomic practices that lie behind their foreign policy and not in the policy itself.[76] Thus, the metaphors in Hos 2 represent no specific referent within the prophet's rhetorical situation but characterize the complex relations among social, political, and cultic realities: "Hosea symbolizes infractions in *any* of these domains through sexual imagery."[77]

---

[72] Stienstra, *YHWH*, 234; Abma, *Bonds*, 1.

[73] Stienstra, *YHWH*, 21; Abma, *Bonds*, 138.

[74] Keefe, "Female Body," 72–73, 93; Keefe, *Woman's Body*, 12–27.

[75] Yee, *Poor Banished Children*, 81–109. See also her earlier study, "'She Is Not My Wife and I Am Not Her Husband': A Materialist Analysis of Hosea 1–3," *BibInt* 9 (2004): 345–83.

[76] Yee (*Poor Banished Children*, 81–83) sees Hosea as a member of a "Yahweh Alone" movement opposed to a "foreign-tributary mode of production" in Israel in the eighth century. This mode of production involved royal latifundialization, political instability, external political treaties, and religious conflicts with polytheism.

[77] Ibid., 91; emphasis added. Similarly, Törnkvist (*Use and Abuse*, 14–15) asserts that the historical interpretation of Hosea's imagery has been overemphasized, and she stresses a social and cultural reading. Other works in this sociological strand of interpretation include M. Chaney, "Agricultural Intensification as Promiscuity in the Book of Hosea," (paper presented at the annual meeting of the AAR/SBL, Washington D.C., 1993); R. Coote and M. Coote, *Power, Politics, and the Making of the*

In light of these works, one can observe three possible interpretations of the main rhetorical issue and metaphorical imagery in Hos 2: 1) cultic interpretation (a Baal fertility cult), 2) socioeconomic interpretation, and 3) historical-political interpretation. Of these three, the first holds nearly complete sway while the third is rarely carefully considered and usually excluded from discussion of the first three chapters of the book.

From this review, one senses that there is currently a dominant way of reading Hos 2 that is rarely challenged or even critically examined. This reading identifies a rhetorical unit that includes only verses 4–25 and does not engage comparative ancient Near Eastern and extrabiblical Jewish texts and traditions beyond the question of genre. Accordingly, the dominant view interprets the chapter's metaphors and imagery in an exclusively religious way and sees the major rhetorical issue and historical situation as an eighth-century religious conflict between the worship of Yahweh and the allegiance to a Baal fertility cult.

3. TOWARD A NEW PROPOSAL

Although the above interpretation represents the dominant view, the preceding review has revealed that recent works are offering several new suggestions that challenge the long-standing consensus. First, as noted above, there have been various unconnected arguments for considering Hos 2:1–3 as an important, and perhaps even original, part of the rhetorical unit.[78] These observations mostly rely on the evidence of linguistic, semantic, and thematic connections among the various parts of chapter 2. They do not usually integrate this discussion with an exploration of larger issues like the rhetorical situation and image-base. Additionally, but independently, there have been arguments for extending the discussion of the ancient Near Eastern and extrabiblical Jewish legal background for the imagery throughout the whole of Hos 2 and not simply with regard to the basic form. For example, Kruger broadens the use of comparative marriage and legal texts, like those from Elephantine, to explain the imagery involving sustenance, provisions, and gifts throughout the text.[79] The

---

Bible: An Introduction (Minneapolis: Fortress, 1990), 43, 49–50; L. Wallis, *God and the Social Process* (Chicago: University of Chicago Press, 1935), 9–10, 155–282.

[78] Most explicitly, see Cassuto, "Second Chapter," 101–3 and Hubbard, *Hosea*, 31–32. But see also suggestions in this direction by Garrett, *Hosea, Joel*, 35, 71 and Snaith, *Mercy*, 27. Yet some new studies continue to reformulate the traditional view (see Vermeylem, "Os 1–3," 24–28).

[79] Kruger, "Marriage Metaphor." Braaten also broadens the discussion to include study of comparative texts from Elephantine, Ugarit, and other parts of the ancient Near East that have implications for the parent-child and disownment/adoption imagery in Hos 1–3 (Braaten, "Parent-Child").

discussions of Kruger and others call into question a strictly cultic interpretation of this part of the text's imagery.

Other recent works have independently challenged the theory of the existence of a widespread Baal fertility cult in Hosea's day. Many of these works question individual elements of this dominant hypothesis and do so from outside Hosea studies.[80] Tigay has even gone so far as to argue that onomastic and inscriptional evidence does not support the existence of any kind of widespread Baal cult in the latter part of the eighth century.[81] These challenges have generated a new interest in studying Hos 2 against its social, historical, and political background.[82]

A final area in which recent works are pushing in new directions involves the interpretation of the major metaphors in Hos 2. Several studies have dealt with the issue of the identity of the wife/mother in the text and have suggested that the proper referent is not the people of Israel as a whole but the capital city Samaria.[83] While not often explicitly connected, these suggestions relate to another set of newer arguments that understand the metaphors of "lovers" and "fornication" as predominantly political rather than religious images.[84] Various studies see these political metaphors in service of larger social or economic critiques but hint at the importance of the political dimension of the text's rhetoric. Yee's recent work especially moves in these directions by emphasizing the convergence of cult, socioeconomics, and politics in Hosea's metaphors.[85] She does not, however, parse the oracle's metaphors in the specific ways allowed by a comparative and comprehensive analysis from a rhetorical perspective.

---

[80] See Yee, *Poor Banished Children*, 85–92 and the works of Oden, Frymer-Kensky, Westenholtz, and Bird referred to in Keefe, "Female Body."

[81] J. Tigay, *You Shall Have No Other Gods: Israelite Religion in Light of Hebrew Inscriptions* (HSS 31; Atlanta: Scholars Press, 1986).

[82] See Sweeney, *The Twelve Prophets*, 1–5 and Yee, *Poor Banished Children*, 85–92. Galambush has also suggested that perhaps political events involving the capital city of Samaria provided the impetus for Hosea's oracle. See J. Galambush, *Jerusalem in the Book of Ezekiel: The City as Yahweh's Wife* (SBLDS 130; Atlanta: Scholars Press, 1992), 49–50.

[83] See J. Schmitt, "The Gender of Ancient Israel," *JSOT* 26 (1983): 115–25; J. Schmitt, "The Wife of God in Hosea 2," *BR* 34 (1989): 5–18; and J. Schmitt, "Yahweh's Divorce in Hosea 2—Who Is That Woman?," *SJOT* 9 (1995): 119–32. See also M. Biddle, "The Figure of Lady Jerusalem: Identification, Deification, and Personification of Cities in the Ancient Near East," in *The Biblical Canon in Comparative Perspective* (eds. K. Younger, W. Hallo, and B. Batto; Lewiston: Edwin Mellen, 1991), 173–94 and A. Fitzgerald, "The Mythological Background for the Presentation of Jerusalem as a Queen and False Worship as Adultery in the Old Testament," *CBQ* 34 (1972): 403–16.

[84] For the clearest connection of the two arguments, see Galambush, *Jerusalem*, 49–50. Cf. Yee, *Composition*, 305–6 and Yee, *Poor Banished Children*, 90.

[85] Yee, *Poor Banished Children*, 94.

The present work attempts to build upon and integrate these new areas of research to investigate the overall rhetorical horizons, situations, and effects of Hos 2. These new independent observations invite a reexamination of the whole of Hos 2 that pays close attention to the unity and legal background of the oracle, as well as to the historical and political events and situations that may have provided the speech's rhetorical need and communicative power.

Consideration of these newer directions helps frame some major questions to explore. An overarching question that guides the present study focuses on the text's metaphors: How does an integrated and comparative analysis of Hos 2's major metaphors, in light of biblical and ancient Near Eastern metaphorical traditions, enable one to understand them and shed light on the overall rhetorical thrust of the chapter? Secondly, how can comparative texts relating to marriage and divorce influence the understanding of the imagery at work throughout the whole of chapter 2? How can the often neglected economic stipulations governing divorce in the Elephantine Jewish texts illuminate the image-base at work in the prophet's speech? Thirdly, can all of Hos 2 be taken as a single, original rhetorical unit, which comes from the same rhetorical situation? And fourthly, can one identify a specific historical background or series of events that illuminates the rhetorical situation presupposed by the text?

The major metaphors in Hos 2 provide the entryway into the overall rhetoric at work. Accordingly, following the discussion of methodology (ch. 2), this study divides into two main parts. Chapters 3 to 5 deal with each of the major metaphors in turn and offer an analysis of their potential meanings in the ancient rhetorical setting. Chapter 3 examines the overarching marriage metaphor and the base from which it is drawn. The discussion focuses on the ancient Near Eastern, especially the Elephantine, texts addressing marriage and divorce and their economic and property legalities. Chapters 4 and 5 investigate the metaphors of the wife/mother, fornication, adultery, lovers, and baal(s) (בעל) and try to identify the entities and actions to which these metaphors refer in Hosea's social context, as well as the various ways they may function rhetorically within the discourse itself.

Chapters 6 to 8 examine the rhetorical dimensions of Hos 2, including the unit and situation, and offer a reading of the oracle itself. Chapter 6 integrates the studies of the metaphors and takes up the question of the original unity of 2:1–25 and what that discourse suggests about the context and conditions against which the prophet spoke. Chapters 7 and 8 offer a comprehensive reading of Hosea's oracle in light of its metaphorical and rhetorical dimensions. Chapter 7 begins with a translation and textual discussion and treats the opening section of 2:1–3, and chapter 8 discusses the remaining section of 2:4–25.

By the end of this investigation, a particular thesis will have emerged. Not only does Hos 2:1–25 represent a unified discourse that contains an identifiable rhetorical aim, but it also addresses a particular rhetorical-historical situation in a theological and metaphorical way. Hosea 2 can fruitfully be understood as the prophet Hosea's metaphorical and theological commentary on the political affairs of Samaria and their implications for both Israel and Judah around the time of the close of the Syro-Ephraimitic war (731–730 B.C.E.).

2

RHETORIC AND METAPHOR IN HISTORICAL PERSPECTIVE

The complementary fields of rhetorical criticism and metaphor theory provide the primary methodology for an analysis of Hos 2 that examines the major metaphors in historical perspective. While the development and range of these fields are complex, the ways in which certain elements of rhetoric, particularly in its classical conception, and metaphor, particularly in its persuasive function, interact provide a useful approach to a text like Hos 2.

1. RHETORICAL CRITICISM AND PROPHETIC INTERPRETATION

Questions concerning Hos 2's aim, setting, audience, and effects naturally connect with the main foci of a rhetorical-critical approach to texts. The study of rhetoric has undergone many varied developments.[1] Nonetheless, the ancient

---

[1] For a recent survey of the history of rhetoric, see G. Kennedy, "Historical Survey of Rhetoric," in *Handbook of Classical Rhetoric in the Hellenistic Period 330 B.C.–A.D. 400* (ed. S. Porter; Leiden: Brill, 1997), 3–42. For an introduction to the classical development of rhetoric in ancient Greece and Rome, see H. Ryan, *Classical Communication for the Contemporary Communicator* (Mountain View, Ca.: Mayfield, 1992), 1–30. For a helpful summary of the basics of classical rhetoric and how one might apply them to biblical texts, see G. Kennedy, *New Testament Interpretation through*

association of rhetoric with persuasion remains central and, as the following discussion hopes to show, correlates most closely with the nature of prophetic texts like Hos 2.

1.1 Classical Rhetoric and Persuasion

The discipline commonly called "classical rhetoric" emerged in the fifth century B.C.E. with Corax of Syracuse and developed through the works of Plato and, most importantly, the formulations of Aristotle.[2] Although later writers like Cicero and Quintilian made important contributions to the study of rhetoric, the views of Aristotle came to be the dominant way of understanding the discipline.[3]

Aristotle's primary work on rhetoric was produced around 335–330 B.C.E. and represented a systematizing of rhetorical study.[4] He offered a definition of rhetoric that focused on the element of persuasion: "The faculty [power] of discovering in the particular case what are the available means of persuasion."[5] Seen in this way, rhetorical criticism was conceived of as the study of the ways in which a discourse attempts to persuade a given audience in a particular

---

Rhetorical Criticism (Chapel Hill: University of North Carolina Press, 1984), 3–38. For a survey of scholarship on rhetoric of various historical periods from the classical period up through the 1980s, see W. Horner, *The Present State of Scholarship in Historical and Contemporary Rhetoric* (Columbia: University of Missouri Press, 1990). For a more thorough and wide-ranging survey of the history and development of rhetoric in view of broader cultural and intellectual developments, especially the study of forms, see M. Buss, *Biblical Form Criticism in Its Context* (JSOTSup 274; Sheffield: Sheffield Academic Press, 1999), 31–155.

[2] E. Corbett, *Classical Rhetoric for the Modern Student* (2d ed.; New York: Oxford University Press, 1971), 595. Cf. Buss, *Biblical Form Criticism*, 41–43; G. Kennedy, *The Art of Persuasion in Greece* (Princeton: Princeton University Press, 1963), 26 and S. Foss, K. Foss, and R. Trapp, *Contemporary Perspectives on Rhetoric* (Prospect Heights, Ill: Waveland, 1985), 1.

[3] Cicero's main work on rhetoric was *De inventione* (87 B.C.E.) and Quintilian's main work was *Institutio oratoria* (93 C.E.). See H. M. Hubbell, ed. and trans., *Cicero, De inventione: De optimo genere dicendi: Topica* (LCL; Cambridge: Harvard University Press, 1949) and H. E. Butler, ed. and trans., *The Institutio Oratoria of Quintilian* (4 vols.; LCL; Cambridge: Harvard University Press, 1920–22).

[4] Kennedy observes ("Historical Survey," 3) that the earliest use of the Greek term ῥητορική is by Socrates in Plato's *Gorgias*, which dates from the second decade of the fourth century B.C.E. In this work, Socrates defines rhetoric as the "worker of persuasion." For a helpful overview and discussion of Aristotle's work on rhetoric, see E. Black, *Rhetorical Criticism: A Study in Method* (2d ed.; Madison: University of Wisconsin Press, 1978), 91–131.

[5] Aristotle, *Rhetoric* (trans. L. Cooper; New York: Appleton, 1932), 1355. Aristotle's understanding of rhetoric primarily restricted it to public oratory given before assemblies, lawcourts, etc., and the majority of later Greek and Roman writers on rhetoric followed him in this regard (Kennedy, "Historical Survey," 4).

situation.[6] Thus, the three main elements that dominated the concerns of classical rhetoric were the speaker or author, the speech or text, and the audience or reader.[7] Additionally, Aristotle highlighted three main aspects of rhetorical study: 1) analysis of types of arguments using ethos, pathos, and logos, 2) the use of topoi or lines of argument, and 3) emphasis on the audience as the guiding principle in persuasive discourse.[8] From these contributions, the other major themes of Aristotelian and later neo-Aristotelian criticism emerged: 1) the types of rhetorical discourses including forensic (judicial), deliberative, and epideictic, 2) the analytical categories of inventio, dispositio, and elecutio, and 3) a focus on the effects of a discourse on an immediate audience.[9]

The classical rhetoric developed in Greece and Rome was expanded slightly in the Middle Ages. The emphasis remained on rhetoric as persuasion but this type of rhetorical criticism came to be applied not simply to oratory but also to letter writing and other types of written discourse.[10] Rhetorical criticism primarily entailed the study of the means of persuasion (potential or actual) of any spoken discourse or written text.

This view of rhetoric as persuasion in terms of the Greek orators remained the dominant understanding of the discipline until the 1960s.[11] Around that time, critics began to suggest a variety of other understandings that shifted the emphasis away from persuasion and pointed to some of the problems with the classical definition.[12] Already in the 1500s, the French scholar Peter Ramus made a significant shift in rhetorical study by separating inventio and dispositio and limiting rhetoric to style and delivery, and many of the newer developments took their cue from this emphasis on stylistics.[13] Suggested broader understandings included an epistemic perspective, which sees rhetoric as the

---

[6] The majority of rhetorical scholars understand this element of persuasion to mean that a discourse is only persuasive in intent and not necessarily in accomplishment, since one is often unable to measure the results. See Black, *Rhetorical Criticism*, 15.

[7] For discussion of these elements in classical rhetoric, see P. Trible, *Rhetorical Criticism: Context, Method, and the Book of Jonah* (GBS; Minneapolis: Fortress, 1994), 8.

[8] Corbett, *Classical Rhetoric*, 599.

[9] Black, *Rhetorical Criticism*, 31; Buss, *Biblical Form Criticism*, 41–43.

[10] Corbett, *Classical Rhetoric*, 31, 603.

[11] See L. Cooper, who asserts, "Rhetoric, not only of Cicero and Quintilian, but of the Middle Ages, of the Renaissance, and of modern times, is, in its best elements, essentially Aristotelian" (quoted in Corbett, *Classical Rhetoric*, 599).

[12] For examples of these critiques, see Black, *Rhetorical Criticism*, x–xiv; 90. Cf. J. Andrews, *The Practice of Rhetorical Criticism* (New York: Macmillan, 1983), 11 and R. Scott and B. Brock, *Methods of Rhetorical Criticism: A Twentieth–Century Perspective* (New York: Harper & Row, 1972), 13.

[13] Corbett, *Classical Rhetoric*, 611; cf. Buss, *Biblical Form Criticism*, 105–7. Several scholars take this development as an indication that there are two fundamentally different traditions within rhetorical study: the Aristotelian/Ciceronian tradition and the Ramistic tradition. For example, see Trible, *Rhetorical Criticism*, vii and M. Nichols, *Rhetoric and Criticism* (Baton Rouge: Louisiana State University Press, 1963), vi–vii.

creation of knowledge rather than the communication of truth, and a fantasy-theme perspective, which assumes that people use rhetoric to construct a social-reality or world view.[14]

These new directions actually served to enhance the classical conception of rhetoric as persuasion rather than to invalidate it.[15] For example, the "new rhetoric" articulated by Perelman and Olbrechts-Tyteca argued against the notion that listeners only play the role of spectators and emphasized an audience-oriented criticism, which focused on the social aspects of the discourse and audience.[16] But this approach focused on dialectical interaction with the audience for the purposes of argumentation and persuasion. Perelman and Olbrechts-Tyteca concluded with a statement that can guide rhetorical analysis of many ancient texts, including those like Hos 2, which make much use of metaphors and symbolic traditions: "All language is language of a community.... The terms used, their meaning, their definition, can only be understood in the *context* of the habits, ways of thought, methods, external circumstances, and *traditions* known to the users of those terms."[17]

One of the most significant aspects of this classical rhetorical tradition is what has come to be designated the "rhetorical situation." This concept emerged from the assumption that, since rhetoric attempts to persuade, it originates within and presupposes a certain situation. The major formulation of the concept of rhetorical situation appeared in the work of Bitzer. He noted that rhetoricians had focused primarily on examining the process through which discourses were

---

[14] For a helpful summary of newer approaches, see Foss, Foss, and Trapp, *Contemporary Perspectives*, 250–56. Cf. Scott and Brock, *Methods*, 15–22; 127; 261–64. There are many examples of these new, broader understandings of rhetorical criticism. For instance, I. A. Richards, already in the 1930s, expressed concern with too limited a focus on persuasion and argued for a new rhetorical study that focused on the laws of the use of language (see discussion in Foss, Foss, and Trapp, *Contemporary Perspectives*, 20–21). More recently, Wayne Booth sought a rhetorical criticism with no strict boundaries, which examines various elements like advertising, television, and fiction to see how they shape people and society. See W. Booth, "The Scope of Rhetoric Today: A Polemical Excursion," in *The Prospect of Rhetoric* (eds. L. Bitzer and E. Black; Englewood Cliffs, N.J.: Prentice-Hall, 1971), 93–114. See further K. Burke, *A Rhetoric of Motives* (New York: Prentice-Hall, 1950); H. Johnstone, "Some Trends in Rhetorical Theory," in *The Prospect of Rhetoric* (eds. L. Bitzer and E. Black; Englewood Cliffs, N.J.: Prentice-Hall, 1971), 78–90; J. Kinneavy, "Contemporary Rhetoric," in *The Present State of Scholarship in Historical and Contemporary Rhetoric* (ed. W. Horner; Columbia: University of Missouri Press, 1990), 186–246.

[15] The main contribution even of twentieth-century rhetoric has been a multidimensional emphasis on relationality and cooperation instead of a single focus on persuasion and manipulation in rhetorical discourse. For example, Burke's concept of "identification" stresses a relational and interactive approach to rhetoric. Cf. Foss, Foss, and Trapp's cooperative rhetoric (*Contemporary Perspectives*, 287–89).

[16] See C. Perelman, "The New Rhetoric," in *The Prospect of Rhetoric* (eds. L. Bitzer and E. Black; Englewood Cliffs, N.J.: Prentice-Hall, 1971), 115–22 and C. Perelman and L. Olbrechts-Tyteca, *The New Rhetoric: A Treatise on Argumentation* (Notre Dame: University of Notre Dame Press, 1969).

[17] Perelman and Olbrechts-Tyteca, *New Rhetoric*, 513; emphasis added.

created without exploring the nature of the situations for which they were created.[18] Bitzer defined a rhetorical situation as

> a complex of persons, events, objects, and relations presenting an actual or potential exigency [i.e., an imperfection, lack, need, etc.] which can be completely or partially removed if discourse, introduced into the situation, can so constrain human decision or action as to bring about the significant modification of the exigency.[19]

This definition identified the situation as the primary factor that calls forth the particular discourse. Bitzer asserted that rhetoric is always situational and does not simply concern itself with the speaker's intention, artistry, or language but with the interaction between persons and their circumstances.[20] Thus, the rhetorical situation contained both objective factors, which are external to the speaker or writer, and subjective factors, which include the speaker's or writer's perspectives, beliefs, etc.[21] The reader must explore these possible factors, contexts, and exigencies and the ways in which they contribute to an understanding of any text's rhetorical aspects.

Some scholars have questioned the relevance of the concept of the rhetorical situation for the reconstruction of the historical situations of biblical texts.[22] Indeed, Bitzer's original concept presents some problems for reading prophetic texts in particular. First, Bitzer asserts that the historical situation is always primary and calls forth a discourse that reflects it.[23] This view does not consider the ability of rhetorical language, even that language within an ancient

---

[18] L. Bitzer, "The Rhetorical Situation," in *Rhetoric: A Tradition in Transition* (ed. W. Fisher; Ann Arbor: University of Michigan Press, 1974), 248; repr. of *Philosophy and Rhetoric* 1 (1968): 1–14.

[19] Ibid., 252.

[20] See L. Bitzer, "Functional Communication: A Situational Perspective," in *Rhetoric in Transition: Studies in the Nature and Views of Rhetoric* (ed. E. White; University Park: Penn State University Press, 1980), 21–38. For examples of other rhetoric scholars who follow Bitzer's views, see Andrews, *Practice*, 9–19 and H. Wichelns, "The Literary Criticism of Oratory," repr. in *Speech Criticism: Methods and Materials* (ed. W. Linsley; Dubuque, Iowa: Brown, 1968), 32.

[21] M. Fox, "The Rhetoric of Ezekiel's Vision of the Valley of the Bones," *HUCA* 51 (1980): 1–15 (repr. in *The Place Is Too Small for Us: The Israelite Prophets in Recent Scholarship* [ed. R. Gordon; SBTS 5; Winona Lake, Ind.: Eisenbrauns, 1995], 176–90).

[22] See T. Olbricht, "Classical Rhetorical Criticism and Historical Reconstructions: A Critique," in *The Rhetorical Interpretation of Scripture: Essays from the 1996 Malibu Conference* (eds. S. Porter and D. Stamps; JSOTSup 180; Sheffield: Sheffield Academic Press, 1999), 108–24 and D. Watson, "The Contributions and Limitations of Greco-Roman Rhetorical Theory for Constructing the Rhetorical and Historical Situations of a Pauline Epistle," in *The Rhetorical Interpretation of Scripture: Essays from the 1996 Malibu Conference* (eds. S. Porter and D. Stamps; JSOTSup 180; Sheffield: Sheffield Academic Press, 1999), 125–51.

[23] For example, Bitzer states, "The presence of rhetorical discourse obviously indicates the presence of a rhetorical situation.... [I]t is the situation which calls the discourse into existence" ("Rhetorical Situation," 248).

text, to create a particular worldview or perceived situation that may be contrary to actual circumstances.[24] For example, Vatz notes that a discourse may be "created" by the rhetor in order to control a situation.[25] One should not simply assume an exact correspondence between a text's rhetorical description and historical setting. This connection must be carefully set out through wide-ranging literary and historical analysis.

A second problem with the application of Bitzer's conception to prophetic texts emerges from his contention that an audience must be capable of being persuaded in order for a discourse to be analyzed as rhetorical.[26] As Jones notes, this definition of a rhetorical situation is too limited and demands an immediate knowledge of the audience not available to readers of prophetic texts.[27] Bitzer's view also seems to exclude consideration of the shared symbolic traditions of the speaker and audience, which may be at play in a richly metaphorical text like Hos 2.[28] Bitzer focuses attention on only one aspect of the interaction among speaker, audience, and situation.[29]

Since there are some problems in applying Bitzer's proposal to prophetic texts, it is necessary to employ a slightly modified concept of the rhetorical situation in the analysis of texts such as Hos 2. Watson argues that the term "rhetorical situation" is not equivalent to a text's historical situation.[30] Rather, the rhetorical situation should be thought of as a distinct textual phenomenon that is "rooted" in the historical situation:

> The rhetorical situation is an evaluative construction derived from and seeking to change the facts of the historical situation. The historical situation has provided the facts from which the rhetor has interpreted and created an exigence based on personal and audience interest.[31]

---

[24] Cf. the "epistemic" and "fantasy-theme" approaches to rhetoric. An example of this critique from within biblical studies can be seen in the study of the book of Revelation. As opposed to the long-standing view that the book's rhetoric *reflects* a situation of persecution, some recent interpreters assert that the language is attempting to create the perception of a crisis in the midst of a situation characterized by complacency and accommodation. See L. Thompson, *The Book of Revelation: Apocalypse and Empire* (New York: Oxford University Press, 1990), 95–170.

[25] R. Vatz, "The Myth of the Rhetorical Situation," *Philosophy and Rhetoric* 6 (1973): 154–61. Cf. Watson, "Contributions," 128.

[26] Bitzer, "Rhetorical Situation," 252–53.

[27] Jones, *Howling*, 225–27.

[28] Ibid.

[29] For example, Bitzer states, "Not the rhetor and not persuasive intent, but the situation is the source and ground of rhetorical activity— and, I should add, of rhetorical criticism" ("Rhetorical Situation," 252).

[30] Watson, "Contributions," 129.

[31] Ibid.

In this view, the "rhetorical situation" denotes a textual phenomenon similar to an implied situation, which one must first reconstruct before examining possible historical situations for a given text.

Watson's use of the label "rhetorical situation," however, seems radically dissimilar from Bitzer's original formulation, which maintained an equivalence between the rhetorical and historical situation. Accordingly, it seems best to distinguish not between a text's rhetorical and historical "situations" but between a text's "rhetorical horizon" and "rhetorical-historical situation." The rhetorical horizon is a construct of the text that uses and reflects certain portions of the data from the rhetorical-historical situation. As Watson affirms, the main goal of rhetorical analysis of a text would then be to offer a "hypothetical construction" of the historical situation by first examining a text's rhetorical horizon.[32] Elements of a text's rhetorical horizon include such things as the genres, problems addressed, types of argumentation, identities of addressees, and values expressed.[33] This rhetorical horizon illuminates the type of rhetorical-historical situation in which the text may have functioned.

The label "rhetorical-historical situation" should thus be understood only in the sense of the general historical occasion believed to provide the context in which the original discourse was constructed.[34] This slight modification takes into account the power of rhetorical language to function in diverse ways in a given situation and respects the unavailability of specific details concerning the cognitive makeup of the original audience. The reader of prophetic texts may focus on reconstructing the rhetorical horizon presupposed by the text and then seek a rhetorical-historical situation that explains the text's rhetorical horizon.[35]

1.2 Classical Rhetoric and Biblical Studies

Rhetorical criticism as a separate discipline within biblical studies came to prominence in the twentieth century with James Muilenburg's 1968 address to the Society of Biblical Literature.[36] Consequently, rhetorical criticism in biblical studies after 1968 has focused nearly exclusively on Muilenburg's approach.[37]

---

[32] Ibid., 131.

[33] Ibid., 132.

[34] Jones, *Howling*, 225–27.

[35] C. Shaw, "The Speeches of Micah: A Rhetorical-Historical Analysis" (Ph.D. diss., Emory University, 1990), 21–25; repr. as *The Speeches of Micah: A Rhetorical-Historical Analysis* (JSOTSup 145; Sheffield: JSOT Press, 1993).

[36] J. Muilenburg, "Form Criticism and Beyond," repr. in *Beyond Form Criticism: Essays in Old Testament Literary Criticism* (ed. P. House; SBTS; Winona Lake, Ind.: Eisenbrauns, 1992), 49–69.

[37] C. Black, "Keeping Up with Recent Studies XVI: Rhetorical Criticism and Biblical Interpretation," *ExpTim* 100 (1988–89): 252–58; Trible, *Rhetorical Criticism*, 48. For examples of the use of various types of rhetorical criticism in the analysis of biblical texts, see the essays in S. Porter and D. Stamps, eds., *The Rhetorical Interpretation of Scripture: Essays from the 1996 Malibu Conference* (JSOTSup 180; Sheffield: Sheffield Academic Press, 1999); S. Porter and T. Olbricht,

Muilenburg's application of rhetorical theory to biblical texts emphasized a transition from a focus on historical background issues to a focus on the text itself. He attempted to supplement form criticism with attention to the unique elements and formulations of specific texts.[38] Nonetheless, Muilenburg's approach included a significant historical aspect tied to the analysis of the interaction between the rhetorical discourse and the original author.[39] He originally emphasized the use of stylistics and aesthetic criticism in order to uncover the "fabric of the *writer's* thought."[40]

In spite of this original historical concern, Muilenburg's rhetorical study developed in such a way as to be primarily defined as the investigation of "the characteristic linguistic and structural features of a particular text in its present form, *apart from* its generic rootage, social usage, or historical development."[41] He himself ultimately defined his approach in this way:

> What I am interested in, above all, is in understanding the nature of Hebrew literary composition, in exhibiting the structural patterns that are employed for the fashioning of a literary unit, whether in poetry or prose, and in discerning the many and various devices by which the predications are formulated and ordered into a unified whole. Such an enterprise I should describe as rhetoric and the methodology as rhetorical criticism.[42]

This type of analysis focused on a text's formal structures and stylistics and simply presented the rhetorical features.[43] In this sense, Muilenburg's approach basically equated rhetorical criticism with all synchronic literary analyses.[44] The work of Trible represents a primary example of Muilenburg's approach. As this approach developed through her and other Muilenburg students, it became more and more detached from historical investigations.[45]

---

eds., *Rhetoric, Scripture, and Theology: Essays from the 1994 Pretoria Conference* (JSOTSup 131; Sheffield: Sheffield Academic Press, 1996); M. Warner, ed., *The Bible as Rhetoric: Studies in Biblical Persuasion and Credibility* (Warwick Studies in Philosophy and Literature; London: Routledge, 1990).

[38] Muilenburg, "Form Criticism," 55.

[39] Ibid., 54–55.

[40] Ibid., 56; emphasis added. One of Muilenburg's main criticisms of form criticism was that it resisted historical commentary on texts and was too skeptical about interpreting texts in their historical contexts (ibid., 54).

[41] W. Roth, "Rhetorical Criticism, Hebrew Bible," *DBI* 2:397; emphasis added.

[42] Muilenburg, "Form Criticism," 57.

[43] Fox, "Rhetoric," 176; cf. Bible and Culture Collective, *Postmodern Bible*, 149–50.

[44] For example, see M. Kessler, "A Methodological Setting for Rhetorical Criticism," *Semitics* 4 (1974): 22–36. See also T. Dozeman, "Old Testament Rhetorical Criticism," *ABD* 5:712–15.

[45] See Trible, *Rhetorical Criticism*, vii–viii. One should also note that the works of Roland Meynet represent another major approach to rhetorical analysis of the Bible that does not focus on history or classical rhetoric yet is different from Muilenburg's criticism (R. Meynet, *Rhetorical Analysis: An*

Although Muilenburg's application of a rhetorical criticism focused on style dominated biblical studies after 1968, some scholars began to challenge it as too narrow and too dissimilar to the ways in which rhetoricians practice their criticism.[46] Accordingly, biblical rhetorical criticism with emphasis on the classical notion of persuasion has more recently made a comeback.

The works of George Kennedy have led the way in this regard.[47] Even though he is not a biblical scholar, Kennedy focuses on rhetorical analysis of the New Testament. He argues that the tendency since the 1960s to identify rhetoric with style is a "distortion of the discipline of rhetoric as understood and taught in antiquity...."[48] Kennedy says that the goal of rhetoric is "the discovery of the author's intent and of how that is transmitted through a text to an audience."[49] He uses this approach to analyze a variety of New Testament texts from both the gospels and the letters. For example, he treats Second Corinthians as a case of judicial rhetoric. In so doing, he establishes a connection between the orations of Greek orators and the epistles of New Testament writers. Kennedy can then show how Paul uses arguments based on ethos and pathos to construct this letter as a defense against charges made against him in the Corinthian community.[50] This approach thus relies on the classical understanding of rhetoric and explores such elements as the rhetorical unit, rhetorical situation, rhetorical style, and overall rhetorical strategy.[51]

These developments demonstrate that both major traditions of rhetorical criticism (style and persuasion) are currently well represented within biblical studies in general and make helpful contributions to the analysis of ancient texts.

1.3 Classical Rhetoric and the Prophets

The tradition of classical rhetoric outlined above is receiving increased attention in the study of Old Testament prophetic texts. Several recent works return to an

---

Introduction to Biblical Rhetoric [JSOTSup 256; Sheffield: Sheffield Academic Press, 1998]). Meynet undertakes a rhetorical analysis that focuses only on dispositio, i.e., the structure and arrangement of the text (ibid., 37–38).

[46] For examples, see Black, "Keeping Up," 254 and Fox, "Rhetoric," 176.

[47] See Kennedy, *Art* and Kennedy, *New Testament Interpretation*.

[48] Kennedy, *New Testament Interpretation*, 3.

[49] Ibid., 12.

[50] Ibid., 86–87.

[51] Ibid., 33–37. Cf. Roth, "Rhetorical Criticism," 398 and Bible and Culture Collective, *Postmodern Bible*, 150–56. Black offers a helpful summary statement of Kennedy's view: "For Muilenburg, 'rhetoric' is virtually synonymous with 'literary artistry'; for Kennedy, the term refers to the disciplined art of persuasion, as conceptualized and practised by Greeks and Romans of the classical and Hellenistic periods" ("Keeping Up," 254). Cf. Warner, *Bible as Rhetoric*, 2. Other names associated with Kennedy's approach include D. F. Watson, Y. Gitay, H. D. Betz, R. Jewett, and W. Wuellner.

emphasis on the study of rhetoric as persuasion and suggest that this methodology is especially fruitful for study of the Israelite prophets.

One finds this rhetorical approach to the prophets as early as 1958 in the work of Ralph Lewis. His work represents a conscious attempt to use classical rhetorical criticism and its analytical categories to analyze the eighth-century prophets as speakers. Lewis explicitly agrees with König's statement that the prophetic literature from 760–460 B.C.E. is the expression of the "Golden Age of Hebrew Rhetoric."[52] He examines Amos, Hosea, and Micah in terms of their stylistic characteristics and emotional appeals yet maintains a significant focus on the interaction of speaker, original audience, and historical situation.[53] From this starting point, Lewis adopts classical rhetoric's analytical categories of proof by logos, ethos, and especially pathos.[54] He then analyzes Amos, Hosea, and Micah by categorizing and comparing their positive appeals (based on faith) and negative appeals (based on fear). Lewis summarizes his approach in an assertion that clearly relies on the intersection of classical rhetorical criticism and prophetic interpretation: "When a prophet speaks, there is an interaction of the speaker, the speech, the audience, and the setting. The persuasive style is determined by these elements."[55]

Michael Fox offers the clearest recent example of this way of working with prophetic texts.[56] He reasserts the premise that rhetoric understood only as analysis of style misses the main point of the rhetorical tradition, and he argues that rhetoric is first and foremost a study of the persuasive force of a discourse. He states, "A study becomes rhetorical only when it removes a text from its 'autonomy' and inquires into the transaction between rhetor and audience, focusing on suasive intentions, techniques, and effects."[57] Fox operates from the previously mentioned view that persuasion may be only potential and the critic can analyze a discourse's "rhetorical force" apart from knowledge of its

---

[52] R. Lewis, "The Persuasive Style and Appeals of the Minor Prophets Amos, Hosea, and Micah" (Ph.D. diss., University of Michigan, 1958), 1. Cf. E. König, "Prophecy (Hebrew)" in *Encyclopedia of Religion and Ethics* (ed. J. Hastings; 12 vols.; New York: C. Scribner's Sons, 1918), 10:388.

[53] Lewis ("Persuasive Style," 2) affirms that even stylistic analysis "necessarily involves, to some degree, the consideration of background information."

[54] Ibid., 4–7.

[55] Ibid., 12. For a similar conclusion concerning Hosea, see Buss, *Prophetic Word*, 59.

[56] Fox, "Rhetoric." For another recent article that approaches prophetic texts as intentional speech acts within particular situations, see W. Houston, "What Did the Prophets Think They Were Doing? Speech Acts and Prophetic Discourse in the Old Testament," in *The Place Is Too Small for Us: The Israelite Prophets in Recent Scholarship* (ed. R. Gordon; SBTS 5; Winona Lake, Ind.: Eisenbrauns, 1995), 133–53; repr. of *BibInt* 1 (1993): 167–88. Houston utilizes the speech act theory of John Austin and does not engage classical rhetorical criticism in an extensive way.

[57] Fox, "Rhetoric," 177–78; cf. Black, *Rhetorical Criticism*, 10–19. Fox notes that his definition of rhetoric is the same as that of the Committee on the Advancement and Refinement of Rhetorical Criticism of the National Development Project in Rhetoric (1970) given in Bitzer and Black, *Prospect*, 220.

immediate effects.[58] He maintains that prophecy is rhetoric and the prophets were primarily interested in attempting to persuade their immediate audience. Therefore, in his view, biblical prophetic texts form a complete corpus of material that can be fruitfully analyzed by all practitioners of rhetorical criticism.[59]

Based on these views, Fox offers a reading of Ezek 37:1–14 against the background of a rhetorical situation in which the exilic generation existed with no hope of returning to their homeland. Abandoning appeals to rational argument, Ezekiel uses an image-laden discourse to persuade his audience to believe in the irrational and unexpected.[60] The prophet's discourse, imagery, and pathos combine in attempting to convince the people that there is hope for the future in the midst of a seemingly limited situation.

Gitay's analysis of Isa 40–48 also follows this approach.[61] He explores these texts by focusing on the rhetorical situation and by investigating all available information including external evidence such as relevant extrabiblical texts.[62] Gitay concludes that, since many prophetic texts originated as oral proclamations, rhetorical criticism in its classical sense provides the most beneficial way to engage texts like Isa 40–48.[63]

An article by Barton further elaborates the close connection between a prophetic text's rhetoric and historical context.[64] Barton examines the rhetoric of prophetic books and concludes that the "genius" of the prophets was their ability to take facts of history, whose implications were ambiguous, and provide an account of them that convinced people that God's hand could be seen in them. The prophets used rhetoric to transform contingencies of history into "divine necessities."[65] They particularly gave political events theological interpretations in order to show that they were not the result of contingencies but the manifestations of God's will in response to national sin. Barton makes the

---

[58] Fox, "Rhetoric," 179.

[59] Ibid., 180.

[60] Ibid., 182.

[61] Y. Gitay, "Rhetorical Analysis of Isaiah 40–48: A Study of the Art of Prophetic Persuasion" (Ph.D. diss., Emory University, 1978). Repr. as *Prophecy and Persuasion: A Study of Isaiah 40–48* (Forum theologiae linguisticae 14; Bonn: Linguistica Biblica, 1981). For other similar works by Gitay, see "Amos's Art of Speech," *CBQ* 42 (1980): 293–309; *Isaiah and His Audience* (Assen: Van Gorcum, 1991); "Oratorical Rhetoric," *ACEBT* 10 (1981): 72–83; "Rhetorical Criticism and Prophetic Discourse," in *Persuasive Artistry* (ed. D. Watson; Sheffield: Sheffield Academic Press, 1991), 13–24.

[62] Gitay, "Rhetorical Analysis," 56, 92–95.

[63] Ibid., 85. Cf. D. Bryant, *Rhetorical Dimensions in Criticism* (Baton Rouge: Louisiana State University Press, 1973), 20.

[64] J. Barton, "History and Rhetoric in the Prophets," in *The Bible as Rhetoric: Studies in Biblical Persuasion and Credibility* (ed. M. Warner; Warwick Studies in Philosophy and Literature; London: Routledge, 1990), 51–64.

[65] Ibid., 52.

important observation that the primary source from which the prophets derived their rhetorical proclamations was the historical and political events unfolding in their day.

The studies of Irvine, Jones, and Shaw also follow this rhetorical approach to prophetic texts and provide a starting point for the study of Hos 2.[66] While treating Isa 6–12, 15–16, and Micah respectively, these works approach the texts by focusing on their persuasive strategies, viewing them as created for oral delivery in specific situations. Picking up on Kennedy's use of Greek oratory to analyze New Testament letters and following suggestions made earlier by Strachey, Duhm, and Buss, these studies interpret the prophets as analogous to ancient Greek political orators and their functions as described by Demosthenes in *De Corona*.[67] Since prophets, like the ancient Greek political orators, functioned primarily to discern the course of events and warn others, prophetic oracles should be considered in terms of persuasive discourse suited to particular events and circumstances.[68]

Rhetorical criticism's contribution to the study of Hos 2 emerges from these newer intersections of classical rhetoric and prophetic literature. Various critiques that have been leveled against this type of rhetorical study, however, should be appreciated. Perhaps the most obvious potential critique concerns the applicability of classical Greco-Roman rhetoric to the Hebrew Bible.[69] For example, Kennedy is able to demonstrate a close connection between the New Testament and Greco-Roman culture and rhetoric, but one cannot do this for the Hebrew Bible.[70] Nonetheless, Kennedy is surely correct in noting that rhetoric is a "universal phenomenon" of the human mind and the oracular nature of some biblical texts highlights the importance of speech.[71] The use of persuasive

---

[66] S. Irvine, *Isaiah, Ahaz, and the Syro-Ephraimitic Crisis* (SBLDS 123; Atlanta: Scholars Press, 1990); Jones, *Howling*; Shaw, "Speeches."

[67] See Shaw, "Speeches," 12. Cf. E. Strachey, *Hebrew Politics in the Times of Sargon and Sennacherib: An Inquiry into the Historical Meaning and Purpose of the Prophecies of Isaiah, with Some Notice of Their Bearings on the Social and Political Life of England* (London: Longman, Brown, Green & Longmans, 1853), 2; B. Duhm, *Die Theologie der Propheten als Grundlage für die innere Entwicklungsgeschichte der Israelite Religion* (Bonn: Adolph Marcus, 1875), 23; Buss, *Prophetic Word*, 116, 125.

[68] Outside of biblical studies, the rhetorician James Darsey approaches an analysis of radical rhetoric in America from the starting point of the Hebrew Bible prophets (J. Darsey, *The Prophetic Tradition and Radical Rhetoric in America* [New York: New York University Press, 1997]). He contends that the prophets functioned like orators and were the primitive source for the rhetoric of reform in America. While he, like Abraham Heschel, primarily takes a psychological approach to the prophets, Darsey adopts the rhetorical categories of logos, ethos, and pathos to analyze the prophets and their practices. Cf. A. Heschel, *The Prophets: An Introduction* (New York: Harper Torch Books, 1962).

[69] See Black, "Keeping Up," 257.

[70] Kennedy, *New Testament Interpretation*, 8.

[71] Ibid., 10–11.

speech forms (lawsuits, trial scenes, etc.) in prophetic texts commends the application of rhetorical analyses to those texts in particular.

A related critique comes from a more postmodern perspective and notes that one cannot simply ignore the "specific ideological effects" of the act of criticism itself.[72] Rhetorical criticism does not simply pass on universal truths; rather, the critic's social location and ideology themselves become a rhetorically powerful discourse. Therefore, any act of rhetorical criticism should include a "self-reflexive" element that exposes the various constraints upon the reading process.[73] This critique is especially significant for a text with imagery like that in Hos 2 as it exposes how readings often serve to reinscribe a text's sexism, violence, and social injustice.[74]

Even while noting the importance of these critiques, the nature of prophetic texts, including Hos 2, warrants a rhetorical-critical approach. These texts possess a verbal and oratorical nature that calls for a method that appreciates them as full oratorical addresses with pragmatic goals.[75] As Gitay observes, rhetoric in the classical sense allows one "to sense the person behind the speech rather than simply regard the book as a literary-theological production. Rhetoric sheds light on our understanding of prophecy in its social-historical context."[76] Thus, this study of Hos 2 uses the long-standing methodology of classical rhetorical criticism but does not limit itself to the specific canons of analysis like inventio, dispositio, and elecutio. The analysis builds upon the underlying views of classical rhetoric that see rhetorical pieces as designed to achieve certain results with a given audience in a particular setting.[77] The focus of this analysis

---

[72] Bible and Culture Collective, *Postmodern Bible*, 162.

[73] Ibid., 166.

[74] Ibid.

[75] Along these same lines, Boadt has offered an analysis of the poetic prose of certain prophetic texts and argued that such poetic prose contains "marks of orality" ("residual orality") that point to an original "public oration and oracular proclamation" that was "oriented toward persuasion to action" (L. Boadt, "The Poetry of Prophetic Persuasion: Preserving the Prophet's Persona," *CBQ* 59 [1997]: 1–21). These markers include such things as formulaic language, repetitions, changes of person, structural unity, and dramatic echoes. He maintains that not only do these markers indicate that extended prophetic discourses were originally delivered as public orations, but they also provide one possible way to identify those sections of prophetic books that are original to the prophet and to help recover the prophet's persona (ibid., 21). Several of the elements that Boadt identifies as indicators of original orality and unity (e.g., structural unity, sequence of drama, repetition, direct address to audience, dramatic echoes between contrasting halves; ibid., 14–15) characterize the poetic address in Hos 2.

[76] Y. Gitay, "The Realm of Prophetic Rhetoric," in *Rhetoric, Scripture, and Theology: Essays from the 1994 Pretoria Conference* (eds. S. Porter and T. Olbricht; JSOTSup 131; Sheffield: Sheffield Academic Press, 1996), 227–28. Cf. Y. Gitay, "Prophetic Criticism—'What Are They Doing?': The Case of Isaiah—A Methodological Assessment," *JSOT* 96 (2001): 101–27.

[77] See Black, *Rhetorical Criticism*, 33.

rests upon the interaction between the rhetor and the audience, including strategies, situations, and potential effects.[78]

More specifically for Hos 2, this type of rhetorical criticism stresses not simply what may have happened but how the speaker and audience interpreted certain events. For example, it can emphasize the ways in which the different parties may have viewed the Syro-Ephraimitic war. This approach also stresses the study of the rhetorical conventions from a particular time and location. For instance, it may focus on prominent metaphors and the metaphorical traditions which gave rise to them. Finally, this method emphasizes the ethical perspectives of the audience concerning right and wrong behavior. In the case of Hos 2, it can explore the significance of metaphors like fornication and adultery within the ethical understanding of a particular setting.[79] With these considerations in mind, this study undertakes an examination of Hos 2's major metaphors in light of their rhetorical function.

2. METAPHOR THEORY AND THE IMAGERY OF HOSEA 2

2.1 Metaphor in Theory and Practice

Over the past five decades, there has been a renewed interest in the critical study of metaphor among literary critics, theologians, rhetoricians, and philosophers.[80] No general agreement has emerged, however, concerning how one identifies metaphors, what and how metaphors communicate, and how one should define metaphor.[81] Almost any contemporary construction can fit some definition of metaphor, and every attempt to find a specific criterion for identifying metaphor has failed.[82]

The term "metaphor" ("to carry over") generally points to the transference of a word or meaning from one element to another.[83] Thus, while differing greatly, many definitions of metaphor focus on the element of interaction between the parts of a metaphorical expression and the possible meanings that emerge from that interaction. For example, Holman and Harmon define a

---

[78] Fox, "Rhetoric," 179.

[79] For these categories of emphasis, see Andrews, *Practice*, 20–24.

[80] For example, writing at the beginning of the 1980s, M. Johnson asserted, "We are in the midst of metaphormania" (*Philosophical Perspectives on Metaphor* [Minneapolis: University of Minnesota Press, 1981], ix). For a recent extensive bibliography on metaphor studies, see J. van Noppen, *Metaphor II: A Classified Bibliography of Publications from 1985–1990* (Amsterdam: Benjamins, 1990).

[81] For discussion of this situation, see M. Abrams, "Metaphor, Theories of," in *A Glossary of Literary Terms* (ed. M. Abrams; 7th ed.; Fort Worth: Harcourt Brace, 1999), 155.

[82] W. Booth, "Metaphor as Rhetoric: The Problem of Evaluation," in *On Metaphor* (ed. S. Sacks; Chicago: University of Chicago Press, 1979), 47.

[83] Abma, *Bonds*, 8.

metaphor as an "analogy identifying one object with another and ascribing to the first object one or more of the qualities of the second."[84] Abma gives a broader definition and says that metaphor is a "literary device in which terms from two different areas of life are brought together in order to achieve a special meaning which goes beyond the ordinary meaning of words or concepts."[85]

Like the rhetorical criticism noted above, the study of metaphor is generally considered to reach back to the work of Aristotle.[86] He was the first to articulate a theory of metaphor by distinguishing between literal and figurative speech. Aristotle defined a metaphorical term as involving "the transferred use of a term that properly belongs to something else; the transference can be from genus to species, from species to genus, from species to species, or analogical."[87] Thus, Aristotle limited metaphor to a concern with the individual word and stressed the notion of transference. This idea of transferring the associations of one word onto another has remained at the heart of most theories of how metaphor works. Scholars have challenged Aristotle's focus on the individual word, however, because it seems to limit a full understanding of how metaphor functions within a larger semantic or literary context. Aristotle seems to have viewed metaphors as primarily decorative devices with no significant cognitive content.[88]

The earliest view of metaphor that emerged from Aristotle's treatment may be called the "substitution view." This view understood a metaphor to be simply a decorative way of saying something that can be equally expressed by a literal statement.[89] The so-called "comparison view" of metaphor was also closely related to Aristotle's initial formulation and viewed a metaphor as a decorative way of expressing a literal comparison.[90] These early theories came under attack

---

[84] H. Holman and W. Harmon, "Metaphor," in *A Handbook to Literature* (eds. H. Holman and W. Harmon; 8th ed.; N.J.: Prentice-Hall, 2000), 315. Cf. J. Soskice, who defines metaphor as a figure of speech that "speaks of one thing in terms which are suggestive of another" (*Metaphor and Religious Language* [Oxford: Clarendon, 1985], 15).

[85] Abma, *Bonds*, 7. Cf. Yee, *Hosea*, 209 and Galambush, *Jerusalem*, 6.

[86] For a survey of the development of metaphor theory from Aristotle through the classical rhetoricians like Cicero and Quintilian up to the modern period, see T. Hawkes, *Metaphor* (London: Methuen & Co., 1972). The main text of Aristotle on metaphor is chapter 21 of the *Poetics*.

[87] *Poetics*, 1457b.

[88] See A. Ortony, "Metaphor, Language, and Thought," in *Metaphor and Thought* (ed. A. Ortony; 2d ed.; Cambridge: Cambridge University Press, 1993), 3 and Stienstra, *YHWH*, 18. E. Kittay has argued, however, that this view misunderstands Aristotle and that he did attach cognitive importance to metaphor (*Metaphor: Its Cognitive Force and Linguistic Structure* [Oxford: Clarendon, 1987], 4).

[89] For example, "Richard is a lion" is understood simply as a decorative way of saying "Richard is brave" (M. Black, "Metaphor," in *Philosophical Perspectives on Metaphor* [ed. M. Johnson; Minneapolis: University of Minnesota Press, 1981], 68; repr. of *Proceedings of the Aristotelian Society* 55 [1954–55]: 273–94).

[90] Ibid., 71.

for their use of the literal statement as an unproblematic standard and their failure to attribute any cognitive content to metaphorical expressions.[91]

Multiple theories of metaphor have emerged from these initial critiques. For the purposes of this study, two theories and their implications for reading prophetic texts are primary: the interaction theory of Richards and Black and the conceptual theory of Lakoff and Johnson. These theories assist the reader in focusing on the historical and rhetorical dimensions of the metaphors in Hos 2. What did the text's metaphors signify in their social context? How do they function rhetorically within the discourse? Why does Hos 2 use metaphor in general and these metaphors in particular?

The "interaction theory" of Richards and Black stands in contrast to the substitution and comparison views by asserting that, in a metaphor, two concepts interact to produce a meaning that goes beyond any literal meaning and affects both parts of the expression.[92] This approach moves away from seeing metaphor as simply a decorative device and sees it as containing real cognitive content. For example, the metaphor "the earth is our mother" calls attention to both the mother-like qualities of the earth and the earth-like qualities of mothers.[93]

Richards introduced the interaction approach by defining metaphor as "two thoughts of different things active together and supported by a single word, or phrase, whose meaning is a resultant of their interaction."[94] He coined two words to describe the two parts of a metaphor: 1) "tenor" refers to the underlying idea or principle subject, and 2) "vehicle" refers to the figurative word in the expression. Richards's main assertion was that the vehicle does not simply restate the tenor but interacts with it in order to produce a new meaning for the expression as a whole.[95]

Black later developed Richards's suggestions in a more substantial manner. He called the two parts of a metaphor the "primary subject" and "secondary subject" and asserted that the latter serves as a "filter" that reorganizes the reader's or listener's perspective of the primary subject. Black added the idea that the principal and secondary subjects carry with them systems of "associated commonplaces," which are placed into interaction by the metaphorical

---

[91] See M. Black, "More about Metaphor," in *Metaphor and Thought* (ed. A. Ortony; 2d ed.; Cambridge: Cambridge University Press, 1993), 22.

[92] See especially, I. Richards, "The Philosophy of Rhetoric," in *Philosophical Perspectives on Metaphor* (ed. M. Johnson; Minneapolis: University of Minnesota Press, 1981), 48–62 (repr. from *The Philosophy of Rhetoric* [Oxford: Oxford University Press, 1936]) and M. Black, *Models and Metaphors: Studies in Language and Philosophy* (Ithaca, N.Y.: Cornell University Press, 1962).

[93] Galambush, *Jerusalem*, 5.

[94] Richards, "Philosophy," 51.

[95] Ibid., 55. Cf. Abma, *Bonds*, 8–9 and Abrams, "Metaphor," 155.

expression.[96] He concluded that a metaphor has its own cognitive content and meaning because the filtering term emphasizes those elements (associated commonplaces) of the principal subject that are most similar to the secondary subject and suppresses the others. Thus, an altogether new meaning emerges when the metaphor is understood.[97] The meaning does not rely on preexisting similarities between the parts of the expression but is created by the metaphor itself. The metaphor does not simply influence a reader's view of one element of the expression but offers a new understanding of both the primary and secondary subjects.[98]

In spite of the interaction theory's fruitful innovations, there are several problems that should be noted.[99] Black's idea of "filtering" is not consistent with his suggestion that metaphors do not use preexisting similarities but create only new ones. He also initially maintained that only the secondary subject (vehicle) brings with it a system of associated commonplaces; yet, this seems to be too limited a view of the role of the primary subject. For the purposes of this analysis of Hos 2, the most significant shortcoming of the interaction theory is the insistence that a metaphor consists of two distinct subjects. This view limits metaphor to the single grammatical form of "A is B" and necessarily excludes all metaphorical expressions in which the tenor is not stated. In response, Soskice, for example, suggests an "interanimative theory" in which a metaphor's meaning emerges from the interplay of the "interpretive possibilities of the whole utterance."[100] Thus, a single metaphorical term could be interacting with an underlying model, and all terms in a metaphorical expression do not need to be present.

Building upon the strengths and weaknesses of the interaction theory, Lakoff and Johnson emphasize that metaphorical expressions stand as parts of

---

[96] Black, "Metaphor," 72–73; cf. Black, *Models*, 39 and G. Eidevall, *Grapes in the Desert: Metaphors, Models, and Themes in Hosea 4–14* (ConBOT 43; Stockholm: Almqvist & Wiksell, 1996), 20–22. Black later came to refer to associated commonplaces as "associated implications" (Black, "More," 28).

[97] Black, "Metaphor," 72; cf. Ortony, "Metaphor," 5. For example, the metaphor "man is a wolf" places the system of associated commonplaces of the wolf onto those of the man, and the wolf acts as a filter that emphasizes those traits of a human that are like a wolf and suppresses those that are not. For a similar view, see N. Goodman, *Languages of Art* (Indianapolis: Bobbs-Merrill, 1968). Goodman argues that metaphors are a crossing of boundaries between categories so that a set of labels from the vehicle is transferred onto the tenor and reorganizes it (*Languages*, 68–85).

[98] See Black, *Models*, 44. Black later abandoned this notion of two-way reshaping ("More," 19–41). Cf. Paul Ricoeur's notion that metaphor creates a new meaning through semantic tension and imagination. See P. Ricoeur, *The Rule of Metaphor* (Toronto: University of Toronto Press, 1977) and "The Metaphorical Process as Cognition, Imagination, and Feeling," in *On Metaphor* (ed. S. Sacks; Chicago: University of Chicago Press, 1979), 141–52.

[99] For discussion, see Soskice, *Metaphor*, 42–43.

[100] Ibid., 44–45.

broader conceptual metaphors operating within a given culture.[101] This "conceptual theory" of metaphor sees language as based on unacknowledged metaphors active in a society. Thus, all metaphors require knowledge of their cultural context for proper understanding. For example, ancient Israelite concepts like a husband's right to his wife's faithfulness may rest upon and require knowledge of the larger metaphorical concept of Yahweh as the husband of his people.[102] Lakoff and Johnson conclude that not only a culture's language but also its entire conceptual system is structured by conventional metaphors. Specific linguistic constructions simply reveal the conceptual metaphors at work in the culture.[103] This view makes it apparent that the study of metaphors like those in Hos 2 must be placed within the broader context of their rhetorical-historical setting.

Lakoff and Johnson further suggest that the broader conceptual metaphors link together to form "systems" through what they call "entailment relationships."[104] Thus, a given cultural metaphor may be intimately bound up with other metaphors that deal with the same concepts.[105] This view identifies three primary domains of conceptual metaphors: 1) structural metaphors, in which one concept is structured in terms of another (e.g., ARGUMENT IS WAR), 2) physical metaphors, which attribute the status of a substance to something that is not a substance (e.g., the brutality of war), and 3) orientational metaphors, which tend to give concepts a spatial orientation (e.g., HAPPY IS UP).[106] The individual metaphorical expression functions in relationship to these larger semantic, historical, and cultural dimensions.[107]

---

[101] See especially G. Lakoff and M. Johnson, *Metaphors We Live By* (Chicago: University of Chicago Press, 1980) and G. Lakoff and M. Johnson, "Conceptual Metaphor in Everyday Language," in *Philosophical Perspectives on Metaphor* (ed. M. Johnson; Minneapolis: University of Minnesota Press, 1981), 286–329; repr. from *The Journal of Philosophy* 77 (1980): 453–86.

[102] Stienstra, *YHWH*, 29.

[103] "Conceptual Metaphor," 290. Lakoff and Johnson illustrate their view with the example of language about argument in American culture. They suggest that such language is structured by the cultural conceptual metaphor of "ARGUMENT IS WAR" (ibid., 288).

[104] Ibid., 291. They refer to the tenor and vehicle as the "target domain" and "source domain" respectively and conceive that the elements of the source domain are "mapped" onto the target domain.

[105] Lakoff and Johnson give the example that the conceptual metaphor TIME IS MONEY "entails" other metaphors like TIME IS A LIMITED RESOURCE and TIME IS A VALUABLE COMMODITY (ibid.).

[106] Ibid., 295–96.

[107] Kittay's "semantic fields theory" also emphasizes the wide-ranging dimensions of meaning. See Kittay, *Metaphor* and E. Kittay and A. Lehrer, "Semantic Fields and the Structures of Metaphor," *Studies in Language* 5 (1981): 31–63. G. Lakoff and M. Turner also pick up much of the terminology and ideas of Kittay in *More Than Cool Reason: A Field Guide to Poetic Metaphor* (Chicago: University of Chicago Press, 1989).

2.2 Metaphor Theory and Biblical Studies

Since the 1970s, there has been a great increase in the use of such metaphor theories in biblical studies. In the last decade or so, several works have drawn upon metaphor theory in the study of a wide range of images, issues, and texts.[108] For example, Perdue relied on certain aspects of contemporary metaphor study to frame a discussion of the rhetorical movement and effects of the book of Job. He especially drew from those theories that emphasize the cognitive content and effect of metaphor and argued that metaphor in Job moves an implied audience from their present structures of linguistic reality to the formulation of a new identity.[109] Camp's work combined certain emphases of metaphor theory with feminist criticism. She primarily used the proposals of Lakoff, Johnson, and Turner in order to argue that metaphor theories grounded in cognitive linguistics provide a theoretical framework for feminist criticism's use of categories like experience and embodiment.[110]

A number of recent works also draw upon metaphor theory in the study of the prophetic literature outside of Hosea.[111] For instance, Newsom picks up the approach of Black's interaction theory in order to analyze Ezekiel's oracles against Tyre. She emphasizes the associated commonplaces of both the ancient and modern reader that are at work within Ezekiel's metaphors. A contemporary reader must engage these aspects of the metaphors and evaluate their relevance for understanding the text.[112]

Several recent works concentrate specifically on the metaphors in Hosea. The majority of these studies focus on Hos 1–3.[113] Some of these analyses

---

[108] Perhaps the most thorough treatment of metaphor in the Bible is P. Macky, *The Centrality of Metaphors to Biblical Thought* (Studies in the Bible and Early Christianity 19; Lewiston: Edwin Mellen, 1990). See also D. Bourguet, *Des métaphores de Jérémie* (EB 9; Paris: J. Gabalda, 1987); C. Camp, "Metaphor in Feminist Biblical Interpretation: Theoretical Perspectives," *Semeia* 61 (1993): 3–36; L. Perdue, *Wisdom in Revolt: Metaphorical Theology in the Book of Job* (JSOTSup 112; Sheffield: JSOT Press, 1991); various articles in *Semeia* 61 (1993), "Women, War, and Metaphor: Language and Society in the Study of the Hebrew Bible."

[109] Perdue, *Wisdom*, 23.

[110] Camp, "Metaphor," 8.

[111] See P. Bird, "To Play the Harlot: An Inquiry into an Old Testament Metaphor," in *Gender and Difference in Ancient Israel* (ed. P. Day; Minneapolis: Fortress, 1989), 75–94; Galambush, *Jerusalem*; K. Nielsen, *There Is Hope for a Tree: The Tree as Metaphor in Isaiah* (JSOTSup 65; Sheffield: Sheffield Academic Press, 1989). For a helpful overview of metaphor theories and their usefulness for the prophetic material, see Galambush, *Jerusalem*, 4–20.

[112] C. Newsom, "A Maker of Metaphors: Ezekiel's Oracles against Tyre," in *The Place Is Too Small for Us: The Israelite Prophets in Recent Scholarship* (ed. R. Gordon; SBTS 5; Winona Lake, Ind.: Eisenbrauns, 1995), 192; repr. from *Int* 38 (1984): 151–64.

[113] For overview discussions of metaphor theory and its application to Hosea, see Eidevall, *Grapes*, 19–49; Nwaoru, *Imagery*, 1–35; Törnkvist, *Use and Abuse*, 35–72. See also Abma, *Bonds*; E. Adler, *The Background for the Metaphor of Covenant as Marriage in the Hebrew Bible* (Berkeley: University of California Press, 1990); G. Baumann, *Liebe und Gewalt: Die Ehe als Metaphor für das*

attempt to operate within the theoretical categories of metaphor theory. For example, Stienstra uses the categories of Lakoff and Johnson to examine the statement "YHWH IS THE HUSBAND OF HIS PEOPLE" as a conceptual metaphor that gives rise to various expressions in Hosea and elsewhere.[114] Baumann also primarily adopts the views of Lakoff, Johnson, and Ricoeur in order to explore the prophetic marriage metaphor as the conceptual image for the relationship between Yahweh and Israel. She attempts to distinguish between explaining the metaphor in its ancient context and interpreting it with an eye toward the contemporary reader, and she uses feminist criticism to expose the sexual violence inherent within the metaphor.[115]

Several other works draw more freely from a wide range of metaphor theories. For example, West focuses on the political and social factors in eighth-century Israel that might have given rise to the metaphors of marriage and the promiscuous woman. He relates this development to political and social events that produced the expansion of an all-male priesthood and the restriction of women's sexual freedom.[116] On the other hand, Landy does not focus on the historical background of Hosea's metaphors but on their literary function within the book as a whole. He stresses that metaphor is less a transfer of properties from one semantic field to another and more an attempt to create an ideal object that establishes identity.[117] He goes on to assert, however, that this explanation overlooks the fact that metaphors can be agents of "disintegration" that may remain ambivalent and change in meaning. Landy concludes that this "disintegration" is the primary feature of the metaphors in Hosea, since they are often shifting and incoherent. Thus, they tend to deconstruct the very identities they are attempting to construct.[118]

Verhältnis JHWH-Israel in den Prophetenbüchern (SBS 185; Stuttgart: Katholisches Bibelwerk, 2000) (Eng. transl. *Love and Violence*); C. Bucher, "The Origin and Meaning of znh Terminology in the Book of Hosea" (Ph.D. diss., The Claremont Graduate School, 1988); H. Hendricks, "Juridical Aspects of the Marriage Metaphor in Hosea and Jeremiah" (Ph.D. diss., The University of Stellenbosch, 1982); P. Kruger, "Prophetic Imagery: On Metaphors and Similes in the Book of Hosea," *JNSL* 14 (1988): 143–51; F. Landy, "In the Wilderness of Speech: Problems of Metaphor in Hosea," *BibInt* 3 (1995): 35–59; J. Lewis, "Metaphors in Hosea," *Evangelical Theological Society Papers* 46 (1995), 1–38; G. Light, "Theory-Constitutive Metaphor and Its Development in the Book of Hosea" (Ph.D. diss., The Southern Baptist Theological Seminary, 1991); B. Seifert, *Metaphorisches Reden von G-tt im Hoseabuch* (FRLANT 166; Göttingen: Vandenhoeck & Ruprecht, 1996); Stienstra, *YHWH*; Weems, "Gomer"; G. West, "The Effect and Power of Discourse: A Case Study of Metaphor," *Scriptura* 57 (1996): 201–12.

[114] Stienstra, *YHWH*, 9.

[115] Baumann, *Liebe*, 15, 38.

[116] West, "Effect," 206.

[117] Landy, "Wilderness," 56.

[118] For example, Landy notes that Yahweh is portrayed in Hosea as a life-giving parent; yet, the book rejects the role of mother and often depicts Yahweh as a bringer of death (ibid., 37, 46).

These different works demonstrate the benefits of drawing from many divergent elements of metaphor theory without adopting a single position and its categories. While approaches like those of Baumann and Landy illustrate reader-response or ideological approaches to analyzing certain metaphors, several of the studies show the potential of exploring the possible rhetorical force of prophetic metaphors for an ancient audience in a particular historical context.[119]

2.3 Metaphor Theory and Hosea 2

Both the interaction and conceptual metaphor theories contribute insights that are relevant to an analysis of Hos 2. The most relevant insight of the interaction theory is its emphasis that metaphors work by causing two concepts to interact. A metaphorical expression can produce a meaning that goes beyond that of the individual elements themselves. Also important is this theory's contention that the terms do not work in isolation but carry with them associated commonplaces connected to both ancient and modern readers. The conceptual theory adds that metaphorical expressions stand as parts of broader conventional metaphors at work in the culture that produced them. Thus, any adequate analysis of a text's metaphors, like those in Hos 2, must explore the larger semantic, cultural, and historical contexts in which the metaphors are operative.

Several general observations on metaphor are also relevant to Hos 2. First, as some theorists note, all metaphor is indeterminate, partial, and unstable.[120] As Black states, "The *very same* metaphorical statement … may appropriately receive a number of different and even partially conflicting readings."[121] The reader must choose which implications and meanings are relevant within a given text. This observation urges attention to the reader's methodologies and presuppositions that are at work in the analysis and opens the possibility for ideological critiques of certain metaphors and their effects.[122] An exploration of Hos 2's metaphors within their ancient context may provide a fruitful starting point for a more ideologically oriented examination.[123]

---

[119] Most notably, Galambush, *Jerusalem*; Newsom, "Maker;" Lewis, "Metaphors;" and West, "Effect." Specifically concerning Hosea, Light observes that most metaphor study has emphasized the effort to put the reader into contact with the historical prophet and reconstruct the historical situation in which the metaphors were operative (Light, "Theory-Constitutive Metaphor," 18).

[120] For example, Lakoff and Johnson note that there are always parts of a metaphor that are not used in a concept or expression ("Conceptual Metaphor," 307). Cf. Newsom, "Maker," 192; Perdue, *Wisdom*, 26.

[121] Black, "More," 25; emphasis original.

[122] For example, Booth asserts that metaphor study should involve analysis and critique of the characters and society that produce and allow certain metaphors ("Metaphor," 67).

[123] Baumann follows this two-step approach to biblical metaphor by stating that she first attempts to "explain" a metaphor according to its ancient setting and then to go on to "interpret" it in the light of modern contexts (*Liebe*, 44–45).

A second general observation concerns the form of metaphor. Contra Black, a number of theorists insist that a metaphor does not always have a particular syntactic form but can even be a single word used as a verb, noun, participle, etc.[124] Metaphors do not always occur in the two-part form "A is B" with two distinct subjects.[125] A given metaphor's tenor or primary subject may be only implicit and not named in the text under consideration.[126] Day provides a helpful example of this phenomenon with the expression "the forest companies are raping the earth." In this metaphor, the primary topic (deforestation) remains implicit.[127] This type of metaphor has the powerful effect of making deforestation equivalent to rape and extending the reader's ideas of the just punishments for rape onto the punishments for deforestation.[128]

The metaphors in Hos 2 are best characterized as this type of metaphor in which the tenor remains only implicit. The text uses metaphors like "mother" and "lovers" without providing full expressions like "A is a mother" or "B are lovers." The present exploration of Hos 2 operates from the conviction that the majority of interpreters have not adequately identified the text's implicit tenors. A comprehensive comparative and historical analysis may shed new light on the primary subjects that stand at the heart of Hosea's oracle.

Two final observations from metaphor theory enable an adequate analysis of Hos 2's metaphors. First, as Eidevall observes, only by interpreting them intertextually does one gain a full appreciation of metaphors and their implicit tenors.[129] In the case of Hos 2, such an analysis necessarily involves both biblical and ancient Near Eastern texts that contain similar expressions and terms. These intertexts can reveal broader metaphorical traditions that may illuminate the particular expressions in the text of Hos 2.

The final observation emphasizes the close relationship between metaphor and rhetoric. One of the main questions for reading metaphors like those in Hos 2 concerns whether metaphor is viewed as simply a linguistic phenomenon or as rhetorical communication.[130] Within metaphor studies, Booth has attempted to connect metaphor with classical rhetorical criticism. He sees metaphor as a "weapon" forged for use in a given rhetorical situation in order to "win" an argument. Given the prominent use of metaphors within acts of *communication*

---

[124] Galambush, *Jerusalem*, 6; Kittay, *Metaphor*, 23; Soskice, *Metaphor*, 18–19, 23; Stienstra, *YHWH*, 37.

[125] Contra Black (see Soskice, *Metaphor*, 43). Cf. Holman and Harmon, "Metaphor," 316; Light, "Theory-Constitutive Metaphor," 52; Riceour, *Rule*, 235.

[126] Kittay notes this is especially prominent in poetic metaphor (*Metaphor*, 171). Cf. Day, "Bitch," 232–33; Eidevall, *Grapes*, 33.

[127] The explicit statement of this metaphor would be "deforestation is raping the earth." Day notes that this type of metaphor is prominent in prophetic texts like Ezek 16 and Hos 2 ("Bitch," 232–33).

[128] Ibid., 234.

[129] Eidevall, *Grapes*, 33; cf. Lewis, "Metaphors," 37–38.

[130] Ortony, "Metaphor," 11.

and their characteristic of being tailored to the cultural conceptions of a society, it seems correct to conclude with Booth that metaphors are not merely decorative devices but are part of intended communication with particular regard for audience and context.[131] The full meaning of a metaphor must be reconstructed from the historical context, rhetorical purpose, and speaker's intentions.[132]

Within biblical studies, Perdue has similarly argued that metaphor exerts a rhetorical force upon a given audience that seeks to cause them to change their previous constructions of reality and structures of experience. Metaphors function to dismantle existing conceptions of reality on the way to constructing new ones.[133] The study of Isa 24–27 by Doyle similarly attempts to "discover why and to what end a biblical author used a particular metaphor or group of metaphors."[134] The work of Macky, perhaps the most thorough treatment of metaphor in the Bible, also insists that interpreting a speech act requires that the interpreter look for the clues given by the speaker/author and the rhetorical situation in order to discover the author's intention.[135]

This rhetorical power of metaphor to construct new structures of experience may explain why Hos 2 employs metaphor in the way that it does. As the following discussion hopes to show, this oracle comes from a rhetorical situation in which the Israelites' basic construction of reality was being reordered due to shifting sociopolitical circumstances. Metaphor in general allows the prophet to construct a new vision of Israel's communal and individual experiences. Hos 2's metaphors in particular permit the text to do this through conventional symbols that stand in dialogue with long-standing metaphorical traditions.

---

[131] Booth, "Metaphor," 51, 55. Cf. Black, *Models*, 29.

[132] As an example, Black notes that an understanding of Churchill's description of Mussolini as "that utensil" requires knowledge of the verbal setting and historical context ("Metaphor," 67).

Ted Cohen also focuses on the close relationship between metaphor and rhetoric. Relying on John Austin's theory of speech acts, he argues that one must consider the context of the "total speech act" in which a metaphor stands. This consideration especially involves knowledge of the "speech situation" of a given speech act (T. Cohen, "Figurative Speech and Figurative Acts," in *Philosophical Perspectives on Metaphor* [ed. M. Johnson; Minneapolis: University of Minnesota Press, 1981], 184–85, 190–91; repr. from *The Journal of Philosophy* 71 [1975]: 669–84). Similarly, Soskice argues that metaphor theories that pay no attention to the "context, speaker's intention, and other extra-utterance factors" are inadequate (*Metaphor*, 36).

[133] Perdue, *Wisdom*, 23. For similar views within biblical studies, see Camp, "Metaphor," 5; Eidevall, *Grapes*, 33; Lewis, "Metaphors," 37–38.

[134] B. Doyle, *The Apocalypse of Isaiah Metaphorically Speaking: A Study of the Use, Function, and Significance of Metaphors in Isaiah 24–27* (BETL CLI; Leuven: Leuven University Press/Peeters, 2000), 5. Doyle's method includes the delimitation of the metaphorical statement, a survey of the indicators of the presence of a metaphor, an analysis of the type of metaphor, and an attempt to uncover the "author's purpose" in using the metaphor (ibid., 6, 140–44).

[135] See Macky, *Centrality*, 17 and M. Black, *The Labyrinth of Language* (New York: Praeger, 1968), 207–8. Cf. Doyle, *Apocalypse of Isaiah*, 100–101.

An analysis of Hos 2's *rhetoric* should thus consider the elements of the speaker, audience, and rhetorical-historical situation. An understanding of Hosea's *metaphors*, however, also involves the knowledge of the larger rhetorical concerns of the oracle itself and how the particular metaphors function within the rhetorical piece and historical situation. Such an analysis should first examine each metaphor through both contextual and intertextual means and then attempt to identify the primary subject or tenor relevant to Hosea's oracle.[136] As Black notes, the goal of such analysis is not to paraphrase the metaphors with a literal statement but to "explicate" the systems of associated commonplaces that give the text's metaphors their communicative power and effect in the ancient rhetorical situation.[137] In the words of Whitt,

> The key to understanding many of the early prophetic oracles from Israel and Judah is the simple observation that the prophets' oracles were delivered before an audience. For our passage in Hosea 2, we must always be aware of Hosea's intended audience and we must constantly ask the question, What would Hosea's audience have thought when he used a particular word or phrase or referred to a particular object?[138]

With these observations in mind, one can now turn to an examination of Hos 2's major metaphors (marriage, wife/mother, fornication, adultery, lovers, and baals) in order to explore the ways in which they illuminate the text's rhetorical features, horizon, and situation.

---

[136] See also Eidevall's approach to Hosea (*Grapes*, 49).

[137] Black, *Models*, 46; cf. Kittay, *Metaphor*, 37.

[138] W. Whitt, "The Divorce of Yahweh and Asherah in Hosea 2, 4–7.12ff," *SJOT* 6 (1992): 31.

PART 1

THE *METAPHORS* OF HOSEA 2

3

THE MARRIAGE METAPHOR

The metaphor of marriage holds the prominent place in both the discourse of Hos 2 and the larger literary context of Hos 1–3. Marriage imagery repeatedly appears to describe relationships among various parties. Although chapters 1 and 3 seem to invite the possibility that the marriage imagery refers to a real-life relationship between two people, the language in Hos 2 is clearly metaphorical. The text depicts Yahweh's relationship with some unnamed group of people as a marriage. Yahweh plays the metaphorical role of a wronged husband, who addresses his description of the situation to his wife's children.

Many recent studies have explored the use of marriage imagery by the Israelite prophets.[1] These scholarly works have produced a construct of a general marriage/adultery metaphor that arises from the speeches of various

---

[1] Abma, *Bonds*, 7; Adler, "Background;" Baumann, *Liebe*; E. Ben Zvi, "Observations on the Marital Metaphor of YHWH and Israel in Its Ancient Israelite Context: General Conclusions and Particular Images in Hosea 1.2," *JSOT* 28 (2004): 363–84; Bucher, "Origin," 7–28; Galambush, *Jerusalem*; E. Matthews, "The Use of the Adultery Motif in Hebrew Prophecy" (Th.D. diss., New Orleans Baptist Theological Seminary, 1987); A. Neher, "Le symbolisme conjugal: Expression de l'histoire dans l'Ancien Testament," *RHPR* 34 (1954): 30–49; H. Ringgren, "The Marriage Motif in Israelite Religion," in *Ancient Israelite Religion* (ed. P. Miller et al.; Philadelphia: Fortress, 1987), 421–28; Stienstra, *YHWH*; A. Weider, *Ehemetaphorik in prophetischer Verkündigung: Hosea 1–3 und seine Wirkungsgeschichte im Jeremiabuch: Ein Beitrag zum alttestamentlichen Gottes-Bild* (FB 71; Würzburg: Echter, 1993); Yee, *Poor Banished Children*.

prophets including Hosea. This metaphor has been identified in such representative texts as Isa 1:21; 50:1–3; 54:1–10; 57:6–13; 62:4–5; Jer 2:1–3, 13; 4:1–31; 13:20–27; Ezek 16; 23; Hos 1–3; 9:1; Mic 1:6–7; Nah 3:4–7; and Mal 2:10–16.

Interpreters have widely assumed that Hosea was the first one to make use of marriage as a metaphor and that this imagery was subsequently adopted by Isaiah, Jeremiah, and Ezekiel.[2] This view developed on the basis of Hosea's early date in comparison to the other prophets and the lack of any biblical or extrabiblical references to the use of such a metaphor before Hosea's time.[3] Furthermore, scholars have typically seen Hosea's marriage metaphor as an intentional foil that co-opts much of the language and imagery of a widespread Baal fertility cult in eighth-century Israel.[4] In this view, Hosea's creation of an exclusive marriage metaphor for Yahweh and Israel (as opposed to a marriage between Baal and the land) served to construct a new picture of God that contrasted with the syncretistic cultic practices of the day. His use of sexual imagery within this exclusive relationship also allegedly served as a foil to sexual rites in the Baal cult. Hosea emphasized Yahweh's lordship as a husband, the exclusivity of Israel's relationship to Yahweh, and Yahweh's forgiving love.[5] According to this common view, the marriage metaphor in Hosea found its primary image-base (i.e., the symbols or practices that fund the prophet's imagination) not in social realities of marriage and divorce but in elements connected with the myths and rituals of a Canaanite fertility cult.

More recent study has produced changes in the treatment of the marriage metaphor. As Baumann observed, prior to the 1980s, scholars viewed the marriage metaphor in general through a theological lens that emphasized themes like the unconditional and personal love of God in contrast to the mechanics of a fertility cult. By contrast, with the rise of feminist biblical studies, the marriage metaphor came to be considered under themes like pornography and violence against women.[6] There has gradually been more emphasis placed not upon the theological affirmations of the metaphor but upon comparative biblical and extrabiblical texts that may shed light on the imagery used. Scholars have also increasingly stressed the social practices of ancient Near Eastern marriage and divorce as a key to understanding the prophetic marriage metaphors.

---

[2] For examples of this view, see Hendricks, "Juridical Aspects," 89; Kruger, "Marriage Metaphor," 7; M. Paolantonio, "God as Husband," *TBT* 27 (1989): 299; Weider, *Ehemetaphorik*, 2; West, "Effect," 201.

[3] For example, Buss observes that, while images of a deity as a husband to a goddess or as a father to another god or a king are widespread in the ancient Near East, there are no descriptions of a deity as the husband of a people (*Prophetic Word*, 111).

[4] I. Rallis, "Nuptial Imagery in the Book of Hosea: Israel as the Bride of Yahweh," *SVTQ* 34 (1990): 200.

[5] See Paolantonio, "God as Husband," 300 and Rallis, "Nuptial Imagery," 201–2.

[6] Baumann, *Liebe*, 17–18.

This study, in keeping with a rhetorical approach, will attempt to identify those historical and social elements in the ancient rhetorical situation that gave the marriage metaphor its communicative power. Such an exploration begins with the assumption that understanding the ancient Israelite concept of marriage is a vital aspect of understanding Hosea's metaphorical usage.[7]

The concept of marriage involves a variety of aspects that may all provide the image-base(s) of Hosea's imagery. These aspects include a multitude of practices connected with marriage as an institution: betrothal, bride price, dowry, marriage gifts, and marital provisions.[8] The marriage metaphor also connects with various elements associated with the realms of adultery and divorce. These elements include philological matters such as Hebrew terms like זנה and נאף, as well as matters such as divorce formulas, adultery punishments, and economic stipulations.[9]

Building on these observations, this chapter examines the specific ways in which marriage imagery is used metaphorically in Hos 2 and explores one of the primary image-bases from which the discourse as a whole draws. The investigation focuses on three central questions: 1) From what image-base does the text draw its metaphorical use of marriage imagery?, 2) What are the characteristics of that image-base?, and 3) How does Hos 2 make use of that image-base in its rhetorical argument? Another question that arises as a byproduct of this investigation asks which parts of Hos 2's language do not rely on the image-base from which the prophet draws his marriage imagery. As these investigations aim to show, the primary image-base that funds Hos 2's marriage metaphor is best viewed as the *actual practices* of marriage and divorce in the ancient Near East and not the myths and rituals associated with a Canaanite fertility religion.

1. THE MARRIAGE METAPHOR IN HOSEA 2 AND ITS PRIMARY IMAGE-BASE

1.1 The Basic Source of the Marriage Imagery

Four major options have emerged from the scholarly discussion about the background of the marriage metaphor: 1) the marriage imagery comes from the prophet's personal, marital experiences, 2) the metaphor relies on and reacts against a Baal fertility cult in eighth-century Israel, 3) the language emerges from the preexisting idea of a covenant between Yahweh and Israel, and 4) the

---

[7] Ibid., 49; cf. Stienstra, *YHWH*, 7.
[8] For a general article on ancient Israelite marriage, see V. Hamilton, "Marriage: Old Testament and Ancient Near East," *ABD* 4:559–69.
[9] For an introductory article on divorce in the ancient Near East, see R. Wall, "Divorce," *ABD* 2:217–19.

imagery comes from the language of curses in ancient Near Eastern vassal treaties.

A first, and most widespread, view regarding the original image-base of Hosea's marriage metaphor locates it in the historical life of the prophet himself. Throughout the history of interpretation, many efforts have been made to reconstruct Hosea's personal life and marriage, and Hosea's own "tragic" relationship with Gomer has often been seen as giving birth to his formulation of the marriage metaphor for Yahweh and the people.[10] This view takes the events narrated in Hos 1 and 3 as actual historical occurrences that depict a broken relationship between Hosea and Gomer due to the latter's adulterous activity. Thus, Hosea came to understand Israel's unfaithfulness to Yahweh as analogous to that of his own wife. The obvious problem with this explanation is that it depends entirely upon the ability to reconstruct successfully the obscure and confusing details of Hosea's personal life.

Secondly, interpreters often read Hos 2 against the background of a supposedly widespread Baal fertility cult in eighth-century Israel. The marriage metaphor, it is concluded, was a direct product of knowledge concerning and reaction to Canaanite mythology and cult present in Israelite society.[11] In this view, the Canaanite mythology and cult are seen as including elements like a sacred marriage, a marital relationship between the god and the land, and sexual practices like cultic prostitution and ritual defloration of virgins, all devoted to the goal of securing fertility for humans, crops, and animals. Hosea, it is argued, developed his metaphor of the marriage of Yahweh and Israel from the image-base of this cult, and the specific imagery within Hos 2 reflects that of fertility rites and sexual practices. Proponents of this view often emphasize those parts of the prophet's speech that focus on agricultural items: "But she has not acknowledged that I myself gave to her the grain and the new wine and the choice oil.... Therefore I will take back again my grain in its time and my new wine in its season, and I will snatch away my wool and my linen ..." (2:10–11). As will be shown in chapter 5, this cultic explanation rests on several assumptions about a Canaanite fertility cult that can no longer be accepted.

A third and more recent explanation of the source of Hosea's marriage imagery asserts that the prophet derived the metaphor from the preexisting idea of a covenant between Yahweh and Israel. The work of Adler represents a

---

[10] For example, see H. H. Rowley, "The Marriage of Hosea," in *Men of God: Studies in Old Testament History and Prophecy* (London: Thomas Nelson, 1963), 66–97; repr. from *BJRL* 39 (1956–57): 200–33. See also Matthews, "Use," 113; Rallis, "Nuptial Imagery," 201–2; Weider, *Ehemetaphorik*, 205.

[11] For examples, see K. Budde, "Der Abschnitt Hosea 1–3 und seine grundlegende religionsgeschichtliche Bedeutung," *TSK* 96/97 (1925): 1–89; Hendriks, "Juridical Aspects," 94; M. Schulz-Rauch, *Hosea und Jeremia: Zur Wirkungsgeschichte des Hoseabuches* (CThM 16; Stuttgart: Calwer, 1996), 27, 157; and the list of names in Adler, "Background," 165.

major formulation of this view.[12] She argues for the priority of the concept of covenant and attempts to set out the factors that led Hosea to liken the covenant relationship of Yahweh and Israel to marriage. She concludes that Israelite marriage and Yahweh's covenant share four common traits: 1) both are legal and artificial relationships, 2) both demand exclusive fidelity from one party, 3) both share the idea of choice/election, and 4) both express the same range of emotions.[13]

The idea of covenant as the source of the metaphor has several deficiencies. For example, Baumann notes that the words for marriage do not usually occur in contexts of and with connotations of covenant and there is more than one concept of covenant within the Hebrew Bible.[14] The covenant explanation also rests on the debatable assumption of an early date (pre-eighth century) for the formulation of the idea of a Yahweh-Israel covenant. As is well-known, a case can be made for considering such a covenant concept to be a seventh-century development within Israel.[15]

A fourth explanation of the image-base of the marriage metaphor appears in works that compare Hosea's imagery with that of the curses in ancient Near Eastern vassal treaties. Hosea, it is concluded, derived both the general idea of a marriage metaphor and the specific imagery therein from the relationship between suzerains and vassals attested in these treaties. For example, Hillers notes that two different ancient Near Eastern treaties attest a metaphorical curse of women becoming prostitutes. A treaty of Ashur-nirari V (ca. 750 B.C.E.) threatens, "Then may the aforesaid become a prostitute, and his warriors women. May they receive their hire like a prostitute in the square of the city."[16] An Assyrian treaty of Esarhaddon also uses a curse in which enemies ravish the

---

[12] See also Abma, *Bonds*, 23–24; C. Fensham, "The Marriage Metaphor in Hosea for the Covenant Relationship between the Lord and His People (Hos 1:2–9)," *JNSL* 12 (1984): 77–78; R. Ortlund, Jr., *Whoredom: God's Unfaithful Wife in Biblical Theology* (New Studies in Biblical Theology; Grand Rapids: Eerdmans, 1996), 9, 25; Rallis, "Nuptial Imagery," 197; Ringgren, "Marriage Motif," 426.

[13] Adler, "Background," 1.

[14] Baumann, *Liebe*, 66–69. See also Hendriks, who specifically refutes the covenant view by asserting that the marriage metaphor is not a substitute for the covenant image but an entirely different way of expressing the relationship ("Juridical Aspects," 94).

[15] See Baumann, *Liebe*, 75.

[16] D. Hillers, *Treaty Curses and the Old Testament Prophets* (BibOr 16; Rome: Pontifical Biblical Institute, 1964), 58. Hillers offers general information on the sources and contents of the ancient Near Eastern treaties, as well as specific analyses of the images that appear in the Hebrew Bible.

The other reference is to the reconstructed, and heavily debated, Sefire I A 40–41: "[And just as a pros]ti[tute is stripped naked], so may the wives of Mati'el be stripped naked ..." (ibid., 59). This text may appear to give some justification for considering actual stripping to be a punishment of harlotry. This conclusion does not seem warranted, however, since prostitution was not illegal in the ancient Near East and the text in no way portrays the act of stripping as a public punishment. More likely, the curse wishes upon the wives of Mati'el the lifestyle of a prostitute, who constantly has her clothes removed by strange men.

wives of the disloyal.[17] Although this image-base has some similarities with the preceding covenant explanation, it is distinguished by a lack of concern with relationship to the divine and a focus on imagery connected with international relations in the political realm.

The identification of these treaty-curses as the source of Hosea's marriage imagery avoids much of the speculation and uncertainty mentioned in connection with the above views. It does not, however, adequately explain all of the marriage imagery in Hosea's oracle (e.g., the reclaiming of provisions, giving of bridal gifts, etc.). None of the above explanations considers the wide range of comparative texts where these other aspects of marriage imagery occur. These views do not look to the *actual practices* of marriage and divorce in the ancient Near East in order to explain the full scope of Hosea's imagery. Rather than dealing with treaty curses or divine covenants, the bulk of available comparative evidence relates specifically to the literal institution of marriage and the actual processes of divorce. Accordingly, the actual laws and customs governing marriage, divorce, and adultery in the ancient Near East may provide a more fruitful and comprehensive place to locate the primary image-base from which Hosea drew his metaphorical imagery. The material practices of marriage in ancient Israel contain the same notions of exclusivity and inequity that Hosea foregrounds in the metaphorical relationship of Yahweh and his "wife."[18]

There is a substantial amount of extrabiblical evidence available for comparison in this regard. Available comparative texts include Babylonian law codes, like the Codex Ur-Nammu, Codex Eshnunna, and Codex Hammurabi, as well as some private Old Babylonian legal documents. Similar stipulations and customs can be found in tablet A of the Middle Assyrian Laws and in the Hittite Laws.[19] Two Ugaritic texts and nearly one hundred Nuzi texts also appear to deal with different aspects of marriage and divorce in those cultures.[20] Perhaps the most fruitful texts, for reasons that will be adumbrated below, are the Jewish "documents of wifehood" from Elephantine. These texts include three primary documents and several other fragmentary ones that reflect Jewish marriage laws and customs in the fifth century B.C.E.[21] One can also compare these various ancient Near Eastern texts with the primary biblical laws regarding adultery (Lev 18:20; 20:10; and Deut 22:22), as well as with the numerous other biblical texts that deal in some way with marriage, divorce, and adultery (e.g., Exod

---

[17] Ibid., 63.

[18] Yee, "Not My Wife," 368.

[19] For discussion of these sources, see R. Westbrook, "Adultery in Ancient Near Eastern Law," *RB* 97 (1990): 543.

[20] See R. Yaron, "A Royal Divorce at Ugarit," *Or* 32 (1963): 21–31 and J. Breneman, "Nuzi Marriage Tablets" (Ph.D. diss., Brandeis University, 1971).

[21] See R. Yaron, "Aramaic Marriage Contracts from Elephantine," *JSS* 3 (1958): 1–39. The three primary texts are Cowley 15, Kraeling 2, and Kraeling 7.

21:10–11; Num 5:11–31; Deut 21:14; 22:13–19; 24:1–4; Prov 6:34–35; 7:5–27).

Across these comparative texts, the basic understanding of marriage is a legal relationship between a man and a woman with adultery being the violation, willingly or otherwise, of a legally attached female. Thus, the most general principle for adultery finds expression in MAL A 13: "If the wife of a man has gone out from her house to a man where he lives and he has had intercourse with her knowing that she is a man's wife, both the man and the woman shall be killed."[22] This basic case of two knowing participants also appears to be the situation in view in the primary biblical laws in Lev 20:10 and Deut 22:22. The ancient Near Eastern texts, however, reflect many different types of divorce and adultery, including the seduction of an unwitting man, a betrothed woman found not to be a virgin, and the rape of a married woman.

The works of Hendriks and Kruger have previously suggested a connection between Hosea's marriage metaphor and the actual practices of marriage and divorce in the ancient Near East. They have specifically highlighted the importance of the legalities governing marriage and divorce for Hosea's imagery, but have done so in treatments that have not been well-known and are not developed in great detail.[23] The following discussions of the divorce formula and punishments for adultery will highlight the paths that these and other scholars have taken and attempt to reformulate them in the context of a comprehensive, comparative analysis of Hos 2.[24]

1.2 The So-Called "Divorce Formula" in Hosea 2:4

Two parts of Hos 2 play a key role in considering the ways in which practices and legalities of marriage may underlie the text's marriage metaphor: the so-called "divorce formula" in 2:4 and the punishments against the wife in 2:4–15. In Hos 2:4 Yahweh states, "For she is not my wife, and I am not her husband." Interpretative questions regarding this verse have centered on whether the above-mentioned phrase should be understood as an actual ancient Near Eastern divorce formula, which would indicate a legal divorce proceeding as part of the image-base drawn upon by Hos 2. The earliest position concerning this issue

---

[22] See Westbrook, "Adultery," 549.

[23] Hendriks, "Juridical Aspects" is an unpublished dissertation, and Kruger, "Marriage Metaphor" is a brief article.

[24] One other theory concerning the source of Hosea's marriage metaphor is related to the comparative approach. Fitzgerald and others assert that the marriage metaphor derives from the ancient Near Eastern practice of seeing capital cities as goddesses who were married to the patron gods (see Fitzgerald, "Mythological Background," 403–16). Adler concedes that the inscriptional and coin evidence does seem to indicate this practice, but she asserts that there is no evidence for referring to a god as "husband" ("Background," 146). Since this argument relates more directly to the question of the personified wife/mother in Hos 2, it will be taken up in the next chapter.

concluded that the verse does indeed contain an ancient Israelite technical divorce formula, or, at the very least, the verse and its context reflect the imagery of real-life legal proceedings against an unfaithful wife. As far back as 1934, Kuhl compared the language of Hos 2:4 with other statements of divorce in Old Babylonian and Elephantine texts and concluded that the verse contains a similar Israelite version of the divorce pronouncement.[25] For example, the typical Old Babylonian divorce pronouncement reads, "You are not my husband" or "You are not my wife." The typical Elephantine statement reads, "I divorce (שׂנא) my wife" or "She will not be my wife."[26] Gordon agreed with Kuhl and offered a representative conclusion that verse four "is simply the Hebrew equivalent of the Akkadian divorce formulae 'thou art not my wife' and 'thou art not my husband.'"[27] Wolff, while not accepting Hos 2:4 as a technical Israelite divorce formula, argued that the verse's language accurately reflects actual legal proceedings against an unfaithful wife.[28]

Against this older view, a majority of interpreters now proposes that, while Hos 2:4 does depend upon the image-base of the legal stipulations for marriage and divorce, it is not an actual Israelite divorce formula.[29] This position seems to rest on the most secure evidence. The words, "She is not my wife, and I am not her husband" are not attested anywhere else in the Hebrew Bible as a formula of divorce, and they are essentially dissimilar from those formulas found in Babylonian and Elephantine texts. Also, as Buss observes, 2:4 has no parallel in Jewish texts, and the rest of Hos 2 is dedicated to convincing the wife to return. Verse 4 is more of a "negated marriage formula" that describes the current situation.[30] Andersen and Freedman further note that too many legal features are missing from Hos 2 for verse 4 to be a technical divorce formula: 1) there is no proper court setting, 2) there is no provision for defense, and 3) there is a failure

---

[25] C. Kuhl, "Neue Dokumente zum Verständnis von Hosea 2:4–15," *ZAW* 52 (1934): 11. Kuhl was not the first, however, to make this observation. The Karaites already recognized Hos 2:4 as a divorce formula, and it appears in their bills of divorce in the Middle Ages. See M. Friedman, "Israel's Response in Hosea 2:17b: 'You are my Husband,'" *JBL* 99 (1980): 199. For similar views, see Cassuto, "Second Chapter," 101–5; M. J. Geller, "The Elephantine Papyri and Hosea 2.3: Evidence for the Form of the Early Jewish Divorce Writ," *JSJ* 8 (1977): 141; Hendriks, "Juridical Aspects," 58; Yaron, "Aramaic Marriage Contracts."

[26] Kuhl, "Neue Dokumente," 11.

[27] C. Gordon, "Hosea 2:4–5 in the Light of New Semitic Inscriptions," *ZAW* 54 (1936): 277.

[28] Wolff, *Hosea*, 32; cf. Mays, *Hosea*, 35.

[29] Abma, *Bonds*, 171; Garrett, *Hosea, Joel*, 76; Harper, *Critical and Exegetical Commentary*, 65; Jeremias, *Der Prophet*, 41; Kruger, "Marriage Metaphor," 12; Macintosh, *Critical and Exegetical Commentary*, 41; Nwaoru, *Imagery*, 138; Rudolph, *Hosea*, 64; Stienstra, *YHWH*, 104; Stuart, *Hosea-Jonah*, 47; Westbrook, "Adultery," 578.

[30] Buss (*Prophetic Word*, 87–88) states, "Rather than instituting divorce, Yahweh is making public the fact that no proper marriage exists and engages in a judicial procedure designed to win her through discipline." So also Kruger, "Marriage Metaphor," 12.

to execute the death penalty for adultery.[31] Accordingly, they conclude that the metaphorical husband and wife in Hos 2 are only separated; therefore, the husband has the ability to take the punitive measures listed throughout the whole of the chapter.[32]

Seen in this way, there is not an exact correspondence between 2:4 and attested ancient Near Eastern divorce formulas, but there remains an essentially legal background for the prophet's metaphor. Another view, however, which builds upon this interpretation and deserves a brief mention, reads the phrase in verse 4 as a question: "Is she not my wife, and am I not her husband?"[33] In this view, 2:4 fits better with a context in which the husband maintains the ability to deal directly with the wife and emphasizes that the purpose of the whole confrontation is reconciliation.

Andersen and Freedman come close to this position when they suggest that the לֹא in 2:4 is an emphatic rather than a negative: "For she is my wife, and I am her husband."[34] Seen in this way, verse 4 asserts that the main controversy in the oracle is that the couple remains married in spite of the wife's indiscriminate behavior. While this third option recognizes the lack of exact correspondence with attested divorce formulas, the rest of the chapter's emphasis on and imagery of future remarriage makes this reading unlikely (cf. 2:18–25).

One additional approach to verse 4 and to the overall image-base of Hos 2 seems to account most thoroughly for both the difficulties cited above and the specific courses of action highlighted throughout the whole of the chapter. Rather than representing a technical divorce formula, the metaphorical language in Hos 2:4 functions well against the background of one specific situation that is addressed by several ancient Near Eastern texts: the circumstance in which a

---

[31] Andersen and Freedman, *Hosea*, 127, 219. On the issue of their assumption of a mandatory death penalty for adultery, see discussion of punishments below.

[32] Ibid., 221. In this regard, some scholars have observed that the primary Hebrew term רִיב in verse 4 does not necessarily imply a court process but may refer to any controversy (cf. Gen 26:19–21; Num 20:3; Judg 11:25). For example, K. Nielsen (*Yahweh as Prosecutor and Judge: An Investigation of the Prophetic Lawsuit (Rib-Pattern)* [JSOTSup 9; Sheffield: JSOT Press, 1978], 25) states that the elements in lawsuit speeches "belong naturally to every sort of quarrel in which one party feels himself to be let down by another." See also Blankenbaker, "Language," 154 and Buss, *Prophetic Word*, 77. J. Limburg ("The Root רִיב and the Prophetic Lawsuit Speeches," *JBL* 88 [1969]: 291–304) concludes that the רִיב terminology of the prophets comes from the language of conflict in international treaties rather than of legal court proceedings. See also M. DeRoche, who argues that the term רִיב denotes a lawsuit only when a dispute is solved by a judge; the word itself is not a technical term for a legal proceeding ("Yahweh's RÎB against Israel: A Reassessment of the So-Called 'Prophetic Lawsuit' in the Preexilic Prophets," *JBL* 102 [1983]: 569).

[33] McKeating, *Books*, 81 and Weems, "Gomer," 91. The NEB has also adopted this reading. See discussion in Light, "Theory-Constitutive Metaphor," 98–99.

[34] Andersen and Freedman, *Hosea*, 223.

wife initiates divorce proceedings against her husband.[35] The majority of these texts prescribe the death penalty for the wife, not only in cases where she is guilty of misbehavior but simply as a punishment for initiating divorce. For example, an OB text states: "Should Tarām-Sagila and Iltani say to Warad-Šamaš, their husband, 'You are not my [*sic*] husband,' they shall throw them from a tower."[36] Another OB text, involving the same name, makes a similar declaration:

> And should Warad-Šamaš say to his wives, 'You are not my wives,' he will pay a mina of silver. And should they say to Warad-Šamaš, their husband, 'You are not our husband,' they will bind them and throw them into the river.[37]

Several other Babylonian texts refer to a woman who initiates divorce and prescribe the penalty of drowning.[38] It seems that wife-initiated divorce, even more so than adultery, is the primary action that warrants the death penalty in ancient Near Eastern marriage laws.

The death-penalty texts, however, do not represent the only course of action available to the husband in this circumstance. There are several cases in which the wife initiates divorce and is simply required to pay a penalty of divorce-money.[39] For example, one OB text reads, "And if one day PN will say unto PN her husband: 'You are not my husband,' she shall forfeit house, field, and property and pay 1/3 mina silver."[40] This alternative financial punishment appears in both Babylonian and Assyrian texts.[41] Even the Hittite laws 26a (ca. 1650–1500 B.C.E.) allow for the wife to initiate divorce without the penalty of death: "If a woman re[fuses] a man, [the man] shall give [her ...] and [the woman shall take] a wage for her seed. But the man [shall take the land] and the children [...]."[42] As Hendriks notes, the ancient Near Eastern texts actually attest a wide *variety* of punitive *options* for a wife who initiates divorce, including both physical and financial: 1) CH §142 says the wife must take her

---

[35] See E. Lipiński, "The Wife's Right to Divorce in the Light of an Ancient Near Eastern Tradition," *JLA* 4 (1981): 9–26.

[36] R. Harris, "The Case of Three Babylonian Marriage Contracts," *JNES* 33 (1974): 365.

[37] Ibid., 367.

[38] For a list of texts, see S. Greengus, "A Textbook Case of Adultery in Ancient Mesopotamia," *HUCA* 40–41 (1969–70): 41, f.n. 22.

[39] CH §142 also allows a wife to divorce her husband without penalty when there is certain justification. For a collection of relevant evidence, see Tal Ilan, "Notes and Observations on a Newly Published Divorce Bill from the Judean Desert," *HTR* 89 (1996): 195–202. Cf. Instone-Brewer, *Divorce*, 19.

[40] Greengus, "Textbook Case," 39.

[41] See ibid.

[42] *COS* 2:109. It is not clear whether this law deals with a wife divorcing her husband or only refusing to comply with the relationship. Hoffner notes, however, that another manuscript of this law reads "divorces" rather than "refuses" (ibid., f.n. 20).

dowry and leave, 2) a Nippur text states that the wife may be enslaved and sold, 3) a second Nippur text prescribes that she must forfeit her dowry and pay divorce money, and 4) an Alalakh text states that the wife must forfeit her bride price.[43]

In light of these diverse texts, there has been much debate over whether the wife was legally permitted to initiate divorce in the ancient Near East.[44] Can the circumstances be considered legal if there are punitive actions attached? The texts just cited suggest that the death penalty prescribed in some cases was meant to function at the husband's discretion and perhaps only as a deterrent to a practice that could legally occur. Thus, the penalties for wife-initiated divorce simply varied in different contexts.[45] When a wife initiated divorce without proper cause (i.e., without wrongdoing by the husband; cf. CH §142), the husband had a set of punitive options available to him, including both physical and financial. While this situation of wife-initiated divorce does not find direct expression in the Hebrew Bible, the law in Exod 21:7–11 appears to stipulate a wife's right to divorce if she has been neglected.[46] By the time of the later Jewish texts from Elephantine in the fifth century B.C.E., the wife appears to have achieved equal power to initiate divorce with or without just cause, and there are no texts that allow the death penalty as a type of deterrent to the practice.[47]

Thus, the evidence indicates that there were cases in which a wife could take the initiative and divorce her husband. On some occasions, this action seems to be legal and associated with typical financial settlements, while on other occasions it appears to be illegal and proscribed via the threat of death. One could perhaps argue that these ancient Near Eastern texts refer only to a wife's refusal to comply with the marital relationship and not her initiation of divorce. Against this interpretation, however, is the fact that the typical language of divorce ascribed to both the husband and wife is exactly the same: "You are not my husband" parallels "You are not my wife" in Old Babylonian

---

[43] Hendriks, "Juridical Aspects," 46–47; cf. E. Goodfriend, "Adultery," *ABD* 1:82–86.

[44] See discussion, especially of positions of Driver, Miles, and van Praage, in R. Westbrook, *Old Babylonian Marriage Law* (AfO 23; Horn, Austria: Ferdinand Berger & Sons, 1988), 79.

[45] See Westbrook, *Old Babylonian Marriage*, 82. Collins notes that the woman's right to divorce is assumed at Elephantine but not yet given in biblical texts (see L. Perdue, J. Blenkinsopp, J. Collins, and C. Meyers, *Families in Ancient Israel* [The Family, Religion, and Culture. Louisville: Westminster John Knox, 1997], 119). He observes that several Babylonian laws allude to this practice but maintains that these are exceptional. In his view, a wife could divorce her husband only if he was at fault in some way (ibid.). In this regard, Collins cites CH §142–143 and counts the texts that prescribe the death penalty as literal laws that serve to prohibit, not deter, wife-initiated divorce. For further discussion, see Lipiński, "Wife's Right to Divorce," 9–26.

[46] See J. Otwell, *And Sarah Laughed: The Status of Women in the Old Testament* (Philadelphia: Westminster, 1977), 120–21.

[47] See R. Yaron, *Introduction to the Law of the Aramaic Papyri* (Oxford: Clarendon, 1961), 46; cf. Instone-Brewer, *Divorce*, 79.

texts. One cannot take the husband's words as signifying divorce while taking the wife's equivalent statement as signifying only refusal. Nonetheless, it is clear that, even on occasions when the wife moves to divorce her husband, the husband retains power over the wife and can decide her fate.

Seen in this way, the actual practices associated with wife-initiated divorce in the ancient Near East may provide a way forward for understanding the prophet's marriage/divorce imagery in Hos 2. Scholars have long acknowledged that it is the wife in Hos 2 whose actions have violated the marriage union. Even so, the statement in Hos 2:4 does *not* present the oracle as a case of wife-initiated divorce. The verse does not contain a technical formula at all, particularly not the technical language for a wife's divorce of her husband. This point is illustrated by Kuhl's effort to emend verse four to include the wife's statement of divorce. Linking the stripping pictured in verse 5 with the stripping stipulated as a punishment for a wife who initiates divorce in two Babylonian texts, he suggests that one should emend verse 4 to include the phrase, "Denn sie hat gesagt: 'Du bist nicht mein Mann.'"[48]

As Kuhl's treatment shows, Hos 2:4 cannot fit the precise image-base of wife-initiated divorce without emendation. Nonetheless, the language in 2:4 and the wife's statements throughout 2:4–15 point to a situation in which the wife refuses to comply with the present marital relationship, that is, she refuses to submit to the husband's authority. Verse 4 in particular, then, functions not as a divorce formula by either partner but as the metaphorical husband's *description* of the present state of the marital relationship. Within the overall metaphorical discourse, Yahweh, the wronged husband, appropriately appeals to his children in the midst of a situation in which their mother is rejecting the relationship.[49] Yahweh's speech in the rest of Hos 2 picks up and explores many of the punitive options noted above in ancient Near Eastern texts dealing with wives who behave improperly, commit adultery, initiate divorce, etc. The conflicting statements of death, punishment, and reconciliation, which run through the chapter, can be understood as drawing upon the imagery of various punitive options available to the husband in these types of situations. As the rest of this study will show, the different sections of Yahweh's speech reflect the various options: death/destruction (2:5–6), confinement/enslavement (2:8–9), divorce with cause (2:11–15), and reconciliation (2:16–25). Seen in this light, Hos 2:4 does not represent a divorce formula but a description of a situation in which the wife refuses to comply with the marital relationship, and this description again suggests that the primary image-base of Hosea's metaphorical language is the actual practices of marriage and divorce in the ancient Near East.

---

[48] Kuhl, "Neue Dokumente," 108.

[49] This view has been briefly suggested by Beeby (*Grace Abounding*, 22–23). He says that the text can be read both as husband-initiated and wife-initiated divorce, i.e., a "dual seeking for divorce."

1.3 The Punishments against the Wife in 2:4–15

The other part of Hos 2 that contributes to the link with the image-base of marriage/divorce practices is the variety of punishments against the wife in 2:4–15. As the metaphorical speech unfolds, Yahweh lists several punitive actions to be taken against his adulterous wife. Hosea 2:5 states, "Lest I will strip her naked and expose her as on the day of her birth." Verse 8 also threatens, "Therefore I will block her path with thorns; I will wall in her wall so that she cannot find her paths." Finally, 2:12 asserts, "And now I will uncover her genitals before the eyes of her lovers."

The first impulse of scholars in trying to understand these actions has been to identify them as actual, legal punishments for adultery, prostitution, and divorce in the ancient Near East. In order to understand the punishment imagery in this way, interpreters must first deal with the issue of whether the death penalty was a mandatory punishment for adultery in Israel and the ancient Near East. The main extrabiblical laws regarding adultery clearly show that there was a wide range of options available to the husband of an adulterous wife.[50] For example, MAL 13 represents the basic case of adultery between two knowing participants, and it prescribes the death penalty for both. Likewise, the Hittite Laws 197, Codex Eshnunna 28, and MAL 15 allow for a husband to kill his wife and her lover on the spot if they are discovered in *flagrante delicto*.[51] The second part of MAL 15, however, states that if the husband brings the wife and her lover to court, he may choose from a variety of options. He is only required to deal with the lover in the same manner in which he deals with his wife: "[I]f the husband of the woman kills his wife, he shall kill the man; if he cuts off his wife's nose, he shall turn the man into a eunuch and his whole face shall be mutilated; but if he frees his wife, he shall free the man."[52] This type of discretion ("whatever the husband states;" "if the wife's master lets his wife live") is also granted to the offended husband in MAL 14 and 16, CH §129, and the Hittite Laws 198.

While none of these texts covers all the different types of adultery, they indicate that the husband could choose from a variety of lesser punishments than death. For the societies outside of Israel, the death penalty was not a mandatory punishment for adultery.[53] The situation within ancient Israel, however, remains debated. The only two biblical laws that deal directly with adultery (Lev 20:10 and Deut 22:22) prescribe death for both the paramour and woman.

---

[50] One can find a survey of these laws in Westbrook, "Adultery," 549–58.

[51] The Codex Ur-Nammu 7 prescribes death for the wife alone if she seduces an unwitting man (Westbrook, "Adultery," 550).

[52] Ibid., 552; cf. *COS* 2:354–55.

[53] Instone-Brewer (*Divorce*, 9) argues that lesser punishments were allowed only in cases of doubt or coercion, but he does not consider MAL 15.

Accordingly, there is a long scholarly tradition of asserting that Israel was unique in its environment because it viewed adultery as a sin against God that was punishable only by death.[54]

The entire sweep of the Hebrew Bible's direct and indirect evidence for adultery punishments, however, indicates that death was simply one possible option. Buss has led the way in this regard, particularly concerning Lev 20:10 and Deut 22:22. He emphasizes that biblical legal expressions using an infinitive absolute and imperfect sometimes clearly mean only "may" and not "shall" (e.g., Lev 21:3). Outside of the laws, the imperfect often carries the sense of permission rather than demand. Thus, death penalty expressions like those in Lev 20:10 and Deut 22:22 can be translated "he may be killed" and may represent a case where civil and criminal law overlap.[55] McKeating also observes that the laws in Leviticus and Deuteronomy are late and do not reflect long-standing social practice.[56] Westbrook further notes that these laws represent only one particular case of adultery: sex between two willing partners.[57] The Hebrew Bible includes several poetic, narrative, and wisdom texts that affirm the possibility of different punishments for other types of adultery.[58]

As interpreters used prophetic oracles like Hos 2, Jer 13, Ezek 16, and Ezek 23 to show that the death penalty was not mandatory for adultery, they noticed that these texts all contain imagery related to stripping in the metaphorical context of marriage, divorce, and adultery. By comparing this imagery with statements in extrabiblical legal texts, many interpreters concluded that the primary legal punishment for an adulterous woman in Israel and elsewhere was public stripping and exposure for humiliation. This view took the punishment

---

[54] The most recent major statement of this position is A. Phillips, "Another Look at Adultery," *JSOT* 20 (1981): 3–25. He argues that, even though the death penalty laws for adultery are found in D and H, they did not originate late. He also asserts that all references to actions besides the death penalty in the Hebrew Bible refer only to illegal practices or metaphorical situations. The only possible exceptions result from the fact that, in his view, D and H were the first to include women in the law and make them liable for adultery. Thus, he concludes that some texts that date before D and H, including Hosea, do allow for other actions besides the death penalty regarding an adulterous woman (ibid, 16).

[55] M. Buss, "The Distinction between Civil and Criminal Law in Ancient Israel," in *Proceedings of the 6th World Congress of Jewish Studies I* (Jerusalem: Academic Press, 1977), 55–56. For Buss, "civil law" deals with relations within a group where settlements are made for the benefit of a private individual. "Criminal law" deals with conflicts between an individual and his group or its leader, which involve other penalties in the community (ibid., 52).

[56] H. McKeating, "Sanctions against Adultery in Ancient Israelite Society, with Some Reflections on Methodology in the Study of Old Testament Ethics," *JSOT* 11 (1979): 57–72.

[57] Westbrook, "Adultery," 549.

[58] For example, Prov 6:32–35 mentions a ransom paid to an offended husband, and Gen 38:26 reports Judah's pardon of Tamar (see ibid., 544–45).

aspects of Hosea's speech as drawing upon the image-base of an established procedure of stripping and humiliating adulteresses.[59]

There are several extrabiblical texts that seem to match the prophetic imagery and support the idea that stripping was an established legal punishment for adultery: 1) a Sumerian text (IM 28051), 2) an OB text from Ḫana (BRM 4 52),[60] 3) four tablets from Nuzi (HSS 5 71; HSS 19 1; HSS 19 10; JEN 444),[61] 4) a late Bronze age text from Emar,[62] 5) an incantation text from Nippar,[63] and 6) a passage from Tacitus's *Germania*.[64] Each of these texts makes some mention of nakedness or loss of clothing for the wife involved. For example, Greengus cites a Sumerian text that deals, in his view, with a case in which a husband has caught his wife in *flagrante delicto* with another man. The relevant portion reads: "The assembly, because with a man upon her she was caught, his/her divorce money ... (they) decided; ... (her) pudendum they shaved; they bored her nose with an arrow (and) to be led around the city the king gave her over."[65] An Akkadian text cited by Huehnergard also refers to loss of clothing, this time upon the occasion of divorce: "If PN my wife would follow a strange man, let her place her clothes on a stool, and go where she will."[66] This last provision also appears in the texts from Ḫana and Nuzi, which prescribe that, in the case of divorce, the woman must go out of the house without her clothes. From this starting point, scholars typically appeal for clarification to a variety of biblical prophetic texts that appear to allude to an established punishment of public stripping for adulteresses. The imagery in Hos 2:5–12 plays a major part

---

[59] See R. Gordis, "Hosea's Marriage and Message: A New Approach," *HUCA* 25 (1954): 20–21; Gordon, "Hosea 2:4–5," 280; Greengus, "Textbook Case," 40; Kuhl, "Neue Dokumente," 102–9; McKeating, "Sanctions," 61; E. Neufeld, *Ancient Hebrew Marriage Laws* (London: Longmans, Green, & Co., 1944), 166; Nwaoru, *Imagery*, 142; S. Paul, "Biblical Analogues to Middle Assyrian Law," in *Religion and Law: Biblical-Judaic and Islamic Perspectives* (ed. E. Firmage, B. Weiss, and J. Welch; Winona Lake, Ind.: Eisenbrauns, 1990), 344; Westbrook, "Adultery," 560.

[60] Kuhl, "Neue Dokumente," 102–9. For original publication, see Clay, *Babylonian Records*.

[61] E. Cassin, "Pouvoirs de la femme et structures familiales," *RA* 63 (1969): 121–48.

[62] J. Huehnergard, "Biblical Notes on Some New Akkadian Texts from Emar (Syria)," *CBQ* 47 (1985): 428–34.

[63] See Paul, "Biblical Analogues," 344.

[64] Some interpreters have also argued that public stripping may have been an established legal action against prostitutes. Evidence for this generally comes from a reconstructed reading of the very fragmentary Sefire Inscription IA 40–41: "[And as a pros]ti[tute is stripped naked], so may the wives of Mati'el, the wives of his offspring and the wives of [his] n[obles] be stripped" (J. Fitzmyer, *The Aramaic Inscriptions of Sefire* [Rome: Biblical Institute, 1967], 14; see also Huehnergard, "Biblical Notes," 433–34; Kruger, "Marriage Metaphor," 15; and P. Day, "Adulterous Jerusalem's Imagined Demise: Death of a Metaphor in Ezekiel XVI," *VT* 50 [2000], 296). However, the fragmentary nature of the Sefire text makes it questionable to derive such theoretical positions from it. It does not appear that general prostitution was considered illegal in the ancient Near East.

[65] Greengus, "Textbook Case," 35; cf. *COS* 3:140.

[66] Huehnergard, "Biblical Notes," 431.

in this argument. Other commonly cited texts include Isa 3:17, Jer 13:22–27, Ezek 23:26, and Nah 3:5.

In one of the most important developments for the study of the metaphorical imagery in Hos 2, however, Day has formulated a detailed critique of the interpretation that the punishment imagery in texts like Hos 2 and Ezek 16 is modeled on the real life punishments for adultery in the ancient Near East.[67] The problem, as she conceives it, is that interpreters have failed to recognize the figurative language of the texts that talk about stripping for adultery and have rushed into a search for supposed social realities.[68]

Day's evidence is persuasive. The ancient Near Eastern texts commonly cited to support the stripping-as-punishment interpretation do not, in fact, do so. For example, the Sumerian text cited by Greengus is the only one that explicitly seems to connect stripping with adultery. It is, however, very unclear and has produced three radically different readings. Remarkably, as Day correctly observes, while all of the remaining ancient Near Eastern texts mention the wife's nakedness in connection with things like initiating divorce, remarrying after her husband's death, and property offenses, there is no mention of adultery.[69]

The commonly cited prophetic texts also fail to establish a secure link between text and social reality. Isaiah 3:17 does not mention adultery at all, and the remaining prophetic texts refer to adultery and stripping only in metaphorical contexts dealing with personified female figures.[70] These textual observations uphold Day's proposal that the imagery of stripping and exposure, like that in Hos 2, does not have its source in the image-base of ancient Near Eastern marriage, that is, in real-life punishments of sexual violence for adultery. Such punitive stripping does not seem to have existed, and it appears that the reader must seek the background of this violent part of Hosea's metaphorical imagery elsewhere.

Thus, one should reconsider exactly what the imagery of a wife leaving her clothes and going out of the house naked symbolizes within ancient Near Eastern divorce customs. The ancient Near Eastern texts that mention this practice, except for the very fragmentary Sumerian document, all involve situations in which the current marriage is ending and the wife is leaving due to inappropriate actions or the desire to follow another man. In the transition from one marital status to another one finds the stipulations that the wife must leave her clothes behind. For example, as noted above, an Akkadian text from Emar notes that, after the death of her husband, a wife who desires to "follow a strange man" must "place her clothes on a stool, and go where she will."

---

[67] Day, "Adulterous Jerusalem," 285–309. Cf. Day, "Bitch," 231–54.

[68] Day, "Adulterous Jerusalem," 286. Cf. McKeating, "Sanctions," 62.

[69] Day, "Adulterous Jerusalem," 296–99.

[70] Ibid., 300–301. Cf. Garrett, *Hosea, Joel*, 78 and Stienstra, *YHWH*, 86.

In all of these texts, the act of stripping is not connected with punishment but has more to do with economics, property, and inheritance. The act of going from the house naked seems to be only a symbolic expression of a legal change in relationship. Huehnergard expresses this idea well:

> While there is in all of these texts undoubtedly an element of humiliation intended in forcing an individual to leave the paternal estate naked, there is clearly also an economic motive: the individual, prohibited from taking even a stitch of clothing, is made to renounce, symbolically, any claim to the estate in question.[71]

Several other documents bear out this interpretation of the act of stripping in general. For example, an Ugaritic royal divorce text (17.396) stipulates that if the son/heir wants to leave with his mother who is departing, "*his* dress upon the throne he shall put and shall go."[72] A Hittite law also notes that the stripping of a son's robe by his mother is a symbolic indication of the breaking of family ties.[73] Even within the Hebrew Bible, one finds a possible reference to the fact that stripping was not for public humiliation but for symbolizing a change of status. Deuteronomy 21:13 stipulates that if a man wants to marry a captive woman, she must shave her head, pare her nails, and discard the clothes she had when captured.[74]

Taken together, the ancient Near Eastern texts seem to indicate that the practice of stripping and going out naked was not a punishment of public humiliation for *adulteresses*. The leaving behind of the clothes could symbolize changes in economic or property connections upon divorce or remarriage after death,[75] but representations of sexual violence, like those in Hos 2:5 and 12, should not be linked with actual legalities concerning adultery.

The so-called divorce formula in 2:4 stands within the chapter's overall marriage metaphor and seconds the notion that this metaphor draws from the image-base of actual ancient Near Eastern practices of marriage and divorce. The sexual violence depicted in Hos 2:4–15 does not. This imagery of physical and sexual violence against a woman thus suggests the presence of another image-base at work within the chapter. More importantly, Hos 2 contains a significant amount of other imagery that is illuminated by the image-base of ancient Near Eastern marriage practices and does not involve metaphorical representations of sexual violence. In order to further understand Hos 2's

---

[71] Huehnergard, "Biblical Notes," 432.

[72] Yaron, "Royal Divorce," 23; emphasis added.

[73] See discussion in Kruger, "Marriage Metaphor," 13.

[74] Cf. Hendriks, "Juridical Aspects," 65.

[75] As Day adds, "[N]akedness may well correspond to as well as symbolize the fact that such a woman would forfeit the goods that she brought into the marriage as a penalty for terminating the marriage" ("Adulterous Jerusalem," 299).

marriage metaphor, let us examine the primary characteristics of its image-base (ancient Near Eastern marriage and divorce practices) before turning to the source of the additional images of sexual violence.

2. THE CHARACTERISTICS OF THE PRIMARY IMAGE-BASE AND ITS USE IN HOSEA 2

Texts that assign various financial penalties upon divorce and describe the symbolic act of leaving clothes behind suggest that aspects related to finances and property occupy the central place in the practices of ancient Near Eastern marriage and divorce.[76] As the following discussion aims to show, the laws that govern these aspects reveal that the image-base of marriage/divorce practices specifically revolves around economic and property issues like compensation and inheritance. Moreover, even though interpreters consistently explain the imagery of verses like Hos 2:10–11, which mention Yahweh's giving and retrieving of things like grain, wine, oil, wool, and linen, by referring to image-bases like that of a supposed Baal fertility cult, the centrality of the economic and property aspects in ancient Near Eastern marriage texts suggests that the practice of divorce itself also involved consideration of such items.

2.1 Economic and Property Aspects of Ancient Near Eastern Marriage

Throughout the ancient Near East, a significant element in the marriage process was the payment of the so-called "bride price" by the groom to the family of the bride. This payment appears in marriage texts from all of the major ancient Near Eastern civilizations.[77] The Hebrew Bible itself, however, contains little direct information concerning the bride price, referred to with the Hebrew word מֹהַר. No biblical law requires a bride price for normal marriages, but the laws governing rape and seduction (Exod 22:16–17; Deut 22:28–29), as well as several narratives, assume this payment.[78] For example, when Shechem asked for Dinah in marriage (Gen 34:12), he offered to pay a large מֹהַר. In such texts, the amount of the bride price varied and remained unspecified except in the case

---

[76] For a detailed study of the contractual and financial nature of marriage in the ancient Near East, see Instone-Brewer, *Divorce*.

[77] For texts from Babylon, Nuzi, Ugarit, and Elephantine, see Braaten, "Parent-Child," 161–67 and Breneman, "Nuzi Marriage Tablets," 22. The major Ugaritic text indicating a bride price transaction is KTU 1.24 (UT 77), which describes the proceedings that lead to the marriage of the moon god Yariḫ and Nikkal.

[78] M. Satlow, *Jewish Marriage in Antiquity* (Princeton: Princeton University Press, 2001), 200.

of marriage after rape (Deut 22:29).[79] The Jewish marriage texts from Elephantine also attested a variety of different amounts for the bride price.[80]

There remains much scholarly debate over exactly what the payment of the bride price signified. Burrows notes several major explanations: 1) the price of establishing the legitimacy of the children,[81] 2) the price of making the woman the mother of the husband's children, 3) remuneration for the expense of having raised the girl,[82] 4) compensation to the bride for the loss of her virginity,[83] and 5) security for the fulfillment of the contract.[84] In any case, the prominent role that these texts assign to the wife's bride price and dowry in situations of divorce suggests that the payment was primarily a provision to be used upon the dissolution of the marriage.

The bride price established a legal married status for the husband and wife with only cohabitation to follow. The payment of the bride price to the bride's father marked the beginning of a period of betrothal leading to the formal marriage ceremony and rendered the marriage legally effective. As Westbrook explains, the payment of the bride price created a state that may be called "inchoate marriage." In the public's view, the couple was married, but the woman remained in her father's house until the actual wedding.[85] Evidence for this practice appears in texts like CH §159–161, which concern cases where marriages do not take place after the payment of the bride price but still refer to the woman as the man's "wife" (*aššassu*).

The aspect of the bride price that is most significant for understanding the imagery of Hos 2 is its close relationship with another financial element of marriage, the wife's dowry. Various texts from Babylon, Nuzi, Ugarit, and Elephantine indicate that the bride's father gave a portion of the bride price to

---

[79] See C. Taber, "Marriage," *IDBSup*, 575. Phillips takes this reference as indicating that the bride price in Israel had become standardized at fifty shekels ("Another Look," 9).

[80] For example, Cowley 15 mentions 5 shekels, Kraeling 7 refers to 1 karsh (= 10 shekels), and Kraeling 2 seems to imply a bride price of 7 ½ shekels. One should note, however, that each of the major Elephantine marriage texts represents a special case and not a normal marriage. In Cowley 15, the bride is a divorcee; in Kraeling 7, she is a freed woman; in Kraeling 2, she is a slave. These complications make it difficult to draw any conclusions from these texts regarding a standard bride price. See Yaron, *Introduction*, 47–48.

[81] See Braaten, "Parent-Child," 137.

[82] Taber, "Marriage," 575; Kruger, "Marriage Metaphor," 19.

[83] C. F. Keil has been the primary one to argue that, in Israel, the bride price was not given to the father but to the bride (see C. F. Keil, *The Twelve Minor Prophets* [Edinburgh: T&T Clark, 1868], 1:69).

[84] M. Burrows, *The Basis of Israelite Marriage* (AOS 15; New Haven: American Oriental Society, 1938), 53–71.

[85] This state appears to represent the meaning of the Hebrew term אֵרַשׂ, which appears in Hos 2:21–22. See Westbrook, "Adultery," 570. Cf. Braaten, "Parent-Child," 188; V. Matthews, "Marriage and Family in the Ancient Near East," in *Marriage and Family in the Biblical World* (ed. K. Campbell; Downer's Grove, Ill.: InterVarsity Press, 2003), 9; Neufeld, *Ancient Hebrew Marriage Laws*, 94; Satlow, *Jewish Marriage*, 69; Stienstra, *YHWH*, 94; Taber, "Marriage," 575.

his daughter as her dowry upon entering the marriage.[86] For example, Elephantine text Kraeling 7 explicitly lists the bride price as part of the wife's dowry that she brought into the marriage. Other texts testify to this practice with reports of the father binding the bride price in the bride's girdle.[87] Since the bride typically gains control of the bride price through her father, the ancient texts seem unclear about who receives the bride price if the wife is on her second marriage. Westbrook notes that OB texts show that on a second marriage after divorce, the divorcee acts independently of her family, so she perhaps receives the bride price.[88] In most OB texts reflecting this situation, however, there is no mention of a bride price. In Elephantine text Cowley 15, the wife is a divorcee, but the husband pays the bride price to her father. Thus, one may imagine that the wife did, in some cases, receive the bride price herself, but the texts do not seem to indicate conclusively a standard practice in this regard.

The wife's dowry denotes the property that the wife brings into the marriage and retains possession of throughout the course of the relationship.[89] The bride typically receives the dowry from her father but could receive it from other members of her family or even the husband himself.[90] The ancient Hebrew marriage laws refer to the dowry as שׁלחים, "parting gifts," and perhaps indicate that the dowry takes the place of the bride's inheritance from her father's house.[91] The wife thus remained the technical owner of the dowry throughout the marriage, since it became her support for life if she outlived her

---

[86] See Braaten, "Parent-Child," 167, 197–98; Breneman, "Nuzi Marriage Tablets," 5; Burrows, *Basis*, 44; J. Fitzmyer, "A Re-Study of an Elephantine Aramaic Marriage Contract (AP 15)," in *Near Eastern Studies in Honor of W. F. Albright* (ed. H. Goedicke; Baltimore: The John Hopkins University Press, 1971), 144; K. Grosz, "Dowry and Brideprice in Nuzi," in *Studies on the Civilization and Culture of Nuzi and the Hurrians* (Winona Lake, Ind.: Eisenbrauns, 1981), 1:163–70; Neufeld, *Ancient Hebrew Marriage Laws*, 105; R. Westbrook, *Property and the Family in Biblical Law* (JSOTSup 113; Sheffield: JSOT Press, 1991), 150; Yaron, "Aramaic Marriage Contracts," 6. Collins uses the textual sources to outline a three-stage history of the bride price in this regard. Originally, the bride price was paid to the bride's father and he kept it. In the second stage, particularly in Elephantine texts, the bride price was converted into part of the bride's dowry. Finally, by rabbinic times, it was paid only upon divorce. See Perdue, Blenkinsopp, Collins, and Meyers, *Families*, 113–14.

[87] See Hendriks, "Juridical Aspects," 22. Understanding this practice helps prevent misunderstandings, like that of Muntingh, that the *terḥatum* and *mhr* in Ugaritic texts must not be bride prices because they seem to be money or property given to the wife by her father (see L. Muntingh, "Married Life in Israel according to the Book of Hosea," in *Studies on the Books of Hosea and Amos* [Die Ou Testamentiese Werkgemeenskap in Suid Afrika 7/8; Potchefstroom: Pro Rege Pers Beperk, 1964–65], 80–81).

[88] Westbrook, *Old Babylonian Marriage*, 61–62. Cf. W. Vogels, "Hosea's Gift to Gomer (Hos 3, 2)," *Bib* 69 (1988): 412–21.

[89] Westbrook, *Property*, 143–44; cf. Instone-Brewer, *Divorce*, 4–6 and Matthews, "Marriage," 14.

[90] For example, two Nuzi texts attest situations in which the brother provided the dowry to his sister (see Grosz, "Dowry and Brideprice," 169).

[91] Neufeld, *Ancient Hebrew Marriage Laws*, 110.

husband.[92] Since the Elephantine texts that detail the dowries do so for the purpose of recording the monetary value of each item, however, it seems that the actual property was shared during the marriage but the wife regained the monetary equivalent of that property upon the dissolution of the marriage.[93]

This picture of the dowry appears widely in ancient Near Eastern texts and, significantly for Hos 2, all of these texts stipulate the property consequences that correspond to different ways of dissolving the marriage (death, divorce with cause, divorce without cause, etc.). For example, Nuzi marriage texts refer to the dowry as *mulûgu* and indicate that its contents vary from household utensils to jewelry to land,[94] while twenty Demotic marriage contracts list the property brought in by the wife and stipulate that the husband cannot later claim that she did not bring it.[95] Within the Hebrew Bible itself, however, the dowry receives little direct mention. The primary term, שׁלחים, appears only in 1 Kgs 9:16, Mic 1:14, and perhaps Exod 18:2.[96] Even so, there are narrative examples of the dowry that occur in the stories of Sarah (Gen 16:1), Rebekah (Gen 24:61), Leah, and Rachel (Gen 29:24, 29), who all seem to have received their handmaidens as part of their dowry.[97]

The practice of bridal gifts, given by the groom to the bride, provides a third financial aspect of marriage and divorce.[98] The general Hebrew term for these gifts is מתּן. While no biblical laws refer to this practice, it does appear in some narrative contexts. The best example is Shechem's marriage proposal to Dinah in Gen 34:12: "Fix (רבה) the bride price (מהר) and gift (מתּן) as high as you like; I will give (נתן) whatever you demand from me."[99] In these contexts, the term seems parallel to the Babylonian and Assyrian *nudunnū*, which appears in the Code of Hammurabi.[100] These texts suggest that the bridal gifts could consist of diverse things, including money, property, and land.[101]

The final financial aspect of the marriage image-base deals with what may be called "bridal provisions." Marriage contracts from the ancient Near East often specify that the husband is required to provide his wife with certain amounts of food, clothing, and personal supplies.[102] These provisions typically

---

[92] Westbrook, *Property*, 144–45; cf. Grosz, "Dowry and Brideprice," 179.

[93] Satlow, *Jewish Marriage*, 205.

[94] See Breneman, "Nuzi Marriage Tablets," 267 and Grosz, "Dowry and Brideprice," 161.

[95] Yaron, "Royal Divorce," 28.

[96] See Westbrook, *Property*, 142.

[97] For this argument, see Hendriks, "Juridical Aspects," 25.

[98] See Burrows, *Basis*, 46; L. Epstein, *The Jewish Marriage Contract: A Study in the Status of the Woman in Jewish Law* (The Jewish People: History, Religion, Literature; New York: Arno, 1973), 78; Kruger, "Marriage Metaphor," 19. There is at least one reference in the Hebrew Bible where the gifts are given to the bride by the groom's father (Gen 24:53) (Otwell, *Sarah*, 37).

[99] See also Eleazer's gifts to Rebekah in Gen 24.

[100] Neufeld, *Ancient Hebrew Marriage Laws*, 113.

[101] For example, MAL 25–26 indicates that gifts may consist of ornaments and jewelry.

[102] Buss, *Prophetic Word*, 88.

appear in the groups of food (e.g., barley), oil, and clothing.[103] One finds these stipulations primarily in ancient Near Eastern laws dealing with the absence of the husband for an extended period of time. For example, MAL A 36 prescribes that a woman must only remain faithful to her husband for five years if he "has gone to the field(s) (and) has left her neither oil nor wood nor clothing nor food nor anything else and has had no provision(?) brought to her from the fields...."[104] The Laws of Lipit-Ishtar also legislate that if a man has had a child with a professional prostitute, "he shall provide grain, oil, and clothing for that harlot...."[105] Even within the biblical laws, the husband's obligation to provide food and clothing appears: "If he takes another woman, he shall not deprive the first of meat, clothes, and conjugal rights" (Exod 21:10 NEB).[106]

This element of legally stipulated bridal provisions emphasizes the centrality that items like food, clothing, and oil have in the practices related to marriage and divorce in the ancient Near East and further strengthens the notion that such practices are characterized by a dominant concern with economic and property issues.

2.2 Legalities Governing Ancient Near Eastern Marriage and Divorce

The financial aspects outlined above operate under certain laws and stipulations that further illuminate this image-base for Hos 2's marriage imagery. Various ancient Near Eastern texts pertaining to marriage and divorce indicate an important distinction between the laws governing divorce without due cause and divorce with just cause. Different financial consequences, regarding both money and property, are connected with different types of divorce, and Old Babylonian, Nuzi, Ugaritic, Middle Assyrian, and Elephantine texts all seem to acknowledge, or at least imply, this distinction.[107]

The work of Westbrook contains the most substantial explanation of this topic, especially as it pertains to ancient Israel.[108] In his article on the prohibition of remarriage in Deut 24:1–4, Westbrook provides a detailed survey of all the ancient Near Eastern laws pertaining to the different types of

---

[103] Hendriks, "Juridical Aspects," 28.

[104] Ibid., 29; cf. *ANET* 183.

[105] *ANET* 160.

[106] Cf. Hendriks, "Juridical Aspects," 30.

[107] For the Elephantine marriage texts, see discussion below. For the primary Ugaritic divorce texts, see Yaron, "Royal Divorce," 21–31. For a list of OB marriage texts, see S. Greengus, "The Old Babylonian Marriage Contract," *JAOS* 89 (1969): 512, f.n. 29. The sources from Nuzi consist of about 100 cuneiform tablets from the fifteenth and early fourteenth centuries B.C.E. See Breneman, "Nuzi Marriage Tablets," 12.

[108] See Westbrook, "Adultery;" Westbrook, *Property*; and Westbrook, *Old Babylonian Marriage*.

dissolution of marriage.[109] The bulk of the texts contain stipulations for dealing with the situation of a husband who wishes to divorce his wife without any specific cause. In these cases, as well as in the case of the death of the husband, the wife was entitled to receive a financial settlement consisting of the dowry (or its monetary equivalent)[110] that she brought into the marriage and generally including additional divorce money also. When divorced without justification, the wife took out everything she brought into the marriage relationship.[111] Westbrook notes that the earliest example of this general practice of compensation for the divorcee comes from the Codex Ur-Nammu 6–7: "If a man divorces his wife, he must pay one mina of silver."[112] CH §138 also grants the wife not only her dowry but her bride price: "If a man divorces his first wife who has not borne children he shall upon divorcing her give her money in the amount of her bride-money (*terḫatum*) and make good to her the dowry that she brought from her father's house."[113]

There is another series of laws, however, that prescribe different financial consequences in cases of divorce with justifiable cause. In these texts, the wife commits some action, perhaps as serious as adultery, which allows the husband to divorce her and escape the regular financial consequences. This type of case would also certainly apply if the wife was refusing to comply with the relationship, seeking other lovers, etc. The husband was entitled to keep all the wife's property and to send her away without anything. It is reasonable to infer that this financial practice functioned as a sort of compensation to the husband for the wrong done to him.[114]

---

[109] R. Westbrook, "The Prohibition on Restoration of Marriage in Deuteronomy 24:1–4," in *Studies in Bible* (ed. S. Japhet; Hierosolymitana 31; Jerusalem: Magnes, 1986), 387–405.

[110] For example, both OB and Elephantine marriage texts list the monetary values of the dowry items, seemingly for the purpose of later restoring to the wife the value of her original dowry.

[111] Westbrook, "Prohibition," 396. So also Instone-Brewer, *Divorce*, 19. One possible piece of contradictory evidence in this regard can be found in MAL 37, which seems to make financial settlement optional: "If a man intends to divorce his wife, if it is his wish, he shall give her something; if that is not his wish, he shall not give her anything, and she shall leave empty-handed" (*COS* 2:357). The following law (MAL 38) seems to draw the distinction that if the woman is residing in her father's house, the husband has no option and must forfeit the bride price upon divorce (*COS* 2:357).

[112] Westbrook, "Prohibition," 394. For texts pertaining to the death of the husband, see CH §171b–172; Neo-Babylonian Laws paragraph 12; *Mishnah* Ketub. 10:1–2.

[113] Westbrook, "Prohibition," 394. Cf. Westbrook, *Old Babylonian Marriage*, 71. In the OB marriage contracts, the stipulations for divorce without cause typically depend on whether the couple has children. For a similar OB marriage contract from Sippar, see Harris, "Case," 364. For similar Ugaritic contracts, see Yaron, "Royal Divorce," 22, 26–27.

[114] Westbrook, "Prohibition," 398. Cf. Westbrook, *Property*, 154–55; Westbrook, *Old Babylonian Marriage*, 77. Epstein offers the same conclusion from the perspective of Jewish law: "In the case of divorce without justifiable cause ... we have seen that if a fine was imposed ... it was imposed on the plaintiff. In the case of divorce on justifiable grounds, if a fine is imposed, it is on the defendant" (*Jewish Marriage Contract*, 207). The Sumerian court case for adultery cited by Greengus seems to

As Westbrook notes, a primary example of this principle in ancient Near Eastern texts is CH §141:

> If the wife of a man ... accumulates a private hoard, scatters her household, slanders her husband—on being found guilty, if her husband pronounces her divorce, he may divorce her without giving her anything, not her journey-money, not her divorce-money.[115]

One may add to this example the texts cited earlier in this chapter prescribing that a misbehaving wife loses her status and must symbolize this by leaving the house naked. Due to the wife's indiscriminate behavior, the divorcing husband is entitled to keep for himself all economic and property assets, including the dowry, provisions, gifts, etc., so that he dismisses the wife "without giving her anything." There is some discretion left to the husband, however, in the form of different punishments prescribed for different offenses. For instance, a Late Bronze Age marriage agreement from Alalakh (*COS* 3:101B) provides for different contexts in which the wife may offend the husband and the settlement of the divorce with cause is different in each case.[116]

The Hebrew Bible rarely mentions legal procedures associated with divorce. In light of this situation, an interpreter should perhaps give special consideration to the terminology used in the relevant texts. In OB marriage texts, the term that often provides the husband's motive for divorcing his wife without cause is *zêrum*, "to hate."[117] The husband has a change of heart, without any justifiable cause, regarding his desire to be married to his wife. The Elephantine marriage texts also attest that the main term in such cases is the Aramaic שנא, "to hate." This term functions with a technical, rather than emotional, meaning in contexts of legal relationships.[118] It consistently occurs, however, in contexts in which the husband is choosing to divorce his wife

---

confirm the notion that the payments involved served as a type of compensation to the wronged husband. In this case, the husband, who caught his wife in the act of adultery, is paid an unknown amount of silver (the text is fragmentary at that point), which is then followed by the punishment of the wife (see Greengus, "Textbook Case," 35 and *COS* 3:140).

[115] Westbrook, "Prohibition," 396. Cf. Greengus, "Textbook Case," 38. See also MAL A 29 and *Mishnah* Ketub. 7:6.

[116] The cases include abuse, insults, and barrenness. For example, lines 10'–14' state, "If the bride pulls at his nose, she(!) must return the bride price but whatever belongs to her father's house [i.e., the dowry] which she(!) brought and was assigned to her, she(!) will keep. She will leave."

[117] Westbrook, *Old Babylonian Marriage*, 22. See also Instone-Brewer, *Divorce*, 7.

[118] Branson offered a major study of the Hebrew term שנא and concluded that, while the basic etymological meaning is "hostility," the secondary meaning in contexts of marriage and politics is the "breaking of covenantal bonds." He especially cited the Elephantine marriage texts as examples of this technical meaning for the term. He did not make an attempt, however, to distinguish between divorce with cause and without cause. See R. Branson, "A Study of the Hebrew Term שנא" (Ph.D. diss., Boston University, 1976), vi–vii, 3, 17–18.

without basis.[119] In light of this evidence, Westbrook is correct to conclude that, throughout the extrabiblical divorce texts, terms meaning "to hate" do not represent the technical term for divorce in general but a type of short-hand that specifies divorce without cause.[120] One of the main marriage texts from Elephantine (Kraeling 7) makes this distinction explicit by including the fuller formulation, "I hate my wife, she shall not be my wife."[121]

These observations shed light on the Hebrew Bible's primary divorce law in Deut 24:1–4. In light of the comparative evidence, Westbrook seems justified in proposing that the text's *terminology* holds the key to its interpretation. Following the ancient Near Eastern conventions, when the first husband divorces the wife with justification, represented by the phrase "he found some indecent thing in her" (מצא בה ערות דבר), he keeps all of the dowry and pays no divorce money. When the second husband divorces her without cause, represented by the term שנא, she receives her dowry and compensation. The first husband is then prohibited from profiting by taking back what he originally declared was unfit.[122] Thus, there is a distinction between, and different

---

[119] The divorce law of Deut 22:13–21 appears to some to be an exception to this conclusion (cf. ibid., 79). This text deals with a man who seeks to divorce his wife on the grounds that he discovered her not to be a virgin when he married her, yet it uses the term שנא to refer to his action. However, the text clearly states that the man first comes to desire a divorce without justification (שנא, 22:13) and then "makes up charges against her" (22:14, JPS).

[120] Westbrook ("Prohibition," 400) derives this technical meaning of שנא from texts that put the term into parallel with general references to divorce. For example, an OB marriage contract states "If [PN] divorces [PN] ... if [PN] hates [PN]," a marriage contract from Alalakh states, "If [PN] hates [PN] and divorces him...," and a Neo-Assyrian text states, "If [PN] hates [PN] (and) divorces...."

[121] Westbrook concludes that the other Elephantine texts have simply shortened the full phrase to just the term שנא. See "Prohibition," 399–401. For an opposing view to Westbrook, see Collins (Perdue, Blenkinsopp, Collins, and Meyers, *Families*, 115–21). He argues that the textual evidence for the term "hate" is not as clear as Westbrook claims and that the term cannot be restricted to divorce without cause. He suggests that the term "to hate" represents the general term for divorce in marriage contracts. For a closer analysis of a relevant Elephantine text that seems to argue against Collins's conclusion and support Westbrook's view, see the discussion below of *TAD* B3.8 (Kraeling 7; Porten B41; *COS* 3:76). Porten, however, suggests that "hate" does not signal divorce at all but only demotion to the status of a secondary (i.e., "hated/repudiated") wife in a polygamous marriage (cf. Leah and Rachel in Gen 29:31–33). See Porten in *COS* 3:155, f.n. 42. This conclusion is contradicted by the repeated emphasis in Elephantine texts that the wife goes out of the house following a declaration of "hatred." The Elephantine texts, which consistently use the term "to hate" (שנא), do not appear to reflect polygamous marriages.

[122] As Westbrook puts it, "The effect would be that the first husband profits twice: firstly by rejecting his wife and then by accepting her. It is a case of unjust enrichment which the law intervenes to prevent" ("Prohibition," 404). One should note that Deut 24:1–4 does not appear in the section of Deuteronomy that deals with sexual relations (22:9–23:18) but in the section that deals with property laws (23:19–24:7). Cf. Instone-Brewer, *Divorce*, 7; Neufeld, *Ancient Hebrew Marriage Laws*, 176; and Stienstra, *YHWH*, 88. For a more traditional treatment of these verses, see J. Tigay, *Deuteronomy* (The JPS Torah Commentary; Philadelphia: Jewish Publication Society, 1996), 220–

financial consequences for, divorce without cause (שׂנא) and divorce with cause
(מצא בה ערות).

The above discussion of the source of Hos 2's marriage metaphor suggests
that the primary image-base is actual practices like those reflected in Deut 24:1–
4. Surprisingly, however, Westbrook suggests that the phrase ערות דבר in
Deut 24 does not include adultery within its provisions. He asserts that adultery
demanded the death penalty and that the only other occurrence of this exact
phrase is in Deut 23:15 (MT), where it refers not to sexual acts but to the
uncleanness of an army camp.[123] The interpretation of this phrase has often been
a contested issue. For example, in the Talmud, the school of Šamai saw it as
referring to sexual unchastity, while the school of Hillel understood it more
broadly including such things as a physical defect.[124] In this regard, Westbrook
fails to consider adequately that the majority of uses of the term ערוה have
sexual connotations.[125] Additionally, as shown above, adultery is not precluded
from leading to divorce because it did not demand the death penalty. Thus,
Neufeld seems correct when he concludes that the term is a general, not a
technical, one, which can denote any kind of impropriety.[126]

The entirety of the preceding evidence favors the conclusion that economic
and property stipulations constitute the primary aspects of ancient Near Eastern
marriage and divorce. As a possible image-base for Hos 2, these elements
revolve around financial consequences, like disinheritance, disownment,
expulsion, and compensation, rather than fertility concerns or physical violence.
Since Hos 2 presents a potential case of divorce with cause, that is, a case in
which the wife has refused to comply with the relationship, engaged illicit
lovers, etc., one may expect these financial penalties to form the operative
image-base for Hosea's marriage metaphor. These material realities of ancient
marriage also presume the dependence and vulnerability of women, which
provides Hosea's metaphor with its images of exclusivity and inequity.[127]

2.3 The Elephantine Marriage Texts: A Jewish Example of Ancient Near Eastern Practices

The majority of the formulations cited to illuminate the legal image-base of Hos
2's marriage metaphor comes from ancient Near Eastern texts that are both
culturally and chronologically separated from ancient Israel. There is, however,

---

22. For a detailed critique of Westbrook, see C. Pressler, *The View of Women Found in the Deuteronomic Family Laws* (BZAW; Berlin: Walter de Gruyter, 1993).
[123] Westbrook, "Prohibition," 396–99.
[124] Neufeld, *Ancient Hebrew Marriage Laws*, 178.
[125] See A. Toeg, "Does Deuteronomy 24, 1–4 Incorporate a General Law on Divorce?," *Diné Israel* 2 (1970): 5–24. See Gen 9:22–23; Exod 28:42; Lev 18:7–10; 20:11, 17; Ezek 22:10; 23:18, 29.
[126] Neufeld, *Ancient Hebrew Marriage Laws*, 179.
[127] Yee, "Not My Wife," 368. Cf. Ben Zvi, "Observations," 370.

a corpus of available marriage texts that was produced by Jews living about three-hundred years after the time of Hosea.[128] Due to the very limited sources for Jewish marriage and divorce practices,[129] these texts from the Jewish colony at Elephantine are an important window into the continuing application of customs that stretch back to eighth-century Israel.[130] They follow the same basic approach to the financial legalities of marriage and divorce as the other ancient Near Eastern texts, some of which are contemporary with Hosea but come from different cultures.[131] The Elephantine texts serve as a complementary and illustrative parallel that comes specifically from Jewish tradition itself.[132]

There are a total of eight relevant Elephantine texts.[133] Three of them are basically complete marriage contracts and provide the primary textual evidence: 1) *TAD* B2.6 (Cowley 15; Porten B28; *COS* 3:63; ca. 441 B.C.E.), 2) *TAD* B3.3 (Kraeling 2; Porten B36; *COS* 3:71; ca. 449 B.C.E.), and 3) *TAD* B3.8 (Kraeling 7; Porten B41; *COS* 3:76; ca. 420 B.C.E.).[134] The remaining texts are more fragmentary in nature: 1) *TAD* B2.5 (Cowley 48; Porten B27), 2) *TAD* B6.1

---

[128] There are no extant divorce texts from Elephantine but only marriage contracts that include references to divorce and two documents (*TAD* B2.8; *TAD* B4.6) that appear to concern payments of the divorce settlement.

[129] As Geller ("Elephantine Papyri," 139) notes, since there is a great paucity of biblical references to divorce, with only occasional mention of a "divorce document," one must depend on postbiblical sources, like the deeds from the Murabba'at caves (first century C.E.), descriptions of the *geṭ* in rabbinic texts, and the Elephantine papyri.

[130] This is, of course, not to say that there is exact continuity between the practices and beliefs of the Elephantine texts and the Hebrew Bible. Such a connection cannot (yet?) be demonstrated. However, the cultural and linguistic relationships at least suggest that the Elephantine texts stand within the legal, social, and religious traditions developed within the Hebrew Bible. For example, Geller is convinced that parallels show that the Elephantine Jews were simply following legal conventions that were already in use in eighth-century Israel (ibid., 147).

[131] Instone-Brewer, *Divorce*, 78.

[132] For another corpus of texts relating to marriage and divorce from the modern period see R. Pummer, *Samaritan Marriage Contracts and Deeds of Divorce* (2 vols.; Wiesbaden: Harrassowitz, 1993). These texts include a very small number of extant deeds of divorce from Samaritan communities between the sixth and twentieth centuries C.E. They reflect many of the same financial stipulations found in the Elephantine and other ancient Near Eastern texts. While the definitions of divorce with cause and without cause are expanded far beyond the issue of adultery, the texts maintain the basic distinction that a woman who is divorced due to infidelity forfeits her right to any dowry or divorce money (ibid., 1:129).

[133] The primary sources for the Elephantine texts are A. Cowley, *Aramaic Papyri of the Fifth Century B.C.* (Oxford: Clarendon, 1923); E. Kraeling, *The Brooklyn Museum Aramaic Papyri: New Documents of the Fifth Century B.C. from the Jewish Colony at Elephantine* (New Haven: Yale University Press, 1953); B. Porten and A. Yardeni, *Textbook of Aramaic Documents from Ancient Egypt* (4 vols., Winona Lake, Ind.: Eisenbrauns, 1986); B. Porten, *The Elephantine Papyri in English: Three Millennia of Cross-Cultural Continuity and Change* (Leiden: Brill, 1996). For the most recent editions of some of these texts, see W. Hallo and K. L. Younger, eds., *The Context of Scripture Vol.3: Archival Documents from the Biblical World* (Leiden: Brill, 2002).

[134] For the dating of these texts, see Yaron, "Aramaic Marriage Contracts," 1.

(Kraeling 14), 3) *TAD* B6.2 (Cowley 36), 4) *TAD* B6.3 (Cowley 46), 5) *TAD* B6.4 (Cowley 18).[135] The main clauses in the contracts deal with similar aspects: 1) the parties, 2) the payment of the bride price (מהר), 3) the list of belongings brought in by the wife, 4) the provisions in case of death of a spouse, 5) the dissolution of the marriage, and 6) the prohibition on the revocation of the dowry.[136] The speaker in these contracts is always the groom, and each of the three major marriage texts contains stipulations for divorce in three typical stages: 1) declaration of divorce, 2) payments to be made, and 3) wife's departure from the house.[137]

The nature of the extant Elephantine contracts, as with other ancient Near Eastern texts, suggests that marriage documents were not written for every marriage but were predominantly used in abnormal situations. Many of the OB texts depict the marriage of a slave-woman.[138] Likewise, the three primary Elephantine texts describe the marriages of a divorcee, a freed woman, and a slave. Clearly, however, the primary purpose for writing these documents was the recording of the wife's dowry for later use upon the dissolution of the marriage. As Satlow concludes, "The purpose of Jewish marriage documents was not to create the marriage, but to clarify and codify *economic obligations* within it."[139]

TAD B2.6 (Cowley 15; Porten B28; *COS* 3:63)[140] details the marriage arrangements of Eshor and Mipta(h)iah. The document relates the typical marriage pronouncement, which is identical in the three main marriage texts (line 4): "She is my wife, and I am her husband" (הי אנתתי ואנה בעלה).[141] The husband then goes on to list the מהר he paid, which consisted of five shekels of silver (lines 4–5).[142] The next ten lines of the document (lines 6–16)

---

[135] One should also note other, more tangentially, related texts: 1) *TAD* B3.11 (Kraeling 10; Porten B44; *COS* 3:79; a dowry addendum), 2) Porten C27 (a Demotic text), 3) Porten C33 (a Demotic text), and 4) Porten D2 (a Greek text). There are two Jewish marriage contracts from the Wadi Murabba'at (ca. first century C.E.), but they are much later and very fragmentary. See A. Mann, "Who Said It First: The Antiquity of 'Be Thou My Wife,'" in *Proceedings of the 9th World Congress of Jewish Studies* (eds. A. Goldberg, et al.; Jerusalem: World Union of Jewish Studies, 1986), 41 and J. Fitzmyer and D. Harrington, *A Manual of Palestinian Aramaic Texts (second century B.C–second century A.D.)* (BibOr 34; Rome: Biblical Institute Press, 1978). There are also ten Demotic divorce texts from Egypt (ca. 542–100 B.C.E.) and several rabbinic divorce texts, both sets of which are farther removed from the relevant time period. See Geller, "Elephantine Papyri," 143.

[136] Yaron, "Aramaic Marriage Contracts," 1–3.

[137] Yaron, *Introduction*, 53.

[138] Greengus, "Old Babylonian Marriage Contract," 512.

[139] Satlow, *Jewish Marriage*, 84; emphasis added.

[140] Cowley dates this text to ca. 441 B.C.E., while Porten dates it to 449 B.C.E. The number of the year in line one is lost.

[141] See also *TAD* B6.1 (Kraeling 14), which is a fragment of the beginning of a marriage document.

[142] Concerning the issue of who receives the bride price on a second marriage, one should note that, although Miptahiah is a widow, her father receives the bride price. This does not correspond to the Babylonian texts mentioned above by Westbrook.

detail the dowry that "[your daughter] Miptahiah brought into me in her hand."[143] This list of possessions at stake in the marriage relationship includes items of money and clothing similar to those in Hos 2: "1 karsh of silver, a woolen garment, shawl, etc." (cf. Hos 2:10–11).[144] Most of the items mentioned, even the woolen garments, are assigned monetary values in silver. For example, lines 7–9 state, "… 1 new woolen garment … worth (in) silver 2 karsh, shekels by the stone(-weights) of the king." These careful calculations seem to support the theory that property items and their economic values played a critical role in the imagery and stipulations associated with divorce. The text notes the monetary values of the items for the purposes of calculation and reimbursement upon the dissolution of the marriage.

Lines 22–26 then deal with a divorce initiated by the wife. Since there is no mention of any wrongdoing by the husband, the text envisions a divorce without justifiable cause. The term שנא represents the wife's desire to end the marriage due to no misconduct of her husband: "Tomorrow o[r] (the) next day, should Miptahiah stand up in an assembly and say: 'I have hated (i.e., divorce without cause; שנאת) Eshor my husband…." Unlike Babylonian and Assyrian texts that allow for the death of the woman who initiates divorce, the Elephantine texts consider men and women equal in this right. In keeping with other ancient Near Eastern texts reflecting divorce without cause, however, the one initiating the divorce (here, the wife) is ordered to pay "divorce money" (שנאה כסף) but is then allowed to leave with "all that she brought in" and to "go away wherever she desires."[145]

Lines 26–29 refer to divorce initiated by the husband and again use the term שנא to indicate a divorce without cause. The husband may dismiss his wife, but he must pay divorce money and cannot claim the bride price, dowry, or bridal gifts for himself.[146] The wife may take out "all that she brought in in her hand." The text specifically notes that when the husband divorces his wife without cause, "her *mohar* [will be] lost" (line 27). While one may reconstruct this line to read "his *mohar* will be lost," in either case the reference is to a penalty paid

---

[143] Cowley apparently failed to understand the importance of the wife's dowry possessions in matters pertaining to marriage and divorce. He interpreted all of the items in lines 6–16 as gifts given to the bride by the groom, and he read line 6 as "I have delivered to *your* daughter Miptahiah into her hand" (italics original).

[144] See also the dowry fragments in *TAD* B6.2 (Cowley 36) and *TAD* B6.4 (Cowley 18) and the well-preserved dowry addendum, given by a father to his daughter, in *TAD* B3.11 (Kraeling 10; Porten B44).

[145] Cowley again seems to have misunderstood the legal imagery at work. He reads, "… all that I have put into her hand she shall give up." Thus, he fails to recognize the woman's right to keep her dowry in any case of divorce without justifiable cause, whether initiated by her or her husband.

[146] See also the stipulations in Porten C27 and Porten C33, two Demotic marriage texts from Elephantine.

by the husband, namely, forfeiture of the bride price he paid.[147] Reconstructing the line "her *mohar*" reminds the reader that the bride price was typically included in the dowry that the wife brought into the marriage.

The other two main Elephantine marriage texts contain the same basic elements as *TAD* B2.6 and further illustrate the legal imagery connected with divorce without justifiable cause. *TAD* B3.3 (Kraeling 2; Porten B36; *COS* 3:71) describes the marriage of Ananiah and Tamet but does not record the bride price paid by the groom, perhaps because Tamet is a slave not a daughter. It does, however, describe a situation of divorce without cause by using the term שׂנא and stipulating that the wife retains possession of her dowry (or its monetary equivalent)[148] and gifts. *TAD* B3.8 (Kraeling 7; Porten B41; *COS* 3:76) reports the marriage of Ananiah to Jehoishma but is addressed to the bride's brother. This text contains a fuller statement regarding divorce, which further suggests that the term שׂנא is not the term for divorce in general but for divorce without cause in particular: "'I hated (שׂנית) my wife Jehoishma, she shall not be my wife.'"[149]

The most distinctive and debated part of this text occurs in lines 33–34 and prohibits Jehoishma from taking another husband:

> But Jeho[ishma] does not have the right [to] acquire another husband be[sides] Ananiah. And if she do thus, it is hatred (i.e., divorce without cause; [שׂ]נא[ה] ה); they shall do to her [the law of ha]tred (i.e., the law of divorce without cause; [שׂ]נאה).

---

[147] For discussion, see Fitzmyer, "Re-Study," 164. Compare the similar penalty against the wife who initiates divorce in *TAD* B3.8 (Kraeling 7), line 25. The fragmentary betrothal contract *TAD* B2.5 (Cowley 48; Porten B27) seems to indicate a similar financial penalty that the groom must pay if he fails to marry the betrothed woman. Porten dates this text to ca. 459 or 449 B.C.E. and argues that it is the betrothal contract of Miptahiah's first marriage prior to that recorded in *TAD* B2.6 (Porten, *Elephantine Papyri*, 176).

[148] For example, note that lines 7–10 prescribe that the husband must pay an unnamed amount of "divorce money" plus a sum of seven shekels, which is the same amount as the total monetary value of her dowry listed in line 6.

[149] See Westbrook, "Prohibition," 399–401. Cf. the wife's divorce statements in lines 24–28. One possible exception to the expected financial stipulations for divorce without cause is that line 25, while discussing divorce initiated by the wife, states that she must pay "divorce money" *and* "her *mohar* will be lost." This latter stipulation is unusual since the Elephantine texts generally include the *mohar* in the wife's dowry, which she is entitled to keep in divorce without cause. Thus, Kraeling suggests reading the line "his *mohar* shall be lost," so that the wife still keeps this part of the dowry (*Brooklyn Museum*, 215). The text goes on, however, to state that the woman may take with her the remaining part of her dowry after the deduction of the monetary equivalent of the bride price paid by the husband and "go out from him with the rest of her money and her goods and her property ..." (lines 26–27). It is perhaps best to explain this unique penalty by recognizing that the different Elephantine contracts adjusted the typical elements to each individual case.

These lines appear to prohibit a form of adultery in which the wife takes a second husband during the lifetime of her first husband or simply leaves her first husband for another.[150] This reading seems to invalidate the comparative evidence, which has suggested that the term שׁנא indicates divorce without cause, because it equates adultery with שׁנא. The immediate context of lines 33–34, however, helps clarify this prohibition. The preceding material in lines 28–32 deals with the death of the husband. This observation suggests that the prohibition in lines 33–34 involves the same context. The prohibition may stipulate that after the death of her husband, if Jehoishma wishes to remarry, the laws of שׁנא apply. Upon her husband's death, the wife inherits all the marital property. If she subsequently chooses to remarry, she may do so, but she must divide the inherited property with her late husband's family as if it were a divorce without cause. She may remarry with her property but not with that of her husband. Put another way, this stipulation prohibits the dead husband's family from treating the widow who wishes to remarry as an adulterer and depriving her of all possessions and inheritance.[151]

There is one document from Elephantine that seems to address the economic and property aspects of divorce *with* justification and thereby provides a more immediate comparison with the imagery of Hos 2. Porten D2 is a Greek text dating to around 310 B.C.E. that describes the marriage arrangements of Herakleides and Demetria. The contract begins by noting the dowry of 1000 drachmas, which Demetria brought into the marriage (line 4). The text then stipulates the financial consequences for a situation in which Demetria brings "shame" upon her husband. These consequences are in keeping with those found in ancient Near Eastern texts like CH §141. Rather than being allowed to leave the house with her dowry, the wife stands to forfeit all bride price, dowry, gifts, and provisions as a form of compensation to the wronged husband. Lines 6–7 state: "If Demetria is discovered dealing deceitfully in any way to the shame of her husband Herakleides, let her be deprived of everything she brought...."[152] The wronged husband may reclaim the bride price, dowry,

---

[150] Geller, "Elephantine Papyri," 141–42. Cf. Kraeling, who sees this text as prohibiting Jehoishma from taking another husband after someone has expelled her from her first husband's house.

[151] R. Yaron ("Aramaic Marriage Contracts: Corrigenda and Addenda," *JSS* 5 [1960]: 69), while not discussing the significance of the term שׁנא, rightly associates this text with widowhood and concludes, "If she remarries, that puts her on the same footing as a divorcee—she will be able to keep her own, but the property of her late husband will revert to his family." This interpretation seems to apply equally well to the prohibition in lines 37–38 that the husband cannot take another wife. Yaron originally interpreted lines 33–34, however, as referring to the wife's taking on a second husband during the lifetime of her first husband (see "Aramaic Marriage Contracts," 27).

[152] This text also includes stipulations pertaining to the misconduct of the husband that would allow the wife to sue for divorce with cause. In this case, lines 10–12 provide that, if her husband has taken another woman, Herakleides must give back to Demetria her dowry and pay her an additional 1000 drachmas.

gifts, and provisions as a means of reckoning his wife's indiscretions. There is no mention of physical violence against the wife.

The relevant Elephantine texts thus reflect situations of divorce both with and without justifiable cause. They do not emphasize physical punishment or public humiliation but the economic and property stipulations governing the different types of divorce. These texts provide a succinct corpus of *Jewish* literature that illustrates the main elements of ancient Near Eastern marriage and divorce practices and further illuminates the potential image-base of Hos 2's marriage metaphor. As Geller concludes, "The Elephantine *ketûbāh* therefore provides the *legal context* behind Hosea's statements, showing that Hosea described his marriage and divorce by alluding to *juridical clauses* from contemporary contracts."[153]

3. SUMMARY AND CONCLUSIONS

This chapter's goal was to identify the comparative image-bases from which Hos 2's marriage metaphor draws. The evidence surveyed suggested that the primary source (image-base) of this imagery is the actual practices of ancient Near Eastern marriage and divorce and not the myths and rituals of a Canaanite fertility cult. These practices primarily consisted of economic and property legalities governing different kinds of marriage and divorce, especially stipulations concerning financial issues like inheritance, dispossession, and compensation that figure prominently in cases of divorce with cause. Such practices did not, however, show evidence of involving physical punishments and public humiliation (stripping, exposure, etc.). The primary image-base of Hos 2's marriage metaphor, namely, ancient Near Eastern marriage and divorce practices, included the possible scenario of a wife refusing to fulfill marital obligations but excluded the notion of physical punishment or humiliation of adulteresses.

In light of the comparative examination, it seems best to resist the typical explanations of Hos 2's marriage imagery and ask the basic questions anew. Along these lines, the statement in 2:4 fits well with laws and provisions for cases in which a wife refuses to comply with the relationship and a husband has various courses of action available in response. Verses like 2:5, "Lest I strip her naked and I exhibit her like the day she was born," do not seem to reflect established practices of physical punishment and public humiliation of adulteresses but economic and property consequences like disinheritance, disownment, and expulsion. Yet these verses have a degree of punitive aggression that one struggles to locate even within this dimension of the marriage image-base. Even 2:10–11, "But she has not acknowledged that I myself gave to her the grain and the new wine and the choice oil…. Therefore I

---

[153] Geller, "Elephantine Papyri," 147; emphasis added.

will take back again my grain in its time and my new wine in its season, and I will snatch away my wool and my linen ...," do not concern the benefits of fertility religion but the financial aspects of bridal gifts, dowries, and provisions, which often take the form of such agricultural and household items. The husband, upon divorce with cause, retains the right to reclaim these items as compensation for the wrong done to him. As this study will show, Hosea's metaphorical rhetoric uses these practices in ways that go well beyond their material realities. Yet the text internalizes real-life relations and the ideologies that support them.[154]

Perhaps the most significant observation that comes from this conclusion is that there is no support for associating Hos 2's language of sexual violence, exposure, etc. with the primary image-base of ancient Near Eastern marriage and divorce customs. The language of verses like 2:12, "And now I will uncover her genitals before the eyes of her lovers," does not seem to come from the marriage metaphor at all. Thus, after properly understanding the legal and economic image-base of the marriage imagery, the reader of Hos 2 is left to search for another metaphorical tradition or image-base that could underlie the oracle's metaphors of physical and sexual violence. The quest for this second image-base leads to the examination of the personified wife/mother in Hosea's speech.

---

[154] Yee, *Poor Banished Children*, 10, 24.

4

THE METAPHORS OF THE WIFE/MOTHER, FORNICATION, AND ADULTERY

The second major metaphor in Hos 2, the wife/mother, is closely connected with two metaphorical terms used to describe the misconduct of which this woman is accused: fornication (זְנוּ) and adultery (נָאַף). As noted concerning the marriage metaphor, biblical and extrabiblical metaphorical traditions underlie and shed light on the possible tenors and meanings of these metaphors.

The preceding discussion of the marriage metaphor indicated that the part of Hos 2's imagery that deals with physical and sexual violence against the woman does not derive from the practices of ancient Near Eastern marriage. By integrating the metaphors of marriage and the wife/mother, however, one may discover another image-base, working in conjunction with the marriage metaphor, which provides the tradition that funds these depictions. This chapter aims to show that the biblical and extrabiblical metaphorical traditions personifying cities as females in the context of their destruction provide an adequate image-base for Hos 2's language of stripping, exposure, and nakedness. This tradition suggests that the wife in Hosea's discourse represents a personified capital city and the metaphors of fornication and adultery offer a theological critique that operates in the political realm.

1. THE METAPHOR OF THE WIFE/MOTHER

1.1 The Consensus View: The Wife as the People of Israel

The long-standing consensus view regarding the identity of Yahweh's metaphorical wife in Hos 2 holds that the wife represents the people of Israel. This view concludes that Hosea personifies Israel as a woman in order to establish a parallel between his marriage to an unfaithful wife and Yahweh's relationship to an unfaithful people.[1] This identification often leads to two other conclusions. First, some interpreters explain that Hosea derived this wife/mother metaphor for Israel from the Pentateuch's practice of describing Israel's religious apostasy as "fornication" (זנה).[2] Hosea 2 develops the imagery, it is claimed, by personifying the people as Yahweh's wife. While the Pentateuch does use the word "fornication" to describe Israel's actions, it does not represent Israel as a female. Israel is never depicted in the Pentateuch as the wife of Yahweh in a way that could give rise to Hosea's metaphor.

Some scholars, on the other hand, draw the conclusion that Hosea was the first to use the image of the people Israel as the wife/mother and that it represents a way of speaking that became unique to Israel. No ancient Near Eastern texts describe the relationship between a deity and a *people* in this way, nor does the image occur clearly in biblical texts that predate Hosea.[3]

Maintaining that the wife/mother represents the people of Israel, however, causes confusion in the metaphor with regard to the children mentioned throughout the chapter. As Wolff notes, the metaphor seems to break down because both the mother and children represent Israel.[4] Additionally, as noted

---

[1] A representative but still not exhaustive list of scholars who hold the consensus view includes the following: Anderson, *Eighth-Century Prophets*, 87; Birch, *Hosea, Joel, Amos*, 10; Buss, *Prophetic Word*, 7; Garrett, *Hosea, Joel*, 28; Harper, *Critical and Exegetical Commentary*, 225; Jeremias, *Der Prophet*, 19; Knight, *Hosea*, 21; Macintosh, *Critical and Exegetical Commentary*, 39; Mauchline, "Hosea," 575; Mays, *Hosea*, 9; McComiskey, *The Minor Prophets*, 32; McKeating, *Books*, 83; Nwaoru, *Imagery*, 14; Pfeiffer, "Hosea," 801; Rudolph, *Hosea*, 64; Snaith, *Mercy*, 33; Sweeney, *The 12 Prophets*, 3; Ward, *Hosea*, 27; Wolff, *Hosea*, 34; Yee, *Hosea*, 197. Some of these scholars offer more subtle interpretations of the wife/mother. For example, Garrett suggests that the wife in Hos 2 represents the leadership, institutions, and culture of ancient Israel while the children in the metaphor represent the ordinary people (*Hosea, Joel*, 39). Wolff further asserts that the wife seems to represent both the people and the land (*Hosea*, 34).

[2] See Garrett, *Hosea, Joel*, 28.

[3] P. Kruger, "Israel, the Harlot (Hos. 2:4–9)," *JNSL* 11 (1983): 107.

[4] Wolff, *Hosea*, 33; cf. Whitt, "Divorce," 53. Recognizing this confusion, Andersen and Freedman explain that Hos 2 represents a dialogue going on within the covenant community (*Hosea*, 219). Another view of the wife as people suggests that the wife/mother and children should not be seen as separate metaphors but as parts of an overarching *familial* metaphor in which Israel is personified as

above, the personification of a people as the wife of a god finds no parallel in any ancient Near Eastern literature. There is no comparative metaphorical tradition that provides a supporting image-base for Hosea's imagery. Given the rhetorical nature of Hos 2, the fact that the metaphor of the wife/mother is unexplained in the text suggests that it relies on a framework that would have been readily understandable to the ancient audience.

Perhaps the most significant critique of the consensus view centers on the issue of the gender of Israel within the Bible. Schmitt argues that the Hebrew Bible consistently portrays the collective Israel as a masculine entity.[5] The term "Israel" names a people, and names of a people, unlike names of countries, are masculine.[6] To demonstrate that Israel is consistently masculine, he notes, for example, that the root זנה never occurs in the Pentateuch in a feminine form referring to Israel. He further points out that all of the eighth-century prophets consistently portray Israel as masculine. Of the forty-one uses of "Israel" in Hosea, twenty reveal gender. Of these twenty, one has a third masculine plural verb (9:7), one has a first common plural verb (8:2), and all the others have a masculine singular verb.[7] In light of this textual evidence, it seems unacceptable to identify the wife/mother with the people of Israel, particularly when seen in the context of the possible comparative metaphorical traditions available in Hosea's day.

1.2 Alternative Identifications: The Wife as Land, Rachel, and Asherah

The difficulties in the consensus view noted above have given rise to alternative understandings. A widely accepted alternative identifies the wife/mother as a metaphor for the land.[8] This identification has the benefit of avoiding the

---

the household of Yahweh. See A. Dearman, "YHWH's House: Gender Roles and Metaphors for Israel in Hosea," *JNSL* 25 (1999): 97–108.

[5] Schmitt, "Gender," 115–25.

[6] Ibid., 116.

[7] Ibid., 119. Schmitt notes two exceptions to his thesis in the Hebrew Bible in places where Israel is feminine. In 1 Sam 17:21 (MT) and 2 Sam 24:9, Israel appears with a third feminine singular verb. These occurrences, however, may represent scribal errors. For example, 1 Chron 21:5 corrects 2 Sam 24:9 to a masculine singular verb (see ibid., 123).

[8] Some of the earliest examples of this view can be found in W. R. Smith, *The Prophets of Israel and Their Place in History to the Close of the Eighth Century B.C.* (London: Adam & Charles Black, 1897), 410–11, f.n. 14 and P. Volz, "Die Ehegeschichte Hoseas," *ZWT* 6 (1898): 323–24. Both of these works viewed the land as a symbol for the people. The earliest major formulation of the land view seems to be a suggestion by an American Jewish psychoanalyst, Efraim Rosenzweig, who argued that ancient Israel suppressed a mother-goddess cult by apotheosizing the feminine land of Israel (E. Rosenzweig, "Some Notes, Historical and Psychoanalytical on the People of Israel and the Land of Israel with Special References to Deuteronomy," *American Imago: Psychoanalytic Journal for the Arts and Sciences* 1/4 [1940]: 50–64). See also Abma, *Bonds*, 5; Birch, *Hosea, Joel, Amos*, 27; Blankenbaker, "Language," 161; B. Duhm, "Anmerkungen zu den Zwölf Propheten," *ZAW* 31

confusion mentioned above between references to the wife/mother and the children in Hos 2. Additionally, it builds upon the feminine gender of "land" (אֶרֶץ) in Hebrew. Scholars often connect this interpretation with the setting of a supposedly widespread Baal fertility cult in Hosea's day and argue that Hosea's portrayal of the land as Yahweh's wife is a polemic against the beliefs of a Baal fertility cult in which, in their view, Baal was married to the land.[9]

The primary evidence for taking the wife/mother to be the land comes from Hos 1:2, where the land is characterized as having "fornicated" (זנה). The punishments described in 2:4–9 also work well as metaphorical actions against a physical land: "make her like the desert; render her like a land of drought," etc. Some passages in the Hebrew Bible do seem to personify the land in feminine terms and use imagery similar to that in Hos 2:4–9.[10]

The relationship between Hos 1:2 and 2:1–25, however, is unclear. Hosea 1:2 is the only place that the land is the subject of זנה, and this may be the result of the joining together of the materials from Hos 1 and 2 at a later date. One should not assume that the prophetic oracle in Hos 2 and the biographical material in Hos 1 have the same rhetorical situation or metaphorical references at work throughout.[11] The original reference would have been primarily determined by the comparative traditions available in the rhetorical situation. As Whitt summarizes, "If ch 1 and 3 postdate the divorce speech, then this speech must be interpreted on its own and the possibility that the language and metaphors in it influenced their use in ch 1 and 3 must be given consideration."[12]

If there was a prominent Baal cult in Hosea's day, it is certainly questionable that the prophet would have so readily embraced the non-Yahwistic idea of a marriage to the land.[13] If Baalism believed that Baal was married to the land, a view that is not clearly evident, it is unlikely that a Yahwistic prophet like Hosea adopted non-Yahwistic categories in this manner without explanation. Additionally, the physical punishments in Hos 2:4–9 (e.g., making into a wilderness or wasteland) specifically appear in the Hebrew Bible

---

(1911): 19; Gowan, *Theology*, 44–45; Harper, *Critical and Exegetical Commentary*, cxlv; Jeremias, *Der Prophet*, 42; Landy, *Hosea*, 37; Lewis, "Persuasive Style," 82; Mays, *Hosea*, 34; O. Steck, "Zion als Gelände und Gestalt: Überlegungen zur Wahrnehung Jerusalems als Stadt und Frau im Alten Testament," *ZTK* 86 (1989): 261–81. For the most recent example of this interpretation, see L. Braaten, "Earth Community in Hosea 2," in *The Earth Story in the Psalms and the Prophets* (ed. N. Habel; The Earth Bible 4; Sheffield: Sheffield Academic Press, 2001), 185–203.

[9] For example, Gowan states, "Hosea thus dared to create an allegory in which it was Yahweh who was the legitimate husband of the land, not Baal" (*Theology*, 45).

[10] See Deut 11:11; Ps 65:10–14; 107:33(MT). Cf. Braaten, "Parent-Child," 16, 282.

[11] For this position, see Schmitt, "Wife," 12.

[12] Whitt, "Divorce," 40.

[13] Baumann, *Liebe*, 94; cf. Wacker, *Figurationen*, 317–18.

as metaphorical descriptions of the destruction of cities not lands (Isa 51:3, 17–23; Jer 6:2–8; Ezek 26:7–21; Mic 1:1–9). Even the texts that seem to personify the land as a woman never portray the land as the wife of Yahweh. The most significant problem with the conclusion that the wife/mother represents the land, however, is that this metaphor is totally absent from other ancient Near Eastern literature.[14] Within Hosea's context, there is no comparative metaphorical tradition that provides an image-base for personifying the land as Yahweh's wife. For instance, Isa 62:4–5 appears to portray the land as married to Yahweh: "[F]or the LORD delights in you(f.sg.), and your(f.sg.) land shall be married" (NRSV). The context and parallelism of this passage make clear, however, that it is the feminine city Zion that is being "married" and not the land itself. Schmitt has clarified that reference to "the land" in such contexts refers specifically to the land immediately surrounding a capital city, which was thought to belong to the capital city.[15]

Dissatisfaction with both the people and land interpretations has given rise to some other less developed views. Yee argues that the wife/mother metaphor now stands in a secondary literary context and the original material in Hosea involved only the image of a mother. She concludes that originally the metaphor of the mother in Hos 2 referred to Rachel, the favored wife of Jacob, who is mentioned in Hos 12:13. Her "children" represent the northern tribes that occupy Hosea's attention.[16] It is unclear, however, what one gains from this position, and the view itself depends upon taking a large amount of the book as secondary in order to avoid portraying Rachel as Yahweh's *wife*.

Whitt begins from a rhetorical perspective that focuses on what Hosea's original audience would have thought when he mentioned a wife for Yahweh and a mother for the people.[17] Based on his reconstruction of Israelite religion in the eighth century, Whitt concludes that the wife/mother in Hosea's speech refers to the goddess Asherah.[18] By relying primarily on the testimony of the Deuteronomistic History, Samarian Ostraca, and inscriptions from Kuntillet 'Ajrud and Khirbet el-Qôm, Whitt defines eighth-century Israelite religion as heavily polytheistic with a prominent place reserved for worship of the goddess Asherah. Thus, he concludes that in Hos 2 Yahweh is divorcing the mother

---

[14] See Nwaoru, *Imagery*, 144.

[15] J. Schmitt, "The Virgin of Israel: Referent and Use of the Phrase in Amos and Jeremiah," *CBQ* 53 (1991): 375.

[16] Yee, *Composition*, 124–25. This view was already suggested in Batten, "Hosea's Message," 266. Similarly, Vermeylem ("Os 1–3," 28, 43–45) suggests that the "mother" metaphor was original and the "wife" metaphor was a deuteronomistic addition. He identifies the original referent of the "mother" metaphor as the city Samaria.

[17] In a move similar to the methodology of this study, Whitt views Hos 2 as "a real speech by the historical Hosea that has been preserved fairly accurately by the original collector ..." (Whitt, "Divorce," 43).

[18] Ibid., 32.

goddess Asherah because the Israelites are acting out rites in which she and
Baal, rather than she and Yahweh, have intercourse to secure the land's
fertility.[19]

The Asherah interpretation suffers from many of the same deficiencies that
plague the land and Rachel interpretations. As Schmitt suggests, it seems
unlikely that Hosea would have drawn on an image that presumed Yahweh's
marriage to a goddess.[20] The worship of Asherah plays no significant role in the
book of Hosea. While there are biblical texts that refer to the worship of
Asherah, there is no clear metaphorical tradition that personifies the goddess as
the wife of Yahweh. Even the extrabiblical texts Whitt cites, like the inscription
from Kuntillet 'Ajrud, are heavily debated and remain unclear.[21]

1.3 The Wife as a Capital City

An additional explanation of the unnamed wife/mother in Hos 2 identifies her as
a metaphor for the capital city Samaria. This discussion developed in articles
that focused on the broader question of female personifications throughout the
Hebrew Bible and was later applied more specifically to Hos 2.[22] In 1972,
Fitzgerald devoted a study to the question of what entities are personified as
females in the Hebrew Bible and concluded that the entity most consistently
personified as such is the city.[23] The evidence in this regard includes a variety of
cases in which at least fourteen cities are clearly personified as women in
prophetic texts.[24] Fitzgerald ultimately maintained that this Hebrew Bible

---

[19] Ibid., 57.

[20] See Schmitt, "Yahweh's Divorce," 123.

[21] For example, it is not clear that this inscription refers to Asherah as Yahweh's consort or even
refers to a goddess called Asherah. For bibliographies on this matter, see W. Dever, "Asherah,
Consort of Yahweh? New Evidence from Kuntillet 'Ajrud," *BASOR* 255 (1984): 34–37; J. Hadley,
"Some Drawings and Inscriptions on Two Pithoi from Kuntillet 'Ajrud," *VT* 37 (1987): 208–11 and
The Cult of Asherah in Ancient Israel and Judah: Evidence for a Hebrew Goddess (University of
Cambridge Oriental Publications 57; Cambridge: Cambridge University Press, 2000).

[22] For a helpful list of recent works devoted to the personification of cities as females, see P. Day,
"The Personification of Cities as Females in the Hebrew Bible: The Thesis of Aloysius Fitzgerald,
F.S.C.," in vol. 2 of *Reading from This Place* (eds. F. Segovia and M. Tolbert; 2 vols.; Minneapolis:
Fortress, 1995), 283, f.n. 1.

[23] Fitzgerald, "Mythological Background," 403–16.

[24] Alice Laffey (*An Introduction to the Old Testament: A Feminist Perspective* [Philadelphia:
Fortress, 1988], 162) notes: Gaza (Amos 1:7), Rabbah (Amos 1:14) and her daughters (Jer 49:3),
Samaria (Amos 3:9) and her daughters (Ezek 16:53, 55), Zion (Isa 1:27) and her daughters (Isa 1:8),
Jerusalem (Isa 51:17) and her daughters (Mic 4:8), the daughter of Gallim (Isa 10:30), the daughter
of Tarshish (Isa 23:10), Sidon (Isa 23:4) and her daughter (Isa 23:12), Tyre (Isa 23:15) and her
daughters (Ezek 26:6, 8), Bethlehem Ephrathah (Mic 5:2), and Sodom (Ezek 16:46, 48–49) and her
daughters (Ezek 16:53, 55). At the same time, Laffey maintains that some prophetic texts do
personify countries as females (ibid., 163). Her list contains, however, several references that are

practice is not simple personification but represents the background of a pattern of West Semitic thought in which cities were seen as goddesses who were married to the patron gods of the cities.[25] Evidence for this thought pattern was found in several sources: 1) Phoenician coins of the Hellenistic period that have representations of and inscriptions about a deified city personified as a woman, 2) similar titles for capital cities and goddesses (e.g., בת), 3) city names that seem to be derived from names of male deities, and 4) Assyrian personal names where the city is seen as feminine (*Aššur-šar-rat*, "Aššur is queen").[26]

In a follow-up article, Fitzgerald emphasized the frequent uses of בת ("daughter") and בתולת ("virgin/maiden") in connection with capital cities in the Hebrew Bible.[27] He concluded that the use of these terms for cities is a natural adaptation of the West Semitic thought pattern in which cities were seen as married goddesses and that one finds evidence of such usage as early as the eighth century. The available evidence in this regard included numerous instances where the terms בת and בתולת are prefixed to cities (e.g., Isa 1:8; 16:1; 47:1; Jer 4:31; Mic 4:8; Lam 2:13) and several places where phrases like עמי ("my people") and בתולת ישראל ("maiden of Israel") clearly require a city interpretation (e.g., Jer 8:19, 21, 22, 23; 18:13; 31:4; Lam 4:3, 6, 10; Amos 5:2).[28]

The work of Biddle argued that a close relationship between cities and goddesses can be found not only in later Hellenistic parallels but also in earlier

---

unclear and debated by scholars as to whether they refer to a city or country (e.g., Jer 3:7–8, 10). The majority of the texts that Laffey cites in this regard refer to the "daughter(s)" or "virgin" of a particular country from which she extrapolates that the country as a whole is personified as a mother (e.g., Isa 16:2; 47:1; Jer 18:13; 46:11; 50:42; Ezek 16:27, 57; 32:18; Amos 5:2). The question revolves around whether the construct expression here is genitival or appositional. As discussed below, these phrases most likely represent a way of speaking about capital cities and do not imply a female personification of the country as a whole. For an extensive argument that these phrases refer to capital cities, see Schmitt, "Virgin," 365–87.

[25] Fitzgerald, "Mythological Background," 404–5. Fitzgerald notes that this thesis was already suggested by J. Lewy, "The Old West Semitic Sun-god Hammu," *HUCA* 18 (1943–44): 436–43.

[26] Fitzgerald, "Mythological Background," 406–13. Fitzgerald concedes, seemingly without basis, that eventually the Hebrew Bible did develop this original tradition to include the female personification of a people (ibid., 405). However, the constructions he cites (like "Maiden Israel" in Jer 18:13) have come to be understood as genitives indicating cities not countries. See F. W. Dobbs-Allsopp, "The Syntagma of *bat* Followed by a Geographical Name in the Hebrew Bible: A Reconsideration of Its Meaning and Grammar," *CBQ* 57 (1995): 451–70.

[27] A. Fitzgerald, "BTWLT and BT as Titles for Capital Cities," *CBQ* 37 (1975): 167–83. For an exhaustive list of where these titles occur, see f.n. 2.

[28] Ibid., 170–73. Fitzgerald argued that constructions with singular terms should be read "daughter Zion" or "Maiden Zion." Dobbs-Allsopp has demonstrated, however, that the grammatical construction is better taken as "daughter of Zion" and reflects an older tradition in which this phrase was a divine epithet for the goddess connected with a given city ("Syntagma," 451). Israel demythologized the expression but maintained the grammatical form. See also Schmitt, "Virgin," 366–67.

Mesopotamian (East Semitic) texts.[29] He maintained, however, that one must recognize distinctions in this imagery among identification, deification, and personification. In the Mesopotamian evidence, cities were masculine (Akk. *ālu*) and neuter (Sum. URU). Nonetheless, in these East Semitic texts, cities were closely "identified" with a goddess, who is their patron.[30] Only in later West Semitic traditions, in which the language for cities is feminine, did the cities themselves become deified as goddesses. In the Hebrew Bible, which had a monotheistic perspective, the writers adopted only the personification, not deification, of cities as feminine personal entities.[31]

The history of research on this issue has focused on discovering the mythological background of the Hebrew Bible's practice of female personification. This background is heavily debated, but the evidence remains that the primary entity that is personified as female in the Hebrew Bible is the city. For example, Day sharply criticizes the thesis of a mythological background of city-goddesses married to patron gods but readily acknowledges the evidence that cities like Samaria and Jerusalem are often portrayed as Yahweh's wives in the Hebrew Bible.[32] One may jettison the idea of a West Semitic goddess background but still affirm that capital cities are often personified as females in both biblical and extrabiblical texts.[33] Throughout the Hebrew Bible, both Israelite and non-Israelite cities appear as wives, brides, and mothers without being described as goddesses, yet the Hebrew Bible, more so than any extrabiblical text, contains the explicit identification of cities as the metaphorical wives of the deity and not just as personified females.[34] Thus, there is a long-standing comparative metaphorical tradition in which cities were personified as various types of female figures.[35]

---

[29] Biddle, "Figure," 173–94.

[30] As examples, Biddle cited goddesses that came to be referred to by the city's name: "Diritum," "the one of Dir" (ibid., 175). He also cited the Mesopotamian city laments in which the goddess of a particular city is described as a "mother" and "queen" and is called upon to lament the destruction of her city (ibid., 176).

[31] Ibid., 174–75.

[32] For a point by point refutation of Fitzgerald's thesis, see Day, "Personification," 282–302.

[33] Cf. Abma, *Bonds*, 22; Steck, "Zion," 261–81. Galambush (*Jerusalem*, 20) suggests that the concept of the city as a goddess married to the patron god may have functioned only as a type of conceptual metaphor that was the unacknowledged source of language about capital cities.

[34] For examples of cities described as brides, wives, mothers, and whores, see Isa 49:14–23; 50:1; 54:6; 62:1–5; Jer 2:2; 3:1, 8; Ezek 16; 23; Lam 1–2. For additional examples, see T. Andersen, "Renaming and Wedding Imagery in Isaiah 62," *Bib* 67 (1986): 75–80.

[35] One may gain an indication of the antiquity of this practice of thinking of cities as feminine from the Amarna letters. In these texts, even though the Akkadian word for city is masculine, the scribes consistently made it feminine to conform to their metaphorical tradition (see Schmitt, "Yahweh's Divorce," 129). As Biddle concludes, the variety of feminine imagery for cities in the Hebrew Bible

Schmitt was the first to apply this tradition in a sustained way specifically to the metaphor of the wife/mother in Hos 2.[36] He demonstrated that several elements within the oracle itself support the view that Yahweh's wife is a city. The image of "mother" most often occurs in prophetic texts that refer to cities (e.g., Isa 49:14–21; 50:1–3), and all the other prophetic texts in which Yahweh divorces a wife have a city in mind.[37] The violent imagery of exposing genitals also only occurs in texts relating to cities and their destruction.[38] This view agrees with the implications of the Targum for Hos 1–3, which seems to have a city in mind for the whole unit: "The Lord said to Hosea, Go and speak a prophecy against the inhabitants of the idolatrous city, who continue to sin" (Hos 1:2).[39]

If the conclusion that the wife/mother is a city holds, it seems obvious that, in Hosea's rhetorical perspective, that city would have been Samaria.[40] Hosea's oracles frequently refer to Samaria (7:1; 8:5–6; 10:5, 7; 14:1), and the prophet displays knowledge of the political intrigue and foreign policies connected with the capital. Additionally, the only other feminine addressee in Hosea occurs in 8:5, where it is the city Samaria, and other prophetic books, like Ezekiel, explicitly personify Samaria, along with Jerusalem, as a wife of Yahweh.

In spite of the arguments in favor of this interpretation, some opposing views should be noted. Abma questions whether the city interpretation accounts for the variations in the biblical imagery and asserts that sometimes nations are personified as females. In this regard, however, Abma cites only Hos 2 and Jer 2–3, two texts which may be seen as referring to cities.[41] Some scholars also conclude that the metaphorical referent in Hos 1–3 is inconsistent and "virtually

---

"is not the result of the whims of individual poets, but rests on well-developed traditions of great antiquity and geographical scope" ("Figure," 186).

[36] Schmitt, "Wife," 5–18. For this view, see also Bucher, "Origin," 136; Galambush, *Jerusalem*, 49; Wacker, *Figurationen*, 323–24.

[37] Bucher also notes that the זנה imagery in the rest of the prophetic books almost exclusively refers to cities, not peoples or nations (e.g., Isa 1:21; 23:17; Jer 2:20; Ezek 16; 23; Mic 1:7) (Bucher, "Origin," 136).

[38] Schmitt, "Wife," 7–10.

[39] K. Cathcart and R. Gordon, *Targum of the Minor Prophets* (*TAB* 14; Wilmington, Del.: M. Glazier, 1989), 29–31. Cf. Schmitt, "Yahweh's Divorce," 131–32.

[40] See Schmitt, "Wife;" "Yahweh's Divorce;" Bucher, "Origin," 136; Galambush, *Jerusalem*, 49. Vermeylem ("Os 1–3," 28, 43), while maintaining that only the "mother" (not the "wife") metaphor is original, identifies its original referent as the city Samaria.

[41] For discussion of Jer 2–3 as referring to cities see Galambush, *Jerusalem*, 49, 51–57; Fitzgerald, "BTWLT and BT," 177; Schmitt, "Gender," 122. Specifically concerning Jer 3:6–11, which names Yahweh as husband of Israel and Judah, Schmitt argues on the basis of grammar that the original referents were the cities of Samaria and Jerusalem called "Apostasy" and "Treachery." In the present form, each of these feminine nouns stands awkwardly beside the masculine noun "Israel" or "Judah." Thus, Schmitt suggests that the masculine country names were later additions used to clarify the referents (see "Gender," 115–25).

impossible to follow."[42] One may perhaps attribute this confusion to the redaction of Hos 1–3 as a unit, which joined an originally independent oracle with the narrative materials in chapters 1 and 3. There does not seem to be any inconsistency or variation in the wife metaphor within Hos 2 itself.[43]

The evidence for the city interpretation given above, however, reveals the existence of a strong metaphorical tradition that personifies cities as different types of female figures. Regardless of the source of this tradition, a prophet like Hosea could draw upon the practice of personifying cities as women and use practically any feminine depiction.[44]

1.4 The Wife/Mother in the Rhetoric of Hosea 2

While previous scholars have explored the arguments for viewing the wife/mother in Hos 2 as the city Samaria, they have not attempted to demonstrate the ways in which this interpretation contributes to a rhetorical analysis of the entire oracle. The interpretation of the wife/mother as the city Samaria seems most fruitful precisely because it has both comparative biblical and extrabiblical metaphorical traditions to support it, and this usage of a shared tradition would have enabled effective communication with the prophet's audience.

The personified female cities in the Hebrew Bible are sometimes taken as metonyms for the nation as a whole.[45] Yet the cities personified as females in prophetic texts are primarily *capital* cities. This phenomenon suggests that the metaphor represents a more precise group. Since the prophetic critiques in these metaphors focus on the seats of power themselves—Jerusalem, Samaria, Nineveh, and Babylon—the cities likely represent the male, ruling elite who sat on their thrones. Thus, the marriage metaphor in the Hebrew Bible expresses not the covenant relationship between Yahweh and the people of Israel but the religious, social, and political activities of those rulers who held office in the seats of power.

This observation prompts one to reconsider the image-bases that fund the prophet's imagination. As noted in chapter 3, several parts of the imagery in Hos 2 cannot be related to the practices of ancient Near Eastern marriage and divorce. These parts include the imagery of sexual and physical violence against

---

[42] Galambush, *Jerusalem*, 45 and Schmitt, "Gender," 120.

[43] Dearman suggests that this literary context should play a determining role in any interpretation and that Schmitt interprets the biblical evidence too strictly on the basis of grammatical form without allowing for instances in which a masculine Israel is associated with feminine imagery ("YHWH's House," 97–108).

[44] Schmitt, "Yahweh's Divorce," 129–30.

[45] So Yee, *Poor Banished Children*, 117.

the wife: "strip her naked" (2:5), "make her like the desert" (2:5), "uncover her genitals" (2:12). A closer analysis of the texts that personify cities as females, however, leads to the observation that there is a link between imagery of physical and sexual violence and descriptions of actual or threatened destruction of cities.

First, examination of the prophetic texts that personify cities as females suggests that the initial observations of Fitzgerald, Schmitt, and others were not sufficiently specific. A more precise characterization of the data is that, within the prophetic corpus, cities are personified as females exclusively in contexts of destruction, even if that destruction takes the form of a present state or threatened action.[46] For example, Jer 49:23–27 personifies Damascus as a mother and states, "Damascus has grown weak, she has turned around to flee; trembling has seized her, pain and anguish have taken hold of her, like a woman in childbirth" (49:24, JPS). Ezekiel 26:7–21 also personifies Tyre as a mother and states, "Your daughter-towns in the country he shall put to the sword; he shall erect towers against you, and cast up mounds against you, and raise [a wall of] bucklers against you" (26:8, JPS). Micah 1:1–9 personifies Samaria as a whore and states, "So I will turn Samaria into a ruin in open country ... and all her harlot's wealth be burned, and I will make a waste heap of all her idols ..." (1:6–7, JPS).[47]

The only prophetic text that seems to personify a city as a female outside of a context of destruction is Isa 16:1, which refers to "the mount of the daughter of Zion." However, the personified Zion is mentioned here only in passing as part of a larger oracle about the destruction of and fugitives from Moab.[48] This observation also holds for the several cases, particularly in Second Isaiah, in which Zion is personified as a wife or mother in promises of hope for the future. While these texts personify Zion in contexts that proclaim a restoration, they imply a present state of destruction. For example, Isa 54:1 addresses Zion and states, "Shout, O barren one, you who bore no child! Shout aloud for joy ... for the children of the wife forlorn shall outnumber those of the espoused—said the Lord" (JPS).[49]

---

[46] As Fitzgerald notes, "For all practical purposes, at least when the imagery [i.e., female personification of a city] is in any way developed, it is limited to a situation in which the city is presented as having suffered or about to suffer a disaster." See Fitzgerald, "Mythological Background," 416; cf. Fitzgerald, "BTWLT and BT," 182; Schmitt, "Wife," 10–11; Galambush, *Jerusalem*, 25–26; Otwell, *Sarah*, 184.

[47] For other prophetic texts that personify cities as females in contexts of imminent or threatened destruction, see Isa 1:8, 21–31; 23:1–18; 34:8–17; 47:1–15; Jer 2:2, 32–37; 3:1–14; 5:7–11; 6:2–8; 13:22–27; 49:2–6; Ezek 16; 23; Nah 3:1–7.

[48] Texts outside the prophetic books do occasionally personify cities in contexts other than destruction, e.g., Ps 48:12.

[49] See also Isa 40:1–11; 49:14–26; 50:1–3; 51:3, 17–23; 52:1–2; 60:1–22; 62:1–12; 66:7–12.

More significantly for Hos 2, when prophetic texts that personify cities *describe* the destruction of the city, they frequently employ language of physical and sexual violence against a woman. Six texts are primary in this regard: Isa 47:1–4; 52:1–2; Jer 13:22–27; Ezek 16:1–63; 23:1–49; Nah 3:1–7. This violent imagery most often takes the form of stripping, exposure, and humiliation. For example, Ezek 23:25–26 threatens Jerusalem, "I will direct my passion against you ... they shall cut off your nose and ears ... they shall strip you of your clothing and take away your dazzling jewels" (JPS). Nahum 3:5 addresses Nineveh and states, "I will lift up your skirts over your face and display your nakedness to the nations and your shame to the kingdoms" (JPS).[50]

The language and imagery of these texts favor the conclusion that they represent a metaphorical tradition of describing the destruction of a city as physical and sexual violence against a woman. The imagery of exposing genitals, for instance, only occurs in texts related to cities.[51] This evidence suggests that such imagery does not represent real violence against a woman but a metaphorical depiction of a personified city's destruction. Ezekiel 16:37–41 provides a helpful illustration because it contains language of stripping and dismemberment yet proceeds to discuss the destruction of towers, platforms, and houses. In commenting on this text, Westbrook attempts to maintain the connection of the sexual punishments with ancient Near Eastern divorce practices and fails to see the distinction between the two types of imagery. He concludes that "reality intrudes" into the metaphor of the city as wife.[52] This text provides a clear example, however, of the metaphorical tradition of describing a city's destruction in terms of physical and sexual violence against a woman.

From this perspective, one may explain Hosea's imagery of stripping and exposing as relying not on the image-base of ancient Near Eastern marriage and divorce practices but on this metaphorical tradition of using language of sexual and physical violence against women to depict the destruction of a city. Thus, there are two primary image-bases that overlap in Hos 2: 1) economic and legal stipulations associated with different types of divorce in the ancient Near East and 2) metaphorical language for the destruction of a city personified as a female. All of the imagery in Hosea's speech can be identified with either divorce legalities or city destruction. For example, the threat "I will strip her naked" (2:4) participates in both image-bases. It draws upon economic

---

[50] This language of sexual violence used metaphorically for a city's destruction is even found in texts outside the prophetic literature. See Lam 1:8–10; 4:21; Rev 17:16.

[51] Cf. Schmitt, "Wife," 10–11.

[52] Westbrook, "Adultery," 560.

provisions of disinheritance in divorce laws, and it reflects the metaphorical "laying bare" of a city and its territory.[53]

Although she focuses on the New Testament text of Rev 17, Rossing treats the imagery of Hos 2 along these lines.[54] She takes the imagery of Hos 2 as exemplary of this metaphorical city-destruction tradition.[55] Accordingly, she translates Hos 2:5 in such a way as to make the city destruction image-base explicit: "... lest I strip it naked ... make it as in the day it was born; and make it like a wilderness, and set it like a parched land...."[56]

1.5 Summary and Conclusions

The interpretation of Yahweh's metaphorical wife in Hos 2 as a personified city provides the only option supported by a wide-ranging comparative metaphorical tradition. If it was to function as a rhetorical discourse that attempted to persuade its original audience, Hos 2's imagery needed such a shared tradition between speaker and audience. The evidence discussed above also suggested, however, that the city in question was the capital city of Samaria. By using the metaphor of Yahweh's wife for Samaria, Hosea not only drew upon a recognizable tradition but also accessed a way of addressing the rulers who were located in the seat of power.

This personification of cities as females within the prophetic texts appears exclusively within contexts of imminent, threatened, or present destruction. In these contexts, the texts evidenced a tradition of using language of sexual and physical violence against a woman (stripping, exposure, etc.) to describe metaphorically the destruction of a personified city. Thus, a second image-base beyond that of ancient Near Eastern marriage practices emerged for Hos 2's language of sexual and physical violence.

These observations aid in beginning to identify the "rhetorical horizon" of Hosea's speech, that is, the construct of the text that uses and reflects certain portions of the data from the rhetorical-historical situation (e.g., values expressed, genres employed, identities of addressees).[57] By discovering that

---

[53] See also Garrett, who concludes that the nakedness motif has more to do with military conquest imagery than divorce law (*Hosea, Joel*, 78).

[54] B. Rossing, *The Choice between Two Cities: Whore, Bride, and Empire in the Apocalypse* (HTS 48: Pennsylvania: Trinity Press International, 1999). She traces the Hebrew Bible's tradition of describing the destruction of cities and specifically associates Rev 17's imagery of physical and sexual violence against the whore with that tradition. For example, she asserts that the punishments against the whore in Rev 17 do not reflect an attack on a woman's body but the "destruction of the city and its landscape through siege and warfare" (ibid., 88).

[55] Ibid., 93. One should note, however, that Rossing fails to extend the metaphorical tradition of city destruction to texts like Ezek 16 and 23 (ibid., 88–89, 93).

[56] Ibid., 93.

[57] See discussion of "rhetorical horizon" and "rhetorical situation" in chapter 2.

Hosea draws upon the metaphorical traditions of the personification of a city as female and the sexual and physical violence imagery for a city's destruction, one gains a clear impression of the focus of his oracle. Not only do his metaphors suggest a rhetorical horizon that centers on the capital city of Samaria, but they also indicate a situation in which Samaria faces imminent or, at least, threatened destruction. The rhetorical force of this metaphorization is already partially apparent. Since the capital cities represent the male ruling elite, the personifications of these cities as females enact an ironic feminization of the ruling hierarchy.[58] The discourse attempts to change the audience's perspective on the political rulers in an ironic way. Within the cultural assumptions and metaphorical traditions of ancient Israel, the most powerful social group, the ruling male elite, is cast as the most helpless social group, the sexually violated female. Due to some action by the city and the rulers she represents, the prophet envisions a situation of looming reversal and punishment for Samaria. The remaining metaphors in Hos 2 make clear how the discourse employs this rhetorical force.

2. The Metaphors of Fornication and Adultery

Near the beginning of his oracle, Hosea, speaking for Yahweh, sets out the misconduct of which the personified Samaria is guilty. He uses nominal and verbal forms of two key words: זנה ("to fornicate") and נאף ("to commit adultery"). While forms of these words appear only three times and one time respectively, they characterize the general actions with which Yahweh's wife is charged.[59] The texts read as follows:

> And let her put aside her fornication (זנוניה) from her face and her adultery (ונאפופיה) from between her breasts (2:4).
> And I will not have compassion on her children because they are children of fornication (זנונים) (2:6).
> For their mother has fornicated … (זנתה) (2:7).[60]

---

[58] Yee, *Poor Banished Children*, 82, 98–99; cf. Yee, "Not My Wife," 368–69. See full discussion below in chapter 8.

[59] The specific action with which the wife is repeatedly charged throughout the oracle is going after "lovers." See discussion in chapter 5.

[60] Hosea 1:2 contains several forms of זנה that appear to be used in the same way but with the subjects of a woman, children, and the land: "a woman of fornication" (זנונים); "children of fornication" (זנונים); and "for the land has indeed fornicated" (זנה תזנה).

The majority of commentators understand זנה and נאף to be metaphors for the entire people's apostasy and idolatry.[61] Some scholars explicitly argue that this religious meaning is incompatible with a political sense that would come from association with a capital city. For example, Kruger asserts, "It is noteworthy that although the whole spectrum of Israel's cultic apostasy in Hosea is described in terms of *znh* the root is not once applied to their external politics."[62] Interpreters often conclude that, because of their sexual connotations, the use of the particular terms "fornication" and "adultery" for religious apostasy is directly related to literal sexual rites performed in Israel's apostate cult. Thus, these terms are not actually metaphorical but reflect literal sexual practices like cultic prostitution. When the wife is accused of "fornication," the prophet is charging the people of Israel with actual sexual infidelity in a cultic context.[63]

If one accepts the interpretation that the metaphor of the wife/mother in Hos 2 represents the city Samaria, however, the focus on such a political entity would appear to draw attention to political relationships and actions. Nonetheless, the determining question remains: Is there a comparative biblical or extrabiblical metaphorical tradition that supports a political interpretation of the metaphors of fornication and adultery?

2.1 The Metaphor of Adultery (נאף)

In Hos 2, the root נאף occurs only in verse 4 as a plural noun that connotes some action or thing that the wife is commanded to "put aside from between her breasts." Perhaps for this reason, many scholars do not interpret ונאפופיה in 2:4 as a metaphorical description at all. Rather, they take this term to refer to an actual object worn by a literal woman in certain situations. For example, Rudolph takes both nouns in 2:4 as referring to the distinctive dress of a professional prostitute such as a veil or jewelry.[64] Wolff suggests the possibility

---

[61] For examples, see Andersen and Freedman, *Hosea*, 48–49; Baumann, *Liebe*, 56; Bucher, "Origin," 20; Buss, *Prophetic Word*, 102; Gowan, *Theology*, 45; Hubbard, *Hosea*, 37; Knight, *Hosea*, 31; Sherwood, *Prostitute*, 138; Sweeney, *The 12 Prophets*, 33; Yee, "Hosea," (*NIB*), 198.

[62] Kruger, "Israel, the Harlot," 109. In order to arrive at this position, Kruger argues that a political meaning for זנה developed only with the later texts in Ezek 16 and 23. He does allow that Hos 8:9–10 "hints" at fornication in a political sense; however, he concludes that there the root should be read as the hapax legomenon תנה, "to hire a harlot" (ibid., 109).

[63] O. Collins, "The Stem ZNH and Prostitution in the Hebrew Bible" (Ph.D. diss., Brandeis University, 1977), 16, 77. For this same view concerning נאף, see D. Freedman and B. Willoughby, "נאף," *TDOT* 9:116–17. For a refutation of Collins's view, see Bucher, "Origin," 1–20.

[64] Rudolph, *Hosea*, 66; cf. Bucher, "Origin," 132. But see J. Assante ("The kar.kid/*harimtu*, Prostitute or Single Woman? A Reconsideration of the Evidence," *UF* 30 [1998]: 75–77), who cites the "Hymn to Inanna-Ninegalla" that refers to the "bead necklace of the kar.kid" worn by Inanna. In Assante's view, this reference indicates that the kar.kid wore such jewelry "to mark her from married women when she was in search of sex in public places" (ibid., 76). The placement of the adultery

of connecting these terms with jewelry or emblems specifically associated with supposed sexual rituals of a Baal fertility cult.[65] A third suggested explanation is that these terms refer to items such as pendants or amulets connected with the Baal cult but not necessarily with sexual activity.[66]

The difficulty with these approaches, however, is that they rely on a literal interpretation of both the woman and the term. They presume the background of an actual woman, who wore these items and participated in some form of literal sexual activity.[67] This woman is then seen as representing the religious apostasy of Israel as a whole. In light of the personification, metaphors, and image-bases observed thus far in Hos 2, however, these explanations seem insufficient. Two things particular to Hos 2 suggest a metaphorical use of the root נאף in this context. First, the term is used in conjunction with זנה, which clearly has a metaphorical meaning throughout the oracle (cf. 2:7). Second, other uses of נאף, both inside and outside Hosea, evidence a tradition of ascribing metaphorical meaning to the term.

Comparative biblical evidence for נאף provides a range of meanings that may be at work in Hos 2.[68] The root occurs thirty-four times in the Hebrew

---

"between her breasts" in 2:4 may refer to such a practice and further serve to depict the woman as acting like a single woman seeking sex.

[65] Wolff states, "These were probably certain marks or emblems, e.g., headbands, belts, rings, necklaces, or similar jewelry, placed on a woman who had participated in the Canaanite sex cult. They could also be scratches on the breast resulting from ecstatic frenzy" (*Hosea*, 33–34). So also Andersen and Freedman, *Hosea*, 224–25.

[66] See Bucher, "Origin," 133.

[67] For example, in his explanation, Wolff assumes that the woman represented in 2:4 is Gomer and that she participated in the ritual defloration of virgins in the Baal cult (*Hosea*, 14–15).

[68] This procedure of investigation raises a general methodological issue. As noted above, only by interpreting metaphors like those in Hos 2 intertextually does one gain a full appreciation of the metaphors and their implicit tenors. These intertextual studies reveal broad metaphorical traditions that shed light on the particular terms. This investigation, however, is always open to the possible objection that such a method of inquiry is not legitimate for understanding the specific terms used within a particular context. Many scholars presume that texts outside of Hos 2, even those elsewhere in Hosea, come from later times and writers and cannot shed light on the ways the metaphors function within this chapter. Additionally, interpreters often object that some of the texts used for comparison, especially those in Ezekiel and Jeremiah, are dependent on Hos 2. Thus, one cannot explain the meaning of terms in chapter 2 by referring to other uses of those terms in texts that may reflect a completely different period and author.

In response to these objections, the method of inquiry used here relies on the assumption that a preexisting, cultural tradition gave rise to the different biblical texts and their use of certain metaphors. This view is intertwined with the conviction of the rhetorical-historical approach to prophetic texts, which affirms the necessity of a shared world of ideas and meanings from which the speaker must draw in order to communicate effectively with his or her audience. Buss's comments provide a way forward in this regard: "It seems to be possible, on the basis of vocabulary and thought, to show that there is a *stream of tradition* which includes Hosea, Deuteronomy, the Asaph psalms, the Deuteronomistic historians, Jeremiah, and Ezekiel" (*Prophetic Word*, 81; emphasis

Bible with twenty-eight of them being outside of the book of Hosea. However, scholars often observe that the majority of these occurrences use the term to refer to the literal act of adultery by a man or woman (sixteen of the twenty-eight uses of the root outside Hosea).[69] No text that is typically dated before Hosea reflects a metaphorical use of נאף. For this reason, many interpreters conclude that Hosea was the first to describe some type of unfaithfulness to Yahweh with the metaphor of adultery. Jeremiah and Ezekiel then develop this metaphor.[70]

The remaining twelve occurrences of נאף outside Hosea that are not literal operate on various levels of meaning. Isaiah 57:3 appears to use the term in a restricted figurative way that disparages the Israelites by calling them illegitimate children, but it does not directly characterize the people's actions.[71] There are four occurrences of נאף, all in the book of Jeremiah, which seem to utilize the root as a religious metaphor for Israel's apostasy from Yahweh (Jer 3:8–9; 5:7; 23:10). For example, Jeremiah 3:8–9 label "Israel" and "Judah" as two sisters married to Yahweh and assert that they have "committed adultery (ותנאף) with wood and stone." The cultic nature of this metaphor is clear not only from the reference to wood and stone but also from the opening description of going up "on every high hill and under every green tree" (3:6).[72]

Alongside these more clearly religious uses of the metaphor, however, one occurrence of נאף outside of Hosea seems to carry an explicitly political meaning. The term functions as a metaphorical description of political alliances and actions that are seen as improper and outside Yahweh's will. Ezekiel 16:32 uses the metaphor of "adultery" within a context that is devoted to Jerusalem's relations with Assyria and Babylon. The text personifies Jerusalem as a female and compares it to "the adulterous wife (האשה המנאפת), who welcomes strangers instead of her husband." This reference is preceded by condemnations of foreign alliances referred to as "playing the whore" (זנה) with the Egyptians (16:26), Assyrians (16:28), and Chaldeans (16:29).

---

added). Buss concludes that there could have been direct knowledge and influence among the writings in this "stream," but the similarities that exist among the texts may equally be the result of a preexistent, shared tradition of meaning for certain terms, images, metaphors, etc.

[69] Exod 20:14; Deut 5:18; Lev 20:10 (4); Job 24:15; Prov 6:32; 30:20; Ps 50:18; Jer 7:9; 9:1(MT); 23:14; 29:23; Ezek 16:38; Mal 3:5.

[70] See Gowan, *Theology*, 44.

[71] For this view of Isa 57:3, see G. Knight (*The New Israel: A Commentary on the Book of Isaiah 56–66* [Grand Rapids: Eerdmans, 1985], 12), who argues that this verse could be taken literally rather than as a metaphor for religious apostasy. Verses 4–5 condemn the people for inappropriate worship of some kind characterized as burning with lust "among the oaks, under every green tree." Verse 3, however, does not use "adultery" as a metaphor for this action but characterizes the people's behavior as that of illegitimate children.

[72] For the possibility of seeing the phrases and names in 3:8–9 as references to cities, see Galambush, *Jerusalem*, 49, 51–57 and Schmitt, "Gender," 122.

Not all of the occurrences of נאף outside Hosea clearly fall into these religious or political categories. On six occasions, the term is ambiguous in meaning and may operate simultaneously on both the cultic and political levels (Jer 13:27; Ezek 23:37[2], 43, 45[2]). For instance, Jer 13:27 makes reference to female Jerusalem's "adulteries" (נאפיך). This reference comes at the climax of a judgment speech that alternates between masculine plural references to the king and queen mother (cf. 13:18) and feminine singular references to the personified Jerusalem (cf. 13:27).[73] This context of an address to the royal house and capital city suggests a political reference for the actions involved. Additionally, as noted above, the text uses metaphorical language of exposure and sexual violence against a woman (13:22, 26) to threaten Jerusalem with destruction, and this language is commonly associated with capital cities. In two of the places where the text refers to specific actions, verse 21 says that Jerusalem ("you," f.sg.) will be ruled by those they have thought to be "allies" (אלפים), and verse 25 states that Jerusalem ("you," f.sg.) has trusted in "deception" (שקר). Both of these statements appear to be overtly political, not cultic, in meaning. The term שקר ("deception") occurs in Isa 28:15 to describe the political actions of the rulers of Jerusalem when they sought foreign and military aid against Assyria (cf. 28:14): "We have made lies our refuge and in falsehood (ובשקר) we have hidden."[74] On the other hand, the final part of Jer 13:27 seems to include cultic behavior in the action referred to as adultery by once again mentioning events that take place "on the hills of the countryside" (cf. Isa 57:3; Jer 3:6). Thus, this text intertwines political and religious meanings for the metaphor of adultery. The situation is much the same for the remaining five occurrences of נאף in Ezek 23.

The above evidence seems to favor the conclusion that the root נאף may be used as either a religious or political metaphor in certain texts and as a multivalent metaphor for combining both meanings in other texts. It is not adequate to conclude, however, that the term always has this multivalent meaning. There are texts outside Hosea that use the term only in the sense of apostasy and idolatry (Jer 3:8–9; 5:7; 23:10). There is also a text that uses it to characterize only improper political actions as tantamount to unfaithfulness in relationship to Yahweh (Ezek 16:32).[75] It is likely impossible to identify which meaning of the metaphor is original, yet the texts suggest that both options were employed in ancient prophetic discourse.[76]

---

[73] Note the switch from 2 m.pl. suffixes in 13:18–20 to 2 f.sg. suffixes in 13:21–27.

[74] Note the similar use of כחש, "lies," in the political context of Hos 7:3. The term שקר, however, does sometimes appear as a reference to cultic misbehavior. See Jer 7:9; 10:14; 51:17.

[75] Cf. Fitzgerald, "Mythological Background," 403.

[76] As the following chapters hope to show, a prophetic text like Hos 2 could draw on the fact that this metaphor can have a religious or political meaning or both and use that tradition to highlight the

The uses of נאף in the book of Hosea outside of chapter 2 provide the most relevant data for analyzing the metaphor's meaning in that discourse. The root occurs six times in Hosea. Two of the six occurrences clearly refer to the literal act of adultery (3:1; 4:2). The occurrences of the term in 4:13 and 14 are unclear and heavily debated. Because they are intimately connected with the metaphor of "fornication" (זנה), these passages will be discussed in the following section. Only two uses of the term in Hosea seem explicitly metaphorical. Since one of these uses is the reference in Hos 2:4, the only text that sheds light on this oracle is Hos 7:4. This occurrence appears in a context that is clearly concerned with Israel's political actions and that addresses the issue of establishing kings and officials: "With their evil they would make the king rejoice, and with their treacheries, the princes. All of them are adulterers (מנאפים)" (7:3–4). In the only other place in which Hosea clearly uses נאף as a metaphor, he utilizes it to characterize political actions and alliances as unfaithful to Yahweh.

In considering this issue, one gains no direct help from extrabiblical texts. There are no ancient Near Eastern texts that describe religious or political misbehavior with the metaphor of adultery or fornication. The rhetoric of ancient Near Eastern political treaties, however, may provide an indirect explanation for such metaphorical political use. Several Assyrian vassal treaties, like the vassal treaties of Esarhaddon, demonstrate the practice of swearing the treaty in the name of divine witnesses and viewing the gods of the different states as guarantors of the political alliance.[77] To be unfaithful to the political treaty could be viewed as being unfaithful to the divine guarantors. If one portrays the divine guarantor as a husband, this unfaithfulness may naturally be characterized as adultery. For Israel, Yahweh's role as guarantor *and* husband means that breaking such a treaty was an offense against him, his name, and his honor.[78]

This metaphor seems even more transparently political if Fitzgerald is correct that there was a mythological background tradition in which cities were seen as married to patron gods.[79] At least within the Hebrew Bible, one certainly witnesses this personification of cities like Samaria and Jerusalem as the wives of the deity. In this tradition, the origin of a metaphor like נאף for inappropriate political actions may be located in the intersection of politics and religion that seems to have accompanied political alliances. The capital city, viewed as the wife of Yahweh, enters a dependent alliance with a foreign power. As Fitzgerald suggests, such alliances may be viewed as the equivalent of false worship

---

significance of one meaning rather than both (i.e., a prophet could focus only on political misdeeds but cast them in such a way that they are depicted as the equivalent of religious apostasy).

[77] For examples of Assyrian texts that display this practice, see M. Cogan, *Imperialism and Religion: Assyria, Judah, and Israel in the Eighth and Seventh Centuries B.C.E.* (SBLMS 19; Missoula: Scholars Press, 1974), 42–64.

[78] Galambush, *Jerusalem*, 34.

[79] Cf. Fitzgerald, "Mythological Background," 403–4.

because they often included token worship given to the suzerain's deities and the acknowledgment of dependence on someone besides Yahweh.[80]

Given the attested political use of the metaphor of נאף and the fact that Hosea's only other clearly metaphorical use of the root appears in a political context, one could understand Hos 2:4 as a political metaphor that condemns inappropriate actions by the city Samaria. Yet נאף is so closely connected with the metaphor of זנה in Hos 2 that a reader cannot fully determine the meaning of one apart from the other.[81]

2.2 The Metaphor of Fornication (זנה)

The root זנה occurs 134 times in the Hebrew Bible with the vast majority of these occurrences (ninety) located in the Latter Prophets.[82] Nearly half of all the occurrences are in Hosea and Ezekiel with forty-two of them being in Ezek 16 and 23. The root appears in a variety of verbal forms as well as three main nominal forms. As noted above, זנה occurs three times in Hos 2 in two nominal forms and one verbal form (2:4, 6, 7).

The discussion surrounding the general meaning of זנה centers on the distinction between the term's literal and figurative meanings.[83] The root's literal meaning seems to involve a sexual relationship outside of a formal union and not a technical act of prostitution (i.e., sex for hire).[84] As Yee explains, "Zānâ is a more inclusive term, covering a wide range of sexual transgressions, including *adultery*, involving a married woman; *fornication*, involving an unmarried daughter, sister, or widow committed under levirate law (see Deut 25:5–6); and *prostitution*, involving women soliciting sex as a means of

---

[80] Ibid. While he concludes that such worship was not forced upon vassal states, Cogan notes several Assyrian texts that suggest that a political treaty with Assyria involved at least token worship of Assyria's gods as well as swearing the treaty in the name of the gods of both the suzerain and vassal (*Imperialism*, 42–64). Adler, however, disputes this idea because there is no evidence in the Hebrew Bible that such political alliances produced religious heterodoxy ("Background," 374).

[81] This close connection between the terms זנה and נאף is evident in several texts in which the terms occur in parallel (Jer 3:8, 9; 5:7, 8; 13:27; Ezek 16:36, 38; 23:43–45; Hos 2:4; 4:13, 14). On this basis, Erlandsson suggests that when a formal union is in view, the two terms are basically synonymous (S. Erlandsson, "זנה," *TDOT* 4:100). Freedman and Willoughby also suggest the terms appear to have "coalesced" in these texts ("נאף," 117). However, Collins maintains that the words do not assimilate even when used in parallel because זנה is never associated exclusively with the context of marriage ("Stem," 7, 180).

[82] For the two major dictionary articles on זנה, see Erlandsson, "זנה" and J. Kühlewein, "זנה," *TLOT* 1:388–90.

[83] For a review of the history of interpretation related to the origin and meaning of זנה terminology in the Hebrew Bible, see Bucher, "Origin," 7–26.

[84] See Erlandsson, "זנה," 100 and Bird, "Harlot," 76.

financial support."[85] By contrast, Galambush argues that זנה in its truly literal meaning refers only to prostitution, but it also has two different levels of metaphorical meaning. The "first level" metaphorical use of זנה refers to a woman's illicit sexual activity (i.e., fornication but not professional prostitution) and functions to assert that such activity is like that of a prostitute. The "second level" metaphorical meaning does not refer to any type of sexual activity but characterizes a variety of other actions of which the most common is the worship of other gods besides Yahweh.[86] This level also includes, however, expressions dealing with trade relations, commercial conduct, etc.[87]

As noted above, scholars often argue that even the metaphorical uses of זנה, particularly in Hosea, have their origin in actual sexual practices within a Baal fertility cult.[88] More recently, however, Bucher calls this conclusion into question and notes that the extrabiblical textual and archaeological sources do not offer firm evidence of the practice of cultic sexual intercourse in Iron Age Syria-Palestine.[89] Accordingly, Hosea's use of this terminology seems to represent a rhetorical move in which the prophet uses a term that describes sexual acts outside of a formal union to characterize the people's behavior as like that of a prostitute.[90] Bird also rejects the notion that such terminology reflects actual cultic sexual rites. She observes that it is only in its metaphorical senses that זנה operates in the cultic sphere. The term's primary metaphorical use occurs with a masculine subject and, in her view, describes the pursuit of other gods besides Yahweh.[91]

In light of this evidence, the metaphorical uses of זנה may refer to a variety of illicit actions, which may not involve literal sexual activity at all. The root implies that an activity is habitual with a motive of personal gain (like a professional prostitute) and that such activity involves a multitude of partners.[92]

---

[85] Yee, "Hosea" (*NIB*), 216; italics original.

[86] Galambush, *Jerusalem*, 27–31. She also notes that the religious metaphorical meaning of the term almost always occurs with a masculine or mixed gender expression and uses the preposition אחרי plus an object of worship to denote the apostasy (ibid., 31). Adler maintains that this construction denotes not a specific act but general infidelity to Yahweh ("Background," 317, 322–23).

[87] For example, Bucher views texts like Mic 1:7 and Isa 23:17 as describing the commercial trade of a city ("Origin," 77). See also Abma, *Bonds*, 4; Adler, "Background," 356–57; Erlandsson, "זנה," 100–104.

[88] The most explicit statement of this position specifically regarding זנה terminology is Collins, "Stem." For another example, see the most thoroughgoing fertility cult interpretation of Hosea: H. May, "The Fertility Cult in Hosea," *AJSL* 48 (1932): 73–98.

[89] See discussion below in chapter 5.

[90] Bucher, "Origin," iii, 20, 78.

[91] Bird, "Harlot," 75–79. Erlandsson cites several texts as ambiguous concerning whether they refer literally to sexual actions or metaphorically to religious apostasy: Num 25:1; Hos 4:13–15; 9:1; Jer 5:7 ("זנה," 100). In light of the above discussion, however, the evidence seems to favor taking even these texts as metaphorical expressions of apostasy.

[92] Adler, "Background," 311–12.

From this starting point, the biblical writers employ the metaphor to describe various levels of estrangement from Yahweh including allegiance to other gods, relationships with people or objects that result in improper worship, and acts of betrayal and unfaithfulness.[93]

Outside of Hosea, זנה appears twenty-seven times in the literal sense of prostitution. This meaning is most widely attested in the narrative and legal literature of the Pentateuch and the wisdom material of Proverbs.[94] Beyond this literal sense, a survey of the occurrences of זנה outside the prophetic books reveals that the term appears only as a metaphor for religious apostasy and never in the sense of commercial or political actions. This predominant metaphorical usage, however, has certain characteristics that accompany it. First, the nonprophetic texts that use זנה as a religious metaphor never involve a personified female city but address a masculine subject, usually the people of Israel. For example, Exod 34:16 admonishes, "When you take wives for your sons from among their daughters, their daughters will fornicate (וזנו) after their gods, and they will cause your sons to fornicate (והזנו) after their gods." Second, these religious uses of זנה almost always have a clarifying preposition that explicitly identifies the object of improper worship.[95] Only two such texts in the Pentateuch and Deuteronomistic History seem to carry a religious meaning without an accompanying preposition (Num 14:33 and 2 Kgs 9:22), but both of these are clearly religious in nature.[96]

In the prophetic literature, however, the metaphorical use of זנה is expanded to include the commercial and political spheres. Outside of Hosea, the term occasionally appears with both a religious and political meaning simultaneously; however, in some cases, it carries either a strictly religious or political connotation.[97] Whereas outside the prophetic texts זנה refers metaphorically only to cultic infidelity, inside the prophets it can be either cultic or political (or perhaps both simultaneously).[98] Within the texts that seem most

---

[93] Ibid., 317.

[94] For example, see Gen 34:31; 38:15; Lev 19:29; 21:7, 9; Deut 22:21; Prov 6:26; 7:10; 23:27; 29:3.

[95] The most frequent preposition is אחרי but others include אל, את, מן, מאחרי, מתחת (see Collins, "Stem," 65–67). For example, see Exod 34:15, 16a, 16b; Lev 17:7; 20:5, 6; Deut 31:16; Judg 2:17; 8:27, 33.

[96] Numbers 14:33 uses the root זנה to describe the people's lack of trust in Yahweh when they initially scouted the land of Canaan. 2 Kings 9:22 accuses Jezebel of engaging in "fornications and sorceries." One also finds texts that seem to carry a religious meaning without prepositions in the later material of Ps 106:39 and 2 Chron 21:11, 13.

[97] For texts that seem to use זנה as a religious metaphor, see Jer 2:20; 3:6, 8, 9; 5:7; Ezek 6:9; 16:15, 16, 17, 20; 20:30. For texts that seem to use the term partially, if not completely, as a political and commercial metaphor, see Isa 23:15, 16, 17; Jer 3:1, 2, 3; Ezek 16:22, 25, 26, 28, 29, 30, 31, 33, 34; 23:3, 5, 7, 8, 11, 14, 17–19, 27, 29, 30, 35, 43, 44; Nah 3:4.

[98] This observation leads Galambush to conclude that the marriage metaphors of the prophetic and extraprophetic books are actually two different but related metaphors because the personification of

evidently political in meaning, however, two important characteristics appear: 1) these texts always involve a personified female city, and 2) they do not have clarifying prepositions that would suggest a religious meaning. Put another way, the vast majority of prophetic texts that use זנה in a religious sense either do not involve a personified female city or use clarifying prepositions and objects of worship. As an example of the evidently political texts, Jer 3:1 accuses a feminine singular subject of "fornicating" (זנית) in a context immediately preceded by the mention of Assyria and Egypt. This verse accuses the female of fornicating specifically with "companions" or "friends" (רעים), a term that is not used to refer to deities but finds its closest referent in the Assyrians and Egyptians mentioned in 2:36. The feminine singular subject "you" finds its clearest referent in the city Jerusalem named at the beginning of the section in 2:1–2,[99] and 3:1 does not contain any reference to other gods as the object of fornication.

Ezekiel 16:22–34 also explicitly uses זנה to describe the city Jerusalem's improper political relationships with Egypt, Assyria, and Babylon: "You (f.sg.) fornicated (ותזני) with the Assyrians in your insatiable lust; you fornicated (ותזנים) but were not satisfied" (16:28; see also 16:22, 25, 26, 29, 30, 31, 33, 34). In the first part of this chapter, there are uses of זנה as a religious metaphor (see 16:15–17, 20). In these instances, the language is explicitly religious (e.g., "shrines," "sacrifice") and, in verse 17, provides the object of worship ("male images"). In 16:22–34, however, not only is there a focus on a personified capital city (Jerusalem), but there are also no objects of worship given and other political entities are named.

Nahum 3:4 uses imagery of sexual violence to address the personified female city of Nineveh: "On account of the multitude of fornication (זנוני) of the fornicator (זונה)...." Once again, this text deals with a personified female city and does not name any objects of worship. The referent here is a foreign city (Nineveh) that would not be condemned for failing to worship Yahweh. Ezekiel 23, the text that most closely resembles the language and imagery of Hos 2, also explicitly uses זנה as a metaphor for political relationships. Ezekiel 23:8 and 9 characterize the city of Samaria's improper political alignments: "She did not give up her fornication (תזנותיה) from Egypt.... Therefore I delivered her into the hands of her lovers, into the hands of the Assyrians, for whom she lusted." In the preceding verse (23:7), the indictment involved a cultic aspect in which Samaria is said to have "defiled herself" with idols. Beginning with verses 8 and 9, the text broadens the indictment to include political misdeeds and explicitly identifies the city's partners in fornication with

---

cities as females does not occur outside the prophets and the phrase זנה plus אחרי plus object, which denotes cultic infidelity, only occurs twice in the prophets, in Ezek 6:9 and 20:30 (*Jerusalem*, 36–37).

[99] For the interpretation of this feminine subject as a city, see Schmitt, "Gender," 122–23.

political entities. Thus, Ezek 23:11 also describes Jerusalem's relations with the Assyrians as "lusting" and "fornicating" without any cultic references: "Her sister Oholibah saw this, yet she was more corrupt than she in her lusting and in her fornication (תזנותיה).... She lusted after the Assyrians." Similarly, Ezek 23:17 describes Jerusalem's political relations with the Babylonians with this metaphor: "And the Babylonians came to her into the bed of love, and they defiled her with their fornication (בתזנותם)." In what is perhaps the clearest demonstration that זנה can, at times, stand as a strictly political metaphor yet is also connected with the realm of religion, Ezek 23:30 offers a summary of the indictment against Jerusalem that has two distinct parts: "These things will be done to you(f.sg.) because you have fornicated (בזנותך) after the nations *and* because you are defiled with their idols."

In light of these instances, it is reasonable to conclude that there is a substantiated tradition of using the metaphor of fornication with a singularly political meaning in the prophetic texts. This political meaning is commonly indicated by reference to a personified female city and lack of prepositions that make a religious meaning explicit. These characteristics may aid in the analysis of the term זנה in Hos 2. There are, however, some texts that do not fit with the general characteristics and so emphasize the importance of context in interpreting the metaphor. For example, Ezek 16:20 uses זנה in a clearly cultic context referring to child sacrifice, but it involves a personified female city (cf. Ezek 16:35, 36, 41).[100] In general, however, if a prophetic text does not make clear through other means whether it uses זנה in a religious or political way, the evidence favors the conclusion that the text is more likely to be political in meaning if it involves a personified female city. Nonetheless, this decision depends heavily on the way in which the metaphor interacts with the other elements of a given text.

In light of the availability of both religious and political meanings for the metaphor of fornication, the reader of Hos 2 should look to the ways in which the metaphor is used elsewhere in the book of Hosea itself. The root זנה occurs twenty-two times in Hosea with three of them being the texts in question in Hos 2.[101] Of the nineteen occurrences outside of Hos 2, six appear to use the term to refer to literal sexual activity outside of a formal union.[102] The other thirteen uses of זנה by Hosea give evidence of *both* religious and political meanings for

---

[100] See Isa 1:21; Jer 13:27; Ezek 16:35, 36, 41; 43:7, 9; Mic 1:7.

[101] Hos 1:2a, 2b, 2c(2); 2:4, 6, 7; 3:3; 4:10, 11, 12(2), 13, 14a, 14b, 15, 18(2); 5:3, 4; 6:10; 9:1.

[102] Hos 1:2a, 2b; 3:3; 4:10, 13, 14a. This judgment contrasts with Stuart, who argues that Hosea uses the term literally only in 4:13–14 (*Hosea-Jonah*, 16). However, due to the association with Gomer and Hosea's children, the occurrences in 1:2a, 2b, and 3:3 appear to refer to actual illicit sex, even if that reference is within a larger allegory. Additionally, 4:10 seems to be a literal threat of punishment against the people of Israel that stands alongside the statement that they will eat and not be satisfied: they will have sex but not be able to multiply.

the metaphorical sense of the term. The five occurrences of the root that seem most transparently cultic in meaning are in Hos 1:2c, 4:12, and 9:1. As expected, however, none of these texts involve a personified female city and all three of them use a clarifying preposition that notes fornication away from Yahweh (מעל, מתחת, מאחרי).

The largest concentration of references to זנה in Hosea is found in chapter 4 (4:10, 11, 12[2], 13, 14a, 14b, 15, 18[2]). The imagery and rhetoric of this chapter are heavily debated, and זנה seems to be employed in a variety of ways within this one particular unit. For example, 4:10 is best taken as a literal curse statement in which the people will "fornicate" but not be allowed to multiply. The reference to זנה at the very beginning of 4:11, however, is more ambiguous. Although it follows a statement that the Israelites have "abandoned Yahweh" (4:10), and thus seems cultic in meaning, the Hebrew text locates it at the head of a list of literal actions like the use of wine and new wine that "take away the understanding" (4:11).[103] The next two occurrences of זנה in 4:12 seem metaphorical and cultic in meaning because they are associated with divinatory practices (4:12a), sacrifices on mountains and hills (4:13a), and a statement about forsaking God: "For a spirit of fornication (זנונים) has led them astray, and they have fornicated (ויזנו) away from (מתחת) their God."

The verses in this chapter that use זנה terminology and have received the most attention are 4:13b–14. Interpreters often argue that the references to fornication in this text refer to literal, cultic sexual rites.[104] For example, following verse 13a's description of sacrifices on the tops of hills and mountains, 4:13b–14 state, "For this reason your daughters fornicate (תזנינה) and your daughters-in-law commit adultery. I will not hold accountable your daughters when they fornicate (תזנינה) and your daughters-in-law when they commit adultery. For they (m.pl.) turn aside with prostitutes (הזנות) and with holy ones they sacrifice." Bird, however, seems correct in suggesting that these זנה references could function equally well to describe a literal consequence for the daughters resulting from the faithless actions of the male population.[105] The references here do not appear, at first blush, to be metaphorical but to describe literal actions being done by the daughters and daughters-in-law of the leaders. Seen in this way, the faithless and disobedient actions of the people outlined in 4:11–13a are presented as the cause of the inappropriate social and sexual behavior described in 4:13b–14 (e.g., fornication, adultery, sacrificing with illegitimate cultic personnel).[106] This description of inappropriate behavior

---

[103] NRSV puts "fornication" here as the final word that finishes the thought of verse 10: "they have forsaken the LORD to devote themselves to whoredom." The Hebrew is unclear but does place זנה at the head of the three-item list that begins verse 11. By its translation, the NRSV invests the term with a metaphorical sense that is cultic in meaning.

[104] For example, see Wolff, *Hosea*, 81–88.

[105] Bird, "Harlot," 85–86; cf. Bucher, "Origin," 148–52.

[106] See discussion of the term קדשה below in chapter 5.

seems to continue in the three remaining occurrences of זנה in 4:15 and 18. For example, verse 18 concludes, "When their drinking has ended, they continually fornicate (הזנה הזנו)."

With regard to the remaining occurrences of זנה in Hosea, the situation changes, and the range of meaning broadens to include the political sense. Hosea 5:3–4 uses the term in a context that is directly concerned with various political entities and does not mention apostasy from Yahweh. Not only does verse 1 refer to "priests" and the "house of Israel," but it also specifically associates the action with the royal house (ובית המלך). Verses 3–4 then state, "I have acknowledged Ephraim and Israel has not been hidden from me. Surely now, O Ephraim, you have caused fornication (הזנית) and Israel has become polluted ... surely a spirit of fornication (זנונים) is in their midst and Yahweh they do not respect." As the Hebrew of 5:5 makes clear, this section deals with the relationships and actions of three separate political entities: Israel, Ephraim, and Judah. The only religious reference in the context (v.6) explicitly states that the people are seeking *Yahweh* not other gods. Thus, "fornication" here appears to refer to illegitimate political actions or relations.

Hosea 6:10, the other remaining use of זנה, also seems to use the term as a social or political metaphor, since it appears in a context that refers to breaking a treaty or covenant, dealing treacherously with Yahweh, and committing murder (6:7–9): "In the house of Israel I have seen a disgusting thing; there is Ephraim's fornication (זנות); Israel has become polluted" (6:10). Although the translation and interpretation of this entire pericope (6:7–11) is highly uncertain, the general sense is not a concern with cultic issues but with acts of violence such as might occur in contexts of war. For example, Gilead, called a "city of evildoers" (6:8), and Shechem, a place associated with "murder" (6:9), were two places involved in the strife of the Syro-Ephraimitic war.[107] The preceding unit of 5:8–6:6 is commonly seen as a speech concerning that conflict around 734–733. Thus, verse 10's reference to Ephraim's "fornication" may function as a summary statement of the civil war and violence that characterized this period.

These various uses of זנה in Hosea demonstrate that the prophet makes use of the terminology in differing ways. Included in these instances are three texts that use the term in an explicitly political context (5:3, 4; 6:10). Although these three texts do not involve a personified female city, in keeping with the observations concerning the prophetic literature in general, neither do the texts that are cultic in meaning. Thus, the sum of this evidence suggests that Hosea was both aware of and used the metaphor of fornication to describe what he viewed as improper political actions that deviated from Yahweh's will.[108] This use complements the term's application in contexts that involve religious

---

[107] See discussion below in chapter 6.
[108] So also Yee, "Not My Wife," 350, 357.

apostasy and social injustice. Keefe seems correct when she concludes that, throughout the whole of Hosea, language of fornication carries political and social connotations and there is no warrant for always seeing it as a metaphor for apostasy since the range of meanings can include any type of faithlessness toward Yahweh.[109] Along these lines, Yee has recently argued for a very broad interpretation of the fornication metaphor in Hosea. She suggests that Hosea's sexual language is a general trope that characterizes misdeeds in any of the realms of religion, politics, and socioeconomics. Yee concludes that the fornication metaphor is ultimately concerned with a system of production that involved the state-run cult, foreign policy, agribusiness, and economic interests.[110] Hosea's sexual metaphors could refer to any and all of these realities. Although Yee rightly avoids restricting the fornication metaphor to cultic critique, she fails to consider, it will be argued, the integration of all the imagery in the specific discourse of Hos 2.

2.3 Adultery and Fornication in Hosea 2

The above exploration of the biblical metaphorical traditions of נאף and זנה has shown that it is certainly possible for these terms to carry a political meaning. There is a well-attested comparative tradition that supports this interpretation. It remains, however, to demonstrate why such a political reading of Hosea's metaphors is more beneficial to understanding his discourse than the religious interpretation of cultic apostasy. In this regard, evidence from other occurrences of these terms both inside and outside Hosea converges.

First, a political interpretation of these metaphors in Hos 2 fits best with the characteristics from other prophetic texts. In Hos 2, the term זנה functions alone and is not linked with the fuller expressions and prepositional phrases that characteristically mark a religious meaning. Furthermore, at the risk of using circular argumentation, if one is convinced by the evidence that the wife/mother in Hos 2 represents the city Samaria, then the chapter's זנה terminology demonstrates the characteristic association with a personified city, which usually carries a political meaning in other prophetic texts. The whole sweep of the comparative evidence suggests that, if a text does not make the meaning of a fornication metaphor explicit, it is most likely to have a political meaning if the text deals with a personified female city (but cf. Ezek 16:15–20).

The second piece of evidence that renders a political interpretation of these metaphors likely is that Hosea himself clearly uses נאף and זנה in this sense elsewhere. Hosea 5:3–4, 6:10, and 7:4 appear to be clearly political in meaning, referring either to internal or external politics. Perhaps on the basis of this evidence, some scholars assert a political meaning for these metaphors

---

[109] Keefe, "Female Body," 90; cf. Keefe, *Woman's Body*, 134–39, 196.
[110] Yee, *Poor Banished Children*, 81, 85, 89, 92, 94. Cf. Yee, "Not My Wife," 359–60.

throughout Hos 4–14; yet they do not do so concerning Hos 2.[111] This view fails to consider, however, the scope and interaction of all the metaphors and rhetoric of Hosea's oracle, including especially the wife/mother as a reference to a capital city and the language of sexual violence as a metaphor for city destruction.

A third piece of evidence that may render a political interpretation of these metaphors likely is the close relationship between Hos 2 and Ezek 23. In rhetoric, subject, and imagery, Ezek 23 forms a close, although chronologically later, parallel to Hosea's oracle.[112] Ezekiel 23 relates the story of the cities of Samaria and Jerusalem, which are personified as two females married to Yahweh. Throughout the text, the prophet uses language of fornication and adultery (cf. 23:3), employs the imagery of physical and sexual violence like stripping and exposure (cf. 23:26), and expresses the desired goal of "knowing" or "acknowledging" Yahweh (cf. 23:49). This imagery in Ezek 23, however, is more clearly political than that of Hos 2. Whereas both Hosea and Jeremiah only imply the nature of the infidelity involved, Ezekiel relates any religious wrongdoing to dependence on foreign overlords and focuses on improper political alliances and their consequences.[113] Thus, one may say that Ezekiel develops Hosea's earlier imagery not by turning an originally religious metaphor into a political one but by making the emphasis on improper foreign relations unambiguous.

These various factors suggest that the metaphors of fornication and adultery in Hos 2 may be fruitfully read as referring to political actions and alliances that Hosea deems to be outside of Yahweh's will. The reason for the close connection of this imagery with that of religious apostasy may be that such political alliances involved at least token worship or commitment in the name of the suzerain's gods. As noted above, several Assyrian vassal treaties demonstrate the practice of swearing the treaty in the name of divine witnesses and viewing the gods of the different states as guarantors of the political alliance.[114] Such treaties often use very personal language of "love" to express the loyalty of a vassal for the suzerain.[115] While some scholars, like Adler, deny that political alliances produced "religious heterodoxy," this conclusion seems

---

[111] Lewis, "Metaphors," 22–23. Cf. Adler, "Background," 364.

[112] For two extended discussions of Ezek 23 in this regard see Galambush, *Jerusalem*, 63–72, 109–24 and Stienstra, *YHWH*, 155–62.

[113] Galambush, *Jerusalem*, 82–83. So also Stienstra, *YHWH*, 158. This way of reading Ezek 23 stands in contrast to the more common religious interpretation. For example, Collins ("Stem," 209, 236–38) argues that Ezekiel connects זנה with cultic terms like טמא and גלולים and that Ezekiel's order of Egypt, Assyria, and Chaldea does not reflect Judah's political realities. But see Galambush, *Jerusalem*, 114.

[114] See complete discussion of this item in chapter 8.

[115] See discussion of "lovers" below in chapter 5.

to overlook the implicit acknowledgment of foreign gods in a treaty situation and the real possibility that ratification of such treaties may have involved a religious ceremony.

Finally, there is no sufficient warrant for concluding that this political use of זנה and נאף developed only in texts later than Hosea.[116] Hosea himself seems to use the metaphors this way in other parts of the book, and several texts that both precede and follow Hosea are unclear and could be read in a political way. The evidence for the development of political and cultic meanings is not sufficiently clear, and one cannot (and does not need to) decide which usage (cultic or political) came first.[117]

2.4 Summary and Conclusions

The second half of this chapter explored the relevant metaphorical traditions that shed light on the metaphors of fornication and adultery in Hos 2. The survey of other occurrences of these metaphors provided a firm context in which to consider Hosea's imagery as relating to the political sphere of Samaria's foreign alliances. Elsewhere in the book of Hosea itself, this same imagery characterized those political actions that the prophet deemed contrary to Yahweh's will and harmful to the people. The close correlation of these metaphors with the female personification of the city Samaria and with the marriage/divorce metaphor in general strengthened the notion that Hos 2 emphasizes the capital city's improper political actions, which constitute a failure to maintain fidelity to Yahweh's direction.

This interpretation of the metaphors of fornication and adultery makes another contribution to the emerging understanding of the rhetorical horizon of Hos 2. Not only does Hosea focus on the political entity of the capital city in the context of looming or threatened destruction, but he also uses the metaphors of fornication and adultery to declare, as the remaining chapters hope to show, that improper *political* alliances and actions are the infidelity that will result in the imminent destruction. Because it has followed a path of concrete actions that lies outside the will of Yahweh, the city Samaria, along with the ruling house it represents, stands at the brink of devastation. Through his metaphors and imagery, Hosea powerfully characterizes these actions as that of a promiscuous wife who engages in illicit activity that warrants legal punishment. With this in mind, it remains to inquire about the partners whom the wanton wife has pursued.

---

[116] For example, Buss (*Prophetic Word*, 103) states explicitly that the *political* meaning is evident in Hosea and may be older than Hosea.

[117] Cf. Galambush, *Jerusalem*, 38.

5

THE METAPHORS OF LOVERS AND BAAL(S)

While the metaphors of fornication and adultery stand as a general description
of the wife/mother's inappropriate behavior, Hos 2 more specifically
characterizes her actions as forsaking Yahweh to go after other "lovers." The
chapter repeatedly uses this metaphor to represent those entities to which
Yahweh's metaphorical wife has given her loyalty:

> For she said, "I will go after my lovers (מאהבי, piel participle) who give me
> my bread and my water, my wool and my linen, my oil and my drink" (2:7).
> And she will chase after her lovers (מאהביה, piel participle), but she will not
> reach them; she will seek them, but she will not find (2:9).
> And now I will uncover her genitals before the eyes of her lovers (מאהביה,
> piel participle), and no one will reclaim her from my hand (2:12).
> And I will make desolate her vine and her fig-tree about which she said, "They
> are gifts for me which my lovers (מאהבי, piel participle) gave to me" (2:14).
> … [S]he adorned herself with her nose-ring and jewelry, and she went after her
> lovers (מאהביה, piel participle) (2:15).

As with the metaphors of marriage, the wife/mother, fornication, and adultery, a
comparative and integrative analysis can inquire as to what this metaphor may

111

have meant in different rhetorical contexts and how it may have functioned in the prophet's overall discourse.

Within Hos 2, the metaphor of lovers is closely connected with the use of the term בעל. The text employs this term as another way of referring to that entity or those entities to which Yahweh's metaphorical wife has now pledged her loyalty:[1]

> I multiplied for her silver and gold that they used for the בעל (2:10).
> I will visit upon her the days of the בעל ים for whom she burned incense ...
> (2:15).
> So it will be in that day, declares Yahweh, you will call me "my husband," and you will no longer call me "my בעל" (2:18).
> I will remove the names of the בעל ים from her mouth ... (2:19).

Scholars nearly unanimously understand this term to be the proper name of the god Baal. This standard interpretation, however, gives practically no consideration to other biblical and extrabiblical uses of בעל and does not examine the way in which the term is integrated into the complex of Hos 2's major metaphors.

Concerning both the terms "lovers" and "baal(s)," one finds a well-substantiated tradition of use both inside and outside the Hebrew Bible. "Lovers" often appears as a metaphor for political allies and, as the following discussion aims to show, there are several strong reasons for understanding the term in this political sense within the rhetoric of Hos 2. The term בעל similarly rests upon a biblical and extrabiblical tradition in which the word can refer to political partners or lords. A reconsideration of both the evidence for a supposedly wide-spread Baal cult in eighth-century Israel and the way in which the term בעל relates to the other metaphors in Hos 2 favors the conclusion that Hosea uses this word in a political sense as well.

1. The Metaphor of Lovers in Hosea 2

1.1 The Consensus View: The Lovers as Other Gods

The common view of the metaphor of lovers in Hos 2 sees this term as a reference to other gods whom the Israelite people have forsaken Yahweh to worship.[2] This position rests on an interpretation of certain evidence discussed

---

[1] The word occurs in both the singular (2:10, 18) and plural (2:15, 19).

[2] A large but still not exhaustive list of scholars who hold this common view includes Birch, *Hosea, Joel, Amos*, 27; Blankenbaker, "Language," 167; E. Bons, *Das Buch Hosea* (Neuer Stuttgarter Kommentar: Altes Testament 23, 1; Stuttgart: Katholisches Bibelwerk, 1996), 44; Cassuto, "Second Chapter," 115; Cheyne, *Hosea*, 51; Davies, *Hosea* (NCB), 65; Harper, *Critical and Exegetical*

below and concludes that Israelite religion in the eighth century was marked by syncretism and constitutes the major area of concern for the prophet's oracle. The common view also generally takes Hosea to be the originator of this metaphor, since it only appears clearly in Hosea, Jeremiah, and Ezekiel.[3] Commentators often associate the metaphorical lovers with various manifestations of the Canaanite god Baal at different cultic places.[4] According to this view, Hosea communicates to his audience by using a metaphor that refers to other gods, especially Baals, as "lovers" with whom the people of Israel have committed adultery against their husband Yahweh.

There are several problems with this consensus view that have produced some alternative interpretations. First, a simple correspondence between Hosea's "lovers" and the Canaanite god Baal is difficult to maintain since the term "lovers" is always plural. The references do not seem to refer to a single rival deity. Second, it is not clear that Hosea's audience would have only understood the metaphor of lovers to be religious in nature. The exploration of the uses of this term in the Hebrew Bible below shows that specific forms of the word are used in different ways that resist easy generalization. Finally, the consensus view does not take sufficient account of the metaphorical use of the terms "love" and "lover" in extrabiblical texts and the ways in which these usages may have provided the background against which Hosea's rhetoric functioned.

1.2 Beyond the Consensus: The Lovers as Political Allies Outside of Hosea

Difficulties with a strictly religious interpretation of the metaphor of lovers suggest the necessity of exploring the question anew. In the Hebrew Bible, the verb forms of אהב ("to love") occur 140 times in the qal, thirty-six times as a qal participle, one time as a niphal participle, and sixteen times as a piel participle. Noun forms of the root also occur fifty-four times.[5] The root is

---

Commentary, 229; Macintosh, *Critical and Exegetical Commentary*, 48; Mays, *Hosea*, 9; Rudolph, *Hosea*, 67; Sellin, *Zwölfprophetenbuch*, 30; Snaith, *Amos*, 56; Stuart, *Hosea-Jonah*, 48; Wolff, *Hosea*, 35; Yee, "Hosea" (*NIB*), 200; Yee, "Hosea" (WBC), 195.

[3] For example, see Mays, *Hosea*, 39.

[4] Wolff, *Hosea*, 35. This notion of a multitude of Baals located at various cultic places seems to be disproved by the bulk of the Ugaritic evidence, a fact that Wolff himself acknowledges (ibid., 38). But see J. A. Dearman, "Baal in Israel: The Contribution of Some Place Names and Personal Names to an Understanding of Early Israelite Religion," in *History and Interpretation: Essays in Honour of John H. Hayes* (eds., P. Graham, W. Brown, J. Kuan; JSOTSup 173; Sheffield: Sheffield Academic Press, 1993), 173–91.

[5] For these and other introductory items related to the root, see the main dictionary article on the subject: G. Wallis, "אהב," *TDOT* 1: 99–118.

employed in an extremely wide variety of ways ranging from the literal to the metaphorical.[6]

Two articles appeared in the 1960s and 1970s that attempted to understand the biblical uses of אהב by studying the terms for "love" and their uses in extrabiblical literature.[7] Moran's 1963 article, for example, proposes the thesis that the book of Deuteronomy does not use the image of parental or conjugal love to talk about the relationship between Yahweh and Israel. Rather, it relies on metaphorical political language of love that finds its source in ancient Near Eastern vassal treaties and loyalty oaths. For example, he notes that love in Deuteronomy can be commanded and is related to fear and reverence. Additionally, Deuteronomy's concept of love must be expressed in loyalty, service, and obedience.[8]

In order to substantiate this thesis, Moran looks to parallel metaphorical language found throughout the ancient Near East across a wide span of time. The specific root אהב, which occurs in the Hebrew Bible, appears only rarely in extrabiblical texts. For example, the root *ʾhb* occurs only twice in the extant Ugaritic literature. In one case it is a noun describing the emotion between Baal and his daughter, and in the other case it is a finite verb describing Baal's carnal action with a heifer.[9] The Elephantine texts have two occurrences of proper names formed with the root.[10] The root also occurs in one Hebrew seal inscription, the Targum of Song of Songs 8:6, and Ben Sira 4:7 and 7:30.[11] While one may argue that these occurrences, especially those in the Ugaritic texts, suggest a close connection between the root and the context of Baalistic religion, such a conclusion rests on very limited evidence.[12]

---

[6] Wallis summarizes the situation well: "The scope of the concept *to love/love* in the OT idiom is very broad. It extends from the affection of members of the opposite sex for one another ... or even conjugal intercourse itself ... to the intimate bonds between father and (favorite) son ... or between mother and her favorite child ... to friendly relationships between men ... even to the intimate relationship between a people and their military leader" (ibid., 104; italics original). The etymology of אהב is unclear and debated. Thomas supports the view of Albert Schultens (1748) that the term comes from the bilateral root הב, which is cognate with an Arabic term meaning "to blow, breathe heavily" (W. Thomas, "The Root אהב 'Love' in Hebrew," *ZAW* 57 [1939]: 61–62). For further discussion, see Wallis, "אהב," 102.

[7] W. Moran, "The Ancient Near Eastern Background of the Love of God in Deuteronomy," *CBQ* 25 (1963): 77–87; J. Thompson, "Israel's 'Lovers,'" *VT* 27 (1977): 475–81. See more recently, S. Ackerman, "The Personal Is Political: Covenantal and Affectionate Love (ʾĀHĒB, ʾAHABÂ) in the Hebrew Bible," *VT* 52 (2002): 437–58. While agreeing with Moran's overall thesis, Ackerman brings out several similarities between the descriptions of political and affectionate love.

[8] Moran, "Ancient Near Eastern Background," 78.

[9] See A. Tushingham, "A Reconsideration of Hosea Chapters 1–3," *JNES* 12 (1953): 150–59 and Thomas, "Root," 58.

[10] Cowley 1:4; 12:107.

[11] See Thomas, "Root," 58. Thomas also notes the appearance of the root *aab* in Samaritan texts.

[12] The scanty occurrences of the root "to love" in Ugaritic religious texts imply that these texts are not the most fruitful place to look for parallels to Hosea's usage.

The articles of Moran and Thompson highlight, however, multiple occurrences of the parallel Akkadian term *ra³āmu* in ancient Near Eastern political texts. These texts demonstrate that there was a conventional use of "love/lovers" as a trope for the relations of vassals or treaty partners within ancient Near Eastern suzerain-vassal treaty language.[13] For example, an eighteenth-century B.C.E. letter to Yasmac-Addu, king of Mari, has the writer describe himself as the king's "lover" (*rā³imka,* "the one who loves you").[14] In the fourteenth-century Amarna letters, "love" clearly refers to international relations. For instance, the pharaoh is instructed to "love" his vassal, and vassals are instructed to "love" their king: "My lord, just as I love the king my lord, so (do) the king of Nuḫašše, the king of Ni³i ... —all these kings are servants of my lord."[15] Another Amarna letter uses verbal forms to address a situation of rebellion in the city of Byblos with similar language: "Behold the city! Half of it loves the sons of ᶜAbd-Ašir-ta [who fostered the rebellion], half of it [loves] my lord."[16]

One can supplement these examples from Moran's article with a variety of texts from the corpus of Assyrian political documents that stretch down to the seventh century B.C.E.[17] For example, Esarhaddon's (680–669 B.C.E.)[18] succession treaty concerning Ashurbanipal commands Humbareš, the city-ruler of Nahšimarti as follows: "... [Y]ou must guard him strongly until one of you, who loves (*i-ra-³a-mu-u-ni*) and feels concern over the house of his lords...."[19] Lines 266–68 of this same treaty also command, "You shall love (*tar-³a-ma-a-ni*) Assurbanipal the great crown prince designate, son of Esarhaddon, king of Assyria, your lord, like yourselves."[20] Ashurbanipal's (668–627 B.C.E.) own political treaties also evidence the metaphorical use of love language. A treaty with Babylonian allies stipulates, "We will love (*ni-ra-³a-a-mu*) [Ashurbanipal], king of Assyria, and [hate his enemy]."[21] This same treaty also contains a more developed pledge of loyalty: "From this day on for as long as we live we will

---

[13] See Keefe, "Female Body," 91. As Moran puts it, these political texts show the use of the term "love" to describe "the loyalty and friendship joining independent kings, sovereign and vassal, king and subject" (Moran, "Ancient Near Eastern Background," 78).

[14] Moran, "Ancient Near Eastern Background," 78. For the Mari text, see G. Dossin, *Correspondence de Iasmaḫ-Addu* (ARM V; Paris: Imprimerie nationale, 1952), 76:4.

[15] Moran, "Ancient Near Eastern Background," 79; cf. Wallis, "אהב," 101. For the Amarna text, see J. Knudtzon, *Die El-Amarna-Tafeln* (Leipzig: J. C. Hinrich, 1915), 53:40–44.

[16] Knudtzon, *Die El-Amarna-Tafeln*, 138:71–73.

[17] For a collection of such materials, see S. Parpola and K. Watanabe, eds., *Neo-Assyrian Treaties and Loyalty Oaths* (SAA 2; Helsinki: Helsinki University Press, 1988).

[18] There is no dispute over the dates of the Assyrian rulers. Dates for Israelite and Judean kings in this study follow J. H. Hayes and P. K. Hooker, *A New Chronology for the Kings of Israel and Judah and Its Implications for Biblical History and Literature* (Atlanta: John Knox, 1988).

[19] Parpola and Watanabe, *Neo-Assyrian Treaties*, 37; l. 207.

[20] Ibid., 39.

[21] Ibid., 66; l. 32.

neither do nor cause anyone to do, nor speak [evil things ... against Assurbanipal], king of Assyria, those who love him (LÚ.*ra-ʾi-ma-ni-šu*), and his land."[22]

These various ancient Near Eastern texts demonstrate that there was a well-substantiated tradition of using love language to refer to a political ally or relationship. While all of the Neo-Assyrian texts that evidence this tradition come from the reigns of Esarhaddon and Ashurbanipal, nearly a century later than Hosea's preaching, the non-Assyrian texts noted above suggest that the practice of using "love/lover" as a political term stretches back as far as the eighteenth century.[23]

Within the Hebrew Bible but outside of the book of Hosea, the terms "love" and "lovers" manifest a wide variety of uses that includes references to parental, conjugal, devotional, and marital love.[24] Mixed in among these uses, however, one also finds clear examples of uses of אהב that carry political meanings. Thompson's 1977 article represents the major exploration of these uses within the Hebrew Bible. He operates from the starting observation that the root אהב in the David and Jonathan stories has political overtones.[25] Thompson then moves beyond Moran's ancient Near Eastern focus and presents evidence that the verb "to love" and the noun "lover(s)" carry political meanings in certain texts throughout the Hebrew Bible. For example, Yahweh's love for Israel is sometimes depicted as that of a suzerain for a vassal.[26] A couple of legal texts also use "love" to describe the relationship between a master and slave.[27] In some texts, the political meaning is made explicit by identifying the lovers as Assyrians and Babylonians (Ezek 16:28–33; 23:5, 9). Nonetheless, Thompson does maintain that some texts use the root אהב to refer to religious apostasy with other deities.[28]

A more specific survey of the occurrences of the root אהב outside of Hosea produces several observations. First, one does find a clear tradition of using the root in a political sense among the qal verb forms in the Hebrew Bible.

---

[22] Ibid; ll. 17–19.

[23] Moran also seems to reach this conclusion and to link this political usage more closely with the time of Hosea by stating, "Since in view of the evidence of the second millennium the oath to love the sovereign hardly arose only in the early seventh century, we may safely assume that kings like Menahem [746–737 B.C.E.] also promised to love their Assyrian lord" ("Ancient Near Eastern Background," 84, f.n. 42).

[24] For examples, see Gen 22:2; 37:3; 44:20; Lev 19:18; Judg 14:16; Ps 119:127.

[25] Thompson, "Israel's 'Lovers,'" 475. See also J. Thompson, "The Significance of the Verb *Love* in the David-Jonathan Narratives in I Samuel," *VT* 24 (1974): 334–38. Cf. P. Ackroyd, "The Verb Love- *ʾāhēb* in the David-Jonathan Narratives: A Footnote," *VT* 25 (1975): 213–14.

[26] See Deut 10:15; 23:5; 1 Kgs 10:9; 2 Chron 2:11; 9:8; Jer 31:3; Mal 1:2.

[27] Exod 21:5; Deut 15:16. Cf. Thompson, "Israel's 'Lovers,'" 478.

[28] Ibid., 476. On this occasion, Thompson makes this assertion but provides no examples. Later, in f.n. 5 on page 477 and again on pages 479–80, he cites only the occurrences of lovers in Hos 2:7, 10, 12, and 13(Eng.) and Jer 8:2 as examples of this religious meaning.

For example, Moran identifies the forms in texts like Deut 6:5, "You shall love (וְאָהַבְתָּ) the LORD your God with all your heart," as carrying a political meaning because the text commands love and connects it with obedience, service, and loyalty.[29] Yet several prophetic texts that use these forms of אהב may be read in either a cultic or political sense or both. For instance, Isa 57:8 states, "[Y]ou have made a covenant with them; you have loved (אָהַבְתָּ) bedding with them...." This statement seems to be religious in nature because verses 7–8a talk about high hills and sacrifices. The verses immediately following, however, concern political alliances in which envoys were sent to other nations. Thus, the JPS translation renders verses 9–10 as a reference to inappropriate contact with a king (as opposed to the god Molech).[30]

The situation is the same when one examines the qal participle forms of the root outside Hosea.[31] The clearest examples of a political meaning can be found in 1 Kgs 5:1, Esther 5:10, Jer 20:4, and Lam 1:2. The most often cited example is 1 Kgs 5:1, "Hiram was a lover (אֹהֵב) of David all the days." Jeremiah 20:4 makes even more explicit the use of the participle to refer to political entities: "I will make you a terror to yourself and to all your lovers (אֹהֲבֶיךָ; NRSV, "friends"), and they will fall by the sword of their enemies...."[32]

Even in the nominal forms of the root אהב outside of Hosea, there is a clear tradition of mixing political usage with other types of meaning. For example, Thompson again associates the noun "love" in the David and Jonathan stories with a political type of loyalty.[33] Additionally, the noun forms in texts like Jer 2:33 seem to refer to an abandonment of Yahweh's will in the political arena, since the context goes on to mention Egypt and Assyria: "Do you trim your ways to seek love (אַהֲבָה)?" (cf. "Egypt" and "Assyria" in 2:36).

The specific form of אהב that occurs in Hos 2 is the piel participle. As a metaphor, the piel participle form is used in the Hebrew Bible only in the sense

---

[29] Cf. the qal forms in Deut 10:12; 11:1, 13, 22; 19:9; 30:6, 16, 20. See also Thompson ("Israel's 'Lovers,'" 475) on the David and Jonathan stories (1 Sam 18:1; 20:17).

[30] For similar texts with a qal verb form that may be read as political or cultic in meaning, see Jer 2:25 and Ezek 16:37 (cf. 16:26, 28, 29). The form in Jer 8:2 appears to be clearly cultic in meaning, "[A]ll the host of heaven which they loved (אֲהֵבוּם) and served and followed, to which they turned and bowed down...."

[31] Examples of a religious meaning include Deut 5:10; 7:9; 13:3; 1 Sam 18:16; 2 Sam 19:7(MT) (see Moran, "Ancient Near Eastern Background," 78, 80).

[32] So also the connection between "lovers" and exile in Jer 20:6: "To Babylon you will go and there you will die and there you will be buried, you and all your lovers (אֹהֲבֶיךָ) to whom you have prophesied deceitfully." Lamentations 1:2 describes the personified city of Jerusalem and refers to her political compatriots: "She has no comforter among all her lovers (אֹהֲבֶיהָ)." Esther 5:10 also clearly seems to use the participle to refer to political allies: "But Haman ... sent for and brought in his lovers (אֹהֲבָיו)...." See also Esth 5:14; 6:13. Perhaps the same usage is intended in Prov 14:20, "But many are the lovers (וְאֹהֲבֵי) of the rich," and Prov 27:6, "Faithful are the wounds of a lover (אוֹהֵב)."

[33] See 1 Sam 18:3; 20:17; 2 Sam 1:26 (Thompson, "Israel's 'Lovers,'" 475).

of adulterous lovers. More importantly, all of the piel participle occurrences of the root elsewhere in the Hebrew Bible are clearly political in meaning, with the exception of an unclear crux in Zech 13:6.[34] For example, Jer 22:20 addresses the coming death of King Jehoiakim and states, "Go up to Lebanon and cry. And lift up your voice in Bashan and cry out from Abarim for all your lovers (מאהביך) are crushed," and 22:22 proclaims, "Your lovers (ומאהביך) will go into captivity."[35] Lamentations 1:19 has the personified female city of Jerusalem admit in the context of destruction, "I called to my lovers (מאהבי); they deceived me." Ezekiel 16:33 addresses the city Jerusalem and stands in the second part of the chapter (16:23–43), which, unlike verses 15–22, focuses on alliances and explicitly refers to committing fornication with Assyria and Babylon: "[Y]ou gave your gifts to all your lovers (מאהביך)." Similarly, Ezek 16:36 draws a distinction between fornicating with lovers and sinning with idols: "Because your lewdness was poured out and your nakedness was bared in your fornications with your lovers (מאהביך) and with the idols of your abominations...."[36] Among these Ezekiel references, however, two uses of the piel participle go beyond merely suggesting a political meaning and explicitly identify the lovers with political entities. Ezekiel 23:5 addresses the personified city of Samaria: "And she lusted after her lovers (מאהביה) to nearby Assyria." Ezekiel 23:9 asserts, "Therefore I have given her into the hand of her lovers (מאהביה), into the hand of the Assyrians on whom she lusted."[37]

The above evidence favors the conclusion that there is a clear and well-substantiated metaphorical tradition, both within and without the Hebrew Bible, of using the language of "love/lovers" to refer to political relationships and allies. The piel participle forms of אהב in particular seem to carry this meaning in every case except one outside the book of Hosea. This metaphorical tradition, while not the only one present in the Hebrew Bible, indicates that a political meaning for the metaphor of lovers in biblical texts is readily possible.[38] The question of its probability for Hos 2 remains to be addressed.

---

[34] Zechariah 13:6 seems to be a reference to the family home: "Those with which I was struck in the house of the ones who loved me (מאהבי)." See Adler, "Background," 371. The piel participle forms are found in Jer 22:20, 22; 30:14; Lam 1:19; Ezek 16:33, 36, 37; 23:5, 9, 22.

[35] See Thompson, "Israel's 'Lovers,'" 477. Cf. Jeremiah 30:14, which speaks of the destruction of Jerusalem and states, "All your lovers (מאהביך) have forgotten you."

[36] See also the piel participle in Ezek 16:37, which occurs in the same context and refers to Yahweh gathering all of Jerusalem's "lovers" (מאהביך). Cf. Thompson, "Israel's 'Lovers,'" 476.

[37] The piel participle in Ezek 23:22 is similar although the identification of the lovers as Babylonians, Chaldeans, and Assyrians appears in the following verse.

[38] Day, "Bitch," 242–43. There are, however, some scholars who object to this reading of the evidence outside of Hosea. For example, Adler ("Background," 371) critiques Moran's view that love terminology in the Hebrew Bible relies on connotations associated with the term *ra'āmu* in ancient Near Eastern texts. She argues that piel participles of אהב simply carry "romantic overtones."

1.3 The Lovers as Political Allies in Hosea 2

In light of the above evidence, it is surprising to note that the majority of
interpreters, even those who argue most strongly for a tradition of connecting
love language with the political sphere, explicitly reject this understanding for
Hos 2.[39] Some commentators suggest that a political meaning may be
secondarily at work in this speech, but very few scholars have suggested that
this meaning of "lovers" is the primary one in the discourse of Hos 2.[40] Yee uses
redaction criticism to conclude that the original material in the book of Hosea
dealt only with political issues and the northern kingdom's pursuit of
inappropriate political allies described as "lovers." Later redactions in the
Josianic and exilic periods altered this original focus to a concern with religious
and cultic elements. Nonetheless, Yee does not consider the majority of the
metaphors and images in Hos 2 to have been part of the original material.[41] The
other treatments of the political aspects of the term "lovers" do not discuss the
occurrences in Hos 2 in detail.[42]

Thus, the primary issue for this metaphor in Hos 2 is not whether the term
can carry a political meaning, since nearly all commentators agree that it can,
but whether that meaning is more probable for this text. In this regard, a number
of factors combine to suggest that the political sense of "lovers" as inappropriate
allies may indeed be the primary meaning of the metaphor in Hosea's oracle.
These factors emerge from the specific analysis of other uses of the root אהב in
the book of Hosea and the interrelation of the different metaphorical imagery
throughout the chapter.

---

[39] For example, Moran ("Ancient Near Eastern Background," 77) argues that there is a fundamental
difference that separates the concept of love in Deuteronomy and Hosea: Hosea speaks only of
Yahweh's love for Israel and not vice versa (cf. Ackerman, "The Personal Is Political," 440–47). It is
difficult to see, however, how this difference precludes Hosea's imagery from being political,
especially given the texts like the Amarna letters, in which suzerains promise to "love" their vassals.
Thompson's ("Israel's 'Lovers,'" 480) only stated reason for maintaining a religious interpretation of
the metaphor in Hos 2 is that the literary context, particularly the presence of the term בעל, demands
it: "It would seem *from the context* that the 'lovers' in question were other deities, the Baalim (verses
8, 13)" (emphasis added; cf. ibid., 477, f.n. 5).

[40] For example, Garrett suggests that "lovers" in Hosea may represent both other deities and foreign
nations with whom Israel has formed alliances (*Hosea, Joel*, 80). Cf. Landy, *Hosea*, 37; Lewis,
"Metaphors," 17; Stuart, *Hosea-Jonah*, 48; Ward, *Hosea*, 38.

[41] Yee, *Composition*, 305–8. She attributes only 2:4aA, 2:4B–5, 2:7B, and 2:12 to Hosea (ibid., 55).
But see her more recent study ("Not My Wife," 368), which reads the "lovers" imagery in Hos 2 as
representing a socially unjust "mode of production."

[42] But see J. H. Hayes, "Hosea's Baals and Lovers: Religion or Politics?" (paper presented at the
annual meeting of the SBL, New Orleans, 1990). Keefe ("Female Body," 76 and *Woman's Body*,
125–30) explores this view but ultimately rejects it in favor of a sociological interpretation (but cf.
Woman's Body, 126). For another investigation of the possible political meaning, see B. Halpern,
"Brisker Pipes Than Poetry: The Development of Israelite Monotheism," in *Judaic Perspectives on
Ancient Israel* (eds., J. Neusner, B. Levine, E. Frerichs; Philadelphia: Fortress, 1987), 77–115.

The root אהב occurs nineteen times in Hosea with fourteen of them being outside of Hos 2. These fourteen other occurrences clearly demonstrate that Hosea used the root in a wide variety of ways, including to carry a political meaning. Eight of the uses employ the term with the connotation of emotion or devotion, especially denoting the love of God. For example, three of these uses appear within Yahweh's instructions to Hosea to go and marry a woman at the beginning of chapter 3: "And Yahweh said to me again, 'Go love (אהב, qal imperative) a woman who is loved (אהבת, qal participle) by a friend and who is an adulteress like the love (כאהבת, noun) of Yahweh for the children of Israel ...'" (3:1).[43]

Hosea uses אהב three times in what appear to be metaphors for religious apostasy. For instance, again in the opening of chapter 3, Hosea describes the people of Israel as "turning to other gods and loving (ואהבי, qal participle) raisin cakes" (3:1). Hosea 9:10 occurs in a context that discusses not the present actions of Hosea's audience but the past actions of their ancestors in an episode with the god Baal-peor (cf. Num 25) and asserts, "And they became hateful like that which they loved (כאהבם, qal infinitive)." The third reference, Hos 4:18, is a very difficult and unclear verse. It appears to be religious in meaning, since 4:17 mentions Ephraim's connection with idols. However, this meaning is far from clear and the text remains ambiguous: "[T]hey have fostered fornication; they have loved (אהבו, qal perfect); shame is its garment."[44] The root also occurs once in Hosea with a seemingly social or ethical connotation: "He [Ephraim] is a trader in whose hands are deceitful weights; he has loved (אהב, qal perfect) to oppress" (12:8).

There are two places in Hosea outside of chapter two, however, that employ forms of אהב in a political sense. Hosea 10:11 appears to characterize the changing alliances and loyalties of the political entity called Ephraim: "And Ephraim was a tethered heifer, loving (אהבתי, qal participle) to thresh...."[45] Although אהב is not a strictly political metaphor here, the context of the verse suggests a political sense for the metaphorical description as a whole. Verse 10 refers to the gathering of people against Israel, verse 13 accuses Israel of trusting in its warriors, and verse 14 predicts the destruction of Israel's fortresses "as Shalman spoiled Beth-arbel in the day of battle." Hosea 8:9

---

[43] For the other literal uses of the root see 9:1, 15; 11:1, 4; 14:4. One should note, however, that Thompson identifies 9:15 and 11:1 with the political imagery of the "love" of a suzerain for a vassal ("Israel's 'Lovers,'" 478).

[44] For a textual discussion of this verse, see Wolff, *Hosea*, 73. In the context, one could easily see how אהב here could carry the political meaning of "they made alliances." Similarly, Thomas has argued that the unclear text in 8:13 (זבחי הבהבי) should be read with the LXX as "the beloved altars" and therefore be viewed as containing a form of אהב ("Root," 63). This argument is not generally followed.

[45] This is an unusual form of the qal participle with a yod attached to the end in construct state. See Wolff, *Hosea*, 179.

represents the clearest political use of the metaphor of lovers in the book of Hosea. This text is the most significant for understanding Hos 2 because it is the only place outside of chapter 2 where the root אהב appears as the plural "lovers." Although the form in 8:9 is a simple noun, as opposed to the participial forms in Hos 2, its presence indicates that the only other use of the word "lovers" in Hosea occurs in a context of international politics and is explicitly political in nature: "Surely they have gone up against Assyria; a wild ass wandering alone is Ephraim; they have hired lovers (אהבים)."[46]

The above survey suggests the likelihood that Hosea was familiar with a variety of uses of this metaphor, including a political use. Given the available ancient Near Eastern evidence, there is no need to suggest that a political use developed only after the time of Hosea.[47] The fact that the only other use of the plural metaphor "lovers" in the book is explicitly political in meaning (8:9) inclines one to read the references in Hos 2 as political as well.[48] Additionally, as noted above, all of the piel participle forms outside of Hosea, with the exception of Zech 13:6, use the metaphor in a clearly and often explicitly political sense, and all five of the appearances in Hos 2 are in the form of a piel participle. Thus, the closest parallels for understanding the lovers in Hos 2 are not the other occurrences in Hosea, but the matching piel forms that occur in Ezekiel, Jeremiah, and Lamentations. These forms consistently employ the metaphor to represent inappropriate political allies. Even the Targum of Hos 2:7 already understood the term in this political tradition and identified the lovers as "nations."

Another factor that suggests a political connotation for the metaphor of lovers in Hos 2 involves the ways in which this reading fits with the entirety of the chapter's imagery. As noted above, Hos 2 relies on violent imagery found elsewhere in the Hebrew Bible only in connection with the political entities of cities. It also employs a long-standing tradition of personifying capital cities as females in the context of their real or threatened destruction. Furthermore, the arguments given above for understanding fornication and adultery as political metaphors, if correct, suggest a connection between the chapter's overall imagery and its use of the term "lovers". The only part of the chapter's discourse that seems, on the surface, to be out of step with the political and city imagery is the use of the term בעל.

---

[46] So also Andersen and Freedman, *Hosea*, 249; Kruger, "Israel, the Harlot," 113; Thompson, "Israel's 'Lovers,'" 477.

[47] Contra Mays, *Hosea*, 39 and Yee, *Composition*, 305–8.

[48] Keefe ("Female Body," 76), taking the qal participle in 3:1 as an object ("lovers of raisin cakes") rather than an action ("loving raisin cakes"), points out that this is the only place in Hosea where lovers are explicitly identified with other gods. Cf. Keefe, *Woman's Body*, 17–18.

1.4 Summary and Conclusions

This discussion of the metaphor of "lovers" in Hos 2 has explored the term in light of its supporting biblical and extrabiblical traditions and its place within the overall rhetorical discourse of the oracle. The common view that the lovers represent illegitimate deities does not take adequate account of the well-substantiated tradition, both inside and outside the Hebrew Bible, of using "lovers" as a metaphor for political allies. Additionally, the use of the term elsewhere in the book of Hosea and its relationship to the other metaphorical imagery in Hos 2 suggest a political meaning for this chapter as well.

This political interpretation of "lovers" provides more insight into the rhetorical horizon constructed by Hos 2 and defines further the type of situation in which the oracle may have functioned as a word from Yahweh. The imagery reinforces the impression that this speech is directly concerned with the political affairs of a capital city that Hosea views as violations of Yahweh's will for the people. When one considers all of Hos 2's major metaphors examined thus far, it appears that the oracle envisions an occasion when the leaders of the northern kingdom, represented by the personified capital city, sought out political relationships with foreign allies that, in the prophet's view, constituted abandonment of Yahweh and brought the city to the point of imminent destruction.

2. The Metaphor of Baal(s) in Hosea 2

The metaphor of lovers in Hos 2 stands in close relationship to the term בעל that occurs in various forms throughout the text. This term is another representation of the entities with whom Yahweh's wife has committed adultery. The precise nature of the relationship between the groups represented by the lovers and baal(s) is unclear. This lack of clarity is due in large part to the fact that בעל occurs in both singular and plural forms in the chapter while "lovers" is always plural. The one verse that uses both terms, however, does appear to equate them: "And I will visit upon her the days of the בעלים for whom she burned incense and she adorned herself with her nose-ring and her jewelry and she went after her lovers (מאהביה)" (2:15).

The majority of interpreters understand Hosea's use of the word בעל in terms of a Canaanite fertility cult and/or religious practices and beliefs that were adopted by the eighth-century Israelites. The prophet's judgments are seen as dealing with Israelite worship of the Canaanite god Baal through the means of sexual and fertility rites. There are two primary features usually associated with the Baal fertility cult: 1) worship of the rain god Baal and the Canaanite goddesses of sex and 2) ritual sex acts in the cult designed to ensure fertility by imitating the sacred marriage of Baal and the earth goddess.[49] According to the common view, Hosea uses the term בַּעַל to refer to the god with whom the Israelites have committed apostasy and mentions fornication and adultery to refer to literal ritual sexual acts performed within the cult dedicated to that god. The comments of Mays are representative of this position:

> From the opening verses of ch. 1 to the concluding oracle in ch. 14, the cult and mythology of the god Baal is the foil of most of Hosea's sayings.... His condemnation of Israel's commerce with Baal and of any syncretistic modification of Yahwism by the influence of Baalism is unyielding. But he also adapts the motifs and rubrics of the fertility cult to portray the relation of Yahweh and his people, to diagnose Israel's sin, and to describe the future which God will create. With daring skill he appropriates the language and thought of Canaanite religion while rejecting Baalism itself.[50]

2.1 Sexual Rites and Fertility Cults in the Ancient Near East

The first major argument that scholars made in attempting to understand the term בַּעַל in Hos 2 rested on belief in the existence of widespread cultic sexual acts and fertility rites in the ancient Near East. The investigation of these sexual elements in the religions of Canaan, Israel, Ugarit, Babylon, etc., typically revolved around four practices that were often not clearly distinguished: 1) cultic or sacred prostitution, 2) ritual defloration of virgins, 3) sacred marriage, and 4) general sexual elements in the cult.[51] Taken individually or together, these alleged practices were understood to provide the general background for the use of בַּעַל in Hos 2. More recently, however, the existence of each of these rites and its relevance for the interpretation of Hos 2 have been called into question.[52]

2.1.1 *Cultic Prostitution.* The alleged sexual rite that has played the most important role in the discussion of Hos 2 was the practice of so-called cultic or sacred prostitution. The standard statement of this notion ran along these lines: part of the religion of the Canaanites, Phoenicians, Babylonians, and perhaps others involved a series of rites in which sacred personnel performed various

---

[49] Keefe, "Female Body," 76.

[50] Mays, *Hosea*, 8.

[51] As Bucher notes, scholars have generally failed to define these elements precisely and have often included evidence for one practice under the heading of another. In this way, a false impression of the weight and breadth of the evidence for ritual sexual practices emerges. Bucher attempts to distinguish more precisely among the categories (see "Origin," 32).

[52] For the overall rejection of sexualized rituals connected with Canaanite religion, see Abma, *Bonds*, 137–42; Ben Zvi, "Observations," 379; Frymer-Kensky, *In the Wake of the Goddess*, 199–202; Keefe, *Woman's Body*, 36–65.

sexual acts primarily to ensure the fertility of the land and its inhabitants.[53] As worshippers engaged in sexual intercourse with temple personnel, the gods were moved to similar action that produced fertility for the land. In the land of Canaan, this type of rite, it was believed, would have been connected with the rain god Baal. Van der Toorn defined such cultic prostitution as "religiously legitimated intercourse with strangers in or in the vicinity of the sanctuary. It had a ritual character and was organized or at least condoned by the priesthood, as a means to increase fecundity and fertility."[54]

This reconstruction primarily emerged from consideration of texts within the Hebrew Bible that seem to denounce the practice of cultic prostitution. For example, while surveying the arguments for this practice, Yamauchi cited Gen 38; Hos 4; Deut 23:17–18; 1 Kgs 14:23–24; 15:12; 22:46; and 2 Kgs 23:6–7 as clear references and Num 25:1–3; 1 Sam 2:22; Jer 13:27; Ezek 16; 23:37–41; and Amos 2:7–8 as possible references to cultic prostitution.[55] Interpreters supplemented the biblical passages with classical texts that made accusations of widespread sexual rites in the ancient Near East. The sources that scholars most frequently cited were the materials in Latin and Greek from Herodotus in the fifth century B.C.E. to Augustine in the fifth century C.E.[56] Within this group, scholars most often relied on the comments of Herodotus concerning Babylon and Cyrpus (I. 199): "The foulest Babylonian custom is that which compels every woman of the land once in her life to sit in the temple of Aphrodite and have intercourse with some stranger."[57] The statements in Strabo's *Geography* XVI. i. 20, which comes from the beginning of the Christian era, have been the second most frequently used source:

---

[53] R. Oden, *The Bible without Theology: The Theological Tradition and Alternatives to It* (San Francisco: Harper & Row, 1987), 131. Cf. O. J. Baab, "Prostitution," *IDB* 3:931–34 and W. von Soden, "Kultische Prostitution," *RGG* 5:642. For an example of a work that incorporates this idea into a full-scale reconstruction of the history of Israelite religion, see W. C. Graham and H. G. May, *Culture and Conscience: An Archaeological Study of the New Religious Past in Ancient Palestine* (Chicago: University of Chicago Press, 1936), esp. 229, 280.

[54] K. van der Toorn, "Cultic Prostitution," *ABD* 5:510. Birch describes the typical understanding behind the practice by stating that, in the winter, Baal was thought to die and go to the netherworld. Later, he was rescued by Anat, and their sexual intercourse provided the spring cycle of fertility. Thus, Canaanite rituals perhaps included cultic sexual intercourse in order to enact this divine union (Birch, *Hosea, Joel, Amos*, 32–33; cf. Knight, *Hosea*, 18 and Stienstra, *YHWH*, 99).

[55] E. Yamauchi, "Cultic Prostitution: A Case Study in Cultural Diffusion," in *Orient and Occident: Essays Presented to Cyrus H. Gordon on the Occasion of His Sixty-Fifth Birthday* (ed. H. A. Hoffner; AOAT 22; Neukirchen-Vluyn: Neukirchener Verlag, 1973), 218. Cf. E. Fisher, "Cultic Prostitution in the Ancient Near East? A Reassessment," *BTB* 6 (1976): 225, 233; Oden, *Bible*, 131; G. Östborn, *Yahweh and Baal: Studies in the Book of Hosea and Related Documents* (LUÅ 51, 6; Lund: C. W. K. Gleerup, 1956), 66.

[56] Oden, *Bible*, 141.

[57] See ibid.; Yamauchi, "Cultic Prostitution," 216.

And in accordance with a certain oracle all the Babylonian women have a custom of having intercourse with a foreigner, the women going to a temple of Aphrodite with a great retinue and crowd....[58]

Along these same lines, scholars found similar references in texts like the *Phoenician History* of Philo of Byblos (ca. 100 C.E.) and *On the Syrian Goddess* by Lucian (ca. 200 C.E.).[59]

The second major set of sources interpreters have used for reconstruction involved terminological evidence from Mesopotamia, Ugarit, and Israel. Scholars examined cognate or equivalent terms in law codes and temple personnel lists. The primary Mesopotamian terms used in this way included *naditu*, *ēntu*, *kezertu*, and *qadištu*.[60] These terms represented classes of female personnel who fulfilled some type of cultic function. From Ugaritic texts, interpreters have emphasized the cultic role of the male group known as the *qdšm*.[61] Writers have drawn connections between these terms and the Hebrew terms קְדֵשָׁה and קָדֵשׁ and identified them as references to female and male cult prostitutes.[62]

In addition to the interpretation of certain biblical texts, classical writings, and ancient Near Eastern terms, the study of the possible practice of cultic prostitution has analyzed a variety of less-developed types of evidence. For example, as noted above, some scholars have not distinguished between different types of sexual activity and thus have considered Mesopotamian texts that refer to a sacred marriage custom as evidence of cultic prostitution.[63] Interpreters also often referred to the Epistle of Jeremiah that mentions a Babylonian custom of women sitting in the streets and then being led away by a

---

[58] Quoted in Oden, *Bible*, 142.

[59] See D. Hillers, "Analyzing the Abominable: Our Understanding of Canaanite Religion," *JQR* 75 (1985): 257.

[60] Fisher, "Cultic Prostitution," 227; Oden, *Bible*, 147.

[61] A. F. Rainey, "The Kingdom of Ugarit," *BA* 28 (1965): 124; Yamauchi, "Cultic Prostitution," 219.

[62] For example, see Yamauchi, "Cultic Prostitution," 219. For discussion, see E. Goodfriend, "Prostitution," *ABD* 5:507 and M. Gruber, "Hebrew *QEDĒŠĀH* and Her Canaanite and Akkadian Cognates," *UF* 18 (1986): 133–48. The term קְדֵשָׁה occurs four places in the Hebrew Bible: Gen 38:21, 22; Deut 23:18; Hos 4:14. The masculine noun קָדֵשׁ appears in Deut 23:18; 1 Kgs 14:24; 15:12; 22:47(MT); 2 Kgs 23:7; Job 36:14.

[63] For example, see Yamauchi, "Cultic Prostitution," 214. Yamauchi also uses as evidence the existence of an independent practice of cultic prostitution in west Africa and India in the twentieth century (ibid., 213).

passerby for sex.[64] Some writers have even investigated evidence from erotic rock art found in the eighth and seventh centuries B.C.E.[65]

The overall course of this examination, however, only produced admittedly "quite fragmentary and somewhat contradictory" evidence for the existence of cultic prostitution in preexilic Israel and Judah.[66] In the years following 1985, scholars have challenged nearly every part of the commonly cited evidence and have convincingly called the existence of the practice into question.[67] Keefe provides a recent example:

> [T]he popular thesis concerning a syncretistic fertility cult in eighth-century Israel does not rest on any firm textual or extra-textual evidence.... [N]one of the key elements of the fertility cult thesis— popular Baal worship, the *hieros gamos* between Baal and the earth goddess, or the practice of sacred prostitution— can be substantiated by reference to the textual or extra-textual sources from eighth-century Syria-Palestine.[68]

An examination of each of the major types of evidence used to support the existence of cultic prostitution shows that Keefe's statement is well-founded. As noted above, the first type of this evidence came from biblical texts themselves.

---

[64] One should note that these events are not placed in a cultic context. See Adler, "Background," 181; cf. C. Moore, *Daniel, Esther, and Jeremiah: The Additions* (AB 44; Garden City, N.Y.: Doubleday, 1977), 347.

[65] For example, see E. Anati, "The Question of Fertility Cults," in *Archaeology and Fertility Cult in the Ancient Mediterranean: Papers Presented at the First International Conference on Archaeology of the Ancient Mediterranean* (ed. A. Bonano; Amsterdam: B. R. Grüner, 1986), 3.

[66] Yamauchi, "Cultic Prostitution," 222. From the earliest inquiries into the notion of cultic prostitution, a major question for investigation involved the attempt to discern what distinctiveness Israel's religion had, if any, from that of its neighbors. For example, William Robertson Smith used the reconstruction of sacred prostitution at non-Israelite temples to contrast the Israelite cult with that of its neighbors. For discussion, see Oden, *Bible*, 136–37.

[67] For example, the 1992 major dictionary article on cultic prostitution by van der Toorn concludes, "In recent years, however, the widely accepted hypothesis of cultic prostitution has been seriously challenged. Various scholars have argued that the current view rests on unwarranted assumptions, doubtful anthropological premises, and very little evidence. At the same time the Ugaritic and Mesopotamian material, often referred to as evidence of cultic prostitution in neighboring civilizations, has been critically reevaluated and shown to be less unambiguous than it has often been assumed" ("Cultic Prostitution," 510).

[68] Keefe, "Female Body," 72, 77; cf. Keefe, *Woman's Body*, 11; 50–65; 89–103. A selective list of recent scholars who have similarly challenged the hypothesis of sacred prostitution includes Adler, "Background;" Anati, "Question;" M. Beard and J. Henderson, "With This Body I Thee Worship: Sacred Prostitution in Antiquity," in *Gender and the Body in the Ancient Mediterranean* (ed. M. Wyke; Oxford, U.K.: Blackwell, 1998), 56–79; Bird, "Harlot;" Bucher, "Origin;" Fisher, "Cultic Prostitution;" Hillers, "Analyzing the Abominable;" S. Hooks, "Sacred Prostitution in Israel and the Ancient Near East" (Ph.D. diss., Hebrew Union College, 1985); Oden, *Bible*; Nwaoru, *Imagery*; J. Westenholtz, "Tamar, Qedeša, Qadištu and Sacred Prostitution in Mesopotamia," *HTR* 82.3 (1989): 245–65; Yee, "Hosea" (*NIB*).

Perhaps the most often cited biblical texts in this regard were Deut 23:18–19 and Hos 4:13–14. The JPS translations of these passages represented the sex-cult interpretation:

> No Israelite woman shall be a cult prostitute (קְדֵשָׁה), nor shall any Israelite man be a cult prostitute (קָדֵשׁ). You shall not bring the fee of a whore (זוֹנָה) or the pay of a dog (כֶּלֶב)[69] into the house of the LORD your God in fulfillment of any vow, for both are abhorrent to the LORD your God (Deut 23:18–19).
>
> They sacrifice on the mountain tops
> And offer on the hills….
> That is why their daughters fornicate
> And their daughters-in-law commit adultery!
> I will not punish their daughters for fornicating
> Nor their daughters-in-law for committing adultery;
> For they themselves turn aside with whores (הַזֹּנוֹת)
> And sacrifice with prostitutes (הַקְּדֵשׁוֹת),
> And a people that is without sense must stumble (Hos 4:13–14).

In a general sense, the overall biblical argument for a sex cult is circular, since the interpretation of relevant biblical passages is often dependent upon the reconstruction of the Canaanite cult while that reconstruction itself depends on the interpretation of the biblical texts.[70] Similarly, as Hillers has noted, the biblical accounts and descriptions of Canaanite religious practices are suspect because they represent the viewpoint of writers who were predisposed to finding such practices inferior and illegitimate.[71]

More specific critiques of the sex-cult interpretations of texts like Deut 23:18–19 and Hos 4:13–14 are well-established in the scholarly literature and do not need to be repeated in detail here. One may note, for instance, that discussions like that of Adler point to the parallelism between קְדֵשָׁה and זֹנָה in Gen 38 and Deut 23:18–19 and argue that this relationship indicates an equivalence between the two terms. Thus, Deut 23:18 simply forbids an Israelite woman from becoming a prostitute. The masculine term *qdšm* appears in Ugaritic texts as a general term referring to all nonpriestly personnel and suggests that Deut 23:18 only prohibits an Israelite man from becoming a "priest in a pagan cult" (קָדֵשׁ). Adler also rejects the common reading of the

---

[69] This term is often translated as "male prostitute" by other English translations like NRSV and NIV. The JPS attaches a note to the word that reads, "I.e., a male prostitute."

[70] Bucher, "Origin," 2.

[71] Hillers, "Analyzing the Abominable," 257.

term כלב as a male prostitute because she finds a lack of extrabiblical evidence for connecting the term with sexuality.[72]

Concerning Hos 4:13–14, Bird takes these verses as a reference to literal sexual activity that was not connected with the cult. Bird notes that the description of the daughters' behavior is not one of the charges against the people but is a consequence of the men's actions. She also rightly observes that these verses simply link the term קדשה with זנה and thus seem to say that these women cultic functionaries should be thought of as equivalent to prostitutes. The text seems to imply a sexual function for the women only because the Israelites, who did not have female cult functionaries, saw women functionaries in the Canaanite cult and wrongly inferred that this practice must involve sexual activity.[73] Nothing in the text warrants seeing Hos 4:13–14 as a reference to cultic prostitution rather than more general, noncultic, inappropriate behavior.[74]

A second type of evidence that scholars used to argue for an ancient Near Eastern practice of cultic prostitution has also been specifically refuted. This evidence deals more particularly with the terms that were viewed as related to the Hebrew קדשה and קדש.[75] In general, evidence from a wide variety of Hebrew and Akkadian texts suggests that the Hebrew term קדשה is simply another word for prostitute, while the Akkadian term refers to a woman who is

---

[72] Adler, "Background," 208–17. In a similar move, Fisher notes that the Mishnah takes the term כלב literally as wages earned from the sale of a dog ("Cultic Prostitution," 234). Similarly, Goodfriend ("Prostitution," 507–8) states that the evidence suggests that קדש refers to a male priestly class rejected by orthodox Yahwists, while קדשה is a synonym for זנה (cf. Gruber ["Hebrew *QEDĒŠĀH*," 133–34], who also takes קדשה as a "poetic synonym" of זנה). Goodfriend suggests that כלב here refers to a servant at a sanctuary in accordance with similar uses of the term in Ugaritic texts.

[73] See Bird, "Harlot," 85–87. This conclusion is similar to Keefe's more general argument that an association developed between cultic functionaries called קדשות and actual prostitutes. This association emerged because prohibited worship was sometimes referred to as prostitution (זנה) so the cultic officials of that worship came to be pejoratively called whores. Thus, in common usage, the term קדשה eventually became equivalent with זנה as in the story of Tamar in Gen 38 ("Female Body," 81–82).

[74] Van der Toorn, "Cultic Prostitution," 510–11; cf. Goodfriend, "Prostitution," 508–9 and Keefe, *Woman's Body*, 9–102. See also Adler, who says that this text reflects the idea that the cultic sins of Israel produced sexual sins but did not involve them ("Background," 232–43). Adler also notes that some scholars consider Isa 57:5–8 to be a reference to cultic prostitution, an interpretation that she calls "disputable" (ibid., 272).

[75] As with the discussion of the biblical texts, the scholarly material on these terms is abundant. For a reflection of the traditional views on such terms in the Hebrew Bible, see B. Brooks, "Fertility Cult Functionaries in the Old Testament," *JBL* 60 (1941): 227–53. For the most concentrated study along these lines, see Gruber, "Hebrew *QEDĒŠĀH*," 133–48. See also Adler, "Background," 173–75; Bird, "Harlot," 87; Bucher, "Origin," 55; Fisher, "Cultic Prostitution," 225–28; Goodfriend, "Prostitution," 507–9; Keefe, "Female Body," 81–82; van der Toorn, "Cultic Prostitution," 512.

dedicated to the service of a deity and functions as a cultic singer or wetnurse.[76] Where terms like *qadištu* occur in Mesopotamian law codes, they do not give any indication of sexual activity, and the law codes and temple records make no mention of a practice of sacred prostitution.[77] Concerning the masculine קָדֵשׁ, none of the four places it occurs in Kings (1 Kgs 14:24; 15:12; 22:47(MT); 2 Kgs 23:7) gives any indication that it refers to a prostitute.[78]

Along these same lines, Oden observes that Akkadian terms like *ēntu* and *nadītu*, previously seen as referring to sacred prostitutes, appear primarily to emphasize chastity and preclude prostitution.[79] Similarly, the Akkadian word *kezertu*, often seen as referring to a ritual prostitute, appears in a Mari letter that mentions this group of women, together with classes called *sekrētum* ("harem women") and *kisalluḫḫatum* ("courtyard sweepers"), as simply low-level cultic officials.[80]

As to possible Ugaritic parallels, the primary term discussed in this regard was *qdšm*, a masculine term that was connected with the Hebrew term קָדֵשׁ (as in Deut 23:18–19) and viewed as referring to a male cult prostitute. Several scholars have reconsidered the Ugaritic evidence and specifically rejected a sexual interpretation. For example, Nwaoru noted the evidence that the Ugaritic texts make no mention of *female* cult prostitutes at all, while Fisher emphasized that the Ugaritic *qdšm* receive a regular income, generally appear in texts after the priests, and give the impression of being a type of male cult personnel associated with priestly functions.[81] Furthermore, one does not find reference to

---

[76] Gruber, "Hebrew *QEDĒŠĀH*," 133. For the relevant Akkadian texts, see ibid., 139–45. Gruber also notes that the idea that קָדֵשׁ is a cult prostitute is unknown to the ancient versions like the LXX of Gen 38 (ibid., 135).

[77] Fisher, "Cultic Prostitution," 226–28. See also Gruber, "Hebrew *QEDĒŠĀH*," 145. The one Hebrew Bible text that seems to give a clear statement of the function of הַקְּדֵשִׁים is 2 Kgs 23:7, and it simply mentions them along with women who wove garments for Asherah (cf. Fisher, "Cultic Prostitution," 235).

[78] On this issue, see M. Gruber, "The qādēš in the Book of Kings and in Other Sources," *Tarbiz* 52 (1983): 167–76 (in Hebrew).

[79] Oden, *Bible*, 148.

[80] Adler, "Background," 174, f.n. 104. Adler does note that Gallery has argued some OB administrative texts seem to indicate that a *kezertu*-woman was obligated to perform nonmarital intercourse on behalf of a goddess (see M. Gallery, "Service Obligations of the *kezertu*-Women," *Or* 49 [1980]: 333–38). However, beyond a mourning rite in the Gilgamesh epic, there is no clear indication of what function these women may have had in the cult (Adler, "Background," 174, f.n. 104).

[81] Nwaoru, *Imagery*, 130–31; Fisher, "Cultic Prostitution," 228. Cf. Goodfriend, "Prostitution," 507. Gruber suggests that the *qdšm* in Ugaritic texts are cultic singers and so usually occur right after priests in administrative lists ("Hebrew *QEDĒŠĀH*," 133). See also J. Day ("Canaan, Religion of," *ABD* 1:831–37), who notes that the available information about Canaanite rituals is scarce and the *qdšm* in Ugaritic texts are not presented as cultic prostitutes.

any kind of orgiastic activity in the texts that contain the most information concerning Baal.[82]

The third main type of evidence that was used to argue for widespread cultic or ritual prostitution, namely the testimony of later classical writers, has also been called into question. Oden summarizes the major problems with using these classical sources for reconstruction.[83] First, most of the sources reflect a late date (e.g., Herodotus in the fifth century B.C.E.), and one cannot assume that the practices they mention existed in Iron Age Israel. This fact raises the possibility that the sources fall victim to the practice of labeling the ancestors as less civilized than their contemporary societies. Second, none of the sources are disinterested or objective but all are apologetic and hostile. Third, all the classical sources seem to be interrelated and interdependent. As Oden put it, "What appears to be a list of more than a dozen sources may in fact be a list of a couple of sources, perhaps even and ultimately a single source: Herodotus."[84] Fourth, Herodotus' observations are superficial, not supported by documents like temple records from Hellenistic Babylon, and overly dependent on his own secondary sources.[85]

When taken together, these critiques call into question the notion that there was cultic or ritual prostitution in Israel and the ancient Near East. Emphasizing the large discrepancy between the apparent denunciations of cultic sex in the Hebrew Bible and the very ambiguous extrabiblical evidence for it, Oden concludes,

> If, however, the existence of sacred prostitution as an element in the liturgical life of several ancient Near Eastern religions and as a continuing temptation for Israelites has achieved the status of a kind of given, it remains true that discovering unambiguous evidence for any such rites among these religions remains quite difficult.[86]

---

[82] Hillers ("Analyzing the Abominable," 258) described this lack of evidence as the "Ugarit-as-embarrassment" motif. For a discussion of the view that Song of Songs reflects "pagan fertility worship" and an exploration of its relationship to Ugaritic mythological and ritual texts, see M. Pope, *Song of Songs* (AB; New York: Doubleday, 1977), 145–53.

[83] Oden, *Bible*, 140–47.

[84] Thus, if Herodotus is unreliable, so are all the later classical and patristic sources. See ibid., 146–47; cf. Bucher, "Origin," 59–60.

[85] For similar critiques concerning these sources, see Bucher, "Origin," 2; Hillers, "Analyzing the Abominable," 254–55; Beard and Henderson, "With This Body," 70; Gruber, "Hebrew *QEDĒŠĀH*," 137.

[86] Oden, *Bible*, 132. Some contrary evidence in support of retaining the concept of cultic prostitution has come in from the field of anthropology. Anthropologists have widely observed sexual behavior in connection with various rituals in different societies. See A. L. Basham, *The Wonder That Was India: A Survey of the History and Culture of the Indian Sub-Continent Before the Coming of the Muslims* (3d rev. ed.; Calcutta: Rupa & Co., 1967), 170–71. For example, temple practice in India in the Middle Ages centered on a god who was treated like an earthly king and thus had various

In spite of the criticisms noted above, a few recent scholars still conclude that the evidence points to the existence of cultic prostitution in ancient Israel. For example, van der Toorn acknowledges the refutations cited above but argues that texts like 2 Kgs 23:7 link prostitutes with the temple yet not with any fertility cult.[87] Accordingly, he redefines cultic prostitution in Israel to include only the money or goods that a prostitute, professional or otherwise, gave to the temple as a means to pay a vow, even if in the form of a one-time act.[88]

In a more traditional way, MacLachlan has recently argued for the existence of cultic prostitution in antiquity but only in connection with Phoenicia, Greece, and Rome and not in association with the worship of Baal.[89] She draws primarily upon the classical texts and argues that the typical scholarly refutations focus too narrowly on individual terms.[90] She cites one Babylonian text that, in her view, provides an unequivocal witness: the civilizing of Enkidu by a "temple courtesian" in the Gilgamesh epic (l. iii). Additionally, MacLachlan contends that Strabo's account of Babylonian sacred sex is similar to Herodotus's but "adds a couple of minor details in his description which indicates that he did not simply copy Herodotus but took the information from an independent source or from an earlier one upon which Herodotus also drew."[91] She also cites a Greek text from 480 B.C.E. that refers to "goddess' women" who offered prayers for the salvation of Corinth and argues that these women were cultic prostitutes.[92]

MacLachlan's arguments are not, however, sufficient to overcome the deficiencies in the traditional evidence outlined above. Her use of the Gilgamesh mythological text to reconstruct a cultic class and practice is questionable in light of the complex nature of the relationship between myth and ritual. The Greek text she cites concerning the goddess's women in Corinth does not contain any direct reference to sexual acts. MacLachlan's interpretation of cultic prostitution as a widespread phenomenon in antiquity, like many such interpretations prior to the 1980s, primarily rests on the problematic testimony of classical writers like Herodotus and Strabo.

Thus, in the final analysis, one must question the notion of widespread cultic or ritual prostitution in ancient Israel and the idea of its powerful

---

attendants, including prostitutes. Basham notes that these prostitutes (devadāsīs) served the male worshippers, who paid their fee to the temple (ibid., 185). There is, however, no clear evidence for such a practice in early sources (ibid).

[87] 2 Kings 23:7 is a very unclear text that refers to women (הנשים) who weave for Asherah and masculine הקדשים who have houses near the temple. There is no clear indication of sexual activity in the verse.

[88] Van der Toorn, "Cultic Prostitution," 511.

[89] B. MacLachlan, "Sacred Prostitution and Aphrodite," *SR* 21/2 (1992): 145–62.

[90] Ibid., 146.

[91] Ibid., 149–50.

[92] Ibid., 158–59.

influence upon texts of the Hebrew Bible. Perhaps Oden provides a helpful way forward in analyzing the problem by suggesting that the biblical and classical texts that seem to make this accusation should be understood as examples of ethical boundary marking between societies, that is, the degradation of an "other" for the sake of establishing one's own identity.[93] The idea of an institution of cultic prostitution that provided the background for texts like Hos 2 can no longer be sustained without great caution and should certainly not be assumed without investigation.

2.1.2 *Ritual Defloration of Virgins.* A second allegedly widespread sexual rite that has sometimes been used to understand the background of the term בעל in Hos 2 is the ritual defloration of virgins. Scholars generally take this practice to mean the required engagement of every female in one act of cultic intercourse at a sanctuary before she is married. According to this view, an eighth-century Israelite woman, like Hosea's wife Gomer, would engage in one act of sexual intercourse at a local shrine dedicated to the fertility god Baal.[94] As with cultic prostitution, however, a strong case can be made against the historical reality of such a practice and its appropriateness for understanding the language of Hos 2.

The primary work on Hos 2 that uses this interpretation is that of Wolff. In discussing the character of Gomer and the descriptions of her as a woman of זנונים (1:2; cf. 2:4), Wolff contends that the language refers not to one who is an ongoing participant in an apostate fertility cult (i.e., a cultic prostitute) but to one who has engaged in a one-time act of ritual sex dedicated to Baal.[95] He cites as evidence, however, the same later extrabiblical texts often cited in connection with the idea of cultic prostitution. In his view, these texts demonstrate that there was a fertility rite in Israel that occurred only once in a woman's lifetime and "must be carefully distinguished from the institution of permanent prostitutes hired for the cult."[96] He draws the conclusion that the type of sexual misconduct alluded to in Hos 1–3 refers to the general practice of "any young

---

[93] Oden, *Bible*, 132. See also Beard and Henderson ("With This Body," 69), who suggest that accusations of cultic prostitution look like "cultural constructions of the Other."

[94] See C. Clemen, *Miszellen zu Lukians Schrift über die syrische Göttin* (BZAW 33; Berlin: Töpelmann, 1918), 89; W. Baumgartner, "Herodots babylonische und assyrische Nachrichten," *ArOr* 18 (1950): 69–109; and Wolff, *Hosea*, 14–15.

[95] Wolff, *Hosea*, 14.

[96] Ibid., 14. For example, he refers to the texts from Herodotus and Lucian mentioned above. He also emphasizes Augustine's statements concerning the goddess Venus in *The City of God* (IV. 10): "[T]he Phoenicians offered the gift of prostituting their daughters, before they married them to husbands" (Wolff's translation; ibid., 14). Further, Wolff notes the *Testament of the Twelve Patriarchs, Judah* 12:2: "It is the custom of the Amorites that those who want to be married must sit in the gate for seven days and engage in prostitution" (ibid). Cf. Lev 19:29; Deut 23:18–19; Judg 11:34, 37–40.

woman ready for marriage (as in 4:13f) who had submitted to the bridal rites of initiation then current in Israel."[97]

The evidence for ritual defloration falters on many of the same grounds as that for cultic prostitution. First, although not cited by Wolff, the earliest evidence for the practice of ritual defloration before marriage comes from a passage in the Gilgamesh epic (IV. 34–36) that refers to a king's right to engage in such an act: "He will have intercourse with the destined wife: he first, the husband afterward."[98] Notwithstanding the issues concerning the relationship of this text to the practice of actual rituals, the passage refers only to the actions of a king and does not present the event as a ritual act of any kind.[99] Second, although Wolff's interpretation of the classical texts as evidence for a one-time, sexual act by women prior to marriage does seem to be an accurate representation of what they describe,[100] he still only finds such evidence in Herodotus, a fifth-century B.C.E. Greek historian writing about Babylon not Canaan; Lucian, a second-century C.E. anti-religious satirist; *The Testament of the Twelve Patriarchs*, a postbiblical Jewish text; and Augustine, a fifth-century C.E. Christian writer.[101] None of these sources are contemporary with Hosea, and there is no clear cuneiform evidence for this type of once-in-a-lifetime prostitution.[102]

2.1.3 *Sacred Marriage.* A third sexual rite that could possibly form part of the background of Hos 2, particularly in view of its marriage metaphor, is the ritual of sacred marriage. This institution primarily involves the ancient Sumerians, almost exclusively revolves around the goddess Inanna (Akk. Ištar; Heb. Aštōret) and her divine spouse Damuzi (Heb. Tammūz), and is attested by clear and contemporary textual evidence.[103] Evidence for this practice in the ancient world comes from three chronological periods: 1) Early Dynastic, Sargonic, and Lagash II periods, 2) Ur III–Isin period, and 3) later OB–first millennium period.[104] The main information about sacred marriage rituals comes from three

---

[97] Wolff, *Hosea*, 15.

[98] For this translation and argument see Yamauchi, "Cultic Prostitution," 216. For discussion see Bucher, "Origin," 57–58.

[99] Cf. Bucher, "Origin," 57–58.

[100] In this regard, Wolff illustrates the problem noted earlier that scholars writing about a supposedly widespread practice of cultic sex in the ancient Near East rely essentially on the same evidence for different cultic reconstructions.

[101] Hillers, "Analyzing the Abominable," 257–58.

[102] Cf. Adler, "Background," 178.

[103] J. Klein, "Sacred Marriage," *ABD* 5:866. Scholars originally applied the term "sacred marriage" (*hieros gamos*) to the union of Zeus and Hera, then extended it to cover other instances of marriage between gods or between a god and a human, especially when ritually reenacted.

[104] J. Cooper, "Sacred Marriage and Popular Cult in Early Mesopotamia," in *Official Cult and Popular Religion in the Ancient Near East* (ed. E. Matsushima; Heidelberg: Universitätsverlag C. Winters, 1993), 82.

types of material: 1) cultic love songs and royal hymns about Inanna and Dumuzi, 2) Sumerian mythological texts describing Dumuzi's rejection by Inanna, death, and descent to the underworld, and 3) laments over Dumuzi's tragic death.[105]

In the earliest period (Early Dynastic, Sargonic, and Lagash II), texts seem to indicate that kings participated in a sacred marriage ritual of some kind, but at this stage, the ritual appears to consist of a locally celebrated marriage between two deities that was not acted out by humans in a sexual way.[106] By contrast, in the second period (Ur III–Isin) one finds the only "sure evidence for ritual copulation" between a goddess and a human ruler.[107] Sumerian hymns of Shulgi of Ur (ca. 2050 B.C.E.) and Iddindagan of Isin (ca. 1950 B.C.E.) refer to the sacred marriage of a named king, in the guise of the god Dumuzi, and the goddess Inanna. For example, one of the hymns refers to Shulgi touching the goddess Inanna's "hair of my loins" and "my pure vulva" and lying in "my sweet womb."[108] In these rituals, the male protagonist is always the king, who represented Inanna's husband Dumuzi, while the identity of the sacred female who engaged in the ritual sex act and represented Inanna remains unclear.[109] The hymns portray an act of physical intercourse between the king and the woman, which represents the marital intercourse of Dumuzi and Inanna.[110] When one considers the evidence for sacred marriage rituals from the first millennium, however, the picture changes dramatically. By the time of the

---

[105] Klein, "Sacred Marriage," 866.

[106] For example, from the Early Dynastic period, a Sumerian tale called "Enmerkar and Ensuḫkeshdanna" has two rival kings (ca. 2400 B.C.E.) who call themselves "spouses of Inanna" (Cooper, "Sacred Marriage," 83). Two inscriptions from Gudea of Lagash (ca. 2150 B.C.E.) report that when he built a temple for the god Ningirsu, he stocked it with bridal gifts for Ningirsu to give annually to the goddess Ba'u (ibid., 84).

[107] Ibid., 83.

[108] Ibid., 84–85.

[109] Suggestions include the queen, the high-priestess, a specially selected votary, a *lukur*-priestess, and various other classes of female clergy (ibid., 87).

[110] The purpose of this physical ritual is debated. The common view is that the ritual served to ensure fertility for plants and animals (see Klein, "Sacred Marriage," 868 and Yamauchi, "Cultic Prostitution," 213). In contrast to this position, one Sumerian text actually proposes a theory of sacred marriage (the hymn of Ishmedagan K57) that suggests the purpose was to regulate relations between people and between the gods and people (Cooper, "Sacred Marriage," 91). The marriage centered on familial relations and kinship ties like establishing the kings of Ur as sons-in-law of the god of their capital. Klein provides a list of commonly considered purposes of the sacred marriage ritual: 1) legitimation and deification of the king, 2) conception of the crown prince, 3) installation of the high priestess, and 4) insurance of fertility for the land ("Sacred Marriage," 868). The study of W. Harmon (*The Sacred Marriage of a Hindu Goddess* [Bloomington: Indiana University Press, 1989], 3, 14, 51), which focuses on a modern sacred marriage festival in India in the 1970s, shows that the marriage in that context primarily functioned to organize perceptions of the relationships between deities and between deities and devotees.

earliest Akkadian evidence, sacred marriage rituals appear to be merely symbolic practices involving only divine images and not persons.[111]

While evidence for a ritual sex act connected with sacred marriage in the ancient Near East does seem to exist in ancient texts, this evidence concerns only the Sumerians and is limited to the second millennium B.C.E. There is nothing in Hos 2 that suggests the union of a goddess and a king other than the supposed correlation noted above between the sexual intercourse of a man and a cult prostitute and the sexual intercourse of Baal and a goddess.

2.1.4 *General Sexual Elements in the Cult.* In light of the above critiques, some scholars see evidence for the existence of only nonspecific sexual elements that were loosely connected with the Israelite cult. This view holds that sexual activity did take place in conjunction with cultic festivals and rituals, but it was not an official part of the religious rites. Both biblically and anthropologically, this conclusion is on surer ground.

The discussions of Fisher and van der Toorn provide recent illustrations of this argument. Fisher thoroughly rejects the notion of cultic prostitution but maintains that there is evidence for general "ritual intercourse" in ancient Israel, that is, sexual activity that took place in conjunction with religious festivals and rituals. The biblical evidence appears primarily in texts that denounce these events (e.g., Num 25; Hos 4:13; 9:10). As ancient Near Eastern evidence for this argument, he notes that this kind of activity was prominent at the Babylonian New Year festival.[112] Van der Toorn similarly suggests that biblical denunciations of debauchery indicate that there was illicit sexual activity that took place at times of religious festivals and ceremonies.[113]

The idea that inappropriate sexual conduct took place at times of congregation for the people seems possible. Anthropologists, for example, widely observe sexual practices in conjunction with religious festivals.[114] There

---

[111] These rituals annually celebrate the sacred marriage of deities but do not involve Dumuzi and Ishtar (Cooper, "Sacred Marriage," 94). The references to the practice are also only sporadic and obscure. For example, Klein notes some references in Neo-Assyrian texts to a sacred marriage between Nabu (god of Borsippa) and his wife Tashmetu ("Sacred Marriage," 869). Even within the material from Ugarit, only the mythological text "Šahar and Šalim" (CTA 23) seems to indicate a ritual performance of a marriage, but such a reconstruction is difficult to maintain (Bucher, "Origin," 64).

[112] Fisher, "Cultic Prostitution," 229.

[113] See van der Toorn, "Cultic Prostitution," 510–11.

[114] For example, in his study of the Lugbara society of Uganda between 1949 and 1952, Middleton observed that a death and burial rite, particularly for an important kinsman, was followed by a period when "many of the obligations of kinship are temporarily in abeyance ... [and there is] permitted license in behavior between kin...." As an example of this behavior, Middleton observed the "normally forbidden seduction of clan-sisters by young men" and occasional reversals of sexual roles with young men wearing women's clothing. See J. Middleton, *The Lugbara of Uganda* (Case Studies in Cultural Anthropology; New York: Holt, Rinehart, & Winston, 1965), 68. See also T.

are two problems, however, that make general cultic sex questionable as a background for texts like Hos 2. First, the majority of evidence cited by scholars like Fisher consists of biblical texts that are ambiguous and heavily debated. Fisher interprets accusations concerning sexual misconduct that appear in the context of language about the cult to represent a denunciation of literal sexual activity engaged in by worshippers during times when they came to a cultic celebration. For example, he follows Mendenhall's argument that the Baal-peor incident in Num 25 refers not to cultic prostitution but to a feast followed by ritual sex acts.[115] The sexual language here, however, is strictly metaphorical and refers to religious apostasy. Additionally, scholars often cite texts like Deut 23:18–19, Hos 4:13–14, and Isa 57:3–10 as referring to general sexual elements that existed in the confines of or in conjunction with cultic occasions.[116] While this may be the case, one cannot take these texts simply at face value as a testimony to general sex any more than as a testimony to cultic prostitution. The possibility remains that the descriptions represent only accusations and rhetorical indictments.

The second and most relevant problem with assuming widespread sexual practices loosely associated with the cult to be the background for Hos 2 is that the available evidence does not specifically connect the practice with any reference to בעל. Even if Israelite worshippers were engaging in excess and illicit sex acts at times of religious festivals, there is nothing to suggest that these actions were particularly associated with the god Baal or provide a background for Hosea's use of the word בעל. They may be only inappropriate activities that represent an illicit form of Yahweh worship. The Baal texts from Ugarit simply do not yield sufficient information about rituals and liturgies.[117]

Hägg (*The Novel in Antiquity* [Berkeley: University of California Press, 1983], 123), who notes that both in Hellenistic poetry and later Greek novels, "a religious festival regularly provides the background for 'love at first sight.'" Cf. A. F. Ide, *Yahweh's Wife: Sex in the Evolution of Monotheism* (Las Colinas, Tex.: Monument, 1991), 26–27, 31–34.

Along these same lines, Marglin offered an anthropological study of a group of devadāsis who, as noted above, appear to be involved in sex in connection with the cult and who were connected with the temple of Jagannātha in Puri, Orissa, India (F. Marglin, *Wives of the God-King: The Rituals of the Devadasis of Puri* [Oxford: Oxford University Press, 1985]). These women engaged in sexual relations that were ideally restricted to the king and the brahmin priests, but this ideal was not strictly enforced and these ritual specialists also commonly engaged in sex with members of the higher castes in Puri (ibid., 90). The sexual relations of the devadāsis were, however, only a private affair and did not take place at public festivals or life-cycle ceremonies (ibid., 89–90).

[115] Fisher, "Cultic Prostitution," 230. Cf. G. Mendenhall, *The Tenth Generation: The Origins of the Biblical Tradition* (Baltimore: The Johns Hopkins University Press, 1974), 105–21.

[116] On Isa 57, see S. Ackerman, *Under Every Green Tree: Popular Religion in Sixth-Century Judah* (HSM 46; Atlanta: Scholars Press, 1992), which argues that this text describes a type of Judahite folk religion.

[117] For example, Day notes that there are no hints toward ritual sex in the Ugaritic texts and such conclusions rely on biblical evidence, disputed terminology, and allusions in classical texts ("Canaan, Religion of," 835). See also J. Day, "Baal (Deity)," *ABD* 1:545–49 and M. Smith,

Only two or three passages in the Ugaritic literature depict sexual activity by Baal (KTU 1.96; KTU 1.10; KTU 1.11). These texts involve sexual intercourse between Anat and Baal, once represented by a heifer and a cow. Nonetheless, as Keefe rightly observes, this textual evidence is too limited to suggest that sexual activity was key to Baal's mythology or played a major role in any ritual devoted to Baal.[118] In the final analysis, texts like Deut 23, Hos 4, and Isa 57 may indeed testify to sexual excess that accompanied times of congregation like cultic festivals, but these do not provide evidence of a widespread practice of ritual sex in Hosea's day, particularly a practice devoted to the god Baal.

2.2 Baal Worship in Ancient Israel

A second major path that scholars have taken in attempting to understand the term בעל in Hos 2 operates from the starting point of the refutations discussed above. Since many interpreters now recognize the lack of evidence for a Baal fertility/sex cult, they no longer suggest the existence of widespread cultic sexual practices like sacred prostitution and ritual defloration. Nonetheless, many scholars still find evidence for the existence of widespread worship of the Canaanite god Baal in Hosea's day, even if this worship did not include sexual rites. According to this view, the background of the term בעל in Hos 2 is a historical situation in which Israelites were either forsaking Yahweh to worship Baal[119] or blending Baal worship with the Yahweh cult.[120] Thus, Hosea's references to sexual acts like fornication constitute only metaphorical descriptions of the Israelites' religious apostasy.[121] As further evidence for this phenomenon, scholars often refer to archaeological and epigraphic evidence like figurines of nude females, seal illustrations, and Baalistic personal names on ostraca.[122]

Several factors suggest, however, that this interpretation still does not deal adequately with the biblical and extrabiblical evidence and that even nonsexual

---

"Interpreting the Baal Cycle," *UF* 18 (1986): 313–39. Smith, in particular, rejects a reading of the Baal cycle that gives a ritualistic interpretation and argues that the cycle's theme is Baal's kingship ("Interpreting the Baal Cycle," 316–18; cf. S. Parker, ed., *Ugaritic Narrative Poetry* [SBL Writings from the Ancient World 9; Atlanta: Scholars Press, 1997], 81–86).

[118] Keefe, *Woman's Body*, 51, f.n. 14.

[119] For example, Garrett, *Hosea, Joel*, 39.

[120] For example, see Clements, "Understanding," 412, which refers to this situation as a subtle "Baalizing" of the Yahwistic cult.

[121] See Stuart, *Hosea-Jonah*, 10. This belief in the prominence of nonsexualized Baal worship in Hosea's day is so widespread that Garrett can assert, "It is a *truism* to say that Hosea presents the *apostasy* of Israel under the metaphor of an unfaithful wife" (*Hosea, Joel*, 39; emphases added). For further discussion, see J. Tigay, "Israelite Religion: The Onomastic and Epigraphic Evidence," in *Ancient Israelite Religion* (eds. P. Miller, P. Hanson, and S. McBride; Philadelphia: Fortress, 1987), 157.

[122] See discussion below.

Baal worship was not widespread in eighth-century Israel: 1) outside of Hosea, no other biblical text shows widespread Baal worship in eighth-century Israel, 2) reconsiderations of the biblical evidence for the history of Israelite religion, particularly that of Kaufmann, demonstrate no evidence for such a Baal cult, and 3) onomastic and epigraphic evidence from the eighth and seventh centuries does not indicate that the god Baal played a significant role in the lives of Israelites. When brought to bear specifically on the oracle under consideration here, these factors raise the possibility that the notion of a background Baal cult of any kind should be dropped as the interpretative framework for Hos 2.

2.2.1 *Baal Worship Outside of Hosea.* When analyzing the question of a prominent Baal cult in eighth-century Israel, the first fact that draws the reader's attention is the lack of any mention of such worship in texts that are contemporary with Hosea.[123] Outside of Hosea, no other biblical text suggests widespread Baal worship in this period. Amos, Micah, and Isa 1–39, three prophetic texts generally considered, at least in part, to be contemporary with Hosea, do not place any emphasis upon a Baal cult. Milgrom offers a recent survey of the biblical evidence and notes that texts which date to the eighth century only accuse Israel of religious apostasy in the form of idolatry fifteen times in comparison with 166 accusations in seventh-century Judean material. Even these fifteen, however, are only references to idolatry broadly defined and not Baal worship in particular.[124] Additionally, some of these texts cited by Milgrom were discussed above and found to be wholly or partially political in meaning.

Clements notes, with regard to Amos, that some interpreters try to connect the references to fathers and sons going to the same girl in Amos 2:7 with cultic sexual acts dedicated to Baal.[125] There is, however, no explicit mention of Baal or rituals in this text. Beyond this verse, interpreters typically view only one passage in the book (5:26) as dealing with idolatry. Even so, this text does not mention Baal, and scholars generally understand it as a reference to astral worship or attempt to excise it as a later addition.[126] Neither Isa 1–39 nor the

---

[123] For scholars who have noticed this fact and used it to question the existence of a widespread Baal cult, see Clements, "Understanding," 412; Kaufmann, *Religion*, 143; Keefe, "Female Body," 78.

[124] See Lev 19:4; 26:1; Amos 5:26; Hos 5:3b–4; 6:10; Isa 2:8, 18, 20; 10:11; 17:8; 27:9; 30:22; 31:7; Mic 1:7; 5:12–13a. The reader should especially note Milgrom's caveat that in order to arrive at this total, he uses a very broad definition of idolatry that includes "the worship of all images, not just of other gods, but also of YHWH" (J. Milgrom, "The Nature and Extent of Idolatry in Eighth–Seventh Century Judah," *HUCA* 69 [1998]: 1, f.n. 1).

[125] Clements, "Understanding," 412.

[126] For examples of those who use the astral interpretation, see S. Paul, *Amos* (Hermeneia; Minneapolis: Fortress, 1991), 194–95 and Kaufmann, *Religion*, 143. For an example of those who see the text as a later addition, see W. H. Schmidt, "Die deuteronomistische Redaktion des Amosbuches," *ZAW* 77 (1965): 190. On the other hand, J. H. Hayes (*Amos: The Eighth-Century Prophet: His Times and His Preaching* [Nashville: Abingdon, 1988], 176–79) argues that 5:26 has

book of Micah names a single foreign deity as an object of popular worship. Additionally, as Keefe observes, even in the stories of Kings, the only clear references to widespread Baal worship occur in texts dealing with the Omride dynasty.[127]

This lack of any concern over the practice of Baalism among relevant texts from Hosea's time must not be overlooked by those attempting to understand the rhetorical background and aim of Hos 2. If Hosea's central concern is the condemnation of Baal worship, it receives very little attention outside of Hos 2. The dearth of correlating evidence from contemporary biblical texts immediately calls into question the adequacy of even nonsexual Baal worship as an interpretative framework for the term בעל in Hos 2.

2.2.2 *The Biblical Picture of Israelite Religion.* Reconsiderations of the wider biblical picture of Israelite religion also raise significant doubts about the existence of widespread Baal worship, even of a nonsexual kind, in the eighth century. The work of Kaufmann represents a major challenge to older assumptions in this regard. Rather than assuming that monotheism within Israel was a late development and that preexilic Israel was characterized by rampant polytheism, an assumption based largely on decisions made by scholars like Wellhausen concerning the late date of certain literature within the Hebrew Bible,[128] Kaufmann concludes that preexilic Israel already had a monotheistic faith dominant throughout the entire nation.[129] As evidence in this regard, he observes that the exceptions to monotheism in the biblical texts describing preexilic times are presented as anomalies and primarily represent "corruptions

---

nothing to do with apostasy but may describe processional items that were traditional elements of the Yahwistic cult. Amos 8:14 contains very unclear references to the guilt of Samaria, the god of Dan, and the way of Beersheba that seem to refer to illegitimate worship but do not involve the god Baal in any way.

[127] Keefe, "Female Body," 78. Cf. Clements, who notes that biblical texts like Jehu's revolt in 2 Kgs 8–9, which react so vehemently to the idea of an established Baal cult, make it unlikely that the northern kingdom ever officially adopted Baalism ("Understanding," 412).

[128] For discussion, see Kaufmann, *Religion*, 1. One may perhaps argue that Kaufmann's conclusions are equally determined by his own scheme of dating for the biblical literature. As a part of his distinct approach, Kaufmann rejects the Wellhausian view that the priestly materials are exilic and the Torah was composed only after the exile. He views the Torah as preceding the prophets (ibid.). In brief, the history of interpretation of the development of monotheism in Israel runs as follows. In the time of Wellhausen, the dominant view was that monotheism developed through a gradual evolution that culminated only in the exilic period. Beginning with Albright in 1940, however, the scholarly consensus adopted the view that there was a Mosaic revolution in which monotheism was introduced into Canaan from the outside. From this starting point, scholars assumed that this pure Yahwism was slowly corrupted by syncretism, in spite of the efforts of reformers like the prophets, Josiah, and Hezekiah. Finally, the restoration of this original, monotheistic Yahwism was accomplished in the exilic period. See R. Gnuse, *No Other Gods: Emergent Monotheism in Israel* (JSOTSup 241; Sheffield: Sheffield Academic Press, 1997), 13, 66.

[129] Kaufmann, *Religion*, 134.

of the worship of YHWH" and not devotion to foreign deities.[130] For example, references to asherahs, high places, pillars, etc. in texts like 1 Kgs 14:22–24 do not explicitly refer to worship of other gods besides Yahweh and may simply be forms of Yahweh worship deemed illegitimate by the biblical writer. In many cases, even the term בעל functions as an epithet for Yahweh.[131] For instance, loyal Yahwistic characters set in the early period (e.g., Saul, David, and Jonathan) gave their sons names with baal elements: Eshbaal, Meribaal, and Beeliada.

Specifically concerning Baal worship in the monarchic period, the biblical texts that describe Israel's religious practices give sufficient evidence for widespread public practice of a Baal cult in only one brief period in Israelite history: the ninth-century reign of Ahab and Jezebel (868–854 B.C.E.).[132] While not precluding the possible existence of private practice of Baalism among the variegated populations of Israel and Judah, the textual evidence clearly indicates that this period was the first time the worship of Baal became officially established and publicly widespread.[133] For example, texts describing the reigns of Saul and David (e.g., 1 Sam 13; 15; 28) do not mention a struggle to remove Baalism from the land but do refer to the removal of mediums, diviners, etc., who may be seen as representatives of Yahweh worship. The widespread, public worship of Baal appears as part of the editorial framework of Judges and Samuel but none of the narratives provides specific information about such worship. Texts referring to the reign of Solomon, including those that mention the worship of Chemosh, Molech, Astarte, and Milcom, do not refer to Baal and present such worship as restricted to the royal house (cf. 1 Kgs 11).[134] Even the narratives relating the reigns of kings like Jeroboam I, Rehoboam, Abijam, and Baasha (1 Kgs 12–16) do not condemn them for worshipping Baal but for what seem implicitly to be corrupt forms of Yahweh worship: high places, pillars, and sacred poles (e.g., 1 Kgs 14:23). As Kaufmann observes, it is not until the narratives of Ahab and Jezebel (and the corresponding prophets Elijah and Elisha) that biblical texts indicate an established Baal cult complete with a temple (1 Kgs 16:32) and prophets (1 Kgs 18:19).[135]

---

[130] Ibid., 139.

[131] Ibid., 138.

[132] Ibid., 140.

[133] Milgrom recently credits Kaufmann with being one of the first to draw a sharp distinction between the official and popular cult (Milgrom, "Nature," 7). However, Milgrom notes that Kaufmann had to stop short of investigating the biblical references sufficiently and clearly identifying the popular religion because the onomastic and archaeological data were not available in the 1930s and 1940s.

[134] See Kaufmann, *Religion*, 134, 138–39.

[135] Similarly, the first direct reference to Baal worship in Judah appears in the stories of Joram son of Jehoshaphat, who was married to Ahab's daughter Athaliah (ibid., 140).

More importantly for the interpretation of Hos 2, Kaufmann also notes that the biblical evidence shows that such widespread Baal worship was limited to this ninth-century period and did not extend down into the time of the eighth-century prophets. Perhaps the best evidence of this reality is that 2 Kgs 8–10 depicts the official Baal cult as small and royally driven and suggests that Jehu exterminated it in its entirety (see 2 Kgs 10:28).[136] Following this act, no texts describing the eighth century in the books of Kings, Isaiah, Micah, or Amos mention the continued existence of official, widespread Baal worship during that period. Neither the described apostasy of Ahaz nor the reform of Hezekiah (1 Kgs 16:1–4; 18:3–9) gives any indication of an established public Baal cult. While private practice of Baalism may have still existed, state-sponsored idolatry is not attested by the time of the eighth-century prophets. As Milgrom suggests, these prophetic texts are not concerned with popular religion but only with the official cult, and in this realm there is no prominence of Baal worship.[137]

From this starting point, Kaufmann offers an interpretation of the book of Hosea in general and of Hos 1–3 in particular. In his view, chapters 1–3 of Hosea do refer to a deep concern with widespread Baal worship.[138] Since these chapters seem to speak of Baalism as a contemporary sin, they must reflect, he argues, a situation for which evidence suggests a prominent practice of Baal worship. In surveying Hos 4–14, Kaufmann stresses that evidence for Baal worship is found in only two places (9:10 and 13:1) and both places depict it as a sin of the past in comparison with the present sins of the calves of Samaria and other images (4:17; 8:5; 10:5; 13:2).[139] Since the biblical evidence indicates that Jehu destroyed Israel's Baal cult once and for all, the other eighth-century prophets do not mention Baal, and Hos 4–14 refers to Baal worship only as a past sin, Kaufmann concludes that Hos 1–3 must be a prophetic collection from the time before Jehu, which was later added to the materials of the eighth-century prophet Hosea.[140]

---

[136] So also B. T. Arnold, "A Pre-Deuteronomistic Bicolon in 1 Samuel 12:21?," *JBL* 123 (2004): 141.

[137] Milgrom, "Nature," 5. Cf. Kaufmann, *Religion*, 141, 369. Milgrom has recently taken up this issue. After surveying the lack of emphasis on idolatry in texts pertaining to eighth-century Israel and Judah, he suggests that the most appropriate explanation for this phenomenon is the answer in the book of Kings, which should be taken literally: "Jehu wiped out the official, royally sponsored, Baal cult from the land" (Milgrom, "Nature," 3). So also Arnold, "Pre-Deuteronomistic," 141.

[138] Kaufmann, *Religion*, 143.

[139] Ibid., 143, 369, 372, 376. In order to maintain that references to Baal worship occur in Hos 4–14 only in 9:10 and 13:1, Kaufmann interprets the reference to the Baals in 11:2 by appealing to similar usage in Jeremiah and arguing that the verse is "no more than a derogatory reference to idol-worship in general, not to actual Baal worship" (ibid., 372). However, this argument seems unnecessary since the context of this verse is also clearly one of historical recital (see discussion below).

[140] Ibid., 369. He sees Hos 1–3 as a prophetic narrative dating to the time of Jehoram (851–840 B.C.E.) that was later joined to oracles of the eighth-century prophet Hosea (ibid., 370, f.n. 5). He

Kaufmann's treatment of the biblical evidence is part of a long-standing debate over the development and nature of monotheism in ancient Israel, a debate that includes many opposing views. The view to which Kaufmann's analysis is most opposed is that of Wellhausen. He maintained that each of the three main documents that make up the Pentateuch (JE, D, RQ) corresponds to a certain phase in the development of Israelite religion toward Mosaic, priestly monotheism. This movement reached completion in the priestly materials of the exilic and postexilic periods, which transformed Israelite religion into a monotheistic institution governed by priests.[141] Whereas Kaufmann assumes the relative reliability of Kings's evaluation of the different rulers and its claim that they (after Ahab) did not endorse a foreign cult, Wellhausen considered all such evaluations to be useless for reconstructing the development of Israelite religion because they are all products of a later revision. In Wellhausen's view, this revision evaluated each ruler on the basis of the "pure religion" that developed initially in the deuteronomic period (i.e., after Josiah) and fully in the exile.[142] The kings were blamed only for "perverted worship of Jehovah," as opposed to the worship of other deities, not because they were monotheistic but because the revisionist(s) evaluated them anachronistically in terms of pure Mosaic religion.[143]

Another alternative reading of the biblical texts suggests that Yahweh and Baal may have been identified completely in Hosea's day and the term בעל functioned simply as an epithet for Yahweh. As evidence in this regard, Day notes the association of Yahweh with a storm theophany in Deborah's song (Judg 5:4), personal names with a Baal element (e.g., Bealiah in 1 Chron 12:6[MT]), and Yahweh's rejection of the term בעל in Hos 2:18.[144] Similarly,

---

dates Hos 4–14 after 732 but before 725 since, in his view, these chapters do not yet view Assyria as the destroyer of Israel (ibid., 372). Following Kaufmann, see also Ginsberg, "Hosea," 1011–17 and Milgrom, "Nature," 1. Several other scholars, however, while not accepting the idea that Hos 1–3 is from a ninth-century prophet, acknowledge the weight of the above evidence for questioning the notion of a widespread Baal cult that forms the primary issue for Hosea's oracles. See Buss, *Prophetic Word*, 82–83; cf. Davies, *Hosea* (OTG), 39; Clements, "Understanding," 412.

[141] J. Wellhausen, *Prolegomena to the History of Israel* (Scholars Press Reprints and Translations; Reprint of the 1885 edition; Atlanta: Scholars Press, 1994), xii–xiv.

[142] Ibid., 277.

[143] Wellhausen sees this revision as deuteronomistic rather than priestly. See ibid., 277–80. For a similar view of the material in Kings, see H. Niehr, "The Rise of YHWH in Judahite and Israelite Religion: Methodological and Religio-Historical Aspects," in *The Triumph of Elohim: From Yahwisms to Judaisms* (ed., D. Edelman; Grand Rapids: Eerdmans, 1996), 45–72. Niehr argues that the "censorship" of biblical texts in the second temple period means that they are only secondary sources for the religion of Israel (ibid., 51).

[144] J. Day, "Yahweh and the Gods and Goddesses of Canaan," in *Ein Gott allein? JHWH-Verehrung und biblischer Monotheismus im Kontext der Israelitischen und altorientalischen Religionsgeschichte* (eds. W. Dietrich and M. Klopfenstein; OBO 139; Göttingen: Vandenhoeck & Ruprecht, 1994), 185–87.

Keel and Uehlinger take the elements *yw-* and *bʿl* in theophoric names as referring to the same deity, namely Yahweh, and as indicating that Yahweh was worshipped "as Baal" in Iron Age IIB Israel.[145] According to this view, Hosea's primary position was that he did not view this identification as acceptable. For example, Jeremias argues that Hosea's polemic against Baal is an inner-Israelite controversy that addresses the fact that, in the time before Hosea (i.e., the wilderness period and the time of Ahab), the Israelites had confused/identified Yahweh with Baal.[146] Hosea's words attempt to set out a sharp contrast/antithesis between Yahweh and Baal, and he refuses to see the two deities in the popular way that equates them.[147]

Given Yahweh's statement in Hos 2:18, which expresses his rejection of the term בעל, this identification interpretation seems to have some force. There are, however, several factors that argue against this understanding of the situation in Hosea's day. First, by and large, the Hebrew Bible's depictions of Yahweh do not seem to reflect a complete identification with Baal in this way. For example, as Day notes, Baal is depicted as a dying and rising god while Yahweh is said neither to sleep nor slumber. Additionally, Baal is not the supreme deity in the Ugaritic pantheon. These discrepancies lead Day to conclude that the most the Hebrew Bible does is appropriate some of Baal's attributes for Yahweh (cf. Ps 29; 104:6–9); it does not portray Yahweh and Baal as the same deity called by two names.[148] While the Hebrew term בעל, "lord," may be used as a title for Yahweh, this practice does not indicate a blending of two distinct deities.

As the following discussion will show, Kaufmann's analysis of the *biblical* evidence, which indicates that there was not a widespread Baal cult, even one devoid of sexual elements, in Hosea's time, finds support in epigraphic and onomastic sources. Nonetheless, this does not mean that one must accept Kaufmann's redactional conclusion of an early date for Hos 1–3, a conclusion that is highly speculative and without adequate grounds when the book of Hosea

---

[145] O. Keel and C. Uehlinger, *Gods, Goddesses, and Images of God in Ancient Israel* (trans., T. Trapp; Minneapolis: Fortress, 1998), 205. For an article that argues there was a gradual development in which Yahweh was identified with the Phoenician high god Baal Šamem, especially in the time of Ahab, see H. Niehr, "JHWH in der Rolle des Baalšamem," in *Ein Gott allein? JHWH-Verehrung und biblischer Monotheismus im Kontext der Israelitischen und altorientalischen Religionsgeschichte* (eds. W. Dietrich and M. Klopfenstein; OBO 139; Göttingen: Vandenhoeck & Ruprecht, 1994), 307–26.

[146] See J. Jeremias, "Der Begriff 'Baal' im Hoseabuch und seine Wirkungsgeschichte," in *Ein Gott allein? JHWH-Verehrung und biblischer Monotheismus im Kontext der Israelitischen und altorientalischen Religionsgeschichte* (eds. W. Dietrich and M. Klopfenstein; OBO 139; Göttingen: Vandenhoeck & Ruprecht, 1994), 441–62. This is how Jeremias understands the references to Baal in Hos 9:10 and 13:1 (ibid., 443). For an effort to relate this view to the discourse of Hos 2, see Yee, *Poor Banished Children*, 86.

[147] Jeremias, "Der Begriff," 444.

[148] Day, "Gods and Goddesses," 187.

is analyzed as a whole.[149] Nor does this conclusion require the claim that Israel was monotheistic (i.e., believed in the existence of only one god) in Hosea's day. Although Kaufmann seems to hold this view, his analysis is significant in so far as it shows that there was no official or widespread worship of the god Baal in the biblical picture of the eighth century. Evidence that was not available to Kaufmann in the 1930s and 1940s, including the use of the term בעל and its cognates in ancient Near Eastern political treaties, provides a way to supplement this purely biblical approach and yet avoid resorting to radical redactional conclusions. Part of this evidence includes other epigraphic and onomastic sources that have come available since the 1930s.

2.2.3 *Onomastic and Epigraphic Evidence.* The main collection of onomastic and epigraphic evidence that bears directly on the issue of Baalism in the preexilic period comes from the city of Samaria in the middle of the eighth century.[150] These Samarian ostraca are primarily tax and shipping records that probably represent the commerce of the male upper class.[151] Although some of the readings are poorly preserved, the records contain theophoric personal names that have been used since their discovery to shed light on the nature of Israelite religion and the identity of the prominent deities.

The theophoric personal names that appear on the Samarian ostraca contain the names of several deities, including Baal. There are seventeen to twenty-one Yahweh names, three to five *ʾēl* names, and five *baʿal* names.[152] Accordingly, the ostraca seem, on the surface, to confirm the notion that polytheism was widespread in ancient Israel and to remove any doubt that Baalism remained common in the northern kingdom down through the eighth century. The mention of at least five individuals whose names contain the element *baʿal* seems to constitute a corrective to the paucity of biblical references emphasized by Kaufmann.

---

[149] For example, in surveying the language, style, and terminology of the whole book in order to assess its unity and originality, Wolff concludes that, while not every word belongs to the *verba ipsissima* of Hosea and some of his original formulations have been joined with language of later editors, "[f]or the most part, however, Hosea's own speech is unmistakable" (*Hosea*, xxiii). As evidence in this regard, Wolff observes that the genres of divine speech and prophetic judgment speech are consistent throughout the book. Additionally, the language is consistently a prose that commonly uses synonymous parallelism, and there is a characteristic rhythm, particularly with the combination of bicola and tricola, that unifies the book.

[150] For the original publication, see G. Reisner, et al., *Harvard Excavations at Samaria* (Harvard Semitic Series; Cambridge: Harvard University Press, 1924), 227–46. For the texts and other introductory discussions, see *ANET*, 321; W. F. Albright, *Archaeology and the Religion of Israel: The Ayer Lectures of the Colgate-Rochester Divinity School 1941* (Baltimore: The Johns Hopkins University Press, 1942), 160.

[151] The ostraca are generally understood to contain the names of court officials and owners of estates. See discussion in Mays, *Hosea*, 48; Whitt, "Divorce," 49; Wolff, *Hosea*, 49.

[152] Whitt, "Divorce," 49.

When the five Baal names on the Samarian ostraca are placed within the context of the entire collection of Israelite theophoric names that occur in extrabiblical texts, however, the Samarian ostraca may actually be seen as strengthening Kaufmann's arguments concerning the biblical literature and further demonstrating that there was no widespread Baal cult of any kind during Hosea's time. Tigay notes that by 1986, scholars had identified the names of more than 1,200 preexilic Israelites in Hebrew and foreign inscriptions that refer to Israel.[153] Accordingly, if there was any kind of widespread polytheism, Tigay suggests, one would expect to find a large number of Israelites named for the rival gods mentioned in various texts of the Hebrew Bible: Baal, Ashtoreth, Asherah, etc.[154] Surprisingly, nearly half of the attested names (557 out of 1,200) contain Yahweh as the theophoric element, and seventy-seven others contain *'ēl* or *'ēlî*, which Tigay takes to be most likely an epithet of Yahweh. By contrast, only thirty-five names seem plausibly to refer to other gods.[155]

More specifically, only six out of 1,200 names contain Baal as the theophoric element, and five of these occur on the eighth-century Samarian ostraca.[156] The other name that contains a Baal element, *tṣb'l*, appears in the seventh-century ostracon from Meṣad Hashavyahu.[157] Thus, the amount of Baal names on the Samarian ostraca constitutes a small minority in comparison with the Yahweh and El names on both those ostraca and in other texts.[158] The ratio

---

[153] See Tigay, "Israelite Religion," and Tigay, *No Other Gods*. The first article represents an earlier compilation of statistics based on a total of 738 Israelite names identified in extrabiblical texts by 1979. The latter work (*No Other Gods*) is a more recent study that updates the statistics based on a total of 1,200 names identified by 1986. For a similar work that draws similar conclusions, see Jeaneane Fowler, *Theophoric Personal Names in Ancient Hebrew: A Comparative Study* (JSOTSup 49; Sheffield: JSOT Press, 1988). For example, she concludes, "Hebrew religion was unique in that it was monotheistic, and no suggestion that it was otherwise can be gained from personal names ..." (ibid., 313).

[154] Tigay, *No Other Gods*, 9 and "Israelite Religion," 162. The reader should keep in mind one of the most significant features of Tigay's approach. In counting names that contain theophoric elements other than Yahweh, he does not count seventy-seven names that contain *'ēl* or *'ēlî* since it is not clear to what god this name refers and it may be simply an epithet for Yahweh ("Israelite Religion," 162; *No Other Gods*, 12). This interpretive decision is a deciding factor in the final outcome of Tigay's statistics (cf. Whitt, "Divorce," 49).

[155] Tigay, *No Other Gods*, 12.

[156] These names and their publications are as follows: *bb'l* (SO 2:4), *b'l* (SO 1:7), *b'lzmr* (SO 12:2–3), *b'lzkr* (SO 37:3), and *mrb'l* (SO 2:7) (see ibid., 65–66). Furthermore, this lack of prominence for Baal names in the eighth century is evidenced again by three more ostraca from Samaria that date to just before 722 B.C.E. and were discovered in 1931 through 1935. These additional finds contain no Baal names at all. See Keel and Uehlinger, *Gods*, 205.

[157] Tigay, *No Other Gods*, 14; cf. Tigay, "Israelite Religion," 163.

[158] In order to maintain this view, Tigay correctly rejects arguments for reconstructing three names on the ostraca as containing Baal elements: 1) *'lb'* (SO 1:6), which Lemaire tries to argue is an abbreviated form of *'lb'l* (A. Lemaire, *Inscriptions Hébraïques 1: Les Ostraca* [LAPO; Paris: Les Éditions du Cerf, 1977], 49), 2) *b'r* (SO 45:2), which Lemaire also takes as an abbreviated Baal name (ibid., 50), and 3) *yrb'[...]* (IR 112), which might be restored as *yrb'l* or *yrb'm*. See Tigay, *No*

of Baal names to clearly Yahwistic or non-Baal names on the Samarian ostraca is about five to eleven.[159] In the larger context, the six total Baal names represent a meager 1.01% of the entire onomastic evidence, while Yahweh names make up 94.1% of the whole.[160] In light of this larger context, eighth-century, extrabiblical evidence for the prominence of Baal names appears restricted to a few isolated occurrences from a particular region and a single period.[161] While the region around Samaria in the eighth century is precisely the ostensible location of the prophet Hosea, when these Baal names are viewed in the context of the dearth of references in the epigraphic corpus more broadly and the lack of other clear artifactual evidence for a Baal cult from the area around Samaria, they do not confirm the presence of widespread Baal worship even in the limited area of Samaria. Additionally, as noted above, several scholars suggest that *ba'al* may be an epithet for Yahweh during the eighth century, and thus the names on the Samarian ostraca may be references to Yahweh.[162]

When one turns to other epigraphic evidence that is not onomastic, the situation is the same. As Tigay notes, epigraphic evidence like salutations in letters, votive inscriptions, and prayers are "exclusively Yahwistic almost without exception."[163] For instance, collections of preexilic letters from Arad and Lachish, a genre in which polytheistic societies include a salutation naming several gods, attest only Yahwistic statements like "I bless you by Yahweh." Oaths in texts from Lachish, also a genre which often invokes several deities in other cultures, swear by Yahweh alone.[164] A possible exception here is represented by some wall inscriptions from Kuntillet ʿAjrud that mention a deity named Baal and date from the early eighth century. These texts, however, come

---

Other Gods, 75. For examples of scholars who argue for more than five Baal names on the Samarian ostraca, see Whitt, "Divorce," 49 and Wolff, *Hosea*, 49.

[159] See I. Kaufman, "Samaria (Ostraca)," *ABD* 5:925.

[160] Tigay, *No Other Gods*, 12–15. As an illuminating comparison, Tigay contrasts this situation with that of the unquestionably polytheistic society in OB Sippar. In the latter case, the chief god, Shamash, appears in only 20% of the names, while the god Sin appears in 15% and other deities appear in steadily decreasing percentages. Thus, the chief god does not overwhelm the others as Yahweh does in Israelite onomastic evidence ("Israelite Religion," 170).

[161] In line with this view, Tigay offers an explanation of the eight personal names in the Hebrew Bible that contain a Baal element. He emphasizes that seven of them come from the period of the judges and the united monarchy described in the books of Judges and Chronicles (*No Other Gods*, 8).

[162] See Buss, *Prophetic Word*, 83 and Stuart, *Hosea-Jonah*, 58. Tigay supports this view by citing Hos 2:18 ("you will call me 'my husband,' and you will no longer call me 'my בעלי'"; Tigay, "Israelite Religion," 163). If this view is correct, the Samarian ostraca do not even indicate the minor presence of popular devotion to a Baal cult.

[163] Tigay, "Israelite Religion," 171–72.

[164] Ibid., 172, 176.

from the area to the south and may not be Israelite, since the script is not Hebrew and may be Phoenician.[165]

The use of onomastic and epigraphical evidence in this way is open to some critiques. The corpus likely represents only the upper strata of society, and one could argue that widespread Baalism existed among the lower classes.[166] Even the Hebrew Bible, however, associates the prominent Baalism of the ninth century with the royal house. One could also maintain that other deities were worshipped without being reflected in people's names.[167] Since many names are only traditional and do not reflect worship practices, the preponderance of Yahwistic names only shows that Yahweh was the most important deity worshipped.[168] While this may be the case, the correspondence between the biblical evidence surveyed above and the onomastic sources available at least suggests that if such unseen Baalism existed, it did not rise to the level of prominence that Yahwism did in both the life and literature of eighth-century Israel. Perhaps the strongest critique of this use of the onomastic evidence is that of Gnuse. He emphasizes that in several states around Israel (e.g., Ebla and Ugarit) the names of popular deities do not frequently occur in personal names.[169] Thus, deities like Baal, El, and Asherah may be absent from the onomastic evidence but still widely worshipped.[170]

In light of these critiques, it must be maintained that the biblical, onomastic, and epigraphic sources should not be relied upon in isolation nor taken as evidence for strict monotheism in eighth-century Israel. A picture of the religious situation in Hosea's day emerges, however, not from any single collection of data but from the totality of the evidence viewed together. The evidence favors the conclusion that there was no officially established or

---

[165] So ibid., 177. See discussion below. R. Hess ("Yahweh and His Asherah? Religious Pluralism in the Old Testament World," in *One God, One Lord: Christianity in a World of Religious Pluralism* [eds., A. D. Clarke and B. W. Winter; Grand Rapids: Baker, 1993], 18) also notes that the Kuntillet 'Ajrud inscriptions may be graffiti and thus may not represent realities of the official state cult. For some of the extensive literature concerning the finds at this location, see W. G. Dever, "Asherah, Consort of Yahweh? New Evidence from Kuntillet 'Ajrud," *BASOR* 255 (1984): 21–37; A. Emerton, "New Light on Israelite Religion: The Implications of Inscriptions from Kuntillet 'Ajrud," *ZAW* 94 (1982): 2–20; Z. Meshel, "The Israelite Religious Centre of Kuntillet ʿAjrud, Sinai," in *Archaeology and Fertility Cult in the Ancient Mediterranean* (ed. A. Bonano; Amsterdam: B. R. Grüner, 1986), 237–40; Z. Meshel, *Kuntillet ʿAjrûd: A Religious Center from the Time of the Judaean Monarchy on the Border of Sinai* (Israel Museum Catalogue 175; Jerusalem: Israel Museum, 1978); cf. Davies, *Hosea* (OTG), 45.

[166] For examples, see J. Day, *Yahweh and the Gods and Goddesses of Canaan* (JSOTSup 265; Sheffield: Sheffield Academic Press, 2000), 227–28; Edelman, *Triumph*, 19; Whitt, "Divorce," 49; Wolff, *Hosea*, 49.

[167] See Tigay, "Israelite Religion," 171.

[168] Day, *Yahweh*, 227.

[169] Gnuse, *No Other Gods*, 107–8.

[170] Ibid.

widespread worship of other gods and, even more clearly, suggests that there was no such worship of the god Baal. All of the sources reveal a lack of evidence for the existence of a widespread, even nonsexual, Baal cult that would provide the background for the use of the term בעל in Hos 2.[171]

2.2.4 *Artifactual and Iconographic Evidence.* In addition to the more direct evidence from biblical, onomastic, and epigraphic sources, there is some artifactual and iconographic data that should be examined for evidence of active Baalism in Hosea's day.[172]

The possible evidence for and identification of Asherah as an active goddess and object of worship has received much attention and is often connected with a supposed Baal cult.[173] This evidence consists of both biblical and extrabiblical material. For example, the well-known references to "Yahweh and his Asherah" at Kuntillet ʿAjrud and Khirbet el-Qom seem to attest the worship of a goddess.[174] Although the meaning of this term in these texts remains debated, several biblical texts suggest the identification of Asherah as a goddess more clearly.[175] Second Kings 23:4 refers to vessels made for Asherah

---

[171] See also Keefe, *Woman's Body*, 118–22.

[172] These sets of data raise questions concerning the relationship between what may be termed "public/official" and "private/domestic" religion. The discussion of this topic is wide-ranging and cannot be easily summarized. It is not clear how to define or distinguish these two spheres. For some works involved in this discussion, see Day, *Gods*; Gnuse, *No Other Gods*; J. Holladay, "Religion in Israel and Judah under the Monarchy: An Explicitly Archaeological Approach," in *Ancient Israelite Religion: Essays in Honor of Frank Moore Cross* (eds., P. Miller, P. Hanson, and S. McBride; Philadelphia: Fortress, 1987), 249–99; Keel and Uehlinger, *Gods*; M. Smith, "Yahweh and Other Deities in Ancient Israel: Observations on Old Problems and Recent Trends," in *Ein Gott allein? JHWH-Verehrung und biblischer Monotheismus im Kontext der Israelitischen und altorientalischen Religionsgeschichte* (eds. W. Dietrich and M. Klopfenstein; OBO 139; Göttingen: Vandenhoeck & Ruprecht, 1994), 197–234.

[173] For a full treatment of the asherim cultic items and the goddess Asherah in Hebrew Bible texts, see S. M. Olyan, *Asherah and the Cult of Yahweh in Israel* (Atlanta: Scholars Press, 1988). For a recent extensive list of secondary literature on Asherah, see Yee, "Not My Wife," 352, f.n. 28.

[174] Evidence from Tel Miqne also includes a storejar inscription from Iron Age II that reads "to/for Asherata" (see Hess, "Yahweh and His Asherah," 28). For an article that contains transliterations and translations of all the relevant Asherah texts, see ibid. A ninth-century cult stand from Taanach also appears to have images that link Yahweh and Asherah. See J. Glen Taylor, "Was Yahweh Worshiped as the Sun?," *BAR* 20:4 (1994): 53–61.

[175] As an example of this scholarly debate concerning definition, Keel and Uehlinger (*Gods*, 232, 240) suggest that there is no evidence to conclude that asherah refers to an actual goddess but only a cult object that functioned as a medium for delivering the blessing of Yahweh. By contrast, Smith ("Yahweh and Other Deities," 206) puts more weight on the biblical references and concludes that the term refers to a goddess figure. Contrast also Dever, "Asherah," 21–37 and P. K. McCarter, "Aspects of the Religion of the Israelite Monarchy: Biblical and Epigraphic Data," in *Ancient Israelite Religion: Essays in Honor of Frank Moore Cross* (eds., P. Miller, P. Hanson, and S. McBride; Philadelphia: Fortress, 1987), 146–49. As Hess ("Yahweh and His Asherah," 23–24) notes, the major scholarly positions in the discussion are that the inscriptions refer to 1) the goddess

in Josiah's day, and 1 Kgs 18:19 mentions prophets of Asherah in the days of Ahab (cf. Judg 3:7; 1 Kgs 15:13 [= 2 Chron 15:16]; 2 Kgs 21:7).[176]

To the biblical and extrabiblical textual evidence, many scholars add the multitude of female figurines discovered at various sites in Israel and Judah.[177] For example, an ivory ointment spoon from Hazor stratum VI seems to depict such a goddess. Similarly, the famous ivory plaque from Samaria showing the motif of the "woman at the window" may be a portrayal of a goddess. Arguments along these lines often also point to multiple images of the "naked goddess" on items like bone amulets, as well as to *terra-cotta* female figurines found in various household dwellings.[178] The nature and meaning of these artifacts, however, are unclear. The images of the "naked goddess," which do appear widely in Syro-Phoenician ivories in Iron Age IIB, do not appear in any material from Israel and Judah. Even the *terra-cotta* female figurines with images of the "naked goddess" are rare in Iron Age IIB and do not begin to appear prominently until the end of the eighth century, perhaps due to Assyrian influence.[179] Moreover, these materials have no explicit connections with the worship of Baal.[180]

Drawing upon this collection of evidence, Day concludes that the Canaanite goddess Asherah, known from extrabiblical texts, was worshipped as a goddess in preexilic Israel. He suggests, however, that Asherah, who is depicted in extrabiblical texts as El's consort, was naturally appropriated for Yahweh when Yahweh came to be equated with El.[181] Thus, although the available data does suggest the active veneration of the goddess, she appears to have been worshipped as a consort of *Yahweh* and not Baal, El, or any other deity. While this evidence argues against the existence of monotheism in monarchic Israel, it does not disrupt the emerging picture that Israel's religion was predominantly *Yahwistic*. Asherah worship was a part of Yahwistic religion, albeit a part condemned by the biblical writers. Texts like those from Kuntillet ʿAjrud

---

Asherah, 2) a symbol of the goddess Asherah, 3) a symbol of Yahweh, or 4) a shrine or sanctuary. For detailed grammatical discussion, see R. Hess, "Asherah or Asherata?," *Or* 65 (1996): 209–19.

[176] Hess ("Asherah or Asherata?," 218) notes that seven passages are generally identified as containing a reference to a deity named Asherah: Judg 3:7; 1 Kgs 15:13; 18:19; 2 Kgs 21:7; 23:4, 7; 2 Chron 15:16.

[177] For discussion, see Keel and Uehlinger, *Gods*, 201–2.

[178] See ibid., 199–202.

[179] Ibid., 201–2.

[180] For further debate over the religious significance of the female figurines, see Holladay, "Religion in Israel," 278 and M. Tadmor, "Female Cult Figurines in Late Canaan and Early Israel: Archaeological Evidence," in *Studies in the Period of David and Solomon and Other Essays* (ed. T. Ishida; Winona Lake, Ind.: Eisenbrauns, 1982), 170–71.

[181] Day, "Yahweh," 184; Day, *Yahweh*, 42–43; 59–61.

("Yahweh and his Asherah") present no problem to the characteristic monolatry of this period because they are, in fact, Yahwistic.[182]

If the above conclusion is correct, it remains to explain those biblical texts in which Asherah is paired with Baal (e.g., Judg 6:25, 28, 30; 1 Kgs 18:19). In previous assessments, scholars have argued that such texts indicate the belief that Baal had formerly displaced El and appropriated Asherah as his own consort.[183] This displacement and appropriation, however, are not attested in any extrabiblical text. As Keel and Uehlinger point out, Baal and Asherah are never paired in inscriptions from the Iron Age, even though they are depicted as interacting sexually on iconography from the Middle Bronze Age IIB.[184] Thus, Day seems correct to conclude that the pairing of Asherah with Baal in some biblical texts is best attributed to "a polemical move" by the writers to "discredit" Asherah, a goddess who was worshipped as a consort of Yahweh in preexilic Israel.[185]

A second set of excavated items that has been connected with a supposed Baal cult portrays a "youthful four-winged god with no beard, most often shown striding, who wears a short loincloth."[186] Keel and Uehlinger point out that the characteristics of youthfulness and a pair of wings are associated with the god Baal during the Late Bronze Age and the doubling of the pairs of wings on Iron Age finds may serve to heighten the "celestial aspects" and omnipotence of the deity. In addition, the blossoms or trees that occur on these items suggest that the god is associated with vegetation. Two of the named owners of seals on which this representation occurs have names with the theophoric element *bꜥl* in them.[187] Items with this portrayal have been found widely in eighth-century Israel and Phoenicia but not in Judah.[188] Surely significant, however, is the fact that the best preserved example of this representation comes only from a domestic setting, namely, a bone carving recovered from a private home in the upper city at Hazor stratum VI (first half of eighth century).

A third collection of archaeological data that is often associated with worship of Baal includes various kinds of bull images from Iron Age Israel. For example, Keel and Uehlinger describe a recently discovered monumental stela from a cultic context at Bethsaida (et-Tell). This stela shows a cultic pole topped by a bull's head and comes from the eighth-century gate of the city. Keel and

---

[182] As McCarter concludes, the religion reflected at places like Kuntillet 'Ajrud, while opposed by prophets and reform movements, was still Yahwistic and involved only the disputed practices of localization (e.g., "Yahweh of Samaria") and a possible consort (McCarter, "Aspects," 138–39).

[183] See discussion in Day, *Yahweh*, 60–61.

[184] Keel and Uehlinger, *Gods*, 201; cf. 37.

[185] Day, *Yahweh*, 60–61.

[186] Keel and Uehlinger, *Gods*, 195.

[187] Ibid.

[188] This same picture of a figure appears on a scarab from Megiddo and on some "silhouette-inlay[s]" in the Samaria ivories. See ibid., 197.

Uehlinger relate the item to the worship of an Aramean moon god.[189] One should note, however, that the cultic area in the city gate most likely catered to travelers. Thus, Keel and Uehlinger are right to question whether this item attests Israelite or non-Israelite worship.[190] Other bull images from Israel in the Iron IIB period (ca. 925–720 B.C.E.) include a seal from Samaria that depicts a worshipper positioned horizontally above a bull.[191] None of the images, however, gives any indication of being connected with a deity other than Yahweh. As Keel and Uehlinger conclude, bull imagery like that of Jeroboam I in 1 Kgs 12 was likely originally connected with the Canaanite god El (not Baal) and appropriated for Yahweh.[192]

The final set of data taken to indicate the presence of Baal worship in the eighth century consists of two of the wall inscriptions from Kuntillet ʿAjrud noted above that offer a blessing in the names of El and Baal. Other fragments of wall inscriptions also contain the names of Yahweh and Baal.[193] These references appear to date to the first half of the eighth century, perhaps to the time of Jeroboam II. More significantly, the attestations of Baal here cannot be easily dismissed as private religion because the wall paintings demonstrate that this site was a "royal/state outpost on a trade route that was under government control."[194] Thus, these texts do seem to represent at least the recognition, if not the veneration, of Baal in an official context. As noted above, however, unlike the storage jars, the wall inscriptions do not seem to be in Hebrew and may be in Phoenician script, and hence it remains unclear whether they are Israelite or Phoenician.[195] Additionally, the inscriptions' character as graffiti strengthens the likelihood that they may not reflect the official state religion.

Overall, then, the sum of the evidence surveyed may be construed to suggest that there was not a prominent, even nonsexual, Baal cult in eighth-century Israel. Even the data that seems to suggest most directly the existence of Baal worship is limited in attestation and often connected with the domestic/private sphere. While the evidence does not indicate the existence of monotheism in eighth-century Israel (contra Kaufmann), it does suggest that Israel's official/state-sponsored religion, the cult with which prophets like Hosea would have presumably been concerned, was not syncretistic but thoroughly Yahwistic.[196] The combination of this negative assessment with the

---

[189] Ibid., ix.

[190] Ibid., 3.

[191] Ibid., 208.

[192] Ibid., 191–94. But see Smith ("Yahweh and Other Deities," 207–8), who argues that the cult of El continued at least until the Iron I period.

[193] See Keel and Uehlinger, *Gods*, 244–45.

[194] Ibid., 245–47.

[195] See ibid., 245 and Tigay, "Israelite Religion," 177.

[196] As Smith concludes, the evidence indicates that the emergence of a centralized, state cult elevated Yahweh to the status of monolatry, a status that later developed into monotheism by definition in the

meanings of the other metaphors in Hos 2 developed thus far questions the notion that Baalistic religion provides the background for the use of the term בעל in Hosea's oracle.

2.3 The Term בעל in the Rhetoric of Hosea 2: A New Alternative

If the above assessments hold, the question emerges anew as to how the reader should understand Hosea's use of בעל if it does not refer to the Canaanite god Baal. A few scholars offer suggestions that hint at a way forward, but they do not pursue the matter far enough or along the most fruitful path. For example, Fisher suggests that much of the confusion about alleged practices like cultic prostitution stems from a failure to consider adequately the metaphorical nature of the terms in Hosea's oracle.[197] Törnkvist, after rejecting the idea of a Baal sex cult in the eighth century, suggests that the primary benefit of dropping this interpretative framework is that one can more clearly observe the "metaphorical character" of the events depicted in Hos 2.[198] Light specifically asserts that the reader of Hos 2 should take בעל seriously as a metaphorical term.[199]

Taking a cue from these approaches that emphasize the metaphorical nature of the word and given the lack of evidence to suggest that Hosea's main concern was a widespread Baal cult, one must examine the term בעל in order to determine the biblical and extrabiblical traditions of usage that may shed light on how the word functions within Hosea's specific rhetorical address. As this examination aims to show, while not strictly a metaphor, בעל is often a general term that can be used in a metaphorical way. This term, as with the metaphorical term "lovers," comes from the language associated with ancient Near Eastern political treaties and fits very well with the overall rhetorical horizon that has been emerging from the study of the text's primary metaphors.

2.3.1 *Biblical Uses of* בעל *Outside of Hosea.* Within the Hebrew Bible, the most well-known and attested use of בעל refers to the personal name of the Canaanite god Baal.[200] This usage of בעל is prominent in the historical books (Judges-2 Kings) and occurs thirty-two times in the books of 1 and 2 Kings alone. The largest concentration of this use of the term in 1 and 2 Kings (twenty-nine out of thirty-two occurrences) appears in the stories describing the ninth-century reign of Ahab and Jezebel and the revolt of Jehu. This religious

---

exile (M. Smith, *The Early History of God* [New York: Harper & Row, 1990], 148). For the use of this evidence to arrive at the opposite conclusion ("official cultic pluralism"), especially for the background of Hosea, see Yee, *Poor Banished Children*, 96.

[197] Fisher, "Cultic Prostitution," 236.

[198] Törnkvist, *Use and Abuse*, 95.

[199] Light, "Theory-Constitutive Metaphor," 67.

[200] As with the use of the term in Hos 2, in this usage בעל is attested in both the singular and plural forms and always appears with the definite article.

use of בעל occurs rarely in the prophetic books and not at all in Isaiah, Ezekiel, Amos, or Micah.

A similar use of the term that is also frequent in the Hebrew Bible connects בעל with another word to denote the title of a foreign deity. Examples include the following: 1) "Baal Berith" in Judg 8:33 and 9:4, 2) "Baal-peor" in Num 25:3, 5; Deut 4:3; and Ps 106:28, and 3) "Baal Zebub" in 2 Kgs 1:2, 3, 6, 16. A third use of בעל that appears in texts outside Hosea includes the term as a place name or part of a place name for a city, town, hill, etc. This usage occurs more than thirty times in the Hebrew Bible. Some examples include "Baal Gad" (Josh 11:17; 12:7; 13:5), "Baal Hermon" (Judg 3:3; 1 Chron 5:23), "Baal Zephon" (Exod 14:2, 9; Num 33:7), and "Baalah" (Josh 15:9, 10, 11, 29; 1 Chron 13:6). One also finds the term בעל in the names of persons in the Hebrew Bible including "Baal" (1 Chron 5:5; 8:30; 9:36), "Baal Hanan" (king of Edom in Gen 36:38, 39; 1 Chron 1:49, 50), and "Baalis" (king of Ammon in Jer 40:14).

Both verbal and nominal forms of בעל also often function in a general way to mean the "act of marriage" or "husband, suitor." The verbal forms of בעל occur with this meaning twelve times and only in qal verbal and participle forms and niphal imperfect forms. For example, Deut 21:13 stipulates, "Then afterward you will go into her and you will marry her (ובעלתה) and she will be a wife to you" (cf. Isa 62:5). Exodus 21:3 uses a nominal form and commands, "If he was the husband (בעל) of a wife, his wife will go out with him." Deuteronomy 24:4 also orders, "[H]er former husband (בעלה) who sent her away cannot take her again to be his wife...."[201]

Significantly for Hos 2, in spite of the prominence of the above uses, the Hebrew Bible also contains several other important ways of using the term בעל. Moving beyond religious and familial realms, one finds a very widespread tradition of employing בעל to refer to an owner or master of something or someone and to a chief or expert practitioner of some trade. The biblical writings frequently use בעל to denote the owner, possessor, or master of an animal, slave, object, and even a quality. The word appears this way twenty-seven times in the Hebrew Bible with the highest concentration in the Covenant Code of Exod 21–22. For example, Exod 21:28 notes, "[B]ut the owner (ובעל) of the ox is innocent," and Exod 22:11 stipulates, "And its owner (בעליו) will take it and he will not pay."[202] The use of the word to refer to a chief practitioner or expert of something is attested fourteen times. Three examples illustrate this usage: 1) "And the masters of arrows (בעלי חצים, i.e., archers) harass him and shoot and lie in ambush for him" (Gen 49:23), 2) "Every master of the lending of his hand (בעל משה ידו, i.e., creditor) who lends will release

---

[201] For other uses of בעל as husband see Gen 20:3; Exod 21:22; Lev 21:4; Deut 22:22; Esth 1:17, 20; Prov 12:4; 31:11, 23, 28; Joel 1:8.

[202] See also Exod 21:29, 34, 36; 22:8, 12, 14, 15; Judg 19:22–23; 2 Kgs 1:8; Job 31:39; Prov 1:17, 19; 3:27; 16:22; 17:8; Eccl 5:11, 13; 7:12; 8:8; Isa 1:3; 41:15; Dan 8:6, 20.

it …" (Deut 15:2), and 3) "And behold the chariots and the masters of horses (ובעלי הפרשים, i.e., horsemen) followed him closely" (2 Sam 1:6).[203]

There are also several uses of בעל in the Hebrew Bible that seem to invest the word with an explicitly political meaning. This usage appears in verbal forms meaning "to rule over" in the sense of a political suzerain and nominal forms designating political lords and chiefs or treaty partners and allies. Verbal forms of בעל carry this overtly political meaning on three occasions. Significantly, two of these three appear in prophetic texts. The text that is most clearly political, however, is 1 Chron 4:22: "and Jokim and the men of Chozeba and Joash and Saraph who ruled (בעלו) over Moab."

The second such usage appears in Isa 26:13 and may initially seem to be religious in meaning: "O Yahweh our god, other lords/masters (אדנים) have ruled (בעלונו) over us beside you…." However, several factors indicate that this verse carries a political meaning. First, the prophet uses the more general term אדנים, which can refer to political masters, rather than the explicitly religious term אלהים.[204] Second, the overall context of Isa 26 focuses on national and political actions like the destruction of the "lofty city" (קריה נשגבה), which may denote not an entire city but a fortified enclosure or military citadel within a city.[205] Third, the prophet goes on in verses 14–15 to mention the destruction of the masters who had ruled over the people and the expansion of Judean territory. These contextual clues signal that the primary concern of the entire unit is with social, political, and military matters and the ways they relate to the favor of Yahweh upon his people.

The third verbal form of בעל that carries a political meaning is very similar to the construction of Hos 2:18. Jeremiah 3:14 records the words of Yahweh: "Return O turning children, declares Yahweh, for I am lord/master (בעלתי) over you…." The context of this verse implies the meaning of one who rules over the people in the fashion of a suzerain. The verse occurs within a unit dedicated to the promise of bringing exiles back to Zion and rescuing them from the hand of those who hold them captive. As Craigie, Kelley, and Drinkard note, the expression here correlates nicely with the larger context in which verses 14b–15 emphasize the political theme of good government and look to the restoration of such a government in Zion.[206] Yahweh asserts his own position as suzerain over the people.

---

[203] See also Gen 37:19; Exod 24:14; 1 Sam 28:7; 1 Kgs 17:17; Ezra 4:8, 9, 17; Eccl 10:11, 20; 12:11; Nah 3:4.

[204] See O. Eissfedlt, "אדון," *TDOT* 1:59–72.

[205] For discussion, see J. H. Hayes and S. Irvine, *Isaiah, the Eighth-Century Prophet: His Times and His Preaching* (Nashville: Abingdon, 1987), 296–97.

[206] P. Craigie, P. Kelley, J. Drinkard, *Jeremiah 1–25* (WBC 26; Dallas: Word Books, 1991), 60. The Tanakh suggests reading בחלתי on the basis of a similar reconstruction in Jer 31:32. However, there does not appear to be any support or need for this reading. Jeremiah 31:32 contains the same

Three nominal forms of בעל also occur with an unambiguously political meaning in the sense of allies, treaty-partners, and overlords. Genesis 14:13 reads, "Then one who had escaped came and told Abram the Hebrew, who was living by the oaks of Mamre, the Amorite, brother of Eschol and Aner; these were treaty-partners (בעלי ברית; lit. "lords of a treaty;" NRSV: "allies") with Abram." Similarly, Neh 6:18 describes the political associates of Tobiah: "For many in Judah were allies/sworn to him (בעלי שבועה, lit. "lords of an oath")...." Finally, Jer 37:13 uses the term to refer to a political and military superior: "And it was, as he was in the gate of Benjamin, a captain of the guard (בעל פקדת, lit. "master of oversight") was there...." In these cases, בעל explicitly functions as a political term that denotes other parties who are compatriots or confederates. These verbal and nominal forms illustrate that בעל could function in a more general way and refer to persons bound in some manner by political relationships. Most significantly for considering Hos 2, this political meaning is primarily indicated by the context within which the term appears.

One may object, however, that the situation is not so straightforward because all of the nominal examples adduced above place בעל in construct with another word in order to achieve a political meaning. In the face of such an objection, one should observe the large number of Hebrew Bible texts that use the term in isolation to denote the political lords/chiefs/leaders of a given city or country. There are at least twenty-two occurrences of בעל that fit this description, with the largest concentration (fifteen out of twenty-two) located in the warfare stories of the book of Judges. All but one of the fifteen occurrences in Judges appear in the story of Abimelech in chapter 9. For example, Judg 9:2 has Abimelech ask, "Please speak in the ears of all the lords/rulers (בעלי) of Shechem: 'What is better for you....'" This same story also contains a description that uses the term in this way twice: "And God sent an evil spirit between Abimelech and the lords/rulers (בעלי) of Shechem. And the lords/rulers (בעלי) of Shechem dealt treacherously with Abimelech" (9:23).[207]

Outside of Judges, the Hebrew Bible attests this political usage of the individual term בעל in various contexts. For example, Num 21:28 states, "For a fire has gone out of Heshbon ... it has consumed Ar of Moab, the lords/rulers (בעלי) of the high places of Arnon." At first blush, this text may seem religious in nature because it mentions "high places." The surrounding verses, however, indicate that the context is a war between the king of the Amorites and the king of the Moabites (cf. 21:21–26). Joshua 24:11 recounts how "the lords/rulers (בעלי) of Jericho" fought against the Israelites, and Isa 16:8 displays this usage

---

verbal form בעלתי, but the context there is clearly religious and concerned with the covenant between Yahweh and the people.

[207] For other texts in Judges see 9:6, 7, 18, 20, 24, 25, 26, 39, 46, 47.

of the term by stating, "For the fields of Heshbon languish, the vines of Sibmah whose cluster made drunk the lords/rulers (בעל) of the nations...."

These examples clearly attest a usage of the term בעל in isolation that carries the meaning of political partners, lords, or rulers. One could perhaps propose that in these instances the word refers simply to the "citizens/people" of a town or city and not particularly to political leaders. Some texts do seem to use בעל in this general way. For example, Judg 9:51 appears to use the term to refer to both the men and women of the city (i.e., the general citizenry). The contexts of the majority of these texts, however, clearly indicate that the word designates those charged with controlling the political affairs of the city.

2.3.2 בעל *and Its Cognates in Ancient Near Eastern Political Treaties and Loyalty Oaths.* The political usage of the word בעל within the Hebrew Bible is not as commonly attested as the religious and familial uses. Extrabiblical occurrences of the word and its cognates, however, demonstrate that there was a widespread and well-established tradition of political usage that deepens the significance of the biblical uses.

Several ancient Near Eastern political treaties and loyalty oaths use the Akkadian term *bēl* (EN) and its cognates to describe various treaty partners and political suzerains. This tradition of use appears in a variety of texts that primarily come from the reigns of the Assyrian kings Sennacherib, Esarhaddon, and Ashurbanipal. An Aramaic treaty (and perhaps an Assyrian copy of the same) that dates to the middle of the eighth century, however, also attests this usage within the general time frame of Hosea's preaching. Taken together, these extrabiblical texts demonstrate a tradition of meaning for the Hebrew term בעל that goes hand in hand with the biblical evidence noted above and strengthens the biblical term's relationship to the language of international politics.

The annalistic account of Sennacherib's third campaign (701 B.C.E.) is the earliest relevant Assyrian text. This text exists in three versions, and each contains a description of the actions of Hezekiah of Judah and his associates that led to the Assyrian campaign.[208] All three versions have the same reading concerning the people of Ekron's act of turning over their king, Padi, to Hezekiah in Jerusalem: "The officials, nobles, and people of Ekron, who had thrown Padi, their king, bound by treaty/oath (*bēl adê*, lit. "lord of oath/treaty")

---

[208] The three versions of this text are as follows: 1) Taylor Prism, first published by Rawlinson and Norris in 1861 (see F. Delitzsch, *Assyrische Lesestücke* [Leipzig: J. C. Hinrichs, 1912], 62–76), 2) Chicago Prism, published in D. Luckenbill, *The Annals of Sennacherib* (OIP 2; Chicago: University of Chicago Press, 1924), 31, and 3) Jerusalem Prism, published in P. Ling-Israel, "The Sennacherib Prism in the Israel Museum- Jerusalem," in *Bar-Ilan: Studies in Assyriology Dedicated to Pinḥas Artzi* (eds. J. Klein and A. Skaist; Ramat-Gan: Bar Ilan University Press, 1990), 213–47. The Jerusalem prism is the most recently discovered text of this campaign. It is a hexagonal prism containing an account of the eight campaigns of Sennacherib (see Ling-Israel, "Sennacherib Prism," 211).

and curse (*māmīt*) of Assyria, into fetters of iron...."[209] Similar to the Hebrew terms noted above in Gen 14:13, this Assyrian treaty uses the term *bēl* to refer to an ally or treaty partner. In this case, Padi, the treaty partner of Assyria, had been overthrown in an act of rebellion against Assyrian rule.

Another example of this tradition of usage appears in a letter from the Assyrian crown prince Ashurbanipal (CT 54 580) that dates to around 672–669 B.C.E. and mentions a treaty between the king of Assyria and the king of Elam.[210] The relevant portion reads: "A message from the Crown Prince to Šulmu-ahu: The king of Elam and the king of Assyria, having repeatedly consulted with each other, have by the command of Marduk made peace with one another and become treaty partners (*bēl adê ša ahāmiš*, lit. "lord of an oath of one another")."[211]

As noted above, one may possibly object to the usefulness of these two examples for the self-standing term בַּעַל in a text like Hos 2. There is a very large number of Neo-Assyrian political texts, however, that employ *bēl* by itself in reference to the dominant party in a political alliance, that is, the political overlord or suzerain, usually the Assyrian king, himself. Five examples provide good illustrations of this well-attested usage. First, the succession treaty of Esarhaddon on behalf of his son Ashurbanipal, like Hos 2, combines the political use of *bēl* with the love imagery (Akk. *râmu*, "to love") noted above (l. 207): "[Y]ou must guard him strongly until one of you, who loves his lord (EN-*šu*) and feels concern over the house of his lords (EN.MEŠ-*šu*)...."[212] Second, this same text contains another example of the political meaning of *bēl* (l. 506): "[W]e will not conceal it but will report it to Assurbanipal, the great crown prince designate, our lord (*be-lí-ni*)."[213]

A third example of this usage appears in a treaty inscription of Esarhaddon referring to a previous political alliance (col. I, ll. 7–8): "At that time, when that treaty was imp[osed] and it was said: 'The king my lord (*be-lí*) has imposed an oath (*ma-mit*) on all [the lands]....'"[214] Similarly, a treaty connected with Ashurbanipal's mother uses the term as a reference to the king (rev. ll. 12–14): "[A]nd if you hear of an ugly [scheme] being elaborated against your lord (*be-lí-ku-nu*) Assurbanipal, king of Assyria...."[215] Finally, Ashurbanipal's own treaty with Babylonian allies shows this meaning (l. 21'): "[We will do]

---

[209] Chicago Prism col. II ll. 73–75 (Luckenbill, *Annals*, 31). Parpola and Watanabe translate, "bound by treaty and oath" (*Neo-Assyrian Treaties*, XXII). Cf. Ling-Israel, "Sennacherib Prism," 227.

[210] For dating issues, see Parpola and Watanabe, *Neo-Assyrian Treaties*, XVIII.

[211] Ibid., XVII.

[212] Ibid., 37.

[213] Ibid., 50.

[214] Ibid., 76.

[215] Ibid., 64. For other examples in this treaty see rev. ll. 4, 7, 9, 11, 17, and 27.

everything that Assurbanipal, king of Assyria, our lord (EN-*a-ni*) tells us....”[216]
Taken together, these texts indicate an established use of *bēl*, standing
independently in political contexts, to refer to the dominant partner of a political
alliance.

As mentioned above, the texts cited thus far all come from the century after
the time of Hosea. This same political use of the term, however, also appears in
the Aramaic Sefire treaties that date from the mid-eighth century B.C.E.[217] These
inscriptions not only represent a closer parallel to Hos 2 in time and language
but also provide further evidence of the use of בעל as an independent term
whose context provides it with a political meaning. The relevant portion refers
to the political relationship between the rulers of “KTK” and Arpad (face A, l.
4): “[A]nd the treaty of the lords (בעלי) of KTK with the treaty of the lords
(בעלי) of Arpad....”[218]

2.3.3 *Uses of* בעל *in Hosea.* Within the book of Hosea, the situation concerning
בעל is complex because the term is not always used in the same manner.
Nonetheless, the occurrences of the term and their contexts within the book shed
light on the way in which the prophet employs the word within the specific
address of chapter 2. The book of Hosea employs, it will be shown, two distinct
traditions of the term בעל. The use of the term in Hos 2 comprises one of those
traditions, while the remaining occurrences in the book constitute the other.

As noted above, the Hebrew word בעל occurs four times in Hos 2 in
alternating singular and plural forms (2:10, sg.; 2:15, pl.; 2:18, sg.; 2:19, pl.).
All of these forms have the definite article with the exception of 2:18, which has
a first-person suffix. Outside of chapter 2, the root appears only three other
times in the book.[219] In Hos 9:10, the text mentions not simply בעל but the
divine name בעל פעור:

---

[216] Ibid., 66. For other examples in this treaty see ll. 23’, 26’, 27’, and 28’. See especially the
extension of the term to refer to any political overlord in line 34’: “[We will not install] nor seek
another king or another lord (EN) for [ourselves] ...” (ibid.).

[217] For the major work on these treaties, see Fitzmyer, *Aramaic Inscriptions.*

[218] Ibid., 43. The relationship between this Aramaic treaty and the Assyrian treaty of Ashur-nirari V
with Mati’-ilu, king of Arpad (see Parpola and Watanabe, *Neo-Assyrian Treaties*, 8–13) remains
debated. There does not seem to be clear evidence for seeing the latter as the Akkadian version of the
former.

[219] This conclusion rejects the BHS text note that suggests reconstructing 11:7 so that it contains an
occurrence of בעל. The text reads, “To the yoke (ואל־על, or “to the Most High”) they call
him....” The translation “yoke” follows the Targum, Vulgate, and some Greek manuscripts while
“Most High” reflects the Syriac and Septuagint. The BHS note suggests reading ואל־בעל, “to Baal
he calls.” There is no textual evidence to support this emendation, and the reference may, in fact, be
to Yahweh and the ineffectiveness of the people’s cries to him because of their divided loyalties.
Wolff follows the emendation but notes, “The text of v 7b remains completely obscure” (*Hosea*,
192). Andersen and Freedman reject the emendation and provide a helpful explanation. They note

Like grapes in the wilderness I found (מָצָאתִי, qal perfect) Israel; like the first fruit on the fig tree in its first season, I saw (רָאִיתִי, qal perfect) your ancestors. They came to (בָּאוּ, qal perfect) Baal-peor (בַּעַל פְּעוֹר), and they dedicated themselves to a shameful thing. They became (וַיִּהְיוּ, qal imperfect vav consecutive) detestable like the thing they loved.

This text clearly uses the term בַּעַל in a religious sense. However, two important factors must dictate the way one uses this verse to understand Hos 2. First, the verse does not use בַּעַל by itself but as a component of a divine name used elsewhere. This name explicitly refers back to the tradition now recorded in Num 25.[220] Second, and most importantly, although this text is clearly religious in meaning, it is not describing the present actions of Hosea's audience. Hosea 9:10 does not accuse the prophet's eighth-century audience of worshipping the god Baal.[221] Rather, within the overall rhetorical structure of Hos 9, verse 10 functions as a retrospective. In order to strengthen the accusations against his contemporary audience, Hosea refers back to the previous generation's apostasy with Baal-peor. The preceding material (9:1–9) does focus on the sins of the present generation but seems to describe them in political rather than religious terms (see 9:6).[222] In order to amplify this message about the present state and impending judgment of the people, the prophet emphasizes the long-standing nature of their rebellion against Yahweh by referring back to the religious rebellion of their earliest ancestors. This meaning

---

that the preposition אֶל suggests that עַל must be a noun while the verb יִקְרָא suggests that עַל designates the name of the god to whom the people call (*Hosea*, 586). The context of Hos 11, however, seems to indicate that the word is a title being ascribed to a rival god (ibid., 587). While a full discussion of the issues and interpretation of this unclear text lies outside the scope of this study, these observations demonstrate that there is no warrant or necessity for emending the text by inserting a ב. The verse can be explained, albeit in a variety of differing ways, without recourse to a mention of the god Baal.

[220] See Num 25:3. This is not to say that Hosea was referring to the pentateuchal material itself, and the influence may have been in the opposite direction. For the evidence that Hos 9:10 predates Num 25:1b–5 and is the earliest of all the references to the Baal of Peor tradition, see G. Boudreau, "Hosea and the Pentateuchal Traditions: The Case of the Baal of Peor," in *History and Interpretation: Essays in Honour of John H. Hayes* (eds., M. P. Graham, W. P. Brown, J. K. Kuan; JSOTSup 173; Sheffield: JSOT Press, 1993), 121–32. For a fuller discussion, see G. Boudreau, "A Study of the Traditio-Historical Development of the Baal of Peor Tradition" (Ph.D. diss., Emory University, 1991).

[221] For a similar interpretive move, see J. Jeremias (*Hosea und Amos: Studien zu den Anfängen des Dodekapropheton* [FAT 13; Tübingen: J. C. B. Mohr, 1996], 87), who argues that the term בַּעַל in Hosea designates a type of divine-human relationship and not a specific deity.

[222] It is not clear whether 9:1–9 constitutes an originally separate rhetorical address followed by an address in 9:10–17. Wolff notes, "It has long been observed that a deep caesura occurs between 9:9 and 9:10" (*Hosea*, 161; cf. Andersen and Freedman, *Hosea*, 537). Even if the two parts were originally separate addresses, they appear at least to relate to the same basic rhetorical situation, namely the rebellion in and siege of Samaria in 724–722 B.C.E.

of verse 10 shows itself most clearly in the preponderance of qal perfect verb forms (with one vav consecutive form) that relate the actions in the verse.[223] After using 9:10's retrospective to reinforce his description of the people's actions and to emphasize their ancestral propensity for unfaithfulness, Hosea concludes the address in 9:11–17 by once again proclaiming the doom that is to come.[224]

The majority of commentators agree with this assessment of Hos 9:10 as a historical retrospect. The mention of the wilderness and Baal-peor clearly directs the reader's thoughts backward in time.[225] Mays expresses the situation best:

> This oracle opens a new section of the book characterized by the repeated use of history to establish the perspective in which the present is to be understood. Up to this point the past has been mentioned, if at all only in passing ... but now references to the historical background become regular and significant. Verse 10 is typical.[226]

Mays's statement is especially significant because the remaining two occurrences of the root בעל in Hosea appear in texts that follow chapter 9, that is, texts in which historical retrospectives play a common and significant role.

The second such occurrence of בעל is in Hos 11:2. The scholarly discussion is not as agreeable, however, because this text uses the word by itself, albeit in the plural form. Nonetheless, like 9:10, this verse employs a reference to Baal only in the context of a historical retrospective and not as a present accusation. Hosea 11:2 reads, "[Others] called to them;[227] thus they walked away because of them;[228] to the baals (לבעלים) they sacrificed and to the images they burned incense." This charge occurs in the context of a

---

[223] Following the retrospective in 9:10, verses 11 and 12 replace the perfect forms with imperfects and a coordinate perfect.

[224] In this regard, Hos 9:15, "All their evil began in Gilgal ...," may also represent a retrospective that employs the name "Gilgal" as a reference to the very first location of the Israelites after crossing into the land of Canaan. The prophet may use this reference to proclaim that the people's evil was present from the very beginning of their existence in the land. But see Andersen and Freedman, *Hosea*, 537.

[225] Andersen and Freedman, *Hosea*, 537; cf. Harper, *Amos and Hosea*, 336–37; Stuart, *Hosea-Jonah*, 151.

[226] Mays, *Hosea*, 132.

[227] This reading follows the MT קראו by taking "others" as an understood subject of the verb and rejects the reading of the LXX from כקראי ("as I called") as without sufficient support. The text refers to those who drew Israel away from Yahweh.

[228] This reading also follows the MT and not the LXX that seems to translate מפני הם ("from before me"). The MT מפניהם can carry the meaning of causation ("because of"), i.e., the Israelites "walked away because of" the influence of these others (cf. Judg 9:21; 1 Sam 21:11; 23:26; Jer 35:11; 37:11; 41:9; 50:16). The normal preposition to indicate defection is מאחרי (contra LXX).

rehearsal of the people's initial abandonment of Yahweh during the journey out of Egypt (see 11:1). Hosea perhaps here refers to the same apostasy with Baal-peor in the wilderness that he mentions in 9:10. As Andersen and Freedman note, if 11:1 describes the exodus then an event soon after, like the apostasy with Baal-peor, would fit the context. Additionally, there are parallels in language between Hos 11:1 and 9:10.[229]

Hosea does not turn to the people's present situation until 11:5: "He will not return to the land of Egypt, but Assyria will be his king because they refused to repent." As in chapter 9, in order to provide a backdrop that strengthens his accusation, the prophet first reflects on how Israel has refused to walk faithfully with Yahweh since the time of the exodus from Egypt (11:1–4). In this context, one finds verse 2's religious accusation that the people have worshipped Baal. Once again, the accusation is not a present charge against Hosea's generation but the sin of a previous generation that highlights the long-standing nature of the people's rebellious attitude toward Yahweh.[230]

The final occurrence of the root בעל in Hosea is in 13:1: "When Ephraim spoke there was trembling; he raised up[231] in Israel. But he became guilty with Baal (בבעל) and he died." This verse stands as a part of a large section of Hosea (12:1–14:1 MT) that deals with the rebellions and punishments of Israel.[232] Within this section, however, the prophet pauses in the midst of charges against his own audience to offer brief historical retrospectives that place the actions of the present generation in the light of those of the ancestors. The first retrospective occurs in 12:4–6 (MT). After describing the political misdeeds of his present-day Israel in relation to Assyria and Egypt (12:1–2) and the resulting punishment from Yahweh (12:3), Hosea reminds his audience of the way their ancestor Jacob sought God until he encountered him at Bethel (12:4–6). In light of Jacob's example, the prophet then calls his own people to turn and seek Yahweh as well (12:7). Following this section, Hosea again describes the sinful actions of his contemporary audience (12:8–12). Beginning in 12:13, however, the prophet offers another historical retrospective that rehearses more elements of the story of Jacob and the people who descended from him. This retrospective seems to extend through 13:1 and describes Jacob's flight to Aram, his descendants' sojourn in Egypt, the exodus from Egypt, and the people's initial abandonment of Yahweh in the wilderness. In

---

[229] Andersen and Freedman, *Hosea*, 578. Contra Harper, who blurs the distinction between past and present by interpreting the reference to the baals here simply as a reference to the golden calves at Dan and Bethel (*Amos and Hosea*, 363). As noted above, while the latter items do seem to be a concern of Hosea about his contemporary audience, Baal worship does not (cf. Hos 8:4–6; 13:2). Cf. Kaufmann, *Religion*, 143, 369, 372.

[230] See also Andersen and Freedman, *Hosea*, 575; Mays, *Hosea*, 152; Wolff, *Hosea*, 193, 197.

[231] Targum and Syriac read this verb as a nifal form, "he was exalted."

[232] For an opposing argument, see Wolff, who concludes that 13:1 begins a wholly new unit because there are "no stylistic or thematic connections with the previous chapter" (*Hosea*, 222).

this latter section (12:14–13:1), the oracle states that, "after Yahweh had brought Israel up from Egypt by a prophet" (12:14), Israel "created bitter provocation" (12:15). The perfect verb form in this verse suggests that it continues the past description of the exodus generation. In this context, Hos 13:1 functions to elaborate more fully the way in which that generation "created bitter provocation," namely, by becoming guilty "with Baal."[233] Immediately following this description, 13:2 explicitly marks a transition back to concern with Hosea's contemporary listeners by equating their actions with the sins of their ancestors: "And *now* (ועתה) they [i.e., Jacob's descendants] are sinning again, and they have made for themselves a molten image...."[234]

Seen in the context of the larger rhetorical unit, the accusation of Baal worship in Hos 13:1 shows itself to be yet another example of Hosea's use of historical retrospective to compare and contrast the behavior of the present and past generations. As in 9:10 and 11:2, the prophet does not accuse his contemporary audience of Baal worship, and the term בעל occurs with that meaning only when he is referring to the apostasy of the wilderness generation.[235] As noted above, Wolff denies the original relationship of the material in Hos 12 and 13. Nonetheless, even he acknowledges that 13:1 refers

---

[233] Andersen and Freedman seem to suggest this retrospective reading of 13:1 when they note that the preposition ב is not used with אשם to identify the partner in sin and probably functions as a locative so that "Baal" is short for "Baal-peor" from Hos 9:10 (*Hosea*, 630). Thus, even from this grammatical perspective, 13:1 seems to refer to the same wilderness generation apostasy as 9:10 and 11:2.

[234] Andersen and Freedman object to this past and present reading of verses 1 and 2 because both ויאשם ("he became guilty") in 13:1 and יוספו ("they are sinning again") are the same form category (imperfects) (ibid., 629). However, this objection overlooks the fact that the verb in the retrospect in 13:1 is an imperfect with a vav consecutive denoting past action while the verb in 13:2 is not in the vav consecutive form. Andersen and Freedman note this difference in form and state that the regular imperfect form in 13:2 "interrupts the continuity in the narrative" (ibid., 631).

[235] These observations concerning Hosea's use of the wilderness tradition challenge the fairly widespread assumption that Hosea, as opposed to the Pentateuch and Ezekiel, consistently views the wilderness period as a positive and ideal time in the life of Israel. This assertion is often based solely on references to the wilderness in Hos 2 that do not necessarily reveal a positive view of the wilderness as a period in Israel's story.

The final retrospective portion of 12:1–14:1 occurs in 13:4–6, which stresses Yahweh's provision for the people in the wilderness and the people's propensity to forget his provisions. However, this retrospect is unlike the others because rather than first speaking of the previous generation and then moving to the present situation, it uses second-person pronouns, intermingled with third-person ones, to identify explicitly the contemporary audience with their ancestors, who received Yahweh's care and fell victim to arrogance. For example, 13:5–6 state, "I knew you in the wilderness, in a land of drought. When I fed them, they were satisfied; and when they were satisfied, their heart was raised up and therefore they forgot me."

to "earlier deeds" and "previous history" while 13:2 proceeds to describe the "present guilt" of which Israel is accused.[236]

Taken together, all of the uses surveyed in this section evidence a consistent characteristic: outside of Hos 2, the book uses בעל in a religious sense but only in historical retrospectives and only to describe the religious sins of the ancestors. These texts need not indicate that worship of the god Baal was a primary issue for Hosea or his eighth-century audience. In fact, Hosea specifically appeals to this sin of the ancestors in order to compare and contrast it with the sins of his own generation.[237]

2.4 Summary and Conclusions

The above discussion has revealed several important elements about the possible background and usage of the term בעל. First, investigation of the available evidence demonstrated that there is no sufficient reason for maintaining the existence of a widespread fertility/sex cult dedicated to the god Baal in eighth-century Israel. Second, the above discussion also showed that there is reason to question the existence of widespread, even nonsexual, Baal worship in Hosea's day. Both biblical and extrabiblical evidence, including eighth-century onomastic and epigraphic items, indicated that Yahwism remained dominant, and thus it stands to reason that there would have been no prevalent concern over Israelites committing apostasy with Baal. Third, an examination of בעל as a more general term revealed that there was a widespread biblical and extrabiblical tradition of using the term with the political meaning of "ally," "treaty-partner," or "overlord." Finally, a survey of the uses of בעל in the book of Hosea outside chapter 2 demonstrated that Hosea used the word only three times, and all three uses appeared in the context of historical retrospectives that described not the behavior of Hosea's audience but the sin of the previous generation.

The above evidence raises the possibility that Hos 2 may use the term בעל in a way that does not involve worship of the god Baal. Since there is no substantial biblical or extrabiblical evidence for a widespread Baal cult, sexual

---

[236] Wolff, *Hosea*, 222, 225. See also Harper, who states that 13:1, in contrast to 13:2, describes Ephraim in the past (*Amos and Hosea*, 395) and Mays, who labels verse 1 "past," verse 2 "present," and verse 3 "future" (*Hosea*, 171).

[237] Kaufmann (*Religion*, 143) reached the same conclusion: "In the last chapters, on the other hand, Baal worship (only in 9:10 and 13:1) [*sic*; cf. 11:2] appears as a sin of the past...." Kaufmann does not include Hos 11:2 as a reference to past Baal worship because he maintains that the use of the term בעלים there, "as often in Jeremiah," is nothing more than a "derogatory reference to idol-worship in general, not to actual Baal worship" (ibid., 372). This argument seems to rest primarily on the fact that the word occurs in the plural in Hos 11:2 and not the singular as in the other Hosea texts. However, such a conclusion is not necessary since, as noted above, the root regularly occurs in alternating singular and plural forms throughout the Hebrew Bible.

or nonsexual, in eighth-century Israel and the rest of the book of Hosea never condemns the Israelites of Hosea's day for practicing Baal worship, apostasy with Baalism should not be seen as constituting the major issue with which Hos 1–3 deals. Rather, factors specific to Hos 2 combine to commend the political sense of "ally," "treaty-partner," or "overlord" for the term in that context.[238]

A first factor is that the language of Hos 2, especially with its combination of the terms "lovers" and "baal(s)" and its emphasis upon devotion and loyalty, is similar to that of the ancient Near Eastern political texts that employ the word *bēl* with a political meaning. Along these same lines, a second factor that suggests a political meaning for בעל in Hos 2 is the similarity of this oracle to other biblical texts that seem to employ the term in a political sense. Two of the three Hebrew Bible texts that use verbal forms of בעל with a political meaning are prophetic texts (Isa 26:13; Jer 3:14), and Jer 3:14 closely resembles the language of Hos 2 in that it has Yahweh assert that he himself will be the lord/master (בעל) over the people (cf. Hos 2:18).

Finally, the interpreter must consider the various elements of the rhetoric of Hosea's speech that have been adumbrated in the preceding chapters. The evidence for understanding Hos 2's references to fornication, adultery, and lovers as political metaphors suggests that בעל would carry a similar meaning and that a purely religious sense of the term would be out of place in the overall context. Even if one is convinced only by the evidence that associates the personified female with the city Samaria, this possibility alone provides a frame of reference from which to interpret the term within the discourse as a whole. As Galambush rightly notes, the interpretation of the word בעל in Hos 2 must stand in close connection with the possible metaphorical identities of the main female subject in the text.[239] If these arguments hold, Hos 2 employs the term בעל, in conjunction with the term "lovers," to refer to those entities who have been involved in the capital city's political actions that Hosea condemns and describes as "fornication" and "adultery."

When one views the term in Hos 2 in the light of all of the uses of בעל in the book, it is possible to suggest an explanation as to how and why Hosea uses this word to characterize those political entities with whom Samaria has gone astray. Through its rhetoric, language, and metaphors, Hosea, similarly to the other prophetic books, takes the contingent political realities of its day and gives them a theological interpretation. Thus, it cannot be said that Hosea operates with a strict distinction between the political and religious realms nor that he is

---

[238] This interpretation has been suggested in passing by Galambush, who does not develop the arguments for it and devotes only one paragraph to discussing it. She suggests, "Hosea may be condemning Samaria's dependence, not on a Canaanite god, but on human 'baalim,' the foreign powers with which she had liaisons" (*Jerusalem*, 49).

[239] Ibid., 49.

interested in simply giving a political commentary on his people's situation.[240] In the context of eighth-century Israel, while there may not have been prominent Baal worship, the term בעל undoubtedly recalled the widespread Baal worship of previous generations. The fact that Hosea elsewhere uses בעל only in historical retrospectives that describe the sin of his audience's ancestors raises the possibility that Hos 2 employs this term to equate political and religious infidelity in a particular way. Given the oracle's rhetoric and metaphors surveyed thus far, the term בעל in Hos 2 serves, on one hand, as a general term that designates Samaria's political allies or overlords. Yet the use of this loaded term simultaneously but subtlely equates the immediate political situation with past (ninth-century) Baal worship. Hosea 2's use of בעל makes the subtle theological statement that the present generation's political misconduct with allies is the theological equivalent of the past generation's religious misconduct with Baal.[241] This explanation fits well with the evidence for the existence of Baal worship in ninth-century Israel and takes seriously the place of Hos 2 within the overall rhetoric and perspective of the book of Hosea. Through the use of this term, Hosea offers a powerful critique that denies the compartmentalization of political and religious life and elevates the ruling house's inappropriate political alliances to the level of a breach in the exclusive relationship with Yahweh. The word בעל functions metaphorically in Hos 2 as it creates a comparison between political alliances and religious apostasy that reformulates the reader's understanding of both.

A proper understanding of the use of בעל in Hos 2 provides additional insight into the text's rhetorical horizon that has been emerging from the analysis of the major metaphors. The בעל imagery once again suggests that this speech is directly concerned with a capital city's political actions that Hosea views as violations of Yahweh's will for the people. As with the metaphor of "lovers," the word בעל further identifies the type of rhetorical-historical situation in which the prophet's oracle may have functioned. When one considers all of Hos 2's major metaphors, it appears that this situation involved an occasion when the leaders of the northern kingdom, represented by the

---

[240] This assertion seems to hold true for the Hebrew Bible in general, since foreign alliances are often seen as simply a prelude to idolatry, e.g., Exod 34:15; 1 Kgs 16:31; 2 Kgs 16:10–12; Ezek 23:7 (ibid., 50).

[241] In this regard, compare the rhetoric of Jer 23:23–27 that offers a condemnation of the present activity of prophets by comparing it to the Baal worship of *previous* generations: "They [the prophets] plan to make my people forget my name ... just as their ancestors forgot my name for Baal" (23:27). Compare also the reference to Baal worship in the past in 23:13 that contrasts with the "more shocking thing" of the present in 23:14. Similarly, 1 Sam 12 compares Israel's request for a king with a previous generation's worship of "the Baals and the Astartes" (see Arnold, "Pre-Deuteronomistic," 141). Yee ("Not My Wife," 363) approaches this position by arguing that Hosea's rhetoric equates that which is foreign (alliances, modes of production, etc.) with the worship of lesser deities.

personified capital city, sought out relationships with foreign powers that Hosea considered to be the equivalent of past generations' apostasy with the Canaanite god Baal. Given the biblical and extrabiblical tradition of using בעל to refer to a suzerain or overlord, the two singular forms of the word in Hos 2 may suggest the presence in the rhetorical horizon of a dominant political ruler to whom Samaria has submitted in conjunction with a variety of other treaty-partners.

Keeping in mind the overall marriage metaphor of Hos 2, one need not translate בעל as "ally" or "lord" because that would remove the term from the overall metaphor. However, one should equally not transliterate it as a personal name. In view of the overarching marriage metaphor containing references to a husband, wife, and lovers, the term seems to refer metaphorically to an illicit sex partner whom the wife pursues in place of her husband. In deference to the political meaning of the word, however, בעל represents a lover/partner who stands as the dominant member of the relationship. Thus, it is perhaps best to translate בעל as "paramour." This term refers not simply to a lover but, more specifically, to one who takes the place, without possessing the accompanying rights, of a husband.[242] In this way, the word points to a rhetorical horizon in which Samaria has attached itself to at least one primary "paramour" and perhaps others (cf. singular and plural uses of בעל), who are usurping its devotion in the sense of political alliances.

---

[242] J. Simpson and E. Weiner, eds., *The Oxford English Dictionary* (20 vols.; 2d ed.; Oxford: Clarendon, 1989), 11:201.

PART 2

THE *RHETORIC* OF HOSEA 2

6

THE RHETORICAL CONTEXT OF HOSEA 2

The preceding investigation of the major metaphors in Hos 2 provides the basis for an analysis of the prophet's speech as a whole. From the standpoint of a rhetorical approach to prophetic texts, such an analysis must begin by considering the larger issues that provide an interpretive context for the specific elements and inner workings of the address: the rhetorical unit, rhetorical horizon, and rhetorical-historical situation.

1. THE RHETORICAL UNIT

Deciding for or against the original unity of a text like Hos 2:1–25 is a difficult task. As Buss observes, it is hard to determine the original units in the book of Hosea as a whole because it lacks a clear inner structure and does not make regular use of prophetic formulas, like "Thus says the Lord," to mark different divisions.[1] In spite of this difficulty, the possible original unit(s) within Hos 2 effects the way one understands the function of all of the metaphors and rhetorical elements within the text's rhetorical horizon. The issue of unity impacts not only the movement within and function of the oracle as a whole but

---

[1] Buss, *Prophetic Word*, 28.

also the scope and nature of the rhetorical-historical context in which the oracle may have functioned.

Several criteria help to establish the rhetorical units within texts like Hos 2. The reader should ask, for instance, whether the chapter makes sense as a whole and whether there are significant elements, like verbal repetition and thematic continuity, which suggest the text reflects a unified composition. Even if these things can be established, however, the observed unity may not be original but only the result of later redaction of originally disparate material.[2] For example, as the reader will see, several scholars defend the unity of all of Hos 2:1–25 but do so only with regard to the final redacted form of the text.[3]

In the face of this quandary, a way forward may be found by beginning not with the effort to determine whether the text is "original" or "authentic" but with the question of to what extent it can be considered the product of a "single act of composition by a single author."[4] One should begin by examining the ways in which a text like Hos 2 reflects a unified act of composition both verbally and thematically. Given the relationship between the text's major metaphors and the thought-world of Hosea's time discussed in the preceding chapters, however, it is reasonable to conclude that if one can establish that Hos 2 reflects a single act of composition, there is no sufficient reason to deny this act to Hosea himself.

While there is no consensus regarding the unit(s) in Hos 2, several positions constitute the primary views on the issue. The most widely accepted scholarly position isolates 2:1–3 as a separate rhetorical unit that was subsequently joined to the material in the rest of chapter 2.[5] Evidence for the independence of 2:1–3 commonly includes several characteristics: 1) these verses interrupt the threat language of both 1:1–9 and 2:4–16,[6] 2) the imperative in 2:4 marks a shift in tone and address by introducing first-person speech,[7] 3) the verb וְהָיָה, "and it will be," seems to envision a scenario in the distant future (cf. 2:20, 23–25),[8] and 4) the notion of a reunited Israel and Judah must come from a late date (at

---

[2] For example, Buss notes that a "major difficulty" appears in determining whether an observable repetition is original, accidental, or redactional (ibid., 29).

[3] For the major statement of this view, see Renaud, "Genèse," 1–20. Cf. Borbone, *Il libro*, 131; Snaith, *Amos*, 56; Snaith, *Mercy*, 27. Yee provides a helpful example of this issue. She identifies 2:1–3 as a unit from the latest (exilic) redactor of Hosea. In the present form, however, she maintains that 2:2–3 forms a strong rhetorical unity with 2:4–25 through the use of common vocabulary so that the rhetorical unit one should consider in the final form is 2:2–25 (*Composition*, 55, 72).

[4] Jones, "Howling," 89.

[5] See Batten, "Hosea's Message," 269; Buss, *Prophetic Word*, 70; Jeremias, *Der Prophet*, 24; Macintosh, *Critical and Exegetical Commentary*, lxix; Mauchline, "Hosea," 565; Mays, *Hosea*, 36; Rudolph, *Hosea*, 55–59; Yee, *Composition*, 55.

[6] Blankenbaker, "Language," 119.

[7] Weems, "Gomer," 94.

[8] Whitt, "Divorce," 33.

least after 720 B.C.E.) due to its similarities with texts like Ezek 37:15–28.[9] Along these lines, several other elements in these verses are often taken as indicators of a late date for the material: 1) the expression "sons of the living God," 2) the use of קבץ, "to gather together," and 3) the positive view of Judah.[10]

Wolff, for example, observes that the style of 2:1–3, with its use of perfect verb forms, stands in contrast to that of 1:2–9, with its use of imperfect consecutives. Nonetheless, he notes that the language and themes of verses 1–3 are originally Hosean. The only reason that these verses should be considered a separate unit is that they deal with the theme of restoration and the benefits of Yahweh's actions. In Wolff's view, 2:1–3 originally stood at the end of the sayings in 2:4–25, but a later editor moved them to their present position to introduce the tension of judgment and restoration in Hosea's message.[11]

There is some variation of views concerning 2:1–3 among interpreters who do not take all of chapter 2 as an original unit. Rather than seeing 2:1–3 as a separate unit, some scholars connect all or part of these verses with the material in Hos 1. This variation stems in large part from the difficulty in determining the conclusion of the story in chapter 1, a difficulty that is reflected in the fact that the Septuagint and Vulgate begin chapter two with verse 3(MT) and place verses 1(MT) and 2(MT) with chapter 1.[12] For example, Blankenbaker follows these ancient versions and sees Hos 2:1–2 as the conclusion to the story of the symbolic children's names in 1:2–9. In his view, the כי clause in 2:2 closes the preceding section while the imperatives at the beginning of 2:3 and 4 link them together.[13] Andersen and Freedman associate all of 2:1–3 with the end of Hos 1 and do not see these verses as an originally self-standing unit. They point out that 2:1–3 share the primary features of the three oracles about the children, especially the first, and that the removal of kingship in 1:4 parallels the new "head" in 2:2.[14]

---

[9] Harper, *Critical and Exegetical Commentary*, 245; Budde, "Der Abschnitt," 23–26. See also Buss, who argues that the word order of Judah followed by Israel in 2:2 indicates a southern origin (*Prophetic Word*, 34).

[10] For summaries of these typical indicators, see H. Wolff, "Der große Jesreeltag (Hosea 2, 1–3): Methodologische Erwägungen zur Auslegung einer alttestamentlichen Perikope," *EvT* 12 (1952–53): 86 and B. Renaud, "Osée ii:2 '*lh mn h'rṣ.* Essai d'interprétation," *VT* 33 (1983): 496–97.

[11] Wolff, *Hosea*, 24–26.

[12] This difficulty also appears in the different chapter divisions in English translations.

[13] Blankenbaker, "Language," 121–22 . Cf. Knight, *Hosea*, 48; McComiskey, *The Minor Prophets*, 4; Pfeiffer, "Hosea," 803; Sweeney, *The Twelve Prophets*, 11–12.

[14] Andersen and Freedman, *Hosea*, 201–2. Cf. Davies, who also takes all of 1:2–2:3 as a rhetorical unit (*Hosea* [OTG], 32). Ibn Ezra had earlier understood 2:1–3 as the conclusion of chapter 1 by taking these three verses as a negative statement about exile at the hands of Sennacherib that continues the doom oracle of 1:8–9 (A. Lipshitz, ed., *The Commentary of Rabbi Abraham Ibn Ezra on Hosea* [New York: Sepher-Hermon, 1988], 32).

There are several difficulties with these positions that separate all or part of
2:1–3 from the rest of Hos 2. First, while these verses interrupt the threat
language of 1:2–9 and 2:4–15, the style and form of 2:1–3, which are distinct
from the biographical material in chapter 1, are consistent with that of 2:4–25
(e.g., compare the language and imagery of 2:1–3 with 2:23–25). Second, verse
3 stands in close connection with verse 4 through the presence of similar
imperative forms that begin both (ריבו‎ ,אמרו‎) and seem to address the same
general (plural) audience. Third, the notion of a reunited Israel and Judah is not
necessarily restricted to exilic times. As noted above, there is much debate about
the nature and authenticity of the references to Judah in the book as a whole, but
the close relationship between Israel and Judah during Hosea's time (see
discussion of history below) suggests that Judah may be well within the
prophet's range of vision. Stuart concludes, for example, that verses 1–3 are
likely original to Hosea because they contain several key words known from
other sections of the book like "children of Israel" (cf. 3:1; 4:5) and "gather
together" (cf. 8:10; 9:6).[15] Fourth, one can perhaps explain the shift in person
and address from 2:3 to 2:4 by assuming a change of speaker from the prophet,
offering an introduction, in 2:1–3 to Yahweh, as portrayed by Hosea, in 2:4–25.
Finally, as will be noted below, there are several strong reasons for considering
2:1, in contrast to 2:4, to be the explicit beginning of a unit.

Most other views concerning the unit(s) of Hos 2 assume the separation of
2:1–3, an assumption that should be challenged. Hence, a second position
excludes 2:1–3 and sees 2:4–17 and 18–25 as the two, originally separate, units
of the chapter.[16] The arguments cited in this regard usually include the
following: 1) the temporal word והיה‎ indicates a new unit in 2:18 that switches
to direct second-person address,[17] 2) the "court metaphor" falls out of use in
2:18–25,[18] 3) the ריב‎ genre is consistently at work throughout 2:4–17 but not in
2:18–25,[19] and 4) the subject of the unfaithful wife fades from view in 2:18–25
and is replaced by a focus on בעל‎ and a new marriage covenant.[20] Whitt
provides a specific example of this position. He asserts that the use of "on that
day" to introduce a promise of restoration and the reference to a ברית‎ are

---

[15] Stuart, *Hosea-Jonah*, 37; cf. Mays, *Hosea*, 31.

[16] For example, see Budde, "Der Abschnitt," 51.

[17] Mays, *Hosea*, 35–37.

[18] Stuart, *Hosea-Jonah*, 45.

[19] Krszyna, "Literarische Struktur," 43. Krszyna also notes that there are two main sections within
2:4–17 and each one has a chiastic structure with inclusios: 2:4–7a and 2:7b–17 (ibid., 46).

[20] Wolff, *Hosea*, 47. Wolff's analysis of 2:18–25 is more complex than the others. He views these
verses not as an original unit but as a "loosely knit series of sayings and fragments of sayings" from
Hosea. The formula "on that day" divides the series into three primary units with two parts each for a
total of six units: 2:18–19, 20–22, and 23–25. The units are now unified, however, by two key
factors: 1) each saying is in the form of a divine speech and 2) each saying offers a description of
"that day" (ibid., 47).

characteristics of late Hebrew. Additionally, he maintains that 2:18–22 employ the metaphor of Yahweh's wife for the people of Israel, a metaphor that, in his view, must be derived from the later works of Ezekiel and Jeremiah.[21]

In addition to the unwarranted exclusion of 2:1–3, several difficulties make this second position's treatment of verses 4–25 problematic. First, the transitional וְהָיָה in 2:18 is not disjunctive, like the וְהָיָה in 2:1, but directly continues the thought of 2:17, which has already begun to describe the "day" to which verse 18 refers. Moreover, the second-person address that begins in 2:18 is not consistent throughout verses 18–25 (cf. the third-person address in 2:19) and may appear earlier in the chapter (cf. 2:8 MT). Second, as noted above, there is no rigid court genre that operates consistently throughout the text or that can be used to establish authenticity.[22] Third, arguments that the repeated use of בַּעַל in 2:18–25 marks a new unit overlook both the preceding appearances of this word in 2:10 and 2:15 and the close connection of this term with the metaphor of "lovers" throughout the beginning part of the chapter. Finally, as the above exploration of the metaphor of Yahweh's wife has shown, there is no sufficient warrant for seeing this metaphor as either a reference to the people of Israel as a whole or as a late development borrowed from Ezekiel.

A third popular position that varies only slightly from the second also excludes verses 1–3 and sees 2:4–15 and 2:16–25 as the two primary units within Hos 2. Scholars who argue for this division generally emphasize that 2:16–17 fit better as a part of the salvation section in 2:18–25 and that the marker "oracle of Yahweh" in 2:15 indicates the original ending point of the oracle.[23] Buss also maintains that 2:16–25 cannot be original because they "can

---

[21] Whitt, "Divorce," 33–34.

[22] Whitt represents an example of the practice of enforcing a rigid divorce theme/genre on the text in order to determine authenticity. He takes the imagery of ancient Near Eastern divorce procedures as determinative and states, "Material that fits what we know of ancient Near Eastern divorce procedure is likely to be original; material that does not is likely to be secondary" (ibid., 35). On this basis, he concludes, for example, that 2:8–9, 10–11, and probably 15 are late because their "ideas" are not consistent with the overall theme of divorce. Accordingly, in his view, the only original verses of the chapter are 4–7, 12–14 (ibid., 34–35, 39).

[23] Braaten, "Parent-Child," 61; Clements, "Understanding," 411; Macintosh, *Critical and Exegetical Commentary*, lxix; Pfeiffer, "Hosea," 803; O. Procksch, *Die kleinen prophetischer Schriften vor dem Exile* (Erläuterungen zum Alten Testament 3; Calwer: Verlag der Vereinsbuch, 1910), 26; Rudolph, *Hosea*, 64–65; Sellin, *Zwölfprophetenbuch*, 33, 38; Ward, *Hosea*, 29, 41; J. Wellhausen, *Die kleinen Propheten: übersetzt und erklärt* (4th ed.; Berlin: de Gruyter, 1963), 100–104. Cf. McKeating, who sees 2:4–15 as consisting of four originally independent units now linked by similar imagery: 2:2–5, 8–9, 6–7, 10–13 (*Books*, 83). Humbert presents a variation on the typical divisions at either 2:15 or 2:17. He suggests that the theme of a return to the ideal relationship of the wilderness unifies all of 2:4–22 and that 2:23–25 is a later, non-Hosean addition (P. Humbert, "La logique de la perspective nomade chez Osée et l'unité d'Osée 2, 4–22," in *Vom Alten Testament: Karl Marti zum siebzigsten Geburtstage gewidmet von Freunden, Fachgenossen, und Schülern* [ed. K. Budde; BZAW 41; Giessen: Töpelmann, 1925], 166).

hardly represent an organic continuation of the declaration of legal process."[24] Andersen and Freedman assert that 2:16–25 employ many more prose particles and have affinities with the priestly style in the Pentateuch.[25] These typical arguments, however, are not sufficient to indicate that 2:4–15 originally stood apart from the material in 2:16–25. There is no need to insist, for example, on the rigid format or imagery of a legal process in order to view verses 16–25 as original. Even Buss allows that 2:16–25 fit with the general imagery of a legal process.[26] The salvation theme in these verses is not out of context in the chapter as a whole and emerges quite coherently from the descriptions of Yahweh's actions in the first part of the oracle. Also, while there are some stylistic differences between the two parts, the content, themes, and imagery are consistent throughout. As Andersen and Freedman conclude, "There is no reason, however, to chop up the unit in terms of literary style … the piece as a whole has a distinctive character and is unified in concept and content."[27] Finally, the marker "oracle of Yahweh" does not always indicate the end of a unit. Even within Hos 2 itself, יהוה־נאם stands near the beginning of a section of the text in 2:18 and occurs near the middle of a verse in 2:23.[28] In both cases, the phrase appears to function emphatically.

One more specific redactional issue on which commentators are divided concerns the original position of 2:8–9. Some interpreters suggest that verses 8–9, which describe Yahweh's actions of "hedging in" and "walling in" and the wife's decision to return to her first husband, originally stood after verse 15, which is the last judgment action of Yahweh.[29] Evidence for this view often includes the suggestions that, in their present position, 2:8–9 break a close juxtaposition between the wife's beliefs and the actual situation in 2:7 and 10 and that the present link between 2:15 and 16 is unclear. The wife's return in 2:9 also appears premature due to the description of further punishments in 2:10–15.[30] Overall, however, the evidence for reordering is weak. As Wolff

---

[24] Buss, *Prophetic Word*, 34.

[25] Andersen and Freedman, *Hosea*, 62.

[26] Buss, *Prophetic Word*, 34.

[27] Andersen and Freedman, *Hosea*, 62.

[28] Contrast Whitt, who argues that יהוה־נאם occurs nowhere else in the "original" Hosea material ("Divorce," 39). He concludes that Hos 2:18, 23, and 11:11 are all late additions. He also dismisses the fact that the phrase is frequent in Hosea's contemporaries Amos (12 times) and Isaiah (4 times). Whitt labels these occurrences as insertions of a Judean phrase (see ibid., f.n. 25).

[29] The first one to suggest this view was H. Oort, "Hozea," *ThT* 24 (1890): 345–64, 480–505.

[30] For these and other arguments for this position, see Yee, *Composition*, 77. Cf. Jerusalem Bible and NAB. For discussion of this issue, see especially Clines, "Hosea 2," 83–86. Several other scholars offer variations of this view. Humbert, for example, suggests that 2:8–9 originally stood after 2:12 ("Logique," 164). Sellin transposes only 2:9b to follow 2:16 (*Zwölfprophetenbuch*, 31). Renaud argues that 2:8–9 are a later addition but have been inserted in the correct place and should not be moved ("Genése," 10). Whitt sees 2:8–9 as late because they contradict the punishment already

notes, the resulting transition from 2:9 to 2:16 is more difficult, and 2:8 is stylistically more connected to 2:7 than to 2:15. Additionally, the wife's speech in 2:9b seems to be intentionally antithetical to the wording in 2:7b.[31]

Perhaps the most significant argument for the relocation of verses 8–9, however, is that the punishments of Yahweh and the return of the wife in these verses seem out of place in the context of more punishments and another return in 2:10–17. In response to this argument, Clines suggests a comprehensive way of understanding the sequence of the text that can illuminate the basic unity of the chapter. He notes that the three "therefores" (לכן) in 2:8, 11, and 16 provide three movements to the arrangement of the text: 1) Yahweh blocks the wife's way, 2) Yahweh removes his gifts, and 3) Yahweh resumes an exclusive relationship with the woman.[32] Accordingly, it is possible to read the three "therefore" statements not as a confusing sequence of actions but a series of *options* from which Yahweh, the wronged husband, may choose. Each of the three "therefore" statements picks up at the end of the woman's defiance in 2:7. This interpretation adequately considers the movement of the text as a whole and accurately recognizes that the wife's statement of return in 2:9 is not actual repentance but only what Yahweh, the speaker, thinks she will say under that circumstance.[33] This interpretation works hand in hand with the earlier observations that, in the imagery associated with a wife's refusal, the husband has a variety of options from which he may choose.

The final position concerning the unity of Hos 2 that has gained some popularity among commentators maintains the independence of 2:1–3 but sees all of 2:4–25 as an original rhetorical unit. Scholars who hold this position typically emphasize the general consistency of theme, imagery, and vocabulary throughout these verses and assert that there is no sufficient reason to deny this consistency to the text's original shaping.[34] One may also consider here those interpreters who deny that the material in chapter 2 comes from a single act of composition but affirm that the whole of 2:1–25 now appears to be unified in theme and content. Thus, all of Hos 2:1–25 is a unity, albeit a *redactional* one. As evidence for this view, Renaud argues that verses 1–25 now possess unity in

---

given in 2:4–5. He also, however, sees 2:10–11 as a later addition so that originally 2:7 continued directly into 2:12 ("Divorce," 37–39).

[31] Wolff, *Hosea*, 35; cf. Macintosh, *Critical and Exegetical Commentary*, 67. See also Krszyna, who argues that going right from the woman's words in 2:7 to the statement in 2:10 is stylistically difficult ("Literarische Struktur," 54).

[32] Clines, "Hosea 2," 83–86.

[33] As is the case throughout other texts like this one, Hos 2 never allows the female character to speak for herself but always speaks for her through the male narrator or male god.

[34] See Andersen and Freedman, *Hosea*, 62. See also Birch, who connects 2:1–3 with the preceding unit in 1:2–9 and views all of 2:4–25 as a single unit (*Hosea, Joel, and Amos*, 24–25). Walter Brueggemann also sets out a point by point correspondence between the first and second halves of 2:4–25, i.e., the latter half (2:16–25) reverses the judgments of the first half (2:4–15) (*Tradition for Crisis: A Study in Hosea* [Atlanta: John Knox, 1968], 110–18).

the form of a chiastic structure that spans the whole chapter. This structure unfolds within the bounds of an inclusio between 2:1–3 and 2:23–25, both of which give positive values to the children's names.[35]

Hosea 2's unifying consistency of vocabulary, themes, and motifs noted by these redactional views calls into question the other positions outlined above. The observations of things like chiastic structures, inclusios, and continuous motifs suggest that many of the decisions about the disunity of Hos 2 have been made on the basis of assumptions about the particular genre, historical setting, and theology that could have been operative in material from Hosea's time. Yet contrary to the common view, these characteristics provide evidence for seeing all of 2:1–25 as an original rhetorical unit that would have made sense in Hosea's context.

A few scholars have previously argued that all of Hos 2 is the product of a single act of composition by a single speaker/author. Cassuto offered the most detailed treatment of this position.[36] He began by affirming that 2:1–3 does not fit easily as a part of the material in 1:2–9 because it does not continue the theme of reproof in those verses. Additionally, he maintained that 2:1–3 contains many parallels with 2:23–25 that indicate the two parts stand within the same rhetorical unit. For instance, both 2:1 and 2:23 begin with the transitional וְהָיָה and both 2:2 and 2:23 refer to "day" (יוֹם) and "land" (אֶרֶץ).[37] By paying attention to these elements, Cassuto concluded that 2:1–3 represents not a later addition but the "prologue" that states the goals of the oracle to follow.[38] He recognized that between the beginning and ending sections, one can identify a chiastic structure of three stanzas (2:4–6), ten stanzas (2:7–17), and finally another group of three stanzas (2:18–22).[39] In addition to these more subjective observations, however, Cassuto also correctly noted that this structural unity is complemented by continuity in the "inner content" of all of chapter 2. The themes, motifs, and language of 2:1–25 constitute a coherent movement and dividing the unit redactionally breaks this movement and renders the individual parts rhetorically powerless.[40]

---

[35] Renaud, "Genèse," 2–3. He maintains, however, that 2:4–7, 10–15 were the original units to which the other parts were added. Cf. Davies (*Hosea* [OTG], 32), who takes all of 1:2–2:3 as a unit compiled by later writers and sees 2:4–25 as a collection of various prophetic sayings from different historical settings that has been unified and structured as a single unit. Buss (*Prophetic Word*, 47) also views Hos 2 as consisting of a number of smaller original units that have now been "welded together into a relatively smooth unit."

[36] Cassuto, "Second Chapter," 101–40. For this same view, see also E. Galbiati, "La Struttura sintetica di Osea 2," in *Studi Sull 'Oriente e la Bibbia* (ed. G. Buccelatti; Genova: Editrice Studio e Vita, 1967), 317–28.

[37] Cassuto, "Second Chapter," 101–3.

[38] Ibid., 118.

[39] Ibid., 106–8.

[40] Ibid., 140.

Hubbard has also previously concluded that all of Hos 2:1–25 is an original rhetorical unit. Like Cassuto, he noted that 2:1–3 forms an original and integral part of the movement of the whole and may represent Hosea's positive view of Judah's dynastic stability in his time.[41] Hubbard further observed that several factors indicate that 2:18–25 functions well as a unified piece with 2:1–17 and should not be seen as a redactional addition: 1) both parts deal with the future, 2) the references to Yahweh and בעל fit with the chapter as a whole, and 3) the covenant language reverses the threats in 2:12.

Several other factors suggest at least the possibility of considering Hos 2:1–25 to be a single rhetorical address from a particular rhetorical situation. First, concerning the often-disputed verses in 2:1–3, one can develop further Cassuto's notion that these verses function as a prologue and thus are integral to the chapter as a whole. As Jeremias observes, the language in 2:1–3 is impersonal and not direct address in which Yahweh declares what he will do.[42] Rather, verses 1–3 seem to function as the prophet's own introduction that sets the stage for Yahweh's direct speech in the rest of the oracle.[43]

Additionally, a close analysis of the text suggests that the clearest division of rhetorical units occurs not between 2:3 and 2:4 but between 1:9 and 2:1. For example, 2:1 has a marked beginning with the transitional term והיה that indicates a change from the temporal setting (past to future), style (prose to poetry), and subject (Hosea's children to the people of Israel and Judah) of 1:9. Unlike its appearance in 2:18, והיה here has a disjunctive function and is not clearly connected as a development of the material in 1:9.[44] Furthermore, 2:1 marks a change in speaker from the address of Yahweh in 1:9 to the speech of the prophet in 2:1. In contrast to Yahweh's speech in 1:9, 2:1 refers to Yahweh in the third-person as the "living god." The first verse of chapter 2 also marks a significant change in mood from judgment to restoration that, again unlike 2:18, is disjunctive and does not follow from what precedes. One should further note that 2:1–3 has no formal link with chapter 1 with the exception of the children's names. The use of these names in 2:1–3, however, forms a much stronger link with their occurrences in 2:24–25.[45]

When taken together, these elements constitute a strong case for considering 2:1 as the beginning of a rhetorical unit.[46] As noted above, however, there are also links that indicate 2:1–3 is of a piece with the material that follows. Both verses 3 and 4 begin with imperatives that link them together

---

[41] Hubbard, *Hosea*, 31–32.
[42] Jeremias, *Der Prophet*, 34.
[43] For further discussion, see chapter 7 below.
[44] Accordingly, some English translations, like the NRSV, render the vav as "Yet."
[45] See Ward, *Hosea*, 24.
[46] Emmerson (*Hosea*, 95) views this evidence as so strong that she asserts, "That 2:1 is clearly marked off from 1:9 and begins a new unit *needs no argument*."

stylistically.[47] Separating 2:1–3 from the following verses breaks both the stylistic and thematic structure of the discourse. Furthermore, the recognition of 2:1–3's importance within the whole unit helps to resolve the difficulty that Landy observes concerning how to reconcile the violence of 2:4–15 with the sudden bliss of 2:16–25.[48] The prophet's introduction in 2:1–3 prepares the reader for the whole movement from judgment to restoration.

There is also an overall consistency of themes, styles, and motifs throughout verses 1–25. The chapter as a whole is bound together by several word repetitions. For example, 2:2–3 and 2:24–25 refer to the three symbolic names of Hosea's children and give them positive interpretations.[49] The use of the metaphor of family relationships (brothers, sisters, mother, wife) to designate certain groups within Israel is also a consistent motif that remains prevalent to the end of the oracle. The primary metaphorical terms of "lovers" and בעל appear throughout the chapter, and the motif of remarriage in 2:21–23 depends upon and refers back to the imagery of divorce in the earlier section of 2:4–6. Moreover, the metaphorical restoration that is envisioned by 2:23–25 depends upon the more explicit description of the nature of that restoration that is provided in the introduction of 2:1–3. The cryptic pronouncement that Yahweh will "sow" his wife in the land (2:25) makes sense only in light of the prophet's introduction that sets forth the restoration of the people (2:1–3).

Finally, research on writing and orality in prophetic texts suggests another indication of unity for Hos 2.[50] In an investigation of poetic elements that indicate both original orality and original unity, Boadt observes the importance of features like structural unity, dramatic sequence/movement, repetition, direct address to the audience, and dramatic echoes between two contrasting halves. In his view, the presence of these elements in a prophetic text makes it likely that the text "reflects in writing what was a style of public oration and oracular proclamation, and was oriented toward persuasion to action (its verbal quality)."[51] These elements suggest that a passage stands close to its "oral origins" and therefore close to the "original prophet."[52] The preceding discussion has highlighted that precisely these characteristics are at work in Hos 2.

In conclusion, while a reader may divide Hos 2 into various subparts for the sake of analysis, there does not appear to be sufficient reason for viewing these parts as originally separate rhetorical units. While it is impossible to say for sure that 2:1–25 was conceived as a unit in its original formation, there does not

---

[47] Wolff, *Hosea*, 32; Sweeney, *The Twelve Prophets*, 11–12; Hubbard, *Hosea*, 72.

[48] Landy, *Hosea*, 31.

[49] Cf. Abma, *Bonds*, 155.

[50] For general treatments of this issue, see E. Ben Zvi and M. Floyd, eds., *Writings and Speech in Israelite and Ancient Near Eastern Prophecy* (SBLSymS 10; Atlanta: SBL, 2000).

[51] Boadt, "Poetry," 10, 14–15.

[52] Ibid., 21.

seem to be adequate warrant for doubting the text's own indications of unity. As noted above, the primary question for this type of analysis is to what extent the text looks like a product of a single act of composition in a particular rhetorical situation. If a text possesses an overall consistency of language, imagery, and themes, it is reasonable to conclude that an interpreter can argue for the presence of a redactional addition only when he or she can see a part of the text that is *not* rhetorically or literarily consistent with the whole. There are no such elements in Hos 2:1–25. The chapter consists of various thematic, metaphorical, and structural elements that cannot and should not be separated from one another. Furthermore, no compelling reason exists to deny this original "act" to the eighth-century prophet Hosea. There are no historical references (like references to Judah) that do not fit his time, and the major metaphors and the meanings they carry are in keeping with the prophet's period. Additionally, as the following chapters will demonstrate more clearly, the terminology and thoughts in the whole unit, which provide a logical movement and development, are not out of place in eighth-century Israel. Even so, as is often the case with rhetorical addresses, 2:1–3 and 2:4–25 *function* as distinct parts of the same speech. The reader should not be surprised that the following analysis deals with the two sections separately. Such organization reflects the parts' distinct rhetorical functions and does not imply their original disunity.

2. THE RHETORICAL HORIZON

In the preceding chapters, each of the oracle's major metaphors has been examined in light of its supporting biblical and extrabiblical traditions and the meaning that those traditions supply for the metaphors in Hosea's speech. At this point, effort must be made to pull together these findings and to examine the overall rhetorical "horizon" of the address. As discussed above in chapter 2, the rhetorical horizon consists of the context and conditions presupposed by and reflected in the text that the reader may attempt to correlate with a particular rhetorical-historical situation. These references, allusions, and images are then examined in light of a reconstruction of historical events drawn from biblical and extrabiblical sources in order that the reader may hypothesize a plausible rhetorical-historical situation in which the text may have originated and initially functioned. The rhetorical horizon is thus a textual phenomenon, that is, the text's "implied situation" that uses and reflects certain portions of the data from a particular historical situation.

The prophet's speech in Hos 2 presupposes and implies several general conditions in its various metaphors, motifs, statements, and allusions. First, a central feature of Hos 2 is the presupposition and indication of a conflict situation. The language of conflict and resolution runs throughout the oracle (e.g., ריב in 2:4, פקד in 2:15, ארש in 2:21). One can also see this conflict situation in the terminology pairs throughout the oracle: "mother-sons," "husband-wife," "husband-lovers." Second, although the conflict in the text most directly concerns Yahweh and his metaphorical wife, several factors point to an inner-Israelite struggle between two competing groups. On the one hand, Yahweh has a conflict with a certain group of Israelites described as his "wife" because they have abandoned him and given their allegiance to other "lovers" (2:4–7). On the other hand, certain statements and allusions point to actions taken within the populations of Israel and Judah. For example, 2:1–3 depicts Israel and Judah campaigning (עלה) in concert in order to bring about the "day of Jezreel," an allusion to inner-Israelite bloodshed of the past (cf. Hos 1:4). The text also calls upon brothers and sisters to address one another (2:3) and children to contend with their mother (2:4). A third condition indicated by the text appears in the references to joint actions undertaken by both Israel and Judah (2:2). These expressions suggest that the text presupposes a time when both states were still in existence and sees both states as somehow involved in the civil strife being addressed.

The major metaphors in Hos 2 make it is possible to describe more specifically the nature of the conflict situation envisaged by the oracle. As noted above, the evidence of comparative traditions indicates that the metaphorical wife/mother represents a personified capital city, likely Samaria. The group of people specifically represented by a personified Samaria would probably be the political officials and the ruling house holding power in the capital city. Thus, the text seems to indicate that the offending party in society is particularly the royal family and political leaders. Additionally, the tendency of the prophetic texts to personify capital cities as women primarily in contexts of imminent, threatened, or present destruction combines with the metaphorical language of stripping and exposure in Hos 2 to expand the focus on the political leaders (e.g., 2:5, 11–12). The prophet's oracle presupposes not only a conflict involving the capital city and its ruling house but also a situation in which that city faces an immediate threat of punishment. Verses 18–25, however, clearly envision restoration to a new status for the people after the judgment. The oracle gives no indication that it presupposes a final destruction of the people on the level of the Assyrian or Babylonian exile or any other major deportation.

Another condition implied by the oracle appears in the metaphors of fornication and adultery. The above discussion of these metaphors emphasized that they rest on a tradition that often uses them to refer to improper political actions. In such a context, זנה and נאף imply an act of disobedience with regard to Yahweh's will in the political realm. One may imagine this disobedience to include actions like the breaking of a Yahweh-sanctioned policy or treaty. In the text's implied situation, these rebellious political acts of the ruling house are the very things that have precipitated the imminent destruction envisaged by the oracle (2:4–7). The text's metaphorical terms "lovers" (אהב) and בעל presuppose a similar situation. The previous discussion of these terms demonstrated that they also draw their meanings from a well-substantiated biblical and extrabiblical tradition that uses them to refer to political allies and/or overlords. The speech thus suggests a rhetorical horizon in which the leaders of the capital city Samaria have sought out illicit political relationships with foreign allies that constitute an abandonment of Yahweh and work to their detriment (2:7, 10). The tradition of using the term בעל to designate a political overlord suggests that the text envisions a situation in which Samaria has become involved with and/or submitted to a dominant political ruler in conjunction with other treaty-partners (cf. the singular use of בעל in 2:10, 18).

These rhetorical elements suggest that political issues are the central concern envisaged by Hosea's speech. Even the reference to burning incense to the בעלים (2:15), the text's only overtly religious reference, does not seem to indicate or presuppose a rampant religious apostasy with other gods but an action dictated by a specific situation. The text never uses terms such as "serve" (עבד) or "bow down" (השתחוה) to characterize Samaria's actions with the lovers or בעלים.[53] Rather, as will be shown, the situationally conditioned actions reflected in verse 15 may presuppose limited cultic activity with other peoples and their deities commonly undertaken as part of political treaty ceremonies among allies in the ancient Near East.[54]

When viewed as a whole, the above considerations provide a clear picture of the rhetorical horizon implied by Hos 2. The capital city Samaria and its ruling house have entered into political relationships with an overlord and/or allies that the prophet deems to be outside of Yahweh's will for the nation. These actions have produced a situation in which competing groups are in conflict within Israel and the capital city itself faces a threat of imminent destruction. Nonetheless, the text also envisions an end to the conflict and a restoration of the capital city to good standing before Yahweh. The approaching conflict seems to be a means to affect change and to rectify a rebellious situation.

3. THE RHETORICAL-HISTORICAL SITUATION

The conditions and presuppositions of Hos 2's rhetorical horizon point most closely to one particular period in Israelite and Judean history: the period of civil war between Hoshea and Pekah at the close of the Syro-Ephraimitic crisis in 731–730 B.C.E. This historical situation centered on the control of Samaria, featured an attack on the capital city, and involved the issue of political relationships/treaties vis á vis Assyria and Damascus. Additionally, the events at the end of the Syro-Ephraimitic war included the inner-Israelite effort to overthrow Pekah, who had executed a coup in Samaria, broken treaty relationships with Assyria, and involved Israel in an alliance with anti-Assyrian

---

[53] Contrast the description of Manasseh's actions with the baals in 2 Kgs 21:3 and 2 Chron 33:3.

[54] See discussion of 2:15 below in chapter 8.

states. Hoshea, who had been designated as the new ruler by the Assyrian king, Tiglath-pileser III, moved to capture Samaria and restore the previous divinely-sanctioned treaty relationship with Assyria. As the following discussion aims to show, although this specific context has never been proposed as the rhetorical-historical situation for *all* of Hos 2:1–25, it accounts for all the elements of the oracle's rhetorical horizon.

Numerous scholarly works offer extensive studies of this particular period.[55] Since the oracle in Hos 2 is directly concerned with the personified capital city of Samaria and the personalities and conflicts that she represents, the present discussion will outline the generally agreed-upon reconstruction of the Syro-Ephraimitic war and the issues connected to it but ultimately proceed to a closer analysis of the specific role and fate of the capital city in these events.

3.1 Reconstructing the Syro-Ephraimitic War

Three primary biblical texts relate to and/or describe the events of the Syro-Ephraimitic war: 2 Kgs 16:1–18, 2 Chron 28:1–25, and Isa 7:1–17.[56] The primary historiographical account in 2 Kgs 16 contains two relevant portions. Verses 5–9 describe the events of the Syro-Ephraimitic crisis. This section is immediately followed by a description of the cultic reforms of Ahaz in verses 10–18. The structure of this chapter gives the impression that the climactic event of the entire crisis was Ahaz's submission to Assyria and that this event resulted in numerous cultic sins on the part of the king. Upon closer analysis, however, the two major sections seem to have been secondarily connected by the deuteronomistic editors.[57] For instance, the two sections use differing ways of

---

[55] For the primary scholarly works on the Syro-Ephraimitic war see A. Alt, "Tiglathpilesers III: erster Feldzug nach Palästina," in *Kleine Schriften der Geschichte des Volkes Israel II* (Munich: C. H. Beck, 1953–1959), 150–63; J. Asurmendi, *La Guerra Siro-Efraimita: Historia y profetas* (Valencia: Institutión San Jerónimo, 1982); J. Begrich, "Der syrisch-ephraimitische Krieg und seine weltpolitischen Zusammenhänge," *ZDMG* 83 (1927): 213–37; H. Cazelles, "Problemes de la guerre syro-ephraimite," *ErIsr* 14 (1978): 70–78; H. Cazelles, "Syro-Ephraimite War," *ABD* 6:282–85; H. Donner, *Israel unter den Völkern: Die Stellung der klassischen Propheten des 8. Jahrhunderts v. Chr. zur Aussenpolitik der Könige von Israel und Juda* (VTSup 11; Leiden: Brill, 1964), 1–63; H. Donner, "The Separate States of Israel and Judah," in *Israelite and Judaean History* (eds. J. H. Hayes and J. M. Miller; Philadelphia: Westminster, 1977), 421–32; S. Irvine, *Isaiah, Ahaz, and the Syro-Ephraimitic Crisis* (SBLDS 123; Atlanta: Scholars Press, 1990); J. Kuan, *Neo-Assyrian Historical Inscriptions and Syria-Palestine* (Jian Dao Dissertation Series 1; Hong Kong: Alliance Bible Seminary, 1995); B. Oded, "The Historical Background of the Syro-Ephraimite War Reconsidered," *CBQ* 34 (1972): 153–65; M. Thompson, *Situation and Theology: Old Testament Interpretations of the Syro-Ephraimite War* (Prophets and Historians 1; Sheffield: Almond, 1982); R. Tomes, "The Reason for the Syro-Ephraimite War," *JSOT* 59 (1993): 55–71.

[56] For an extensive comparative analysis of these texts and their role in the reconstruction of this period, see Irvine, *Isaiah*, 75–95.

[57] Ibid., 79.

referring to Ahaz ("Ahaz" in 16:5–9; "King Ahaz" or "the king" in 16:10–18) and different spellings of the name "Tiglath-pileser" (פלסר תגלת in 16:7; תגלת פלאסר in 16:10). The editors appear to have joined these two sections in order to connect Ahaz's religious apostasy with his political allegiance to Assyria. Several commentators rightly conclude that the passage as a whole is not a reproduction of official court records but a rewritten source from a deuteronomistic editor.[58]

Second Kings 16:5–9 would then appear to offer the most useful material for historical reconstruction since it does not center on theological evaluations of Ahaz's cultic policies. These verses describe the Syro-Ephraimitic attack by noting that Rezin and Pekah besieged Ahaz but "were not able to fight" (16:5, יכלו להלחם). Since verse 5 also makes clear that they did "advance on Jerusalem," the Hebrew לחם here must have the meaning of "to prevail" or "to conquer" as it does in Isa 7:1.[59] Verses 5–9 also mention that Rezin captured the Judean city of Elath for Aram and that Edomites came to settle there. Verse 6 states, "At that time, Rezin the king of Aram restored Elath to Aram; he drove out the Judeans from Elath, and Edomites came to Elath and settled there until this day." This verse presents many problems for both translation and interpretation. For example, several versions read the term "Edomites" as "Arameans" and suggest that Damascus had previously held the Judean city of Elath and Rezin recaptured it.[60] On the other hand, some scholars remove Rezin as a gloss and read "Edom" (אדם) for "Aram" (ארם) throughout the verse.[61] Irvine, however, argues on the basis of the historical evidence for Syria's prominence at this time that Rezin may be original and that he may have aided the Edomites in taking Elath at this time.[62] Whatever the exact referent of this verse, it testifies to the loss of Judean territory during Judah's conflict with Damascus and Israel. The account in 2 Kgs 16:5–9 concludes by mentioning that Ahaz appealed for help to Tiglath-pileser III by sending him a "bribe" (שחד) consisting of gold and silver from the temple and palace. According to verse 9, Tiglath-pileser's siege and capture of Damascus was the direct result of Ahaz's appeal.[63]

---

[58] H. Tadmor and M. Cogan, "Ahaz and Tiglath-Pileser in the Book of Kings: Historiographical Considerations," *Bib* 60 (1979): 506; cf. Irvine, *Isaiah*, 88.

[59] Isaiah 7:1 includes the clarifying preposition עליה ("against it").

[60] The MT ketib and some manuscripts of the Syriac, Targum, and Vulgate presuppose the Hebrew וארמים ("Arameans"). By contrast, the MT qere, LXX, and other manuscripts of the Targum and Vulgate presuppose ואדמים ("Edomites").

[61] J. Gray, *I and II Kings* (OTL; Philadelphia: Westminster, 1963), 573 and G. H. Jones, *1 and 2 Kings* (2 vols.; NCB; Grand Rapids: Eerdmans, 1984), 2.535.

[62] Irvine, *Isaiah*, 84–85.

[63] The language and construction of the verse makes this causal relationship clear by placing the actions in an imperfect-imperfect verb sequence in which the second verb denotes the consequence of the first: "And the king of Assyria listened/responded (וישמע) to him; so the king of Assyria campaigned (ויעל) against Damascus ..." (16:9).

The second major biblical text relating to the Syro-Ephraimitic war is 2 Chron 28:1–25. The writer of Chronicles reports a series of separate yet related events that devastated Judah. First, the text describes a Syrian attack against Ahaz in which the king of Aram took many captives (28:5). Next, the writer mentions an attack against Judah by Pekah, who is reported to have killed 120,000 Judeans (28:5–6). Following these events, 2 Chron 28 reports an event not mentioned in any other text. Verse 7 states that Zichri, an Ephraimite, killed Ahaz's son, the commander of the palace, and the second-in-command of the king. Thereupon, 28:8–15 describes another attack against Judah by the Israelites who captured 200,000 Judeans and took a large amount of spoil. The text reports, however, that the Samarian army subsequently returned the captives and booty upon the advice of a prophet named Oded. Finally, verses 16–18 state that Ahaz appealed for help to Tiglath-pileser specifically with regard to the aggressive actions of the Edomites and Philistines, who were taking Judean territory. Ironically, 28:20 reports that the king of Assyria actually marched against Ahaz rather than supported him. Throughout the Chronicler's account, the writer adumbrates the religious causes of these events (cf. 28:19) and presents Ahaz's religious apostasy as the primary reason for the historical-political circumstances.[64] The Chronicler has subsumed all historical considerations under the controlling framework of his theological evaluation of Ahaz as a Davidic king.

The third major biblical text that deals with the Syro-Ephraimitic crisis is Isa 7:1–17. This text is primarily a presentation of a series of encounters between Isaiah and Ahaz with the attack of Rezin and Pekah[65] as a backdrop. The chapter's opening verses are parallel to the report in 2 Kgs 16:5–6. Verses 1–2 summarize the events by reporting that Rezin and Pekah marched against Jerusalem but were "unable to prevail against it (ולא יכל להלחם עליה)." This text adds the detail of the reason for the Syro-Ephraimitic attack: Rezin and Pekah intended to replace Ahaz with "the son of Tabeel."[66] Perhaps the most important contribution that Isa 7:1–17 makes to the historical reconstruction of these events, however, is that it makes no mention of an appeal or payment made by Ahaz to the Assyrian king.

---

[64] Irvine (*Isaiah*, 93–94) observes that the writer's theological interests have shaped this account to make three primary affirmations: 1) the religious sins of Ahaz made him the worst king of Judah, 2) the attacks of these enemies were punishments by Yahweh for Ahaz's religious apostasy, and 3) Ahaz did not repent in the time of trouble.

[65] Perhaps for rhetorical reasons, Isaiah never calls Pekah by his name but only by the title "son of Remaliah."

[66] The debate concerning this name and the identity of the historical person referred to lies beyond the scope of this discussion. See J. Blenkinsopp, *Isaiah 1–39* (AB 19; New York: Doubleday, 2000), 230 and J. A. Dearman, "The Son of Tabeel (Isaiah 7.6): History of Interpretation and Extra-biblical Sources," in *Prophets and Paradigms: Essays in Honor of Gene M. Tucker* (ed. S. Reid; JSOTSup 229; Sheffield: Sheffield Academic Press, 1996), 33–47.

In addition to these three major texts, scholars often attempt to relate other selected passages to the general background of the Syro-Ephraimitic conflict. Perhaps the most well-known of such proposals concerns Hos 5:8–6:6. In an article originally published in 1919, Alt argues that this text reports on a Judean counterattack against Israel immediately following the end of the siege of Jerusalem.[67] There is, however, no evidence for such a Judean counterattack, and Arnold has recently offered a detailed refutation of Alt's theory while maintaining the connection of this text with the general background of the Syro-Ephraimitic war.[68] He particularly examines the place names and geographical detail and suggests that the oracle describes the initial Israelite march against Jerusalem.[69]

As the above discussion shows, texts like 2 Kgs 16 and 2 Chron 28 relate only those events that directly concern the kingdoms of Israel and Judah and focus on theological matters and ideological evaluations. Because of this fact, the Assyrian historical inscriptions of Tiglath-pileser III provide important supplementary information for historical reconstruction.[70] Several of these inscriptions relate to events in Syria-Palestine leading up to and during the Syro-Ephraimitic conflict. The relevant Assyrian inscriptions include the following:

1. Layard 45b+III R 9, 1 (Tadmor Ann. 21): This text is the earliest relevant text of Tiglath-pileser III and dates to around 743–740 B.C.E.[71] The inscription details the tribute paid by Rezin of Damascus and other neighboring states but does not mention Samaria. Nonetheless, some scholars maintain that the inscription has lost the phrase "Menahem of the land of Samaria" and it should be restored in the available space.[72]

---

[67] Alt, "Hosea 5, 8–6, 6," 537–68. One of the main reasons for this view is that the order of the cities listed appears to form a line moving northward toward Samaria from the area of Jerusalem. So also Mays, *Hosea*, 85–89; Jeremias, *Der Prophet*, 80–82; Wolff, *Hosea*, 103–30.

[68] P. Arnold, *Gibeah: The Search for a Biblical City* (JSOTSup 79; Sheffield: JSOT Press, 1990), 112–15.

[69] In addition to this Hosean text and Hos 2:1–25, two other texts also likely reflect the rhetorical-historical situation of the Syro-Ephraimitic war. Micah 4:9–5:14 is an oracle of Micah proclaiming the ultimate failure of the coalition's siege of Jerusalem (see Shaw, "Speeches," 243–49). Deuteronomy 32 (the "Song of Moses") is an oracle from the prophet Hosea delivered on the occasion of Hoshea's assault on Pekah at the close of the war (see J. H. Chong, "The Song of Moses [Deuteronomy 32:1–43] and the Hoshea-Pekah Conflict" [Ph.D. diss., Emory University, 1990]).

[70] See H. Tadmor, *The Inscriptions of Tiglath-Pileser III King of Assyria* (Jerusalem: Israel Academy of Sciences and Humanities, 1994). Tadmor classifies the inscriptions as follows: 1) annals which are chronologically arranged (including series A with seven lines per column, series B with twelve lines per column, and series C with more lines per column) and 2) summary inscriptions that are geographically arranged (ibid., 10, 22–23).

[71] There is no consensus regarding the date of this text, but it appears to predate the Iran Stela, which is more securely dated to 739–738 (for full discussion of dating see Kuan, *Neo-Assyrian Historical Inscriptions*, 141).

[72] See Tadmor, *Inscriptions*, 276.

2. Iran Stela: This text is a fragmentary summary inscription found in western Iran.[73] Column II, lines 1–23 preserve a list of Anatolian and Syro-Palestinian rulers on whom Tiglath-pileser III imposed tribute. This list includes "Menahem of the land of Samaria." The inscription seems to date to the time of Tiglath-pileser's Ulluba campaign in 739–738 because it presupposes a period when the Assyrian army was in Iran and names Tubail as the king of Tyre rather than Hiram, who was involved in the 734–732 campaign.[74]

3. Layard 50a+50b+67a: This inscription is a fragmentary annals text that consists of twenty-four lines recording Tiglath-pileser's military achievements in his eighth and ninth palê (738–737 and 737–736). The discussion of these achievements includes the receipt of tribute from western states in Syria-Palestine and mentions "Menahem of the city of Samaria." The text is nearly identical to the Iran Stela and scholars are virtually unanimous in dating the tribute list to 738–737 because of the text's later reference to the ninth palû.[75]

4. II R 67: This text is a fragment of a long summary inscription of Tiglath-pileser that summarizes the king's achievements in his first seventeen palê. Line 11 of the reverse contains a tribute list that mentions "Jehoahaz of the land of Judah." The tribute list should be dated prior to 733 because it refers to "Mitini of the land of Ashkelon," who was deposed by 733–732.[76] This text is the only reference to Judah in the Assyrian inscriptions prior to 720 B.C.E.

5. Layard 29b: There is much debate about whether to reconstruct this text to include a reference to the northern kingdom. The inscription describes Tiglath-pileser's campaign against Syro-Ephraimitic states after he left Philistia in 733. The relevant portion of the text is broken but refers to Assyria's capture of a certain district's territories in the Galilee region (ll. 230ff). The text may be reconstructed to indicate that these territories belonged either to "Bit-[Hazael]" or "Bit-[Humri]."[77] The reconstruction has implications concerning the size and status of the northern kingdom in the waning years of the conflict.

6. Layard 66: This text describes events at the end of the Syro-Ephraimitic war. The inscription is a fragmentary annals text that records Assyrian campaigns in the west from 732 to 731, including the subjugation of Queen

---

[73] For the original publication, see T. Levine, *Two Neo-Assyrian Stelae from Iran* (Toronto: Royal Ontario Museum, 1972). For a complete reading of the stela, see Tadmor, *Inscriptions*, 91–110.

[74] The text must precede Layard 50a+50b+67a because that text names Hiram as the king of Tyre. See also the Mila Mergi Rock Relief and the Eponym Chronicle. Kuan dates the text to 739–738 (*Neo-Assyrian Historical Inscriptions*, 151) while Levine dates it to the 737 campaign to Media (*Two Neo-Assyrian Stelae*, 14).

[75] See T. Levine, "Menahem and Tiglath-Pileser: A New Synchronism," *BASOR* 206 (1972): 40–42.

[76] For discussion of dating, see Irvine, *Isaiah*, 40–44.

[77] For example, Tadmor reconstructs "Bit-Humri" but allows that "Bit-Hazael" is possible (*Inscriptions*, 80–81).

Shamshi of Arabia.[78] The description in line 228 refers to Tiglath-pileser's treatment of "the city of Samaria."

7. III R 10, 2: This summary inscription from Nimrud also relates to the close of the Syro-Ephraimitic war. However, the text is not chronologically but geographically arranged and comes not from the time of the events themselves but from the period after Tiglath-pileser had settled affairs in Syria-Palestine.[79] At this stage in the course of events, the Assyrian scribes refer to the land of "Bit-Ḫumri."

8. ND 4301+4305: This final relevant text consists of two fragments of a clay tablet and essentially parallels III R 10, 2.[80] Since this text mentions Hoshea's payment of tribute to Tiglath-pileser at Sarrabanu in Babylon (l. 10), it seems to come from the time after Tiglath-pileser had settled affairs in Syria-Palestine and left the region. As with III R 10, 2, this inscription refers to the border of the land of "Bit-Ḫumri" (ll. 3–4).

By utilizing the above biblical and extrabiblical texts, scholars have outlined a generally agreed-upon reconstruction of the main events of the Syro-Ephraimitic war between the years of 734 and 731 B.C.E.[81] The starting point of this course of events was a widespread anti-Assyrian movement in Syria-Palestine in the years leading up to 734. The various Assyrian lists of those who paid tribute and those who were subjugated during this period indicated that the primary anti-Assyrian participants in this conflict included Rezin of Damascus, Pekah of Israel, Hiram of Tyre, Mitini of Ashkelon, Shamshi of Arabia, and possibly Hanno of Gaza. These Assyrian texts consistently ascribed the prominent role in the rebellion to Rezin of Damascus (e.g., Layard 23b and ND 4301+4305), and the Eponym Chronicle noted that the Assyrian army remained in the Damascus region for the span of two consecutive New Year's festivals (733–732 and 732–731 B.C.E.).[82]

Perhaps in response to this rebellion or perhaps for other reasons,[83] Tiglath-pileser III campaigned to the west in 734–733 B.C.E. and moved down the coast to attack Philistia (Eponym List and ND 400). This assault was immediately followed by campaigns to Gaza and the "brook of Egypt" (Wadi Besor; ND

---

[78] See ibid., 202–3.

[79] For discussion, see H. Tadmor, "The Southern Border of Aram," *IEJ* 12 (1962): 116 and Kuan, *Neo-Assyrian Historical Inscriptions*, 177.

[80] For the original publication, see D. J. Wiseman, "A Fragmentary Inscription of Tiglath-pileser III from Nimrud," *Iraq* 18 (1956): 117–29.

[81] For a concise, point-by-point listing of the consensus views, see Irvine, *Isaiah*, 69–72.

[82] A. Millard and H. Tadmor ("Adad-nirari III in Syria: Another Stele Fragment and the Dates of His Campaigns," *Iraq* 35 [1973]: 62) have argued that the location given on the Eponym list is that of the army at the time of the Akitu festival and not the target of the military campaign. So also Kuan, *Neo-Assyrian Historical Inscriptions*, 99. Millard has clarified that the location is specifically that of the army, with or without the king. See A. Millard, *The Eponyms of the Assyrian Empire 910–612 BC* (SAAS 2; Helsinki: The Neo-Assyrian Text Corpus Project, 1994), 4–5.

[83] See discussion below.

400). Around this time, according to the inscription II R 67, Ahaz of Judah and several other local rulers offered tribute. Rezin and Pekah, as well as others, apparently did not pay tribute but continued their resistance to Assyria for at least two more years. The Assyrian army besieged Damascus from 733–731 B.C.E. (Eponym List) and captured the capital city (Layard 72b+73a; ND 4301+4305), seized cities in Bashan, Golan, and Galilee (Layard 29b), and provincialized all territories previously held by Damascus (III R 10, 2). They also moved against Shamshi of Arabia (Layard 66; ND 400; ND 4301+4305; III R 10, 2) and Hiram of Tyre (ND 4301+4305), both of whom submitted and were allowed to remain on the throne, as well as against Mitini of Ashkelon, who was deposed and killed by his own subjects (Layard 29b). By the time of the close of the campaign, however, the Assyrians had not moved against Pekah of Israel. Rather, a rebellion broke out in Israel led by Hoshea sometime around 732 B.C.E., apparently with the approval of the Assyrian king.[84] Samaria was eventually captured, Pekah was deposed, and Hoshea sent tribute to Tiglath-pileser in Babylon (Layard 66; ND 4301+4305; III R 10, 2; 2 Kgs 15:30).

Within these general points of agreement concerning the course of events, there are some finer points of disagreement. The three most prominent of these issues concern the purpose of the Syro-Ephraimite attack on Jerusalem, the purpose and timing of Tiglath-pileser's campaign to Philistia, and Ahaz's so-called appeal (or "bribe," cf. 2 Kgs 16:8) for Assyrian intervention.

Regarding the question of the purpose of the Syro-Ephraimitic attack against Ahaz and Jerusalem, Begrich popularized the idea that there was an intimate connection between the attack on Jerusalem and anti-Assyrian activities in Syria-Palestine.[85] In this regard, he was initially arguing against scholars like Meissner, who saw the Syro-Ephraimitic war as a purely inner-Palestinian conflict.[86] In Begrich's view, the purpose of Rezin and Pekah's siege of Jerusalem was to force Judah into a coalition being formed to rebel against Assyrian vassalage and resist the Assyrians when they returned to the west.[87] Although Donner conceived of a slightly different sequence of events, he also argued that the purpose of the attack against Ahaz was to solidify and/or force Judah's participation in the growing anti-Assyrian coalition led by Damascus.[88]

---

[84] Cazelles argues that Hoshea assassinated Pekah before Damascus fell to the Assyrians, i.e., around 733 ("Syro-Ephraimite War," 284; cf. Cazelles, "Problemes," 70–78).

[85] See Begrich, "Der syrisch-ephraimitische Krieg," 213–37.

[86] See B. Meissner, *Könige Babyloniens und Assyriens* (Leipzig: Quelle & Meyer, 1926), 164. Tomes ("Reason," 59) has recently pointed out that although Begrich popularized this position, the first to make the connection with Assyrian activities was August Knobel in the first edition (1853) of his Isaiah commentary (*Der Prophet Jesaia* [2d ed.; Kurzgefasstes exegetisches Handbuch zum Alten Testament 5; Leipzig: S. Hirzel, 1854], 52–53).

[87] Begrich, "Der syrisch-ephraimitische Krieg," 216–20.

[88] Donner, *Israel unter den Völkern*, 61–63 and "Separate States," 429–32. So also Irvine, *Isaiah*, 104.

Oded, however, picked up the older view of Meissner and maintained that the Syro-Ephraimitic war was strictly an inner-Palestinian conflict that had no relation to Assyria.[89] In his view, the conflict was the result of a battle among Syria, Israel, and Judah for control of territories in the Transjordan.[90] Tomes has recently revitalized Oded's position and argued that no Assyrian text indicates the reason for the Syro-Ephraimitic attack on Jerusalem and the reason must be surmised from the biblical texts.[91] Even these texts, however, described different reasons for the event. In this regard, he emphasized that if there had been an anti-Assyrian coalition, one would expect the Assyrians to mention it as they did with the previous coalition that included Hadadezer of Damascus and Ahab of Israel in the time of Shalmaneser III.[92]

A similar debate has surrounded the issue of the timing of Tiglath-pileser's campaign to the west in 733 B.C.E. in relationship to the Syro-Ephraimitic attack on Jerusalem. Begrich initially argued that the siege of Jerusalem must have taken place before the Assyrian campaign to Philistia in order to solidify the coalition for resistance.[93] Yet Donner, who also understood the aim of the attack to be forcing Judah's participation in a coalition, concluded that such a move took place only after (i.e., in response to) the Assyrian campaign to Philistia.[94] His primary evidence for this conclusion was that the Assyrian texts do not indicate that Tiglath-pileser's campaign was a response to an anti-Assyrian rebellion. Donner reconstructed a sequence of events in which the Assyrians campaigned to Gaza in 734–733 B.C.E. but then left Syria-Palestine for approximately a year. This reconstruction, although unsupported by the inscriptional evidence, allowed Donner to shift the siege of Jerusalem to after the initial Assyrian campaign to the west.

The final issue on which there is some disagreement, the so-called payment or bribe of Ahaz in order to secure Assyrian intervention, has not received the same amount of attention. Regardless of their views of the purpose and timing of the campaigns, the majority of scholars have taken the biblical presentation that Ahaz made a special appeal for an Assyrian campaign to the west (cf. 2 Kgs 16; 2 Chron 28) as the key to explaining Assyrian actions against Damascus and Samaria in 733–731 B.C.E. For example, although Oded explained the Syro-Ephraimitic war as a land dispute that had nothing to do with Assyrian interests, he maintained that Tiglath-pileser got involved because of a request from the king of Judah.[95]

---

[89] Oded, "Historical Background," 153–54. Budde had also earlier argued at length against Begrich's view (K. Budde, "Jesaja und Ahaz," *ZDMG* 84 [1931]: 125–38).

[90] Oded, "Historical Background," 155–61.

[91] Tomes, "Reason," 61, 64–65.

[92] See Shalmaneser III's Monolith Inscription.

[93] Begrich, "Der syrisch-ephraimitische Krieg," 216–20.

[94] Donner, *Israel unter den Völkern*, 61–63 and "Separate States," 429–32.

[95] Oded, "Historical Background," 160–65. Cf. Cazelles, "Syro-Ephraimite War," 284.

Irvine, however, suggests that Ahaz's tribute mentioned in the biblical and Assyrian texts should not be seen as a special request for Assyrian intervention but a regular tribute paid only after Tiglath-pileser was present in the area.[96] On this point he notes that if Ahaz had made a special appeal, one would expect to see mention of it or at least a reference to special treatment afforded to Ahaz in the Assyrian texts. In II R 67, which records Ahaz's submission, however, Tiglath-pileser receives tribute from him like everyone else, and 2 Kgs 16:8 suggests that the tribute was very high. One may add to Irvine's evidence the observation that this Assyrian inscription's tribute list dates to the time after the Assyrians are in the area (733) and includes several rulers whom no one presumes paid their tribute in advance. The idea of an appeal (literally a "bribe") in 2 Kgs 16 is more readily explained as a product of the deuteronomistic editors, who paint a very negative portrait of all of Ahaz's actions.[97]

The available evidence seems to suggest the conclusion that the attack of Rezin and Pekah on Jerusalem had the aim of forcing Judah and its territories into a rebellious coalition. While there is no direct evidence from the Assyrian texts concerning such a coalition, the group of states absent from the tribute list of 733 B.C.E. (II R 67) suggests there was a broad-based anti-Assyrian movement at the time.[98] There is also no strong evidence for doubting the biblical indication that Rezin and Pekah intended to replace Ahaz with a cooperative king (Isa 7:6), especially since the biblical writers elsewhere attest to even earlier actions in concert by Rezin and Pekah against Judah (2 Kgs 15:37). These texts consistently bear witness to a coalition between Rezin of Damascus and Pekah of Samaria, both of whom held out against Assyria between 734 and 731 B.C.E.

This growing anti-Assyrian resistance in the west is also the most logical explanation for Tiglath-pileser's campaign to Philistia in 734–733 B.C.E. The Assyrian campaign does not make sense as a simply empire-expanding venture since western states including Damascus and Samaria are recorded as paying tribute to Tiglath-pileser as early as 743–740, 739–738 and 738–737 B.C.E.[99] By the time of the Philistia campaign, however, these states are absent from the list of those voluntarily paying tribute to Assyria (II R 67).

---

[96] Irvine, *Isaiah*, 107–8. Stephanie Dalley ("Recent Evidence from Assyrian Sources for Judean History from Uzziah to Manasseh," *JSOT* 28 [2004], 388) has recently suggested that Judah had an "established alliance" with Assyria that stretched back to Uzziah and that this provides the explanation for Ahaz's appeal. This suggestion relies on the familial terminology ("your son") in Ahaz's appeal in 2 Kgs 16:7.

[97] Irvine, *Isaiah*, 107–8. The account in 2 Chron 28 may suggest the unhistorical nature of an "appeal" from Ahaz in that it declares that Tiglath-pileser actually attacked Ahaz when he arrived in the area.

[98] See discussion of II R 67 below.

[99] See Layard 45b+III R 9, 1 (Tadmor Ann. 21), Iran Stela, and Layard 50a+50b+67a respectively.

Finally, with regard to the so-called appeal of Ahaz for Assyrian intervention, the case for seeing that event as a deuteronomistic motif seems convincing. No extrabiblical evidence gives any indication that a full-scale Assyrian campaign to the west was the direct result of a Judean king's appeal. Prior to 733 B.C.E., Judah never even appears in Assyrian texts and may have functioned only as a vassal state to the larger northern kingdom.[100] The notion that Assyria responded to the appeal of a state with whom they had had no prior direct diplomatic contact seems unlikely. Ahaz's payment of tribute fits best as a response to Tiglath-pileser's western campaign around 733 B.C.E., a campaign

---

[100] See M. Haran, "The Rise and Decline of the Empire of Jeroboam ben Joash," *VT* 17 (1967): 266–97; B. Kelle, "What's in a Name? Neo-Assyrian Designations for the Northern Kingdom and Their Implications for Israelite History and Biblical Interpretation," *JBL* 121 (2002): 639–66; M. Vogelstein, *Jeroboam II: The Rise and Fall of His Empire* (Cincinnati: self-published, 1945); H. Winckler, *Geschichte Israels in Einzeldarstellung* (2 vols.; Leipzig: Pfeiffer, 1895–1900), 1. 88–95, 145–48, 176–80. But compare Dalley, "Recent Evidence," 388.

One sees this reality as early as Israel's first appearance in Assyrian texts. Shalmaneser III's Monolith Inscription mentions "Ahab of Israel" as a member of an anti-Assyrian force at the battle of Qarqar (853 B.C.E.). In this description, Ahab is said to possess a force of 2,000 chariots and 10,000 soldiers, a force that represents more than two-thirds of the resistance and contains a chariotry equal to that of Assyria. This size and strength for Israel is generally out of keeping with what is known about Israel in the 850s. Although some scholars have attempted to explain the text by resorting to emendation (e.g., N. Na'aman, "Two Notes on the Monolith Inscription of Shalmaneser III from Kurkh," *TA* 3 [1976]: 99–101), an explanation that does not require emendation is available. The Monolith Inscription makes no reference to Judah, Moab, Edom, Tyre, or Sidon, and several texts suggest Israel (under Omri then Ahab) may have acted as a dominant partner to many of these states. Specifically concerning Judah, 1 Kgs 22:4 depicts Jehoshaphat (877–853 B.C.E.) making peace with Ahab and functioning as subservient to him (cf. 2 Kgs 3:7; see W. Hallo, "From Qarqar to Carchemish: Assyria and Israel in the Light of New Discoveries," *BA* 23 [1960]: 37). Jehoshaphat also came to be remembered as the Judean king who gave unqualified support to Israel (2 Chron 18:3). This situation of Israelite dominance may also be reflected in the later Tel Dan inscription on which "Israel" still seems to represent an entity that includes Judah, so that the two are portrayed as basically one unit and the Aramean king fought against both of them.

The inclusion of Judah as a vassal state to the larger northern kingdom continued throughout the rest of the reign of Shalmaneser III. For example, although the Black Obelisk switches from "Israel" to "Bit-Humri," it does not mention Judah. Unlike the Mesha Inscription concerning Moab, there is nothing to suggest that Judah had broken out from under the north's sphere of control, and the biblical story of Jehu (2 Kgs 9:27–29) presents him as killing both Joram of Israel and Ahaziah of Judah. The biblical texts seem to point even more explicitly to the vassaldom of Judah throughout the following period of 810–800 B.C.E. After Assyria's return to power in the west under Adad-nirari III and Joash of Samaria's payment of tribute, Israel moved to recover territory lost to Aram (2 Kgs 13:24–25). During this time, 2 Kgs 14:8–14 indicates that King Amaziah of Judah challenged Joash to battle, but no reason is given for the dispute. However, the text's rhetoric (e.g., "the cedar in Lebanon" versus "the thistle in Lebanon," 14:9) suggests that Amaziah was making a bid for Judean independence after successfully defeating Edom and capturing Sela (14:7). Verses 11–14 note that Joash of Samaria captured Amaziah, breached the wall of Jerusalem, plundered the Jerusalem temple and palace, and carried off Judean prisoners.

undertaken to quell a broad-based anti-Assyrian rebellion led by Rezin of Damascus.

3.2 The Fate of Samaria and the End of the Syro-Ephraimitic War (731–730 B.C.E.)

Given Hos 2's rhetorical horizon, the most important aspect of the Syro-Ephraimitic war for understanding this text is the role and fate of the capital city Samaria, especially at the close of the war around 731–730 B.C.E. Fortunately, several of the Assyrian inscriptions related to this conflict refer explicitly to Samaria and its role in the events. These inscriptions, together with relevant biblical texts, provide the most direct historical background for Hos 2.

3.2.1 *Samaria and Assyria 734–730 B.C.E.* In the Assyrian inscriptions reflecting events in the decade leading up to the beginning of the Syro-Ephraimitic war (745–734 B.C.E.), Samaria (under Menahem), Tyre, Arabia, and even Aram-Damascus (under Rezin) are recorded as paying tribute to Tiglath-pileser III and maintaining an official policy of submission to Assyria (see Layard 45b+III R 9, 1 [Tadmor Ann. 21], Iran Stela, Layard 50a+50b+67a).[101] By the time of the first relevant inscription of Tiglath-pileser III after his Philistia campaign in 734–733 B.C.E., the situation has changed dramatically. As noted above, II R 67 is a tribute list that dates from 733 B.C.E. In contrast to previous tribute lists, Samaria, Aram-Damascus, Tyre, and Arabia are noticeably absent from the list of those submitting voluntarily. Moreover, other inscriptions of Tiglath-pileser that relate to the following years attest that his campaigns were directed against precisely these states. While Samaria is suddenly absent from the tribute list, II R 67 includes the first appearance of a Judean king in Assyrian texts (rev. l. 11): "[Mi]tini of the land of Ashkelon, Jehoahaz of the land of Judah (*ia-u-ḫa-zi* KUR *ia-u-da-a-a*), Kaušmalaka of the land of Edom...."

These observations favor the conclusion that II R 67 reflects the situation in Syria-Palestine after Tiglath-pileser's campaign to Philistia when Damascus and

---

[101] Dalley ("Recent Evidence") has argued that this pro-Assyrian stance was in fact a cooperative alliance between Judah and Assyria that stretches back to the time of Uzziah. Her argument primarily relies on the names of two queens discovered in an eighth-century tomb at Nimrud. Dalley argues that the queens' names contain Yahwistic theophoric elements and thus these queens of Tiglath-pileser III and Shalmaneser V were Judean princesses. The presence of Judean women in the Neo-Assyrian court, as well as other texts from the reign of Sargon II that mention Judeans in contexts of Assyrian campaigns, suggest, in her view, that there was a long-standing patron-client relationship between Judah and Assyria. For challenges to Dalley's arguments about the theophoric elements, see K. L. Younger, "Yahweh at Ashkelon and Calah? Yahwistic Names in Neo-Assyrian," *VT* 52 (2002): 207–18.

Samaria were in open rebellion.[102] The combination of biblical and extrabiblical texts provides a possible explanation for this sudden shift in Samaria's policy. Second Kings 15:25 notes that Pekah—the king who was on the throne during the events of 734–731 B.C.E.—assassinated the reigning Pekahiah after two years in an attack specifically placed "in the royal palace in Samaria" (JPS). Second Kings 15:27 also provides a crucial clue for interpretation of the events by assigning Pekah a reign of twenty years. Yet evidence from Assyrian texts fixes Menahem on the throne in 738 and Hoshea in 730 B.C.E. Accordingly, many scholars view the biblical assignment of twenty years to Pekah as a mistake and reduce his rule.[103] As early as 1888, however, Lederer suggested that Pekah may have ruled as a rival king for a number of years before his usurpation of the central throne in Samaria.[104] Cook gives the most comprehensive supporting argument for this view and demonstrates that several biblical texts indicate this course of events.

Evidence in this regard includes 2 Kgs 15:27 and 37. These texts indicate that Pekah was active as an anti-Assyrian rival "king" as early as the reign of Jotham and the last years of Jeroboam II. Since these biblical texts attest to close ties between Pekah and Rezin of Damascus (see also Isa 7:1), one can conclude that when Rezin usurped the throne in Damascus, Pekah, perhaps a Transjordanian, collaborated with him. Consequently, Pekah emerged as a puppet ruler over the Transjordan and Galilee territories as Rezin grew in strength and the central government in Samaria diminished in size.[105] This state of affairs may explain the references to two distinct entities, "Israel" and "Ephraim," and accompanying internal civil strife throughout the book of Hosea.[106] Thus, when Pekah assassinated Pekahiah sometime around 734 B.C.E., Samaria, as the seat of the northern kingdom's central government, underwent a significant change. For the first time in over a century (i.e., since Jehu in 841 B.C.E.), Samaria's political alignment shifted from pro- to anti-Assyrian. Perhaps more importantly, the evidence suggests that Samaria did not undertake this

---

[102] The sudden appearance of Judah in this text also favors the conclusion that Judah asserted its independence from Israel for the first time around 734–733 B.C.E. If this conclusion is correct, it further strengthens the previous indications that Judah functioned primarily as a vassal to Israel throughout the years of 841–734 B.C.E.

[103] For examples, see H. J. Cook, "Pekah," *VT* 14 (1964): 121–22. Tetley offers the most recent attempt to deal with this issue (M. C. Tetley, "The Date of Samaria's Fall as a Reason for Rejecting the Hypothesis of Two Conquests," *CBQ* 64 [2002]: 59–77). Based on a readjustment of the dating of Hoshea, she offers the unsubstantiated speculation that the original number of Pekah's reign was "twenty-nine" and the "nine" was omitted by a copyist (ibid., 74).

[104] C. Lederer, *Die biblische Zeitrechnung vom Auszuge aus Ägypten bis zum Beginne der babylonischen Gefangenschaft* (Speier: F. Kleeberger, 1888), 135–38.

[105] For further discussion of this course of events, see J. M. Miller and J. H. Hayes, *A History of Ancient Israel and Judah* (Philadelphia: Westminster, 1986), 324.

[106] See Cook, "Pekah," 121–55.

action alone but threw its lot in with the anti-Assyrian political ringleader of the region, Rezin of Damascus.[107]

Between 734 and 731 B.C.E., several texts show that Tiglath-pileser moved against and subjugated each of the major states engaged in the rebellion.[108] Three Assyrian inscriptions provide information about the specific fate of Samaria at the end of the conflict, and these texts suggest several important things about the larger situation in both Israel and Judah. The first is the Assyrian text Layard 66, which succinctly reports the ultimate fate of Samaria as Tiglath-pileser finished his campaigns around 731 B.C.E. The text as a whole does not center on Samaria but affords the city a mention only in the last line, probably because of the unusual treatment the capital city received (l. 228): "... and Samaria (URU *sa-me-ri-na*) alone I le[ft ...] their king [...]."[109] The inscription suggests that, unlike all the other anti-Assyrian states, the Assyrians did not directly attack Samaria and Pekah.

The historical implications of this comment become clear when Layard 66 is compared to the next relevant inscription relating to the events in 731 B.C.E. III R 10, 2 is a summary inscription that provides two significant pieces of information concerning the northern kingdom. In order to understand this text, particularly its two different designations for the northern kingdom, however, one must note with Tadmor that it is not arranged chronologically but geographically.[110] The inscription does not come from the period when the events described took place but represents a retrospective description from the period after Tiglath-pileser had settled affairs.

As with Layard 66, III R 10, 2 contains a specific reference to the unusual treatment of the northern kingdom at the close of the war (ll. 15–18):

---

[107] Layard 29b is the other relevant inscription of Tiglath-pileser that comes from the middle of the Syro-Ephraimitic war. Scholars debate whether this text should be reconstructed to contain a reference to the northern kingdom. Because the text has significance for understanding what territory was left for Hoshea at the close of the war, it will be discussed below.

[108] For the campaign against Philistia (particularly Gaza), see ND 400 and III R 10, 2; for Tyre, see ND 4301+4305; for Aram-Damscus, see Layard 72b+73a, ND 4301+4305, and III R 10, 2; for Arabia, see Layard 66, ND 400, ND 4301+4305, and III R 10, 2; for Ashkelon, see Layard 29b. The systematic assault against these states strengthens the notion that they were not acting in isolation but had formed, however loosely, an anti-Assyrian coalition. Furthermore, the protracted campaign against Rezin and Damascus (the Eponym List indicates the action lasted two years) and the fact that only Damascus's holdings were provincialized further indicate that Rezin was the most powerful figure involved and the veritable ringleader of the coalition.

[109] Cf. the reconstructions in Kuan, *Neo-Assyrian Historical Inscriptions*, 174; Tadmor, *Inscriptions* 202–3; and *ANET*, 283.

[110] Tadmor, "Southern Border," 116.

Bit-Ḫumri (KUR É *ḫu-um-ri-a*) […] the entirety of its people [… together with their possessions to] Assyria I led away. Pekah their king (LUGAL-*šunu*) *they* deposed and Hoshea [… for king]ship over them I appointed.[111]

These two inscriptions together make it clear that Tiglath-pileser took several decisive actions in Syria-Palestine at the close of the war. After eliminating Rezin and Damascus, as well as subduing the other rebellious states, he did not move against Pekah and Samaria. Rather, Tiglath-pileser undertook to reorganize the remaining political entities in the region. As a part of this reorganization, the Assyrian king apparently recognized Hoshea as the new Israelite monarch whose task it was to overthrow Pekah and possess the kingdom in Samaria.[112] Furthermore, 2 Kgs 16:10a suggests that King Ahaz of Judah, probably along with other rulers in the area, met with Tiglath-pileser in Damascus after the defeat of Rezin. This meeting may well have been a general one at which Hoshea was also present. The Assyrian king may have used this meeting to establish the new political boundaries and make the final arrangements for vassal states in Syria-Palestine.[113] In any case, the emphasis of these inscriptions is clear: The people themselves, led by Hoshea, were left with the task of overthrowing the anti-Assyrian rebel, Pekah, and reclaiming the capital of Samaria; Tiglath-pileser did not attack the city.

III R 10, 2 contains a second significant factor that has historical implications. The apparent name of Hoshea's new vassal state is "Bit-Ḫumri." Some of the earlier lines in the inscription also make this fact clear (ll. 6–7): "… Gal'az[a], Abil-[…], which are on the border of Bit-Ḫumri (KUR É *ḫu-um-ri-a*).…" As noted above, this text is a summary inscription that comes from the period after Tiglath-pileser had made final arrangements and departed from Syria-Palestine. None of Tiglath-pileser's tribute lists from the years of the war refer to the northern kingdom in this way, and the Assyrians never claim to have taken "Bit-Ḫumri." Given this fact, it seems reasonable to suggest that the references to an entity called "Bit-Ḫumri" do not represent a state that was involved in the Syro-Ephraimitic war. The designation "Bit-Ḫumri" recalls, however, the primary name for the northern kingdom as a steadfast Assyrian vassal in extrabiblical texts from the time of Shalmaneser III to Adad-nirari III (ca. 841–803 B.C.E.). Thus, it seems reasonable to conclude that Tiglath-pileser or Hoshea reintroduced the old designation "Bit-Ḫumri" to define the newly

---

[111] Cf. the reconstructions in Tadmor, *Inscriptions*, 140–41 and *ANET*, 283.

[112] Tiglath-pileser's claim to have exiled the "entirety" of Bit-Ḫumri's people (III R 10, 2) must be exaggeration since he goes on to note that the people themselves deposed Pekah (so Irvine, *Isaiah*, 68).

[113] For discussion and argumentation of this idea and its relationship to biblical texts, see Chong, "The Song of Moses," 320, 329.

constituted Assyrian vassal kingdom that would be led by the Assyrian-appointed Hoshea.

Thus, at the close of Tiglath-pileser's campaign in 731–730 B.C.E., Pekah remained in control of Samaria, and the Assyrians had not taken the city. The Assyrian king designated Hoshea as the new ruler of "Bit-Ḫumri," who was to lead the people themselves in taking Samaria. The deposing of Pekah, the capture of Samaria, and the reestablishment of the north as a pro-Assyrian vassal state was an inner-Israelite conflict. III R 10, 2 emphasizes this perspective as the text remarks in retrospect that "Pekah their king *they* deposed and Hoshea [... for king]ship over them I appointed." Second Kings 15:30 also seems to reflect this course of events by stating, "Hoshea son of Elah conspired (וַיִּקְשָׁר קֶשֶׁר) against Pekah son of Remaliah and attacked him (וַיַּכֵּהוּ), killed him, and became king in his place...." The final Assyrian inscription relevant to this time, ND 4301+4305, provides the conclusion of this course of events. Lines 10–11 note that Hoshea, apparently after the successful reclaiming of Samaria, sent a first payment of tribute to Tiglath-pileser after he had left the area: "[... Hoshea as ki]ng over them [I set ...] Sarrabanu before me [...]."[114] As is the case with III R 10, 2, the text reflects a time after the king had settled matters in the west and left the area.[115] This inscription suggests Hoshea's or his

---

[114] This line is commonly restored on the basis of III R 10, 2.

[115] Accordingly, the preceding lines make use of the designation "Bit-Ḫumri" as a geographical indicator (ll. 3–4): "[...] the widespread [land of Bit-]Hazael in its entirety from [... which is on the bor]der of Bit-Ḫumri (KUR É *ḫu-um-ri-a*)...."

In the most recent article addressing the course of the Syro-Ephraimitic war, Tetley ("Date," 59–77) offers a completely different reconstruction. She adjusts downward Hoshea's accession to 727 by concluding that Tiglath-pileser III campaigned twice in the west between 734 and 727 B.C.E. (ibid., 66–70). As the Eponym List indicates, Tiglath-pileser campaigned to Damascus in 733/732 and 732/731 B.C.E. Tetley emphasizes, however, that the Assyrian inscriptions related to these campaigns do not explicitly mention the capture of Damascus or the overthrow of Pekah. She correlates this initial campaign with 2 Kgs 15:29, which mentions cities in northern Israel that fell to Tiglath-pileser III. She then stresses that 2 Kgs 16:5–9 *subsequently* refers to Rezin and Pekah as still active and besieging Jerusalem (ibid., 66). She also takes Tiglath-pileser's references to former campaigns against Israel on texts like Layard 66 and III R 10, 2 as forming a chronological sequence that distinguishes an earlier campaign from the latter one in which Pekah was overthrown by his own subjects (ibid., 67–68). In her view, these biblical and extrabiblical texts suggest that Tiglath-pileser campaigned once to the west in 733/732 through 732/731 B.C.E. but did not destroy Rezin or Samaria. Subsequently, however, Pekah and Rezin attacked Ahaz in Jerusalem, Ahaz appealed to Assyria for help, and Tiglath-pileser returned to the west on a campaign in which Rezin was killed and Pekah was replaced by Hoshea (ibid., 69). In order to date this supposed later campaign, Tetley looks to the Eponym List's broken place name for 728/727, which she reconstructs as "Di" for "Damascus," and missing place name for 727/726 B.C.E. Thus, in her view, Ahaz's appeal to Assyria, Hoshea's eventual overthrow of Pekah, and Tiglath-pileser's second western campaign should be dated to 728/727 B.C.E. (ibid., 69–70).

Several pieces of evidence, however, argue against Tetley's proposal. For example, she does not consider Layard 29b, which seems to contain the actual reference to the death of Rezin and is dated by most scholars to 733 B.C.E. because it mentions Mitini of Ashkelon (see Irvine, *Isaiah*, 32–

ambassadors' appearance before the Assyrian king at Sarrabanu in southern Babylon in order to pay tribute.

One final significant question related to the historical events of the close of the Syro-Ephraimitic war builds on the observations about the new entity "Bit-Ḫumri" made above. As noted previously, II R 67, a tribute list dating from the middle of the conflict (733 B.C.E.), contains the first appearance of the name "Judah" in Assyrian records. The previous absence of such references perhaps finds its best explanation in the possibility given above that Judah existed only as a vassal state to the larger northern kingdom from the 840s on and did not operate independently in the realm of international relationships. Upon Pekah's coup and Samaria's sudden shift to an anti-Assyrian partnership, the evidence suggests that Ahaz asserted Judah's independence for the first time in over a century.

Surprisingly, however, there are no further references to Judah in Assyrian texts from Tiglath-pileser III or any other Assyrian king until after Sargon's final destruction of Samaria in 720 B.C.E. What explanation accounts for this lack of continued reference? Perhaps an explanation can be found in the constitution of Hoshea's postwar territory. But what should the reader understand Hoshea's newly-formed entity called "Bit-Ḫumri" to include? The Assyrian text, Layard 29b, which comes from the middle of the Syro-Ephraimitic war, has a significant impact on this question. Scholars debate whether this text should be reconstructed to include a reference to the northern kingdom. In general, the text relates to Tiglath-pileser's activities in Syria-Palestine after his departure from Philistia. The inscription refers to the king's trek across the Galilee to attack Israel, Arabia, and Damascus and describes the capture of a certain entity's territories (ll. 230ff): "… [prisoners of …] districts of Bit-[… l] took away [… prisoners of …] … Ḫinatuna … Aruma, Marum…."[116] The general scholarly consensus agrees that the cities mentioned here are located in the Galilee. The question concerns whether they were under Israel's or Aram's control at this time, and whether the fragmentary "Bit" in line 230 should be reconstructed as "Bit-Hazael" or "Bit-Ḫumri." Second Kings 15:29 refers to the Assyrian annexation of the Galilee region in these years but

---

33). Additionally, texts like Layard 66 and III R 10, 2, on which she finds references to former and latter campaigns against Israel, are widely taken to be geographical in organization and unable to be used for chronological reconstruction (cf. Tadmor, "Southern Border," 116). In any case, the lines immediately following the reference to Hoshea's accession in III R 10, 2 refer to Shamshi of Arabia, who figured prominently in the events of 733/732 not 727/726 B.C.E. (cf. Layard 72b + 73a). Most problematic of all for Tetley's argument, however, is that she never mentions the inscription II R 67, which records Ahaz's payment of tribute to Tiglath-pileser that she dates to a second campaign in 727. On the contrary, the tribute list portion of this text (rev. 7–13), or at least the second half of the list, is securely dated to 734/733 because line 11 refers to "[M]itinni of Ashkelon" and Layard 29b shows that he was off the throne by 733/732 B.C.E. (cf. Irvine, *Isaiah*, 41–42).

[116] See Kuan's reconstruction in *Neo-Assyrian Historical Inscriptions*, 168.

does not say that Israel was in possession of this territory. Rezin's widespread expansion and Israel's diminished status suggest that Damascus was in control of this territory, that the central government in Samaria was limited to the city's immediate vicinity even prior to 734, and that one should reconstruct line 230 as "Bit-Hazael." The parallel reference to the "16 districts of the land of Damascus" in Layard 72b–73a strengthens this restoration.[117]

If this reconstruction is accurate, it indicates that Damascus, not Israel, was in control of the region of Galilee during the course of the war. The consequence of this view is that, upon the defeat of Rezin, the Assyrians would have seen this territory as belonging to Syria and annexed it as an Assyrian province (cf. 2 Kgs 15:29). In addition, III R 10, 2 makes a reference to the "border of Bit-Ḫumri" (line 6). Tadmor reconstructs this text so that the southern-most border of Aram with Bit-Ḫumri was at Abel-Beth-Maacah and Ramoth-gilead.[118] According to his view, all of Gilead south of Ramoth-gilead belonged to Israel. Irvine, however, has challenged Tadmor and argued that Aramean territory extended deep into traditionally Israelite areas.[119] He concludes that the border between Aram and Israel at the time of the war extended into the Transjordan and Aramean territory included Bashan, the Golan, and the Galilee region from the Yarmuk to the Jabbok and beyond. The Syrian border west of the Jordan included not only Galilee but also the Jezreel Valley, the northern edge of the Ephraimite hill country, and the Plain of Sharon. Consequently, if this view is correct, these territories, under Aram's control at the end of the war, would have been incorporated into the Assyrian provinces and would not have been part of Hoshea's kingdom.

The above evidence indicates that Tiglath-pileser's new entity "Bit-Ḫumri" consisted only of the area west of the Jordan and south of Jezreel, that is, primarily the territory south of Samaria. Combining this limited span of territory available to Hoshea with the disappearance of Judah from Assyrian records after this time, it seems reasonable to conclude that the kingdom over which Hoshea was appointed once again included the smaller state of Judah. Thus, the Judean independence reflected in II R 67 was only temporary until Tiglath-pileser reorganized Syria-Palestine, and Israel once again assumed the role of the dominant partner. The Assyrian king seems to have reestablished essentially the old entity "Bit-Ḫumri" mentioned on Shalmaneser III's Black Obelisk as a pro-Assyrian satellite including both Israel and Judah, but with greatly reduced territory.

---

[117] For the opposite view, see Tadmor, "Southern Border," 114–22 and *Inscriptions*, 80–81.

[118] "Southern Border," 118. In his more recent work, Tadmor states that the reading "Abel-Beth-Maacah" can no longer be sustained and suggests "Abel-Shittim." He retains the reading "Gilead" (*Inscriptions*, 139).

[119] Irvine, *Isaiah*, 65–67.

This conclusion makes a significant contribution to the understanding of affairs in Israel and Judah at the close of the Syro-Ephraimitic war. Although Ahaz remained on the Judean throne, the northern and southern kingdoms approximated one kingdom with two separate but not equal heads. Consequently, Hoshea's campaign to retake Samaria likely started from and enlisted the help of Judah. The people of Israel and the people of Judah rallied their support behind one leader, Hoshea, and attempted to carry out the concerted action of reclaiming the capital city of Samaria. In so doing, both kingdoms could be liberated from the scourge of Pekah and the anti-Assyrian proponents, who had brought the wrath of Assyria down on the promised land.

4.   Summary and Conclusions: Hosea 2's Rhetorical Horizon and Historical Situation

This chapter examined the general rhetorical elements of Hos 2. On the basis of unifying vocabulary, themes, motifs, and images that bind the material together, it was proposed that 2:1–25 represents a single rhetorical address by the prophet Hosea. By examining the relevant metaphors and images, the chapter identified indications of a general "rhetorical horizon" presupposed by and reflected in the text. The historical analysis just completed attempted to provide details concerning a specific situation that may aid in understanding Hos 2: the period of civil war between Hoshea and Pekah at the close of the Syro-Ephraimitic war (731–730 B.C.E.).

When placed into dialogue with Hos 2, this rhetorical-historical situation accounts most adequately for all the elements in the oracle's rhetorical horizon. First, as noted above, the rhetorical horizon of Hos 2 presupposes a conflict situation, and, more particularly, alludes to an inner-Israelite conflict between two competing groups. This characteristic fits precisely with the situation in Israel at the close of the Syro-Ephraimitic war when Hoshea led a pro-Assyrian faction in an attack on Samaria's own ruling house in an attempt to overthrow Pekah. The oracle's rhetorical horizon also envisions some type of joint action by both Israel and Judah (2:1–3). The situation of 731–730 B.C.E. accounts for this feature through the nature and make-up of Hoshea's "Bit-Ḫumri" and the likely role played by Judeans in the move against Pekah. A third aspect of the rhetorical horizon also finds fulfillment in the course of events involving Hoshea and Pekah: Hos 2 personifies a capital city in the context of imminent or threatened destruction. Such an imminent threat of violence is surely characteristic of Samaria's situation after Tiglath-pileser had isolated it and designated Hoshea to assume its leadership.

The fourth element of chapter 2's rhetorical horizon noted above consists of the theological statement that Yahweh plans to execute judgment against an offending party. This statement may plausibly represent a theo-political interpretation of the failure of Pekah's rebellious plans and the approaching overthrow of Samaria's government. The speech's horizon also attests, however, the assumption that this judgment will be followed by the people's restoration to a new status. This specific detail fits especially well with Hoshea's likely intentions at the close of the war: the attack on Samaria had the express aim of recovering the capital in order to establish the new entity called "Bit-Ḥumri."

If the above analyses are correct, they suggest that even the final two parts of Hos 2's rhetorical horizon that were outlined earlier find an appropriate historical setting in the Hoshea-Pekah conflict. The text's use of the metaphors of "fornication" and "adultery" characterize the improper political actions that violate the will of Yahweh. Additionally, Hosea's metaphors of "lovers" and "paramours," which seem to allude to the presence and involvement of political allies in general and a political overlord in particular, tie into the northern kingdom's entanglement with an anti-Assyrian coalition controlled by the dominant leader Rezin of Damascus.

Thus, the historical events in Israel and Judah at the close of the Syro-Ephraimitic war provide well for the overall rhetorical horizon presupposed by and reflected in Hos 2. The capital city Samaria and its ruling house had entered into political relationships with an overlord (Rezin) and allies (the coalition), and these actions have produced a situation in which two competing groups (Hoshea's pro-Assyrian and Pekah's anti-Assyrian group) are in conflict over the capital city of Samaria. Nonetheless, the text also envisions an end to the conflict and a restoration of the capital city to good standing. Against this backdrop, the prophet Hosea uses metaphor and rhetoric to proclaim his message, rally support behind Hoshea's cause, and provide a theological interpretation of these events designed to communicate Yahweh's will to the people.

7

THE RHETORICAL ADDRESS OF HOSEA 2
(PART 1):
TRANSLATION AND THE PROPHET'S INTRODUCTION
(2:1–3)

The general rhetorical elements of Hos 2 yield a number of insights that can be pulled together to offer a reading of the oracle as Hosea's address within a particular rhetorical situation. This reading, which is contained in the present and following chapters, depends upon the proposals suggested above concerning the meaning of the text's major metaphors, the unity of the speech's composition, and the nature of the oracle's rhetorical-historical situation. Simultaneously, it offers further evidence to support the preceding conclusions. There is, of course, a danger here of circular argumentation. No interpretation, however, avoids entirely a certain degree of circularity. Thus, the following discussion first offers a translation of Hos 2:1–25 that reflects the conclusions reached through a rhetorical-historical analysis of the text's metaphors and rhetorical horizon. The remainder of this chapter then begins the examination of Hos 2 as a full oratorical address that can be fruitfully engaged, even if only as an interpretive exercise, as a rhetorical speech designed to provide a theological statement about social and political events in Israel and Judah at the close of the Syro-Ephraimitic war.

1. TRANSLATION AND TEXTUAL NOTES

The following translation attempts to represent the meaning and function of the text's major metaphors within the discourse as a whole. The translations are not as smooth as they might be but attempt, as often as possible, to recapture rhetorical devices like wordplays, repetitions, etc. The translation does not, however, replace the metaphors with literal statements reflecting their meaning within the rhetorical situation but leaves the metaphorical discourse in tact wherever possible.[1]

(2:1) And the number of the children of Israel will be like the sand of the sea that cannot be measured and cannot be counted. So it will be, in the place in which it was said to them, "You (m.pl.) are not my people," it will be said to them, "Children of the living God." (2:2) And the children of Judah and the children of Israel will be gathered together and they will set over themselves one head, and they will march up from the land for great will be the day of Jezreel. (2:3) Say to your (m.pl.) brothers, "My People" and to your (m.pl.) sisters, "Compassion."

(2:4) Contend with your (m.pl.) mother, contend, for she is not my wife and I am not her husband. And let her put aside her fornication from her face and her adultery from between her breasts. (2:5) Lest I strip her naked and I exhibit her like the day she was born. I will make her like the desert and I will render her like a land of drought. And I will kill her with thirst. (2:6) And I will not have compassion on her children because they are children of fornication.

(2:7) For their mother has fornicated. The one who conceived them has acted shamefully. For she said, "I will go after my lovers who give me my bread and my water, my wool and my linen, my oil and my drink." (2:8) Therefore, behold, I will hedge her way with briers and I will wall-in her wall, and she will not find her paths. (2:9) And she will chase after her lovers, but she will not reach them; she will seek them, but she will not find. Then she will say, "I will go and I will return to my first husband for it was better for me then than now."

(2:10) And she herself has not acknowledged that I myself gave to her the grain and the new wine and the choice oil. I multiplied for her silver and gold that they used for the paramour. (2:11) Therefore, I will take back again my grain in its time and my new wine in its season, and I will reclaim my wool and my linen in order to reckon her indiscretion. (2:12) Now I will uncover her genitals before the eyes of her lovers, and no one will reclaim her from my hand. (2:13) I will bring to an end all her rejoicing, her festivals, her new

---

[1] The translation and analysis also do not attempt to provide a comprehensive text-critical study of Hos 2 and do not discuss all the variants found in the text. For more comprehensive textual analyses, see the major commentaries (Wolff, *Hosea*; Andersen and Freedman, *Hosea*, etc.) and Borbone, *Il libro*.

moons, her sabbaths, and all her appointed times. (2:14) And I will make desolate her vine and her fig-tree about which she said, "They are gifts for me that my lovers gave to me." I will make them (m.pl.) into a forest, and the beast of the field will devour them (m.pl.). (2:15) I will visit upon her the days of the paramours when she burned incense for the sake of/with them and she adorned herself with her earring and her jewelry and went after her lovers. But me she forgot, declares Yahweh.

(2:16) Therefore, behold, I am about to seduce her and bring her into the wilderness, and I will speak to her heart. (2:17) And I will give to her her vineyards from there and the valley of Achor for a doorway of hope. And she will respond there as in the days of her youth and as on the day of her coming up from the land of Egypt.

(2:18) So it will be in that day, declares Yahweh, you (f.sg.) will call me "my husband," and you (f.sg.) will no longer call me "my paramour." (2:19) I will remove the names of the paramours from her mouth so they will no longer be remembered by their (m.pl.) names.

(2:20) And I will make for them (m.pl.) a covenant in that day with the beasts of the field, with the birds of the sky, and with the creeping things of the earth. I will banish the bow and sword and warfare from the land, and I will make them (m.pl.) lie down in safety. (2:21) And I will wed you (f.sg.) to myself forever. I will wed you (f.sg.) to myself with righteousness and with justice and with kindness and with compassion. (2:22) I will wed you (f.sg.) to myself with faithfulness, and you (f.sg.) will acknowledge Yahweh.

(2:23) And it will be on that day, I will respond, declares Yahweh, I will respond to the heavens and they themselves will respond to the earth. (2:24) And the earth will respond to the grain and to the new wine and to the choice oil, and they themselves will respond to Jezreel. (2:25) And I will sow her to myself in the land, and I will have compassion on "No-Compassion." I will say to "Not-My-People," "You (m.sg.) are my people," and he will say, "My God."

Verse 1

"And the number ... will be" (וְהָיָה מִסְפַּר): Mays begins this verse by translating the *vav* as an adversative ("yet") in order to emphasize the contrast with the ending of 1:9.[2] Along these same lines, LXX translates וְהָיָה with the past tense καὶ ἦν, which makes an intentional connection with 1:9. This past tense reading, however, is not supported by 4QXII[d].[3] Even the LXX renders

---

[2] Mays, *Hosea*, 30; cf. Wolff, *Hosea*, 24.

[3] The primary Qumran texts pertaining to Hos 2 are 4QXII[d], which contains fragments of 1:7–2:5, 4QpHos[a], which is a fragmentary commentary with the text of 2:8–14, 4QXII[c], which contains fragments of 2:13–15, and 4QXII[g], which has portions of 2:1–2, 4–5, 15–19, and 22–25. Overall, the Qumran evidence for Hos 2 seems to reflect the MT in all essential features and suggests that Hos 2 is

וֹהָיָה with καὶ ἔσται in 2:1b ("so it will be, in the place in which ..."), and the overall context of verse one seems to call for the future translation "and the number ... will be."[4]

"the children of Israel" (בְּנֵי יִשְׂרָאֵל): Hosea uses this phrase six times with five of them occurring in chapters 1–3: 2:1, 2; 3:1, 4, 5; 4:1.

"in the place in which ..." (בִּמְקוֹם אֲשֶׁר): This phrase may be understood as a reference to a literal or figurative place or as a locative relative adverb meaning "where."[5] The phrase might also be rendered as "instead of" (equivalent to תַּחַת).[6] Yet, as Mays notes, there are no valid parallels for equating this construction to תַּחַת אֲשֶׁר.[7]

"it will be said to them" (יֵאָמֵר לָהֶם): 4QXII[d] reads the third person singular "he shall say," apparently as a reference to Yahweh.

Verse 2

"together" (יַחְדָּו): Kuhnig emends the MT into the verb form *yēḥādû* on the basis of Ugaritic parallels.[8] Stuart observes, however, that the term יַחְדָּו commonly occurs at the end of poetic lines (cf. Amos 1:15).[9]

"they will march up from the land" (וְעָלוּ מִן־הָאָרֶץ): See discussion below.

"for great" (כִּי גָדוֹל): The כִּי in this phrase is grammatically ambiguous and could be read as the preposition "for" or as an intensifying element meaning "how great." For example, Andersen and Freedman translate "how great" because they conclude that there is no logical connection between the two parts of the verse.[10] The LXX, however, translates כִּי with the preposition ὅτι ("for, because"). The emphatic translation misses the connection with the military imagery in the first part of the verse and the association of "Jezreel" with military conflict in 1:4–5.

"will be the day of Jezreel" (יוֹם יִזְרְעֶאל): This final phrase does not contain a verb. The context, however, seems to call for a future-tense translation.[11]

---

one of the few textually stable parts of the book. See M. Abegg, P. Flint, and E. Ulrich, *The Dead Sea Scrolls Bible* (San Francisco: Harper, 1999), 419 and Stuart, *Hosea-Jonah*, 13.

[4] So Andersen and Freedman, *Hosea*, 143; Garrett, *Hosea, Joel*, 71; Mays, *Hosea*, 30; Stuart, *Hosea-Jonah*, 35; Wolff, *Hosea*, 24. The Syriac seems to presuppose the negative construction וְלֹא יִהְיֶה.

[5] See Andersen and Freedman, *Hosea*, 203.

[6] So *KBL*, 560; *BDB*, 880; Wolff, *Hosea*, 24; Sellin, *Zwölfprophetenbuch*, 27.

[7] Mays, *Hosea*, 31. Cf. Stuart (*Hosea-Jonah*, 35), who also rejects the translation "instead of."

[8] W. Kuhnig, *Nordwestsemitische Studien zum Hoseabuch* (BibOr 27; Rome: Pontifical Biblical Institute, 1974), 5–6.

[9] Stuart, *Hosea-Jonah*, 39.

[10] Andersen and Freedman, *Hosea*, 209. See also Stuart, *Hosea-Jonah*, 36.

[11] So Garrett, *Hosea, Joel*, 71; Mays, *Hosea*, 30; Stuart, *Hosea-Jonah*, 35. Wolff inserts a present-tense verb: "great is the day of Jezreel" (*Hosea*, 24).

Verse 3

"Say" (אִמְרוּ): Qal imperative m.pl. The LXX considers 2:3 as the opening verse of the unit 2:3–25. Andersen and Freedman translate "you will say" and take this command as directed to the child Jezreel even though the imperative is plural.[12]

"brothers ... sisters" (לַאֲחֵיכֶם ... וְלַאֲחוֹתֵיכֶם): The LXX translates with singular forms, linking the phrase with the specific children mentioned in Hos 1. The MT should be retained, however, since the plurals are not likely to have developed from the singulars. Even the LXX contains plural pronouns throughout the rest of the verse.[13]

Verse 4

"Contend" (רִיבוּ): 4QXII^g has a singular imperative unlike the plural in the MT and LXX.

"for she is not" (כִּי־הִיא לֹא א): See discussion below.

"let her put aside" (וְתָסֵר): The LXX presupposes a 1 c.sg. verb and a 1 c.sg. pronominal suffix, "I will put aside ... from my face." Thus, in this rendering, the threat begins already in verse 4. The MT is confirmed, however, by the "lest" (פֶּן) in 2:5 that indicates the clear beginning of the threat.[14]

Verse 5

"I exhibit her" (וְהִצַּגְתִּיהָ): The verse's initial imperfect verb "I will strip" (אַפְשִׁיטֶנָּה) serves as the governing verb for the perfects that follow. This translation of the hifil of יצג follows the suggestion of Brown, Driver, and Briggs concerning this verse and relies on other occurrences of the word that appear to carry the meaning "to exhibit" (e.g., Judg 8:27; Gen 47:2).[15]

"I will render her" (וְשַׁתִּהָ): This verb is a common synonym for שׂים and its most usual parallel in poetic couplets.[16]

Verse 6

"children of fornication" (בְּנֵי זְנוּנִים): See discussion below.

Verse 7

"has acted shamefully" (הֹבִישָׁה): The verbs זָנְתָה ("has fornicated") and הֹבִישָׁה ("has acted shamefully") form a perfect-perfect verb sequence in which the second verb denotes sequence or consequence. Andersen and Freedman point out that the hifil verb "does not make sense here in either of its usual

---

[12] Andersen and Freedman, *Hosea*, 212.
[13] Ibid.
[14] See Wolff, *Hosea*, 30.
[15] *BDB*, 426.
[16] Stuart, *Hosea-Jonah*, 44.

meanings—causative ('to put to shame'), for it has no object, or stative ('to be ashamed'). The verb here must have the active force...."[17]

"*I will go after*" (אלכה אחרי): This verb is used elsewhere of commitment both to Yahweh (Deut 13:5; 1 Kgs 14:8) and to false gods (Deut 4:3; 6:14). The cohortative here should be understood as "conveying resolution."[18]

"*linen*" (פשתי): Outside of Hos 2, this word appears only in the plural form in the Hebrew Bible (thirteen times). Since this form is not the regular pattern of the word, Freedman suggests that the original reading was *pištay* rather than *pišti*.[19] He observes that three of the four cola in verse 7 end in -*ay* with the only exception being פשתי. Thus, originally, the word must have been vocalized as *pištay*.[20]

Verse 8

"*I will hedge*" (הנני־שך): This exact form of the verb occurs elsewhere only in Job 1:10, where it expresses the idea of keeping attackers outside. Macintosh, however, suggests that the verb is a variant form of סוך II and should be connected with the root שכך II/ סכך II and the Arabic *skk*, "to close up, stop up." In this form, the verb also occurs in Job 3:23 and 38:8. In these cases, as well as in the case of the noun form in Isa 5:5 (משוכה), the term denotes an enclosure like a protective hedge.

"*her way*" (דרכה): The MT reads "your (f.sg.) way" (דרכך). This third-person translation follows the LXX and Syriac and makes better sense with the other suffixes in the verse.[21]

"*I will wall-in her wall*" (וגדרתי את־גדרה): This phrase is unclear as to whether the pronoun "her/its" refers to the roadway or the wife ("her wall" or "its wall"). Some commentators follow the Vulgate in separating the pronominal suffix from the direct object and read "I will wall her in with its wall."[22] Macintosh explains, however, that since the participle of גדר is attested with the meaning "wall builder" (cf. 2 Kgs 12:13[MT]; 22:6), the translator should consider the verb here to be a denominative.[23]

---

[17] Andersen and Freedman, *Hosea*, 229.

[18] Macintosh, *Critical and Exegetical Commentary*, 48.

[19] D. Freedman, "פשתי in Hosea 2:7," *JBL* 74 (1955): 275. This view was originally suggested by W. F. Albright ("The Gezer Calendar," *BASOR* 92 [1943]: 22, f.n. 34).

[20] Freedman, "פשתי," 275. Contrast K. Tangberg, "A Note on *pištî* in Hosea II 7, 11," *VT* 27 (1977): 222–24.

[21] Cf. Wolff, *Hosea*, 30 and Buss, *Prophetic Word*, 8. Stuart and Kuhnigk suggest that the MT consonants should simply be repointed and vocalized with an emphatic כי, "(her) very way" (Stuart, *Hosea-Jonah*, 44; Kuhnigk, *Nordwestsemitische Studien*, 14).

[22] E.g., Andersen and Freedman, *Hosea*, 237.

[23] Macintosh, *Critical and Exegetical Commentary*, 50–51.

Verse 9

"she will not find" (*ולא תמצא*): The LXX and Syriac supply the missing accusative 3 m.pl. pronoun "them."

Verse 10

"But she has not acknowledged" (*והיא לא ידעה*): For the translation of ידע as "to acknowledge," see discussion below.[24]

"silver and gold" (*וכסף* ... *וזהב*): In terms of the poetry, one should split the lines as "and silver I multiplied for her" and "gold that they used for the paramour" (3 words per line). The MT accents, however, place "gold" with the former line so that the last line consists only of the phrase "they used for the paramour."[25]

"that they used for the paramour" (*עשו לבעל*): The BHS notes suggest that this last phrase is a later addition. Wolff also argues that these two final Hebrew words in the verse are late glosses.[26] This view does have some force since the change to a 3 m.pl. verb in a passage that otherwise consistently speaks of the wife/mother in the 3 f.sg. invites question. Stuart, noting the syntactical difficulty with the 3 m.pl. verb, suggests emending the word to an infinitive absolute and reading "and provided her with gold." He also proposes emending the final Hebrew word to *לא בעל* and explaining the present form as the result of "anomalous orthography by reason of the omission of the 'aleph."[27] Macintosh suggests identifying two separate clauses here: "the silver which I multiplied for her, and the gold they have consecrated to Baal."[28] However, the words "silver and gold" here seem to function as a double accusative.

Buss translates *עשו לבעל* as "they made into Baal."[29] The usual meaning of the construction *עשה ל* is indeed "to make into."[30] In the case of Hos 2:10, however, there does not seem to be an idol or any physical object under

---

[24] For this verb as "to admit" or "to confess," see H. Huffmon, "The Treaty Background of the Hebrew YĀDAᶜ," *BASOR* 181 (1966): 31–37. Cf. H. Huffmon and S. Parker, "A Further Note on the Treaty Background of Hebrew YĀDAᶜ," *BASOR* 184 (1966): 36–38. See also *BDB*, 394 and Macintosh, *Critical and Exegetical Commentary*, 54. Andersen and Freedman (*Hosea*, 242) similarly observe that the issue here is not ignorance but a rejection of knowledge. For the classic study of ידע, see E. Baumann, "YDᶜ und seine Derivate: Ein sprachlich-exegetische Studie," *ZAW* 28 (1908): 22–41; 110–43.

[25] Abma, *Bonds*, 130.

[26] Wolff, *Hosea*, 31; cf. Macintosh, *Critical and Exegetical Commentary*, 54.

[27] Stuart, *Hosea-Jonah*, 44; so also Kuhnigk, *Nordwestsemitische Studien*, 19.

[28] Macintosh, *Critical and Exegetical Commentary*, 54. 4QpHosᵃ indicates that two or more letters preceding עשו have been erased. The last letter appears to have been a ה, but the word זהב is present (ibid., 57).

[29] Buss, *Prophetic Word*, 9. So also Andersen and Freedman, *Hosea*, 244; Garrett, *Hosea, Joel*, 82; Wolff, *Hosea*, 37.

[30] See Exod 27:3; Deut 9:14; Judg 8:27; Isa 44:17, 19; Jer 37:15.

consideration. As McComiskey maintains, the presence of the definite article on
לבעל precludes reading this as the making of images.[31] In this regard, verse
10's construction is similar to the use of עשה ל to mean "used for" in 2 Chron
24:7: "For the children of the wicked Athaliah had violated the House of God
and had even used (עשו) the sacred things of the House of the LORD for the
Baals (לבעלים)" (JPS). Exodus 38:24 reflects a similar usage: "All the gold
that was used for the work (העשוי למלאכה) ..." (JPS).[32]

Verse 11

"I will take back again" (אשוב ולקחתי): Literally, "I will turn and take
back." These terms form a verbal hendiadays. The verb אשוב here denotes not
only the repetition of an action but also the return to a previous condition or
status.[33]

"in order to reckon" (לכסות): This translation takes לכסות as a rare
form of the qal geminate infinitive from כסס rather than כסה. The supporting
arguments can be found in the discussion below.

"her indiscretion" (ערותה): The Targum renders this "shame" (קלנה).
The term also appears as a euphemism (e.g., Gen 9:22–23).[34] For the meaning of
"improper behavior" or "indecency" the Hebrew Bible consistently attests the
construct phrase ערות דבר, as in Deut 23:15 and 24:1. Hence, the translation
"indiscretion" here is not the common meaning of this word when used
independently but derives largely from the immediate literary and metaphorical
context.[35]

Verse 12

"her genitals" (נבלתה): Stuart observes that, although this term is often
translated "her genitals," there is no actual lexical evidence for such a
meaning.[36] The use of euphemisms is so common in the Hebrew Bible,
however, that this word "may be intended to imply the parts of the female body
normally covered out of propriety."[37] Andersen and Freedman also note that,
since this word appears only here in the Hebrew Bible, "we derive no help from

---

[31] McComiskey, *The Minor Prophets*, 36.

[32] For others who translate 2:10 as "used for," see Davies, *Hosea* (NCB), 74; Harper, *Amos and Hosea*, 230; Mays, *Hosea*, 41; McComiskey, *The Minor Prophets*, 36.

[33] See Wolff, *Hosea*, 31; *BDB*, 998; cf. Deut 23:14 and 2 Kgs 24:1.

[34] For the translation "indiscretion" see *BDB*, 789. Cf. Andersen and Freedman, *Hosea*, 246.

[35] For example, while Deut 24:1 uses the full phrase cited above, it does so in the context of describing the behavior that meets the condition for a divorce with cause. This is the same overall context in which the term in Hos 2:11 appears.

[36] For a discussion of the etymology and function of this term, see S. Olyan, "'In the Sight of Her Lovers': On the Interpretation of *nablūt* in Hos 2, 12," *BZ* 36 (1992): 255–61.

[37] Stuart, *Hosea-Jonah*, 44; cf. Buss, *Prophetic Word*, 9.

other usages in setting its precise meaning."[38] The LXX renders this Hebrew term with ἀκαθαρσίαν ("uncleanness," "impurity"), and the Targum translates it with קְלָנָה ("shame").[39] See discussion below.

Verse 13

"*I will bring to an end*" (וְהִשְׁבַּתִּי): This verb forms a play on words with the following noun וְשַׁבַּתָּהּ ("her sabbaths").

"*her appointed times*" (מוֹעֲדָהּ): The nouns in this verse are singular collectives. מוֹעֵד seems to be a general term used of passover (Lev 23:4–5), new moon (Ps 104:19[MT]), the feast of unleavened bread (Lev 23:4–6), and the feast of booths (Deut 31:10) and functions as an inclusio here with the other general term מְשׂוֹשָׂהּ ("rejoicing"). This four-term expression (festivals, new moons, sabbaths, and appointed times) occurs only here and in Ezek 45:17 in the Hebrew Bible, while the three-term expression without חַג is more common (cf. 1 Chron 23:31; 2 Chron 2:3[MT]; 31:3).

The last piece of the pesher in 4QpHos[a] follows the citation of this verse.[40] The pesher reads, "The interpretation of it is that they make [the fe]asts go according to the appointed times of the nations. And [all joy] had been turned for them into mourning." Bernstein concludes that the reference to "walking in the festivals of the gentiles" in this pesher is modeled on a similar passage in *Jubilees* 6:34–35.[41]

Verse 14

"*gifts*" (אֶתְנָה): This word occurs only here in the Hebrew Bible. The translation "gifts" follows the BHS text note and makes the noun into the more common masculine form in order to match the masculine plural demonstrative pronoun (הֵמָּה) and the masculine plural suffixes in the rest of the verse (cf. Deut 23:19; Mic 1:7; Hos 9:1). One may then explain the presence of the masculine plural suffixes by noting that one of the multiple antecedents is masculine. The unusual MT form seems to be prompted by the word-play with "fig tree" (וּתְאֵנָתָהּ) and "they gave" (נָתְנוּ).[42]

---

[38] Andersen and Freedman, *Hosea*, 248.

[39] For further discussion of etymology, see Macintosh, *Critical and Exegetical Commentary*, 58–60.

[40] For a study of this part of the pesher, see M. Bernstein, "'Walking in the Festivals of the Gentiles': 4QpHosea[a] 2.15–17 and *Jubilees* 6:34–38," *JSP* 9 (1991): 21–34.

[41] Ibid., 25. To the writers of the pesher and of *Jubilees*, the issue was an incorrect calendar in Israel. 4QpHos[a] addresses the Qumranites in relation to their opponents in the matter of the calendar (see ibid., 33).

[42] See Macintosh, *Critical and Exegetical Commentary*, 63–64.

Verse 15

This verse appears in a fragmentary state in 4QXII^g. The verse is also cited in the Qumran text "Barki Nafshi" as a general reference to God's goodness to Israel.[43]

Verse 16

"*I am about to seduce her and bring her*" (והלכתיה מפתיה אנכי): These terms form a participle and perfect verb sequence that denotes two impending future actions. In several places the hifil of הלך describes the journey of the Israelites through the desert under Yahweh's leadership (e.g., Deut 8:2, 15; 29:4; Jer 2:17; Ps 106:9[MT]).[44] The LXX has a substantially different reading of this verse: "Therefore I will cause her to err, and I will make her as desolate...."

Verse 17

"*doorway of hope*" (תקוה פתח לְ): This phrase functions as the second of two accusatives for the main verb, both of which are marked with the sign of the direct object. As Buss notes, one may also read the verb נתן plus the preposition לְ as "to make ... into...."[45]

"*she will respond*" (וענתה): Macintosh observes that at least four meanings are attested for this verb in biblical Hebrew. He translates, "she will be attentive."[46] Wolff adds a sense of motion and action to the verb and reads, "she shall willingly follow."[47] The LXX seems to follow another possible meaning of the verb and reads, "she shall be afflicted" (ταπεινωθήσεται). The more common sense of ענה meaning "to respond, answer," however, fits well with the overall context of marriage and remarriage language.[48]

Verse 18

"*you will call me*" (תקראי): The MT contains a qal imperfect 2 f.sg. verb with the 1 c.sg. object understood in the first verb but explicit in the second one (תקראי־לי). The BHS note suggests emending these verbs to 3 f.sg. forms ("she will call"), assuming that a preposition and object have been omitted from the first part of the statement (cf. LXX, Syriac, and Vulgate).[49] For other uses of a second-person form in this context, however, see verse 21. Stuart concludes that

---

[43] See Abegg, Flint, Ulrich, *The Dead Sea Scrolls Bible*, 419.

[44] Andersen and Freedman, *Hosea*, 272.

[45] Buss, *Prophetic Word*, 9.

[46] Macintosh, *Critical and Exegetical Commentary*, 72–73.

[47] Wolff, *Hosea*, 31.

[48] So Buss (*Prophetic Word*, 9), who reads, "she will answer."

[49] For example, Buss reads, "she will say" with the LXX because he says that the MT "you" is not euphonic (ibid.).

it is ultimately impossible to decide whether the second- or third-person form is original.[50]

Verse 19

"*they will no longer be remembered*" (עוד יזכרו ולא): Macintosh gives this verb a cultic meaning and reads, "they will not be invoked."[51] For this usage, see also Jer 3:16 and Ps 20:8(MT).

Verse 20

"*for them*" (להם): The masculine plural suffixes in this verse seem most clearly to function resumptively and to refer to the group of beasts, birds, and creeping things included in the covenant of mutuality, since the preceding and following verses use third- and second-person *feminine* singular forms respectively to refer to the wife/mother.[52]

Verse 21

"*And*" (ו): BHS note suggests that this verse may continue 2:18 and that 2:19–20 may be an intrusion. This conclusion, however, breaks the thematic movement and unity of the oracle outlined above.

"*I will wed you*" (וארשתיך): The translation of this verb follows Wolff, who demonstrates that the "pi⁽c⁾el denotes the legal act constituting marriage. The customary translation 'to betroth,' as we use the term, incorrectly separates the act described here from the time of the public act of marriage."[53] In the ancient context, this term places the emphasis on the finality of the act of engagement. As Beeby notes, this emphasis on finality is indicated by the following word "forever" (לעולם).[54]

"*forever*" (לעולם): This term appears only here in the book of Hosea but also occurs in the legal parlance of the Elephantine marriage contracts. See discussion in chapter 3 above.

Verse 22

"*Yahweh*" (יהוה): The Vulgate and several Hebrew manuscripts read "that I am Yahweh."

Verses 23–24

"*respond*" (ענה): This verb occurs five times in these verses. The LXX (ἐπακούσομαι) and Vulgate (*exaudiam*) use the same translation in all five

---

[50] Stuart, *Hosea-Jonah*, 55.

[51] Macintosh, *Critical and Exegetical Commentary*, 80.

[52] See further discussion of this issue below.

[53] Wolff, *Hosea*, 46. Cf. Deut 20:7. Contrast Andersen and Freedman, *Hosea*, 283.

[54] Beeby, *Grace Abounding*, 30.

occurrences. The Targum, however, omits one of the occurrences and translates
the others in four different ways: "I will *listen* to their prayer, and I will
command the heavens that they *send down rain* upon the earth; and the earth
shall *make abundant* (תרבי) the corn, wine, and oil; and they shall *supply
enough for* (יספקון) the exiles of my people."[55]

Verse 25

"And I will sow her" (וזרעתיה): This verb forms a play on words with
"Jezreel" from verse 24, which means "God sows." Macintosh takes this phrase
as an agricultural metaphor "of the repopulation of the land by Israel." He does
not, however, translate the following preposition "to me" (לי), which seems to
argue against this position.[56] The BHS note also proposes changing the 3 f.sg.
suffix to 3 m.sg. ("I will sow him"). Stuart notes that it is not clear to what the
present feminine suffix refers. Only if it refers to Jezreel, the immediate
antecedent, is an emendation to "him" required.[57] Within the overall context,
however, the pronoun seems most naturally to refer to the wife/mother.

"You are my people" (עמי־אתה): The masculine gender here is probably
the result of the reference to Hosea's male child "Not-My-People" (cf. 1:9).

2. THE PROPHET'S INTRODUCTION (2:1–3)

Hosea 2 opens with three verses of prophetic speech that introduce and set the
stage for the divine speech that follows. At this point, the oracle does not use the
major metaphors of the wife, lovers, fornication, adultery, and בעל. Rather,
verses 1–3 rely on military imagery that envisions several joint actions
undertaken by the people of Israel and Judah. The opening section of Hosea's
oracle does not rely on such things as the legal background of ancient Near
Eastern divorce or the metaphorical traditions of sexual violence. While the
arguments given in the preceding chapters suggest that 2:1–3 stand as a unified
piece of the whole oracle in 2:1–25, these verses seem to *function* as a group in
a way that is different from the divine address in verses 4–25.

If these verses were not added later nor relocated from another original
position, how do they function as the opening of the extended oracle? The
observations made by commentators like Wolff concerning the differences
between 2:1–3 and 2:4–25 are accurate. The opening three verses do contain
things like passive constructions and third-person rather than first-person
references to Yahweh. An analysis of the rhetorical address of 2:1–3 illuminates
these areas and suggests not only a way to integrate the verses into the larger

---

[55] A. Guillaume, "A Note on Hosea II. 23, 24 (21, 22)," *JTS* 15 (1964): 57–58. Guillaume argues that
the Targum correctly interprets the "play on the nuances" of ענה (ibid., 58).

[56] Macintosh, *Critical and Exegetical Commentary*, 89.

[57] Stuart, *Hosea-Jonah*, 56.

whole but also a way to understand them more fully against Hosea's own rhetorical situation.

2.1 The Rhetorical Address of 2:1–3

2.1.1 *Restoration and Rejuvenation (2:1).* Hosea begins his oracle by proclaiming a grand recovery and reversal for the people of the northern kingdom of Israel: "And the number of the children of Israel will be like the sand of the sea that cannot be measured and cannot be counted" (2:1). The prophet uses a reference to sand that is similar to the traditions of Yahweh's promises to the patriarchs to announce this turning point in the story of the people.[58] The future that he proclaims includes a rejuvenated existence for Israel that fulfills Yahweh's intentions for them.

Both sentences of verse 1 begin with the same Hebrew verb (וְהָיָה, "and will be"), which gives the proclamation a future orientation.[59] Although the following verse includes the people of Judah in the events that will take place, the opening of the oracle assigns the central role to the northern kingdom. The phrase "children of Israel" in 2:1 does not function as a traditional or inclusive label for a united kingdom, since this same label appears side by side with "children of Judah" in verse 2. Hence, the opening words of the address clearly locate the prophet's focus on the northern kingdom, with an accessory role envisioned for Judah.[60] The extent to which the recovery and restoration that Hosea envisions remain in the future, however, is not as clear. The opening verses of the oracle contain no explicit indications that the prophet is looking to a distant time. These verses contain no references to the children of Israel dwelling "many days without king and without prince and without sacrifice" (cf. Hos 3:4). Neither do they contain "on that day" phrases that project the prophet's message into another era. Rather, the two appearances of וְהָיָה in verse 1 combine with the commands to speak to a contemporary audience in verse 3 to present a recovery and resurgence that is already underway.

---

[58] See Gen 15:5; 22:17; 32:13(MT). This observation does not presume the priority of Genesis. As with the discussion of Baal-peor in chapter 5, it is possible that Hosea's references preceded and contributed to the formation of the pentateuchal traditions. Additionally, "sand of the sea" is a common ancient Near Eastern metaphor.

[59] Within the literary context, several scholars have observed the contrast between the pessimistic pronouncement of 1:9 and the hopeful proclamation of 2:1 and have translated verse 1's opening *vav* as an adversative ("but the number of the children of Israel will be," e.g., Rudolph, *Hosea*, 55 and Mays, *Hosea*, 30). While this translation is helpful in illuminating the literary context, the preceding discussion of the rhetorical unit of Hos 2 has argued that 2:1 begins a new speech that was not originally connected to the material in 1:9.

[60] Cf. Landy, who emphasizes that the phrase "children of Israel" in 2:1 matches the phrase "children of Israel" in 2:2 (*Hosea*, 29).

The second part of 2:1 states the reversal motif more specifically: "So it will be, in the place in which it was said to them, 'You (m.pl.) are not my people,' it will be said to them, 'Children of the living God.'" Once again, the language makes clear that the group that is in need of restoration, the group that has been previously told they are not Yahweh's people, is specifically the inhabitants of the northern kingdom of Israel. The only available referent for the masculine plural pronouns in this sentence is the phrase "children of Israel." The "children of Judah" are not mentioned until the beginning of verse 2. In this proclamation, the same Hebrew word (אמר) appears in both a past and future sense in order to emphasize the changing fortunes of the people of Israel: "it was said … it will be said."

The restoration of Israel as God's people will occur in a particular "place." The scholarly discussion of the unnamed "place" (מקום) in which this reversal is set has varied greatly. At the outset, it is not clear whether Hosea has a specific place in mind or whether this term simply functions as a type of prepositional phrase (e.g., "instead of"). The majority of commentators assume the former. For example, Garrett and Andersen and Freedman suggest that the unnamed place may be the wilderness mentioned as the place of reconciliation in 2:16, but McKeating argues that the place refers to Shechem, the traditional site where Joshua made the covenant (Josh 24) and the Israelites rejected the House of David under Reheboam (1 Kgs 12).[61] On the other hand, Wolff does not consider the term to refer to a place at all but to carry the meaning of "instead."[62] Within the context of the traditions and oracles of Hosea, however, the most apparent place that could function in the symbolic role of reversal is Jezreel.[63] The phrase "blood of Jezreel" appears in 1:4 as a condemnation of the house of Jehu, and the phrase "valley of Jezreel" appears in 1:5 as the place of judgment upon the northern kingdom. "Jezreel" also appears in both chapters 1 and 2 as the name of Hosea's son and in 2:24 as one of the entities that receives Yahweh's restoration. The joint "march" of Judah and Israel in 2:2 also culminates in a great "day of Jezreel" that appears to have both positive and negative connotations. What is significant about this language for a rhetorical-historical analysis of Hosea's speech is that the use of the term "Jezreel" again emphasizes that the focus of both the condemnation and restoration is the northern kingdom, particularly the royal house (cf. 1:4, 5).[64] Additionally, the references to the area of Jezreel fit well with the historical situation of the Syro-

---

[61] Garrett, *Hosea, Joel*, 71–72; Andersen and Freedman, *Hosea*, 203; McKeating, *Books*, 80.

[62] Wolff, *Hosea*, 27; so also Garrett, *Hosea, Joel*, 72 and Mauchline, "Hosea," 574.

[63] Cf. Mays, *Hosea*, 32.

[64] For a study of the threat against Jezreel in Hos 1 and its relationship to the rhetoric and context of Hosea, see S. Irvine, "The Threat of Jezreel (Hosea 1:4–5)," *CBQ* 57 (1995): 494–503.

Ephraimitic war in which this region played a role in various stages of the conflict.[65]

Regardless of the precise identification of the unnamed place in verse 1, Andersen and Freedman are certainly correct to note that the significance of the "place" is symbolic: the place where the Israelites were once rejected as the people of God is the place where they will be reclaimed, that is, "redemption by recapitulation."[66] This opening proclamation does not yet contain the actual changing of the symbolic names for the people, which comes at the conclusion of chapter 2. The reclamation remains in the future. Neither the sentence "You are not my people" nor the phrase "Children of the living God" is a name per se (cf. 2:25).[67] Rather, the opening seems to introduce the overall movement of restoration that will occur in the verses that follow. In so doing, Hosea uses a phrase that appears to be an originally Hoseanic formula: "Children of the living God," and describes the restoration in passive language: "it will be said to them."[68] As Jeremias rightly emphasizes, one should note that this language is impersonal and not direct speech by Yahweh like that which appears in 2:4–25.[69] This lack of direct speech continues throughout verses 1–3 and gives verse 1 in particular an introductory quality within the whole of 2:1–25. Beginning in verse 1 and continuing throughout verses 2 and 3, Hosea provides an overview that sets out the intended results of Yahweh's actions in 2:4–25.

2.1.2 A New Leader and a New Mission (2:2). After presenting the general picture of restoration for the people of Israel in 2:1, Hosea offers a much more specific commentary on the events of that restoration in 2:2. This verse begins by mentioning the "children of Judah" before the "children of Israel." Since this order mirrors that of the superscription in 1:1, some interpreters suggest that this verse is part of a later Judean redaction.[70] As noted above, however, the prophet's speech that began in verse 1 has already established the northern kingdom of Israel as the focus of the oracle. Hosea now mentions Judah as playing an accessory role in the events that center on Israel. The speeches of Hosea often refer to Judah's status in actions involving the northern kingdom

---

[65] For example, Macintosh says that the unnamed place in 2:1 refers to Jezreel and reverses the memory of Tiglath-pileser's deportations from the area after his 733 B.C.E. campaign (*Critical and Exegetical Commentary*, 36).

[66] Andersen and Freedman, *Hosea*, 203.

[67] For example, Andersen and Freedman observe that these are statements based on the name of the third child and that the word order in 1:9, when the phrase, "you are not my people," is a name, has the second-person subject ("you") first not last (ibid., 204).

[68] It is not clear whether the phrase "living God" originated with Hosea as well.

[69] Jeremias, *Der Prophet*, 34.

[70] E.g., Buss, *Prophetic Word*, 34 and Blankenbaker, "Language," 143.

(e.g., 1:7).[71] In 2:2, for example, the word order seems to invert that of 1:6b–7a, and Andersen and Freedman conclude that this verse suggests nothing about the inferiority or superiority of Judah in the course of events.[72] Most importantly, the events at the close of the Syro-Ephraimitic war constitute a rhetorical-historical situation in which both Judah and Israel played a significant role. Due to the previous encroachments of Damascus on Israelite territory, the area placed under Hoshea's control by Tiglath-pileser III would have most likely included Judah. Thus, any action around this time would have involved both kingdoms.

In the remaining part of verse 2, Hosea proclaims that the people of Israel and Judah will undertake three joint actions: 1) "they will be gathered together," 2) "they will set over themselves one head," and 3) "they will march up from the land." As Mays observes, each of these three actions appears to be military in character.[73] The first action is in the form of a niphal perfect verb (וְנִקְבְּצוּ) that produces a passive voice. At first blush, this term may appear to be a reference to a return from exile (post 586 B.C.E.). The verb קבץ often functions as a sort of technical term in prophetic books for bringing people home from exile.[74] On the other hand, some commentators suggest that the language in 2:2 should not be understood as part of a promise but as part of a threat.[75] The other occurrences of קבץ in Hosea do not have the meaning of returning from exile but have negative connotations and could produce a meaning of being gathered in order to go into exile (8:10; 9:6).[76] In contrast to both of these interpretations, the rhetorical context of the Syro-Ephraimitic war provides another way to understand the prophet's statement as a part of the larger discourse of 2:1–25. Due to territorial restraints and the organization imposed by the Assyrian king, Israel and Judah seem to have been temporarily reunified under the leadership of Hoshea around 731 B.C.E. This situation contrasted sharply with the hostility between the northern and southern kingdoms that had existed from 734–731 B.C.E. According to Hosea, the first joint action undertaken by Israel and Judah ("gathering together") characterizes their new relationship at this time. It is not

---

[71] Garrett concludes that none of the references to Judah in Hosea is secondary, and each of them is "integral to the structure or message of the texts in which they appear" (*Hosea, Joel*, 25).

[72] Andersen and Freedman, *Hosea*, 207.

[73] Mays, *Hosea*, 32.

[74] E.g., Isa 40:11; Jer 31:8–10; Ezek 34:11–13. Cf. Abma, *Bonds*, 162.

[75] Gowan, *Theology*, 40–41.

[76] This interpretation goes back at least to Ibn Ezra, who resisted the typical medieval Jewish commentators' view that this verse is a messianic prophecy. He argued that "they will be gathered" is a reference to the destruction of Judah by Sennacherib, who is referred to in this text as the "one head." Thus, to "go up from the land" was originally a reference to going into exile. These arguments seem to have been driven by Ibn Ezra's conclusion that 2:1–3 was a negative oracle that continued the doom oracle of 1:8–9 (see Lipshitz, *Ibn Ezra*, 5–6, 27).

clear whom Hosea has in mind as the one gathering Judah and Israel together, and the referent may be Hoshea, Tiglath-pileser, or even Yahweh.

Hosea's reference to the "gathering" of Israel and Judah connects closely with the second action in 2:2: "they will set over themselves one head." First Samuel 8:4–5 also uses the verb קבץ to describe the elders of the people gathering before Samuel to request a king. In Hosea's address, he describes this second action of the people with very particular vocabulary: ושמו להם ראש אחד. Many commentators take the text's use of the term ראש ("head") and failure to employ the word מלך ("king") as an intentional polemic against the institution of the monarchy. Mays argues that the use of ראש is an implicit polemic against the king, since the use of this word as a title often occurs in relation to nonroyal offices (e.g., Num 14:4; Judg 11:8).[77] Similarly, Wolff maintains that ראש appears in this positive context because Hosea only uses מלך in judgment speeches.[78] These interpretations generally presume that the writer or speaker of verse 2 considered the premonarchic time to be ideal and envisioned the postexilic situation as a return to that state. Thus, it is concluded, the text avoids the word מלך because the new postexilic leadership will transcend the old institution of the monarchy.[79] Jeremiah 30:9, Ezek 34:23–24, and 37:22–23 use similar imagery to depict the postexilic reunion of Israel and Judah under a leader from the house of David.

If one does not presume a postexilic setting for this verse, however, the language itself does not preclude the possibility that Hosea is in fact speaking of an actual king. The use of the phrase שׂים ל ("to appoint") has a parallel in 1 Sam 8:5 where the people ask Samuel specifically for a king.[80] Isaiah 7:8–9 also clearly demonstrate that the term ראש can be used as a figure of speech for a king, and 1 Sam 15:17 and Job 29:25 use ראש as a parallel term for מלך.[81] Psalm 18:44 even uses the exact language of Hos 2:2 and refers to the king as "head": "You appointed me (תשׂימני) as head (לראש) of nations." Most likely on the basis of this type of textual evidence, there is a tradition, especially among older commentaries, which understands Hos 2:2 as a reference to an actual monarch. These interpretations are heavily influenced, however, by the notion of a postexilic date for 2:1–3 and thus typically consider the king to be a

---

[77] Mays, *Hosea*, 32.

[78] Wolff, *Hosea*, 27; cf. Birch, *Hosea, Joel, Amos*, 25.

[79] Bons, *Buch*, 36; Davies, *Hosea* (OTG), 62; Garrett, *Hosea, Joel*, 73; Macintosh, *Critical and Exegetical Commentary*, lxxxviii, 30; Stuart, *Hosea-Jonah*, 39. For discussion of Hosea's supposed interpretation of the wilderness and premonarchic periods as ideal, see chapter 5 above.

[80] Andersen and Freedman state, "The same idiom is used in 1 Sam 8:5 for the selection of a monarch, which makes it possible that the 'one head' is a king" (*Hosea*, 208). Cf. Deut 17:15: "You will indeed set up over yourselves a king (שׂום תשׂים עליך) whom Yahweh your God will choose...."

[81] For the purposes of this work, it is interesting to note that the Isaiah reference also comes from a prophet describing the kings involved in the Syro-Ephraimitic war.

surviving member of the Davidic dynasty. For example, Cheyne compares 2:2 with the reference to a king in 3:5 and concludes that the figure called רֹאשׁ is "doubtless the Davidic King."[82]

Building upon the above evidence, the rhetorical context of the Syro-Ephraimitic war and the literary context of all of 2:1–25 help illuminate this second action of the people. As noted above, due to various restraints and necessities, the people of Israel and Judah were joined together in the vassal state called "Bit-Ḫumri," which Tiglath-pileser established around 731 B.C.E. Hoshea was the ruler designated by Assyria both to oversee that territory and to lead the final removal of Pekah from Samaria. Against the background of these developments, the prophet's words here may be seen as proclaiming at least a temporary unification of Israel and Judah in a joint effort under the leadership of Hoshea. This unification, however, existed for the particular, cooperative, military-type action that is described in the last part of verse 2. Accordingly, Hosea may indeed have deliberately chosen the word רֹאשׁ to describe Hoshea because it both refers to one who is a king and reflects the situation in which Israel and Judah, two states with two kings (Hoshea and Ahaz), are joined under one designated leader (Hoshea) in order to accomplish a particular military task. The language of the story of Jephthah in Judg 11:5–11 is instructive in this regard as it describes a leader specifically chosen to lead in battle with the words שִׂים רֹאשׁ. Hoshea did not assume the kingship of Judah but served as the "head" of the two cooperating states in this particular joint venture.

Seen in this way, one can conceive differently the relationship between Hos 2:2 and exilic texts like Ezek 34:23–24.[83] Although Ezek 34:23–24 uses similar imagery of appointing one leader who will restore the exiled community, it is not necessary to conclude that Hos 2:2 borrows this imagery and comes from the exilic or postexilic period.[84] To the contrary, these later texts may be exilic appropriations of features in Hosea's preaching, namely, the language of "one head" and the positive view of Davidic leadership (cf. Hos 3:5).

The specific action that the combined people of Israel and Judah will take under Hoshea's leadership appears in the last part of verse 2: וְעָלוּ מִן־הָאָרֶץ. While the language itself is straightforward, the translation of this construction remains highly debated, and scholars' renderings are often governed by their redactional conclusions about the date and reference of the verse. The traditional

---

[82] Cheyne, *Hosea*, 46. So also Harper, *Critical and Exegetical Commentary*, 247; Knight, *Hosea*, 49; Rudolph, *Hosea*, 57. Some newer studies that have picked up this idea include Blankenbaker, "Language," 144–45 and Ward, *Hosea*, 45. Some interpreters have argued that 2:2 should be read as a messianic passage that does not refer to a human leader of any kind and perhaps considers Yahweh to be the "head" (e.g., McComiskey, *The Minor Prophets*, 29). Rudolph (*Hosea*, 57) explicitly rejects this interpretation.

[83] See also Jer 30:9 and Ezek 37:22–23.

[84] See Gelston, "Kingship," 77.

interpretation before 1899 understood it as a reference to the return from exile.[85] This interpretation goes back at least to the Targum (מארע גלותהון, "land of their exile") and has continued among some modern commentators.[86] Recent scholarship, however, has widely rejected this exilic interpretation. There is no precedent in the Hebrew Bible for referring to foreign nations as "the land," (i.e., the single term הארץ without any construct phrase).[87] The prophetic books in particular do not use הארץ to refer to foreign lands.

In the twentieth century, five primary views of this phrase have emerged. First, as early as 1899, Lambert argued that the phrase carries the meaning of "to gain ascendancy/take possession of the land."[88] Wolff initially adopted a view of this verse that related it to a pilgrimage up to a covenant shrine but later followed Lambert's suggestion and translated, "they will take possession of the land."[89] This view relied on the evidence of Exod 1:10, which expresses the Egyptians' fears that the Hebrews will become too numerous and "go up from the land" (ועלה מן־הארץ). Wolff saw Hos 2:2 as a reference to the Israelites recapturing territory lost after the events of the Syro-Ephraimitic war. As Andersen and Freedman emphasized, however, the preposition "from" (מן) in this phrase argues against this reading of "take possession of."[90] Perhaps because of this difficulty, as early as 1912, Theis suggested a second approach to the verse. He considered the preposition מן to be a comparative on the basis of the line in Exod 1:10 and understood the phrase to mean that the people will increase more than the land.[91]

A third proposal for understanding this phrase reads Hos 2:2 in light of Gen 2:6, which describes how a primordial river continually went up over the land (יעלה מן־הארץ). From this parallel, some interpreters translate Hosea's

---

[85] For example, Wellhausen omits the word "land" from his translation and renders עלה with zurückkehren, "to come back" (Wellhausen, *Die kleinen Propheten*, 11). For discussion, see K. Rupprecht, "עלה מן הארץ (Ex 1:10, Hos 2:2): sich des Landes bemächtigen?," *ZAW* 82 (1970): 442–47.

[86] E.g., Abma, *Bonds*, 162; Duhm, "Anmerkungen," 18–19; Harper, *Critical and Exegetical Commentary*, 247; Jeremias, *Der Prophet*, 35; Mauchline, "Hosea," 576; Stuart, *Hosea-Jonah*, 38–39.

[87] Emmerson, *Hosea*, 98; Garrett, *Hosea, Joel*, 73; Macintosh, *Critical and Exegetical Commentary*, 30; Mays, *Hosea*, 33; Wolff, *Hosea*, 27–28.

[88] M. Lambert, "Note exégétique," *REJ* 39 (1899): 300.

[89] Contrast Wolff, "Der große Jesreeltag," 95 with Wolff, *Hosea*, 24. Wolff later conceded that the notion of an eschatological pilgrimage does not fit the context (see *Hosea*, 28). Contrast Ward (*Hosea*, 46), who argues that this verse refers to a pilgrimage to a national sanctuary and thus is a reversal of 2:13 where Yahweh takes away the national festivals. Cf. Sweeney (*The Twelve Prophets*, 24), who sees this phrase as terminology for going up to Jerusalem and Snaith (*Amos*, 55), who says the phrase may refer to Israel and Judah coming up from the country to the city of Jerusalem for the great feasts. For the "take possession of" translation following Lambert, see also Birch, *Hosea, Joel, Amos*, 17 and McKeating, *Books*, 79.

[90] Andersen and Freedman, *Hosea*, 208–9.

[91] J. Theis, *Sumerisches im Alten Testament* (Trier: Paulinus-Druekerei, 1912), 14.

statement in terms of a resurgence of Israelite strength: "they will flood/swamp the earth."[92] This interpretation, however, does not appear to have any connections with the immediate context of the phrase in Hos 2. A fourth view of this phrase also relies upon Gen 2:6 and draws parallels with Ugaritic uses of the term *ʾereṣ*. Holladay suggests interpreting הארץ here as one of a small number of places in the Hebrew Bible where the term means "underworld."[93] He argues that this meaning is especially prevalent when ארץ occurs in conjunction with the phrase עלה מן ("to go up from"). For example, Holladay takes the reference noted above in Gen 2:6 as describing "ground-water" that rises up "out of the underworld."[94] He also places the story of Saul's summoning of the spirit of Samuel in 1 Sam 28:13 into this category: "a spirit I have seen coming up from the underworld." Finally, Holladay adds the reference in Exod 1:10 and interprets it metaphorically: "lest … he [Israel] be added to our enemies, and he gain a resurrection (עלה מן־הארץ)." This proposal understands Hos 2:2 in similar terms of a national resurrection: "they shall arise from the underworld."[95] In response to this view, however, one may observe not only that such a meaning for הארץ is rare in the Hebrew Bible but also that the immediate context of Hos 2 does not suggest a literal or metaphorical resurrection from the dead.[96]

A final major proposal for understanding the people's joint action in verse 2 draws upon the agricultural imagery present in the chapter as a whole. This view takes the phrase in question as an agricultural metaphor meaning "to grow/sprout up from the earth."[97] The agricultural reading fits well with the imagery at the end of the oracle in 2:25 ("I will sow her"). Additionally, the verb עלה occasionally describes the springing up of vegetation (e.g., Gen 41:5, 22; Deut 29:22[MT]; Isa 15:13). These facts do not, however, provide a convincing case for interpreting the particular phrase in Hos 2:2 in this metaphorical way. The clear agricultural imagery that appears at the end of the chapter is not present in these opening verses.

In response to these various explanations of the joint action in Hos 2:2, two particular studies have argued that the literal sense of "going up from the land" best represents the function of this phrase within the text's overall discourse.

---

[92] See H. Gressmann, *Der Messias* (FRLANT 43; Göttingen: Vandenhoeck & Ruprecht, 1929), 235.

[93] W. Holladay, "ʾEREṢ-'Underworld': Two More Suggestions," *VT* 19 (1969): 123–24 and Kuhnigk, *Nordwestsemitischen Studien*, 8–10. For a list of biblical texts where ארץ possibly means "underworld," see M. Dahood, *Psalms I: 1–50* (AB 16; Garden City, N.Y.: Doubleday, 1979), 106.

[94] Holladay, "ʾEREṢ," 123.

[95] Ibid., 123–24. The most recent major commentary to follow this view is Andersen and Freedman, *Hosea*, 208–9.

[96] For critique, see Rupprecht, "עלה," 495.

[97] This view goes back to Rudolph, *Hosea*, 58. See also Bons, *Buch*, 36; Davies, *Hosea* (NCB), 62; Emmerson, *Hosea*, 98; Garrett, *Hosea, Joel*, 73; Macintosh, *Critical and Exegetical Commentary*, 30; McComiskey, *The Minor Prophets*, 28.

Rupprecht specifically analyzes the relationship between Hos 2:2 and Exod 1:10 and concludes that one cannot glean a special meaning for one from the other. Both phrases make the most sense when translated literally within their own contexts, and they do not mean the same thing.[98] Particularly in the case of Hos 2:2, Rupprecht maintains that the different proposals outlined above provide no better understanding than the literal sense of a group of people going up from some territory. He does not, however, go on to explore what the historical implications and rhetorical function of the phrase in verse 2 might be if seen in this way.

Along these same lines, Renaud concludes that a literal translation should be retained.[99] Unlike Rupprecht, however, Renaud goes on to explore the possible implications and function within the discourse as a whole. Since he operates with the view that 2:1–3 comes from a postexilic redactor and describes the return from exile, he asserts that the phrase deliberately draws upon the typology of the exodus from Exod 1:10. Thus, in spite of the fact that the exilic interpretation is without precedent in the Hebrew Bible, Renaud revitalizes the traditional view of Hos 2:2 as a description of the return from exile by arguing that it draws upon the imagery of Exod 1:10 to depict the return as a second exodus.[100] He concludes that both Hos 2:2 and Exod 1:10 should be read literally as the reversal of the descent (ירד) of the Israelites into Egypt (cf. Gen 12:10; 42:2, 38).

Rupprecht's and Renaud's conviction that one should deal with the literal meaning of the phrase "go up from the land" specifically in light of its function in the context of Hos 2:1–3 provides a way forward. The translations of Lambert and Wolff, although plagued by the presence of the preposition מן, correctly observe and emphasize the military nature of the phrase and its context. The presence of the particular verb עלה in this verse is even more significant in this regard. The term עלה often occurs in the context of military actions with the meaning of "to march/campaign."[101] When the subject of this verb is an army, the term specifically means to mount a campaign and the verse typically names the target.[102] Although Hos 2:2 does not contain an explicit reference to an army or an attack, the overall context and imagery of verses 1–3 is that of a series of

---

[98] Rupprecht, "עלה," 446–47. Most interestingly in relation to this study, Macintosh has concluded that if one insists that Hos 2:2 and Exod 1:10 have the same meaning, the only meaning of עלה that fits both is "to mount an attack" (*Critical and Exegetical Commentary*, 32).

[99] Renaud, "Osée ii:2," 495.

[100] Renaud considers הארץ in 2:2 to represent the diaspora or land of captivity. He also takes ראש as a new leader who is cast in the role of a second Moses (ibid., 496–98).

[101] See *KBL*, 705; *BDB*, 748; Mays, *Hosea*, 33.

[102] Andersen and Freedman, *Hosea*, 208.

military actions. On this basis alone, several commentators conclude that the action expressed by עלה here must also be military in nature.[103]

When carrying this military/warfare meaning, עלה typically stands with the preposition אל or על.[104] There are, however, some occurrences in which the verb carries the meaning of a military campaign without the presence of a preposition. In Num 13:30 Caleb adjures the people, "Let us by all means go up (עלה נעלה), and we shall gain possession of it...." Second Kings 17:5 uses the verb to indicate an attack on Samaria: "And he (Shalmaneser) marched against (ויעל) Samaria and he besieged it three years."[105] Isaiah 7:1 describes an attack of Rezin of Damascus and Pekah of Samaria by saying that they "marched up" (עלה) to Jerusalem to fight against it. Isaiah 21:2 also calls forth military action against Babylon by commanding, "March up (עלי) O Elam!" The common military meaning of the verb עלה is even clearer in texts that combine the term with the preposition מעל in order to indicate retreat from battle.[106] More importantly for the phrase in Hos 2:2, however, three occurrences of the verb in Josh 10 use the whole phrase עלה מן to express a military campaign and its point of origin. Joshua 10:7 and 9 state that Joshua and the people "marched up from Gilgal" (ויעל ... מן־הגלגל) to attack Gibeon. Joshua 10:36 also uses the phrase to narrate the attack against Hebron: "Then Joshua marched up ... from Eglon (ויעל ... מעגלונה) to Hebron and made war against it." These examples suggest that there was a common tradition of using the verb עלה, with or without a preposition, to describe a military action of some sort, namely, a march or campaign.[107]

In Hosea's statement in verse 2, the point of origin for the apparent military campaign is simply called "the land." This word (הארץ) appears with various meanings throughout the Hebrew Bible. Analysis of the term's meaning in Hos 2, however, should focus on the specific form of the word found therein: the case of ארץ with a definite article and independent of any construct phrase. Throughout the Hebrew Bible, this particular form refers on some occasions to "the earth" in a broad sense. This usage is especially prevalent in the Primeval History.[108] Yet, already in the Genesis material dealing with Abram, הארץ

---

[103] See for example Blankenbaker, "Language," 147; Cheyne, *Hosea*, 46; Knight, *Hosea*, 49; McComiskey, *The Minor Prophets*, 30.

[104] For examples, see Num 13:31; Judg 1:1; 6:3; 12:3; 15:10; 18:9; 1 Sam 7:7; 14:10; 1 Kgs 14:25; 16:17; 20:22; 2 Kgs 17:3; 18:25; Isa 36:10; Joel 1:6; Nah 2:2. There are no examples in which the preposition מן indicates the object of the campaign. This observation is not relevant for Hos 2:2, however, because the preposition is not used in this verse to indicate the object of the attack but to indicate the geographical location from which the attack originated.

[105] This lack of preposition contrasts with 2 Kgs 17:3 which uses על.

[106] See 1 Kgs 15:19; 2 Kgs 12:19; 2 Chron 16:3; Jer 21:2; 34:21.

[107] For an exploration of how עלה functions with a military meaning in prophetic language, see R. Bach, *Die Aufforderungen zur Flucht und zum Kampf im alttestamentlichen Prophetenspruch* (WMANT 9; Neukirchen: Neukirchen Verlag, 1962), 63.

[108] For examples, Gen 1:1, 2, 15, 17; 2:1; 6:4–5; 7:3; 9:1.

functions as a more specific reference to the land of Canaan in particular.[109] The repeated references to the "people of the land" provide good examples of this usage.[110] This specific referent for הארץ becomes clearer and more exclusive in the legal materials of Leviticus and Deuteronomy and continues throughout the historical books like Joshua and Kings.[111]

Beginning in 2 Kings, however, הארץ occurs frequently in references to another group also called "the people of the land."[112] This usage seems to indicate a meaning for the term that refers specifically to the land of Judah and not simply to all of Canaan. Even prior to this material, the last part of 1 Kgs 4:19 contains one of the clearest uses of "the land" to refer specifically to Judah. While listing the officers appointed by Solomon, verse 19 states, "and one officer was in the land (בארץ)."[113] When one turns to the prophetic books, he or she finds both the use of הארץ in the broader sense of "the earth" and the use of the term as a specific reference to the land of Judah. For example, Jer 41:2 and 18 describe the assassination of Gedeliah, the leader of Judah after 586 B.C.E., by noting that the king of Babylon had appointed him over "the land" (בארץ). Jeremiah 1:14–15 also uses the term in this way while describing a coming attack on the land of Judah: "From the north shall disaster break loose upon all the inhabitants of the land (הארץ)."[114]

Within the book of Hosea, the situation is complex. Hosea often uses the specific form of ארץ with the definite article in the broad sense of the whole "earth" or in the agricultural sense of the "ground."[115] In the latter case, the term הארץ never refers to a specific foreign land of any kind but always to some portion of the land of Canaan.[116] Similarly, in the context of chapter 2 there is nothing that suggests a foreign land.[117] Verses 20 and 23–25 employ an agricultural metaphor and use "the land" in the broad sense of the earth or ground. The occurrence of הארץ in Hos 2:2, however, seems to be a special case because of its literary context.[118] This appearance is the only place in the book where הארץ stands in a verse that focuses on and names Judah as well as

---

[109] See Gen 12:6, 10.

[110] Cf. Gen 23:7, 12, 13.

[111] See Lev 18:25, 27, 28; Deut 12:1; 15:4; Josh 1:11; Judg 1:2; 2 Kgs 15:19; 23:35.

[112] Cf. 2 Kgs 11:14, 18, 19, 20; 15:5; 21:24; 23:30. The issue of the historical identity of this group lies outside the scope of this work.

[113] To clarify the meaning, the LXX inserts "Judah" (cf. NRSV).

[114] See also Isa 16:1; Jer 3:2, 9; Ezek 15:8; 36:28.

[115] For the broad sense, see Hos 1:2; 2:20. For the agricultural imagery, see 2:23, 24, 25; 6:3.

[116] Cf. 4:1, 3. See Andersen and Freedman, *Hosea*, 209; Emmerson, *Hosea*, 98; Hubbard, *Hosea*, 67; Mays, *Hosea*, 33; Wolff, *Hosea*, 94.

[117] As Cheyne concluded, the referent of this term in Hos 2 "can only be Palestine since there is nothing in the context to suggest that either the land of captivity (as Kimchi, following the Targum) or the earth in general is intended" (*Hosea*, 46).

[118] Harper observes this difference and concludes that הארץ in 2:2 does not refer to the land of Israel in general as it does in 2:20 (Harper, *Amos*, 245).

Israel. Furthermore, the references to עלה and ראש in this verse suggest that it is heavily nationalistic and militaristic (i.e., not agricultural) in nature. One should also note that the perspective and action of verse 2 reflect the standpoint of Judah. For example, the verse places the "children of Judah" in the first position before the "children of Israel." Taken together with the uses of the term as a shorthand for Judah in other parts of the Hebrew Bible, these contextual considerations suggest that the use of הארץ in Hos 2:2 is neither a broad reference nor an agricultural term but reflects the predominant meaning of the word in other prophetic texts: the land of Judah. In verse 2, the prophet describes a group of Judeans and Israelites marching up out of the land of Judah. Thus, a translation of 2:2 should render this term not as "the earth" or "the ground" but simply "the land."

When one places this reading of Hos 2:2 against the backdrop of the prophet's rhetorical-historical situation, several conclusions emerge. First, the text's indications of a joint military campaign by Israel and Judah that is to begin in the land of Judah fit well with what is known of the period around 731 B.C.E. when Hoshea was appointed to lead the new territory designated "Bit-Humri" and to oust Pekah from Samaria. Because of the territorial reduction of the northern kingdom outlined earlier in chapter 6, a joint campaign of this kind would most likely have had to move northward from the stable territory of Judah that had remained loyal to Assyria throughout 734–731 B.C.E. Thus far in his introduction, Hosea employs his rhetoric in order to proclaim that this action is sanctioned by Yahweh and will result in a time of restoration and rejuvenation for the people of the northern kingdom of Israel, who have suffered the consequences of Pekah's inappropriate political actions and open rebellion against Assyria.[119] In so proclaiming, the prophet describes these events at the close of verse 2 by exclaiming, "great will be the day of Jezreel."[120] This final phrase recalls the judgment against Israel described in 1:4–5, which brings violence against the house of Jehu in the same symbolic place that they perpetrated earlier atrocities. As Mays notes, the phrase "day of Jezreel" functions like the "day of Midian" in Isa 9:3(MT), which emphasizes that the battle will be Yahweh's not the people's.[121] This reference to the symbolic place of Jezreel once again suggests that the focus of the oracle's rhetoric is specifically the ruling house in the northern kingdom.

2.1.3 *A Family Reunion (2:3).* The final verse of the opening section of Hos 2 consists of a specific command for the people to address members of their own

---

[119] Knight offers a similar interpretation of Hos 2:2 and argues that the imagery represents Israel and Judah marching north from the land of Judah to the plain of Esdraelon, where Jezreel was located. However, he dates the verse to the period after the death of Josiah (Knight, *Hosea,* 49).

[120] See text critical notes above for the future-tense translation of this verbless phrase.

[121] Mays, *Hosea,* 33; cf. Blankenbaker, "Language," 148.

community. In contrast to 2:4, this verse does not yet contain divine speech by Yahweh in the first person but the conclusion of Hosea's description of the course of events: "Say (אִמְרוּ) to your (m.pl.) brothers, 'My People,' and to your (m.pl.) sisters, 'Compassion.'" One of the most significant features of Hosea's statement is that it is addressed to plural subjects (m.pl. imperative and m.pl. pronouns). The objects with whom the subjects are to speak are also plural ("brothers" and "sisters"). Because the identity of these groups is not immediately clear, proposals range across a vast spectrum.[122] Several interpreters follow the LXX, which contains the singular forms "brother" and "sister," and attempt to relate this verse to the actual personal life of Hosea. They take the word "Jezreel" at the end of verse 2 as a reference to Hosea's son from 1:4, who is now called upon to speak to his sister "No-Compassion" (1:6) and his brother "Not-My-People" (1:9).[123] Similarly, but more speculatively, McComiskey explains the groups being addressed here as "adoptive children born to Gomer before her marriage to Hosea," while Knight suggests that they represent the "Canaanite peoples of various nations who dwelt in the plain of Esdraelon...."[124] These proposals are influenced heavily by the authors' interpretive decisions concerning the priority of the family traditions in chapter 1 over the oracular materials in chapter 2. If, however, the family traditions in Hos 1 developed later and under the influence of Hosea's preaching, these interpretations are less likely. In either case, the above readings overlook the fact that both the subjects and objects in verse 3 are plural.

Hosea's statement seems to involve a conversation among the members of the people of Israel and Judah. The historically hostile brothers and sisters of Judah and Israel speak to each other in a type of new covenant. Along these lines, Wolff and Rudolph rightly recognize the connection between this imagery and the rhetorical situation of the Syro-Ephraimitic conflict. Wolff interprets 2:3 as repentant northerners speaking to southerners, while Rudolph understands it as forgiving Judeans speaking to Israelites.[125] While these readings fit with the overall rhetorical horizon and situation of the oracle, the text does not support a clear-cut distinction between Israelites and Judeans. Hosea's introduction has already suggested that a combined group of northerners and southerners is undertaking a joint campaign directed against Samaria. The historical situation surrounding Hoshea's ultimate overthrow of Pekah in Samaria also suggests a period in which some Israelites were aligned with Judeans while others stood

---

[122] For surveys of the various interpretations, see Harper, *Critical and Exegetical Commentary*, 247 and Davies, *Hosea* (NCB), 63.

[123] Andersen and Freedman, *Hosea*, 212; Mauchline, "Hosea," 575; Sellin, *Zwölfprophetenbuch*, 26; Ward, *Hosea*, 26.

[124] McComiskey, *The Minor Prophets*, 32; Knight, *Hosea*, 51.

[125] Wolff, *Hosea*, 33; Rudolph, *Hosea*, 58–59; cf. Blankenbaker ("Language," 151), who understands the speakers as only the faithful Israelites.

with the ruling house in Samaria. Thus, in his rhetorical situation, Hosea's statement may operate on two levels. He not only encourages the sanctioned cooperation between Israelites and Judeans, but he also suggests a reclaiming or rescuing of those "brothers" and "sisters" who remain under the influence of Pekah and the rulers in Samaria. Those very Israelites who had previously been disowned by Yahweh (cf. "it was said to them, 'You[m.pl.] are not my people,'" 2:1) are the very ones to be welcomed back as "brothers" and "sisters."

In order to persuade his audience in this regard, Hosea employs familial language. By addressing those Israelites who have been caught up in Pekah's rebellious actions as "your brothers" and "your sisters," the prophet emphasizes the intimate relationship that remains between those who are undertaking the campaign against Pekah and those whom they will encounter. His command to address the "brothers" as "My People" also signifies a restored relationship for them with Yahweh. Hosea's language even reasserts the united tradition and shared history that existed between the "brothers" and "sisters" of Israel and Judah. This verse does not yet contain, however, any representation of the actual restoration of the people or the full reversal of the symbolic names. That reversal appears in the divine speech in 2:16 and 25. At this point, Hosea sets the stage for Yahweh's dramatic discourse that follows by providing an overview of the events and their significance.

3. SUMMARY AND CONCLUSIONS

The first three verses of Hos 2 function in a way that is different from the divine oracle that follows. In these verses, there is no talk of the legalities of divorce or the metaphors of lovers. There are no references to fornication, adultery, or punishment. On the contrary, 2:1–3 outlines a broad movement of divine reversal that results in a cooperative effort between northerners and southerners and a reconciliation between Yahweh and those people who were estranged from him. Thus, verses 1–3 have a clear and intimate connection as the opening of the larger rhetorical address that spans the entirety of chapter 2. Only with these verses in place is the reader prepared for the full movement of Hos 2 from judgment to restoration.[126]

When taken together, the elements of verses 1–3 indicate a situation that fits well with the sequence of events known to have taken place concerning Israel, Judah, and Samaria at the close of the Syro-Ephraimitic war. These verses may indeed represent the prophet's theological explanation and exhortation addressing and endorsing the cooperative effort of Hoshea of Israel and Ahaz of Judah to carry out the Assyrian command to overthrow Pekah and restore Samaria to its status as a pro-Assyrian vassal state. In verses 1–3, Hosea specifically addresses the joint effort as well as the positive results he believes it

---

[126] So also Landy, *Hosea*, 31.

will accomplish. The people of Israel and Judah will be restored to the status of heirs to the patriarchal promises (2:1) through their successful execution of the day of judgment ("day of Jezreel") on Pekah and the anti-Assyrian rulers that remain in Samaria (2:2). Under Hoshea, the newly appointed ruler of the Assyrian territory that included both the northern and southern kingdoms, the cooperative force will campaign from Judah and take Samaria. As a result, the divided "brothers" and "sisters" throughout the lands of Israel and Judah will be reunited under the banner of political rest and religious faithfulness. Through his words, Hosea depicts this entire course of historical-political events as the divinely appointed reversal of judgment and restoration of right-relationship between the people and Yahweh.[127]

Seen in this way, Hos 2:1–3 functions as a type of overture to the extended metaphorical discourse in 2:4–25. Verses 1–3 provide a general overview of the events and the prophet's understanding of their theological implications. Verses 4–25 then elaborate on the particular workings of the situation by emphasizing Yahweh's perspectives, actions, and even thoughts. The first three verses function as Hosea's own introduction to the divine oracle, which sets the stage for Yahweh's direct address.

The prophetic oracle in Mic 6:1–8 provides an instructive parallel to the function of Hos 2:1–3. In Mic 6, the opening two verses are a prologue given by

---

[127] The historical situation reflected in Hos 2:1–3 may also shed light on the explicit comments made about King Hoshea of Israel elsewhere in 2 Kgs 17:2: "He did evil in the eyes of Yahweh though not like the kings of Israel who were before him." This verse's uniquely positive evaluation of a northern king by the Judean editors has produced a wide range of explanations from both ancient and modern interpreters. This anomaly suggests that the editorial assessment comes from editors living close to Hoshea's time, since the editors living in the exilic or postexilic period would have presumably had no knowledge of events in Hoshea's reign that could lead to a positive evaluation of him by Judeans unless these events were preserved in earlier written sources. Rabbinic writers attributed this positive assessment to Hoshea's practice of allowing northerners to worship in Jerusalem by removing the roadblocks to the southern city (e.g., b. *B. Bat.*, 121a; b. *Git.*, 88a; b. *Ta'an.*, 30b. Cf. M. Cogan and H. Tadmor, *II Kings: A New Translation with Introduction and Commentary* [AB 11; Garden City, N.Y.: Doubleday, 1988], 196). Modern commentators have continued the tradition of giving a cultic explanation of the Judeans' positive evaluation of Hoshea. For example, van der Kooij suggests that, since Assyria had captured Dan, Hoshea retained only one golden calf in his kingdom (A. van der Kooij, "Zur Exegese von II Reg. 17, 2," *ZAW* 96 [1984]: 109–12). Snaith also proposes that the Judean editors viewed Hoshea's later anti-Assyrian rebellions (2 Kgs 17:3–4) as examples of righteousness (N. Snaith, "II Kings," in *IB* III: 278; cf. W. Brueggemann, *1 & 2 Kings* [Smyth and Helwys Bible Commentary; Macon: Smyth & Helwys, 2000], 475–76).

In contrast to these explanations, the comments of the Judean editors may reflect the fact that Hoshea played a unifying role in the affairs of Israel and Judah at the close of the Syro-Ephraimitic war. Hoshea himself spearheaded the cooperative movement to remove Pekah and reclaim Samaria. In so doing, he removed the very one that had threatened to conquer Jerusalem only a few years earlier. Thus, the positive evaluation of Hoshea in 2 Kgs 17:2 may find its explanation in the shared pro-Assyrian stance and joint military effort between Hoshea and Ahaz around 731 B.C.E. (see J. H. Hayes and J. K. Kuan, "The Final Years of Samaria (730–720 BC)," *Bib* 72 [1991]: 177–78).

the prophet that speaks of Yahweh in the third-person and introduces the themes and motifs of the unit as a whole. This prologue is then followed by the direct divine address in verses 3–8. In the same manner, the opening verses of Hos 2 contain the prophet's prologue that lays the thematic and theological foundations for the divine contention that follows.[128] The prophet's words serve both to introduce Yahweh's specific explanation of the situation that begins in verse 4 and to frame the actions being undertaken by Hosea's audience as part of a larger theological movement in which Yahweh restores his estranged "wife" to a right-relationship.

This reading of Hos 2:1–3 necessarily sees a close relationship between the prophet's general statements and the situation's specific events. Hence, Wolff is correct when he argues that these verses come from the period after the Syro-Ephraimitic war (for him, after 733 B.C.E.). As mentioned earlier, however, Wolff goes on to conclude that the language and imagery of 2:1–3 are eschatological in nature and do not reflect actual historical events from this period.[129] To the contrary, the analysis given above suggests that Hosea is specifically addressing the social and political actions being undertaken in Israel and Judah around 731 B.C.E. The prophet's task in his opening remarks is to overview the whole movement of the oracle, to show the theological implications of these actions, and to persuade his audience to work toward the realization of Yahweh's goals among his people. After having established this framework, Hosea can allow the audience to hear Yahweh's own passionate presentation in verses 4–25 of the ultimate significance of these local events.

---

[128] Micah 6:1–8 also forms an instructive parallel in another way. Like Hos 2, Mic 6 emphasizes the Hebrew term רִיב and centers on a contention or accusation that Yahweh makes against some portion of his people.

[129] Wolff, *Hosea*, 24–29.

8

THE RHETORICAL ADDRESS OF HOSEA 2 (PART 2):
The Divine Speech (2:4–25)

Unlike the general introduction in the chapter's first three verses, beginning in 2:4, Hosea presents his audience with a divine oracle in which Yahweh himself speaks in the first person. The voice of Yahweh purports to reveal some of the inward thoughts and emotions that constitute the divine perspective on what has transpired regarding Samaria and the people of Israel in the years of the Syro-Ephraimitic crisis. Through this oracle, the prophet's audience can see not only the divine decision-making process but also the ultimate goal of Yahweh's purpose in this situation. To communicate these things to his audience, Hosea puts a metaphorical speech into Yahweh's mouth that is complex and violent. The speech describes marital unfaithfulness, divorce procedures, retributive punishments, and ultimate reconciliation. Through all these complexities, the rhetoric offers a metaphorical and theological commentary on Samaria's (and its rulers') political actions during this critical time in Israelite and Judean history. Thus, with the beginning of Yahweh's first-person speech in verse 4, the major metaphors examined in the preceding chapters provide the primary communicative effect.

As this chapter will show, the speech in 2:4–25 recasts the social and political events in Israel from 734–731 B.C.E. as a complex relationship between

Yahweh and his unfaithful wife. The city of Samaria, personified as the wife of the deity, is presented as committing fornication and adultery by seeking out political alliances and policies that lie outside the will of Yahweh. The voice of Yahweh characterizes the political allies and overlords who have led Samaria astray as lovers and paramours, who lure away the loyalty of Yahweh's wife. Thus, 2:4–25 uses the form, process, and property arrangements of ancient Near Eastern divorce laws to depict this estrangement between Yahweh and the capital city. Ultimately, however, the text envisions the city's restoration by using the metaphor of remarriage. The realms of politics and religion are inextricably interwoven in Hosea's metaphors and rhetoric. Thus, Hosea's oracle imparts to a series of events a significance that may not yet be clear to the general audience. Samaria's political infidelity to Assyria is essentially equivalent to religious apostasy to Yahweh. Through his commentary, the prophet attempts to compel his hearers to do their duty in relationship to Yahweh's will.

1. OPENING SUMMONS (2:4–6)

1.1 The Call to Contend (2:4)

The major section of Hos 2 opens by introducing both the dominant metaphor of the marriage relationship between Yahweh and Samaria and the dominant point of view of Yahweh's perspective. Yahweh speaks as a husband and instructs his children to "contend" (רִיבוּ) with their mother. Yahweh's speech uses parallelism to present the situation that calls for such contention: "Contend with your (m.pl.) mother, contend, for she is not my wife and I am not her husband." As demonstrated above, this expression does not represent an actual divorce formula but depicts a situation in which the wife refuses to comply with the relationship.[1] The text indicates a metaphorical circumstance in which Yahweh and his wife are currently estranged and the husband faces several options available within that context.

The opening summons to contend with or accuse Yahweh's metaphorical wife is explicitly directed to her children ("your [m.pl.] mother"). The employment of the children in the confrontation of a wife who has chosen to leave her husband draws upon the image-base of ancient Near Eastern divorce practices. For example, Gordon notes the links between this verse and a divorce text from Nuzi in the second millennium in which the husband's sons are called upon to remove the clothes of the wife if she marries another.[2] As Stuart observes, the bluntness and repetition of the imperative רִיבוּ suggest that these

---

[1] See discussion above in chapter 3.

[2] Gordon, "Hosea 2:4–5," 279–80. For a discussion of this action as a symbolic economic act rather than a punishment for adultery, see discussion in chapter 3.

children are envisioned as hostile witnesses.[3] Nonetheless, this repetition expresses a close relationship between the children and their mother, which produces a sense of urgency for the children.[4]

If the arguments for understanding the wife/mother here as the city Samaria hold, then there is no confusion between the speakers referred to as "children" and the addressee referred to as "mother." The personified city represents Samaria's ruling house. As discussed above, referring to the inhabitants of a city as the "children" of the "mother" city is common in biblical and extrabiblical city traditions.[5] This distinction between the capital city and the people governed from that city appears verbally and conceptually throughout the Hebrew Bible, most notably in the distinction of designations like "Judah and Jerusalem" (e.g., Isa 1:1; 2:1; 36:7; Jer 4:4) and "he reigned over Israel in Samaria" (1 Kgs 16:29; 22:52; 2 Kgs 3:1; 10:36).[6] Failing to recognize this distinction produces confusion. For example, Wolff concludes that the marriage metaphor breaks down in 2:4–6 because both the mother and children represent the people of Israel.[7] While avoiding ambiguous categories like Harper's identification of the mother as the whole nation and the children as the individual Israelites, recognizing the personification of the capital city as the wife/mother illuminates the conflict presupposed by Hosea's discourse.[8] Yahweh's address draws an initial distinction between the people outside of the ruling house, whether in Samaria or elsewhere and most probably including those Israelites and Judeans involved in Hoshea's effort to recapture Samaria, and Samaria's rulers who have rebelled against Yahweh's plans. The speech metaphorically commands those not represented by the personified city to confront the errant wife/mother.

The specific action that Yahweh instructs the children to take is represented by the imperative רִיבוּ, "contend." The language here is not the technical terminology of an actual court case. As Garrett points out, there is nothing in the context that denotes a trial or courtroom setting; rather, the word seems to have a "quasi judicial" meaning here.[9] The term רִיב is best understood as denoting a

---

[3] Stuart, *Hosea-Jonah*, 47. Cf. Andersen and Freedman, who note that this verb never describes a call to repentance but always a hostile confrontation (*Hosea*, 219).

[4] Blankenbaker, "Language," 156.

[5] See chapter 4.

[6] For discussion and further examples, see Schmitt, "Virgin," 378–79.

[7] Wolff, *Hosea*, 33. Andersen and Freedman also reach this conclusion and suggest that the text envisions a dialogue within the covenant community (*Hosea*, 219). Ibn Ezra explored the possibility that this text addressed exiles in the hope that they would repent (see Lipshitz, *Ibn Ezra*, 28). Contrast Bucher ("Origin," 134–35), who asserts that one should look for two different referents for the wife/mother and the children.

[8] Harper, *Critical and Exegetical Commentary*, 226; so also Birch, *Hosea, Joel, Amos*, 28; Limburg, *Hosea-Micah*, 10; McComiskey, *The Minor Prophets*, 33.

[9] Garrett, *Hosea, Joel*, 75; cf. Andersen and Freedman, *Hosea*, 219.

"prelegal" or "extra legal" controversy prior to its presentation in a court.[10] The only other occurrence of this verb in Hosea is in 4:4 where it is parallel to a hifil form of נכה, "to reprove, correct."[11] Thus, in this opening summons, the prophet's rhetoric is drawing upon the legal background and imagery of ancient Near Eastern marriage and divorce customs, but it is using those traditions in a metaphorical way. Hosea 2 is neither a divorce document nor a post-divorce document but draws upon divorce traditions as only one among several image-bases at work in the metaphorical discourse. Nonetheless, as argued previously, the image-base most clearly reflected here seems to be that of a circumstance in which a wife has refused to comply with the marital relationship. Yahweh's command in 2:4 emphasizes this type of situation by stating that the children are to contend with their mother "for (כי) she is not my wife and I am not her husband." Although some scholars suggest reading כי here as a relative particle ("that") introducing the content of the threat or accusation rather than the reason for it,[12] the presence of the particle פן ("lest") in 2:5 indicates that the threat begins there.[13] At this point, Yahweh sets forth the circumstance that the rest of his speech addresses.

In the remainder of verse 4, Yahweh calls for his wife to turn away from those practices that have led to the present circumstance of estrangement: "And let her put aside (ותסר) her fornication (זנוניה) from her face and her adultery (ונאפופיה) from between her breasts." With these words, the text envisions a wife who has been unfaithful and has perhaps decided to break the marriage relationship for good. This accusation should be viewed, however, in light of the previous discussion of "fornication" and "adultery" as metaphors for improper political actions. There are several elements here that place the emphasis squarely upon the capital city Samaria and its political activities. For instance, although the verb סור does appear in connection with the act of putting away foreign gods (e.g., Gen 35:2; Josh 24:14, 23; 1 Sam 7:3), it stands here only as part of the larger metaphor of adultery.[14] As noted above, several commentators identify זנוניה and ונאפופיה in this command as actual cultic objects placed upon the face or breast and connect these actions with a Canaanite sex cult.[15]

---

[10] Buss, *Prophetic Word*, 76–77. For ריב as a general term that can denote any controversy, see Nielsen, *Yahweh as Prosecutor*, 25; Limburg, "Root," 291–304; DeRoche, "Yahweh's RÎB," 569.

[11] Cf. Schmitt, "Yahweh's Divorce," 124; contra Whitt ("Divorce," 52), who takes the term in 2:4 as meaning "to defend."

[12] Macintosh, *Critical and Exegetical Commentary*, 39; Stuart, *Hosea-Jonah*, 44. This reading follows the Targum.

[13] So Andersen and Freedman, *Hosea*, 223.

[14] Blankenbaker, "Language," 157.

[15] Mauchline, "Hosea," 577; Mays, *Hosea*, 38; Wolff, *Hosea*, 34. Yee ("Hosea" [*NIB*], 224) suggests that these terms refer only to a woman's use of cosmetics or jewelry to make herself attractive and not to items from a Baal cult. But see Assante ("The kar.kid/ḫarimtu," 75–77), who cites the "Hymn to Inanna-Ninegalla" that refers to the "bead necklace of the kar.kid" worn by Inanna and suggests that the kar.kid wore such jewelry "to mark her from married women when she was in search of sex

Yet several things argue against this conclusion. First, this view rests upon assumptions and speculative reconstructions about the existence and prevalence of a Baal fertility cult, as well as its relevance to Hosea's oracles. Second, this interpretation attempts to make the metaphor too concrete and fails to consider the metaphorical traditions that invest "fornication" and "adultery" with political meanings. Finally, as Nwaoru observes, items for adornment are usually specifically named whenever they occur in the imagery of harlotry (e.g., Jer 4:30; Ezek 23:40).[16] Hosea's terms, on the other hand, function more clearly as references to behaviors or practices that are simply described by references to parts of the body.[17] In the metaphorical discourse of Hos 2, the words may be taken as addressing the political unfaithfulness that has characterized the capital city and its leaders and produced the current situation of conflict.

1.2 A Potential Reaction (2:5–6)

Following the opening charge to the children, Yahweh presents a possible two-part course of action to be undertaken if his metaphorical wife does not put aside her fornication and adultery. The first part, described in 2:5, uses synthetic parallelism to build the intensity of Yahweh's threats: "Lest I strip her naked and I exhibit her … I will make her like the desert … I will kill her with thirst." The imagery in this verse is striking. The opening conjunction (פֶּן) governs five clauses of increasing severity. Additionally, the imagery here finds an illuminating parallel in an Ugaritic text (UT 68:27–28) in which the complete destruction of an enemy is described by three verbs of mounting intensity that also use *šit* (שִׁית) as the second verb.[18]

Using similar imagery, Hosea, speaking on behalf of Yahweh, declares one potential outcome of the present estrangement. As discussed above, in a situation where the wife fails or refuses to fulfill the obligations of a relationship, the husband retains several options for dealing with the situation. Yahweh's speech in 2:4–25 seems to be an elaboration of these different options for dealing with his metaphorical wife rather than a sequential procession of events.[19] Verse five, for example, sets out the first of these options as a threat ("lest"): the execution of the wife. In this verse, the metaphorical imagery describes both the stripping and exposure of the wife as well as her

---

in public places" (ibid., 76). The imagery of Hos 2:4 may draw upon this distinctive marker of a single woman in search of sex.

[16] Nwaoru, *Imagery*, 143.

[17] So Macintosh, *Critical and Exegetical Commentary*, 39–40. Compare Yee (*Poor Banished Children*, 103), who suggests the terms here may be "eroticized idioms for the luxury goods the elite derived from their agribusiness and foreign affairs (cf. Isa 1:21–23; 23:17–18)."

[18] See Andersen and Freedman, *Hosea*, 226.

[19] See discussion of Clines, "Hosea 2" and the "therefore" structuring of Hos 2 in chapter 6.

transformation into a desert wasteland.[20] The verse gives no indication of myths or rituals associated with a Canaanite fertility cult.[21] The metaphorical imagery here can be fully associated with the personification of capital cities as women.[22] The previous discussion of physical and sexual violence against women has demonstrated that the punishment of literal stripping or public exposure was not associated with adultery in the ancient Near East. Rather, within the prophetic texts of the Hebrew Bible, it was concluded, the metaphorical depictions of such physical and sexual violence occur exclusively in contexts of the destruction of cities.[23]

Yahweh's threat in 2:5 is one of the places in Hos 2 that explicitly links the metaphorical action of stripping with city imagery. As many commentators recognize, this punishment is primarily directed to a physical place and not a person or people.[24] The motif of turning into a desert in the Hebrew Bible often occurs with cities that are either conquered or stand as objects of God's judgment.[25] Additionally, the primary examples of the stripping and desolation of women in the context of adultery all have cities as their subjects (Ezek 16; 23; Nah 3:4–6). Thus, within the metaphorical rhetoric of Hos 2, the first potential action of the wronged husband is described as the total destruction of the capital city personified as Yahweh's wife. Within the prophet's rhetorical-historical situation, these words begin to build the case that Yahweh could rightly allow Samaria to be destroyed as a consequence of the events of the past years. In the hearing of a joint-military group embarking on a mission of reclamation at the close of the Syro-Ephraimitic war, however, Hosea shows this fatal option only to pass it by on the way to describing Yahweh's ultimate goal of reconciliation and restoration. On the level of both the audience he is encouraging to support the campaign and the people who are its targets, the discourse serves to create the realization that Yahweh's exacting of this decisive option would be justified. Nonetheless, the prophet, speaking on behalf of the deity, has more to say.

The final verse of the opening summons (2:6) adds a further ramification of Yahweh's first potential response: Yahweh will disown his wife's children. The message of Yahweh's words is that the first option of ultimate punishment on the adulterous wife includes the severing of the relationship between father and

---

[20] The phrase צִיָּה אֶרֶץ ("land of drought") also occurs in Jer 2:6 and Ezek 19:13 to describe a wilderness setting.
[21] For Hos 2:14, which mentions vines and fig-trees that seem to relate to the issue of fertility, see discussion below.
[22] For example, Blankenbaker concludes that Hosea is not relying here on the form of a Canaanite Baal myth but on sanctions associated with treaties ("Language," 162).
[23] See discussion of stripping and the Hebrew Bible texts above in chapter 4.
[24] E.g., Braaten, "Parent-Child," 262; Macintosh, *Critical and Exegetical Commentary*, 44; Stienstra, *YHWH*, 106.
[25] Cf. Isa 14:17; 27:10; Jer 4:23–26; 9:11–13; 22:6.

children. With this inclusion of the potential disownment of children, the discourse again draws on the image-base of ancient Near Eastern laws concerning marriage, divorce, and inheritance. For example, both Buss and Braaten note the link between this imagery and ancient Israelite and ancient Near Eastern cases of disownment based on the low status of the mother.[26] Yahweh's words seem to have the force of a disinheritance formula.[27] While there are no ancient Near Eastern parallels that speak of the disinheritance of children specifically during the divorce of an adulterous or obstinate wife, some biblical texts do indicate disinheritance based on the mother's status (Gen 21:10–14; Judg 11:3, 7). A threat of disinheritance makes sense in response to a wife's refusal to comply with the marital relationship.

The exact identity of the children and the reason for their guilt, however, remain uncertain. The text describes them as זְנוּנִים בְּנֵי. It is unclear whether this phrase identifies the children as offspring of one who has fornicated or as ones who are also guilty of fornication. For example, Stuart reads this phrase as "prostituting children" and portrays the children themselves as guilty, while Andersen and Freedman read "children of promiscuity" and view the children simply as having been disgraced by the actions of their mother.[28] As noted above, the children commanded to confront their mother in verse 4 seem to represent those living throughout Israel and Judah not associated with Pekah and the ruling house. Since the group in verse 6 is depicted as receiving Yahweh's potential judgment against the city, it is possible that the children here may refer more specifically to those associated with Samaria.[29] The text's emphasis is on their association with the mother and not on their actions. On one hand, it is possible that the children envisioned here represent the inhabitants of the capital city, who are not members of the ruling house but are endangered by the sinful actions of the rulers. Jeremiah 21:3–9 may be helpful in this regard, since it portrays a similar situation and distinction by highlighting the potential suffering of Jerusalem's inhabitants due to the rebellion of King Zedekiah against the Babylonians (see 21:6–7). On the other hand, given the metaphorical tradition of personifying cities connected to the capital city as "children" of the "mother" city, it is possible that the "children" in this verse represent those

---

[26] Buss, *Prophetic Word*, 88–89 and Braaten, "Parent-Child," 5, 8, 134.

[27] Schmitt, "Yahweh's Divorce," 125 and Whitt, "Divorce," 60. For this interpretation of Yahweh refusing to acknowledge the children, see the discussion of this text and the verb רחם as "to acknowledge [as one's own child]" in S. Sperling, "Biblical *rḥm* I and *rḥm* II," *JANES* 19 (1989): 149–59.

[28] Stuart, *Hosea-Jonah*, 48; so also Wolff, *Hosea*, 34. Compare Andersen and Freedman, *Hosea*, 228; so also Macintosh, *Critical and Exegetical Commentary*, 46 and Wellhausen, *Die kleinen Propheten*, 11.

[29] Along these lines, for example, Blankenbaker suggests the religious distinction that the children in 2:4 are the faithful ones while those in 2:6 are the unfaithful ones ("Language," 158). Wolff (*Hosea*, 34) and Jeremias (*Der Prophet*, 42) argue that 2:6 is a later gloss drawn from 1:2 and 6.

towns that were still supportive of Pekah and Samaria in 731 B.C.E. In the end, the metaphorical children never speak as at least some of them are commanded in 2:4; rather, their very presence seems to be a sign of the mother's fornication and adultery.[30] Yet, within the rhetoric of Yahweh's oracle, this threatened disownment of the children stands as only one potential option available to the rejected husband.

2. THE WIFE'S ACTION AND A SECOND POTENTIAL REACTION (2:7–9)

2.1 The Wife's Action (2:7)

After describing the current state of separation and presenting one possible course of action, Yahweh speaks again as the wronged husband in 2:7–9. At this point in the oracle, the metaphor of fornication assumes the central place in Yahweh's description of the wife's actions. As explored in detail in the previous discussion, the metaphor of זנה in Hos 2 refers to those improper political actions and alliances that have been undertaken by the ruling house in Samaria and have produced the present state of conflict at the close of the Syro-Ephraimitic war.[31] Yahweh reiterates the political unfaithfulness of his wife, who is here described again as the "mother" of and the "one who conceived" the children. In Hosea's view, the personified city and the rulers she represents have acted in the manner of a prostitute, who offers herself to whomever will provide for her needs.

The text goes further, however, than a general description of behavior and details the wife's own words and thoughts. Through the voice of Yahweh, the prophet puts words into the mouth of the wife that ostensibly represent her viewpoint and express her determination: "For she said, 'I will go after my lovers who give me my bread and my water, my wool and my linen, my oil and my drink'" (2:7). This verse's accusation works on several levels. First, the first-person cohortative verb and the repeated use of first-person pronouns communicate a sense of independence and determination. As Wolff observes, this imagery of the wife seeking out her lovers heightens the discourse's condemnation by contrasting typical prostitutes, who wait for their lovers to come to them, with Yahweh's wife, who chases down improper relationships with great determination.[32] On another level, this verse highlights a central issue that runs throughout all of Hos 2: the wife's refusal to acknowledge that it is

---

[30] In this regard, Sherwood provides an illuminating comparison with Nathaniel Hawthorne's *The Scarlet Letter* in which Hester Prynne is marked with a scarlet letter "A": "Her daughter Pearl, the offspring of her sexual liason, becomes, similarly, a 'living hieroglyphic,' a scarlet letter endowed with life" (Sherwood, *Prostitute*, 139).

[31] See discussion above in chapter 4.

[32] Wolff, *Hosea*, 35. Ezekiel 16:34 also depicts a city, Jerusalem, soliciting her "lovers" rather than waiting for their solicitation.

Yahweh, not other allies or overlords, who provides the necessities of life. In the prophet's presentation of the wife's statement in 2:7, an emphatic first-person pronoun stands on each item mentioned: "my bread and my water, my wool and my linen, my oil and my drink." At this point, the text holds open the question of whether the wife's lack of realization is due to ignorance or stubbornness.

On a third level, the condemnation of 2:7 serves to introduce the parties with whom Yahweh's wife has committed fornication: "my lovers" (מאהבי, piel participle). As explored above, this term functions in the discourse of Hos 2 as a metaphorical reference to those political allies with whom the leaders of Samaria have entered into alliances that violate the will of Yahweh. The prophet's rhetoric equates those political allies with adulterous lovers to whom an unfaithful wife turns in exchange for the payment of a prostitute. One may perhaps even translate the participle נתני ("the ones who give me") here as "the ones who pay me" for sexual services (cf. Gen 38:16). In the hopes of securing a better situation for herself, the personified Samaria looks to other providers than Yahweh.

This imagery of a city that receives what it possesses directly from the hands of its allies fits very well with the rhetorical-historical situation of Pekah's rule. As mentioned earlier, various biblical and extrabiblical texts suggest that Pekah and his compatriots were set in power by Rezin of Damascus and the other anti-Assyrian forces. For example, the historiographical notice relating to the Syro-Ephraimitic crisis in Isa 7:2 could be translated, "Syria has descended on (נחה על) Ephraim." This translation resists various proposed emendations and takes the verb as the well-attested sense of נוח, "to settle, descend on."[33] Seen in this way, Syria's "descent" on Ephraim may be a reference to Damascus's participation in Pekah's coup in Samaria. Along these same lines, the language of Hos 2:7 has the personified city itself characterize its provisions as gifts received from adulterous lovers. The same set of circumstances can also illuminate the wife's more specific description in verse 14, which labels her vine and fig-tree as "gifts" that her lovers gave to her.

Finally, Yahweh's description of the wife's action in 2:7 once again draws upon the image-base of ancient Near Eastern marriage and divorce traditions. Some commentators attempt to associate the provisions in this verse (bread, water, wool, linen, oil, drink) with the cultic and agricultural language of a supposed Baal fertility cult in eighth-century Israel.[34] The language here, it is assumed, reflects Israel's abandonment of Yahweh and participation in Baal

---

[33] See Irvine, *Isaiah*, 138–39. For other attestations of this sense of the verb, see Exod 10:14, 2 Sam 17:12, and Isa 7:19.

[34] See Andersen and Freedman, *Hosea*, 230; Blankenbaker, "Language," 169; Stuart, *Hosea-Jonah*, 46. Van Selms offers another option and suggests that this imagery comes from parallels with the love poetry of Song of Songs (A. van Selms, "Hosea and Canticles," *OTSWA* 7/8 [1966]: 85–89).

worship in order to secure the fertility of the land, crops, and animals. As discussed in chapter 5, however, there is no compelling evidence for the existence and practice of Baal worship in Hosea's day or within the rhetorical scope of Hosea's preaching. Rather, the wife's statement of provisions makes sense against the legal background of ancient Near Eastern marriage stipulations. As Buss observes, "Marriage contracts in the Near East (especially in Egypt) specified that the husband furnish his wife with certain, sometimes carefully stipulated, amounts of food, clothing, and personal supplies."[35] In the marriage texts, these provisions are the responsibility of the husband and possession of them often constitutes the central issue in divorce.[36] For example, MAL A 36 stipulates,

> If a woman is residing in her father's house, or her husband settles her in a house elsewhere, and her husband then travels abroad but does not leave her any oil, wool, clothing, or provisions, or anything else, and sends her no provisions from abroad— that woman shall still remain (the exclusive object of rights) for her husband for five years.... [A]t the onset of(?) six years, she shall reside with the husband of her choice.... [S]he is clear for her second husband.[37]

This comparative evidence suggests that the language of Hos 2:7 does not reflect that of the participation in a Baal fertility cult but draws upon the image-base of ancient Near Eastern marriage legalities. The provisions under consideration here are those that a husband must give to his wife.

Taken as a whole, the language and imagery in 2:7 presents a detailed description of the metaphorical wife's action. Yahweh condemns the wife/mother for behaving like a prostitute and initiating acts of fornication with various "lovers" in order to provide for her own wellbeing. The use of direct quotation functions rhetorically to emphasize the wife's deliberate rebellion. Nonetheless, the words of the wife that appear here and throughout the entire chapter do not represent the actual words or perspectives of the woman but only the husband's representation of her point of view (cf. 2:9, 14).[38] These quotations, though perhaps unfairly representing the thoughts and intentions of the personified wife, constitute a powerful rhetorical move by allowing the husband to put the desired words into the woman's mouth and to speak for her.

---

[35] Buss, *Prophetic Word*, 88.

[36] See Kruger, "Marriage Metaphor," 16.

[37] *COS*, 2:357; cf. *ANET*, 183. The Laws of Liput Ishtar 27 likewise reads, "If a man's wife does not bear him a child but a prostitute from the street does bear him a child, he shall provide grain, oil, and clothing rations for the prostitute ..." (*COS*, 2:413; cf. *ANET*, 160). See also discussion of Assyrian, Babylonian, and Elephantine texts above in chapter 3.

[38] See Yee, "Hosea" (*NIB*), 224.

2.2 A Second Potential Reaction (2:8–9)

In the opening verses of the divine speech (2:4–6), Yahweh presents the possibility that he could punish and humiliate his wife because of her actions. After further describing her behavior in 2:7, Yahweh's speech now presents another possible course of action in 2:8–9. Verse 8 begins with the transitional word לכן ("therefore"), which also appears before each of Yahweh's following reactions to his wife's behavior (cf. 2:11, 16). As Buss notes, this term often serves to mark the transition from accusation (description of action) to threat (description of reaction).[39] The preceding discussion of the unity of Hos 2 in chapter 6 suggested that the three "therefores" are keys to the overall structure of the text and provide three movements to the arrangement of the oracle.[40] Seen in this way, the three "therefore" statements are not a convoluted sequence of actions but a series of alternatives from which the wronged husband may choose.[41] If one follows this reading, then there is no need to relocate 2:8–9 to after 2:10–15. Some commentators suggest this relocation because the woman's change of heart in 2:9 seems premature in relation to the additional punishments that follow.[42] The structural device of the term לכן provides the clue that the argument is not following a strict logical or chronological order.[43] Additionally, as noted above, this understanding of the movement of Yahweh's speech accords well with the image-base of various divorce situations in which the husband had several courses of action from which to choose.

Verse 8 thus follows the further description of the personified Samaria's actions in verse 7 with another possible reaction of Yahweh, the wronged husband. The text uses synthetic parallelism to build the list of Yahweh's potential actions and their consequences. First, rather than threatening to kill his

---

[39] Buss, *Prophetic Word*, 120; Andersen and Freedman (*Hosea*, 235) also note that each "therefore" in Hos 2 follows the pattern of being preceded by an accusation. Cf. Blankenbaker, "Language," 167.

[40] Clines, "Hosea 2," 83–86.

[41] So also Andersen and Freedman, *Hosea*, 236. They suggest comparing Lev 26:14–25 as a similar list of possible or optional punishments from which Yahweh may choose. This text, however, does not rely on the term "therefore" for structure and does seem to envision a historical sequence of events in which each successive judgment is seen as ineffective before the next commences. This type of sequence is confused in Hos 2, since the text at times envisions the wife's return and repentance only to be followed by descriptions of more punishments.

[42] For example, see Harper, *Critical and Exegetical Commentary*, clxxvi; Snaith, *Mercy*, 56; cf. discussion above in chapter 6.

[43] As Clines notes, the wording of 2:9b is deliberately antithetical to the wording of 2:7b (Clines, "Hosea 2," 84–85). Other scholars, who neither attempt to rearrange the text nor adopt the reading of potential actions, are forced to offer less-satisfactory explanations. For example, Braaten concludes that 2:8–9 must represent a past judgment that has failed ("Parent-Child," 258). The text, however, in no way presents these actions as past events. Yee explains the three "therefores" as "signposts" of the final redactor with only the occurrence in 2:11 as original to Hosea (*Composition*, 81).

wife as in 2:4–6, Yahweh threatens to block her paths with thorns and enclose her within a wall: "I will hedge her way with briers and I will wall-in her wall" (2:8).[44] The goal of this action is to prevent the wife from continuing to seek out her lovers: "… she will not find her paths." The imagery of taking the wife captive here can function directly against the background of divorce in the ancient Near East. For example, the Code of Hammurabi 141 allows a husband to keep an adulterous wife as a slave in his house.[45]

Along with the destruction imagery in 2:5, however, verse 8 provides one of the other places in which Hosea's marriage metaphor intersects clearly with city imagery. This connection is most evident in Yahweh's statement that he will "wall-in her wall" (וגדרתי את־גדרה). This phrase has produced much scholarly discussion, but, as noted in the translation discussion above, the third-person feminine suffix makes sense in connection with the noun גדר and functions to denote a wall "pertaining to" or "around" her.[46] The term גדר occasionally indicates a heaped-up rampart of stone used as a fence to mark the boundaries for vineyards (Isa 5:5; Ps 80:13).[47] In this sense, verse 8's reference appears to be agricultural in nature: Yahweh will build a protective hedge around his wife resembling a small stonewall around a vineyard, a structure that is, at times, employed to restrict movement (Job 3:23; 19:8; Prov 15:19).[48]

This same Hebrew term (גדר), however, also serves to indicate a city wall (Mic 7:11; Ezra 9:9), and, given the metaphorical context, the imagery here may better reflect a siege wall placed around a city.[49] The text presents an option in which Yahweh could "wall-in" Samaria's wall in the manner of a second wall built around a target city's own wall in the midst of a siege. For example, the Assyrian king Sennacherib states that he shut up Hezekiah "like a bird in a cage" by surrounding the city of Jerusalem with earthwork.[50] In a description even closer to the imagery of 2:8, the stela of Zakkur, king of Hamath describes a siege on the city by saying, "and they raised a wall higher than the wall of

---

[44] Although the text-critical evidence outlined in chapter 7 favors emending the MT's "your way" to "her way," de Regt ("Person Shift," 214–16) notes that sudden changes of person in prophetic texts often serve to mark the start of a new section by addressing the subject anew. Cf. the structuring function of לכן in this verse.

[45] Cf. Greengus, "Textbook Case," 40. This observation is against Westbrook, who asserts that the actions in verse 8 do not have any legal content or background but rely wholly on city-destruction imagery ("Adultery," 579). Rudolph represents a common interpretation of Yahweh's actions by regarding this verse as a reference to God blocking the way to the Baalistic cult places (*Hosea*, 68).

[46] McComiskey, *The Minor Prophets*, 34.

[47] Wolff, *Hosea*, 36.

[48] See discussion in Macintosh, *Critical and Exegetical Commentary*, 51.

[49] Schmitt ("Wife," 15) also notes that the image of a vineyard wall does not function well in the discourse since people could easily climb such a small wall.

[50] *COS*, 2:303; *ANET*, 288. Esarhaddon's vassal treaty 582–84 also contains a treaty-curse that refers to catching people like a bird in a trap. See discussion in Hillers, *Treaty Curses*, 69.

Hazrach...."[51] Lamentations 3:7–9 also forms a close parallel to the language of Hos 2:8: "He has built a wall (גדר) around me so that I cannot escape ... he has walled-in my ways (גדר דרכי) with stones and made my paths crooked." Rather than repeating the verb גדר, Hos 2:8 employs the synonym שׂך ("to hedge"). Nonetheless, the Lamentations text occurs in the context of a first-person speech by a figure who represents the city of Jerusalem. Yahweh's action of walling-in that personified city so that it cannot escape appears as a punishment for the people's past unfaithfulness (cf. Lam 3:42). Yahweh's statement in Hos 2 similarly combines the metaphor of the adulterous wife with the imagery of the siege of a city and serves the purpose of prohibiting the wife from freely seeking out contacts with others.

Considering the totality of the imagery of Yahweh's possible reaction in verse 8, Kruger observes that this verse possesses a "multiplicity of meaning."[52] First, the imagery works on the level of the overall marriage metaphor and shows the husband taking actions to restrict the movements of the adulterous wife. The imagery also functions, Kruger argues, on the level of larger religious themes by restricting the wife's cultic movements and blocking access to high places. Thirdly, verse 8 operates intertextually with other images of the world of nature and animals used to describe the people in the book of Hosea (4:16; 8:9). Along with these levels, one finds the level of political metaphor. This verse describes the harsh consequences of war and the siege of a city. Kruger especially emphasizes the long-standing tradition of this interpretation and notes that the medieval commentator Kimchi already interpreted 2:8 in relation to a city. Ultimately, however, in Kruger's view, this evidence demands that an interpreter resist restricting the language to any single interpretation.[53] Although a modern reader can certainly trace the operation of all of these levels in the final canonical form of Hos 2, a rhetorical-historical analysis of Hosea's oracle, given both its generative rhetorical situation and supporting metaphorical traditions, leads to the conclusion that the punishments described in 2:8 originally served the prophet's attempt to address the city Samaria's situation near the end of Tiglath-pileser's campaign in 731 B.C.E.

Following verse 8's description of Yahweh's potential actions, 2:9 goes on to relate the intended results: "And she will chase after her lovers, but she will not reach them; she will seek them, but she will not find." The imagery of verses 8 and 9 does not match in a strict way. Yahweh's action of walling-in his wife should prevent her even from chasing or seeking her lovers. Nonetheless, the point of the rhetoric is clear. The result of Yahweh's punitive imprisonment is that his wife will no longer achieve her stated goal of interacting with other

---

[51] *COS*, 2:155; *ANET*, 501–2.
[52] P. Kruger, "'I Will Hedge Her Way with Thornbushes' (Hosea 2, 8): Another Example of Literary Multiplicity?," *BZ* 43/1 (1999): 92–99.
[53] Ibid., 99.

lovers.[54] The final part of 2:9, however, provides the ultimate intended result of the actions: "Then she will say, 'I will go and I will return to my first husband for it was better for me then than now.'" The wife, who is denied access to the lovers she seeks, will resolve to return to her first husband (שׁיא). The use of the term שׁיא here anticipates the final change in terminology in 2:18–19. This second part of verse 9 also corresponds to the language of verse 7 ("I will go after") and thus sets up a contrast between the "lovers" in the former and the "first husband" in the latter.[55] Yet, as with the portrayal of the wife's words in 2:7, the quotation of the wife's repentance in 2:9 represents only the desired result and not an actual event. The statement is a "fantasy" of Yahweh that depicts a future possibility.[56] The wife herself does not speak; her response to Yahweh's punishment is provided only by the male voice.

Interpreters struggle with how to incorporate this imagined response into the oracle's overall context of marriage and divorce imagery. The phrase "return to my first husband" seems to envision a situation in which a divorce has taken place. Several scholars resist this reading, however, on the basis of Deut 24:1–4, which forbids the return of a wife to her first husband.[57] Stuart suggests the alternative that this phrase does not imply an actual divorce but only a separation.[58] Jeremias retains the idea that the verse envisions a divorce followed by remarriage but argues that this movement intentionally contradicts Deut 24:1–4 in order to demonstrate that the humanly impossible is possible with God.[59] As noted previously, however, the prohibition against the restoration of marriage in Deut 24:1–4 envisions a very specific circumstance that revolves around the distinction between divorce with and without cause and the rule of estoppal.[60] Yahweh's hoped for response from his wife makes good sense within Hos 2's presentation of a wife who refuses to comply with the relationship. Whether or not the imagery suggests that the wife has remarried to (an)other husband(s), the imagined response centers on her decision to return to the husband from whom she separated herself. The "lovers" in the literary

---

[54] Landy notes that this text has an "erotic substratum" because of echoes with Song 3:1–4 where the woman seeks her lovers at night ("Fantasy," 151). Cf. Buss, *Prophetic Word*, 89. For three major studies of Hosea and Song of Songs, see M. Buss, "Hosea as a Canonical Problem: With Attention to the Song of Songs," in *Prophets and Paradigms: Essays in Honor of Gene M. Tucker* (ed. S. Reid; JSOTSup 229; Sheffield: Sheffield Academic Press, 1996), 79–93; van Dijk-Hemmes, "Imagination," 35–39; and van Selmes, "Hosea and Canticles," 85–89.

[55] Abma, *Bonds*, 174.

[56] Ibid., 175.

[57] Andersen and Freedman, *Hosea*, 239; McComiskey, *The Minor Prophets*, 36; Stuart, *Hosea-Jonah*, 49; Sweeney, *The Twelve Prophets*, 31; Wolff, *Hosea*, 36.

[58] Stuart, *Hosea-Jonah*, 49.

[59] Jeremias, *Der Prophet*, 43.

[60] See discussion of Westbrook and others in chapter 3.

context clearly assume the role of at least "pseudo-husbands" who have taken the place of the wife Samaria's true husband.[61]

The first two sections of Yahweh's speech (2:4–6, 7–9) provide a metaphorical picture of the state and affairs of Samaria at the close of the Syro-Ephraimitic war. In this first-person speech by the deity, Hosea purports to give his audience a glimpse into the thoughts and feelings of Yahweh himself. These verses introduce the inappropriate actions of Samaria and the ruling house it represents by characterizing them as examples of "fornication" committed with other "lovers." This opening section also begins to move through Yahweh's potential reactions to Samaria's rebellion by drawing upon the image-base of possible punitive actions by a wronged husband toward a wife who has rejected the relationship. Thus, the opening movement of Yahweh's address begins to construct a theological framework for understanding the contemporary events of Hosea's time. Yahweh considers but passes over two punitive options on the way to a decision for reconciliation.

3. THE WIFE'S ACTION AND A THIRD POTENTIAL REACTION (2:10–15)

3.1 The Wife's Action (2:10)

Up to this point in the oracle, Yahweh describes two possible courses of action that he could take against his adulterous wife: punishment through humiliation and destruction (2:4–6) or restriction through confinement and imprisonment (2:7–9). In 2:10–15, Yahweh offers a further metaphorical elaboration of his wife's inappropriate actions and presents another potential reaction. Picking up on the description of the wife's stubbornness in 2:7, Yahweh characterizes the wife's actions in a different but related way: "But she has not acknowledged that I myself gave to her the grain and the new wine and the choice oil" (2:10). The verb יָדַע, which is used as the primary description of the wife's action, can carry the more intentional sense of "to acknowledge" rather than simply "to know."[62] The immediate literary context of verse 10, particularly the statement attributed to the wife in verse 7, suggests that the issue is not one of ignorance but rebellion. The wife's transgression centers on her refusal to "acknowledge" her dependency on her original husband rather than on competing lovers and paramours. The oracle does not present the problem as a lack of intimacy between husband and wife but as the existence of other loyalties that are competing for the wife's confessed dependence. This motif of the proper acknowledgment of Yahweh later resurfaces as the climactic result of Yahweh's

---

[61] So Andersen and Freedman, *Hosea*, 239.

[62] *HALOT*, 2:390; *DCH*, IV:99; *TDOT*, 5:456–57; *TLOT*, 2:512, 515; *BDB*, 394; Macintosh, *Critical and Exegetical Commentary*, 54. Cf. Gen 18:19; Exod 33:12; Isa 19:21; 59:12; Jer 2:8; 3:13; 14:20; Amos 3:2; Hos 4:1; 5:4.

redemptive actions: "I will wed you to myself with faithfulness, and you will acknowledge (וְיָדַעַתְּ) Yahweh" (2:22).

Huffmon offers a definitive treatment of the term יָדַע in light of the role played by "knowing" in ancient Near Eastern political treaties.[63] The term "to know" is used in a technical manner in Hittite and Akkadian texts. The primary technical use is with regard to mutual legal acknowledgment between a suzerain and vassal. For example, in a treaty between the Hittite king Suppiluliumas and Ḫuqqanas, the king states, "... son (of) whom I, the Sun, say 'This one everyone should know (šakdu),' ... you, Ḫuqqanas, know him (apūn šā[k])! ... Moreover, another lord ... do not ... know (lē ... šakti)!"[64] In each case where such usage is attested, the technical sense of "to know" is "to recognize/acknowledge" as legitimate. As Huffmon points out, the Hebrew Bible also attests this technical sense of "to know." This meaning appears in reference to Yahweh's recognition of Israel or individuals (cf. Gen 18:19).[65] More importantly, several passages in the Hebrew Bible use יָדַע to refer to a vassal's acknowledgment of Yahweh as legitimate suzerain, and every example of this usage cited by Huffmon comes from the book of Hosea (2:22; 4:1; 5:4; 8:2; 13:4).[66]

Thus, the reality represented by the language of 2:10 contrasts sharply with the wife's statement in 2:7 and emphasizes Yahweh as the true husband. In presenting Yahweh's speech, Hosea introduces the contention with the emphatic combination of a first-person pronoun followed by a first-person verb: "I myself gave her" (אָנֹכִי נָתַתִּי). This statement not only forms a contrast with the wife's attribution of provisions to her lovers in 2:7 but also balances the third-person emphatic statement about the wife's refusal that opens that verse: "she herself has not acknowledged" (וְהִיא לֹא יָדְעָה). Additionally, the language for the specific items mentioned in verse 10 does not merely replicate the wife's statement in verse 7. Rather, Yahweh describes the commodities he gives as "*new* wine" (וְהַתִּירוֹשׁ) and "*choice* oil" (וְהַיִּצְהָר), items that are more valuable than normal oil (שַׁמְנִי) and drink (וְשִׁקּוּיָי). In this way, the discourse achieves the subtle rhetorical effect of implying that the gifts for which the wife has abandoned Yahweh are ironically of less value than those she already possessed but failed to acknowledge. The three specific terms (וְהַיִּצְהָר, וְהַתִּירוֹשׁ, דָּגָן) in the first part of 2:10 also often occur in later descriptions of

[63] Huffmon, "Treaty Background," 31–37. Cf. Huffmon and Parker, "Further Note," 36–38.
[64] Huffmon, "Treaty Background," 31–32. The treaty between Muwattallis and Alaksandus, the Hittite king, provides an example of the same usage within the context of rebellion: "I the [Su]n, will know only you (tukpat ... ša-ag-ga-aḫ-ḫi)" (ibid., 32). Additionally, Huffmon notes the Amarna text in which the king of Amurru, Abdi-Aširta, requests aid from his suzerain and says, "May the king my lord know me (lu-ú yi-da-an-ni)" (ibid.). In the follow-up study of Huffmon and Parker ("Further Note," 36–38), the authors provide two additional texts that display the technical meaning of "know" in international treaties: 1) an Akkadian text from Mari and 2) an Ugaritic text from Ras Shamra.
[65] Huffmon, "Treaty Background," 34.
[66] Ibid., 35–36.

the richness of Yahweh's covenant provisions. For example, Deut 7:13 employs all three terms in a covenant blessing, and Deut 28:51 uses them in covenant curses.[67]

Commentators have wrestled with how to understand the nature and function of the commodities listed in 2:10 within the overall metaphorical discourse. The items mentioned by the wife in verse 7 (bread, water, wool, linen, oil, and drink) represent basic provisions for everyday life. The wife stands accused of seeking the essential needs of life in a source other than Yahweh. By contrast, verse 10 appears to be addressing a different issue. Against the oracle's image-base of ancient Near Eastern marriage traditions, the items enumerated in 2:10 are best understood not as basic provisions but as bridal or wedding gifts originally given by Yahweh that his wife has now used in her interactions with other lovers.

This interpretation of the terms becomes clearer when considered in light of the last part of the verse, which mentions the commodities of silver and gold: "I multiplied for her silver and gold that they used for the paramour" (2:10). As discussed in the preceding translation section, the construction in the last phrase of this verse (עָשׂוּ לַבַּעַל) functions in this context as a reference to "using" rather than "making" certain materials, since there does not seem to be an idol or any physical object under consideration.[68] In connection with this act, the text introduces the other major metaphorical term for those allies with whom Yahweh's wife has been unfaithful: בַּעַל, "paramour."

Seen in this context, the commodities in verse 10, especially silver and gold, may represent gifts that Yahweh's wife has taken and used in her relationships with her adulterous lovers. Both biblical and extrabiblical texts use similar language to refer specifically to the bridal gifts given to a bride by her husband at marriage and the bride price paid to the father that became part of the wife's dowry. For example, Gen 24:47 and 53a describe the giving of gifts of silver and gold to Rebekah upon her agreement to be Isaac's wife. Other biblical and extrabiblical texts use "silver" as a general reference to the bride price. Exodus 22:16 states, "[H]e must weigh out silver according to the bride price of virgins," while KTU 1. 24:20 reads, "I shall give as her bridewealth [*mhrh*] to

---

[67] See also Deut 11:14; 12:17; 14:23; 18:4; and Joel 2:19. Whitt argues that these terms are late additions to Hos 2 because, in his view, the presence of the triplet in deuteronomistic material represents the earliest usage. Accordingly, the truly predeuteronomistic material like Hos 7:14 and 9:1–2 contains only the pair "grain and new wine" ("Divorce," 37). In order to maintain his view, however, Whitt must discount the presence of the same triplet in Hos 2:24 by arguing that it also is a postexilic addition. He also has to take Deut 33:28, which contains only the pair of terms, as a predeuteronomistic text. Whitt seems to assume that Hos 2:10–11 are later additions because they repeat the future tense of the punishment even after the wife's repentance in 2:9 (ibid.).

[68] Cf. Exod 38:24 and 2 Chron 24:7. So also Davies, *Hosea* (NCB), 74; Harper, *Critical and Exegetical Commentary*, 230; Mays, *Hosea*, 41; McComiskey, *The Minor Prophets*, 36.

her father a thousand (shekels) of silver and ten thousand shekels of gold."[69] Various Middle Assyrian Laws further indicate that bridal gifts could consist of personal ornaments and jewelry.[70] As Kruger observes, the root רבה ("to multiply") in 2:10 also occurs as a technical term related to the bride price in Shechem's marriage proposal concerning Dinah (Gen 34:12) and should perhaps be understood as "to fix": "Fix (הרבו) for me a bride price (מהר) ever so high...."[71] In light of this comparative evidence, it seems reasonable to conclude that the distinction between the accusations of verses 7 and 10 is rhetorically deliberate. In 2:7, Yahweh puts words into the wife's mouth that describe how she has sought out the basic provisions of life from providers other than her true husband. In the last part of 2:10, if not in the whole verse, Yahweh turns his attention to the bridal gifts given to his wife at the time of her first marriage and declares that, in her unfaithfulness, she has used these very gifts to consort with competing paramours.[72]

Thus, Yahweh's words in 2:10 add to his earlier condemnations the accusation that his wife has taken the marriage gifts and used them for other lovers. Since this accusation occurs after the wife's apparent change of heart in verse 9, some scholars suggest that it represents a relapse of the woman to her previous ways.[73] As noted above, however, Clines's proposal about the structural function of the three "therefores" provides a way to see verse 10 as another characterization of the wife's actions to be followed by an alternative, potential reaction. Within the rhetorical-historical situation of Hos 2, this second description once again portrays the city Samaria as acting improperly by seeking out alliances with political treaty-partners. Furthermore, the use of the singular, definite term בעל here suggests that the prophet has a specific political figure in mind, a figure who stands as more than a simple ally. In the context of the Syro-Ephraimitic war, the "paramour" or "overlord" with whom Samaria became involved was primarily Rezin of Damascus.

Yet the statement in 2:10 also broadens the scope of Yahweh's condemnation beyond Samaria as an entity. The final phrase of this verse shifts from consistent second-person feminine singular to third-person plural ("they used"). On the basis of this switch, Wolff and others conclude that the phrase is foreign to the oracle and originated as a late gloss.[74] Throughout the discourse, however, the personified female figure of Samaria consistently represents not

---

[69] Braaten, "Parent-Child," 266–67. Cf. Andersen and Freedman (*Hosea*, 242), who seem to agree that the items in 2:10, particularly silver and gold, represent gifts rather than provisions.

[70] E.g., MAL 25–26; see Kruger, "Marriage Metaphor," 20.

[71] Kruger, "Marriage Metaphor," 19.

[72] The language of Ezek 16:17, which is addressed to the personified city of Jerusalem, provides an illustrative parallel of using silver and gold given by Yahweh to his wife in the act of "fornication." Unlike Hos 2:10, however, this text does explicitly mention using the items to make images.

[73] Nwaoru, *Imagery*, 64; Andersen and Freedman, *Hosea*, 241.

[74] Wolff, *Hosea*, 37 and Harper, *Critical and Exegetical Commentary*, 230.

only the city itself but also Pekah and the ruling house within the capital. The speech in verse 10 momentarily shifts from the corporate image of the wife/mother Samaria to the individuals who make up the ruling house.[75] This dual vision characterizes both the threat and promise portions of the divine address (cf. 2:20).

3.2 A Third Potential Reaction (2:11–15)

Following the accusation in 2:10, the transitional word לָכֵן introduces another possible reaction of Yahweh. This reaction takes the form of a series of related events described in 2:11–15. In addition to the punishments of destruction and confinement in 2:4–9, Yahweh now outlines another potential punishment for his unfaithful wife. Verse 11 provides the substance of the reaction and verses 12 to 15 relate its consequences: "Therefore, I will take back again (אָשׁוּב וְלָקַחְתִּי) my grain in its time and my new wine in its season, and I will reclaim (וְהִצַּלְתִּי) my wool and my linen in order to reckon (לְכַסּוֹת) her indiscretion (עֶרְוָתָהּ)" (2:11). The use of the verb שׁוּב in Yahweh's statement plays upon the wife's expression in 2:9 that she will "return" (וְאָשׁוּבָה) to her first husband. The repeated use of first-person possessive pronouns attached to each commodity listed also contrasts sharply with the wife's statement in 2:7. Yahweh's speech emphasizes that he alone is the true owner of the things that his wife has viewed as her own. The description of what Yahweh will "take back" includes items that appear in both the list of basic provisions in 2:7 (wool and linen) and the list of bridal gifts in 2:10 (grain and new wine) and thus encompasses both aspects of the marriage relationship as well as the entities typically involved in cases of divorce with cause.

The majority of commentators understand verse 11 against the background of a supposedly widespread Baal fertility cult in Hosea's day. According to this view, Yahweh's punitive action consists of withholding the fertility of the land in order to expose the true powerlessness of the Baals.[76] Given the active image-bases and traditions at work in Hos 2, however, the language permits a different interpretation, and the final phrase of the statement in particular holds the key to a proper understanding.[77]

A survey of ancient and modern readings shows that לְכַסּוֹת is unanimously considered to be the piel infinitive construct of כסה meaning "to

---

[75] This explanation is similar to that of Blankenbaker, who suggests that the corporate image represents the mother while the individuals represent her children ("Language," 173). De Regt ("Person Shift," 216) proposes that such references could refer to different generations of Israelites, but that does not seem to fit the context of verse 10.

[76] Macintosh, *Critical and Exegetical Commentary*, 61; Mays, *Hosea*, 41; Sweeney, *The Twelve Prophets*, 32–33.

[77] For an expanded version of the following discussion, see B. Kelle, "A Reconsideration of *kĕkassôt* in Hosea 2, 11(MT)," *ZAW* 116, 3 (2004): 334–347.

cover." This reading then naturally understands the final word, עֶרְוָתָהּ, to be "nakedness." From a strictly grammatical standpoint, this is an adequate reading. The infinitive has the normal form for the piel of III-He verbs and the form לְכַסּוֹת appears thirteen times in the Hebrew Bible as the piel infinitive of כסה.[78] The problem with this reading, however, is that it makes no sense in the context of the verse in particular or the address in general. The grammatically straightforward rendering of לְכַסּוֹת as "to cover" is confusing because it produces the reading, "I will reclaim my wool and my linen in order to cover her nakedness." The typical purposive meaning of the preposition לְ with an infinitive construct renders the phrase unintelligible. Additionally, the remaining commonly attested uses of לְ with an infinitive construct do not seem to fit this case.[79]

In light of the problems with the straightforward reading, scholars have suggested a variety of explanations and emendations. The most widely accepted explanation assumes the presence of an elliptical construction in the MT and thus connects the infinitive לְכַסּוֹת with the objects of "wool" and "linen" by inserting a relative pronoun: "my wool and my linen which were to cover her nakedness." This rendering goes back to the Targum and Peshiṭta. The Targum exhibits the elliptical explanation by inserting the relative pronoun דִּי ("that," "which,") and an additional verb and preposition with a suffix: דִּיהֲבִית לַהּ לְכַסָּאָהּ ("which I gave her to cover her").[80] Similarly, the Peshiṭta inserts a relative pronoun and a verb: *dyhbt lh.*[81]

The major English translations of the Hebrew Bible continue the dominant trend of assuming the presence of an elliptical construction in the MT, associating לְכַסּוֹת with the objects "wool" and "linen," and translating the phrase as a relative clause. The RSV translation is representative, "I will take away my wool and my flax which were to cover her nakedness" (2:11).[82] The only apparent deviations from this practice are English translations that still assume the presence of an ellipsis but insert words other than a relative pronoun.[83] Modern critical commentaries that offer their own translations also

---

[78] Exod 26:13; 28:42; Num 4:15; 1 Kgs 7:18, 41, 42; 2 Chron 4:12, 13; Ezek 24:7; 38:9, 16; Ps 104:9, and most scholars also include Hos 2:11.

[79] For example, the לְ plus infinitive as a temporal clause, result clause, gerundive clause, modal clause, etc. For full discussion, see B. Waltke and M. O'Connor, *An Introduction to Biblical Hebrew Syntax* (Winona Lake, Ind.: Eisenbrauns, 1990), 598–611. Cf. I. Soisalon-Soininen, "Der Infinitivus Constructus mit לְ in Hebräischen," *VT* 22 (1972): 82–90.

[80] See A. Sperber, *The Bible in Aramaic* (Leiden: Brill, 1962): 3:388 and Cathcart and Gordon, *Targum*, 33.

[81] A. Gelston, *The Peshiṭta of the Twelve Prophets* (Oxford: Clarendon, 1987), 186. So also the Vulgate ("*quae operiebant ignominiam eius*") and Luther's German translation ("damit sie ihre Schaam bededet").

[82] Cf. JPS, Jerusalem Bible, and NRSV.

[83] E.g., as early as 1560, the Geneva Bible read, "and wil recouer my woll and my flaxe *lent* to couer her shame" (italics original to show an insertion). Cf. KJV and NIV.

predominantly follow the ellipsis and relative clause explanation. For example, Wolff reads, "I will remove my wool and my flax which were to cover her nakedness."[84]

While an ellipsis such as this is a common syntactical phenomenon and presents no grammatical problems for understanding this phrase, there is a significant issue that problematizes the explanation. Although the elliptical explanation goes back to the Targum and Peshiṭta, the earliest witnesses to Hos 2:11 do not understand the text in this way. In a fragmentary commentary on Hosea from Qumran (4QpHosᵃ), the text given for 2:11 presents the verse in a different light by not assuming an ellipsis but by inserting a preposition and making the phrase negative: "and I shall take away my wool and my flax, from covering (מלכסות) [her nakedness]."[85] The interpretation that follows this text reinforces the negative rendering of the infinitive: "Its interpretation: he has punished them with hunger and with nakedness so they will be sham[e] and disgrace in the eyes of the nations on whom they relied."[86] Similarly, the LXX does not assume an ellipsis but renders the infinitive as a negative: τοῦ μὴ καλύπτειν ("so as not to cover"). Even a few major commentaries do not assume the presence of an ellipsis in the MT but suggest that the infinitive may have a privative sense meaning "to lay bare."[87] These readings link the infinitive with the verb, "I will reclaim," and not with the objects of "wool" and "linen." Even so, these versions and commentaries still consider לכסות to be a form of כסה and are not satisfactory because they functionally emend the text by interpreting the infinitive in negative fashion. The divergent witness of these versions and commentaries demonstrates, however, that the current scholarly consensus does not adequately account for all available textual evidence. These differences also highlight the difficulty in attempting to relate any form of the verb כסה to the context of Hos 2:11. If this root must be retained, no explanation offers a way to read the text in a straightforward manner without emending it in some way. Thus, the translator is seemingly at an impasse because he or she lacks any meaningful way to adjudicate between alternatives of emendation like the ellipsis and negative renderings.

This situation raises the possibility that the cause of the confusion in interpreting the punishment in 2:11 may be the effort to read לכסות as an infinitive form of כסה. One may perhaps attribute this dominant view to the

---

[84] Wolff, *Hosea*, 31. So also Blankenbaker, "Language," 175; Garrett, *Hosea, Joel*, 81; Macintosh, *Critical and Exegetical Commentary*, 57; Mays, *Hosea*, 35; Stuart, *Hosea-Jonah*, 44.

[85] 4QpHosᵃ is the only Qumran text that bears directly on Hos 2:11. See J. M. Allegro, "A Recently Discovered Fragment of a Commentary on Hosea from Qumran's Fourth Cave," *JBL* 78 (1959): 142–48.

[86] F. Martinez and E. Tigchelaar, eds., *The Dead Sea Scrolls Study Edition* (2 vols.; Leiden: Brill, 1997), 1:331.

[87] E.g., Andersen and Freedman (*Hosea*, 215) render, "to uncover her nakedness." Cf. Stuart, *Hosea-Jonah*, 44 and Borbone, *Il libro*, 129.

presence of גלה ("to uncover") in the following verse (2:12). The language of the two verses, then, would revolve around the imagery of covering and uncovering. As noted above, however, verses 12 to 15 seem to function as separate but related consequences of the primary punishment in 2:11 rather than as one extended description of the same act. Yet, there may be a way to accept the straightforward grammatical sense of the infinitive without emendation and to fit it even more closely into the immediate context and imagery of the prophet's address. This goal can be met by taking לְכַבֹּותֹ as an infinitive, not of כסה but of the geminate root כבב. This approach makes sense of the context insofar as כבב has a number of important connections with ancient Near Eastern marriage and divorce legalities and imagery that underscore the verse's rhetorical and communicative effect.

The root כבב has a range of meanings including "to count, calculate, apportion."[88] It appears rarely in the Hebrew Bible, and all known occurrences are found within the Pentateuch. The only verbal occurrence of the root is the qal imperfect in Exod 12:4, which also contains a noun form of the root, and this appearance provides the basic definition that scholars have adopted for the term. For example, the NRSV reads, "If a household is too small for a whole lamb, it shall join its closest neighbor in obtaining one; the lamb shall be divided (תָּכֹסּוּ) in proportion to the number of (בְּמִכְסַת) people who eat of it." According to this rendering, the root כבב, in both its verbal and nominal forms, possesses the basic meaning of "to apportion, count" in dividing the sacrifice.[89] Appropriate weight should be given to this restricted use of the verb in a verse dealing with sacrificial animals. However, while the verbal form occurs only here in the Hebrew Bible, the noun form מִכְסַת also appears in Lev 27:23 in the context of instructions for dealing with payment for a house in the year of Jubilee: "the priest will reckon to it the calculation [i.e., amount or price; מִכְסַת] of your estimation up to the year of Jubilee."[90] In this context, the root כבב does not deal with the dividing of sacrificial animals but has a clear financial meaning that refers to a calculated amount to be paid. This additional attestation should be considered more closely when attempting to understand and translate the verbal reference in Exod 12:4. The use of כבב in the Exodus text makes equally as much sense as a reference to payment for the sacrificial lamb. The instruction of 12:4 might just as well be concerned with a small family's inability to afford the loss of a whole lamb. Thus, there is no leap to be made from apportioning something to payment; the "division" or "calculation"

---

[88] See *BDB*, 493; *DCH*, IV:445; *HALOT*, 2:490.

[89] The reading "divide" may be explained as the result of an overdependence on proposed etymological roots like the Akkadian *kasāsu*, perhaps meaning "to chew, gnaw, cut in two." See *CAD*, 8:242–43. West Semitic seems to derive the meaning "to proportion" from this etymology; see *HALOT*, 2:490 and *BDB*, 493.

[90] Author's translation.

envisioned in this text is done for the purpose of payment. Some English translations seem to adopt this financial interpretation of Exod 12:4 (KJV, JPS, RSV). Seen in this way, one could render Exod 12:4 as follows: "If a house is too small for a whole lamb, then it and its neighbor closest to the house will take one; according to the calculation [or number; בְּמִכְסַת] of the ones who eat, you will calculate [i.e., for payment; תָּכֹסּוּ] regarding (עַל) the lamb."[91] Such a translation underscores the text's emphasis that rests not simply on apportioning the meat among members of one house but on the sharing of the same lamb by *multiple* households. The law stipulates that no single household will bear full responsibility for providing the lamb. Rather, one household will volunteer a lamb, but the other will pay a calculated amount to help cover the loss. This financial reading of Exod 12:4 fits better with the sense of the only other occurrence of the noun form מִכְסָה in Lev 27:23.

In addition to the above correlation, the dictionaries also connect another noun, מֶכֶס, with the root כסס. This nominal form occurs six times in Num 31 in the context of instruction concerning booty in holy war (31:28, 37, 38, 39, 40, 41). Each of these uses carries the meaning of an amount required to be paid: "From the warriors who went out to battle, you will set aside as a calculation [or tribute, payment; מֶכֶס] to Yahweh one out of every five-hundred ..." (31:28). While it may not immediately be clear that these noun forms are related to the verbal root כסס, the corresponding Arabic terms favor that conclusion. The Arabic nouns *maksun*, "tax," and *makasun*, "tax collector," which carry a clearly financial meaning, are securely tied to the Arabic verbal root *kss*. Taken together with the use of מִכְסָה in Lev 27:23 and the financial sense of תָּכֹסּוּ and בְּמִכְסַת in Exod 12:4, these occurrences demonstrate that, contrary to the common definitions, the root כסס typically carries meanings like "proportion to be paid, tax, tribute." The basic definition of the root is "to calculate," but the sense is to calculate *for payment*.

In relation to the form in Hos 2:11, there remains some grammatical difficulty in reading לְכַסּוֹת as an infinitive form of כסס. The normal form for such a piel infinitive follows the *qattēl* pattern. Additionally, piel infinitives of III-He verbs do typically take a form like לְכַסּוֹת. The appearance of the latter form in Hos 2:11, however, may be explained as a rare form of the qal geminate infinitive. These infinitives generally occur in the reduced form (סֹב) and occasionally in the triliteral form (לִסְבֹּב). Nonetheless, Ezek 36:3 attests the alternative form שַׁמּוֹת as the qal infinitive construct of שׁמם. While some lexica and commentators argue against this reading in Ezekiel and propose emendations, Zimmerli maintains the word's identification as a qal infinitive. He argues that the immediate context demands that one retain the root שׁמם and

---

[91] Author's translation.

not emend it to something like נשׁם.[92] Even Greenberg, who argues for the latter emendation, concedes that the text is pointed as a geminate infinitive.[93]

Zimmerli goes on to point out two other words that attest this form of qal geminate infinitives. Psalm 77:10 attests חַנּוֹת as a qal infinitive form of חנן, and Ps 77:11 attests חַלּוֹתִי as a qal infinitive of חלל. On the basis of what appears to be a more secure form in Ezek 36:3, these words provide further examples of an unusual qal geminate infinitive form.[94] Thus, in spite of their rarity, these forms demonstrate the grammatical possibility of understanding לְכַסּוֹת in Hos 2:11 as a qal infinitive form of the geminate כסס. The identification of this term as a qal finds further support in the fact that the only clear verbal attestation of כסס outside of Hosea is also a qal form (Exod 12:4).

If one follows the reading of Hos 2:11 outlined above, then one can posit a translation of the final phrase along the lines of "I will reclaim my wool and my linen in order to calculate...." This reading seems to move verse 11 into a discourse about property, payment, and legal calculation. Given the image-base of ancient Near Eastern divorce traditions that has been shown to be at work throughout the prophet's address, the benefits of this translation are apparent. Rather than linking Yahweh's punitive action to a toppling of confidence in a Baal fertility cult, the above proposal locates it firmly within the stipulations governing marriage and divorce.[95] As discussed in chapter 3, one of the possible punishments for divorce due to infidelity was the total loss of property and the driving away of the wife from the husband's juridical responsibility and provision. More specifically, the marriage and divorce laws reviewed above stipulate that, if the woman has committed some wrong that justifies a divorce, then she forfeits all of her dowry and leaves the husband's home with no quittance or provision. Upon an official divorce with cause, there was a financial calculation or reckoning to be made concerning properties, gifts, and provisions. It is not clear whether this financial stipulation represents a type of compensatory payment in proportion for the wronged husband,[96] but the reclaiming of property certainly stands as a direct consequence of divorce with

---

[92] W. Zimmerli, *Ezekiel 2: A Commentary on the Book of the Prophet Ezekiel Chapters 25–48* (Hermeneia; Philadelphia: Fortress, 1983), 228. So also L. Allen, *Ezekiel 20–48* (WBC 29; Dallas: Word Books, 1990), 168. But see, for example, W. Gesenius, *Hebrew Grammar* (ed. E. Kautzsch; trans. A. E. Cowley; Oxford: Clarendon, 1910), §67r and §113e, which take this as a III-He verb.

[93] Greenberg argues that the context does not call for the meaning of an infinitive of שׁמם and uses Isa 42:14 to argue for a qal infinitive of נשׁם (M. Greenberg, *Ezekiel 21–37* [AB 22a; New York: Doubleday, 1997], 718).

[94] Zimmerli, *Ezekiel*, 228. As with the occurrence in Ezek 36:3, some scholars deal with these forms in other ways. For example, see M. Tate, *Psalms 51–100* (WBC 20; Dallas: Word Books, 1990), 270 and Dahood, *Psalms II*, 228–29.

[95] Hendriks, "Juridical Aspects," 38.

[96] This conclusion is a possible inference that can be drawn from the legal texts.

cause. Divorce with cause is exactly the type of possible action that fits the imagery of Hos 2.

The previous discussion of ancient Near Eastern divorce laws demonstrated that this action of official divorce with cause was an option available to a husband whose wife had refused to comply with the relationship in various ways. He could grant her a divorce and was entitled to treat her as one being divorced with cause. Thus, in keeping with the marriage metaphor of the entire chapter, Yahweh's words in Hos 2:11 outline another potential reaction to his wife's behavior: he can officially divorce his wife with justification in the pattern of ancient Near Eastern divorce stipulations. Because it is a divorce with cause, Yahweh, the wronged husband, may reclaim all bridal gifts, dowry (grain and new wine; cf. 2:10), assets, and provisions (wool and linen; cf. 2:7) in order to tally and settle the wrong. Accordingly, לְכַסּוֹת here may perhaps best be rendered with the English "to reckon." By definition, "reckon" encompasses both the aspects of making a calculation or computation and settling an account or penalty.

This interpretation of לְכַסּוֹת has direct implications for a proper understanding of the meaning and rhetorical function of the final word in verse 11: עֶרְוָתָהּ. As mentioned earlier, scholars generally understand this term to be "nakedness." This understanding often serves to strengthen the elliptical relative clause translation of לְכַסּוֹת, which sees Hos 2:11 as Yahweh's declaration that he will remove those items that have served as clothing and expose his wife. This action is often assumed to reflect the actual stripping and public humiliation of adulteresses in the ancient Near East, a notion that has proved to be unsubstantiated.[97] In addition to this lack of evidence for the practice of stripping, the context of Hos 2 itself argues against this understanding of verse 11. The symbolic language of nakedness and exposure appears not in verse 11 but in the following verse. The presence of וְעַתָּה ("and now") at the beginning of verse 12 clearly signals a new action that is not equivalent with that of verse 11. Understanding 2:11 as a reference to the removal of the wife's clothes makes 2:12 redundant and lessens its rhetorical impact in the context. More significantly, wool (צֶמֶר) and linen (פֵּשֶׁת) never occur together in the Hebrew Bible to represent clothes, and only the elliptical translation of לְכַסּוֹת identifies them as items that cover a person's nakedness.

The above considerations suggest that the common understanding of עֶרְוָתָהּ in Hos 2:11 may not be adequate. This word has strong connections to the legal image-base at work in the discourse. The discussion of marriage texts in chapter 3 explored Westbrook's proposal that Deut 24:1–4, the prohibition on the restoration of marriage, has as its rationale the property rules expressed in the ancient Mesopotamian and Elephantine texts. Westbrook specifically claims

---

[97] See discussion above in chapter 3.

that 24:1–4 makes the necessary distinction between divorce with and without justification by using the expression עֶרְוַת דָּבָר to indicate that the husband has found some "indecent thing" in his wife that justifies the divorce.[98] Yahweh's speech in Hos 2:11 uses the precise word that expresses divorce with justification: עֶרְוָתָה. This term does not occur in the other places in Hos 2 that refer to simple nakedness (2:5, 12). Rather, this specific word seems to denote a type of indecency or indiscretion. As suggested in the preceding translation section, the full phrase that connotes indecency or improper behavior is עֶרְוַת דָּבָר. Deuteronomy 24, however, connects this phrase explicitly with the issue of divorce, and the overall legal context of Hos 2:11 suggests that the word in isolation may also function as a technical description of the wife's actions. This technical sense seems to explain the word's function at the climax of verse 11. In this situation of divorce with cause, the text idiomatically expresses Yahweh's right to reclaim certain gifts and provisions "in order to reckon [i.e., tally and settle] her indiscretion."[99]

In summary, Hos 2:11 introduces another possible punishment by Yahweh. Although the MT is unclear, some early textual evidence from Qumran and the LXX and various ancient Near Eastern legal texts dealing with divorce stipulations lead to the conclusion that the verse's infinitive (לְכַסּוֹת) should not be taken from the common root כסה, "to cover," but from the root כסס, "to calculate, reckon." This reading sets the verse nicely within the rhetorical address's marriage/divorce metaphor as it draws upon one of the primary traditions found in the juridical principles of the ancient Near Eastern divorce texts. The potential punishment of this verse envisions Yahweh officially divorcing and disowning his unfaithful wife and laying claim to all marital property: "Therefore I will take back my grain in its time and my new wine in its season; I will reclaim my wool and my linen in order to reckon her indiscretion" (2:11).

After presenting the possibility of a technical divorce, Hosea has Yahweh relate this action's consequences for the personified city of Samaria in 2:12–15. These verses repeatedly use first-person verb forms to stress divine, personal participation in the actions, and a first-person verb stands at the beginning of every sentence in verses 11–15. The first consequence brings to the fore the other prominent image-base that this study has identified for Hosea's discourse, namely, the metaphorical description of physical and sexual violence against a woman: "Now I will uncover her genitals (נַבְלֻתָה) before the eyes of her lovers, and no one will reclaim her (לֹא־יַצִּילֶנָּה) from my hand" (2:12). In this declaration, Yahweh repeats his word "reclaim" (נצל) from 2:11 to emphasize the inability of any lover to help the adulterous wife.

---

[98] See Westbrook, "Prohibition," 395.
[99] *BDB*, 789 and Andersen and Freedman, *Hosea*, 246 also raise this possibility.

At first blush a reader is tempted to view this verse as a reference to the alleged practice of stripping as an ancient punishment for adultery. This literal interpretation seems to be based upon the misreading of verse 11 as the removal of clothes "which were to cover her nakedness." On the contrary, the discussion of comparative biblical texts revealed the existence of a tradition in which this language of physical and sexual violence against a woman consistently appeared metaphorically in conjunction with a city personified as a female and specifically referred to that city's imminent or threatened destruction. Even within Hosea's address, verse 5 has already explicitly intertwined the imagery of women, nakedness, and cities.

Seen in this light, Yahweh's words in 2:12 do not repeat the metaphorical punishment in 2:11 because that punishment deals with financial and property arrangements and divorce settlements not physical exposure. Rather, verses 12–15 make the connection between the metaphorical wife and the capital city explicit. The consequences in these verses do not make sense in reference to an individual but to a city. Verse 12 in particular employs the typical, metaphorical language for describing the destruction of a personified city. Physical consequences of this kind follow logically from the metaphorical action in which Yahweh officially divorces, that is, permanently casts off, his wife Samaria. In the very sight of her political allies ("lovers"), Samaria will experience the consequence of destruction. Should Yahweh divorce his metaphorical wife with cause and withdraw all of his support, the city will not survive.

In keeping with the supporting metaphorical traditions, Hosea, speaking for Yahweh, portrays this consequence of destruction as the uncovering or disclosure of the wife's נבלתה. This term is a *hapax legomenon* and inspires much scholarly discussion. The main interpretations of this term fall into four categories. First, the most widespread view understands נבלתה as a reference to genitalia based on a comparison with the Akkadian word *baltu/baštu*.[100] Second, Wellhausen suggests that this term functions only as a general reference to the nakedness of the adulteress.[101] Third, as opposed to the sexual connotations of the preceding views, Rudolph maintains that נבלתה derives from the word נבל, "to wither," and suggests that Yahweh will expose the weak state of his metaphorical wife.[102] Fourth, a growing number of commentators now associate this term with the Hebrew root נבל II, which means "to be

---

[100] This view goes back to P. P. Steininger, "Nablŭt: Ein Beitrag zur hebräischen Grammatik und Lexicographie," *ZAW* 24 (1904): 141–42. Cf. Wolff, *Hosea*, 37. Whitt also understands this term to be "genitals" but argues that it is not related to the Akkadian *baltu*. He suggests that this meaning derives from the use of the Hebrew root נבל to denote an oblong vessel like a jar, pitcher, etc. ("Divorce," 63).

[101] Wellhausen, *Die kleinen Propheten*, 13.

[102] Rudolph, *Hosea*, 64, 70. Rudolph also sees "foolishness" ("Torheit") as a plausible translation (ibid., 70).

foolish," with or without sexual connotations.[103] For example, Andersen and Freedman explicitly reject the proposed connection between נבלתה and the Akkadian root *baltu/baštu* because derivation from נבל II is more likely.[104]

In the face of these various possibilities, Olyan offers some evidence that may provide a way forward.[105] He observes that נבלתה in Hos 2:12 is not limited to a single meaning but functions on multiple levels in the literary context. As noted above, the themes of the wife's nakedness and the physical destruction ("nakedness") of land/territory stand together throughout the discourse. Because of the reference to nakedness in 2:5, one is inclined to translate נבלתה as "genitals" and to see it as another metaphorical description of the imminent or threatened destruction of the capital city Samaria. Linguistically, however, נבלתה most probably represents a noun with an abstract ending derived either from נבל II, "to be foolish" or *nābel*, "to wither."[106]

Within the specific metaphorical discourse of Hosea's address, this relationship of נבלתה to נבל II ("to be foolish") provides another important level of meaning. As Olyan notes, while נבלתה is a *hapax*, the noun נְבָלָה comes from נבל II and means "foolishness." In several occurrences in the Hebrew Bible, however, this noun has an explicitly sexual application and often describes an act of sexual misconduct.[107] For instance, Gen 34:7 characterizes the rape of Dinah as an act of נְבָלָה.[108] Biblical texts also describe both adultery and fornication as נְבָלָה (cf. Jer 29:23; Deut 22:21). Thus, נבלתה in Hos 2:12 functions well as a reference to a wanton act of sexual behavior: "And now I will reveal her sexual misconduct in the sight of her lovers...."[109] This translation fits nicely with the reason for Yahweh's potential punishment in verse 11 and strengthens the translation of ערותה as "indiscretion" in that verse.

On the basis of the above possibilities, it is reasonable to conclude that נבלתה functions on two levels within the discourse of Hos 2. The immediate literary context contains metaphorical imagery of both nakedness (2:5) and indiscretion (2:11). Thus, on one level, the first consequence of Yahweh's potential punishment involves the public revelation of his wife's inappropriate

---

[103] This nonsexual interpretation appears as early as the Vulgate's rendering, "*stultitia*," meaning "foolishness."

[104] Andersen and Freedman, *Hosea*, 248.

[105] Olyan, "'In the Sight of Her Lovers,'" 255–61.

[106] Ibid., 257–58.

[107] Ibid., 259.

[108] See also the descriptions of the rape of Tamar (2 Sam 13:12), the loss of virginity before marriage (Deut 22:21), adultery with a neighbor's wife (Jer 29:23), the proposed intercourse with the Levite traveler (Judg 19:23–24), and the rape of the Levite's concubine (Judg 20:6, 10).

[109] Olyan, "'In the Sight of Her Lovers,'" 260. See also Macintosh, *Critical and Exegetical Commentary*, 58 ("lewd behavior/ vile corruption") and McComiskey, *The Minor Prophets*, 39.

behavior that is characterized within the overarching marriage metaphor as sexual misconduct. On another level, the consequence listed in 2:12 again invokes the metaphorical tradition of describing the threatened destruction of capital cities as physical and sexual violence against a woman. This verse's verb גלה often appears with the image of exposing a woman's genitals in connection with the destruction of a city (e.g., Nah 3:5–6; Ezek 16:37; Isa 47:3). To the prophet's audience in his rhetorical situation, Yahweh's words in 2:12 raise the possibility of the ultimate consequence for Samaria should Yahweh choose to disown the city completely. When placed within the full movement of the discourse that ends with Yahweh's choice of reconciliation, this verse's stark language highlights both the severity of Samaria's rebellion and the graciousness of Yahweh's plan.

Verse 13 adds to the consequence of potential destruction and envisions the end of the entire cultic calendar of seasonal, monthly, and weekly celebrations. To accomplish this rhetorical effect, Yahweh's speech uses a play on words between the verb והשבתי ("I will bring to an end") and the noun ושבתה ("her sabbaths"). Additionally, the verse produces a tone of comprehensiveness by placing a list of singular collectives between the general terms משושה ("her rejoicing") and מועדה ("her appointed times"). This second consequence flows directly from the possible reaction described in 2:11. If Yahweh were to divorce officially his metaphorical wife, not only would the wife Samaria suffer destruction, but part of that destruction would involve the end of the people's cultic life.[110]

The vast majority of commentators associates this verse only with the termination of a widespread Baal cult in Israel and identifies these cultic occasions as Baal festivals. Macintosh's statement is representative: "All the state's religious observances were tainted by idolatry ... with the Baals...."[111] The actual language of the verse, however, makes no mention of apostasy and does not indicate in any way that the cultic occasions listed have any connection with a supposed Baal fertility cult. When placed within the discourse as a whole, there is no compelling reason not to understand this consequence as the end of the normal, Yahwistic cultic life of Samaria and its people. Verse 13's actions have no legal content or juridical background in the realm of marriage and divorce laws but simply represent an extrapolation of the city-destruction imagery.[112] This threatened action thus parallels some ancient Near Eastern political treaty curses that threaten "the removal of joyful sounds from a

---

[110] Harper is so convinced that the imagery here represents the climactic punishment for the people that he relocates the verse to follow 2:14 so that it connects with the similar cultic references in 2:15 (*Critical and Exegetical Commentary*, 231).

[111] Macintosh, *Critical and Exegetical Commentary*, 62. So also Jeremias, *Der Prophet*, 45; Mays, *Hosea*, 42; Wolff, *Hosea*, 38.

[112] So also Westbrook, "Adultery," 579.

land."[113] Moreover, Yee notes that the end of these festivals has a specifically political dimension as a punishment against the ruling elite. The festivals serve as a major source of income for the religious and political establishment.[114]

The third consequence that the prophet envisions for verse 11's potential punishment appears in verse 14. This verse intensifies the threatening consequences by relating Yahweh's purpose of desolating his metaphorical wife's "vine" and "fig-tree." The language here matches that in 2:5 where Yahweh threatens to make Samaria like a "desert;" the exact same Hebrew verb forms appear in both verses.[115] These physical objects of Yahweh's judgment once again make the connection with the city of Samaria explicit. Should Yahweh permanently divorce his wife, the resulting destruction would include not only the cessation of the cultic calendar but also the desolation of agricultural resources.[116] Contra Whitt, there is no reason to speculate that the prophet includes these physical objects because they had "some role in the cultic rituals [i.e., fertility rituals] devoted to Asherah."[117] On the contrary, the motif of destroying vines and fig-trees reverses a common formula for peace and prosperity.[118] Furthermore, this verse uses language similar to that of treaty-curses that refer to the destruction of trees and the establishment of a jungle with wild animals.[119]

In relating this consequence, Yahweh's speech reiterates the wife's claim that the fruitful land represents gifts from her lovers: "They are gifts (אֶתְנָה) for me that my lovers gave to me" (2:14). Yahweh's words then relate further destruction: "I will make them (m.pl.) into a forest, and the beasts of the field will devour them (m.pl.)." The term אֶתְנָה ("gifts"), which is placed on the wife's lips to describe her assets, is another *hapax*. As Yee notes, this anomalous term is very similar to the more common word, אֶתְנַן, which is the technical term for a prostitute's wages.[120] The unusual MT form perhaps results from the word-play with וְהַתְּאֵנָה ("fig-tree") and נָתְנוּ ("they gave").[121] If one follows the BHS note's suggestion and makes the noun into the more common masculine form, then it matches the pronoun הֵמָּה that immediately follows it and clarifies the antecedent of the masculine plural suffixes in the rest of the

---

[113] Hillers, *Treaty Curses*, 57. E.g., Sefire Treaty I A 29; cf. Jer 7:34; 16:9.

[114] Yee, "Not My Wife," 378.

[115] Landy, "Fantasy," 149.

[116] The pair "vine and fig-tree" occurs in Jer 5:17 and Joel 2:22 as a specific symbol for abundance.

[117] Whitt, "Divorce," 63. Mauchline also views the reference to turning vines and fig-trees into a forest as strange and so follows the LXX by reading "into a witness" (from לְעֵד) rather than "into a forest" (from לְיַעַר) ("Hosea," 585).

[118] Sweeney, *The Twelve Prophets*, 32; cf. Isa 36:16; Mic 4:4; and Zech 3:10 for peace and prosperity formulas with this imagery.

[119] See Blankenbaker, "Language," 178.

[120] Yee, "Hosea" (*NIB*), 225; cf. Mays, *Hosea*, 42. Note Hosea's use of this technical term in 9:1. Deuteronomy 23:18 prohibits the use of this fee to pay a vow to Yahweh.

[121] Macintosh, *Critical and Exegetical Commentary*, 63–64.

verse. Without this emendation, the masculine plural pronouns and suffixes do not match the gender of "vine" and "fig-tree" and have no apparent antecedent in the verse.[122] With this emendation, however, the force of Yahweh's words becomes clear. One of the consequences of an official divorce with cause would be Yahweh's desolation of the very things the wife has viewed as benefits of her relationship with adulterous lovers. This description relies on the common motif in prophetic literature that divine judgment results in the transformation of cultivated areas into desert wastelands.[123]

Within the context of the prophet's address, the audience once again hears a metaphorical reference to the political allies ("lovers") upon whom Pekah and the rulers of Samaria have relied for provision and prosperity. Hosea, speaking for Yahweh, presents the personified city's voice in order to contrast it with Yahweh's own statement. If Yahweh chooses the option of complete disownment of the city, the very signs of a prosperous and beneficial relationship between Samaria and its political "lovers" will fall victim to the ravages of the wild. In Hosea's context, the reference to vines and fig-trees makes sense as something that political allies may have provided to Samaria. As noted above in the discussion of the historical setting, Pekah most likely gained or was given increased amounts of territory as Rezin expanded his power. From this perspective, members of the royal house could indeed view the territory gained, particularly that of Samaria itself, as gifts given to them by their political overlord. This language is similar to that of political treaties where a political power refers to his ability to take away land, destroy trees, and transform a place into a jungle.[124]

At the conclusion of a sequence of five emphatic, first-person declarations by Yahweh, verse 15 summarizes the consequences of Yahweh's metaphorical divorce. This verse's statement encompasses all the consequences of Yahweh's potential action by characterizing them as holding his wife accountable for the days of her unfaithfulness: "I will visit upon her the days of the paramours (הבעלים) when (אשר) she burned incense for them and she adorned herself with her earring and her jewelry and went after her lovers. But me she forgot, declares Yahweh" (2:15). In this summary, the discourse once again employs the metaphorical terms בעל ("paramour") and מאהביה ("lovers") to represent those political overlords and allies with whom Samaria and its leaders have been

---

[122] For example, Andersen and Freedman emphasize that the masculine plural suffixes do not match and suggest that the masculine plural suffixes refer to the wife/mother's children and that the verse threatens the killing of these children by wild animals (*Hosea*, 252–53). Another possible explanation is to identify the antecedent of the pronouns as the masculine plural "lovers." However, the vine and fig-tree clearly stand as the central focus of both the wife's and Yahweh's statements.

[123] Ibid., 252; cf. Jer 4:23–26; Mic 3:12.

[124] See Blankenbaker, "Language," 178.

unfaithful to Yahweh.[125] In contrast to 2:10, however, this verse uses the plural form בעלים to identify the parties involved in the "days" when Yahweh's metaphorical wife engaged in her inappropriate actions (cf. בעל in 2:18 and בעלים in 2:19). Scholars commonly attempt to explain this plural reference through hypothetical reconstructions of the Baal cult known from Ugaritic texts. For example, Mays suggests that the plural term intentionally refers to the variety of epithets for the god Baal, who was worshipped at various shrines, and that this description fits with the multiple Hebrew Bible references like Baal of Peor (Num 25:3), Baal Berith (Judg 8:33), and Baal of Carmel (1 Kgs 18).[126] As Mays himself acknowledges, however, the evidence regarding Baal from Ugaritic texts argues against the idea of a variety of Baals at separate shrines. According to this evidence, the plural בעלים must simply denote various manifestations or characteristics of a single deity.[127]

As discussed in chapter 5 above, this alternation of singular and plural forms of בעל in Hosea's address, combined with the consistently plural references to "lovers," creates problems for the conclusion that religious apostasy with the god Baal is the discourse's central underlying issue. Such a supposition is weaker in light of the available evidence concerning the Baal cult. These plural forms make more sense as references to the various political allies with whom the personified Samaria has consorted in her actions that violated Yahweh's will. As noted previously, the singular בעל in 2:10 may be a metaphorical reference to Rezin of Damascus, the leader of the anti-Assyrian coalition in the west. The plural forms in verses 15 and 19, however, seem to be parallel references to "lovers" and perhaps represent other political partners with whom Samaria has aligned itself. The alternating singular and plural terms present no problems in the political realm. Even so, as chapter 5 made clear, Hosea deliberately draws upon language from the religious sphere, not to make another religious reference, but to equate the political misdeeds of the present with the religious apostasy of the past.[128]

Perhaps the part of Yahweh's statement in verse 15 that sways most commentators to characterize the issue as religious in nature is the description of the wife's actions on these days of the paramours. Yahweh specifically accuses

---

[125] As most commentators observe, this verse seems to identify explicitly the "lovers" with the בעלים. This identification itself does not suggest in any way, however, that these terms have a religious rather than political meaning within the metaphorical discourse.

[126] Mays, *Hosea*, 43.

[127] Ibid. Cf. Stuart, *Hosea-Jonah*, 52 but contrast Dearman, "Baal in Israel," 173–91. Andersen and Freedman (*Hosea*, 257) seem to acknowledge the problem with correlating verse 15's reference with a reconstructed Baal cult by suggesting that the term under consideration may not be plural at all. Rather, they propose that בעלים in 2:15 may be the singular form with a suffixed enclitic mem or simply a plural of majesty.

[128] See above discussion in chapter 5 of the other uses of בעל in historical retrospectives throughout the rest of Hosea.

his wife of burning incense and adorning herself with earring and jewelry. These actions, particularly the burning of incense, seem to be cultic in nature and to represent the explicit worship of other gods by Yahweh's wife. The description of these actions raises two crucial questions that begin to pull together the overall rhetorical function of Hos 2's metaphors. First, if the prophet's main concern is political, why does he refer to these religious activities? The first step in explaining this verse is to recognize that the Hebrew phrase itself is not clear. Following the phrase "the days of the paramours," the text tersely offers the words אֲשֶׁר תַּקְטִיר לָהֶם.[129] Most interpreters take the relative pronoun (אֲשֶׁר) and prepositional phrase (לָהֶם) as a clear reference to the wife worshipping other gods by burning incense to them. Wolff translates, "I will call her to account for the feast days of the Baals, when she burns incense to them...."[130] On the contrary, the preposition לְ may also have a sense of cause or motive ("because of," "for the sake of") or accompaniment ("with") and denote more of a corporate, cultic event between the wife and the בְעָלִים.[131] Macintosh rightly observes that the pronoun אֲשֶׁר in this phrase modifies "days" rather than בְעָלִים and should be translated accordingly.[132] Thus, one may render the phrase as "the days of the paramours when she burned incense for the sake of/with them."

Regardless of the translation, the vast majority of scholars see the phrase "the days of the בְעָלִים" as a reference to particular times of worship that specifically involved the Canaanite god Baal. Some interpreters identify these "days" as Canaanite religious festivals that Israel had been observing alongside the major Yahwistic celebrations. Wolff represents this view and proposes that the text's reference is to "the Canaanite cultic feasts, with their outdoor festivities upon the sacred high places and underneath the holy trees (4:13)."[133] On the other hand, several commentators, seemingly acknowledging the lack of evidence for an established Baal cult in Hosea's day, conclude that verse 15 refers not to separate Baalistic celebrations but to syncretistic Baal worship that took place during Yahwistic holy days. For example, Harper sees this verse as a

---

[129] Andersen and Freedman (*Hosea*, 259) note that the construction in this verse is unusual because the first part has an imperfect verb (תַּקְטִיר) while the second part has a vav-consecutive form (וַתַּעַד). They suggest that the first verb refers to a past period of continual action. Cf. McComiskey, *The Minor Prophets*, 40.

[130] Wolff, *Hosea*, 31.

[131] For the causative sense, see *HALOT*, 2:510 and *DCH*, IV:484; cf. Gen 4:23. For the sense of accompaniment, see *DCH*, IV:484; cf. 1 Kgs 22:34.

[132] Macintosh, *Critical and Exegetical Commentary*, 65.

[133] Wolff, *Hosea*, 40. He also associates verse 15's phrase "went after her lovers" with participation in processions within the sanctuary (ibid.). Cheyne (*Hosea*, 52) also sees these "days" as actual holy days of the Baals.

reference to Baal worship conducted at the major Yahwistic festivals mentioned in 2:13.[134]

These explanations overlook one aspect of political alliances in the ancient world that may explain the explicitly religious language used to describe the personified Samaria's actions. A proper understanding of the metaphorical nature of the terms בעל and בעלים in Hos 2 eliminates the need to relate the wife's actions to a supposed Canaanite cult. Nonetheless, verse 15 does represent the one place in the discourse where the prophet condemns Samaria for cultic activities. Yet the process of political treaty-making in the ancient Near East clearly attests to the prominence of a religious component in the course of explicitly political acts. Particularly in the Neo-Assyrian period, political treaties enacted between states evidence the practice of swearing the treaty in the names of both sets of gods.[135] The evidence for this practice comes primarily from Assyrian "*adê*" documents. As Cogan points out, these oaths of political loyalty do not require vassals to worship Assyria's gods but do involve another state acknowledging the Assyrian gods, as well as their own, as guarantors of the treaty.[136] For example, Sargon's reference to his vassal Ullusunu in a text from his eighth campaign states, "As for king Ullusunu, their lord (*bēlišunu*), I set a rich table before him.... They, together with the soldiers of Assyria, I seated at a festive table, and *before Ashur and the gods of their country*, they blessed my rule."[137] Neo-Assyrian treaties consistently appear as pacts that are not only witnessed by but also sworn in the names of the gods of *both* parties.[138] A state's participation in a political alliance seems necessarily to have involved acknowledgment of the power of gods other than their own.

Assyrian texts also attest a secondary practice that developed from the well-known occurrence of swearing treaties in the names of the gods of both parties. The basic practice of swearing seems to have led to token worship (mostly through the giving of gifts) of a treaty-partner's gods for the sake of solidifying the political relationship. One should not identify such worship as an imposition of religious activities upon vassals, a practice for which there is no evidence in Assyrian texts. Rather, as Cogan states concerning treaties with Assyria, "It is

---

[134] Harper, *Critical and Exegetical Commentary*, 233. So also Rudolph, *Hosea*, 71.

[135] For full discussion and additional examples of this practice, see M. Tsevat, "The Neo-Assyrian and Neo-Babylonian Vassal Oaths and the Prophet Ezekiel," *JBL* 78 (1959): 199–204.

[136] See Cogan, *Imperialism*, 44, 48.

[137] Ibid., 48–49; emphasis added; cf. *TCL* 3: 63–64. Other examples of this practice include the following: 1) Esarhaddon's nonaggression pact with Urtaku of Elam, which states, "[T]hey dispatched their messengers of friendship and peace ... and swore an oath by the great gods," (Parpola and Watanabe, *Neo-Assyrian Treaties*, XVII), 2) Ashurbanipal's instruction to an Elamite vassal, which states, "[K]eep the [treaty] that I have made you swear before the gods of heaven and earth!" (ibid., XXI), and 3) Aššur-nerari V's treaty with Mati'-ilu of Arpad, which states, "You are sworn by Aššur, king of heaven and earth!" (l. 6; ibid., 13).

[138] Parpola and Watanabe, *Neo-Assyrian Treaties*, XXXVII.

conceivable, however, that in the interest of good relations with the Assyrian suzerain, a vassal's occasional gifts might have included donations to the suzerain's gods.... Gifts to a god other than one's own apparently carried political overtones...."[139] An example of this related practice can be seen in an Assyrian text in which a border guard relates having intercepted a gift of horses sent from the Elamites to Uruk in order to solidify an alliance. The guard's inquiry specifically notes that the Elamite gift was addressed to Ishtar the goddess of Uruk: "On the bronze 'turner' of the trappings was written: [From] Tammaritu [...] the *teppir*-official of the king of Elam to Ishtar of Uruk."[140]

Beyond the giving of gifts, a third cultic dimension of political alliances seems to have taken place at the inception of a treaty. Some texts attest that the consummation of a political treaty involved not simply swearing in the names of both sets of gods but also actively acknowledging the authority of your partner's deity/deities. For example, the Vassal Treaty of Esarhaddon specifically requires the vassal to accept not only Assyria's supremacy but also that of its god, Ashur (ll. 393–94): "In the future and forever Aššur will be your god, and Assurbanipal, the great crown prince designate, will be your lord (EN-*ku-nu*)."[141] Parpola and Watanabe observe that this treaty, as well as some other loyalty oaths, suggests that a cultic ceremony, perhaps including shared worship of all gods involved, took place at the consummation of a treaty.[142] Esarhaddon's treaty stipulates (l. 153): "You shall not take a mutually binding oath with (any)one who installs (statues of) gods in order to conclude a treaty before gods...."[143] Again, this treaty refers to the presence of gods at the inception of the oath (ll. 494–95): "May these gods be our witnesses: We will not make rebellion or insurrection against Esarhaddon, king of Assyria...."[144]

Even the eighth-century Sefire treaties, which come from the general period of Hosea's preaching, allude to the prominent place of religious activity in the making of political treaties. The opening section of the text (ll. 6–12) provides an extensive list of both states' deities, who are portrayed as witnesses and guarantors of the alliance. This list concludes with the summarizing statement (ll. 12–13), "[A]ll the god[s of KTK and the gods of Ar]pad (are) witnesses (to it). Open your eyes, (O gods!), to gaze upon the treaty of Bar-Ga'yah [with Mati'el, the king of Arpad]."[145] The text ultimately goes on to characterize the alliance as an agreement enacted between the gods themselves (ll. 6–8): "This is

---

[139] Cogan, *Imperialism*, 56. For a detailed discussion of this cultic aspect of political treaties with Assyria, see ibid., 42–61.

[140] Ibid., 56; cf. *ABL*, 268, obv. 13–rev. 1.

[141] Parpola and Watanabe, *Neo-Assyrian Treaties*, 44.

[142] Ibid., XXXVII.

[143] Ibid., 35.

[144] Ibid., 50. See also *ABL*, 213:7, which states, "let the gods come for the treaty."

[145] Fitzmyer, *Aramaic Inscriptions*, 43.

the treaty of gods, which gods have concluded.... [And all the gods] shall guard [this] treaty."[146]

The above Assyrian and Aramaic texts point to the conclusion that religious activities were a vital part of ancient Near Eastern treaty-making throughout the eighth and seventh centuries B.C.E. Not only did such treaties involve swearing in the names of and acknowledging the authority of multiple gods, but also they seem to have often included token worship of various gods in order to solidify the alliance. It seems reasonable to conclude that the establishment of a political treaty may have specifically included a cultic ceremony in which the relevant parties engaged in cooperative worship, at least with respect to the deities of the more powerful partner. The realms of religion and politics (even gods and nations) intertwine in such imagery. This background sheds light on the condemnation of the personified Samaria in Hos 2:15. The "days of the paramours" may be yet another reference to the enacting of political alliances that violated Yahweh's will. In this particular verse, Yahweh plays the role of both the wronged husband and the wronged deity. The issue, however, is not that the wife has committed religious apostasy by worshipping a Canaanite fertility god. Rather, she has entered into inappropriate political alliances that were sealed with cultic acts like the burning of incense.

The second major question that emerges from this imagery concerns its relationship to the portrayal of Yahweh as the wronged husband. If, as Hosea's rhetorical-historical situation suggests, verse 15's activities represent the establishment of political treaties with other nations in rebellion against a previous vassal treaty with Assyria, why are these actions seen as sins against *Yahweh*? How does the act of political disloyalty to Assyria become disloyalty to Yahweh? On the basis of the above evidence for the religious dimension of political treaty-making, it is reasonable to conclude that Samaria's previous treaty arrangement with Assyria was also sworn in Yahweh's name. Thus, such a treaty could be seen as Yahweh's treaty, and disloyalty to that treaty would constitute disloyalty to Yahweh (in whose name the treaty was sworn) and not simply to Assyria (the entity with whom the treaty was made). Ezekiel 17:11–21 provides an example of this perspective.[147] Verses 13–15 note that the king of Judah entered into a covenant/treaty with the king of Babylon but subsequently broke it by conspiring with Egypt. But in verse 19, the rhetoric changes and identifies the treaty in question as *Yahweh's* treaty: "Therefore, thus says the Lord God, as I live, my oath which he despised and my covenant which he broke, I will visit upon his head."[148] Similarly, in verse 20, Yahweh identifies the king's unfaithfulness as "unfaithfulness in which he acted unfaithfully

---

[146] Ibid., 48–49.
[147] So also Ezek 21:23–29 and 29:14–16. For full discussion, see Tsevat, "Vassal Oaths," 201–4.
[148] Author's translation.

against me."[149] Hence, if a treaty between Israel and Assyria like that in Hosea's day was enacted with the participation of Yahweh, Hosea could assume that it was Yahweh's treaty and could proclaim that its violation violated Yahweh. When this rhetoric is placed within Hos 2's overall marriage metaphor, Yahweh becomes the wronged husband and the wronged deity.

While drawing upon the cultic background of ancient Near Eastern treaty-making, Yahweh's words in 2:15 continue to employ the overall metaphor of Samaria as the adulterous wife who has abandoned her husband. The term נִזְמָהּ ("her earring") often appears as an engagement gift given to a young woman by a suitor in order to signify betrothed status. For instance, Gen 24:22 describes how Abraham's servant gave Rebekah an earring (נֶזֶם) and bracelets after identifying her as a bride for Isaac, and Ezek 16:12 says that Yahweh gave the personified Jerusalem a "ring (נֶזֶם) on your nose" to mark her betrothal.[150] Accordingly, the image in 2:15 is that of a wife who uses her original bridal gifts in the service of adulterous lovers (cf. silver and gold in 2:10). As Sweeney remarks, "If this is the case, then the terms are employed sarcastically here to signify both the wife's married state and the adultery with which the husband charges her."[151]

At the close of this verse, Yahweh summarizes the situation with a succinct characterization: "But me she forgot, declares Yahweh." The unusual placement of the object ("me") in the first position puts the emphasis on Yahweh as the wronged husband, interrupts the sequence of actions, and places the first-person reference side by side with "her lovers."[152] Adding to this emphatic ending is the reminder that this statement is the word of Yahweh in the first-person: "declares Yahweh (נְאֻם־יְהוָה)." This phrase occurs four times in Hosea (2:15, 18, 23, and 11:11), but only once does it mark the end of a speech unit (11:11). Here, as in the rest of chapter 2, the phrase functions to emphasize that the prophet is presenting Yahweh's perspective.[153]

With these words, verse 15 marks the end of Yahweh's description in 2:10–15. In keeping with the marriage metaphor, Yahweh presents the option of the wronged husband to divorce his wife with cause according to the imagery of ancient Near Eastern legal traditions. The text describes a variety of consequences that such a disownment would have upon the personified Samaria. In the list of threatened destruction, cultic collapse, and natural

---

[149] Author's translation.

[150] Sweeney, *The Twelve Prophets*, 29; Andersen and Freedman, *Hosea*, 260. Wolff notes that the term נֶזֶם also appears in Exod 32:2 to denote the earrings used in the golden calf episode (*Hosea*, 40).

[151] Sweeney, *The Twelve Prophets*, 29.

[152] Andersen and Freedman, *Hosea*, 262.

[153] Stuart, *Hosea–Jonah*, 53; Wolff, *Hosea*, 41; Yee, *Composition*, 82.

devastation, Yahweh does not yet give any hint of a course of action that could lead to reconciliation.

4. THE INTENT TO REMARRY (2:16–17)

Following immediately upon this pessimistic picture, verse 16 marks a sudden turning point in the speech. Once again, Yahweh's words begin with "therefore" (לכן), but the logical connection with the rest of the passage is surprising. The transitional term לכן combines with the preceding phrase נאם־יהוה to form a "hinge" that both separates and connects the halves of chapter 2.[154] Since the preceding uses of this transitional term introduce punitive actions, the reader expects such a judgment in this verse as well. Rather than presenting another sequence of the wife's action followed by a potential punishment, however, Yahweh ironically asserts an intent to reunite with his unfaithful wife: "Therefore, behold, I am about to seduce her (מפתיה) and bring her into the wilderness (והלכתיה המדבר), and I will speak to her heart (ודברתי על לבה)." Thus, 2:16 concludes Yahweh's review of the options for dealing with the situation of estrangement and rejection. The wronged husband will not punish his wife through humiliation, destruction, confinement, or formal divorce; he will renew his wedding vows. If the oracle's various descriptions of punishments represent a series of options available to the husband, then, as Clines concludes, Yahweh chooses the final option because the others lead only to a fixation of the current state of affairs.[155] Seen in this way, verse 16 surprisingly proclaims a restoration without any hint of required reform on the part of the wife. Considering the prophet's theological vantage point, Buss is right to associate such positive turns of events with the type of Israelite prophecy that "does not ground its prediction in human activity … but [in] an occurrence based in God."[156] The series of restorative actions that begins in 2:16 provides the rhetorical effect of explicitly reversing or eliminating the threats made up to this point in Yahweh's speech.[157] The covenant with the beasts in 2:20 eliminates the threat to the vine and fig-tree in 2:14, and the giving of grain and new wine in 2:24 reverses the reclaiming of these items in 2:11. Even Yahweh's opening statement in verse 16 overturns the earlier threat of making the wife into a wilderness/desert (מדבר) in 2:5.

---

[154] Landy, *Hosea*, 39. McComiskey suggests that "therefore" in 2:16 is not the "logical consequence" of the preceding verse but of the whole speech up to this point (*The Minor Prophets*, 42). Garrett also describes the "therefore" here as deliberately paradoxical (*Hosea, Joel*, 87).

[155] Clines, "Hosea 2," 99.

[156] Buss, *Prophetic Word*, 126. Buss also notes that this unexpectedly positive "therefore" statement represents the ironic tension between tragedy and comedy that runs through the book as a whole (M. Buss, "Tragedy and Comedy in Hosea," *Semeia* 32 [1984]: 76).

[157] Andersen and Freedman, *Hosea*, 264.

Yet the imagery of verse 16 is striking. Yahweh declares that he is about to "seduce" or "lure" (מְפַתֶּיהָ) her into the wilderness. The combination of the participle ("seduce") and the perfect ("I will bring her") gives the sense of two impending future actions, but the first of these actions ("seduce") is described with a word that seems to have negative connotations associated with seducing a woman for rape. Exodus 22:15 uses this term to describe the seduction and rape of a virgin. For this reason, some commentators see Yahweh's statement as yet another threat of violence against the wife. As Landy observes, however, the term פתה in the context of verse 16 does not have negative connotations but simply refers to a type of sexual "enchantment" or attraction.[158] Yahweh sets out to enchant his wife both sexually and verbally into a situation of reconciliation.

Another aspect of verse 16 that leads some to see the imagery as negative is the location of the act of restoration.[159] In Yahweh's statement of his intent to remarry, the place of reconciliation and reconsummation is the "wilderness" (הַמִּדְבָּר). While the image of the wilderness is prominent in romantic literature like the Song of Songs (e.g., Song 4:8; 7:12),[160] its only other occurrence in Hos 2 is negative (2:5). Given this fact, why does Yahweh choose this location as the scene of reconciliation? One long-standing view that attempts to explain texts like 2:16 asserts the existence of a desert or nomadic ideal in the prophetic literature. According to this view, prophetic texts use a motif of the return to the wilderness in order to express a return to the ideal time in the relationship between Yahweh and Israel. The earliest scholar to propose this concept of a nomadic ideal in the prophets was Budde.[161] Even so, he did not see Hos 2:16 as an example of this motif. Rather, Budde maintained that this verse represented punishment on Israel and the turning of the land into a wilderness.[162] Building upon Budde's work in another direction, however, Humbert soon applied the concept of a desert ideal to Hosea's notion of a return to the wilderness.[163]

In a thorough study of the wilderness motif in the prophetic literature, Riemann rejects the older view and demonstrates that there is no motif of a return to the ideal wilderness setting in the prophetic texts.[164] On the contrary,

---

[158] Landy, "Wilderness," 50.

[159] So H. Ginsberg, "Studies in Hosea 1–3," in *Yehezkel Kaufmann Jubilee Volume* (ed. M. Haran; Jerusalem: Magnes, 1960), 66 and Landy, "Wilderness," 48. Jeremias (*Der Prophet*, 47) considers the statement to be indeterminate as to whether it is positive or negative. The negative interpretation also goes back to the Rabbinic commentators Ibn Ezra, who understands the referent to be the land of Israel turned into a wilderness, and Rashi, who sees the verse as an allusion to the exile (see Macintosh, *Critical and Exegetical Commentary*, 70).

[160] Garrett, *Hosea, Joel*, 90.

[161] K. Budde, "The Nomadic Ideal in the Old Testament," *The New World* 4 (1895): 726–45.

[162] Ibid., 734.

[163] P. Humbert, "Osée le prophète bédouin," *RHPR* 1 (1921): 97–118; cf. Humbert, "Logique," 158–66.

[164] See P. Riemann, "Desert and Return to the Desert in the Pre-Exilic Prophets" (Ph.D. diss., Harvard University, 1964).

he concludes that the preexilic prophets had a negative view of the wilderness and saw it as a threatening region into which an entity could be turned as punishment.[165] Thus, although Riemann rejects Budde's general conclusion, he agrees with his specific interpretation of Hos 2:16: the reference in this verse is negative and says nothing positive about the wilderness.[166]

The use of the term "desert/wilderness" to indicate a state of desolation in Akkadian texts adds to the negative evaluation of the imagery. In these texts, "desert/wilderness" is not a place to which one is taken but a condition into which something is turned. For example, a Nimrud letter uses the term "desert" (*mu-da-bi-ri*) to describe a postwar condition: "the towns ... are ... desert (*mu-da-bi-ri*)."[167] This descriptive use of the term in Akkadian texts also fits with the references in Isa 13:21–22 and 34:11–14 that use מדבר to refer to the abode of demons. Seen in this way, Yahweh's statement in Hos 2:16 contains a threat to bring a condition of postbattle destruction upon the personified city of Samaria.

The problem with these negative interpretations of verse 16, however, is that the specific wilderness image here functions rhetorically to represent a new beginning.[168] One cannot ignore the positive tone that takes over at this point in the overall rhetorical address. Thus, the reconciliation of Yahweh and his wife may be set in the location of the wilderness simply in order to reverse symbolically the metaphorical judgment of 2:5 in which the city was turned into a desolate wasteland. Another possibility is that verse 16's imagery of remarriage draws upon the traditions associated with the exodus from Egypt and the wilderness wanderings, so that Yahweh's relationship with his wife will symbolically return to the place in which it started. Unlike the understanding of the nomadic ideal interpretation, the point is not to return to the wilderness existence for good but simply to recapitulate the divine-human relationship from its point of origin. Hosea may be drawing here upon a tradition that envisions Yahweh's first marriage to have taken place at the time of the wilderness journey from Egypt.[169] As Andersen and Freedman observe, the hifil form of הלך found in verse 16 is often used in descriptions of Israel's journey through the wilderness.[170]

If this wilderness tradition of Israel coming out of Egypt is being utilized, it may seem to undermine the identification of the metaphorical wife as the city of Samaria in Hos 2. It appears that Hosea draws not only on the tradition of the

---

[165] Ibid., 60–61.

[166] Ibid., 124, 159–62.

[167] H. W. F. Saggs, "LXX-ND 2766, Plate XIV," *Iraq* 25–26 (1963–64): 70–80. For further discussion, see Chong, "Song," 257–60.

[168] For example, Buss (*Prophetic Word*, 132), while rejecting the nomadic ideal interpretation and suggesting that the wilderness here represents a "Sheol" or negative "state of disorder," maintains that the text presents a recreation.

[169] Anderson, *Eighth-Century Prophets*, 86.

[170] Andersen and Freedman, *Hosea*, 272. Cf. Deut 8:2, 15; 29:4 (MT); Ps 136:16.

exodus from Egypt but also on that of the entrance into the land (e.g., "valley of Achor" in 2:17). Yet there is a version of these traditions that is peculiar to prophetic texts and revolves around capital cities. In the era after Hosea, the prophet Ezekiel relates a metaphorical tradition in which Yahweh first discovers and then betroths his wife in the open field (Ezek 16:1–14). In this particular account, the wife of Yahweh discovered in the wild is not the entire nation but the personified city of Jerusalem (Ezek 16:2). Ezekiel 23 also draws on this tradition. In this context, both Jerusalem and Samaria are portrayed as wives of Yahweh whom he found in Egypt and betrothed as his own (Ezek 23:1–4). Jeremiah 2:2 similarly declares that Yahweh's original engagement to his wife took place "in the wilderness," and, once again, the wife under consideration is the personified city of Jerusalem.

Since the oracles of Jeremiah and Ezekiel date from the time after the fall of the northern kingdom, it is not surprising that they focus on Jerusalem as the personified wife of Yahweh. Rather than assuming that these later prophets created the notion that Yahweh's marriage to the capital cities began in the wilderness between Egypt and Canaan, however, it is reasonable to conclude that Hosea's marriage imagery already drew upon and contributed to that tradition. Yahweh's speech in 2:16 perhaps makes use of a tradition that specifically associated the capital city's initial engagement to Yahweh with the wilderness setting. Thus, Yahweh proclaims neither a return to permanent living in the wilderness nor a judgment of desolation on the land but a recapitulation of the beginning of his marital relationship with Samaria.

In this wilderness setting, Yahweh declares that he will undertake several actions that express the intent to remarry his estranged wife. The first of these actions appears in the expression, "I will speak to her heart." This phrase has generated much scholarly discussion and has produced two primary interpretations. First, the majority of commentators understand this expression to represent speaking kindly, comfortably, or romantically in order to influence the addressee in a positive way. This explanation generally relies on the appearances of this phrase in the context of courtship in the Hebrew Bible (e.g., Ruth 2:13).[171] Even the Targum explicitly adopts this reading of Hos 2:16 by inserting the word "comfort": אמליל תבחומין על לבה ("I will speak comfort to her heart"). A closer examination of the specific occurrences of this phrase in the Hebrew Bible, however, leads some feminist scholars to propose a

---

[171] For this view, see Harper, *Critical and Exegetical Commentary*, 239; Mays, *Hosea*, 44; McComiskey, *The Minor Prophets*, 42; Pfeiffer, "Hosea," 804; Rudolph, *Hosea*, 75; Wolff, *Hosea*, 42. Some commentators suggest the phrase may have the more specific meaning of "to make love to" (Knight, *Hosea*, 56; Macintosh, *Critical and Exegetical Commentary*, 69; Snaith, *Amos*, 56). For an example of the romantic interpretation in the service of a larger theological project, see M. Diaz, "I Will Speak to Their Hearts," *SEDOS Bulletin* 28 (1996): 271–76. The phrase occurs nine times in the Hebrew Bible: Gen 34:3; 50:21; Judg 19:3; Ruth 2:13; 2 Sam 19:8 (MT); 2 Chron 30:22; Isa 40:2; Hos 2:16; 2 Chron 32:6.

second interpretation. This proposal observes that the phrase often appears in the context of sexual violence. The expression indicates that the subject "acts in a deceitful manner by manipulating her sexually."[172] In the context of Shechem's rape of Dinah, for example, Gen 34:3 states that "he loved the young woman, and he spoke to the heart (וידבר על־לב) of the young woman."

These common explanations overlook another possible meaning for this expression that fits very well with the legal and juridical image-base at work in Hosea's address. In various legal agreements from Elephantine, the similar expression, "to please the heart" (טב לבב), functions as a technical phrase that denotes "to reach an agreement, satisfy, convince."[173] While this is not an exact parallel to the expression in Hos 2:16, it is close in both form and function. For example, a contract dealing with withdrawal from a piece of land uses this phrase to express resolution (*TAD* B2.2; Cowley 6; *COS* 3.60). After the questioning party ("Dargamana") received an oath sworn to Yahweh by Mahseiah indicating that the latter had not taken land belonging to the former, Dargamana states (l. 12), "You swore to me by YHW and satisfied my heart (הוטבת לבבי) about that land." The expression also functions in this manner in another text dealing with a suit over goods (*TAD* B2.8; Cowley 14; *COS* 3.65). In this text, after the suing party ("Pia") receives an oath from the other person concerning the goods, he concludes (l. 5), "And my heart was satisfied (וטיב לבב) with that oath." Similar uses of this expression occur throughout the legal texts in various contexts dealing with property and possessions.[174]

Even more importantly for understanding Hos 2:16, the above expression occurs in some Elephantine "Documents of Wifehood." In these contexts, the phrase represents the reaching of a satisfactory agreement between two parties entering into a marriage relationship. For instance, *TAD* B2.6 (Cowley 15; *COS* 3.63) provides the groom's ("Eshor's") description of the bride price (מהר) that he paid to his bride's father. Following this description, the groom concludes (l. 5), "your heart was satisfied (וטב לבבך)." Later in the same text, the groom lists the dowry brought into the marriage by the bride and then declares (l. 15), "my heart was satisfied (וטיב לבבי)." The "Document of Wifehood" for Ananiah and his wife follows a similar pattern (*TAD* B3.8; Kraeling 7+15+18; *COS* 3.76). After listing the bride price given to the wife's brother, Ananiah states (l. 5), "your [heart was satis]fied (וטי[ב ל]בב[ך]) herein." Finally, the fragmentary beginning of a marriage agreement also attests this usage (*TAD*

---

[172] Törnkvist, *Use and Abuse*, 157. This view seems to go back to van Dijk-Hemmes ("Imagination," 84), who relies primarily upon the occurrences of the phrase in Gen 34:3 and Judg 19:3.

[173] According to the index in Porten and Yardeni (*TAD*, xxxii), the term "heart" (לבב) occurs nineteen times in the corpus. All but two of these appear in a form of the expression, "to please the heart."

[174] See *TAD* B2.9:8, 9 (Cowley 20; *COS* 3.66); *TAD* B4.3:8 (Cowley 3); *TAD* B4.4:9 (Cowley 2); *TAD* B5.2:7 (Cowley 65); *TAD* B5.5:7 (Cowley 43); *TAD* B3.2:4 (Kraeling 1; *COS* 3.70); *TAD* B3.4:6 (Kraeling 3; *COS* 3.72); *TAD* B3.12:6, 14, 26 (*COS* 3.80); *TAD* B5.6:3.

B6.1; Kraeling 14). Once again, the husband lists the bride price given to the bride's father and concludes (l. 5), "[your heart was satisfied] ([טיב לבבך])."

Four of the nine occurrences of the phrase "speak to the heart" in the Hebrew Bible seem to be simply a way of stating that someone encouraged or comforted another person.[175] Yet some appearances of this phrase also attest the technical meaning of "to reach an agreement, satisfy." Particularly the uses in the context of a relationship between a man and woman are perhaps best understood not as romantic or violent language but as the man's attempt to reach an agreement, convince, or satisfy the woman to some end. This seems particularly to be the case in Shechem's words in Gen 34:3 and the Levite's words in Judg 19:3. In both cases, the man attempts to convince or satisfy the woman in order to achieve a certain type of relationship. Particularly in Judg 19:3, the phrase occurs within the context of the Levite attempting to persuade his estranged concubine to return to the previous relationship. Even the occurrences of this phrase in Gen 50:21, where Joseph's arrangement of provisions satisfies his brothers, and 2 Sam 19:8(MT), where David attempts to convince his troops to remain with him, fit this technical usage.

The above biblical and extrabiblical evidence suggests another way to understand Yahweh's statement in 2:16 within the context of the chapter's overarching marriage metaphor. The first action that Yahweh takes toward his estranged wife is to take her back to the point of their initial betrothal and convince her to enter into an agreement that begins the marriage relationship anew. Yahweh enchants her sexually and offers her terms designed to persuade her to a certain course of action.

The expression of Yahweh's intent to remarry continues in the statements and imagery of verse 17. Yahweh adds two more actions that he will undertake in the wilderness in order to reestablish the marriage relationship: "And I will give to her her vineyards from there and the valley of Achor for a doorway of hope." In keeping with the image-base of ancient Near Eastern marriage procedures, these items may symbolize bridal gifts given on the occasion of remarriage. Like the gifts given to a woman by a suitor, Yahweh's gifts serve the symbolic function of sealing the new relationship.[176] While a reference to vineyards does not occur in the earlier lists of items in verses 7, 10, and 11, verse 14's image of destroying the personified city's "vine" and "fig-tree" casts

---

[175] For example, the phrase occurs in parallel with the command to "comfort" (נחמו) the people in Isa 40:1–2. The same situation occurs in Ruth 2:13 where Ruth says, "… you have comforted me (נחמתני) and you have spoken to my heart." Second Chronicles 30:22 and 32:6 also use the phrase to depict Hezekiah offering a word of encouragement to Levites and commanders.

[176] So also Wolff, *Hosea*, 42; Andersen and Freedman, *Hosea*, 272–73; Kruger, "Marriage Metaphor," 20.

the gift in 2:17 as an explicit reversal of an earlier threat.[177] Furthermore, Andersen and Freedman observe that the Ugaritic text "Nikkal and the Moon" (UT 77) portrays a marriage situation and lists vineyards as a part of the items given by the groom to the bride's father.[178]

The symbolic transformation of the valley of Achor into a "doorway of hope" may also represent a bridal gift given to initiate the new marriage.[179] In this statement, the prophet once again draws upon the traditions of the wilderness and entrance into the land.[180] The exact location of this valley is unknown. King suggests the Buqe'a valley in the Judean desert, west of the Dead Sea. This valley appears to have had seventh-century outposts that guarded the route by which resources came to Jerusalem.[181] Perhaps for this reason, the text presents the valley as a "doorway." On a broader level, however, Josh 7 presents Achor both as the location through which Israel entered the promised land and as the site of the first instance of the people's rebellion after crossing the Jordan. As Wolff notes, the sound of the word "Achor" (עכור) may function more prominently than its location in this context since "Achor" recalls Achan's act of bringing "misfortune" (עכר) in Josh 7:25.[182] Seen against this background, one of Yahweh's bridal gifts is the symbolic transformation of this traditional location into a positive place from which Yahweh's wife can once again reenter life in the land.

Yahweh's declaration of intent to remarry in 2:16–17 ends with the anticipation that his goal will be achieved and his wife will "respond (וענתה) there as in the days of her youth and as on the day of her coming up from the land of Egypt" (2:17). The critical term in this statement is ענה. As Macintosh notes, the sense of this term is difficult to ascertain because at least four meanings are attested in the Hebrew Bible.[183] Some commentators read verse 17

---

[177] For another reference to vineyards found in the wilderness, see Song 1:14. The symbol of the vine or vineyard is a common prophetic allegory for the relationship between Yahweh and the people (see Isa 5:1–7; Jer 2:21; Ps 80:9–17[MT]).

[178] Andersen and Freedman, *Hosea*, 272–74; cf. Kruger, "Marriage Metaphor," 20.

[179] Buss notes that the expression נתן ... ל may be read as "to make ... into...." (*Prophetic Word*, 9). Ginsberg follows Sellin and connects לפתח with the verb פתח in the sense of "to plow" (cf. Isa 28:24). Accordingly, he reads, "into a promising plow land" ("Studies," 66–67).

[180] Stuart (*Hosea–Jonah*, 53) observes that Hosea's statement emphasizes two themes from the wilderness experience that represent reconciliation: the gift of the land (Josh 24:13) and the valley of Achor (Josh 7:24–27).

[181] P. King, *Amos, Hosea, Micah: An Archaeological Commentary* (Philadelphia: Westminster, 1988), 26–27. So also Anderson, *Eighth-Century Prophets*, 88. Wolff suggests the Wadi en-Nuwēʿime, northwest of Tell es-Sultan (*Hosea*, 42). For discussion see Macintosh, *Critical and Exegetical Commentary*, 74–75, f.n. 13.

[182] Wolff, *Hosea*, 43. Garrett (*Hosea, Joel*, 91) observes that the term "hope" (תקוה) has a homonym in Josh 2:18, 21 that means "cord" and refers to Rahab's scarlet cord.

[183] Macintosh, *Critical and Exegetical Commentary*, 72–73.

as indicating that the wife will "be wholly attentive,"[184] "play and sing,"[185] or "respond sexually."[186] In the context of the marriage imagery at work in the text, however, the verb ענה can function as a reference to the wife's "response" to the husband's marriage proposal.[187] As Friedman suggests, one can imagine that the marriage ceremony involved oral pronouncements by the bride and groom similar to those attested in the ancient Near Eastern texts discussed earlier: "You are my wife;" "You are my husband."[188] Seen in this way, the usage in Hos 2:17 parallels Yahweh's description of the people as a "kingdom of priests" in Exod 19:5–6, 8 in which all the people "responded (ויענו) as one."[189] After the speaking of words and giving of gifts, Yahweh anticipates that his wife will "respond" affirmatively. The verse states that the wife will respond as she did at the initial wedding. In these last two phrases, the prophet continues to draw upon the tradition noted above that imagines the wilderness as the location of the initial relationship. Once again, however, Hosea relies on the particular version of that tradition that is made explicit in the later oracles of Jeremiah and Ezekiel and that associates capital cities, even Samaria (cf. Ezek 23:3–4, 8), with the exodus and wilderness experience.[190]

5. THE DECLARATION OF REMARRIAGE AND THE MARRIAGE COVENANT (2:18–22)

5.1 The Declaration of Remarriage (2:18)

Verses 18–22 develop further the theme of Yahweh's metaphorical remarriage to Samaria by describing some related events. Verse 18 begins this process by abruptly shifting to the second-person (f.sg.) and addressing the wife directly. As noted above, this type of shifting of perspective and person occurs more than once in the prophet's address (cf. 2:21–22) and does not indicate a separate rhetorical unit. Person shifts in Hosea function rhetorically in conjunction with other markers like "therefore" and "on that day" to mark a new section within the same discourse and a new address to or situation for the same addressee

---

[184] Ibid., 73.

[185] Ibn Ezra suggests this reading so that the wife's actions parallel those of Miriam in Exod 15:21 (Lipshitz, *Ibn Ezra*, 30).

[186] Landy ("Wilderness," 50) notes that the verb has sexual connotations in Exod 21:10, which uses the term to refer to both cohabitation and rape.

[187] Friedman, "Israel's Response," 200–203; so also Kruger, "Marriage Metaphor," 21.

[188] Friedman, "Israel's Response," 203. Friedman suggests that although the Elephantine texts have only the husband's declaration, the texts serve primarily as legal documents and thus may not reflect fully what was said orally.

[189] Ibid., 202; Yee, *Composition*, 81.

[190] For the city interpretation of this imagery, see also Schmitt, "Gender," 120.

envisioned throughout the discourse (cf. Hos 2:21–22; 11:8–9).[191] As Clines observes, if the emendation of the MT in 2:8 ("her way") is correct, verse 18 indicates that Yahweh addresses his metaphorical wife directly only at the time of restoration.[192] At this climactic moment in the metaphorical portrayal of reconciliation, the wronged husband targets his words directly to his estranged wife and thus offers her a new address and a changed situation. With these words, Yahweh describes an act of renaming that both accompanies and symbolizes the remarriage: "So it will be in that day (וְהָיָה בַיּוֹם הַהוּא), declares Yahweh, you (f.sg.) will call me 'my husband,' (אִישִׁי) and you (f.sg.) will no longer call me 'my paramour' (בַעְלִי)."

The verse begins with the transitional phrase, "So it will be in that day," which delineates a new thought in Yahweh's speech. This precise phrase also marks the transition to the next stage of the remarriage process in 2:23.[193] In verse 18, the expression also forms a link with the statement of Yahweh's intent to remarry, the verbal persuasion, and the giving of gifts in 2:16–17. One need not understand the phrase "in that day" in the sense of the traditional concept of the "day of Yahweh," an eschatological day of final salvation for Israel (cf. Amos 5:18).[194] Rather, in its literary context, the day of reconciliation and remarriage envisioned in 2:16–17 provides the clearest referent for the "day" about which Yahweh speaks in 2:18 and again in 2:23.

Yahweh's words in verse 18 set forth the first thing that will take place upon the day of reconciliation: the wife's own words will signify a change of status for Yahweh from בַעַל to אִישׁ. The language of this verse plays on the common Hebrew words for husband. The standard scholarly interpretation considers אִישׁ to be an expression that indicates a deep, personal relationship while בַעַל emphasizes the legal and impersonal position of the husband as owner. Verse 18 uses these terms, it is argued, to depict a change in relationship that restores the intimacy of an estranged husband and wife.[195] Yet this view assumes that the marriage relationship was never broken and the only change of status needed is in the level of intimacy. Such an understanding does not fit with the overall imagery of divorce and punishment throughout the chapter. As Yee

---

[191] For a full discussion of this rhetorical feature and examples from other prophetic books, see de Regt, "Person Shift," 214–31.

[192] Clines, "Hosea 2," 90.

[193] Outside of chapter 2, this phrase occurs elsewhere in Hosea only at 1:5 where it denotes the time when Israel's military power will be broken.

[194] Contra Wolff, *Hosea*, 49.

[195] See Birch, *Hosea, Joel, Amos*, 36; Jeremias, *Der Prophet*, 49; Mays, *Hosea*, 49; Wolff, *Hosea*, 49. Wellhausen (*Die kleinen Propheten*, 12) considers this verse to be a later gloss but portrays the typical distinction with his words "Eheherr" (wedded lord) and "Mann" (husband). Knight (*Hosea*, 58) argues that a man was called a "*baal*" if he was the head of a household with more than one wife but "*ish*" if he was in a monogamous relationship. As Blankenbaker observes, however, 1 Sam 1:8 clearly indicates that "*ish*" may be used to describe a man who has more than one wife ("Language," 187).

notes, this view reads modern marriage conceptions back upon Hosea, whose marriage imagery functions to emphasize the inequity not mutuality of the relationship with Yahweh.[196] Moreover, upon closer examination, this common distinction does not hold. Other uses of the term בעל in the context of intimacy, compassion, and love argue against this interpretation (e.g., 2 Sam 11:26; Isa 54:5–8; Joel 1:8).[197]

Even without this typical distinction between terms, the majority of scholars drop all metaphorical considerations and read verse 18 as a literal statement about the Israelites' worship of Baal.[198] The most serious problem with both the intimacy distinction and Baal worship explanation is that they lose sight of the *metaphorical* function of the term בעל in this verse in particular and in the chapter as a whole.[199] Verse 18 should be kept within the metaphorical imagery and not extracted as a literal description. Additionally, if, as argued above, the discourse of Hos 2 repeatedly draws upon the tradition in which בעל functions as a metaphorical term and denotes a political entity such as an ally or overlord, the interpretation of this verse remains unclear. Although the common view does not seem to be adequate, only a tentative proposal can be offered in its place. Perhaps Hosea, speaking for Yahweh, maintains the overall metaphor of a wife and her (political) lovers but expands it in order to comment specifically on the status of her first husband. By asserting that the wife had come to see Yahweh as a "paramour" (בעל), Hosea indicates a situation in which the wife had assigned Yahweh to the status of one sex partner among many. In response, Yahweh's words in this verse declare that the first action on the day of remarriage will be a change in status in which Yahweh moves from being one among many partners to being her exclusive relationship partner. This depiction fits well with the address's rhetorical-historical situation in which Samaria, rather than engaging in some form of Baal worship, had entered into relationships with various political allies, who represent competing loyalties to Yahweh.

5.2 The Marriage Covenant (2:19–22)

The second action that will take place on the day of Yahweh's remarriage appears in 2:19. In contrast to the preceding verse that described Yahweh as a "paramour" (בעל), verse 19 refers to the removal of all other "paramours" who have been competing for the wife's loyalty: "I will remove the names of the paramours (את־שמות הבעלים) from her mouth so they will no longer be

---

[196] Yee, *Poor Banished Children*, 107.

[197] So Abma, *Bonds*, 190; Emmerson, *Hosea*, 26; and Rudolph, *Hosea*, 75, 78.

[198] For example, although Wolff maintains the distinction based on levels of intimacy, he also sees this verse as a reflection of actual Baal worship being practiced in Hosea's day (*Hosea*, 49).

[199] Light, "Theory-Constitutive Metaphor," 65.

remembered (ולא־יזכרו) by their names." Since this action is not one to be taken directly by the wife, the language once again switches to the third-person (f.sg.) ("her mouth"). Rather than demanding that the wife "put aside her fornication" (2:4), Yahweh takes the initiative.[200] In this way, verse 19 begins an extended section (2:19–22) that functions as the marriage covenant for the reconciliation of Yahweh and his wife. Following the declaration of a new relationship in 2:18, verses 19–22 describe several actions that Yahweh takes on behalf of his wife. These acts lead up to the exchange of responses and consummation of the marriage depicted in 2:23–25.

Some commentators reach the decision that the imagery in 2:19 demands a strictly religious interpretation. For example, Andersen and Freedman conclude that the action here is one in which Yahweh eliminates the "liturgical recitation of the names of Baal in formal worship."[201] Seen in this way, the verb זכר in the final phrase carries the meaning, "to invoke" (cf. Exod 23:13; Ps 20:8[MT]). This expression, however, is not the common way of invoking a god in the Hebrew Bible (קרא בשם).[202] Furthermore, scholars like Andersen and Freedman are not able to cite any texts that attest this Baalistic practice of liturgical recitation. Given these drawbacks, it seems reasonable to conclude that בעל continues to function as a political metaphor that depicts those allies and overlords with whom Samaria has consorted as competing romantic callers. On the day of remarriage, the restored relationship between Yahweh and his wife will eliminate any consideration of competing loyalties.

Yahweh's words in 2:20 add another action that is included in his remarriage commitment to his wife. The prophet, speaking for Yahweh, uses hyperbole to assert that the new relationship with the personified Samaria will include peaceful relations for all of creation: "And I will make for them (m.pl.) a covenant in that day with the beasts of the field.… I will banish the bow and sword and warfare from the land, and I will make them (m.pl.) lie down in safety." Once again, the phrase "in that day" associates these actions with the envisioned day of remarriage and not with an eschatological event (cf. 2:18). Additionally, the language here reverses the threat of destruction by wild beasts in 2:14.[203] Andersen and Freedman thus suggest that Yahweh's covenant is not with the people but with the animals for the sake of the people.[204] This covenant, however, does not seem to involve Yahweh directly as a covenant partner at all. On the people's behalf, Yahweh enacts a covenant between the animals and the people that will result in an end to violence ("I will make *for*

---

[200] Nwaoru, *Imagery*, 65.

[201] Andersen and Freedman, *Hosea*, 279. Cf. Macintosh, *Critical and Exegetical Commentary*, 80; Snaith, *Amos*, 58.

[202] Stuart, *Hosea-Jonah*, 58.

[203] The breaking of the bow in 2:20 also reverses the threat in 1:5 that represents the destruction of Israel's army in the Jezreel Valley.

[204] Andersen and Freedman, *Hosea*, 280–81.

them a covenant"). Yahweh serves as more than just a witness but fills the role of the guarantor of a covenant between two parties.

The imagery in verse 20 draws heavily upon the image-base of ancient Near Eastern political treaties. The phrase "to make a covenant" (כרת ברית) occurs elsewhere in Hosea at 10:4 and 12:2, where it refers to an international political treaty. As Hillers points out, the language of a covenant with wild animals reverses a common curse or threat in ancient Near Eastern treaties, several of which say that wild animals will come upon a land as punishment.[205] The statement "I will banish (אשבור) the bow and sword and warfare" resembles another common curse in ancient Near Eastern treaties that a god will "break a man's weapons, usually the bow."[206] Seen in this light, Yahweh's remarriage pledge not only presents the metaphorical picture of a harmonious creation but also signifies a return to right-relationships within the political realm.

The use of third masculine plural pronouns in verse 20 appears out of place in a speech dealing with the wife/mother. There are several possible explanations for this usage. First, Hosea may shift here from the corporate image of the wife to the individuals who are associated with her (cf. 2:10). On the other hand, the pronouns may function resumptively and refer to the group of animals involved in the covenant. The second of the masculine plural suffixes clearly seems to refer to this group as a whole. The referents may also be the metaphorical children who were directed to contend with their mother in 2:4.[207] The realization of Yahweh's hope for remarriage results in the ability of the children to "lie down in safety." Regardless of the explanation one chooses, 2:20 broadens the benefits of reconciliation to the sphere of all creation.

Yahweh's statement in 2:21–22 represents the climax of his remarriage covenant that precedes the exchange of responses in 2:23–25. Yahweh declares that he will indeed enter into marriage with his estranged wife. This declaration once again takes up the direct address of second-person speech, a person shift that marks a new address to or changed situation for the main subject of the discourse.[208] Additionally, the verb, ארש ("to wed"), begins three consecutive lines in this section and holds the key to understanding the imagery at work: "And I will wed you (f.sg.) (וארשתיך) to myself forever. I will wed you (f.sg.) (וארשתיך) to myself with righteousness ... I will wed you (f.sg.) (וארשתיך) to myself with faithfulness ..." (2:21–22). As discussed in the translation section above, the piel form of ארש denotes the legal act that constitutes a

---

[205] Hillers, *Treaty Curses*, 54–56. E.g., Sefire Treaty I A 30–32; cf. Jer 5:6; Hos 13:7–8. The idea of peaceful relations with animals also appears several times in Hebrew Bible texts (e.g., Lev 26:6; Isa 11:6–9; Ezek 34:25; Job 5:23).

[206] Hillers, *Treaty Curses*, 60. E.g., Sefire Treaty I A 38–39. For a list of references to "breaking" (שבר) war, see Friedman, "Israel's Response," 201, f.n. 11.

[207] Andersen and Freedman, *Hosea*, 281.

[208] See de Regt, "Person Shift," 214–19.

marriage. The term indicates the final act in which a marriage is solidified by the payment of the bride price; it represents the end of premarital status and is followed by cohabitation.[209] In this regard, the verb functions as the conclusion of Yahweh's marriage covenant by signifying his decision to seal the marriage. The term לְעוֹלָם ("forever"), which stands immediately after the first occurrence of the verb, emphasizes the finality of the act. As Wolff notes, this term can occur in legal contexts to denote a lifelong commitment.[210]

Following this declaration, Yahweh lists five things with which he will carry out the act of remarriage: righteousness, justice, kindness, compassion, and faithfulness. Rather than having significance as individual words, these terms function together as the qualities that mark Yahweh's remarriage. Yet the realm of meaning for these terms within the context of 2:21–22 is legal and contractual.[211] The vast majority of commentators rightly emphasize the connection between the use of these terms in verses 21–22 and the references to the payment of the bride price by the husband in descriptions of marriage arrangements. For instance, 2 Sam 3:14 also combines the verb אֵרַשׂ with the preposition בְּ ("with") to indicate the bride price paid by David for his marriage to Michal.[212] Seen in this way, the five nouns in 2:21–22 do not simply represent kind actions that characterize the reconciliation of Yahweh and his wife but function explicitly within the overall legal and marital imagery at work in the discourse. Yahweh states his intention to wed his wife through the typical, legal means of the payment of a new, albeit symbolic, bride price.

Abma maintains, however, that these items cannot represent a new bride price because they are presented as being given directly to the wife rather than to her father. Hence, he argues they should be connected only to the concept of bridal gifts.[213] This objection overlooks the observation made in chapter 3 that, in the case of the remarriage of a divorced woman, the bride price may go directly to the bride. Although the evidence on this point is not clear, Westbrook notes that the OB texts seem to attest this practice of a price paid to the wife. Furthermore, it is logical that a widow or divorcee would receive such payment

---

[209] Wolff (*Hosea*, 46, 52) notes that this verb should be distinguished from לְקַח ("to take;" Deut 20:7) and שָׁגַל ("to lie with;" Deut 28:30) because it marks the conclusion of premarital status. See also Humbert, "Logique," 165; Mays, *Hosea*, 50; McKeating, "Sanctions," 88; Satlow, *Jewish Marriage*, 69; Stienstra, *YHWH*, 219; Stuart, *Hosea-Jonah*, 59; Sweeney, *The Twelve Prophets*, 36. Contra Andersen and Freedman (*Hosea*, 283), who argue that this term refers only to an engagement prior to marriage.

[210] E.g., Exod 21:6. See Wolff, *Hosea*, 52. Cf. E. Jenni, "Das Wort ʿōlām im AT," *ZAW* 64 (1952): 235–39.

[211] Hubbard, *Hosea*, 87.

[212] The NRSV renders בְּ with the correct legal meaning: "Give me my wife Michal, to whom I became engaged at the price of (בְּ) one hundred foreskins of the Philistines."

[213] Abma, *Bonds*, 192. Buss also considers these entities to be bridal gifts (*Prophetic Word*, 111).

independently.[214] It is precisely this imagery of remarriage that is at work in 2:21–22. Thus, one may view verses 21–22 as using the typical language of marriage law (בְ plus bride price; cf. 2 Sam 3:14) to depict the symbolic bride price Yahweh gives for remarriage.[215]

Yahweh concludes his remarriage covenant by asserting that his actions will finally produce the reaction he has sought from his wife: "and you (f.sg.) will acknowledge (וְיָדַעַתְּ) Yahweh" (2:22). Through these actions, Yahweh's wife will finally come to comply with the relationship. As with the use of the verb יָדַע in 2:10, the text again employs the technical sense drawn from ancient Near Eastern political treaties. This verb does not function here as a euphemism for the sexual consummation of the marriage or for the simple reestablishment of intimacy between the husband and wife.[216] Rather, Yahweh declares that the end result of his gracious choice of remarriage will be his estranged wife's ultimate recognition of him over all competing paramours. As Huffmon translates, "you will know (*wĕyādaʿat, recognize as suzerain*) Yahweh."[217] The product of Yahweh's act explicitly reverses the condemnation leveled against the wife in 2:10.

The presentation of Yahweh's marriage covenant in 2:19–22 uses a broad range of imagery to describe a metaphorical reconciliation of Yahweh and the personified city Samaria. Yahweh relates his intention to remove the enticement of competing paramours, to offer a covenant of mutuality that even produces peaceful relations in the realm of nature, and to engage in the technical act of remarriage by paying a new bride price. By depicting these words of Yahweh, the prophet further emphasizes that a gracious choice has been made concerning

---

[214] Westbrook, "Adultery," 580. As discussed in chapter 3, the lack of clarity on this matter comes from the fact that most OB texts describing the remarriage of a divorced woman do not mention a bride price. The Elephantine text Cowley 15 describes the remarriage of a divorcee in which the husband pays the bride price to her father. Thus, there does not seem to have been one standard practice in this matter.

[215] Wolff, *Hosea*, 52. So also Andersen and Freedman, *Hosea*, 283; Blankenbaker, "Language," 190; Braaten, "Parent-Child Imagery," 267; Garrett, *Hosea, Joel*, 93; Harper, *Critical and Exegetical Commentary*, 243; Knight, *Hosea*, 59; Macintosh, *Critical and Exegetical Commentary*, 83; Mays, *Hosea*, 51; Rudolph, *Hosea*, 80–81; Snaith, *Mercy*, 70. Vogels compares the bride price listed here to the entities given in Hos 3:2 for Hosea's acquiring of the woman: "I acquired her (וָאֶכְּרֶהָ) to myself with (בְ) fifteen shekels of silver and a homer of barley and a measure of wine" (Hos 3:2) (Vogels, "Hosea's Gift," 417). The verb in this context, however, does not deal with marriage. McKeating also suggests that another option besides the idea of bride price is to understand the five nouns in 2:21–22 as indicating that Yahweh will remarry his wife "according to the proper forms of law and custom" (*Books*, 88). As Ginsberg notes, the notion of bride price in this verse has a particular rhetorical function, namely, Yahweh offers this price in order to insure the wife's future fidelity ("Studies," 56, f.n. 21).

[216] For these views, see Birch, *Hosea, Joel, Amos*, 38; Hubbard, *Hosea*, 76; Knight, *Hosea*, 30; Landy, *Hosea*, 45; Macintosh, *Critical and Exegetical Commentary*, 84–85; Stuart, *Hosea-Jonah*, 60.

[217] Huffmon, "Treaty Background," 36; emphasis added. So also Wolff, *Hosea*, 53.

the future of Samaria. Rather than destruction, confinement, or disownment, the personified Samaria's future will consist of return, reconciliation, and restoration. The only remaining event in the metaphor is the marriage's consummation.

6. THE GIFTS, RESPONSES, AND REUNION (2:23–25)

Yahweh concludes the metaphorical remarriage with Samaria by undertaking three actions: 1) he sets in motion a series of agricultural blessings, 2) he enacts the consummation of the marriage, and 3) he reunifies the brothers, sisters, and mother described at the beginning of oracle (2:2–3). First, in 2:23–24, Yahweh "responds" to the heavens and begins a series of events that results in benefits for the wife:

> And it will be on that day, I will respond (אֶעֱנֶה), declares Yahweh, I will respond (אֶעֱנֶה) to the heavens and they themselves will respond (וְהֵם יַעֲנוּ) to the earth. And the earth will respond (תַּעֲנֶה) to the grain and to the new wine and to the choice oil, and they themselves will respond (וְהֵם יַעֲנוּ) to Jezreel.

Like the description of the marriage declaration and covenant in verses 18 and 20, this first action by Yahweh is set "on that day" (בַּיּוֹם הַהוּא). As noted above, however, this phrase refers not to an eschatological day of salvation but to the time of remarriage that is envisioned by Yahweh's words throughout this section. Speaking on behalf of the deity, the prophet imagines that the metaphorical day of reconciliation will include not only the wife's recognition of Yahweh (2:18) but also Yahweh's actions on behalf of his wife (2:23–24).

Several commentators observe that 2:23–24 describe a full agricultural cycle in which the sky waters the earth which then responds with grain, wine, and oil.[218] Surprisingly, this beneficial action is presented as the result of Yahweh's "response" (עֲנָה) to the heavens. Thus, the description here picks up the language of 2:17 in which Yahweh projected that the wife would "respond" (עֲנָה) on the day of remarriage as she had in the days of her youth. As noted above, this verb can carry the legal meaning of a testimony or answer given in the course of a marriage agreement.[219] Nonetheless, each of the entities named also "responds" to another. This figurative language seems to employ the technical marriage term "respond" as a shorthand description of each entity's appropriate action. Consequently, the Targum renders each occurrence of עֲנָה in this verse with a different verb in order to make explicit the different nuances

---

[218] Stuart, *Hosea-Jonah*, 60; Wolff, *Hosea*, 53.

[219] Cf. Sweeney, *The Twelve Prophets*, 37 and Macintosh, *Critical and Exegetical Commentary*, 86. For the use of this term in legal contexts, see Exod 20:16; Deut 5:20; 31:21; 1 Sam 12:3; Isa 3:9; Mic 6:3; Job 9:14–15.

of meaning.[220] This use of language presents Yahweh's actions as a groom's response within the metaphorical remarriage ceremony. Once again, however, the voice of the personified wife does not appear in the text (cf. 2:7, 9, 14). The reader encounters only the "response" of Yahweh (2:23), who does not even direct his response to the wife, and his description of what he will do *to* the wife (2:25). The text simply assumes the correctness of Yahweh's assertion at the end of verse 22 that his wife will acknowledge him.

Yahweh's "response" to the heavens sets in motion a series of events that results in the production of grain, new wine, and choice oil. This production cycle represents a reversal of typical threats of judgment like that in Deut 11:17: "[H]e will shut up the heavens, so that there will be no rain and the land will yield no increase; and you will perish quickly off the good land that the LORD is giving you." More importantly for the context of Hos 2, verse 24 names the same three entities of grain, new wine, and choice oil that verses 10–11 describe as Yahweh's original gifts to his wife. The agricultural cycle described as Yahweh's "response" to the remarriage in 2:23–24 functions as the giving of new bridal gifts and provisions that inaugurate the second marriage. There is no simple emphasis on fertility here but on the restoration of a city, namely, Samaria, to the normal cycle of agricultural productivity.

As with the ceremonial response, there is no prominent focus on Yahweh's wife in the giving of the gifts. The bridal gifts and provisions do not go directly to the personified woman. Rather, 2:24 once more uses the technical term עָנָה to relate that the gifts of grain, new wine, and choice oil will "respond" to "Jezreel." The verse effects an explicit transformation of this symbolic name. At first blush, the language in the rest of verses 24 and 25 depends upon the tradition of Hosea's three children given in chapter 1. It is possible, however, to explain this imagery from within the discourse of Hos 2 itself. The use of "Jezreel" as a term with negative connotations appears independently of chapter 1's tradition in 2:2: "great will be the day of Jezreel." As argued above, this reference in 2:2 alludes to a traditional place of bloodshed and judgment associated with northern kingdom politics rather than to a particular child. Even the naming of the child in 1:4 is associated with this older tradition of Jezreel as a symbolic place of judgment in 1:5. Hence, "Jezreel" in 2:24 functions as a reference to the symbolic place of judgment depicted in 2:2, a place that will now be the recipient of the transforming gifts of grain, new wine, and choice oil in the day of Yahweh's remarriage.[221] The final phrase of verse 24 is not part of

---

[220] The Targum offers the following explanations: 1) God responds: "I will listen," 2) heavens respond: "they send down rain," 3) earth responds: "it makes abundant," and 4) they respond to Jezreel: "they shall supply enough for." See Guillaume, "Note," 57.

[221] Some scholars argue that "Jezreel" in 2:24 cannot be a reference to a geographical location because of the presence of "land" in 2:25 (e.g., Mays, *Hosea*, 53; Emmerson, *Hosea*, 33). This view stems from the unnecessary attempt to connect "Jezreel" with the 3 f.sg. pronominal suffix in 2:25

the actions that follow but forms the climax to Yahweh's description of bridal gifts by asserting that even the traditional place of judgment will be turned into a place of hope.

Following this description of the bridal gifts in 2:23–24, the final verse of the oracle relates two other actions to be taken by Yahweh upon remarriage. The first action represents the metaphorical consummation of the reunion: "I will sow her to myself in the land" (2:25). The verb "I will sow her" (וזרעתיה) in this verse forms a play on words with "Jezreel" (יזרעאל, "God sows") from the end of verse 24. Within the marriage metaphor of Hosea's address, this language appears to have an explicitly sexual connotation so that the "insemination of a woman is like the sowing of a field."[222] In this regard, some scholars question the feminine singular object "her" in this phrase. For example, Wolff suggests that a protasis has been lost from the beginning of the verse because the pronoun has no apparent antecedent.[223] Yet throughout the oracle, Yahweh's speech regularly moves back and forth between second- and third-person references to places, children, and the wife/mother. Additionally, as noted above, the opening phrase of 2:25 is not a continuation of the giving of gifts in 2:23–24 but a new action undertaken by Yahweh. It is thus reasonable to conclude that the feminine pronoun here refers once more to the personified wife.

The imagery of sowing in 2:25 also functions on another level within the literary context of Hos 2. Not only does the text envision the ultimate consummation of the marriage, but it also picks up the theme of the wife's return from the wilderness to which she was taken in 2:16. The agricultural sense of the term, together with the provided location of "in the land," suggests that זרע may be a metaphor for repopulation.[224] Yahweh's "sowing" of his wife "in the land" symbolizes both her reentry into a marital relationship and her return to the land after her period of seduction in the wilderness.

In the third and final act of restoration, Yahweh broadens the scope of the reconciliation to include those who have previously been addressed in the discourse of chapter 2: "[A]nd I will have compassion on 'No-Compassion.' I will say to 'Not-My-People,' 'You (m.sg.) are my people,' and he will say, 'My God'" (2:25). These verses again seem to refer explicitly to the symbolic names of Hosea's children in chapter 1. While it is possible that this tradition of children may be at work in the discourse, the precise language of verse 25 appears earlier in Hos 2 itself. The prophet's own introduction in 2:3 describes

---

and to make "Jezreel" the object of the verb "to sow." The MT correctly preserves, however, the 3 f.sg. suffix so that 2:25 constitutes a final reference to the personified wife rather than a continuation of the description of the bridal gifts in 2:23–24.

[222] Andersen and Freedman, *Hosea*, 288.

[223] Wolff, *Hosea*, 54.

[224] Macintosh, *Critical and Exegetical Commentary*, 89.

the reunification of the group coming up from Judah with the survivors in and around Samaria by instructing the former to call their brothers "My People" and their sisters "Compassion." In 2:25 Yahweh himself takes up this language of reversal. The same group that is to receive the reconciling words of the prophet's audience here receives the reconciling proclamation of Yahweh. The earlier reference in 2:3 may also explain the masculine pronouns "you" and "he" in this verse, since verse 3 identifies the phrase "My People" with the "brothers."[225] This climax to Yahweh's acts of restoration also reverses the threat made against the wife's children in 2:6: "And I will not have *compassion* on her children because they are children of fornication."

The final results of Yahweh's actions go well beyond his personified wife. Verse 22 depicted the ultimate response of the wife as she "acknowledged" Yahweh. Verse 25 concludes the speech by proclaiming that even the group represented by "Not-My-People" will respond affirmatively and grant the acknowledgment that Yahweh has sought all along: "and he will say, 'My God.'" As seen previously, the text again shifts between the image of the wife/mother and the individual children connected to her. In this way, the final section (2:23–25) moves from the description of bridal gifts in 2:23–24, to the consummation of the remarriage in 2:25a, to the benefits of that metaphorical reconciliation for the people involved in 2:25b. Yahweh's extended address in 2:4–25 ends in the same way as Hosea's introduction in 2:1–3. Both proclaim an ultimate restoration that goes beyond the personified city of Samaria and embraces the people of both Israel and Judah.

7. SUMMARY AND CONCLUSIONS: THE IMPORT OF HOSEA'S METAPHORS

Yahweh's address in 2:4–25 serves as a metaphorical commentary that communicates the divine passion and perspective on the events involving the capital city of Samaria at the close of the Syro-Ephraimitic war. Hosea relies on the form, process, and property arrangements of ancient Near Eastern divorce texts to depict the possible actions available to Yahweh, the wronged husband. He also uses the tradition of personifying cities as females and employs the metaphors of fornication and adultery to describe Samaria's political alliances that violate Yahweh's will. The prophet labels the city's political allies and overlords as "lovers" and "paramours," who attempt to lure Yahweh's wife away. For the audience who is to be intimately involved in the retaking of Samaria and the overthrow of Pekah, this speech metaphorically communicates both the specific sins of Samaria and the rulers it represents as well as the ultimate goal of Yahweh's will. The political misdeeds of Samaria and her

---

[225] The typical explanation for these masculine pronouns in 2:25 is that chapter 1 presents "Not-My-People" as a male child (cf. 1:8–9) (e.g., Macintosh, *Critical and Exegetical Commentary*, 89).

rulers are equivalent to the religious apostasy of previous generations and constitute a complete abandonment of Yahweh. Nonetheless, the divine oracle clearly indicates that the mission against Samaria is not to be understood as one of punishment or destruction but restoration.

At the end of this reading of Hos 2, the question remains as to why metaphor in general and these metaphors in particular make this speech effective in a way that other rhetorical devices would not. On the general level, the earlier methodological discussion noted that metaphors use the combination of two words or entities to produce a new meaning that recasts the primary and secondary subjects in a new light. Metaphors function to change existing conceptions of reality and replace them with new ones. In the situation of Israel and Judah at the close of the Syro-Ephraimitic war, it was precisely the present conceptions of political and social realities that were under negotiation and that the prophet sought to recast. In Hosea's view, the events involving the overthrow of Pekah and the reestablishment of Samaria as an Assyrian vassal needed to be viewed through a theological lens that emphasized Yahweh's role and purpose. Hosea 2 accomplishes this reenvisioning through the particular metaphors of the wife/mother, fornication, adultery, lovers, and paramours. As outlined in chapters 3 to 5, these metaphors rest upon traditions from Hosea's social context, which are intricately concerned with political affairs, but also have resonances with the realms of religion and family. The import of these metaphors takes, however, different forms in relation to both the target of the prophet's condemnations and the audience who receives his exhortations.

7.1 Yahweh the Wronged Husband as a Political Metaphor

In dealing with Hos 2's metaphorical depictions of Samaria's wrongful actions, this chapter suggests that Hosea employed the marriage metaphor in general and the image of Yahweh as a wronged husband in particular to condemn political actions that constituted a breach in Samaria's agreement with Assyria, actions that the prophet sees as outside Yahweh's will for the nation. The use of marital metaphors like fornication and lovers, which have widespread traditions of political meanings like alliances and allies, fits nicely within such a metaphorical discourse. At the close of this discussion, it is useful to consider how Hos 2 connects these images of Yahweh as Samaria's husband, the "lovers" as anti-Assyrian political allies, and "fornication" as political disloyalty to Assyria. How does the prophet make what he sees as inappropriate political actions by the ruling house toward Assyria into acts of unfaithfulness toward Yahweh, which place Samaria under the threat of divine judgment? If Hosea's complaint is that Samaria has violated its agreement with Assyria, why does he call it to return to a relationship with Yahweh? The metaphorical referents at work in this speech, if interpreted correctly, seem to push the metaphor to its breaking point.

The answer to this question lies in a prophetic perspective on politics that is reflected in language like that in Hos 2:15, language echoed in texts like Ezek 17:11–21; 21:23–29; and 29:14–16.[226] The above discussion argues that verse 15's worship imagery reflects religious elements present in the practices of treaty-making in the ancient Near East. Political treaties, presumably including the one which existed between Samaria and Assyria prior to 734 B.C.E., were typically sworn in the names of and identified with the deities of the nations involved. The gods were seen as personal guarantors of the treaty arrangements. In the perspective of prophets like Hosea and Ezekiel, since the original treaty was sworn in Yahweh's name, it became Yahweh's treaty and loyalty to that treaty constituted loyalty to Yahweh (see Ezek 17:19). The realms of religion and politics (gods and nations) were intertwined in such practices. Hence, the rebellious actions of the leaders represented by the personified capital city are a departure from Yahweh, a departure in need of a return in Hosea's view, since they represent unfaithfulness to the treaty sworn in Yahweh's name.

When these theological conceptions are placed into the context of the metaphorical tradition in which capital cities were portrayed as the wives of deities, acts of political wrongdoing can be readily described with marital metaphors like fornication, adultery, and lovers. Thus, Hos 2's discourse puts Yahweh in the place of Assyria as the true object of Samaria's disloyalty and thereby achieves its rhetorical effect: the ruling house's inappropriate political involvement constitutes a form of apostasy against Yahweh to which Yahweh must respond.

7.2 The Rhetorical Function of Hosea's Metaphors

As demonstrated throughout this study, Hos 2 employs the biblical and extrabiblical conventions of personifying cities as females within contexts of destruction and describing city destruction with language of physical and sexual violence against a woman. The effect of the chapter's specific marital and sexual metaphors is their significance for the conception of the ruling house and the imagination of the listening audience. Perhaps the key to the rhetoric's function here is the fact that in Hosea, as in the majority of such cases of female personification, the text personifies a *capital* city. This combination of symbolic conventions and capital cities suggests that as the female represents the city, the city metonymically represents the ruling house and political elite that sat on its throne. Hence, the full force of this metaphorical rhetoric attempts to change the audience's perspective on the ruling elite in an ironic way. The political elite, who in the ancient rhetorical context of the prophet and his audience would have likely been all male, are cast as physically threatened and sexually violated

---

[226] See above discussion of verse 18 and Tsevat, "Vassal Oaths."

females. Relying upon the assumptions and conventions of a patriarchal society, a society in which women were thought of as subordinate and vulnerable to a powerful, particularly a conquering male, the metaphors in Hos 2 reenvision the most powerful social group— the male ruling elite— as the most helpless social group— the sexually violated female. The male rulers who seem to hold unimpeachable power are feminized as vulnerable, shamed, and subordinate.[227]

Hosea 2's use of these particular marital and sexual metaphors has another rhetorical effect on the audience. Not only does the discourse feminize the political rulers in a way that removes their seeming invincibility, but it also serves to change the audience's perspective on Yahweh by employing irony against the political elite. By metaphorizing Yahweh as the husband of the personified Samaria, Hos 2 casts Yahweh as the truly powerful male, who holds the fate of the subordinate female in his hands and can punish, shame, and even destroy. The power of this simultaneous metaphorization of Yahweh is especially poignant in the rhetorical-historical context of ancient Israel in which Yahweh was frequently coopted by the political elite and portrayed as not only sanctioning their actions but being inextricably committed to their preservation. With subversive rhetoric, Hos 2's marital metaphors transform the audience's imagination by liberating Yahweh from the ruling house and casting it into the position of the subordinate female, who may suffer shame and violence at the hands of the truly powerful, conquering male. Hosea recasts Samaria and its political rulers in a way that frees his audience to become involved against them: the ruling house represented by Samaria is a shamed entity, which is subject to justifiable, violent punishments by a divine authority.

As discussed in this chapter, however, the rhetoric of Hos 2 passes by the options of violence and destruction in favor of ultimate reconciliation. Hosea portrays his audience as remaining connected to the capital city of Samaria, and its place in Yahweh's will, in important ways. Hence, the particular metaphors used in Hos 2 offer a way to emphasize that the actions concerning the city of Samaria intimately involve more than just the political rulers in the capital. The broader metaphors of marriage, family, and children are uniquely personal metaphors that involve the audience in Hosea's theological critique. The familial nature of such marital metaphors forces the reader or hearer to conceive of seemingly impersonal political events in the most intensely personal and emotional way. Through these metaphors, Hosea recasts the social and political events in Israel from 734–731 B.C.E. as the complex relationship between Yahweh and his metaphorical wife in which every Israelite and Judean is an

---

[227] For a similar discussion of the feminizing function of Hosea's rhetoric, see Yee, *Poor Banished Children*, 82, 99, 117. Portraying male rulers as married to a male deity undermines the norms of masculinity and thereby gives rise to a variety of social and ideological issues. For a discussion of the issues connected with this practice, see H. Eilberg-Schwartz, *God's Phallus and Other Problems for Men and Monotheism* (Boston: Beacon, 1994), 20–27, 97–105.

involved and vulnerable family member. The rhetoric of Hos 2 serves to set out the implications of a situation before they would have been readily apparent to the common people and to compel the people to see that situation, as well as their involvement in it, in light of Yahweh's purposes.

9

CONCLUSION:

SUMMARY AND IMPLICATIONS

The investigation of Hos 2 offered in this book adds a frequently neglected voice to the interpretive conversation. Through a rhetorical analysis that treats the text's metaphors in historical perspective, one can see Hos 2:1–25 as the prophet's theological and metaphorical commentary on the events surrounding Samaria and their implications concerning the people of Israel and Judah at the close of the Syro-Ephraimitic war (731–730 B.C.E.). It is hoped that what has been presented in this study can be taken together with other discussions to provide future lines of inquiry into Hos 2. Toward that end, the discussion below summarizes the full sweep of this study and sets forth two implications that arise from a rhetorical engagement with this prophetic speech.

1. SUMMARY

Chapter 1 began by demonstrating that, although there has been a paucity of full-scale, comprehensive treatments of Hos 2, there is a dominant way of reading that is rarely challenged: Hos 2 consists of a unit that includes only verses 4–25 (or less), relies upon religious imagery of sex and fertility, and deals with the central issue of Israel's religious unfaithfulness to Yahweh through participation in a cult dedicated to the god Baal. Chapter 1 also observed, however, that several more recent works have included arguments for the unity of all of Hos 2:1–25, critiques of the notion of a widespread Baal cult in Hosea's day, considerations of the role of political events and forces in shaping Hosea's preaching, and examinations of the text's major metaphors in light of their possible referents in the ancient rhetorical setting.

Chapter 2 started from the observation that the classical conception of rhetoric, which examines texts as persuasive discourses designed to achieve certain results with a given audience in a particular setting, has found a home in scholarly treatments of the biblical prophetic literature. The chapter emphasized that texts like Hos 2 can similarly be thought of in terms of public addresses that functioned with pragmatic goals in specific rhetorical situations.[1] In conjunction with this understanding, the discussion of metaphor theory emphasized Booth's observation that metaphors are not simply linguistic devices but function as rhetorical "weapon[s]" within certain circumstances.[2] Implied in this observation was the methodological principle that in order to understand a metaphor adequately, the reader must attempt to comprehend the ancient speaker's semantic and cultural context.

Chapter 3 began the primary task of investigating each of the major metaphors of Hos 2 by means of a comparative, historical, and integrated analysis. This chapter dealt with the text's overarching metaphor of marriage and divorce. After challenging the common explanations that the marriage metaphor relies upon Hosea's personal experience or the practices of a Baal fertility cult, the investigation presented the possibility that the ancient Near Eastern and Elephantine legal texts dealing with marriage and divorce constitute the oracle's primary image-base. These texts emphasized not physical punishments like stripping and exposure but financial and property stipulations concerning inheritance and possessions. The texts also set forth different consequences for divorces with justification and those without justification. The language of sexual and physical violence in Hos 2, it was concluded, cannot be traced back to the text's marriage metaphor but must be identified with a different image-base.

Chapter 4 then examined the metaphors of the wife/mother, fornication (זנה), and adultery (נאף) by investigating their use in comparative biblical and extrabiblical texts. The purpose of this investigation was to identify the metaphorical traditions available to Hosea and his audience in the ancient

---

[1] The functions of the later political orators of ancient Greece provided a helpful analogy: "But for what is he [an orator] responsible? For discerning the trend of events at the outset, for forecasting results, for warning others…. Further, he ought to reduce to a minimum those delays and hesitations, those fits of ignorance and quarrelsomeness … and to promote unanimity and friendliness, and whatever impels a man to do his duty" (Demosthenes in *De Corona*, 246).

[2] Booth, "Metaphor," 51; cf. Black, *Models*, 29.

context that could have provided the meaning for these terms. Concerning the metaphor of the wife/mother, the discussion demonstrated that the interpretation of this "wife" as the personified capital city Samaria is the only one supported by a wide-ranging comparative metaphorical tradition. Hosea drew upon a recognizable tradition of personifying cities as females in order to address the rulers and inhabitants of the capital city. This chapter further pointed out that the prophetic texts of the Hebrew Bible evidence a tradition of using the metaphorical language of sexual and physical violence against a woman to describe the destruction of such a personified city. Concerning the metaphors of fornication and adultery, chapter 4 also provided a firm context in which to consider these terms as relating to the political sphere of Samaria's foreign alliances: the prophet used the metaphors of fornication and adultery to characterize those political actions that he deemed contrary to Yahweh's will and harmful to the people.

Chapter 5 turned to the metaphors of lovers (אהב) and baal(s) (בעל) and attempted to identify the metaphorical traditions that were available to Hosea's audience in his social setting. The discussion challenged the common view that the "lovers" represent illegitimate deities with whom Israel had committed apostasy and revealed the existence of a well-substantiated tradition in both biblical and extrabiblical texts that uses "lovers" as a metaphor for political allies or treaty-partners. This chapter also found reason to question the common assumption that the term בעל in Hosea's oracle represents the proper name of the Canaanite god Baal and signals the existence of widespread participation in a Baal fertility cult. On the contrary, the comparative and historical analysis demonstrated that the evidence for such eighth-century Baal worship is lacking and that this term too should be seen in light of a widespread, biblical and extrabiblical tradition in which it connotes a political ally or overlord. Hosea's use of this term bridged the gap between the religious and political spheres by characterizing the political actions of Hosea's audience as equivalent to the religious unfaithfulness of an earlier generation.

Chapter 6 set the stage for a reading of Hos 2 by integrating the findings of the preceding investigations and examining the broader issues of the rhetorical unit, rhetorical "horizon," and rhetorical-historical situation. The discussion of the rhetorical unit made the case that all of Hos 2:1–25 can be seen as the product of a single act of composition by the prophet Hosea and that the text is a thematically consistent, unified discourse with a coherent rhetorical purpose. The investigation of the rhetorical "horizon," that is, the contexts and conditions reflected in and presupposed by the text itself, revealed several characteristics: 1) a time of inner-Israelite conflict, 2) a joint action undertaken by both Israelites and Judeans, 3) a focus on the capital city Samaria and its improper political actions, and 4) a relationship with political allies and a political overlord. In light of this rhetorical horizon, the chapter concluded that the period of civil war in Israel between Hoshea and Pekah at the close of the Syro-

Ephraimitic conflict in 731–730 B.C.E. most closely matches all the elements presupposed by and reflected in Hos 2.

Finally, chapters 7 and 8 combined to offer a reading of Hos 2 in light of its metaphorical traditions and rhetorical situation. Chapter 7 specifically analyzed the translation issues of the speech and provided an interpretation of 2:1–3. This section of the text was identified as the prophet's introduction, which outlines a broad movement from judgment to restoration and reflects the situation of a cooperative effort between Israelites and Judeans to execute Yahweh's will and overthrow Pekah. Chapter 8 dealt with Yahweh's first-person speech that begins in 2:4 and traces the possible actions that Yahweh might take concerning the personified Samaria and the rulers she represents. Through the use of image-bases like ancient Near Eastern marriage legalities and the metaphorical language of sexual violence for the destruction of personified cities, the divine oracle addressed Pekah's political alliances that broke Samaria's treaty with Assyria and got Israel involved in a Damascus-led rebellion. In the end, the address proclaimed Yahweh's ultimate goal of reconciliation with his metaphorical wife.

The totality of the investigations undertaken in these chapters suggests that Hos 2:1–25 is an extended rhetorical discourse, which represents Hosea's theological and metaphorical commentary on the political affairs of Samaria and their implications for the people of Israel and Judah at the close of the Syro-Ephraimitic war (731–730 B.C.E.). The text's genres, metaphors, and traditions find a suitable rhetorical-historical context in this set of circumstances yet work together to demonstrate how intimately the political and religious spheres intersect in the prophet's rhetoric and theology.

2. IMPLICATIONS

It remains to overview briefly two possible implications of the present study. A first implication concerns the understanding of the nature of ancient Israelite prophets and their discourse. Since the nineteenth century, there has been a tendency among many scholars to define Israel's prophets primarily as forthtellers rather than foretellers and as creative innovators of genius apart from tradition. These descriptions have often included the conclusion that the primary task of prophets like Hosea, Amos, and Micah was ethical teaching concerning social justice.[3]

If the above examination of Hos 2 holds, however, the conclusions of this study suggest that the long-standing interpretation of the nature of prophecy in ancient Israel may be in need of reformulation. The present study certainly

---

[3] For the standard discussion of these classical positions and the history of the interpretation of prophets, see J. Blenkinsopp, *A History of Prophecy in Israel* (rev. and enl. ed.; Louisville: Westminster John Knox, 1996).

strengthens the notion that prophets like Hosea were not predictors of the future but spoke messages that addressed the events of their own day. The preceding analysis raises questions, however, about the identification of social (and even cultic) behavior as the primary focus of the prophetic texts. Hosea's speech in 2:1–25 does not deal with issues like the treatment of the poor and widow but focuses on the political affairs and policies of the central government in relation to Yahweh's perceived will for the people. This characteristic also seems to hold true for the rest of the book of Hosea. While other prophetic books like Amos and Micah possess a more explicitly ethical dimension, the example of Hos 2 may provide impetus for reexamining the ways in which those ethical pronouncements function within a larger rhetorical project devoted to addressing national and international political affairs and their implications for Yahweh's people.

Perhaps interpreters should extend the guiding paradigm outlined above in chapter 2 beyond the limits of the speech in Hos 2. A paradigm that understands ancient Israel's prophets as analogous to ancient Greece's political orators, rather than as socially marginal, ethical teachers, may provide new and fruitful ways to engage all the prophetic books in the Hebrew Bible. In this analogy, there is an ethical dimension, but it stands as only one part of an overall prophetic focus on the constitutive affairs of the nation as a whole. As with the orators of ancient Greece, the prophets of Israel seem to be concerned with using rhetoric to discern the meaning of contemporary events before they are evident to the common people, to foresee what is coming, to forewarn others, to judge a society's ills, and to call people to do their duty.[4] Thus, prophets in ancient Israel may perhaps be viewed most fruitfully as public orators, who used speech to address audiences in specific historical situations, in order to persuade them to some action on the basis of theological belief.

A concomitant implication of this understanding of the nature of prophecy in ancient Israel concerns the interpretation of prophetic discourse itself. The dominant way of reading prophetic texts like Hos 2 relies on redaction criticism and attempts to dissect the texts by identifying a multitude of later additions to the prophet's original words.[5] If the above understanding of Hosea and his speech in 2:1–25 holds, however, it implies that the prophetic texts in the Hebrew Bible may not always represent collections of fragmentary sayings from a variety of historical settings but extended rhetorical addresses with pragmatic goals. This notion may provide the impetus for considerations of other prophetic texts both inside and outside Hosea in terms of public addresses that revolve

---

[4] See the Demosthenes quote from *De Corona* given above and the discussion in chapter 2.
[5] For a ready example of this practice with Hos 2, see Wolff's (*Hosea*, 24–55) treatment of the chapter and its constitutive parts.

around the interaction of a speaker, discourse, and audience and use persuasive strategies within particular rhetorical situations.[6]

A second implication of this exploration of Hos 2 deals with the construction and arrangement of the book of Hosea as a whole. Scholars have long recognized the significant differences in style, tone, and imagery between Hos 1–3 and 4–14. On the one hand, as described above in chapter 5, the work of Kaufmann and Ginsberg used these differences to suggest that chapters 1–3 came from another prophet who lived prior to the reign of Jehu in a time when Baalism was prominent in Israel.[7] On the other hand, in contrast to the sharp division suggested by Kaufmann and Ginsberg, many scholars have dated various parts of Hos 1–3 and 4–14 to the same historical situations and thus implied that the present form of the book is a disorganized collection in which materials related to a single setting or event have been separated and relocated based upon thematic concerns. Commentators have often concluded that Hos 1–3 in particular is a thematically based compilation, which contains traditional or legendary material that dates from a wide-range of settings, while Hos 4–14 is a chronologically arranged collection that proceeds from the 740s to the fall of Samaria. According to this view, the present form of the book contains no identifiable structure for the whole.

Wolff's commentary represents this approach well. He treats chapters 1–3 as a collection of diverse material that came together around the theme of Hosea's personal life, marriage, and divorce. Wolff dates parts of chapter 1 to Jeroboam's years of 747–746 B.C.E. (1:2–4, 6) and other parts to the period after 733 B.C.E. (1:5), but he also assigns portions of chapter 2 to this time after 733 (2:4–17) as well as to the reign of Shalmaneser V after 727 B.C.E. (2:18–25).[8] Furthermore, while again associating the imagery and language of Hos 3:1–4 with the years after 733 B.C.E., he concludes that 3:5 comes from a "relatively early Judaic redaction ... connected with the late phase of Hosea's activity...."[9] Beginning with Hos 4:1–3, however, Wolff understands the remaining oracles to cover once again the period from Hosea's early preaching in the 740s to the last period of the northern kingdom in the 720s B.C.E.[10]

---

[6] For some analyses of prophetic texts that have moved in this direction, see Fox, "Rhetoric," Gitay, "Rhetorical Analysis," Irvine, *Isaiah*, and Shaw, "Speeches."

[7] Kaufmann, *Religion*, 368; cf. Ginsberg, "Hosea," 1011–17 and Milgrom, "Nature," 1.

[8] Wolff, *Hosea*, 12, 47–48.

[9] Ibid., xxxi, 57–59.

[10] Ibid., xxxi, 66, 110–11, 234. Wolff's scheme for the composition of the book actually involves three transmission complexes (chapters 1–3, 4–11, 12–14) that developed independently, were supplemented by two later Judean redactions, and ultimately came together at some point in the exilic or early postexilic period (ibid., xxx–xxxii). Nonetheless, his view considers Hos 1–3 to be a compilation of independent materials from different settings while Hos 4–11 follows an essentially chronological order.

If the present work's arguments for the connection between Hos 2:1–25 and the close of the Syro-Ephraimitic war are correct, they may suggest a way to conceive an overall arrangement of the book that accounts for both the significant differences between chapters 1–3 and 4–14 and the apparent overlaps in the historical backgrounds of various oracles.[11] As early as 1957, Hellmuth Frey suggested in a general way that the book as a whole is arranged in two *parallel* chronological sections (chapters 1–3 and 4–14), which both include references to the fall of Samaria.[12] In this view, Hos 1–3 follows a chronological structure that begins with the time of Jeroboam II in chapter 1 and stretches to the fall of Samaria in chapter 3. Rather than picking up after the fall of Samaria, however, Hos 4 then takes the reader back to the time of Zechariah, just after the death of Jeroboam II, and proceeds once more from there to the fall of Samaria in chapter 14.[13]

The dating of Hos 2:1–25 to the close of the Syro-Ephraimitic war and its consequent overlap with materials in the later sections of Hos 5 and 6, which also seem to reflect the period of the late 730s, invite further study of the possibility that the book may, in fact, be arranged in two panels that overlap chronologically (chapters 1–3 and 4–14).[14] This possibility demonstrates a need for future studies of the exact details of this structure, including analyses of the historical background of various sections that may differ from Frey's general

---

[11] For example, combining the present analysis with the common view of Hos 5 and 6, 2:1–25 would then reflect the same period of the Syro-Ephraimitic war as the material in 5:8–6:6. Cf. Alt, "Hosea 5, 8–6, 6," 537–68 and Arnold, *Gibeah*, 112–15.

[12] H. Frey, "Der Aufbau der Gedichte Hoseas," *WD* Neue Folge 5 (1957): 102–3; H. Frey, *Das Buch des Werbens Gottes um seine Kirche: Der Prophet Hosea* (BAT 23, 2; Stuttgart: Calwer, 1957), 79. As Frey states his proposal concerning the whole of Hosea, "These speeches are put together in two parallel collections [zwei parallelen Sammlungen] 1–3 and 4–14, which both presuppose the end of Samaria in 722 …" ("Aufbau," 103; writer's translation from the original German).

[13] Frey summarizes his position as follows: "If in chapters 1–3, the prophetic acts of Hosea from his first appearance until his last deed, which he accompanied with speeches and oracles, were collected, chapters 4–14 offer an exclusive collection of speeches and oracles that are not all situated early but correspond to the same time of Hosea's public actions, that is, perhaps until about the time of Samaria's destruction" (*Buch*, 79; writer's translation from the original German). Frey dates Hos 1 to the time of Jeroboam II (ibid., 1) and Hos 3 to the period of the fall of Samaria in 722 B.C.E. (ibid., 71). He then dates Hos 4 to the time just after Jeroboam II's death (ca. 748 B.C.E.) (ibid., 79) and Hos 14 to the fall of Samaria in 722 B.C.E. (ibid., 282–83).

[14] The most direct suggestion of this possibility appears in a brief footnote in Hayes and Kuan, "Final Years," 164, f.n. 23. They state, "The book of Hosea is arranged in two panels: chaps. 1–3 and 4–14. Within each panel the materials are arranged chronologically. Chaps. 1–3 cover a period from the last years of Jeroboam II (late 750s) until after the arrest of Hoshea (725). The second panel covers from the years of Shallum's coup until the capture of Samaria by Sargon. Chaps. 4–7 derive from the time before King Hoshea's arrest; chaps. 8–9 from the time between Hoshea's arrest and the capture of Samaria in 722; and chaps. 10–14 from the time of Sargon's activity in the west." As an example of this overlapping arrangement, they propose that both Hos 3:4 and 10:15 allude to the arrest of Hoshea and looting of Bethel in 725 B.C.E.

proposals. For example, the possibility exists that chapters 1–3 follow sequentially the movement of speeches and actions relating to situations from the final years of Jeroboam II through the Syro-Ephraimitic war to a capture of Samaria by Shalmaneser V (ca. 725 B.C.E.), while chapter 4 returns to the mid-740s B.C.E. but extends the same chronological movement down to the fall of Samaria and perhaps beyond. Thus, the book consists of two panels that are not identical but overlap on both chronological endpoints: chapter 1 (ca. 750) begins earlier than chapter 4 (ca. 747), and chapter 3 (ca. 725) ends earlier than chapter 14 (ca. 720). Rather than identifying Hos 1–3 as a compilation devoid of chronological structuring, future study may indicate that these chapters represent a sequential panel that follows the same basic ordering as chapters 4–14 but presents the situations and events specifically from the viewpoint of Hosea's utilization of the marriage metaphor and his symbolic actions. The grouping of these three chapters highlights one particular dimension of the prophet's rhetoric that he used to address audiences in these circumstances from the 740s to the 720s B.C.E. It remains for further studies to examine not only the ways in which various other individual speeches can be related to specific rhetorical situations but also how those relationships influence the understanding of the present form of the book.

3. CONCLUSION

The conclusion that Hos 2 constitutes a speech given by the prophet Hosea in order to provide a metaphorical and theological commentary on the political affairs of Samaria at the end of the Syro-Ephraimitic war represents a decidedly historical interpretation. Due to the violent nature and tone of many of the text's metaphors, however, Hosea's oracle has often been viewed as deeply problematic for theological reflection on God and God's relationship with humanity. Within biblical scholarship, particularly among feminist interpreters, such an analysis typically takes the form of reception-oriented approaches, which focus on the intersection of the text's language with contemporary concerns. Yet the historical undertaking of this study operates with an intentionally *inception*-oriented approach, which seeks to determine the function of Hos 2's language within the contexts and structures of a foreign thought-world. Far from negating the importance of reception-oriented analyses, it is hoped that the present type of rhetorical analysis will provide a meaningful dialogue partner for other types of reading, a dialogue partner that offers a broader historical and cultural context from which to view both the prophet's words and their continuing functions among readers of the text. Such a rhetorical analysis helps to remind all readers that biblical texts come from the crucible of real situations and the lives of real people. An appreciation of the rhetoric of a text like Hos 2, which relies on the cultural and comparative metaphorical traditions of another time, highlights this dimension of the biblical literature all the more.

BIBLIOGRAPHY

Abegg, M., P. Flint, and E. Ulrich. *The Dead Sea Scrolls Bible*. San Francisco: Harper, 1999.

Abma, R. *Bonds of Love: Methodic Studies of Prophetic Texts with Marriage Imagery (Isaiah 50:1–3 and 54:1–10, Hosea 1–3, Jeremiah 2–3)*. Studia Semitica Neerlandica. Assen: Van Gorcum, 1999.

Abrams, M. "Metaphor, Theories of." Pages 155–58 in *A Glossary of Literary Terms*. Edited by M. Abrams. 7th ed. Fort Worth: Harcourt Brace College Publishers, 1999.

Ackerman, S. "The Personal Is Political: Covenantal and Affectionate Love (ʾAHĒB, ʾAHABÂ) in the Hebrew Bible." *Vetus Testamentum* 52 (2002): 437–58.

―――. *Under Every Green Tree: Popular Religion in Sixth-Century Judah*. Harvard Semitic Monographs 46. Atlanta: Scholars Press, 1992.

Ackroyd, P. "The Verb Love- ʾāhēb in the David-Jonathan Narratives: A Footnote." *Vetus Testamentum* 25 (1975): 213–14.

Adler, E. "The Background for the Metaphor of Covenant as Marriage in the Hebrew Bible." Ph.D. diss., University of California, 1989.

Albright, W. F. *Archaeology and the Religion of Israel: The Ayer Lectures of the Colgate-Rochester Divinity School 1941*. Baltimore: The Johns Hopkins University Press, 1942.

―――. "The Gezer Calendar." *Bulletin of the American Schools of Oriental Research* 92 (1943): 22.

Allegro, J. "A Recently Discovered Fragment of a Commentary on Hosea from Qumran's Fourth Cave." *Journal of Biblical Literature* 78 (1959): 142–48.

Allen, L. *Ezekiel 20–48*. Word Biblical Commentary 29. Dallas: Word Books, 1990.

Alt, A. "Hosea 5, 8–6, 6: Ein Kreig und seine Folgen in prophetischer Beleuchtung."
     Neue kirchliche Zeitschrift 30 (1919): 537–68. Repr. pages 163–87 in *Kleine
     Schriften II.* Munich: C. H. Beck, 1959.

———. "Tiglathpilesers III erster Feldzug nach Palästina." Pages 150–63 in *Kleine
     Schriften II.* Munich: C. H. Beck, 1959.

Anati, E. "The Question of Fertility Cults." Pages 2–15 in *Archaeology and Fertility Cult
     in the Ancient Mediterranean: Papers Presented at the First International
     Conference on Archaeology of the Ancient Mediterranean.* Edited by A.
     Bonano. Amsterdam: B. R. Grüner, 1986.

Andersen, F. and D. Freedman. *Hosea.* Anchor Bible 24. New York: Doubleday, 1985.

Andersen, T. "Renaming and Wedding Imagery in Isaiah 62." *Biblica* 67 (1986): 75–80.

Anderson, B. *The Eighth Century Prophets.* Proclamation Commentaries. Philadelphia:
     Fortress, 1978.

Andrews, J. *The Practice of Rhetorical Criticism.* New York: Macmillan, 1983.

Aristotle. *Rhetoric.* Translated by L. Cooper. New York: Appleton, 1932.

Arnold, B. "A Pre-Deuteronomistic Bicolon in 1 Samuel 12:21?" *Journal of Biblical
     Literature* 123 (2004): 137–42.

Arnold, P. *Gibeah: The Search for a Biblical City.* Journal for the Study of the Old
     Testament Supplement Series 79. Sheffield: JSOT Press, 1990.

Assante, J. "The kar.kid/ḫarimtu, Prostitute or Single Woman? A Reconsideration of the
     Evidence." *Ugarit Forschungen* 30 (1998): 5–96.

Asurmendi, J. *La Guerra Siro-Efraimita: Historia y profetas.* Valencia: Institutión San
     Jerónimo, 1982.

Baab, O. "Prostitution." Pages 931–34 in vol. 3 of *The Interpreter's Dictionary of the
     Bible.* Edited by G. A. Buttrick. 4 vols. Nashville: Abingdon, 1962.

Bach, R. *Die Aufforderungen zur Flucht und zum Kampf im alttestamentlichen
     Prophetenspruch.* Wissenschaftliche Monographien zum Alten und Neuen
     Testament 9. Neukirchen: Neukirchen Verlag, 1962.

Barton, J. "History and Rhetoric in the Prophets." Pages 51–64 in *The Bible as Rhetoric:
     Studies in Biblical Persuasion and Credibility.* Edited by M. Warner. Warwick
     Studies in Philosophy and Literature. London: Routledge, 1990.

Basham, A. L. *The Wonder That Was India: A Survey of the History and Culture of the
     Indian Sub-Continent before the Coming of the Muslims.* 3d ed. Calcutta: Rupa
     & Company, 1967.

Batten, L. "Hosea's Message and Marriage." *Journal of Biblical Literature* 48 (1929):
     257–73.

Baumann, E. "YDᶜ und seine Derivate: Ein sprachlich-exegetische Studie." *Zeitschrift
     für die alttestamentliche Wissenschaft* 28 (1908): 22–41, 110–43.

Baumann, G. *Love and Violence: Marriage as a Metaphor for the Relationship between
     YHWH and Israel in the Prophetic Books.* Translated by L. Maloney.
     Collegeville, Minn.: Liturgical Press, 2003. Translation of *Liebe und Gewalt:
     Die Ehe als Metaphor für das Verhältnis JHWH-Israel in den
     Prophetenbüchein.* Stuttgarter Bible Studien 185. Stuttgart: Katholisches
     Bibelwerk, 2000.

Baumgartner, W. "Herodots babylonische und assyrische Nachrichten." *Archiv
     Orientální* 18 (1950): 69–109.

Beard, M. and J. Henderson. "With This Body I Thee Worship: Sacred Prostitution in Antiquity." Pages 56–79 in *Gender and the Body in the Ancient Mediterranean*. Edited by M. Wyke. Gender and History. Oxford: Blackwell, 1998.

Beeby, H. *Hosea: Grace Abounding*. International Theological Commentary. Grand Rapids: Eerdmans, 1989.

Begrich, J. "Der syrisch-ephraimitische Krieg und seine weltpolitischen Zusammenhänge." *Zeitschrift der deutschen morgenländische Gesellschaft* 83 (1927): 213–37.

Ben Zvi, E. "Observations on the Marital Metaphor of YHWH and Israel in Its Ancient Israelite Context: General Considerations and Particular Images in Hosea 1.2." *Journal for the Study of the Old Testament* 28 (2004): 363–84.

———. "Studying Prophetic Texts against Their Original Backgrounds: Pre-Ordained Scripts and Alternative Horizons of Research." Pages 125–35 in *Prophets and Paradigms: Essays in Honor of Gene M. Tucker*. Edited by S. Reid. Journal for the Study of the Old Testament Supplement Series 229. Sheffield: Sheffield Academic Press, 1996.

———. and M. Floyd, eds. *Writings and Speech in Israelite and Ancient Near Eastern Prophecy*. Society of Biblical Literature Symposium Series 10. Atlanta: SBL, 2000.

Bernstein, M. "'Walking in the Festivals of the Gentiles': 4QpHosea[a] 2.15–17 and Jubilees 6:34–38." *Journal for the Study of the Pseudepigrapha* 9 (1991): 21–34.

Bible and Culture Collective. *The Postmodern Bible*. New Haven: Yale University Press, 1995.

Biddle, M. "The Figure of Lady Jerusalem: Identification, Deification, and Personification of Cities in the Ancient Near East." Pages 173–94 in *The Biblical Canon in Comparative Perspective*. Edited by K. Younger, W. Hallo, and B. Batto. Scripture in Context 4. Ancient Near Eastern Texts and Studies 11. Lewiston: Edwin Meller, 1991.

Birch, B. *Hosea, Joel, and Amos*. Westminster Bible Companion. Louisville: Westminster John Knox, 1997.

Bird, P. *Missing Persons and Mistaken Identities: Women and Gender in Ancient Israel*. Overtures to Biblical Theology. Minneapolis: Fortress, 1997.

———. "To Play the Harlot: An Inquiry into an Old Testament Metaphor." Pages 75–94 in *Gender and Difference in Ancient Israel*. Edited by P. Day. Minneapolis: Fortress, 1989.

Bitzer, L. "Functional Communication: A Situational Perspective." Pages 21–38 in *Rhetoric in Transition: Studies in the Nature and Uses of Rhetoric*. Edited by E. White. University Park: Penn State University Press, 1980.

———. "The Rhetorical Situation." *Philosophy and Rhetoric* 1 (1968): 1–14. Repr. pages 247–60 in *Rhetoric: A Tradition in Transition*. Edited by W. Fisher. Ann Arbor: University of Michigan Press, 1974.

———. and E. Black, eds. *The Prospect of Rhetoric*. Report of the National Development Project of the Speech Communication Association. Englewood Cliffs, N.J.: Prentice-Hall, 1971.

Black, C. "Keeping Up with Recent Studies XVI: Rhetorical Criticism and Biblical Interpretation." *Expository Times* 100 (1988–89): 252–58.

Black, E. *Rhetorical Criticism: A Study in Method.* Madison: University of Wisconsin Press, 1978.

Black, M. *The Labyrinth of Language.* New York: Praeger, 1968.

———. "Metaphor." *Proceedings of the Aristotelian Society* 55 (1954–55): 273–94. Repr. pages 63–82 in *Philosophical Perspectives on Metaphor.* Edited by M. Johnson. Minneapolis: University of Minnesota Press, 1981.

———. *Models and Metaphors: Studies in Language and Philosophy.* Ithaca, N.Y.: Cornell University Press, 1962.

———. "More about Metaphor." Pages 19–41 in *Metaphor and Thought.* Edited by A. Ortony. 2d ed. Cambridge: Cambridge University Press, 1993.

Blankenbaker, G. "The Language of Hosea 1–3." Ph.D. diss., The Claremont Graduate School, 1976.

Blenkinsopp, J. *A History of Prophecy in Israel.* Philadelphia: Westminster, 1983. Rev. and enl. ed. Louisville: Westminster John Knox, 1996.

———. *Isaiah 1–39.* Anchor Bible 19. New York: Doubleday, 2000.

Boadt, L. "The Poetry of Prophetic Persuasion: Preserving the Prophet's Persona." *Catholic Biblical Quarterly* 59 (1997): 1–21.

Bonano, A., ed. *Archaeology and Fertility Cult in the Ancient Mediterranean: Papers Presented at the First International Conference on Archaeology of the Ancient Mediterranean.* Amsterdam: B. R. Grüner, 1986.

Bons, E. *Das Buch Hosea.* Neuer Stuttgarter Kommentar: Altes Testament 23, 1. Stuttgart: Katholisches Bibelwerk, 1996.

Booth, W. "Metaphor as Rhetoric: The Problem of Evaluation." Pages 47–70 in *On Metaphor.* Edited by S. Sacks. Chicago: University of Chicago Press, 1979.

———. "The Scope of Rhetoric Today: A Polemical Excursion." Pages 93–114 in *The Prospect of Rhetoric.* Report of the National Development Project of the Speech Communication Association. Englewood Cliffs, N.J.: Prentice-Hall, 1971.

Borbone, P. *Il libro del profeta Osea.* Torino: Silvio Zamorani, 1987.

Botterweck, G. J. and H. Ringgren, eds. *Theological Dictionary of the Old Testament.* 7 vols. Grand Rapids: Eerdmans, 1974–.

Boudreau, G. "Hosea and the Pentateuchal Traditions: The Case of the Baal of Peor." Pages 121–32 in *History and Interpretation: Essays in Honour of John H. Hayes.* Edited by M. Graham, W. Brown, and J. Kuan. Journal for the Study of the Old Testament Supplement Series 173. Sheffield: JSOT Press, 1993.

———. "A Study of the Traditio-Historical Development of the Baal of Peor Tradition." Ph.D. diss., Emory University, 1991.

Bourguet, D. *Des métaphores de Jérémie.* Echter Bibel 9. Paris: J. Gabalda, 1987.

Braaten, L. "Earth Community in Hosea 2." Pages 185–203 in *The Earth Story in the Psalms and the Prophets.* Edited by N. Habel. The Earth Bible 4. Sheffield: Sheffield Academic Press, 2001.

———. "Parent-Child Imagery in Hosea." Ph.D diss., Boston University, 1987.

Branson, R. "A Study of the Hebrew Term נשׂא." Ph.D diss., Boston University, 1976.

Breneman, J. "Nuzi Marriage Tablets." Ph.D. diss., Brandeis University, 1971.

Brenner, A., ed. *A Feminist Companion to the Latter Prophets*. Sheffield: Sheffield Academic Press, 1995.

Brooks, B. "Fertility Cult Functionaries in the Old Testament." *Journal of Biblical Literature* 60 (1941): 227–53.

Brown, F., S. R. Driver, and C. A. Briggs. *A Hebrew and English Lexicon of the Old Testament*. Oxford: Clarendon, 1907.

Brueggemann, W. *1 & 2 Kings*. Smyth and Helwys Bible Commentary. Macon: Smyth & Helwys, 2000.

———. *Tradition for Crisis: A Study in Hosea*. Atlanta: John Knox, 1968.

Bryant, D. *Rhetorical Dimensions in Criticism*. Baton Rouge: Louisiana State University Press, 1973.

Bucher, C. "The Origin and Meaning of znh Terminology in the Book of Hosea." Ph.D. diss., The Claremont Graduate School, 1988.

Budde, K. "Der Abschnitt Hosea 1–3 und seine grundlegende religionsgeschichtliche Bedeutung." *Theologische Studien und Kritiken* 96/97 (1925): 1–89.

———. "Eine folgenschwere Redaktion des Zwölfprophetenbuchs." *Zeitschrift für die alttestamentliche Wissenschaft* 39 (1922): 218–26.

———. "Jesaja und Ahaz." *Zeitschrift der deutschen morgenländischen Gesellschaft* 84 (1931): 125–38.

———. "The Nomadic Ideal in the Old Testament." *The New World* 4 (1895): 726–45.

Burke, K. *A Rhetoric of Motives*. New York: Prentice-Hall, 1950.

Burrows, M. *The Basis of Israelite Marriage*. American Oriental Series 15. New Haven: American Oriental Society, 1938.

Buss, M. *Biblical Form Criticism in Its Context*. Journal for the Study of the Old Testament Supplement Series 274. Sheffield: Sheffield Academic Press, 1999.

———. "The Distinction between Civil and Criminal Law in Ancient Israel." Pages 51–62 in *Proceedings of the 6th World Congress of Jewish Studies I*. Jerusalem: Academic Press, 1977.

———. "Hosea as a Canonical Problem: With Attention to the Song of Songs." Pages 79–93 in *Prophets and Paradigms: Essays in Honor of Gene M. Tucker*. Edited by S. Reid. Journal for the Study of the Old Testament Supplement Series 229. Sheffield: Sheffield Academic Press, 1996.

———. *The Prophetic Word of Hosea*. Beihefte zur Zeitschrift für die alttestamentliche Wissenschaft 111. Berlin: Töpelmann, 1969.

———. "Tragedy and Comedy in Hosea." *Semeia* 32 (1984): 71–82.

Butler, H., ed. and trans. *The Institutio Oratoria of Quintilian*. 4 vols. Loeb Classical Library. Cambridge: Harvard University Press, 1920–1922.

Camp, C. "Metaphor in Feminist Biblical Interpretation: Theoretical Perspectives." *Semeia* 61 (1993): 3–36.

Cassin, E. "Pouvoirs de la femme et structure familiales." *Revue d'assyriologie et d'archaeologie Orientale* 63 (1969): 121–48.

Cassuto, U. "The Second Chapter of the Book of Hosea." Pages 101–40 in *Biblical and Oriental Studies*. Translated by I. Abrahams. 2 vols. Jerusalem: Magnes, 1973.

Cathcart, K. and R. Gordon. *Targum of the Minor Prophets*. Vol. 14 of *The Aramaic Bible*. Wilmington, Del.: Glazier, 1989.

Cazelles, H. "Problemes de la guerre syro-ephraimite." *Eretz-Israel* 14 (1978): 70–78.

————. "Syro-Ephraimitic War." Pages 282–85 in vol. 6 of *The Anchor Bible Dictionary*. Edited by D. N. Freedman. 6 vols. New York: Doubleday, 1992.

Chaney, M. "Agricultural Intensification as Promiscuity in the Book of Hosea." Paper presented at the annual meeting of the Society of Biblical Literature. Washington, D.C., 1993.

Cheyne, T. *Hosea*. The Cambridge Bible for Schools and Colleges. London: Cambridge University Press, 1884.

Chong, J. H. "The Song of Moses (Deuteronomy 32:1–43) and the Hoshea-Pekah Conflict." Ph.D. diss., Emory University, 1990.

Clay, A. T., ed. *Babylonian Records in the Library of J. Pierpont Morgan IV*. New Haven: Yale University Press, 1923.

Clemen, C. *Miszellen zu Lukians Schrift über die syrische Göttin*. Beihefte zur Zeitschrift für die alttestamentliche Wissenschaft 33. Berlin: Töpelmann, 1918.

Clements, R. "Understanding the Book of Hosea." *Review and Expositor* 72 (1975): 405–23.

Clines, D. J. A., ed. *Dictionary of Classical Hebrew*. Sheffield: Sheffield Academic Press, 1993–.

————. "Hosea 2: Structure and Interpretaton." Pages 83–103 in *Studia Biblica: Sixth International Congress on Biblical Studies*. Edited by E. Livingstone. Journal for the Study of the Old Testament Supplement Series 11. Sheffield: University of Sheffield Press, 1979.

Cogan, M. *Imperialism and Religion: Assyria, Judah and Israel in the Eighth and Seventh Centuries B.C.E.* Society of Biblical Literature Monograph Series 19. Missoula: Scholars Press, 1974.

————. and H. Tadmor. *II Kings: A New Translation with Introduction and Commentary*. Anchor Bible 11. Garden City, N.Y.: Doubleday, 1988.

Cohen, T. "Figurative Speech and Figurative Acts." *The Journal of Philosophy* 71 (1975): 669–84. Repr. pages 182–99 in *Philosophical Perspectives on Metaphor*. Edited by M. Johnson. Minneapolis: University of Minnesota Press, 1981.

Collins, O. "The Stem ZNH and Prostitution in the Hebrew Bible." Ph.D. diss., Brandeis University, 1977.

Cook, H. J. "Pekah." *Vetus Testamentum* 14 (1964): 121–35.

Cooper, J. "Sacred Marriage and Popular Cult in Early Mesopotamia." Pages 81–96 in *Official Cult and Popular Religion in the Ancient Near East*. Edited by E. Matsushima. Heidelberg: Universitätsverlag C. Winter, 1983.

Coote, R. and M. Coote. *Power, Politics, and the Making of the Bible: An Introduction*. Minneapolis: Fortress, 1990.

Corbett, E. *Classical Rhetoric for the Modern Student*. 2d ed. New York: Oxford University Press, 1971.

Cowley, A. *Aramaic Papyri of the Fifth Century B.C.* Oxford: Clarendon, 1923.

Craghan, J. "The Book of Hosea: A Survey of Recent Literature on the First of the Minor Prophets." *Biblical Theology Bulletin* 1 (1971): 81–100, 145–70.

Craigie, P., P. Kelley, J. Drinkard. *Jeremiah 1–25*. Word Biblical Commentary 26. Dallas: Word Books, 1991.

Dahood, M. *Psalms I: 1–50*. Anchor Bible 16. Garden City, N.Y.: Doubleday, 1979.

Dalley, S. "Recent Evidence from Assyrian Sources for Judean History from Uzziah to Manasseh." *Journal for the Study of the Old Testament* 28 (2004): 387–401.

Darsey, J. *The Prophetic Tradition and Radical Rhetoric in America.* New York: New York University Press, 1997.

Davies, G. *Hosea.* New Century Bible Commentary. Grand Rapids: Eerdmans, 1992.

——. *Hosea.* Old Testament Guides. Sheffield: Sheffield Academic Press, 1993.

Day, J. "Baal (Deity)." Pages 545–49 in vol.1 of *The Anchor Bible Dictionary.* Edited by D. N. Freedman. 6 vols. New York: Doubleday, 1992.

——. "Canaan, Religion of." Pages 831–37 in vol. 1 of *The Anchor Bible Dictionary.* Edited by D. N. Freedman. 6 vols. New York: Doubleday, 1992.

——. *Yahweh and the Gods and Goddesses of Canaan.* Journal for the Study of the Old Testament Supplement Series 265. Sheffield: Sheffield Academic Press, 2000.

——. "Yahweh and the Gods and Goddesses of Canaan." Pages 181–96 in *Ein Gott allein? JHWH-Verehrung und biblischer Monotheismus im Kontext der israelitischen und altorientalischen Religionsgeschichte.* Edited by W. Dietrich and M. Klopfenstein. Orbis Biblicus et Orientalis 139. Freiburg: Universitätsverlag, 1994.

Day, P. "Adulterous Jerusalem's Imagined Demise: Death of a Metaphor in Ezekiel XVI." *Vetus Testamentum* 50 (2000): 285–309.

——. "The Bitch Had It Coming to Her: Rhetoric and Interpretation in Ezekiel 16." *Biblical Interpretation* 8 (2000): 231–54.

——. "The Personification of Cities as Female in the Hebrew Bible: The Thesis of Aloysius Fitzgerald, F.S.C." Pages 283–302 in *Reading from This Place.* Edited by F. Segovia and M. A. Tolbert. 2 vols. Minneapolis: Fortress, 1995.

——. "The Son of Tabeel (Isaiah 7.6): History of Interpretation and Extra-biblical Sources." Pages 33–47 in *Prophets and Paradigms: Essays in Honor of Gene M. Tucker.* Edited by S. Reid. Journal for the Study of the Old Testament Supplement Series 229. Sheffield: Sheffield Academic Press, 1996.

——. "YHWH's House: Gender Roles and Metaphors for Israel in Hosea." *Journal of Northwest Semitic Languages* 25 (1999): 97–108.

——., ed. *Gender and Difference in Ancient Israel.* Minneapolis: Fortress, 1989.

Dearman, J. A. "Baal in Israel: The Contribution of Some Place Names and Personal Names to an Understanding of Early Israelite Religion." Pages 173–91 in *History and Interpretation: Essays in Honour of John H. Hayes.* Eds. P. Graham, W. Brown, J. Kuan. Journal for the Study of the Old Testament Supplement Series 173. Sheffield: Sheffield Academic Press, 1993.

Delitzsch, F. *Assyrische Lesestücke.* Leipzig: J. C. Hinrichs, 1912.

Demosthenes. *Demosthenes on the Crown (De Corona).* Translated by S. Usher. Warminster: Aris & Phillips, 1993.

DeRoche, M. "Yahweh's RÎB against Israel: A Reassessment of the So-Called 'Prophetic Lawsuit' in the Preexilic Prophets." *Journal of Biblical Literature* 102 (1983): 563–74.

Dever, W. "Asherah, Consort of Yahweh? New Evidence from Kuntillet 'Ajrud." *Bulletin of the American Schools of Oriental Research* 255 (1984): 21–37.

Diaz, M. "I Will Speak to Their Hearts." *SEDOS Bulletin* 28 (1996): 271–76.

Dietrich, M., O. Loretz, and J. Sanmartín, eds. *Die Keil alphabetischen Texte aus Ugarit: Teil 1 Transkription.* Alter Orient und Altes Testament 24/1. Kevelaer: Butzon & Bercker, 1976.

Dietrich, W. and M. Klopfenstein, eds. *Ein Gott allein? JHWH-Verehrung und biblischer Monotheismus im Kontext der israelitischen und altorientalischen Religionsgeschichte.* Orbis Biblicus et Orientalis 139. Freiburg: Universitätsverlag, 1994.

Dijk-Hemmes, F., van. "Imagination of Power and the Power of Imagination: An Intertextual Analysis of Two Biblical Love Songs: The Song of Songs and Hosea 2." *Journal for the Study of the Old Testament* 44 (1989): 75–88.

Dille, S. "God as Father and Mother in the Interplay of Deutero-Isaiah's Metaphors." Ph.D. diss., Emory University, 1999.

Dobbs-Allsopp, F. W. "The Syntagma of *bat* Followed by a Geographical Name in the Hebrew Bible: A Reconsideration of Its Meaning and Grammar." *Catholic Biblical Quarterly* 57 (1995): 451–70.

Donner, H. *Israel unter den Völkern: Die Stellung der klassischen Propheten des 8. Jahrhunderts v. Chr. zur Aussenpolitik der Könige von Israel und Juda.* Supplements to Vetus Testamentum 11. Leiden: Brill, 1964.

———. "The Separate States of Israel and Judah." Pages 421–32 in *Israelite and Judean History.* Edited by J. H. Hayes and J. M. Miller. Philadelphia: Westminster, 1977.

Dossin, G. *Correspondence de Iasmah-Addu.* Archives royales de Mari 5. Paris: Imprimerie nationale, 1952.

Doyle, B. *The Apocalypse of Isaiah Metaphorically Speaking: A Study of the Use, Function, and Significance of Metaphors in Isaiah 24–27.* Bibliotheca Ephemeridum Theologicarum Lovaniensium CLI. Leuven: Leuven University Press, 2000.

Dozeman, T. "Old Testament Rhetorical Criticism." Pages 712–25 in vol. 5 of *The Anchor Bible Dictionary.* Edited by D. N. Freedman. 6 vols. New York: Doubleday, 1992.

Duhm, B. "Anmerkungen zu den Zwölf Propheten." *Zeitschrift für die alttestamentliche Wissenschaft* 31 (1911): 1–43.

———. *Die Theologie der Propheten als Grundlage für die innere Entwicklungsgeschichte der Israelite Religion.* Bonn: Adolph Marcus, 1875.

Edelman, D., ed. *The Triumph of Elohim: From Yahwisms to Judaisms.* Grand Rapids: Eerdmans, 1996.

Eidevall, G. *Grapes in the Desert: Metaphors, Models and Themes in Hosea 4–14.* Coniectanea Biblica Old Testament Series 43. Stockholm: Almqvist & Wiksell, 1996.

Eilberg-Schwartz, H. *God's Phallus and Other Problems for Men and Monotheism.* Boston: Beacon, 1994.

Emerton, A. "New Light on Israelite Religion: The Implications of Inscriptions from Kuntillet 'Ajrud." *Zeitschrift für die alttestamentliche Wissenschaft* 94 (1982): 2–20.

Emmerson, G. *Hosea: An Israelite Prophet in Judean Perspective.* Journal for the Study of the Old Testament Supplement Series 28. Sheffield: JSOT Press, 1984.

Enos, R. and A. Blakeslee. "The Classical Period." Pages 9–44 in *The Present State of Scholarship in Historical and Contemporary Rhetoric*. Edited by W. B. Horner. Rev. ed. Columbia: University of Missouri Press, 1990.

Eph'al, I. "'The Samarian(s)' in the Assyrian Sources." Pages 36–45 in *Ah Assyria: Studies in Assyrian History and Ancient Near Eastern Historiography Presented to Hayim Tadmor*. Edited by M. Cogan and I. Eph'al. Scripta Hierosolymitana 33. Jerusalem: Magnes, 1991.

Epstein, L. *The Jewish Marriage Contract: A Study in the Status of the Woman in Jewish Law*. The Jewish People: History, Religion, Literature. New York: Arno, 1973.

Ewald, H. *Amos, Hosea, and Zechariah*. Vol. 1 of *Commentary on the Prophets of the Old Testament*. Translated by J. Smith. London: Williams & Norgate, 1875.

Fensham, C. "The Marriage Metaphor in Hosea for the Covenant Relationship between the Lord and His People (Hos 1:2–9)." *Journal of Northwest Semitic Languages* 12 (1984): 71–78.

Fisch, H. "Hosea: A Poetics of Violence." Pages 137–58 in *Poetry with a Purpose: Biblical Poetics and Interpretation*. Edited by H. Fisch. Bloomington: Indiana University Press, 1988.

Fisher, E. "Cultic Prostitution in the Ancient Near East? A Reassessment." *Biblical Theology Bulletin* 6 (1976): 225–36.

Fitzgerald, A. "*BTWLT* and *BT* as Titles for Capital Cities." *Catholic Biblical Quarterly* 37 (1975): 167–83.

———. "The Mythological Background for the Presentation of Jerusalem as a Queen and False Worship as Adultery in the Old Testament." *Catholic Biblical Quarterly* 34 (1972): 403–16.

Fitzmyer, J. *The Aramaic Inscriptions of Sefire*. Biblica et Orientalia 19. Rome: Pontifical Biblical Institute, 1967; rev. ed., 1995.

———. "A Re-Study of an Elephantine Aramaic Marriage Contract (AP 15)." Pages 137–68 in *Near Eastern Studies in Honor of W. F. Albright*. Edited by H. Goedicke. Baltimore: The Johns Hopkins University Press, 1971.

———. and D. Harrington. *A Manual of Palestinian Aramaic Texts (second century B.C.–second century A.D.)*. Biblica et Orientalia 34. Rome: Biblical Institute Press, 1978.

Fontaine, C. "A Response to 'Hosea.'" Pages 60–69 in *A Feminist Companion to the Latter Prophets*. Edited by A. Brenner. Sheffield: Sheffield Academic Press, 1995.

Foss, S., K. Foss, and R. Trapp. *Contemporary Perspectives on Rhetoric*. Prospect Heights, Ill.: Waveland, 1985.

Fowler, J. *Theophoric Personal Names in Ancient Hebrew: A Comparative Study*. Journal for the Study of the Old Testament Supplement Series 49. Sheffield: JSOT Press, 1988.

Fox, M. "The Rhetoric of Ezekiel's Vision of the Valley of the Bones." *Hebrew Union College Annual* 51 (1980): 1–15. Repr. pages 176–90 in *The Place Is Too Small for Us: The Israelite Prophets in Recent Scholarship*. Edited by R. Gordon. Sources for Biblical and Theological Study 5. Winona Lake, Ind.: Eisenbrauns, 1995.

Freedman, D. "פשׁתי in Hosea 2:7." *Journal of Biblical Literature* 74 (1955): 275.

Frey, H. "Der Aufbau der Gedichte Hoseas." *Wort und Dienst* Neue Folge 5 (1957): 9–103.

———. *Das Buch des Werbens Gottes um seine Kirche: Der Prophet Hosea.* Die Botschaft des Alten Testamentes 23, 2. Stuttgart: Calwer, 1957.

Friedman, M. "Israel's Response in Hosea 2:17b: 'You Are My Husband.'" *Journal of Biblical Literature* 99 (1980): 199–204.

Frymer-Kensky, T. *In the Wake of the Goddess: Women, Culture, and the Biblical Transformation of Pagan Myth.* New York: Free Press, 1992.

Galambush, J. *Jerusalem in the Book of Ezekiel: The City as Yahweh's Wife.* Society of Biblical Literature Dissertation Series 130. Atlanta: Scholars Press, 1992.

Galbiati, E. "La Struttura sintetica di Osea 2." Pages 317–28 in *Studi sull 'Oriente e la Bibbia.* Edited by G. Buccelatti. Geneva: Editrice Studio e Vita, 1967.

Gallery, M. "Service Obligations of the *kezertu*-Women." *Orientalia* 49 (1980): 333–38.

Garrett, D. *Hosea, Joel.* The New American Commentary 19a. Nashville: Broadman & Holman, 1997.

Gelb, I. et al., eds. *Assyrian Dictionary of the Oriental Institute of the University of Chicago.* Chicago: University of Chicago Press, 1956–.

Geller, M. J. "The Elephantine Papyri and Hos. 2, 3: Evidence for the Form of the Early Jewish Divorce Writ." *Journal for the Study of Judaism in the Persian, Hellenistic, and Roman Periods* 8 (1977): 139–48.

Gelston, A. "Kingship in the Book of Hosea." Pages 71–85 in *Language and Meaning: Studies in Hebrew Language and Biblical Exegesis.* Edited by J. Barr. Oudtestamentische Studien 19. Leiden: Brill, 1974.

———. *The Peshitta of the Twelve Prophets.* Oxford: Clarendon, 1987.

Gesenius, W. *Hebrew Grammar.* Edited by E. Kautzsch. Translated by A. E. Cowley. Oxford: Clarendon, 1910.

Ginsberg, H. "Hosea." Columns 1010–24 in *Encyclopedia Judaica* 8. Jerusalem: Encyclopedia Judaica/ Macmillan, 1971.

———. "Studies in Hosea 1–3." Pages 50–69 in *Yehezkel Kaufmann Jubilee Volume.* Edited by M. Haran. Jerusalem: Magnes, 1960.

Gitay, Y. "Amos's Art of Speech." *Catholic Biblical Quarterly* 42 (1980): 293–309.

———. *Isaiah and His Audience.* Assen: Van Gorcum, 1991.

———. "Oratorical Rhetoric." *Amsterdamse Cahiers voor Exegese en bijbelse Theologie* 10 (1981): 72–83.

———. "Prophetic Criticism—'What Are They Doing?': The Case of Isaiah—A Methodological Assessment." *Journal for the Study of the Old Testament* 96 (2001): 101–27.

———. "The Realm of Prophetic Rhetoric." Pages 218–29 in *Rhetoric, Scripture, and Theology: Essays from the 1994 Pretoria Conference.* Edited by S. Porter and T. Olbricht. Journal for the Study of the Old Testament Supplement Series 131. Sheffield: Sheffield Academic Press, 1996.

———. "Rhetorical Analysis of Isaiah 40–48: A Study of the Art of Prophetic Persuasion." Ph.D. diss., Emory University, 1978. Repr. as *Prophecy and Persuasion: A Study of Isaiah 40–48.* Forum theologiae linguisticae 14. Bonn: Linguistica Biblica, 1981.

———. "Rhetorical Criticism and Prophetic Discourse." Pages 13–24 in *Persuasive Artistry.* Edited by D. Watson. Sheffield: Sheffield Academic Press, 1991.

Gnuse, R. *No Other Gods: Emergent Monotheism in Israel.* Journal for the Study of the Old Testament Supplement Series 241. Sheffield: Sheffield Academic Press, 1997.

Goldingay, J. "Hosea 1–3, Genesis 1–4 and Masculist Interpretation." *Horizons in Biblical Theology* 17 (1995): 37–44.

Goodfriend, E. "Adultery." Pages 82–86 in vol. 1 of *The Anchor Bible Dictionary.* Edited by D. N. Freedman. 6 vols. New York: Doubleday, 1992.

———. "Prostitution." Pages 505–10 in vol. 5 of *The Anchor Bible Dictionary.* Edited by D. N. Freedman. 6 vols. New York: Doubleday, 1992.

Goodman, N. *Languages of Art.* Indianapolis: Bobbs-Merrill, 1968.

Gordis, R. "Hosea's Marriage and Message: A New Approach." *Hebrew Union College Annual* 25 (1954): 9–35.

Gordon, C. H. "Hosea 2:4–5 in the Light of New Semitic Inscriptions." *Zeitschrift für die alttestamentliche Wissenschaft* 54 (1936): 277–80.

Gordon, R., ed. *The Place Is Too Small for Us: The Israelite Prophets in Recent Scholarship.* Sources for Biblical and Theological Study 5. Winona Lake, Ind.: Eisenbrauns, 1995.

Gowan, D. *Theology of the Prophetic Books.* Louisville: Westminster John Knox, 1998.

Graetz, N. "God Is to Israel as Husband Is to Wife: The Metaphoric Battering of Hosea's Wife." Pages 126–45 in *A Feminist Companion to the Latter Prophets.* Edited by A. Brenner. Sheffield: Sheffield Academic Press, 1995.

Graham, W. and H. May. *Culture and Conscience: An Archaeological Study of the New Religious Past in Ancient Palestine.* Chicago: University of Chicago Press, 1936.

Gray, J. *I and II Kings.* Philadelphia: Westminster, 1963.

Greenberg, M. *Ezekiel 21–37.* Anchor Bible 22a. Garden City, N.Y.: Doubleday, 1997.

Greengus, S. "The Old Babylonian Marriage Contract." *Journal of the American Oriental Society* 89 (1969): 505–32.

———. "A Textbook Case of Adultery in Ancient Mesopotamia." *Hebrew Union College Annual* 40–41 (1969–1970): 33–44.

Gressmann, H. *Der Messias.* Forschungen zur Religion und Literatur des Alten und Neuen Testaments 43. Göttingen: Vandenhoeck & Ruprecht, 1929.

Grosz, K. "Dowry and Brideprice in Nuzi." Pages 161–82 in vol. 1 of *Studies on the Civilization and Culture of Nuzi and the Hurrians.* Edited by D. Owen and M. Morrison. Winona Lake, Ind.: Eisenbrauns, 1981.

Gruber, M. "Hebrew *QEDĒŠĀH* and Her Canaanite and Akkadian Cognates." *Ugarit Forschungen* 18 (1986): 133–48.

———. "The qādēš in the Book of Kings and in Other Sources." *Tarbiz* 52 (1983): 167–76.

Guillaume, A. "A Note on Hosea II. 23, 24 (21, 22)." *Journal of Theological Studies* 15 (1964): 57–58.

Hadley, J. *The Cult of Asherah in Ancient Israel and Judah: Evidence for a Hebrew Goddess.* University of Cambridge Oriental Publications 57. Cambridge: Cambridge University Press, 2000.

———. "Some Drawings and Inscriptions on Two Pithoi from Kuntillet 'Ajrud." *Vetus Testamentum* 37 (1987): 208–11.

Hägg, T. *The Novel in Antiquity.* Berkeley: University of California Press, 1983.

Hallo, W. "From Qarqar to Carchemish: Assyria and Israel in the Light of New Discoveries." *Biblical Archaeologist* 23 (1960): 33–61.

——— and K. L. Younger, eds. *The Context of Scripture*. 3 vols. Leiden: Brill, 1997–2002.

Halpern, B. "Brisker Pipes Than Poetry: The Development of Israelite Monotheism." Pages 77–115 in *Judaic Perspectives on Ancient Israel*. Edited by J. Neusner, B. Levine, and E. Frerichs. Philadelphia: Fortress, 1987.

Hamilton, V. "Marriage: Old Testament and Ancient Near East." Pages 559–69 in vol. 4 of *The Anchor Bible Dictionary*. Edited by D. N. Freedman. 6 vols. New York: Doubleday, 1992.

Haran, M. "The Rise and Decline of the Empire of Jereboam ben Joash." *Vetus Testamentum* 17 (1967): 266–97.

Harmon, W. *The Sacred Marriage of a Hindu Goddess*. Bloomington: Indiana University Press, 1989.

Harper, R., ed. *Assyrian and Babylonian Letters Belonging to the Kouyunjik Collections of the British Museum*. 14 vols. Chicago: University of Chicago Press, 1892–1914.

Harper, W. *A Critical and Exegetical Commentary on Amos and Hosea*. International Critical Commentary 23. Edinburgh: T&T Clark, 1905.

Harris, R. "The Case of Three Babylonian Marriage Contracts." *Journal of Near Eastern Studies* 33 (1974): 363–69.

Hawkes, T. *Metaphor*. London: Methuen & Company, 1972.

Hayes, J. H. *Amos: The Eighth-Century Prophet: His Times and His Preaching*. Nashville: Abingdon, 1988.

———. "Hosea's Baals and Lovers: Religion or Politics?" Paper presented at the annual meeting of the Society of Biblical Literature. New Orleans, 1990.

———. and J. K. Kuan. "The Final Years of Samaria (730–720 BC)." *Biblica* 72 (1991): 153–81.

———. and P. K. Hooker. *A New Chronology for the Kings of Israel and Judah and Its Implications for Biblical History and Literature*. Atlanta: John Knox, 1988.

———. and S. Irvine. *Isaiah, the Eighth-Century Prophet: His Times and His Preaching*. Nashville: Abingdon, 1987.

Hendriks, H. "Juridical Aspects of the Marriage Metaphor in Hosea and Jeremiah." Ph.D. diss., The University of Stellenbosch, 1982.

Heschel, A. *The Prophets: An Introduction*. 2 vols. New York: Harper Torch Books, 1962.

Hess R. "Asherah or Asherata?" *Orientalia* 65 (1996): 209–19.

———. "Yahweh and His Asherah? Religious Pluralism in the Old Testament World." Pages 13–42 in *One God, One Lord: Christianity in a World of Religious Pluralism*. Edited by A. D. Clarke and B. W. Winter. Grand Rapids: Baker, 1993.

Hillers, D. "Analyzing the Abominable: Our Understanding of Canaanite Religion." *Jewish Quarterly Review* 75 (1985): 253–69.

———. *Treaty Curses and the Old Testament Prophets*. Biblica et Orientalia 16. Rome: Pontifical Biblical Institute, 1964.

Holladay, J. "Religion in Israel and Judah under the Monarchy: An Explicitly Archaeological Approach." Pages 249–99 in *Ancient Israelite Religion: Essays in Honor of Frank Moore Cross.* Edited by P. Miller, P. Hanson, and S. McBride. Philadelphia: Fortress, 1987.

Holladay, W. "'EREṢ—'Underworld': Two More Suggestions." *Vetus Testamentum* 19 (1969): 123–24.

Holman, H. and W. Harmon, eds. "Metaphor." Pages 315–16 in *A Handbook to Literature.* Edited by H. Holman and W. Harmon. 8th ed. New Jersey: Prentice-Hall, 2000.

Hooks, S. "Sacred Prostitution in Israel and the Ancient Near East." Ph.D. diss., Hebrew Union College, 1985.

Horner, W. *The Present State of Scholarship in Historical and Contemporary Rhetoric.* Columbia: University of Missouri Press, 1990.

Houston, W. "What Did the Prophets Think They Were Doing? Speech Acts and Prophetic Discourse in the Old Testament." *Biblical Interpretation* 1 (1993): 167–88. Repr. pages 133–53 in *The Place Is Too Small for Us: Israelite Prophets in Recent Scholarship.* Edited by R. Gordon. Sources for Biblical and Theological Study 5. Winona Lake, Ind.: Eisenbrauns, 1995.

Hubbard, D. *Hosea: An Introduction and Commentary.* Tyndale Old Testament Commentaries. Leicester: InterVarsity Press, 1989.

Hubbell, H. M., ed. and trans. *Cicero, De inventione: De optimo genere dicendi: Topica.* Loeb Classical Library. Cambridge: Harvard University Press, 1949.

Huehnergard, J. "Biblical Notes on Some New Akkadian Texts from Emar (Syria)." *Catholic Biblical Quarterly* 47 (1985): 428–34.

Huffmon, H. "The Treaty Background of Hebrew YĀDAᶜ." *Bulletin of the American Schools of Oriental Research* 181 (1966): 31–37.

———. and S. Parker. "A Further Note on the Treaty Background of Hebrew YĀDAᶜ." *Bulletin of the American Schools of Oriental Research* 184 (1966): 36–38.

Humbert, P. "La logique de la perspective nomade chez Osée et l'unité d'Osée 2, 4–22." Pages 158–66 in *Vom Alten Testament: Karl Marti zum siebzigsten Geburtstage gewidinet von Freunden, Fachgenossen und Schülern.* Edited by K. Budde. Beihefte zur Zeitschrift für die alttestamentliche Wissenschaft 41. Giessen: Töpelmann, 1925.

———. "Osée le prophète bédouin." *Revue d'histoire et de philosophie religieuses* 1 (1921): 97–118.

Ide, A. F. *Yahweh's Wife: Sex in the Evolution of Monotheism.* Las Colinas: Monument, 1991.

Ilan, T. "Notes and Observations on a Newly Published Divorce Bill from the Judean Desert." *Harvard Theological Review* 89 (1996): 195–202.

Instone-Brewer, D. *Divorce and Remarriage in the Bible: The Social and Literary Context.* Grand Rapids: Eerdmans, 2002.

Irvine, S. *Isaiah, Ahaz, and the Syro-Ephraimitic Crisis.* Society of Biblical Literature Dissertation Series 123. Atlanta: Scholars Press, 1990.

———. "The Threat of Jezreel (Hosea 1:4–5)." *Catholic Biblical Quarterly* 57 (1995): 494–503.

Jenni, E. "Das Wort ᶜōlām im AT." *Zeitschrift für die alttestamentliche Wissenschaft* 64 (1952): 235–39.

———. and C. Westermann, eds. *Theological Lexicon of the Old Testament.* Translated by M. Biddle. 3 vols. Peabody: Hendrickson, 1997.

Jeremias, J. "Der Begriff 'Baal' im Hoseabuch und seine Wirkungsgeschichte." Pages 441–62 in *Ein Gott allein? JHWH-Verehrung und biblischer Monotheismus im Kontext der Israelitischen und altorientalischen Religionsgeschichte*. Edited by W. Dietrich and M. Klopfenstein. Orbis Biblicus et Orientalis 139. Freiburg: Universitätsverlag, 1994.

———. *Hosea und Amos: Studien zu den Anfängen des Dodekapropheton*. Forschungen zum Alten Testament 13. Tübingen: J. C. B. Mohr, 1996.

———. *Der Prophet Hosea*. Das Alte Testament deutsch 24. Neur Göttingen Bibelwerk. Göttingen: Vandenhoeck & Ruprecht, 1983.

Johnson, M., ed. *Philosophical Perspectives on Metaphor*. Minneapolis: University of Minnesota Press, 1981.

Johnstone, H. "Some Trends in Rhetorical Theory." Pages 78–90 in *The Prospect of Rhetoric*. Report of the National Development Project of the Speech Communication Association. Englewood Cliffs, N.J.: Prentice-Hall, 1971.

Jones, B. *Howling Over Moab: Irony and Rhetoric in Isaiah 15–16*. Society of Biblical Literature Dissertation Series 157. Atlanta: Scholars Press, 1996.

Jones, G. *1 and 2 Kings*. 2 vols. Grand Rapids: Eerdmans, 1984.

Kaufman, I. "Samaria (Ostraca)." Pages 921–26 in vol.5 of *The Anchor Bible Dictionary*. Edited by D. N. Freedman. 6 vols. New York: Doubleday, 1992.

Kaufmann, Y. *The Religion of Israel: From Its Beginnings to the Babylonian Exile*. Translated by M. Greenberg. Chicago: University of Chicago Press, 1960.

Keefe, A. "The Female Body, the Body Politic, and the Land: A Sociopolitical Reading of Hosea 1–2." Pages 70–100 in *A Feminist Companion to the Latter Prophets*. Edited by A. Brenner. Sheffield: Sheffield Academic Press, 1995.

———. *Woman's Body and the Social Body in Hosea*. Gender, Culture, Theory 10. Journal for the Study of the Old Testament Supplement Series 338. Sheffield: Sheffield Academic Press, 2001.

Keel, O. and C. Uehlinger. *Gods, Goddesses, and Images of God in Ancient Israel*. Translated by T. Trapp. Minneapolis: Fortress, 1998.

Keil, C. F. *The Twelve Minor Prophets*. 2 vols. Edinburgh: T&T Clark, 1868.

Kelle, B. "What's in a Name? Neo-Assyrian Designations for the Northern Kingdom and Their Implications for Israelite History and Biblical Interpretation." *Journal of Biblical Literature* 121 (2002): 639–666.

Kennedy, G. *The Art of Persuasion in Greece*. Princeton: Princeton University Press, 1963.

———. "Historical Survey of Rhetoric." Pages 3–42 in *Handbook of Classical Rhetoric in the Hellenistic Period 330 B.C.–A.D. 400*. Edited by S. Porter. Leiden: Brill, 1997.

———. *New Testament Interpretation through Rhetorical Criticism*. Chapel Hill: University of North Carolina Press, 1984.

Kessler, M. "A Methodological Setting for Rhetorical Criticism." *Semitics* 4 (1974): 22–36.

King, P. *Amos, Hosea, Micah: An Archaeological Commentary*. Philadelphia: Westminster, 1988.

Kinneavy, J. "Contemporary Rhetoric." Pages 186–246 in *The Present State of Scholarship in Historical and Contemporary Rhetoric*. Columbia: University of Missouri Press, 1990.

Kittay, E. *Metaphor: Its Cognitive Force and Linguistic Structure*. Oxford: Clarendon, 1987.

———. and A. Lehrer. "Semantic Fields and the Structures of Metaphor." *Studies in Language* 5.1 (1981): 31–63.

Klein, J. "Sacred Marriage." Pages 866–70 in vol. 5 of *The Anchor Bible Dictionary*. Edited by D. N. Freedman. 6 vols. New York: Doubleday, 1992.

Knight, G. *Hosea: God's Love*. Torch Commentaries. London: SCM, 1960.

———. *The New Israel: A Commentary on the Book of Isaiah 56–66*. Grand Rapids: Eerdmans, 1985.

Knobel, A. *Der Prophet Jesaia*. 2d ed. Kurzgefasstes exegetisches Handbuch zum Alten Testament 5. Leipzig: S. Hirzel, 1854.

Knudtzon, J. *Die El-Amarna-Tafeln*. Leipzig: J. C. Hinrich, 1915.

Koehler, L., W. Baumgartner, and J. Stamm. *The Hebrew and Aramaic Lexicon of the Old Testament*. Translated and edited by M. Richardson. 4 vols. Leiden: Brill, 1994–99.

König, E. "Prophecy (Hebrew)." Page 388 in vol. 10 of *The Encyclopedia of Religion and Ethics*. Edited by J. Hastings. 12 vols. New York: C. Scribner's Sons, 1918.

Kooij, A., van der. "Zur Exegese von II Reg. 17, 2." *Zeitschrift für die alttestamentliche Wissenschaft* 96 (1984): 109–12.

Kraeling, E. *The Brooklyn Museum Aramaic Papyri: New Documents of the Fifth Century B.C. from the Jewish Colony at Elephantine*. New Haven: Yale University Press, 1953.

Krszyna, H. "Literarische Struktur von Os 2, 4–17." *Biblische Zeitschrift* 13 (1969): 41–59.

Kruger, P. "'I Will Hedge Her Way with Thornbushes' (Hosea 2, 8): Another Example of Literary Multiplicity?" *Biblische Zeitschrift* 43 (1999): 92–99.

———. "Israel, the Harlot (Hos. 2:4–9)." *Journal of Northwest Semitic Languages* 11 (1983): 107–16.

———. "The Marriage Metaphor in Hosea 2:4–17 against Its Ancient Near Eastern Background." *Old Testament Essays* 5 (1992): 7–25.

———. "Prophetic Imagery: On Metaphors and Similes in the Book of Hosea." *Journal of Northwest Semitic Languages* 14 (1988): 143–51.

Kuan, J. *Neo-Assyrian Historical Inscriptions and Syria-Palestine*. Jian Dao Dissertation Series 1. Hong Kong: Alliance Bible Seminary Press, 1995.

Kuhl, C. "Neue Dokumente zum Verständnis von Hosea 2:4–15." *Zeitschrift für die alttestamentliche Wissenschaft* 52 (1934): 102–109.

Kuhnigk, W. *Nordwestsemitische Studien zum Hoseabuch*. Biblica et Orientalia 27. Rome: Pontifical Biblical Institute, 1974.

Laffey, A. *A Feminist Introduction to the Old Testament: A Feminist Perspective*. Philadelphia: Fortress, 1988.

Lakoff, G. and M. Johnson. "Conceptual Metaphor in Everyday Language." *The Journal of Philosophy* 77 (1980): 453–86. Repr. pages 286–329 in *Philosophical Perspectives on Metaphor*. Edited by M. Johnson. Minneapolis: University of Minnesota Press, 1981.

———. *Metaphors We Live By*. Chicago: University of Chicago Press, 1980.

————. and M. Turner. *More Than Cool Reason: A Field Guide to Poetic Metaphor.* Chicago: University of Chicago Press, 1989.

Lambert, M. "Note exégétique." *Revue des études juives* 39 (1899): 300.

Landy, F. "Fantasy and the Displacement of Pleasure: Hosea 2:4–17." Pages 146–60 in *A Feminist Companion to the Latter Prophets.* Edited by A. Brenner. Sheffield: Sheffield Academic Press, 1995.

————. *Hosea.* Readings: A New Biblical Commentary. Sheffield: Sheffield Academic Press, 1995.

————. "In the Wilderness of Speech: Problems of Metaphor in Hosea." *Biblical Interpretation* 3 (1995): 35–59.

Lederer, C. *Die biblische Zeitrechnung vom Auszuge aus Ägypten bis zum Beginne der babylonischen Gefangenschaft.* Speier: F. Kleeberger, 1888.

Leith, M. Joan Winn. "Verse and Reverse: The Transformation of the Woman, Israel, in Hos 1–3." Pages 95–108 in *Gender and Difference in Ancient Israel.* Edited by P. Day. Minneapolis: Fortress, 1989.

Lemaire, A. *Inscriptions Hébraïques 1: Les Ostraca.* Littératures anciennes du Proche-Orient. Paris: Les Éditions du Cerf, 1977.

Levine, T. "Menahem and Tiglath-Pileser: A New Synchronism." *Bulletin of the American Schools of Oriental Research* 206 (1972): 40–42.

————. *Two Neo-Assyrian Stelae from Iran.* Toronto: Royal Ontario Museum, 1972.

Lewis, J. "Metaphors in Hosea." *Evangelical Theological Society Papers* 46 (1995): 1–38.

Lewis, R. "The Persuasive Style and Appeals of the Minor Prophets Amos, Hosea, and Micah." Ph.D. diss., University of Michigan, 1958.

Lewy, J. "The Old West Semitic Sun-god Hammu." *Hebrew Union College Annual* 18 (1943–1944): 436–43.

Light, G. "Theory-Constitutive Metaphor and Its Development in the Book of Hosea." Ph.D. diss., The Southern Baptist Theological Seminary, 1991.

Limburg, J. *Hosea-Micah.* Interpretation. Atlanta: John Knox, 1988.

————. "The Root ריב and the Prophetic Lawsuit Speeches." *Journal of Biblical Literature* 88 (1969): 291–304.

Ling-Israel, P. "The Sennacherib Prism in the Israel Museum-Jerusalem." Pages 213–48 in *Bar Ilan Studies in Assyriology Dedicated to Pinḥas Artzi.* Edited by J. Klein and A. Skaist. Ramat-Gan: Bar Ilan University Press, 1990.

Lipiński, E. "Fertility Cult in Ancient Ugarit." Pages 207–16 in *Archaeology and Fertility Cult in the Ancient Mediterranean: Papers Presented at the First International Conference on Archaeology of the Ancient Mediterranean.* Amsterdam: B. R. Grüner, 1986.

————. "The Wife's Right to Divorce in the Light of an Ancient Near Eastern Tradition." *Jewish Law Annual* 4 (1981): 9–27.

Lipshitz, A., ed. *The Commentary of Rabbi Abraham Ibn Ezra on Hosea.* New York: Sepher-Hermon, 1988.

Luckenbill, D. *The Annals of Sennacherib.* Oriental Institute Publications 2. Chicago: University of Chicago Press, 1924.

Macintosh, A. A. *A Critical and Exegetical Commentary on Hosea.* International Critical Commentary. Edinburgh: T&T Clark, 1997.

Macky, P. *The Centrality of Metaphors to Biblical Thought.* Studies in the Bible and Early Christianity 19. Lewiston: Edwin Mellen, 1990.

MacLachlan, B. "Sacred Prostitution and Aphrodite." *Studies in Religion/Sciences Religieuses* 21/2 (1992): 145–62.

Mann, A. "Who Said It First: The Antiquity of 'Be Thou My Wife.'" Pages 39–45 in *Proceedings of the 9th World Congress of Jewish Studies.* Edited by A. Goldberg, et al. Jerusalem: World Union of Jewish Studies Press, 1986.

Marglin, F. *Wives of the God-King: The Rituals of the Devadasis of Puri.* Oxford: Oxford University Press, 1985.

Martinez, F. G. and E. Tigchelaar, eds. *The Dead Sea Scrolls Study Edition.* 2 vols. Leiden: Brill, 1997.

Matthews, E. "The Use of the Adultery Motif in Hebrew Prophecy." Th.D. diss., New Orleans Baptist Theological Seminary, 1987.

Matthews, V. "Marriage and Family in the Ancient Near East." Pages 1–32 in *Marriage and Family in the Biblical World.* Edited by K. Campbell. Downer's Grove, Ill.: InterVarsity Press, 2003.

Mauchline, J. "Hosea." Pages 553–725 in vol. 6 of *The Interpreter's Bible.* Edited by G. Buttrick, et al. Nashville: Abingdon, 1956.

May, H. "The Fertility Cult in Hosea." *American Journal of Semitic Languages and Literature* 48 (1932): 73–98.

Mays, J. *Hosea.* Old Testament Library. London: SCM, 1969.

McCarter, P. K. "Aspects of the Religion of the Israelite Monarchy: Biblical and Epigraphic Data." Pages 137–56 in *Ancient Israelite Religion: Essays in Honor of Frank Moore Cross.* Edited by P. Miller, P. Hanson, and S. McBride. Philadelphia: Fortress, 1987.

McComiskey, T., ed. *The Minor Prophets: An Exegetical and Expository Commentary.* 2 vols. Grand Rapids: Baker Book House, 1992.

McKeating, H. *The Books of Amos, Hosea and Micah.* Cambridge Bible Commentary. Cambridge: Cambridge University Press, 1971.

———. "Sanctions against Adultery in Ancient Israelite Society, with Some Reflections on Methodology in the Study of Old Testament Ethics." *Journal for the Study of the Old Testament* 11 (1979): 57–72.

Meissner, B. *Könige Babyloniens und Assyriens.* Leipzig: Quelle & Meyer, 1926.

Melugin, R. "Prophetic Books and the Problem of Historical Reconstruction." Pages 63–78 in *Prophets and Paradigms: Essays in Honor of Gene M. Tucker.* Edited by S. Reid. Journal for the Study of the Old Testament Supplement Series 229. Sheffield: Sheffield Academic Press, 1996.

Mendenhall, G. *The Tenth Generation: The Origins of the Biblical Tradition.* Baltimore: The Johns Hopkins University Press, 1974.

Meshel, Z. "The Israelite Religious Centre of Kuntillet ᵓAjrud, Sinai." Pages 237–40 in *Archaeology and Fertility Cult in the Ancient Mediterranean: Papers Presented at the First International Conference on Archaeology of the Ancient Mediterranean.* Edited by A. Bonanno. Amsterdam: B. R. Grüner, 1986.

———. *Kuntillet 'Ajrûd: A Religious Center from the Time of the Judean Monarchy on the Border of Sinai.* Israel Museum Catalogue 175. Jerusalem: Israel Museum Press, 1978.

Meynet, R. *Rhetorical Analysis: An Introduction to Biblical Rhetoric.* Journal for the Study of the Old Testament Supplement Series 256. Sheffield: Sheffield Academic Press, 1998.

Middleton, J. *The Lugbara of Uganda.* Case Studies in Cultural Anthropology. New York: Holt, Rinehart, & Winston, 1965.

Milgrom, J. *Leviticus 17–22: A New Translation with Introduction and Commentary.* Anchor Bible 3a. New York: Doubleday, 2000.

———. "The Nature and Extent of Idolatry in Eighth–Seventh Century Judah." *Hebrew Union College Annual* 69 (1998): 1–13.

Millard, A. *The Eponyms of the Assyrian Empire 910–612 BC.* State Archives of Assyria Studies 2. Helsinki: The Neo-Assyrian Text Corpus Project, 1994.

———. and H. Tadmor. "Adad-nirari III in Syria: Another Stele Fragment and the Dates of His Campaigns." *Iraq* 35 (1973): 57–64.

Miller, J. M. and J. H. Hayes. *A History of Ancient Israel and Judah.* Philadelphia: Westminster, 1986.

Moore, C. *Daniel, Esther, and Jeremiah: The Additions.* Anchor Bible 44. New York: Doubleday, 1977.

Moran, W. "The Ancient Near Eastern Background of the Love of God in Deuteronomy." *Catholic Biblical Quarterly* 25 (1963): 77–87.

Muilenburg, J. "Form Criticism and Beyond." *Journal of Biblical Literature* 88 (1969): 1–18. Repr. pages 49–69 in *Beyond Form Criticism: Essays in Old Testament Literary Criticism.* Sources for Biblical and Theological Study. Edited by P. House. Winona Lake, Ind.: Eisenbrauns, 1992.

Muntingh, L. "Married Life in Israel according to the Book of Hosea." *Die Oud Testamentiese Werkgemeenskap in Suid Afrika* 7/8 (1964–65): 77–84.

Musée du Louvre. *Textes Cunéiformes.* Paris: P. Geuthner, 1910–67.

Na'aman, N. "Two Notes on the Monolith Inscription of Shalmaneser III from Kurkh." *Tel Aviv* 3 (1976): 99–101.

Naumann, T. *Hoseas Erben: Strukturen der Nachinterpretation im Buch Hosea.* Beiträge zur Wissenschaft vom Alten und Neuen Testament 131. Stuttgart: Kohlhammer, 1991.

Neher, A. "Le symbolisme conjugal: Expression de l'histoire dans l'Ancien Testament." *Revue d'histoire et de philosophie religieuses* 34 (1954): 30–49.

Neufeld, E. *Ancient Hebrew Marriage Laws.* London: Longmans, Green, & Company, 1944.

Newsom, C. "A Maker of Metaphors: Ezekiel's Oracles against Tyre." *Interpretation* 38 (1984): 151–64. Repr. pages 191–204 in *The Place Is Too Small for Us: The Israelite Prophets in Recent Scholarship.* Edited by R. Gordon. Sources for Biblical and Theological Study 5. Winona Lake, Ind.: Eisenbrauns, 1995.

Nichols, M. *Rhetoric and Criticism.* Baton Rouge: Louisiana State University Press, 1963.

Niehr, H. "JHWH in der Rolle des Baalšamem." Pages 307–26 in *Ein Gott allein? JHWH-Verehrung und biblischer Monotheismus im Kontext der Israelitischen und altorientalischen Religionsgeschichte.* Edited by W. Dietrich and M. Klopfenstein. Orbis Biblicus et Orientalis 139. Freiburg: Universitätsverlag, 1994.

———. "The Rise of YHWH in Judahite and Israelite Religion: Methodological and Religio-Historical Aspects." Pages 45–72 in *The Triumph of Elohim: From Yahwisms to Judaisms*. Edited by D. Edelman. Grand Rapids: Eerdmans, 1996.

Nielsen, K. *There Is Hope for a Tree: The Tree as Metaphor in Isaiah.* Journal for the Study of the Old Testament Supplement Series 65. Sheffield: Sheffield Academic Press, 1989.

———. *Yahweh as Prosecutor and Judge: An Investigation of the Prophetic Lawsuit (Rîb-Pattern)*. Journal for the Study of the Old Testament Supplement Series 9. Sheffield: JSOT Press, 1978.

Nissinen, M. *Prophetie, Redaktion und Fortschreibung im Hoseabuch: Studien zum Werdegang eines Prophetenbuches im Lichte von Hos 4 und 11*. Alter Orient und Altes Testament 231. Kevelaer: Butzon & Bercker, 1991.

Noppen, J., van. *Metaphor II: A Classified Bibliography of Publications from 1985– 1990*. Amsterdam: J. Benjamins, 1990.

Nwaoru, E. *Imagery in the Prophecy of Hosea*. Ägypten und Altes Testament 41. Wiesbaden: Harrassowitz, 1999.

Nyberg, H. *Studien zum Hoseabuche*. Uppsala Universitet Årsskrift 6. Uppsala: Almquist & Wiksells, 1935.

Oded, B. "The Historical Background of the Syro-Ephraimitic War Reconsidered." *Catholic Biblical Quarterly* 34 (1972): 153–65.

Oden, R. *The Bible without Theology: The Theological Tradition and Alternatives to It.* San Francisco: Harper & Row, 1987.

Olbricht, T. "Classical Rhetorical Criticism and Historical Reconstructions: A Critique." Pages 108–24 in *The Rhetorical Interpretation of Scripture: Essays from the 1996 Malibu Conference*. Edited by S. Porter and D. Stamps. Journal for the Study of the Old Testament Supplement Series 180. Sheffield: Sheffield Academic Press, 1999.

Olyan, S. *Asherah and the Cult of Yahweh in Israel*. Society of Biblical Literature Monograph Series 34. Atlanta: Scholars Press, 1988.

———. "'In the Sight of Her Lovers': On the Interpretation of nablūt in Hos 2, 12." *Biblische Zeitschrift* 36 (1992): 255–61.

Oort, H. "Hozea." *Theologisch tijdschrift* 24 (1890): 345–64, 480–505.

Ortlund, Jr., R. *Whoredom: God's Unfaithful Wife in Biblical Theology*. New Studies in Biblical Theology. Grand Rapids: Eerdmans, 1996.

Ortony, A. "Metaphor, Language, and Thought." Pages 1–18 in *Metaphor and Thought*. Edited by A. Ortony. 2d ed. Cambridge: Cambridge University Press, 1993.

Östborn, G. *Yahweh and Baal: Studies in the Book of Hosea and Related Documents*. Lunds Universitets Årsskrift 51, 6. Lund: C. W. K. Gleerup, 1956.

Otwell, J. *And Sarah Laughed: The Status of Women in the Old Testament*. Philadelphia: Westminster, 1977.

Paolantonio, M. "God as Husband." *The Bible Today* 27 (1989): 299–303.

Parker, S., ed. *Ugaritic Narrative Poetry*. Society of Biblical Literature Writings from the Ancient World 9. Atlanta: Scholars Press, 1997.

Parpola, S. and K. Watanabe, eds. *Neo-Assyrian Treaties and Loyalty Oaths*. The State Archives of Assyria 2. Helsinki: Helsinki University Press, 1988.

Paul, S. *Amos*. Hermeneia. Minneapolis: Fortress, 1991.

————. "Biblical Analogues to Middle Assyrian Law." Pages 333–50 in *Religion and Law: Biblical-Judaic and Islamic Perspectives*. Edited by E. Firmage, B. Weiss, and J. Welch. Winona Lake, Ind.: Eisenbrauns, 1990.

Pentiuc, E. *Long-Suffering Love: A Commentary on Hosea with Patristic Annotations*. Brookline, Mass.: Holy Cross Orthodox Press, 2002.

Perdue, L. *Wisdom in Revolt: Metaphorical Theology in the Book of Job*. Journal for the Study of the Old Testament Supplement Series 112. Sheffield: JSOT Press, 1991.

————., J. Blenkinsopp, J. Collins, and C. Meyers. *Families in Ancient Israel*. The Family, Religion, and Culture. Louisville: Westminster John Knox, 1997.

Perelman, C. "The New Rhetoric." Pages 115–22 in *The Prospect of Rhetoric*. Report of the National Development Project of the Speech Communication Association. Englewood Cliffs, N.J.: Prentice-Hall, 1971.

————. and L. Olbrechts-Tyteca. *The New Rhetoric: A Treatise on Argumentation*. Translated by J. Wilkinson and P. Weaver. Notre Dame: University of Notre Dame Press, 1969.

Pfeiffer, C. "Hosea." Pages 801–18 in *The Wycliffe Bible Commentary*. Edited by C. Pfeiffer and E. Harrison. Chicago: Moody, 1962.

Phillips, A. "Another Look at Adultery." *Journal for the Study of the Old Testament* 20 (1981): 3–25.

Porten, B. *The Elephantine Papyri in English: Three Millennia of Cross-Cultural Continuity and Change*. Leiden: Brill, 1996.

————. and A. Yardeni. *Textbook of Aramaic Documents from Ancient Egypt*. 4 vols. Winona Lake, Ind.: Eisenbrauns, 1986.

Porter, S. and T. Olbricht. *Rhetoric, Scripture, and Theology: Essays from the 1994 Pretoria Conference*. Journal for the Study of the Old Testament Supplement Series 131. Sheffield: Sheffield Academic Press, 1996.

————. and D. Stamps, eds. *The Rhetorical Interpretation of Scripture: Essays from the 1996 Malibu Conference*. Journal for the Study of the Old Testament Supplement Series 180. Sheffield: Sheffield Academic Press, 1999.

Pressler, C. *The View of Women Found in the Deuteronomic Family Laws*. Beihefte zur Zeitschrift für die alttestamentliche Wissenschaft. Berlin: Walter de Gruyter, 1993.

Pritchard, J., ed. *Ancient Near Eastern Texts Relating to the Old Testament*. 3d ed. Princeton: Princeton University Press, 1969.

Procksch, O. *Die kleinen prophetischer Schriften vor dem Exile*. Erläuterungen zum Alten Testament 3. Calwer: Verlag der Vereinsbuch, 1910.

Pummer, R. *Samaritan Marriage Contracts and Deeds of Divorce*. 2 vols. Wiesbaden: Harrassowitz, 1993.

Rainey, A. F. "The Kingdom of Ugarit." *Biblical Archaeologist* 28 (1965): 102–25.

Rallis, I. "Nuptial Imagery in the Book of Hosea: Israel as the Bride of Yahweh." *St. Vladimir's Theological Quarterly* 34 (1990): 197–219.

Regt, L. J. "Person Shift in Prophetic Texts: Its Function and Its Rendering in Ancient and Modern Translations." Pages 214–31 in *The Elusive Prophet: The Prophet as Historical Person, Literary Character, and Anonymous Artist*. Edited by J. C. de Moor. Oudtestamentische Studiën. Leiden: Brill, 2001.

Reisner, G., C. Fisher, and D. Lyon, eds. *Harvard Excavations at Samaria.* Harvard Semitic Series. Cambridge: Harvard University Press, 1924.

Renaud, B. "Genèse et unité redactionnelle de Os 2." *Revue des sciences religieuses* 54 (1980): 1–20.

———. "Osée ii:2: *'lh mn h'rṣ.* Essai d'interprétation." *Vetus Testamentum* 33 (1983): 495–500.

Richards, I. *The Philosophy of Rhetoric.* Oxford: Oxford University Press, 1936. Repr. in part pages 48–62 in *Philosophical Perspectives on Metaphor.* Edited by M. Johnson. Minneapolis: University of Minnesota Press, 1981.

Ricoeur, P. "The Metaphorical Process as Cognition, Imagination, and Feeling." Pages 141–57 in *On Metaphor.* Edited by S. Sacks. Chicago: University of Chicago Press, 1979.

———. *The Rule of Metaphor.* Toronto: University of Toronto Press, 1977.

Riemann, P. "Desert and Return to the Desert in the Pre-Exilic Prophets." Ph.D. diss., Harvard University, 1964.

Ringgren, H. "The Marriage Motif in Israelite Religion." Pages 421–28 in *Ancient Israelite Religion: Essays in Honor of Frank Moore Cross.* Edited by P. Miller, P. Hanson, and S. McBride. Philadelphia: Fortress, 1987.

Rosenzweig, E. "Some Notes, Historical and Psychoanalytical on the People of Israel and the Land of Israel with Special References to Deuteronomy." *American Imago: Psychoanalytic Journal for the Arts and Sciences* 1/4 (1940): 50–64.

Rossing, B. *The Choice between Two Cities: Whore, Bride and Empire in the Apocalypse.* Harvard Theological Studies 48. Harrisburg, Pa.: Trinity Press International, 1999.

Roth, W. "Rhetorical Criticism, Hebrew Bible." Pages 396–99 in vol. 2 of *The Dictionary of Biblical Interpretation.* Edited by J. H. Hayes. 2 vols. Nashville: Abingdon, 1999.

Rowley, H. H. *Men of God: Studies in Old Testament History and Prophecy.* London: Thomas Nelson, 1963.

Rudolph, W. *Hosea.* Kommentar zum Alten Testament 13. 1. Gütersloh: G. Mohn, 1966.

Rupprecht, K. "עלה מן הארץ (Ex 1:10, Hos 2:2): Sich des Landes bemächtigen?" *Zeitschrift für die alttestamentliche Wissenschaft* 82 (1970): 442–47.

Ryan, H. *Classical Communication for the Contemporary Communicator.* Mountain View, Ca.: Mayfield, 1992.

Saggs, H. W. F. "LXX-ND 2766, Plate XIV." *Iraq* 25–26 (1963–64): 70–80.

Satlow, M. *Jewish Marriage in Antiquity.* Princeton: Princeton University Press, 2001.

Schmidt, W. "Die deuteronomistische Redaktion des Amosbuches." *Zeitschrift für die alttestamentliche Wissenschaft* 77 (1965): 168–93.

Schmitt, J. "The Gender of Ancient Israel." *Journal for the Study of the Old Testament* 26 (1983): 115–25.

———. "The Virgin of Israel: Referent and the Use of the Phrase in Amos and Jeremiah." *Catholic Biblical Quarterly* 53 (1991): 365–87.

———. "The Wife of God in Hosea 2." *Biblical Research* 34 (1989): 5–18.

———. "Yahweh's Divorce in Hosea 2– Who Is That Woman?" *Scandinavian Journal of the Old Testament* 9 (1995): 119–32.

Schulz-Rauch, M. *Hosea und Jeremia: Zur Wirkungsgeschichte des Hoseabuches.* Calwer Theologische Mongraphien 16. Stuttgart: Calwer, 1996.

Scott, R. and B. Brock. *Methods of Rhetorical Criticism: A Twentieth-Century Perspective.* New York: Harper & Row, 1972.

Seifert, B. *Metaphorisches Reden von G-tt im Hoseabuch.* Forschungen zur Religion und Literatur des Alten and Neuen Testaments 166. Göttingen: Vandenhoeck & Ruprecht, 1996.

Sellin, D. *Das Zwölfprophetenbuch übersetzt und erklärt.* Kommentar zum Alten Testament. Leipzig: A. Deichertsche Verlagsbuchhandlung, 1922.

Selms, A., van. "Hosea and Canticles." *Oud Testamentiese Werkgemeenschap in Suid Africa* 7/8 (1966): 85–89.

Setel, T. "Prophets and Pornography: Female Sexual Imagery in Hosea." Pages 86–95 in *Feminist Interpretation of the Bible.* Edited by L. Russell. Philadelphia: Westminster, 1985.

Shaw, C. "The Speeches of Micah: A Rhetorical-Historical Analysis." Ph.D. diss., Emory University, 1990. Repr. as *The Speeches of Micah: A Rhetorical-Historical Analysis.* Journal for the Study of the Old Testament Supplement Series 145. Sheffield: JSOT Press, 1993.

Sherwood, Y. *The Prostitute and the Prophet: Hosea's Marriage in Literary-Theoretical Perspective.* Journal for the Study of the Old Testament Supplement Series 212. Sheffield: Sheffield Academic Press, 1996.

Shields, M. "An Abusive God? Identity and Power/Gender and Violence in Ezekiel 23." Pages 129–52 in *Postmodern Interpretations of the Bible: A Reader.* Edited by A. Adam. St. Louis: Chalice, 2001.

Simpson, J. and E. Weiner, eds. *The Oxford English Dictionary.* 2d edition. 20 vols. Oxford: Clarendon, 1989.

Smith, M. *The Early History of God.* New York: Harper & Row, 1990.

———. "Interpreting the Baal Cycle." *Ugarit Forschungen* 18 (1986): 313–39.

———. "Yahweh and Other Deities in Ancient Israel: Observations on Old Problems and Recent Trends." Pages 197–234 in *Ein Gott allein? JHWH-Verehrung und biblischer Monotheismus im Kontext der israelitischen und altorientalischen Religionsgeschichte.* Edited by W. Dietrich and M. Klopfenstein. Orbis Biblicus et Orientalis 139. Freiburg: Universitätsverlag, 1994.

Smith, W. R. *The Prophets of Israel and Their Place in History to the Close of the Eighth Century B.C.* London: Adam & Charles Black, 1897.

Snaith, N. "II Kings." Pages 187–338 in vol. 3 of *The Interpreter's Bible.* Edited by G. A. Buttrick, et al. 12 vols. New York: Abingdon-Cokesbury, 1951–57.

———. *Amos, Hosea, and Micah.* Epworth Preacher's Commentaries. London: Epworth Press, 1956.

———. *Mercy and Sacrifice: A Study of the Book of Hosea.* London: SCM, 1953.

Soden, W., von. "Kultische Prostitution." Page 642 in vol. 5 of *Religion in Geschichte und Gegenwart.* Edited by K. Galling. 7 vols. 3d ed. Tübingen: Mohr Siebeck, 1957–65.

Soisalon-Soininen, I. "Der Infinitivus Constructus mit ל in Hebräischen." *Vetus Testamentum* 22 (1972): 82–90.

Soskice, J. *Metaphor and Religious Language.* Oxford: Clarendon, 1985.

Sperber, A. *The Bible in Aramaic.* 4 vols. Leiden: Brill, 1962.

Sperling, S. "Biblical *rḥm* I and *rḥm* II." *Journal of the Ancient Near Eastern Society of Columbia University* 19 (1989): 149–59.

Steck, O. "Zion als Gelände und Gestalt: Überlegungen zur Wahrnehung Jerusalems als Stadt und Frau im Alten Testament." *Zeitschrift für Theologie und Kirche* 86 (1989): 261–81.

Steininger, P. "Nablūt: Ein Beitrag zur hebräischen Grammatik und Lexicographie." *Zeitschrift für die alttestamentliche Wissenschaft* 24 (1904): 141–42.

Stienstra, N. *YHWH Is the Husband of His People.* Kampen: Kok Pharos, 1993.

Strachey, E. *Hebrew Politics in the Times of Sargon and Sennacherib: An Inquiry into the Historical Meaning and Purpose of the Prophecies of Isaiah, with Some Notice of Their Bearings on the Social and Political Life of England.* London: Longman, Brown, Green, & Longmans, 1853.

Stuart, D. *Hosea-Jonah.* Word Biblical Commentary 31. Waco: Word Books, 1987.

Sweeney, M. *The Twelve Prophets.* 2 vols. Berit Olam. Collegeville: The Liturgical Press, 2000.

Taber, C. "Marriage." Pages 573–76 in *The Interpreter's Dictionary of the Bible Supplementary Volume.* Edited by K. Crim. Nashville: Abingdon, 1976.

Tadmor, H. *The Inscriptions of Tiglath-Pileser III King of Assyria.* Jerusalem: Israel Academy of Sciences & Humanities, 1994.

———. "The Southern Border of Aram." *Israel Exploration Journal* 12 (1962): 114–22.

———. and M. Cogan. "Ahaz and Tiglath-Pileser in the Book of Kings: Historiographical Considerations." *Biblica* 60 (1979): 491–508.

Tadmor, M. "Female Cult Figurines in Late Canaan and Early Israel: Archaeological Evidence." Pages 139–73 in *Studies in the Period of David and Solomon and Other Essays.* Edited by T. Ishida. Winona Lake, Ind.: Eisenbrauns, 1982.

Tangberg, K. "A Note on *pištî* in Hosea II 7, 11." *Vetus Testamentum* 27 (1977): 222–24.

Tate, M. *Psalms 51–100.* Word Biblical Commentary 20. Dallas: Word Books, 1990.

Taylor, J. G. "Was Yahweh Worshiped as the Sun?" *Biblical Archaeology Review* 20:4 (1994): 53–61.

Tetley, M. C. "The Date of Samaria's Fall as a Reason for Rejecting the Hypothesis of Two Conquests." *Catholic Biblical Quarterly* 64 (2002): 59–77.

Theis, J. *Sumerisches im Alten Testament.* Trier: Paulinus-Druekerei, 1912.

Thomas, W. "The Root אהב 'Love' in Hebrew." *Zeitschrift für die alttestamentliche Wissenschaft* 57 (1939): 57–64.

Thompson, J. A. "Israel's 'Lovers.'" *Vetus Testamentum* 27 (1977): 475–81.

———. "The Significance of the Verb *Love* in the David-Jonathan Narratives in I Samuel." *Vetus Testamentum* 24 (1974): 334–38.

Thompson, L. *The Book of Revelation: Apocalypse and Empire.* New York: Oxford University Press, 1990.

Thompson, M. *Situation and Theology: Old Testament Interpretations of the Syro-Ephraimitic War.* Prophets and Historians 1. Sheffield: Almond, 1982.

Tigay, J. *Deuteronomy.* The JPS Torah Commentary. Philadelphia: Jewish Publication Society, 1996.

———. "Israelite Religion: The Onomastic and Epigraphic Evidence." Pages 157–94 in *Ancient Israelite Religion: Essays in Honor of Frank Moore Cross.* Edited by P. Miller, P. Hanson, and S. McBride. Philadelphia: Fortress, 1987.

———. *You Shall Have No Other Gods: Israelite Religion in the Light of Hebrew Inscriptions.* Harvard Semitic Studies 31. Atlanta: Scholars Press, 1986.

Toeg, A. "Does Deuteronomy 24, 1–4 Incorporate a General Law on Divorce?" *Diné Israel* 2 (1970): 5–24.

Tomes, R. "The Reason for the Syro-Ephraimitic War." *Journal for the Study of the Old Testament* 59 (1993): 55–71.

Toorn, K., van der. "Cultic Prostitution." Pages 510–13 in vol. 5 of *The Anchor Bible Dictionary*. Edited by D. N. Freedman. 6 vols. New York: Doubleday, 1992.

Törnkvist, R. *The Use and Abuse of Female Sexual Imagery in the Book of Hosea: A Feminist Critical Approach to Hos 1–3*. Uppsala Women's Studies A. Women in Religion 7. Uppsala: Acta Universitatis Uppsaliensis, 1998.

Trible, P. *Rhetorical Criticism: Context, Method, and the Book of Jonah*. Guides to Biblical Scholarship. Minneapolis: Fortress, 1994.

Trotter, J. *Reading Hosea in Achaemenid Yehud*. Journal for the Study of the Old Testament Supplement Series 328. Sheffield: Sheffield Academic Press, 2001.

Tsevat, M. "The Neo-Assyrian and Neo-Babylonian Vassal Oaths and the Prophet Ezekiel." *Journal of Biblical Literature* 78 (1959): 199–204.

Tushingham, A. "A Reconsideration of Hosea, Chapters 1–3." *Journal of Near Eastern Studies* 12 (1953): 150–59.

Vatz, R. "The Myth of the Rhetorical Situation." *Philosophy and Rhetoric* 6 (1973): 154–61.

Vermeylem, J. "Os 1–3 et son histoire littéraire." *Ephemerides theologicae Lovanienses* 79 (2003): 23–52.

Vogels, W. "Hosea's Gift to Gomer (Hos 3, 2)." *Biblica* 69 (1988): 412–21.

Vogelstein, M. *Jeroboam II: The Rise and Fall of His Empire*. Cincinnati: self-published, 1945.

Volz, P. "Die Ehegeschichte Hoseas." *Zeitschrift für wissenschaftliche Theologie* 6 (1898): 323–24.

Wacker, M. *Figurationen des Weiblichen im Hosea-Buch*. Herder's Biblische Studien 8. Freiburg: Herder, 1996.

Wall, R. "Divorce." Pages 217–29 in vol. 2 of *The Anchor Bible Dictionary*. Edited by D. N. Freedman. 6 vols. New York: Doubleday, 1992.

Wallis, L. *God and the Social Process*. Chicago: University of Chicago Press, 1935.

Waltke, B. and M. O'Connor. *An Introduction to Biblical Hebrew Syntax*. Winona Lake, Ind.: Eisenbrauns, 1990.

Ward, J. *Hosea: A Theological Commentary*. New York: Harper & Row, 1966.

Warner, M., ed. *The Bible as Rhetoric: Studies in Biblical Persuasion and Credibility*. Warwick Studies in Philosophy and Literature. London: Routledge, 1990.

Watson, D. "The Contributions and Limitations of Greco-Roman Rhetorical Theory for Constructing the Rhetorical and Historical Situations of a Pauline Epistle." Pages 125–51 in *The Rhetorical Interpretation of Scripture: Essays from the 1996 Malibu Conference*. Edited by S. Porter and D. Stamps. Journal for the Study of the Old Testament Supplement Series 180. Sheffield: Sheffield Academic Press, 1999.

Weems, R. "Gomer: Victim of Violence or Victim of Metaphor?" *Semeia* 47 (1989): 87–104.

Weider, A. *Ehemetaphorik in prophetischer Verkündigung: Hos 1–3 und seine Wirkungsgeschichte im Jeremiabuch: Ein Beitrag zum alttestamentlichen Gottes-Bild*. Forschung zur Bibel 71. Würzburg: Echter, 1993.

Wellhausen, J. *Die kleinen Propheten: Übersetzen und Erklärt*. 4th ed. Berlin: Walter de Gruyter, 1963.

———. *Prolegomena to the History of Israel*. Scholars Press Reprints and Translations. Repr. of 1885 ed. Atlanta: Scholars Press, 1994.

West, G. "The Effect and Power of Discourse: A Case Study of a Metaphor." *Scriptura* 57 (1996): 201–12.

Westbrook, R. "Adultery in Ancient Near Eastern Law." *Revue Biblique* 97 (1990): 542–80.

———. *Old Babylonian Marriage Law*. Archiv für Orientforschung 23. Austria: Ferdinand Berger & Sons, 1988.

———. "The Prohibition on Restoration of Marriage in Deuteronomy 24:1–4." Pages 387–405 in *Studies in Bible: Scripta Hierosolymitana 31*. Edited by S. Japhet. Jerusalem: Magnes, 1986.

———. *Property and the Family in Biblical Law*. Journal for the Study of the Old Testament Supplement Series 113. Sheffield: JSOT Press, 1991.

Westenholtz, J. "Tamar, Qedeša, Qadištu, and Sacred Prostitution in Mesopotamia." *Harvard Theological Review* 82. 3 (1989): 245–65.

White, E., ed. *Rhetoric in Transition: Studies in the Nature and Views of Rhetoric*. University Park: Penn State University Press, 1980.

Whitt, W. "The Divorce of Yahweh and Asherah in Hos 2, 4–7.12ff." *Scandinavian Journal of the Old Testament* 6, 1 (1992): 31–67.

Wichelns, H. "The Literary Criticism of Oratory." Pages 181–216 in *Studies in Rhetoric and Public Speaking in Honor of James A. Winans*. Edited by A. Drummond. New York: Century, 1925.

Wilson, R. "The City in the Old Testament." Pages 3–14 in *Civitas: Religious Interpretations of the City*. Edited by P. Hawkins. Studies in the Humanities. Atlanta: Scholars Press, 1986.

Winckler, H. *Geschichte Israels in Einzeldarstellung*. 2 vols. Leipzig: Pfeiffer, 1895–1900.

Wiseman, D. "A Fragmentary Inscription of Tiglath-pileser from Nimrud." *Iraq* 18 (1956): 117–29.

Wolff, H. "Der große Jesreeltag (Hosea 2, 1–3): Methodologische Erwägungen zur Auslegung einer alttestamentlichen Perikope." *Evangelische Theologie* 12 (1952–53): 78–104.

———. *Hosea*. Hermeneia. Philadelphia: Fortress, 1974.

Yamauchi, E. "Cultic Prostitution: A Case Study in Cultural Diffusion." Pages 213–22 in *Orient and Occident: Essays Presented to Cyrus H. Gordon on the Occasion of His Sixty-fifth Birthday*. Edited by H. A. Hoffner. Alter Orient und Altes Testament 22. Neukirchen-Vluyn: Neukirchener Verlag, 1973.

Yaron, R. "Aramaic Marriage Contracts: Corrigenda and Addenda." *Journal of Semitic Studies* 5 (1960): 66–70.

———. "Aramaic Marriage Contracts from Elephantine." *Journal of Semitic Studies* 3 (1958): 1–39.

———. *Introduction to the Law of the Aramaic Papyri*. Oxford: Clarendon, 1961.

———. "A Royal Divorce at Ugarit." *Orientalia* 32 (1963): 21–31.

Yee, G. *Composition and Tradition in the Book of Hosea: A Redaction Critical Investigation.* Society of Biblical Literature Dissertation Series 102. Atlanta: Scholars Press, 1987.

———. "Hosea." Pages 195–202 in *The Women's Bible Commentary.* Edited by C. Newsom and S. Ringe. Louisville: Westminster John Knox, 1992.

———. "Hosea." Pages 195–298 in vol. 7 of *The New Interpreter's Bible.* Edited by L. Keck et al. Nashville: Abingdon, 1996.

———. *Poor Banished Children of Eve: Woman as Evil in the Hebrew Bible.* Minneapolis: Fortress, 2003.

———. "'She Is Not My Wife and I Am Not Her Husband': A Materialist Analysis of Hosea 1–3." *Biblical Interpretation* 9 (2004): 345–83.

Younger, K. L. "Yahweh at Ashkelon and Calah? Yahwistic Names in Neo-Assyrian." *Vetus Testamentum* 52 (2002): 207–18.

Zimmerli, W. *Ezekiel 2: A Commentary on the Book of the Prophet Ezekiel Chapters 25–48.* Hermeneia. Philadelphia: Fortress, 1983.

INDEX OF ANCIENT SOURCES

Note: The footnotes are not separately indexed. Hence a reference to page 6 could refer to the body or a footnote on that page. Similarly, multiple instances on a page are not indicated.

INDEX OF AUTHORS

Note: The footnotes are not separately indexed. Hence a reference to page 6 could refer to the body or a footnote on that page. Similarly, multiple instances on a page are not indicated.

INDEX OF SCRIPTURE REFERENCES

Note: The footnotes are not separately indexed. Hence a reference to page 6 could refer to the body or a footnote on that page.

Printed in the United States
36904LVS00005B/1-78